# AIRCRAFT
## FOR
# THE MANY

*Other books by the same author:*

FORCE FOR FREEDOM
The USAF in the UK since 1948

ACTION STATIONS
1: Military airfields of East Anglia

ACTION STATIONS
6: Military airfields of the Cotswolds and Central Midlands

AIRCRAFT FOR THE FEW
The RAF's fighters and bombers in 1940

THE BATTLE OF BRITAIN
50 Years On

THE SPITFIRE
50 Years On

AIR RAID!
The enemy air offensive against East Anglia 1939–45

Patrick Stephens Limited, an imprint of Haynes Publishing, has published authoritative, quality books for enthusiasts for more than a quarter of a century. During that time the company has established a reputation as one of the world's leading publishers of books on aviation, maritime, military, model-making, motor cycling, motoring, motor racing, railway and railway modelling subjects. Readers or authors with suggestions for books they would like to see published are invited to write to: The Editorial Director, Patrick Stephens Limited, Sparkford, Nr Yeovil, Somerset, BA22 7JJ.

# AIRCRAFT
## FOR
# THE MANY

## A DETAILED SURVEY OF THE RAF'S
## AIRCRAFT IN JUNE 1944

## MICHAEL J. F. BOWYER

Patrick Stephens Limited

© Michael J.F. Bowyer 1995                    11/07

First published in 1995

British Library cataloguing-in-
publication data:
A catalogue record for this book is
available from the British Library.

ISBN: 1 85260 427 1

Library of Congress
catalog card no. 94 79678

Patrick Stephens Limited is an imprint of
Haynes Publishing, Sparkford,
Nr. Yeovil, Somerset BA22 7JJ.

Typeset by G&M,
Raunds, Northamptonshire.
Printed and bound in Great Britain by
BPC Hazell Books Ltd

# Contents

# Glossary

**NOTE** The code letters used to record damage levels, the cause of the damage and the fate of the aircraft have been taken from official records in which the combination of such letters was not necessarily consistent eg FA AC means the same as AC FA. Some combinations appear below. The damage code letter was sometimes preceded by Cat (Category). The letters in the tables are reproduced in the combinations in which they appear in the original documents.

**21/34** effective sorties/total sorties

**(42.35)** total number of hours and minutes flown by an aircraft

**A** Category A damage; the lightest category

**ABC** *Airborne Cigar*; Lancaster with three transmitters manned by German speakers to interfere with German fighter controllers' instructions to night-fighters

**AC** category A damage repaired by the Contractor; or Air Commodore

**ACAST** Assistant Chief of the Air Staff (Training)

**ADGB** Air Defence of Great Britain

**ADLS** Air Despatch Letter Service

**AEAF** Allied Expeditionary Air Force

**AFC** Air Force Cross

**AFDU** Air Fighting Development Unit

**AFEE** Airborne Forces Experimental Establishment

**AFV** armoured fighting vehicle

**AI** Airborne Interception; radar

*Albany* drop of US 101st Airborne Division on the Cotentin Peninsular on 6.6.44

**ALG** Advanced Landing Ground

*anti-diver* patrol to shoot down V-1s

**AOP** Air Observation Post

**API** air position indicator

**ARF** Aircraft Reception Flight

**AS** anti-submarine (bomb)

*Ascension* operation to establish airborne radio contact with Resistance organizations

**AST** Air Service Training

**ASV** Air to Surface Vessel radar

**ATTDU** Airborne Tactical Transport Development Unit

**AWA** Armstrong Whitworth Aircraft

**B1, B2 etc** Advanced Landing Grounds in Normandy, around Bayeaux

**B** bomber; or Category B damage

**Baedeker raids** German bombing raids on British cities noted as tourist destinations

**BAFO** British Air Forces of Occupation

**BBOC** brought back on charge, having been previously written off

**Beau-bomber** bomb-carrying Beaufighter

*Beaune* special duty operation

*Bell Weather* AOP operation prior to D-Day

*Bodenplatte* Luftwaffe operation against 2nd TAF and other Allied airfields on 1.1.45

**bogey** unidentified aircraft (slang)

**Bomphoon** Typhoon with bombs (slang)

*Boston* drop of US 82nd Airborne Division on the Cotentin Peninsular on 6.6.44

**BS** Bomber Support

*Bullseye* night training exercise for bombers and anti-aircraft units

**C** Category C damage; or repaired by Contractor

*Camaraderie* special duty operation

*Carpetbagger* special duty supply operation to Resistance forces

**casevac** casualty evacuation

**Cat E** Category E damage; a write-off

**CFE** Central Fighter Establishment

*Channel Stop* operation to close Channel to enemy shipping

*Charitaitie* special duty operation

*Chicago* operation to take gliderborne troops of US 101st Airborne Division to the Cotentin Peninsular on 6.6.44

*Circus* fighter-escorted bomber operation to entice enemy fighter response

*Colossus* British airborne operation in southern Italy in February 1941

*Coney* airborne operation dropping paratroops behind enemy lines

**cookie** 4,000lb light case bomb

**CRD** Controller Research and Development

**CRO** Civilian Repair Organisation

*Darwin* special duty operation

*Daviston* special duty operation

*Deadly* patrols against small surface warships

*Deadstick* part of Operation *Tonga*

*Detroit* operation to take gliderborne troops of the 82nd Airborne Division to the Cotentin Peninsular on 6.6.44

**D/H** direct hit

*Donald* special duty operation

**DP** deep penetration

*Draw String* Main Force in Operation *Flashlamp*

**DTD** Director of Technical Development, a department of the Air Ministry and subsequently of MAP

*Dutch Coast* patrols against small surface warships

**DWI** directional wireless installation

**E.1, E.2 etc** operations

airlifting squadron personnel from Britain to ALGs in Normandy then returning with casualties

**ELG** Emergency Landing Ground

**ELINT** electronic intelligence

*Elmira* operation to take US gliderborne troops to the Cotentin Peninsular on 6.6.44

*Epicure* weather reconnaissance sortie over the Atlantic

*Eureka* ground beacons used by paratroop pathfinders

**FA** flying accident

**FB** flying battle

*Flashlamp* operation by RAF heavies to bomb 10 gun batteries in the Seine Bay on 5/6.6.44

*Flowers* night-intruder operation against specific night-fighter airfields

*Forsythia* special duty operation

*Freeport* resupply operation to US airborne troops

*Freya* German early warning radar

**FS** full supercharger

**FTR** failed to return

**FX** Fritz X, a German radio-controlled glider bomb

**GA** ground accident

**GAL** General Aircraft Ltd

*Galverston* operation to take US gliderborne troops to the Cotentin Peninsular on 7.6.44

**GCI** Ground-Controlled Interception

*Gee* a medium-range navigation aid using ground transmitters and airborne receivers

*Gee-H* blind-bombing device

*Gilbey* patrols against surface warships

*Glimmer* window-dropping operation

*Gold* code-name for British assault beach adjacent to the American beaches

*Gondolier* special duty operation

*Goodwood* British offensive in July 1944 on the Bourgébus Ridge SW of Caen

**GR** general reconnaissance

**Grand Slam** 22,000lb deep penetration bomb; also called earthquake bomb

**GSU** Group Support Unit

**GT** Glider Tug

**H2S** airborne radar

**H2X** American version of H2S

*Hackensack* operation to take US gliderborne troops to the Cotentin Peninsular on 7.6.44

*Harlech* special duty operation

**HC** high capacity (bomb); 80% explosive

*Hermit* special duty operation

**HF** high flying

**HGCU** Heavy Glider Conversion Unit (formerly the Heavy Glider Training Unit)

**HGSU** Heavy Glider Support Unit

**H-hour** time at which bombing was to start

*Highball* bouncing anti-shipping bomb designed to be fitted to the Mosquito

*Historian* special duty operation

**IAS** indicated air speed

**IFF** Identification Friend or Foe

*Intruder* operation to attack a night-fighter airfield

**IR** immediate reserve ie number of aircraft in a unit's reserve

*Japonica* special duty operation

*Jim Crow* shipping reconnaissance fighter sortie

*Jostle* jamming operation

*Jubilee* the Dieppe raid, 19.8.42

*Juno* code-name for British assault beach between *Gold* and *Sword* beaches

*Keokuk* resupply operation to US airborne troops

**KG** Kampfgeschwader (German bomber wing)

**Ladder Plan** order in which squadrons re-equipped

**LB** long burn (target indicator)

**LCT** Landing Craft, Tank

**Leigh Light** searchlight for anti-submarine operations

**LF** low flying

**LL** low level

**lodgement area** the area beyond the beachhead taken from the enemy and made secure

**LRB** long range bomber

**LZ** landing zone

*Mahmoud* night-fighter sortie to seek out enemy night-fighters in a specific area

*Mallard* gliderborne landings of 6th Airlanding Brigade on 6.6.44

*Mandrel* airborne radar-jamming device

**MAP** Ministry of Aircraft Production created in May 1940, superseding the Air Ministry

**Marker Force** aircraft using target indicators

**MC** medium case (bomb; 40% explosive) or Military Cross

*Memphis* resupply operation to US airborne troops

**Met Recce** Meteorological Reconnaissance

**MI** major inspection

**MLO** military liaison officer

*Monica* warning radar to show the approach of a German night-fighter

**MR** major repair

**MS** medium supercharger

**MU** Maintenance Unit

*Mulberry* prefabricated artificial harbour

**NA** North American Inc

*Neptune* the code-name for the seaborne phase of *Overlord*

**NFT** night flying training

*Nightlight* exercise in April 1944; pathfinding by Mitchells

**NJG** Nachtjagdgeschwader (German night-fighter unit)

*Noball* V-1 launch site

**NS** Nova Scotia

**OADU** Overseas Aircraft Despatch Unit

*Oboe* blind bombing aid

*Omaha* code-name for US assault beach adjacent to *Gold*

**op(s)** operational or operation(s)

*Orange* special duty operation

**ORB** Operations Record Book

**ORC** Operational Requirements Committee

*Outmatch* standing night patrols over English Channel shipping and some areas of the intended beachhead on 5/6.6.44

*Overlord* the code-name for the invasion of Normandy

**pack howitzer** compact artillery piece for air transportation

*parametta* blind ground-marking technique used by PFF

**PFF** Pathfinder Force

**POL** petrol, oil, lubricant

*Politician* special duty operation

**PRU** Photographic Reconnaissance Unit

*Prank* combined services exercise around Studland Bay in March 1944

**PTS** Parachute Training School, Ringway

**RAAF** Royal Australian Air Force

**RAE** Royal Aircraft Establishment, Farnborough

*Ramrod* fighter-escorted bomber daylight raid

*Ranger* deep penetration operation to a specified area, seeking targets of opportunity

**R-boat** Raumboot; German minesweeper

**RCAF** Royal Canadian Air Force

**RCM** Radio countermeasures

*Rebecca* navigation equipment for locating Eureka beacons

**Red Horsa** rear-unloading Horsa with quick-release bolts

**remarked** target marked a second or third time with target indicators

*Rhubarb* low-level sortie over enemy territory

**RIW** repaired in works

**RNAS** Royal Naval Air Station

**RNZAF** Royal New Zealand Air Force

*Roadstead* fighter operation against enemy shipping in the Channel

*Rob Roy* air-dropped resupply operation for airborne units

**ROC** Royal Observer Corps

*Rodeo* fighter sweep over enemy territory

**ROS** repaired on site

*Roundup* plan for the invasion of Europe in 1943

*Rover* Coastal Command patrol to seek out and destroy enemy shipping

**RP** rocket projectile

**RSF** red spotfire; type of target indicator

**RSU** Repair and Salvage Unit

**SAL** Scottish Aviation Ltd

**SCI** Smoke Curtain Installation fitted to Bostons to lay smoke to conceal the invasion fleet

**SCR** American airborne search radar

**SD** special duty

**SEAC** South East Asia Command

**SEF** single-engined fighter

*Serrate* German radar detection equipment

**SHAEF** Supreme Headquarters Allied Expeditionary Force

*Sledgehammer* British plan for gaining a foothold in France of which *Jubilee* was a part.

**SO** special operations

**SOC** struck off charge (written off)

**SOE** Special Operations Executive; responsible for helping Resistance movements

**Sparrow** HP Harrow (Transport Conversion); slang

*Spartan* an exercise in 1943 to establish how to make an entire airfield unit mobile

**special duty** dropping/landing agents and/or supplies to Resistance groups and collecting agents

**spotfire** type or target indicator

*Starkey* operation in September 1943; a fake invasion of the Pas de Calais

*Stationer* special duty operation

*St Edmund* special duty operation

**stick** paratroopers carried by a single aircraft

**SU** Servicing Unit

*Sunflower* dropping of reconnaissance parties of SAS troops

**Super Roundup** as *Roundup* but including the Americans

**sweep** general term for fighter operation

*Sword* code-name for British assault beach on the right flank of the invasion area

**T** trainer

**Tac/R** tactical report

**TAF** Tactical Air Force

**Tallboy** 12,000lb deep penetration bomb

**TAS** true air speed

*Taxable* window-dropping operation

**TBR** torpedo bomber reconnaissance

**TDU** Torpedo Development Unit

**TEF** twin-engined fighter

**tennis court** a specific location patrolled by a Mosquito FB looking for ground targets

**Tetrarch** air-transportable light tank

**TF** torpedo fighter

*TFN* air patrol along French coast

**TFU** Telecommunications Flying Unit

**TI** target indicator

*Titanic* operation to drop dummy paratroops on 5/6.6.44

**TOBA** Time Over Beach Area

*Tonga* airborne drop and gliderborne landings of 3rd and 5th Parachute Brigade Groups with other 6th Airborne Division troops on the night of 5/6.6.44

**Torbeau** torpedo carrying Beaufighter

*Torch* Allied landings in French North Africa in 1942

**TOT** time on target

**Transportation Plan** bombing of transport centres prior to D-Day

**TRE** Telecommunications

Research Establishment, Defford

**Tsetse** Mosquito armed with 57 mm Molins gun (slang)

**TT** target tug

**TTC** Technical Training Command

*Turbinlite* a searchlight fitted to the nose of a Havoc to illuminate enemy aircraft at night

**Universal Carrier** also known as Bren Gun Carrier; small, tracked infantry vehicle

**UP** unrotated projectile (type of rocket)

**USAAC** United States Army Air Corps

**USAAF** United States Army Air Force

**USAF** United States Air Force

**USS** United States Ship

*Utah* code-name for American assault beach on the left flank of the invasion area

**V-1** Vergeltungswaffe 1 (revenge weapon); Fiesler 103 flying bomb

**WAAF** Women's Auxiliary Air Force

**wads** sandwiches (slang)

*Westminster* special duty operation, radio listening

**White Horsa** fixed-rear Horsa with side access doors

*Window* metalized strips of paper dropped in great quantity to swamp enemy radar with false images

**x-raid** approaching unidentified aircraft

**Yagi** directional aerial array

*Zenit* German reconnaissance flight

**ZG** Zerstörergeschwader (twin-engined fighter unit)

9

# Introduction

Summer 1994 saw the 50th anniversary of Operation *Neptune*, the greatest sea and airborne invasion of all time, and summer 1995 sees the Second World War fall half a century away. Even so, it continues to impact upon our lives. As for the Normandy landings, they produced the most important stepping-stone to victory; the foothold from which much of mainland Europe was freed from Nazi domination. The force required to achieve that – and which included a higher proportion of British and Commonwealth personnel than is often supposed – was then available to serve in the Far East where bombing involving the use of US atomic bombs dealt the most horrendous blow of any wartime deed. That was achieved without the assistance of the other Services; in sharp contrast to the invasion of Normandy which called for the most extensive and finely-tuned inter-service and international co-operation possible. Yet even the enormous force which assaulted France on 6 June 1944 was not officially regarded as having fully secured even the lodgement area until 3 July, the date originally and sensibly chosen in 1994 to commemorate Operation *Neptune*.

It was surely unfortunate that the commemoration of the events of 6 June 1944 dwelt so very heavily just upon the initial landings in Normandy, very courageous though they were. Their success depended much upon the skill of the navies and in particular upon the preparations carried out by the Allied air forces, and many of these are outlined within this book. The air operations during just that one day involved about 40,000 flying personnel, a considerable number by any reckoning, and not unusual on many days in 1944. The contribution to the overall campaign by the independent air forces was vast.

The part played by the American air forces differed considerably from that of the British. The US 9th Troop Carrier Command fielded an enormous transport force whereas RAF strength rested in a large number of fighters. RAF Bomber Command operated much of its front-line strength on 5/6 June and again on 6/7 June, directing around 10,000 tons of bombs at coastal guns and, during the following night, on transport targets adjacent to the battle area. *Oboe* radio-controlled blind marking enabled reasonably accurate bombing whereas H2X radar equipment used by the US 8th AF for attacks much closer to land forces meant that extreme caution was demanded. During 6 June the 600 A-20s and B-26s of the 9th Bomber Command repeatedly carried out heavy raids in direct support of the invading troops; then the RAF's No. 2 Group tactical bombers opened a night interdictor campaign that continued to the end of the war. Coastal Command, the Royal Navy and a few PB4Y-1 Liberators of the US Navy sealed the sea approaches to Normandy, providing vital protection from April until July 1944. The air forces complemented each other, continuing to do so to the end of hostilities.

*AIRCRAFT FOR THE MANY* not only describes the RAF's part in D-Day; it represents a companion volume to *AIRCRAFT FOR THE FEW* (PSL, 1991). For as well as reviewing the RAF's contribution on 5/6 June 1944 and D-Day itself, it outlines the development histories of aircraft types involved and lists those on strength for Operation *Neptune*. Although some continued operating to VE-Day, the listing of Halifaxes and Lancasters highlights the heavy losses Bomber Command endured to the end of hostilities.

A major problem in preparing such collations surrounds the aircraft of the tactical and some home defence squadrons. Beginning six weeks prior to the invasion many were not placed on squadron strength but were assigned instead to back-up units – at least on paper. In substance many were fed into squadrons. The purpose of all this was to allow rapid positioning within units incurring heavy losses during the early days of *Neptune*. On 8 June, with casualties lighter than expected, aircraft were positively assigned to squadrons, in many cases those with which they were already serving. This policy was particularly evident in respect of Typhoon squadrons, and was also applicable to No. 2 Group squadrons. Dating aircraft on each squadron's strength is thus difficult. Readers who can verify individual aircraft flown by the squadrons are invited to contact the author.

Within RAF Official records relating to D-Day the anomalies are many, but it must be realized that the squadrons and organizations which prepared them existed to fight and not to record information! Sorting and correlating material relative to merely this day in the RAF's war has proven a demanding, concentrated, grand-scale exercise undertaken over a number of years. The result does not necessarily accord with what often purports to relate to the D-Day operations, possibly because parameters governing statistics are sometimes uncertain. This becomes clear when one attempts to relate the 'aircraft on strength' returns at 18:00 hrs on 5 June to the listing of individual aircraft likely to have been held.

For the purposes of this book I have worked from the RAF's Form 540/541s, and Operations Records Books of the relevant Commands, Groups, Squadrons, Flights and assorted other units. I have also, over many decades, perused a large number of Official and unoffical files, returns and intelligence assessments. I acknowledge Crown Copyright within Official material, some of which now resides in the Public Record Office, Kew.

My research and recording of D-Day started very soon after the first Allied troops set foot ashore on 6 June, for I began logging the air movements that day as Lancasters of No. 3 Group landed back from Ouistreham at around 07:00 hrs. Those were soon followed by a swarm of B-24s which took 40 minutes to complete passage overhead, thundering over my home town and providing a splendid view of some of the participants. I certainly did not imagine then that half a century later I would be publishing any recollections of that great day. How worthwhile it can prove to keep a diary.

Photographs of the RAF at or around the time of D-Day are far from common. For this book some fine examples have been contributed by Bruce Roberston, Ray Sturtivant and Andrew Thomas, who have kindly dug deeply into their collections to provide excellent and rare illustrations. I am much indebted to them. More came after the Editor of the *Newcastle Chronicle* published a letter to which John Sigmund very kindly responded. He contacted a Czech friend who produced unique photographs of Czech Spitfires, and of activity at the Wing's base at Appledram. Some of the ground views I have included because of the rarity of such pictures. To these have been added Imperial War Museum photographs supplementing some from my own collection.

As the Second World War slides into what, for many, is ancient history, the sacrifice it forced from millions must never be forgotten. Had victory not been ours the European Community as we have come to accept it would be non-existent. Achieving it demanded, to the bitter end, multitudinous displays of courage from many who, in civilian life, would never have faced the type of ghastly moments that were a daily occurrence. Disembarking under shellfire on to the flooded and mined shore of Normandy, suddenly finding oneself engulfed in the flames of a blazing Typhoon, jumping into the darkness of a Norman night, skimming low over a glassy sea seeking E-boats and, for so many, the daunting prospect of facing fierce hand-to-hand combat after a terrible bout of sea-sickness – all were experiences impossible to eradicate from memory. How inconsequential by comparison are the so-called 'problems' of the 1990s, and how grateful we should be that the young are unlikely to face a repeat of those terrible occasions – at least in the forseeable future.

And what of the overall military lessons generated? Some by chance – or automatically – were drawn upon for Operation *Desert Storm* which displayed many ingredients inserted into the campaign to free Europe. Of more importance is a perceptible swing of the military pendulum, yet again showing that while history does not repeat itself it throws up variations derived from the past. Combined army-air operations in the First World War preceded the need for home air defence, after which came the formation of a strategic bomber force and an independent air force. In the 1920s and 1930s that pattern of events was largely repeated and included civil wars and peripheral conflicts on the edges of Europe. Hostilities brought a swing to ever higher fighting before an abrupt change to low attack as the air forces responded to the need to support the armies and defeat the radar challenge. Similar changes of tactics have been a post-war feature. With combined operations presently paramount, our government would be well advised not to ignore a possible, almost probable need for strong home air defence, unlikely as that currently seems. Few power blocs comprised of contrasting, dissimilar nations somewhat unwillingly thrown together last for long, and when they fall apart the consequences are usually laced with bloodshed. We over-dilute our Armed Services at our peril.

Scanning the pages of this book, how apparent is it that in the 1940s British aircraft were undoubtedly the finest in many fields. One could not, sadly, substantiate any such claims in the 1990s. The reasons for that are highly complex, but political will, common sense and self-control are very much lacking. All are prerequisites to most necessary change – along with an enormous improvement in the whole education system. Only time will tell whether history's lessons have again been ignored, and yet another terrible round has to be fought in Europe.

Michael J.F. Bowyer
Cambridge 1994

# Preludes

As the last British soldier left France in 1940, one thing was certain – to win the war the British Army must return to liberate the nation which had so rapidly capitulated, and then go on to release the rest of Europe from a tyrannical regime. Easy to say, so difficult to achieve. Fortunately the English Channel had halted advancing hordes who had devised no plan for its crossing in order to force the British Isles into submission. By that failure they helped considerably to bring about their own downfall. By October 1940 it was abundantly clear that no invasion of Britain could be mounted without many months of planning, and the destruction of Britain's infrastructure as much as of its armed services and an enormous collection of purpose-built military might. While the Luftwaffe waged its unplanned, erratic night offensive the British carefully set the seed from which Operation *Roundup*, the liberation of France and the Benelux countries and ultimate victory would grow.

By late 1941 Operation *Roundup* envisaged the establishment of a lodgement area in France during the second half of 1943. Meanwhile, the Soviet Union, under savage assault by the Nazis, repeatedly asked that a 'second front' be opened. The best that could be done was to persist with the bombing campaign and the war in the North African desert. But suddenly all changed – the Americans were forced into war by the Japanese. Within days of the Pearl Harbor attack the British were revealing to the Americans details of Operation *Roundup*, and a few weeks later it transformed itself into *Super Roundup*, and the Americans were onboard.

During a Combined Chiefs of Staff meeting on 2 March 1942 the decision was taken to make a foray across the Channel. It would to a degree placate the USSR, might encourage the Germans to increase their forces in the West, but far more important would provide valuable experience of what was involved in a cross-Channel combined-forces excursion. As Operation *Jubilee*, it went ahead, part of a new overall plan called Operation *Sledgehammer*, which was a British idea for the establishment of a foothold in France. Operation *Jubilee*, the Dieppe raid of 19 August 1942, highlighted the extreme difficulties involved in landing even a relatively small force on the French shore just to briefly hold a lodgement area. Sustaining it long enough to establish a bridgehead base for an elaborately equipped army would be far harder, and demand overwhelming air and naval superiority which the Allies had still to achieve.

*Jubilee* certainly emphasized what was involved. Air superiority was vital, to protect assembling shipping and assault convoys. Ideally the Channel would need to be sealed at both ends – below as well as above the water. All enemy airfields within a radius of about 100 miles of a landing would need to be destroyed, thus preventing fighter response. Railways leading to the assault area needed closure to prohibit arrival of troop reinforcements. Bridges, too, must be destroyed – and they were small, difficult targets. Coastal defences in the assault area would have to be neutralized. Not least in the initial planning stage, the most suitable stretch of coastline needed to be chosen, then minutely studied. With so much to be done the Allies, in 1942, decided to first clear the Germans out of the whole of North Africa while simultaneously training their forces and starting a carefully planned campaign to reduce the enemy's power.

As early as 1941 the British Combined Chiefs of Staff had chosen the coast between the River Orne and the Vire as the most suitable strip for a landing. The angle of repose of the beach, tidal rise and fall, position relative to British launching havens, proximity of French ports, possibility of providing constant fighter cover and extent of enemy coastal defences – all confirmed the Normandy coast as the most likely for a lodgement to be achieved.

On 26 May 1943 the plan embracing the overall destruction of the Nazi fighting machine in northern Europe was named Operation *Overlord*. During the summer its many components were considered and on 7 September 1943 the latest version of the seaborne landing in France was named Operation *Neptune*. It called for three divisions of troops to land at high tide on a 'narrow front' in Normandy and to be followed by another two on the following tide. Two artificial *Mulberry* harbours would be towed across the Channel and assembled off-shore, allowing constant

*Making plans: General Montgomery and ACM Sir Trafford Leigh-Mallory discuss operations. (IWM CL136)*

support and avoiding the need to capture deep water ports.

On 6 December 1943 came the announcement that an American, Gen Dwight D. Eisenhower, had been appointed Supreme Commander Allied Forces. His deputy, appointed on 17 January 1944, was ACM Sir Arthur W. Tedder GCB, which at least showed the importance attached to the air forces. An assortment of reasons led to Eisenhower being in command, not all of them military. Already commanding the Allied Expeditionary Air Force (AEAF) was ACM Sir Trafford Leigh-Mallory of Battle of Britain fame. The RAF and USAAF were almost equal in strength and complementary, with the USAAF having much superiority in the airlift field and the British in strike aircraft and a vastly more potent bomber force. Into the line-up came the British Army's masterful General Montgomery, 'Monty', veteran of the 1940 French débâcle and victor at El Alamein. A most experienced warrior and a superb leader, he was quick to appreciate that the 30-mile landing front proposed was tactically unsound, for it had no precise edges. The front, he insisted, must extend from the Orne to high ground at the southern extremity of the Cotentin Peninsula. He was right, and his plan meant that two more trained army divisions were needed, and that meant finding more ships, more sailors to man them, more equipment. Had a foreseeing Supreme Commander been appointed earlier, such aspects would have been resolved sooner.

By early 1944, and after months of intricate planning, it was estimated that Operation *Neptune*'s aim to 'secure a lodgement' needed 4,000 assorted vessels just to transport sufficient troops to Normandy for the first day's assault. No military venture before or since has been so extensively and so skilfully planned as *Neptune*. The Operations Order merely for giving details to those manning the ships making the sea crossing filled 700 pages with great detail, and the complexity and extent of signals planning remains breathtaking. No date for the adventure having yet been named, the day was merely designated 'D-Day' until 8 May 1944 when 5 June was chosen for the invasion.

By January 1944 refinement of the assault phase called for the dropping of two airborne divisions to seal the flanks before the seaborne landing of five divisions between Ouistreham and St Martin de Vareville. Two more divisions of troops would join them on the next tide. The British would race inland to take Caen and its airfield, the Americans to the west would have the capture of Cherbourg as an early aim.

Not since 1066 had a largely uninvited army sailed across the English Channel to achieve a successful military invasion – and that had taken place a thousand years after the previous one!

Seaborne invasions have throughout history been fraught with problems – not least of which has been the inability of the landing force to cope with a rough sea. Seasickness is surely the last thing any invader would wish to combat. The possibility of inclement weather hampering Operation *Neptune* had long influenced planning. Indeed, destruction of railways in northern and central France by RAF Bomber Command commenced in April 1944, in case of last-minute bad weather.

Much had to be achieved in the weeks left before *Neptune*. Road and rail bridges, particularly across the Seine below Paris and the Loire below Orléans, certainly had to be smashed. Commenced in earnest on D -30 (D-Day minus 30 days), that was difficult and hazardous, for light AA guns protected many. When V-1 flying-bomb sites mushroomed in north-east France extremely accurate attacks had to be launched in the face of similar defences. By comparison, bridges seemed relatively bold aiming points. Post-war assessment showed that 640 tons of bombs from 'heavies' were needed to achieve success. Fighter-bombers were just as successful using 100–200 tons dropped in about 100 sorties. Typhoons began a dedicated anti-bridge campaign on 21 April 1944 and Spitfire IX dive-bombers also helped, but mainly it was the US 9th AF that undertook the task. Analysis of the AEAF effort against bridges showed:

| Rail | Sorties | Load Bombs/RP |
|------|---------|---------------|
| 78   | 3,897   | 2,784 tons/904 x 60-lb RP |

| Road | Sorties | Load Bombs/RP |
|------|---------|---------------|
| 28   | 987     | 1,210 tons/495 x 60-lb RP |

Essential, too, was the disabling of coastal gun defence batteries, radar stations, radio communication centres and military camps.

Overlooking the assault area were 49 gun batteries, some still under construction. Bombing thickly casemented guns seemed unlikely to be effective, but in the Cherbourg area some weapons were only partly protected. Locating such small targets was difficult, but on 28/29 May seven Mosquitoes accurately marked St Martin de Vareville for attack by 64 Lancasters. Of its four bunkers No. 3 received a direct hit and the others were considerably damaged. Attacks were also carried out by the AEAF on 16 of 18 assault area gun sites, nine effective hits on emplacements being recorded. Of 48 batteries listed for attention from Bomber Command, 14 outside the invasion area could have harmed assembling convoys. Five in the beachhead zone were hit, and 10 attacked on the night of 5/6 June. Attacks on coastal gun batteries between 10 April and 5 June 1944 attracted the following effort:

| | Within assault area | | Outside assault area | |
|---|---|---|---|---|
| | (Sorties) | (Tons) | (Sorties) | (Tons) |
| AEAF | 1,755 | 2,886.5 | 3,244 | 5,846 |
| | | 495 x 60-lb RP | | |
| Bomb C'd | 556 | 2,438.5 | 1,499 | 6,785 |
| 8th AF | 184 | 579 | 1,527 | 4,559 |
| **Total** | **2,495** | **5,904** | **6,270** | **17,190** |

Radars surveying the English Channel were essential pre-invasion targets. Some, controlling coastal gun batteries, would also detect an airborne invasion. On 10 May attacks upon them started in earnest, and also on radar stations controlling Luftwaffe night-fighters. By D-Day, Typhoons during 604 low-level sorties had launched 4,517 rockets against radars, while Spitfire Mk IX bombers and 'Bomphoons' had carried out 759 dive attacks hurling 1,258 x 500-lb bombs onto these well-defended targets. Several skilled attack leaders were, however, shot down. During the three days prior to D-Day the 12 most important of 39 radar sites in the invasion area were intensively raided, as well as two navigation stations – Sortosville and Lanmeur – and four W/T stations. Only 18 out of 92 radar stations usually operating functioned during the invasion, and none was active between Le Havre and Barfleur. Of the large airborne force flying along the west side of the Cherbourg Peninsula the enemy had no warning, and no fighters challenged it.

Other targets were large military camps and vehicle concentration areas. One was the tank depot at Mailly-le Camp, attacked on 3/4 May by Bomber Command Lancasters, and with heavy losses: the raid Main Force Controller's VHF radio was jammed by an American broadcast. As the bombers orbited, awaiting attack orders, German fighters homed in on the No. 5 Group force. They dealt even more severely with No. 1 Group following, resulting in 42 Lancasters failing to return. Mosquitoes, without loss, meanwhile delivered 13 tons of bombs, most spectacularly, to an ammunition dump at Châteaudun, and over 300 Lancasters successfully raided the large military camp at Bourg-Leopold on 27/28 May.

In the face of an ever-increasing onslaught, enemy fighter reaction was remarkably absent. Possible conservation of forces suggested that a fighter-bomber onslaught against the invasion was certain. Accordingly, airfields within a 130-mile radius of the assault area were chosen for destruction mainly by A-20 and B-26 bomb groups of the USAAF, supported by level-bombing Bostons and Mitchells of the RAF's No. 2 Group. The belief was that a week of intensive air battles would still be fought over the beachhead, bringing heavy losses to both sides. To ensure rapid replacement, from early April RAF fighters and fighter-bombers were, on paper, assigned to pool support organizations although retained by squadrons. They could then, if necessary, be ordered where they were urgently needed. German single-engine fighter production between November 1943 and March 1944, planned to total 7,065, actually resulted in only 2,950 examples. RAF night intruders further weakened the German fighter force by concentrating upon operational training stations to reduce crew replacement. No utterly indisputable figures concerning German fighters destroyed or damaged in the invasion run-up period ever became available. Post-war RAF assessment was that between 1 April 1944 – when the lead-in to the invasion was fully launched – and 5 June 1944, 2,655 were put out of action during combat by aircraft operating from Britain. It seems logical to conclude that the enemy did try to conserve stock.

With air superiority essential for *Neptune*, 40 main airfields likely to be used were earmarked for destruction in a campaign commencing on 11 May 1944. A dozen were allocated to Bomber Command and the remaining 28 to the AEAF and the US 8th AF. Another 59 – bomber bases beyond the tactical area – were also listed for attention. Eventually, 91 raids were directed at airfields – 56 by the 9th AF, 17 by the 8th AF, 12 by 2nd TAF and six by Bomber Command. Between them they dropped 6,717 tons of bombs during 3,915 sorties. Although heavily hit, airfields near the lodgement area were repeatedly visited by RAF fighters on D-Day.

Much hinged upon the effectiveness of fighter protection over the beach-head. Extending their duration, Spitfire Mk Vs

*Meeting the Men: Gen Eisenhower, Supreme Commander, visits the Czech Fighter Wing. (via John Sigmund)*

carried slipper tanks while the LF Mk IXs had 90 gal cylinder tanks slung beneath the fuselage. Extensive use of Mk Vs may provoke surprise, but they were quite suitable for low-level protection patrols. RAF fighters flew low- to medium-level sorties over the entire beachhead from 6 June until 3 July, while the USAAF provided top cover.

Fighters covering the assault area on D-Day were given five main tasks, *viz.* cross-Channel convoy protection; neutralization of coastal and beach defences, in part carried out by Typhoons; prevention of air attacks upon the beachhead; dislocation of communications inward of the assault area; and prevention (by ground attack) of supplies and reinforcements reaching enemy ground forces.

The numbers of tactical aircraft in the AEAF, RAF and US 9th AF were complementary and closely matched, as these figures for 1 April 1944 show:

|  | RAF | 9th AF |
| --- | --- | --- |
| Light bombers | 38 | 96 |
| Medium bombers | 70 | 496 |
| Fighters/fighter-bombers | 1,764 | 607 |
| Transports | 225 | 865 |
| Gliders | 351 | 782 |
| Reconnaissance aircraft | 156 | 63 |
| AOP | 164 | 0 |
| **Total** | **2,768** | **2,909** |

As D-Day approached, attacks on rail facilities around the chosen landing area were increased. Some 17 rail focal points still needed to be destroyed, and seven were added – to disguise the area of interest. Then from D -7 (seven days before D-Day), fighter-bombers waged an intensive campaign against the remaining rail tracks, bridges, junctions, tunnels, crossovers – anything connected with railways. Between 9 February and 5 June 1944 the Allied air forces despatched 21,949 sorties against 80 main rail targets, dropping 66,517 tons of bombs in a highly successful campaign.

On 21 May 1944 Allied fighters began another intensive campaign, this time against locomotives in France and the Low Countries. On the first day alone 504 P-47s, 233 Spitfires, 16 Typhoons and 10 Tempests between them claimed 67 locomotives destroyed and 97 damaged; while in Germany 131 P-38s, 135 P-47s and 287 P-51s of the US 8th AF claimed another 91 destroyed and 134 damaged.

During a fortnight of such activity 1,388 'loco-busting' sorties were flown by the AEAF, 3,932 by the Allies in total.

Over many months photographic reconnaissance aircraft roamed across Europe, returning with a vast number of superb photographs of wide-ranging subjects. For over a year they repeatedly photographed the coast between Spain and the German border. Between Granville and Flushing they gathered an amazing array of photographs, including wave-top views of the coastline from three to four miles out from the shore – useful for landing craft commanders. For platoon leaders they obtained zero feet offshore photographs, while for the planners they brought back obliques and verticals taken from 2,000 ft of many tactical items such as selected DZs and LZs, flooded areas and POL dumps. Medium- and low-level photography was particularly the province of RAF and USAAF Mustangs, some armed, supplementing the day and night work of RAF Mosquitoes and high-flying Spitfires.

The belief was strong that the Luftwaffe would have no choice but to attack the 2,000+ ships assembled for the main assault in south coast harbours, and more than 6,000 landing craft and small ships scheduled to join them in the week before *Neptune* was launched. From the Bristol Channel to the Thames Estuary they filled every available parking slot, while ashore thousands of troops gathered in a host of camps. Embarkation practices were necessary, and they surely provided beckoning targets. What was the response of the Luftwaffe to all this?

On 25/26 April 40 aircraft raided Portsmouth, 80 repeating the operation the next night, and instead of concentrating on the harbour they roamed over the Portsmouth–Needles–Basingstoke triangle. On 29/30 April 35 attacked the Plymouth area. Southampton was raided by 100 aircraft on 14/15 May, Weymouth by 80 on 15/16 May. After a pause, 33 bombers operated over the Dartmouth–Start Point area on 28/29 May, and small forces made dispersed, indiscriminate attacks on the two following nights. In total, a pathetic, wasted effort during which night fighters claimed 22 bombers shot down, six probables and five damaged. Two more were credited to AA gunners.

During daylight high-level, low-level

*Tented accommodation at Appledram, and common on southern England's Advanced Landing Grounds. (via John Sigmund)*

and anti-reconnaissance standing patrols protected the assembling armada. Over the six weeks prior to the big day the enemy attempted 125 English Channel reconnaissances and four over the Thames Estuary. Allied fighters responded by patrolling 40 to 50 miles out from the Isle of Wight, and intruders repeatedly raided the enemy reconnaissance aircraft base at Dinard.

Completely ignored by the enemy was the easiest, most vulnerable target of all: those thousands of wooden gliders gathered on the airfields of southern England, and which could have been so easily devastated by incendiary attack. Hardly a bomb fell anywhere near them, or indeed any air transport bases.

And what of the Kriegsmarine's part in thwarting the invasion? The fear was that U-boats might slip into the Channel, so between 1 April and 5 June RAF Coastal Command flew 4,340 anti-U-boat sorties and attacked submarines 22 times. In addition, 103 attacks were delivered on coastal shipping. E- and R-boats constituted a considerable threat, so the entrances to their bases at Boulogne, Le Havre and Cherbourg were mined, by which time the invasion forces – like the storms – were arriving in force: the bad weather, 'that damned British weather!' as Eisenhower called it.

For the invasion to be carried out as scheduled on 5 June, the ships needed to start sailing to their embarkation and assembly areas a week before. But the weather, oh that stormy weather! So far all the preparatory action had gone extremely well, and now, at the vital moment, in rolled deep depressions. On 3 June at Advance HQ, Portsmouth, with the Channel sea state 'rough' and a very low pressure system moving eastwards, an urgent conference was convened for 21:00 hrs. Postponement of Operation *Neptune* would involve mighty upheaval – yet the weather was so *very* bad that at 23:59 hrs the decision was taken; the invasion would be postponed, and the conference would reconvene at 04:00 hrs on 4 June. Whether those involved slept that night is surely unlikely!

By 04:00 hrs the weather was so atrocious that the air forces would have been unable to perform their vital tasks. Therefore, further postponement had to be ordered, and for 24 hrs, with another appraisal to be undertaken at 21:00 hrs. Conditions by then had slightly moderated. The high state of readiness could not be sustained much longer and repeated embarkation and disembarkation of the troops was asking too much of them – and there was an ever-increasing risk of security breaches.

*'Bathroom, ALG, Mk 1'! (via John Sigmund)*

At 04:30 hrs on 5 June, the commanders met once more. They concluded that although the storm on 5/6 June would include a Force 5 wind and remain below that offering minimal conditions for such a vast enterprise, delay would inevitably extend over many days because of the need for suitable tidal conditions. Bad weather, it was argued, also handicapped enemy response, and then consensus was reached. Despite the conditions the operation was just practicable, *Neptune* was on and would open with paratroop and glider landings. Crossing the English Channel would be 1,700 ships carrying the American force and protected by 10 cruisers, three battleships and 35 destroyers. To the east was the British and associated force aboard 2,426 vessels and guarded by 13 cruisers, three battleships and 44 destroyers. Vast arrays indeed, from which, as the high tide of 6 June swept in along the five-Division front, seaborne troops would storm ashore.

At 05:30 hrs five groups of warships began pounding 23 batteries – usually four guns each of between 4.9-in and 6.1-in calibre in 7-ft-thick domes – to produce the heaviest ship-to-shore naval bombardment in history, supported by fearsome rocket barrages released from LCTs. There was amazingly little enemy response. Sunrise came at 06:00 hrs DBST as the high tides

*Tea and 'wads' at Appledram's Cafe Royal! (via John Sigmund)*

*'Airfield No. 134' packed and ready to move. (via John Sigmund)*

began closing in at the western end of the Seine Bay, to be full at 09:45 hrs DBST and again at 00:45 hrs DBST on 7 June. The 1st American Army, seaborne, started storming ashore at 06:30 hrs in the rough water between Varreville and Colleville-sur-Mer, on *Omaha* and *Utah* beaches. The 2nd British Army, five brigades strong, received the signal to go ashore from two midget submarines flashing 'green'. Between Asnelles and Ouistreham the British Army returned, as it vowed it would in 1940,. landing on *Sword* and *Gold* beaches at 07:25 hrs, on *Juno* between 07:35 hrs, and to the left at 07:45 hrs when the tide covered rocks. A mistake had been made for the 'rocks' turned out to be a large bank of seaweed – such is war! Gliders would bring more support during the evening, then follow-on forces would come ashore on the second tide. All went to plan, and the enemy was unable to stop it.

Throughout, the RAF, in close partnership with the Royal Navy and thousands of courageous soldiers of the British Army and their Commonwealth companions, played a highly significant, vital part. For four-and-a-half years, and alone of all the services, it was almost continuously in combat, and in the thick of a fight demanding enormous courage and the endurance of horrendous casualties. For its part in D-Day the RAF relied upon vast numbers of aircraft of unequalled quality, among them the Spitfire, Mosquito and Lancaster. As for its men, many had chosen to come thousands of miles to fight for freedom – from Australia, New Zealand, Canada, South Africa and many Empire lands. The contribution of the Poles, as during the Battle of Britain, was outstanding, for they manned 14 of their own squadrons and were also found in others. Czechs and Norwegians each manned another four squadrons, the Dutch and Belgians another two each. From the large, nearby population of France sufficient airmen had come to man only three fighter squadrons and two bomber squadrons.

All had one aim – to liberate their homelands. To achieve that the English Channel had to be safely crossed. How precious to our well-being that narrow stretch of water has proven. Although history does not repeat itself, it certainly produces alarming equivalents to previous situations. Thus we must never overlook learning about events of the past. Lessons on offer must be appreciated, explored – especially when, as seems feasible in the future, even the strongest political associations are likely to fall apart, plunging Europe once more into tremendously turbulent times.

But now, with the greatest military adventure of all time underway, let Bomber Command – which had paved the way to victory at such great cost in lives and from the very start of hostilities – open this account of the part played by the Royal Air Force during Operation *Neptune*.

# Part One
# The Bombers

In January 1944 the AEAF Bombing Committee unanimously agreed that while no heavy bombers would be transferred to the AEAF, RAF and USAAF strategic forces should, from 14 April 1944, come under the control of the Combined Chiefs of Staff.

Four roles were chosen for the heavyweights: (1) continuance of the strategic offensive against Germany; (2) neutralization of railways, guns, harbours and airfields within 130 miles of Caen, Brest and Nantes; (3) protection of shipping crossing the English Channel; and (4) prevention of enemy reinforcements from reaching the lodgement area. Using 'heavies' against rail targets in direct support of *Overlord* started first. Bomber Command would operate at night to cripple 75 major railway installations in Belgium and France, despite strong political criticism pointing to likely civilian casualties around rail centres, and just when their support would be most needed. HQ Bomber Command also disagreed with the 'misuse' and 'diversion of its strength' from the strategic offensive.

By the beginning of March 1944 sufficient agreement had been reached regarding 'The Transportation Plan' for a trial attack to be mounted where civilian casualties were thought unlikely to exceed 150. On the night of 6/7 March 263 aircraft attacked Trappes, SW of Paris, dropping 1,258 tons in a devastating attack. Widely repeated, that would certainly shatter the entire rail network of north-west Europe. Eight more such attacks were unleashed that month, and more during April and May 1944. Amiens, Aulnoye, Juvisy, Le Mans, Lille, Noisy-le-Sec, Villeneuve-St-Georges, all were hit. Although damage was

extensive a few tracks through the centres soon reopened only to be closed by tactical forces. Overall the effect was devastating, with truck repair facilities and rolling stock hard-hit too.

Although the USAAF was allocated 45 targets, only one had been raided by the end of April, but by D-Day the USAAF had bombed 23, dropping 11,648 tons of bombs. Combined Allied heavy bomber forces had, by 5 June, hurled 66,517 tons of bombs onto 80 rail targets of which 51 were reckoned completely put out of use, 25 required further attention and only four had been little damaged. RAF Bomber Command, at a cost of 203 aircraft out of 8,795 sorties despatched between 6/7 March and 2/3 June, had put 22 in the first and 15 in the second grouping. The enemy's ability to move by rail had been severely curtailed, and repairable lines were fairly easy targets for Allied tactical aircraft. French civilians showed more readiness to accept the loss of their dear ones in the common cause than the politicians had forecast.

Despite the protestations, Bomber Command was ordered to support *Neptune* directly. Prior to D-Day it must destroy four important W/T stations and two radar navigation stations near the forthcoming battle area. Immediately prior to June 1944 coastal gun batteries would be raided, and 10 main batteries would each be bombed by 100 aircraft shortly before the first troops waded ashore in Normandy. Early on 4 June 96 Lancasters of No. 5 Group operating in cloudless conditions destroyed, with a 509 ton load, the Signals Intelligence Station at Ferie D'Urville in the Cherbourg Peninsula, while No. 1 Group bombed the Wimereux heavy guns and No. 3 Group called on the Calais battery. On the night of 4/5 June 69 bombers and 10 pathfinders again raided the Calais battery, 53 Lancasters bombed Sangatte's heavy railway-mounted guns and 63 Halifaxes hit at guns near Boulogne. Although far from Normandy, all could interfere with assembling and passing convoys. Confusion was also generated when 52 Lancasters, through ample cloud, attacked the Maisy battery situated between *Omaha* and *Utah* beaches earmarked for American landings. As a diversion, 20 Mosquitoes bombed Cologne and six more set out for the Argentan railway junction near the intended lodgement area.

The backbone of Bomber Command on the eve of D-Day was its 896 Lancasters. Second most numerous, totalling 549 examples, were the Halifaxes, whose maker was destined to have aircraft in RAF service from its birth in April 1918 to October 1993; an unequalled achievement. Mosquito bombers equipped seven squadrons, while ever fewer Stirling IIIs and the handful of Fortress IIs would play a greater part on 5/6 June than their numbers might suggest.

Bomber Command consisted of seven operational Groups. No. 1 Group, Lancaster-equipped, was based south of Humberside. No. 3 Group, the East Anglian, flew assorted Lancasters, and held the remaining three Stirling bomber squadrons. Additionally, it controlled Nos. 138 and 161 (Special Duty) Squadrons, Tempsford-based and flying Halifaxes supplemented by a handful of Lockheed Hudsons and Westland Lysanders. No. 4 Group and No. 6 (Canadian) Group, Yorkshire-based, were both Halifax-armed. No. 6 (Canadian) Group also held two squadrons of Lancaster Xs. No. 5 Group, Lincolnshire-based, while considering itself *the* Lancaster Group, also had a squadron of Mosquito IVs for low-level spot marking. More Mosquito bombers were found within No. 8 Group, the Pathfinder Force (PFF), which operated Lancasters for bombing as well as back-up marking. Its Mosquito high-speed light night bomber diversion force, which had only existed for some four months was, like the Lancasters, able to deliver 4,000-lb bombs. More Mosquitoes equipped Nos. 105 and 109 Squadrons, relying upon *Oboe* for marking and to repeatedly spearhead

Bomber Command attacks. Still more Mosquitoes – fighters and fighter-bombers found in No. 100 Group – specialized in supporting bomber operations by mounting *Intruder* attacks upon night-fighter aerodromes and engaging airborne enemy fighters. No. 100 Group also carried out radar jamming and 'spoofing' to mislead German radar operators, for which purpose it flew Fortress IIs, Halifaxes, Mosquitoes and Stirling IIIs.

At 18:00 hrs on 5 June, Bomber Command's equipment and strength was as follows:

**MOSQUITO Mk IV/XX**
bombers

| Sqn | Estab | Type/Mark | Serviceable Op | Non-op | Un |
|---|---|---|---|---|---|
| 109 | - | IV | - | - | 1 |
| 139 | 18 | { IV | 6 | - | - |
| | | XX | 3 | - | 2 |
| 627 | 18 | IV | 10 | - | 1 |
| 692 | 18 | IV | 9 | - | 2 |
| **Totals** | **54** | | **28** | **-** | **6** |

**MOSQUITO Mk IX/XVI**
bombers

| Sqn | Estab | Type/Mark | Serviceable Op | Non-op | Un |
|---|---|---|---|---|---|
| 105 | 30 | { XVI | 10 | - | 3 |
| | | IX | 14 | | 2 |
| 109 | 30 | { XVI | 19 | - | 5 |
| | | IX | 6 | - | 1 |
| 139 | - | { XVI | - | - | 2 |
| | | IX | 3 | - | 1 |
| 571 | 20 | { XVI | 15 | - | 5 |
| | | IX | - | - | 1 |
| 692 | - | XVI | 2 | - | 1 |
| **Totals** | **80** | | **68** | **-** | **20** |

**MOSQUITO Mk VI**
bombers

| Sqn | Estab | Type/Mark | Serviceable Op | Non-op | Un |
|---|---|---|---|---|---|
| 617 | - | - | - | - | 1 |
| **Overall** | **134** | | **96** | **-** | **26** |

| Type/Mark | Sqn | Estab (IE + IR) | Serviceable Op | Non-op | Un |
|---|---|---|---|---|---|
| **HALIFAX** | | | | | |
| No. 4 Group (Merlins) | | 16 + 4 | | | |
| II | 77 | - | - | - | 1 |
| II | 78 | - | - | - | - |
| II | 346 | - | - | - | 1 |
| II | 428 | - | 15 | - | 3 |
| V | 346 | 20 | 19 | - | 3 |
| **Totals** | **2 (+3)** | **20** | **34** | **-** | **8** |
| No. 4 Group (Hercules) | | 24 + 6 | | | |
| III | 10 | 30 | 28 | - | - |

| | | | | | |
|---|---|---|---|---|---|
| III | 51 | 30 | 30 | - | - |
| III | 76 | 30 | 24 | - | 3 |
| III | 77 | 30 | 21 | - | 1 |
| III | 78 | 30 | 26 | - | 2 |
| III | 102 | 30 | 27 | - | 5 |
| III | 158 | 30 | 25 | - | 2 |
| III | 466 | 20 | 15 | - | 4 |
| III | 578 | 30 | 29 | - | 2 |
| III | 640 | 20 | 17 | - | 1 |

**No. 6 Group**

| | | | | | |
|---|---|---|---|---|---|
| III | 420 | 20 | 19 | - | 1 |
| III | 424 | 20 | 19 | - | 1 |
| III | 425 | 20 | 20 | - | - |
| III | 426 | 20 | 18 | - | 2 |
| III | 427 | 20 | 17 | - | 1 |
| III | 428 | 20 | 19 | - | 1 |
| III | 431 | 20 | 19 | - | 2 |
| III | 432 | 20 | 20 | 5 | 3 |
| III | 433 | 20 | 20 | - | 1 |
| III | 434 | 20 | 18 | - | 3 |
| **Totals** | **20** | **480** | **431** | **5** | **35** |
| **OVERALL 21(25)** | | **500** | **465** | **5** | **43** |

## LANCASTER I/III
**No. 1 Group**

| | | | | |
|---|---|---|---|---|
| 12 | 20 | 22 | - | - |
| 100 | 20 | 20 | - | - |
| 101 | 30 | 28 | 1 | 1 |
| 103 | 20 | 19 | - | 1 |
| 166 | 30 | 28 | - | 1 |
| 300 | 20 | 19 | - | 1 |
| 460 | 30 | 26 | 4 | 7 |
| 550 | 20 | 19 | - | - |
| 576 | 20 | 19 | - | 1 |
| 625 | 20 | 18 | - | 1 |
| 626 | 20 | 16 | - | 5 |

**No. 3 Group**

| | | | | |
|---|---|---|---|---|
| XV | 20 | 15 | - | 6 |
| 75 | 30 | 27 | - | 3 |
| 90 | 30 | 7 | - | 4 |
| 115 | 30 | 24 | - | 5 |
| 622 | 20 | 16 | - | 7 |

**No. 5 Group**

| | | | | |
|---|---|---|---|---|
| 9 | 20 | 19 | - | - |
| 44 | 20 | 17 | - | 3 |
| 49 | 20 | 21 | - | 1 |
| 50 | 20 | 17 | - | 3 |
| 57 | 20 | 18 | - | 2 |
| 61 | 20 | 19 | - | 1 |
| 83 | 20 | 21 | - | - |
| 97 | 20 | 19 | - | 3 |
| 106 | 20 | 16 | - | 2 |
| 207 | 20 | 16 | - | 6 |
| 463 | 20 | 19 | - | 3 |
| 467 | 20 | 18 | - | 1 |
| 617 | 20 | 32 | - | 1 |
| 619 | 20 | 18 | - | 2 |
| 630 | 20 | 18 | - | 2 |

**No. 8 Group**

| | | | | |
|---|---|---|---|---|
| 7 | 20 | 18 | - | 4 |
| 35 | 20 | 17 | - | 6 |
| 156 | 20 | 16 | - | 4 |
| 405 | 20 | 17 | - | 2 |
| 582 | 20 | 18 | - | 3 |
| 635 | 20 | 18 | - | 1 |
| **Totals** | **37** | **800** | **715** | **5** | **93** |

**Mk II**

| | | | | | |
|---|---|---|---|---|---|
| No. 3 Group | 514 | 30 | 23 | - | 1 |
| No. 6 Group | 408 | 20 | 23 | 2 | 5 |
| **Totals** | **2** | **50** | **46** | **2** | **6** |

**Mk VI**

| | | | | | |
|---|---|---|---|---|---|
| No. 8 Group | 7 | - | - | - | - | 1 |
| | 105 | | 2 | | |
| **Totals** | **2** | **-** | **-** | **2** | **-** | **1** |

**Mk X**

| | | | | | |
|---|---|---|---|---|---|
| No. 6 Group | 419 | 20 | 20 | - | - |
| | 428 | 20 | 1 | - | 5 |
| **Totals** | **2** | **40** | **21** | **-** | **5** |
| **OVERALL** | **41** **(44½)** | **890** | **784** | **7** | **105** |

## STIRLING III
**No. 3 Group**

| | | | | |
|---|---|---|---|---|
| 90 | - | 15 | - | 6 |
| 149 | 20 | 16 | - | 4 |
| 218 | 20 | 16 | - | 4 |
| **Totals** | **3** | **40** | **47** | **-** | **14** |

## No. 100 (Bomber Support) Group

**FORTRESS II**

| | | | | | |
|---|---|---|---|---|---|
| | 214 | 14 | 5 | 4 | 4 |

**MOSQUITO**

| | | | | | |
|---|---|---|---|---|---|
| NF Mk II | 141 | 18 | 13 | - | 3 |
| | 157 | - | - | - | 3 |
| | 169 | 18 | 11 | - | 4 |
| | 239 | 18 | 12 | - | 4 |
| FB Mk VI | 23 | 18 | 16 | - | 2 |
| | 515 | 18 | 15 | - | 3 |
| NF Mk XVII | 85 | - | - | - | 4 |
| NF Mk XIX | 85 | 18 | 16 | - | 2 |
| | 157 | 18 | 13 | - | 5 |

**STIRLING III**

| | | | | | |
|---|---|---|---|---|---|
| | 199 | 20 | 19 | - | 1 |
| **Totals** | **9** | **160** | **120** | **4** | **35** |

**No. 192 Squadron (Mixed)**

| | | | | |
|---|---|---|---|---|
| Anson | 1 | - | 1 | - |
| Halifax III | 10 | 7 | - | 3 |
| Mosquito IV | 7 | 4 | - | ? |
| Wellington X | 7 | 5 | - | 3 |
| **Totals** | **25** | **16** | **1** | **6** |
| **OVERALL** | **10** | **185** | **136** | **5** | **41** |

## No. 3 Group (Special Duties)

**No. 138 Sqn**

| | | | | |
|---|---|---|---|---|
| Halifax V | - | - | 13 | - | 5 |
| Stirling IV | 16 | - | - | - |
| **Totals** | **16** | **13** | **-** | **5** |

**No. 161 Sqn**

| | | | | |
|---|---|---|---|---|
| Halifax V | 6 | 7 | - | 1 |
| Hudson I | - | - | - | 2 |
| Hudson III | 6 | 5 | - | - |
| Lysander | 15 | 13 | - | - |
| **Totals** | **27** | **25** | **-** | **3** |
| **OVERALL** | **2** | **43** | **38** | **-** | **8** |
| **OVERALL GRAND TOTAL** | **82** | **1,792** | **1,566** | **17** | **237** |

## OPERATIONS – 5/6 JUNE 1944

Immediately preceding the Normandy landings the RAF's 'heavies' unleashed Operation *Flashlamp*, the bombing of 10 gun batteries around Seine Bay. Five overlooked the British beach areas, including that by the mouth of the River Orne. The remainder, along the eastern side of the Cherbourg Peninsula, could have interfered with American landing forces. All needed neutralizing, which was far from easy for the guns and their fire control systems were within thick concrete bunkers. Finding and accurately marking these small targets in moonlight would have been a formidable task. Destroying them by bombing through cloud was well nigh impossible – and that was the task that eventually confronted the bombers.

Four Groups would each dispatch two 100-bomber forces to bomb two allocated targets. One of the other two batteries would be tackled by a No. 8 (PFF) Group Main Force, the other by Lancasters of No. 3 Group which would be last in, to attack a battery overlooking Ouistreham beach where British troops would land. Each two-phase Main Force attack followed marking by three Mosquito B Mk IX/XVIs drawn from Nos. 105 and 109 Squadrons, PFF. Ideally, special bombs able to penetrate thick concrete should have been used, but they were few in number and costly. Instead, the bombers would employ British or American GP or MC 1,000 lb and 500 lb high explosive conventional weapons released from between 9,000 and 12,000 ft, to at least 'discourage' the gunners even if the guns could not be destroyed. Bomber Command would also undertake assorted specialized activities.

Secrecy being essential, no bomber aircrews were briefed prior to 18:15 hrs on 5 June. Even then, no mention was made of an invasion of France, but the need for extremely accurate flying was stressed. *Oboe* Mosquito crews headed out from Bourn or Little Staughton to Debden then followed the track Hastings–50° 20'N/00° 00'W–target, thence to 49° 40'N/02° 30'W–Reading–back to bases. Five *Oboe*-equipped Mosquitoes ordered to each target carried out 'parametta' marking, three aircraft making the drops leaving two available in reserve. Flying at between 8,000 and 20,000 ft, these Mosquitoes would each carefully place three long-burn

(LB) red smoke target indicators, one at H -3 minutes with the other two releasing at H -2 and H -1. 'H-hour' was the time on target (TOT) for the Main Force. If *Oboe* failed in each Mosquito at any one target, back-up Lancasters relying upon *Gee* or *H2S* would, at H -1, drop 1,000 lb green TIs.

The Main Force would comprise two waves of approximately 50 aircraft each attacking over four-minute periods to allow for mid-strike remarking if necessary. The entire operation was spread over a six-hour period to limit the number of aircraft over the forthcoming beachhead at any one time. The complexity of the night's activity demanded careful routeing and adherence to signals orders. Crews attacking westerly targets were routed from Bridport east of Cherbourg or south-east from Lyme Bay to follow a course of 70 miles heading for Fecamp, and 20 miles north of Cap Barfleur, before turning southerly along the eastern shore of the Cherbourg Peninsula. Those attacking on the eastern section of Seine Bay flew out southerly from Kent before turning on to a westerly heading at the eastern edge of the Bay to pass Le Havre, and then turning west to pass south of Cherbourg before flying towards the Channel Islands and Sidmouth. Thus, all were kept away from air and sea invasion forces. Correlating the bombing raids with the activities of the many transport aircraft had been a major task. No instructions could be ignored, including a strict order not to fly below 6,000 or above 12,000 ft. Any crew ignoring these instructions was liable to be shot down by Allied forces.

Bomber Command's ability to destroy the gun batteries during fine weather was questionable. To shatter them by bombing through thick cloud layers was expecting too much. Yet despite the very awful conditions, the night's operations proceeded as planned.

Surviving records suggest that Lancaster III *ND990* of 103 Squadron, Elsham Wolds, piloted by Flt Lt D. Allwood and which took off at 21:06 hrs was the first bomber airborne. Its target was at Crisbecq and moments later Plt Off G.W. Chase (Canadian) took off in *ME674* for St Martin de Vareville. Mosquito B Mk IX *LR508*, which left Bourn at 22:03 hrs flown by Sqn Ldr L.W. Millett bound for Crisbecq, was the first marker to set forth. At the latter target, in the Cherbourg Peninsula, bombs began falling at 23:35 hrs DBST. Each Lancaster was minimally loaded with 1,265 gal of petrol, 11 x 1,000 lb bombs and 4 x 500 lb MC bombs. An exception was *Worm Cast*, the Master Bomber's aircraft, operating from 12 Base. Use of IFF during early attacks was banned, and no *Window* was carried. Of the 97 Lancasters drawn from the three No. 1 Group Bases, 93 bombed through thick cloud through which TIs glowed. That scenario was to be repeated at each target.

The second attack involved the remainder of No. 1 Group led by Master Bomber 'Curley'. Beginning at 23:43 hrs the target was St Martin de Vareville, next to the Crisbecq battery, and which had been raided on 29 May. All crews were told not to orbit or hold off, and the *Draw String* Main Force ran in slightly too soon, starting bombing two minutes early. Later that night Lt Col Robert G. Cole led 75 paratroops to the St Martin battery, found wrecked by bombing and unmanned.

As No. 1 Group opened the night's bombing, Lancasters of No. 101 Squadron set forth upon an eventful night of special activity: electronic and voice interference with the German night-fighter control network. The squadron's tactics, devised by No. 14 Base Commander, were planned to ensure that *Airborne Cigar* (*ABC*) equipment aboard the Lancasters would come into play at 23:50 hrs and continue until 04:05 hrs, when the last aircraft needed to quit the patrol area. Reached by way of Gravesend and Bexhill, the patrol zone was within the arc 50° 45'N/00° 50'E to 50° 30'N/00° 20'E and 49° 20'N/02° 00'E to 49° 40'N/02° 30'E. Instead of bombs the 24 Lancasters each carried around 2,154 gal of petrol.

By the time they had reached Bexhill the Lancasters were at 15,000 ft and climbing to patrol heights of between 20,000 and 23,000 ft. First away had been Lancaster I *LL833-O* which, between 22:17 hrs and 05:28 hrs, completed a successful sortie, although thick 10/10 cloud between 12,000 and 25,000 ft brought a very bumpy ride to many other crews and trouble to some equipment. Those aboard *LM479-C*, second to take off, found that their Lancaster could not even attain the ordered patrol height and so aborted. *LL774-U* turned back with navigation aids

unserviceable, and very rough weather made the special duty operator aboard *DV301-Y* very airsick. Unable to coax the aircraft above the turbulent conditions, the pilot aborted the sortie.

After the crew of *DV245-S* had flown a patrol circuit their *Gee* and *ABC* equipment became unserviceable, so they too abandoned their sortie. In icy conditions the ASI aboard *LM472-T* became useless after only two patrol tracks and, with the D/R compass and API both out of action, their sortie was aborted. Intercom trouble later that night forced *LL771-L* to return to base early, which meant that only 16 crews completed the operation according to plan. All managed to land at around 05:00–05:30 hrs – except for *Q-Queenie* which was missing.

At 22:51 hrs Lancaster *ME565-Q* flown by Plt Off E.J. Steele, a New Zealander, had taken off from Ludford Magna. The starboard outer constant speed unit was soon giving trouble and the propeller had to be feathered. In the atrocious weather the aircraft was unable to maintain height, so at 00:44 hrs the crew sent an SOS and called for a position fix. They were given two bearings before ditching at 00:50 hrs some 25 miles south of Beachy Head. HMS *Orwell* rescued them at 02:00 hrs.

No. 101 Squadron's crews reported five sightings of enemy aircraft, three combats over the sea and a Ju 88 as damaged. Radio transmissions during German air activity had been heard from around Montdidier and Neuchatel.

Lancaster crews of No. 101 Squadron were not the only listeners patrolling that night, for at 27,000 ft – and higher – No. 214 Squadron, No. 100 Group, fielded five of its relatively new Boeing B-17F Fortress IIs. Although 14 had reached the Oulton-based squadron only five were available, and the first took off at 22:50 hrs carrying a crew of nine. All five were away within 10 minutes for what proved to be an eventful night in which only *SR381-F* and *SR388-H* completed the planned four runs in either direction along individual patrol lines over the English Channel. Aboard *SR377-M* the crew decided to abandon their sortie after an hour's flying, and at position 50° 47'N/00° 54'E, because the essential intercom system was unserviceable. Sqn Ldr S.R. Jeffrey and crew aboard *SR382-B* were also forced home when, at position

52° 00'N/00° 40'E, their port outer engine caught fire. Even greater trouble was encountered by Wg Cdr D.J. McGlinn and crew when, soon after 02:00 hrs, *SR386-N* was fired upon by what was thought to be an Me 410 whose shots hit their No. 2 engine's turbo-supercharger. That prevented the Fortress from regaining the height lost during combat and, since they were low and off track, the crew abandoned their sortie and landed at Oulton at 03:20 hrs. Returning fire, they claimed to shoot down the Me 410 into the sea. The 38 to 42 megacycle range had been 'one solid mass of *Jostle* jamming'.

While the airborne forces headed for Normandy, Grp Cpt Leonard Cheshire VC, in *LM482-W*, led 16 crews of the famous No. 617 'Dambusters' Squadron undertaking Operation *Taxable*. In two formations, the rear one seven miles behind the leaders, the aircraft within each group flew two miles apart and on a straight seven-mile track, turning on to a reciprocal course; then after seven miles they turned again along the former route, advancing it very slightly towards Cap d'Antifer. Every 12 seconds, 24 bundles of *Window* were released in an operation that began very soon after dusk and continued non-stop through the night. This activity was designed to simulate a large convoy of ships approaching on a 14-mile-wide front a point on the French coast where no invasion was going to occur. Several German radar stations had been left intact, allowing them to detect the feint which was made all the more realistic by including 18 small ships. Some flew Mk VI balloons while others carried reflectors to increase the likelihood of radar detection. Six Stirlings of No. 218 Squadron flew Operation *Glimmer*, a similar feint off Boulogne.

More bizarre still were the activities of 22 Stirlings of Nos. 90 and 149 Squadrons and Halifaxes of Nos. 138 and 161 Squadrons. After taking off at short intervals beginning at 22:22 hrs, they carried out Operation *Titanic* by repeatedly dropping around Yvetot, Malton and Marigny, dummy paratroops filled with fused firecrackers to simulate rifle fire.

A *Mandrel* screen to cloak Allied air activity and confuse enemy radar was produced by Stirlings of No. 199 Squadron, and *Serrate* Mosquito II fighters sought out Luftwaffe night-fighters.

While these specialists exercised their talents, bombing of the gun batteries continued. The third attack involved half of No. 6 Group and comprised five squadrons of Halifaxes and 13 Lancaster Xs of No. 419 Squadron. They tackled Merville/Franceville overlooking the Orne Estuary. Confirming their superior load capacity, the Lancasters each carried 13,440 lb bomb loads and 1,175 gal of fuel whereas the Halifaxes (Mks II and III) managed 10,200 lb or 11,280 lb bomb loads and 1,315 gal or 1,360 gal of fuel respectively. This time, three bundles of *Window* were dropped every minute from position 50° 20'N to the French coast. Some of the bombers passed outwards over Low Zone barrage balloon-protected areas. That caused Billingham's 10-balloon barrage to be close-hauled between 21:30 and 23:00 hrs and again between 01:00 and 08:00 hrs. Over the Thames Estuary the barrage was lowered to 1,500 ft as a safety measure, and at Barry, Bristol, Cardiff, Newport, Port Talbot, Swansea and Weston-super-Mare balloons were flown at 500 ft between 01:15 and 06:00 hrs.

Merville's four field guns, manned by 130 men of the 1716th Regiment and including 75 mm weapons, were protected by thick concrete casements surrounded by machine-gun posts and minefields. Because of its tactical siting the Merville battery had to be neutralized before Allied troops stormed ashore at Ouistreham. Mosquito crews, on arrival over the target, found dense clouds and had to unload their TIs blind, trusting the accuracy of *Oboe*. Lancasters of No. 7 Squadron provided back-up, the mixture of burning TIs and flares producing an indeterminate glow into which bombs rained from 70 of the 86 No. 6 (Canadian) Group Halifaxes and 10 out of 13 Lancaster Xs. No. 6 Group had been chosen to bomb because Canadian troops were to take part in a land assault on the battery. The bunkers in which the guns and control systems were housed still remain largely complete, giving a chance for visitors to understand the task Bomber Command faced.

Sited south of Merville village, the battery had spasmodically been assaulted since March 1944, and 382 tons of bombs from this latest onslaught fell mainly on the

*A Merville gun battery casement, a target for Halifaxes on 5/6 June 1944, photographed in July 1987.*

village of Gonneville-sur-Merville. More exploded among the vanguard of the 9th Battalion, 3rd Parachute Brigade, 6th Airborne Division under the leadership of Lt Col Otway. His contingent of 35 officers, 500 British and 100 Canadian troops had parachuted from Dakotas into the area to take the guns by storm soon after the bombing. Only from 17 of the 108 RAF Dakotas did the troops parachute onto the intended DZ 'V', and two-thirds of the Brigade landed over a wide area. Some of the paratroops arrived too far away to participate in the assault, and by 02:50 hrs Otway's group, numbering only about 150 men, was still 2¹/₂ km from the battery. Reinforcements in Horsa gliders were expected at 04:30 hrs, but one-third of these gliders failed to arrive and mortars for

firing smoke bombs to mark the LZ had earlier been destroyed. One glider succumbed to AA fire, one landed 7 km away and another had a tow failure on take-off.

Nevertheless, and knowing the importance of their task, Otway's small force pressed on. After a fierce 30-minute battle in which some 70 of his men were lost, the Germans gave in and 22 became PoWs. Allied troops destroyed two of the guns and put the others out of action. It transpired that the gunners had been briefed not to fire upon ships but engage any troop advance from the coast.

Halifaxes of No. 4 Group attacked batteries around Maisy-la-Perruque, raided the previous night. Five 155 mm heavy guns here were housed in three large

*General view across the Merville gun battery.*

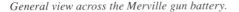

*Mosquito B Mk IV DZ516-O of No. 627 Squadron, undergoing a major 'health check' and, unusually for a bomber, wearing 'invasion stripes', never applied to No. 8 Group's marker Mosquitoes. (via A.S. Thomas)*

concrete casements, and four similar emplacements protected 90 mm guns at Maisy-la-Martiniere. An early casualty was *NA511-C* of No. 77 Squadron, captained by Plt Off C.S. Baldwin, which crashed during take-off, killing the crew.

Assorted Halifaxes participated in this attack, Mk IIIs carrying 8 x 1,000 lb and 7 x 500 lb HEs while Mk Vs, like the Halifax IIIs fitted with H2S, were loaded with 7 x 1,000 lb and 8 x 500 lb bombs. Halifaxes with 13 bomb stations were loaded with 9 x 1,000 and 4 x 500 lb bombs. There were also variations in the number of fuel tanks fitted.

Two thick cloud layers covered the Maisy area, one of 1/10 to 2/10 at 5,000 to 6,000 ft, the other 8/10 to 10/10 extending between 17,000 and 22,000 ft. Cloud breaks allowed the Main Force to undertake fairly concentrated visual bombing, on burning TIs, which began a minute early and overran the TOT by two minutes. Pathfinders responded by carrying out their back-up for nine minutes.

La Pernelle, most northerly of the Cherbourg Peninsula batteries and overlooking *Utah* beach, was to have been raided by No. 4 Group. Because of its importance No. 5 Group, with its low-level marker Mosquito force backing the PFF, was substituted, and the nine-squadron force set out at around 01:20 hrs. Wg Cdr Jendwine acted as Master Bomber for 122 Lancasters of which only 108 eventually bombed. Moments after the second of the

*Oboe* Mosquito crews released their markers, four Mosquitoes of No. 627 Squadron flew low, illuminating the target with 'spotfires'. Two 54 Base Lancasters then followed, dropping green TIs. Marking, at first scattered, soon became concentrated. Instructions called for the Main Force to arrive on target at H +2 min, and to attack in four three-minute waves. Instead, the loads of 11 x 1,000 lb and 4 x 500 lb HEs per aircraft began falling at 03:35 hrs – several minutes early – before marking was perfected, and through 6/10 to 10/10 cloud which again penalized accuracy.

As the seaborne force closed in on Normandy, raids were mounted in quicker succession. The remaining strength of No. 6 Group made for the Houlgate battery overlooking *Sword* beach. Six squadrons, in subjecting the battery to a 10-minute bombardment, crossed the target at between 9,000 and 12,000 ft, with 15 aircraft operating at each 50 ft separation level. Carrying 1,360 gal of petrol, each of the Halifax IIIs forming the bulk of the force carried 7 x 1,000 lb and 8 x 500 lb HEs, those with additional wing tanks carrying two fewer 500 lb bombs. Aircraft not fitted to carry 'thousand-pounders' conveyed 18 x 500 lb bombs.

Half an hour separated the Houlgate operation from the bombing of Longues, a battery E of Cabourg and Dives and near to Arromanches, where the *Mulberry* harbour would be assembled. Almost an all-8

*Production Lancaster IIs had swollen bomb bay doors to accommodate conventional 8,000 lb bombs, plus provision at their aft end for the FN 64A ventral turret. (AWA)*

Group affair, it also included 18 crews of No. 408 Squadron and seven of No. 419 Squadron – both No. 6 Group Lancaster squadrons – the bombing taking place between 04:14 and 04:28 hrs.

Around 02:20 hrs, the next bomber force to attack had begun taking off from Yorkshire, and 15 minutes after the Longues raid Mont Fleury's guns were assaulted by 101 of the 114 Halifaxes which No. 4 Group had despatched. Four of the Group's squadrons – Nos. 10, 51, 76 and 78 – were fielding their entire serviceable strength. Many German gunners had become casualties or were stunned by the ferocious bombing which effectively put their batteries out of action. Two more remained to be bombed.

St Pierre du Mont overlooked the route of the American forces, and was attended to by 105 Lancasters of seven squadrons of No. 5 Group. Mosquitoes of No. 627 Squadron again backed up No. 8 Group's marking, but the bombing mainly undershot the gun emplacements.

The final round was scheduled for 05:05 hrs DBST, equivalent to 03:05 hrs GMT and which, on a very fine, clear morning would have provided a glimmer of daylight. Instead, 6 June 1944 brought a damp, drizzly dawn, so that even as the last Lancasters in the final wave were landing at their bases, they were doing so in very poor light. Led again by PFF Mosquitoes and this time by five Lancasters of No. 635 Squadron, 105 of the 106 No. 3 Group Lancasters operating dropped their loads.

The bombers were a mixed bunch, for Nos. 115 and 514 Squadrons were still operating some Lancaster IIs whereas the other No. 3 Group squadrons – Nos. XV and 622 up from Mildenhall, No. 75 (New Zealand) Squadron from Mepal and 8 Group's No. 635 Squadron – fielded a mixture of Mk Is and Mk IIIs and hybrids variously modified. Some Mk IIs retained FN 64 ventral turret provisioning and dished bomb doors allowing carriage of 8,000 lb HC bombs. The Lancaster Is and IIIs also featured a variety of radio and radar bombing and protection aids. No. 3 Group was never afforded the glamour of some others, yet it took to Ouistreham that morning the most meritorious of the remaining early Lancasters. One, very special, was *L7566-Z* of No. XV Squadron which on 3 March 1942 had participated in the first Lancaster operation, the mining of Kiel Bay. Among No. 622 Squadron's contributors were *L7576-K* and *R5625-B* – both very elderly operators. Mildenhall's participants were quite the most outstanding for they also included *LL806-J*, a sortie record holder. Attracting these and others in the final onslaught was a variety of guns including four of 105 mm calibre in casements near the waterworks at Pointe du Siège, and set between the Caen Canal and the River Orne and near Ouistreham. In just two hrs' time British forces would land nearby on an open, flat beach area liberally supplied with pernicious items to prevent just such a venture. Thin, patchy cloud allowed some visual identification of

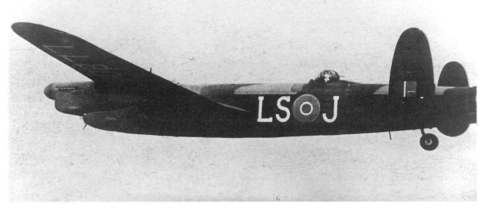

*LL806-J of No. XV Squadron, illustrated in post-war trim, took part in the Ouistreham raid of 5/6 June and attacked Lisieux the following night. It eventually completed 134 operational sorties.*

the Ouistreham guns and two huge explosions were caused in ammunition stores.

Some 5,267 tons of bombs were dropped by the RAF bombers during the 10 raids. Bomber Command research teams, after interrogating surviving gunners, found it impossible to rate the effectiveness of the raids. Conventional bombs could never have penetrated the concrete bunkers, but half of the batteries had been unable to perform. Several of the others ineffectually fired, only to be shelled at first light by naval gunners.

# Summary of attacks by Bomber Command during Operation *Flashlamp*, 5/6 June 1944

NB: Aircraft used are, where known, listed. Some Operations Record Books are incomplete, some entries are without doubt in error. Overall sortie records also differ in detail and totalling. Where possible, all have been checked against other sources.

**1. CRISBECQ (49° 29'N/01° 18'W); by No. 1 Group**
No. 8 Group: 2/5 Mosquitoes marked
 from 23:31–23:32 hrs
No. 1 Group: 93/97 Lancasters bombed
 from 23:35–23:41 hrs

### SQUADRONS AND AIRCRAFT INVOLVED
**Marker Force**
No. 105 Sqn – 3 Mosquitoes:
*ML902-S* released; *LR508-G* and *ML999*
 no release
No. 109 Sqn – 2 Mosquitoes:
*ML997* released; *ML991-S* no release
**Main Force**
No. 12 Sqn – 7 Lancasters:
*LL910-A, LL917-C, LM106-H, LM509-M,*
 *ND528-B, ND799-L* and *PA986*
No. 100 Sqn – 10 Lancasters:

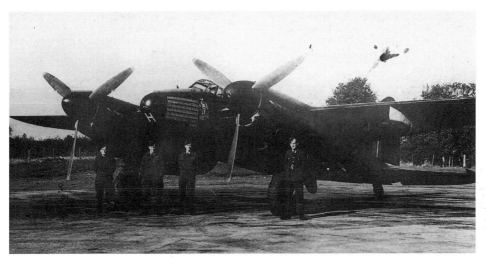

*Mosquito B Mk IX LR504 of No. 105 Squadron marked for the bombing of St Martin's guns, Black undersurfaces were a feature of early Oboe-equipped Mosquitoes.*

ED749-B, JB557-U, LL898-L, LL958-H,
LM321-K, ND388-G, ND413-R,
ND458-A, ND644-N and ND972-W

No. 103 Sqn – 6 Lancasters:
JB655, LM116, LM132, ND990, ND993
and NE173

No. 166 Sqn – 9 Lancasters:
LL896, LM550, ME746, ME812, ME829,
ND614, ND707, NE113 and NE170

No. 300 Sqn – 6 Lancasters:
LL804-F, LL807-N, LL856-O, LM488-D,
??124-M and ??286-C

No. 460 Sqn – 13 Lancasters:
JB700, LL905, LL952, LL957, ME698,
ME744, ME776, ME784, ND656,
NE163, NE164, NE174 and one
uncertain

No. 550 Sqn – 18 Lancasters:
W5005-N, DV279-M, ED562-G, EE193-
C, LL747-P, LL748-D, LL796-O,
LL800-A, LL811-J, LL831-U, LL837-Q,
LL838-S, LL850-L, LM134-H, LM455-
F, LM460-R, ME556-F and PA991-E

No. 576 Sqn – 7 Lancasters:
JA868-J2, LL799-N2, LM122-X2, LM532-
A2, NE115-B2, PB128-S2 and one
uncertain

No. 625 Sqn – 8 Lancasters:
LL897, LL962, LM103, LM512, ME682,
ND459, ND619 and ND742

No. 626 Sqn – 10 Lancasters:
W4967-G2, LM112-A2, LM113-F2,
LM136-D2, ME750-X2, ME830-K2,
ND952-E2, PA990-R2, PA993-H2 and
one uncertain

NB: Sqn identity of a further three
Lancasters used is unknown.

## 2. ST MARTIN DE VARREVILLE (42° 26'N/01° 15'W); by No. 1 Group

No. 8 Group: 5/5 Mosquitoes marked
from 23:43–23:48 hrs

No. 1 Group: 94/95 Lancasters bombed
from 23:48–00:01 hrs

### SQUADRONS AND AIRCRAFT INVOLVED

**Marker Force**

No. 105 Squadron – 3 Mosquitoes:
LR504, ML923-Z and ML982 released

No. 109 Squadron – 2 Mosquitoes:
LR511-R and ML989-C released

**Main Force**

No. 12 Sqn – 13 Lancasters:
JB462, JB716, LL909, LM106, LM137,
ME645, ME758, ME786, ME788,
ND627, ND699, ND749 and ND842

No. 100 Sqn – 10 Lancasters:
JB289-T, JB603-E, LL915-V, LM584-Q,
LM585-S, ME828-F, ND326-J, ND356-
O, ND594-P and PA969-N

No. 103 Sqn – 11 Lancasters:
JB746, LM124, ME674, ME799, ND381,
ND632, NE136, PA985, PA999 and two
uncertain

No. 166 Sqn – 16 Lancasters:
W4994, JB649, LM135, LM386, LM388,
LM581, ME647, ME806, ND399,
ND621, ND626, ND628, ND635,
ND678, ND757 and NE112

No. 460 Sqn – 13 Lancasters:
*JB743, LL907, LL957, LL964, LM547,
ME649, ME696, ME785, ME793,
ND392, ND615, ND864* and one
uncertain
No. 576 Sqn – 11 Lancasters:
*JB460-V2, LM594-G2, ME735-P2,
ME792-Q2, ME800-W2, ME801-C2,
ME810-K2, ND859-L2, ND903-R2,
ND994-F2* and *PA997-D2*
No. 625 Sqn – 10 Lancasters:
*DV278, ED814, ED938, LL956, ME594,
ME733, ND639, ND992, ND995* and
one uncertain
No. 626 Sqn – 8 Lancasters:
*W4990-V2, LL895-Y2, LL961-S2, LM102-
Z2, LM105-P2, ME774-L2, ME830-K2*
and one uncertain
NB: Sqn identity of a further three
Lancasters used is unknown

## 3. MERVILLE/FRANCEVILLE (49° 16'N/00° 12'W); by No. 6 Group
No. 8 Group: 5/5 Lancasters and 3/5
Mosquitoes marked from 00:25–00:31
hrs
No. 6 Group: 70/86 Halifaxes and 10/13
Lancasters bombed from 00:29–00:39
hrs

### SQUADRONS AND AIRCRAFT INVOLVED
**Marker Force**
No. 7 Sqn – 5 Lancasters:
*ND590-B, ND852-D, ND897-C, NE126-R*
and *NE129-G* dropped 53 x 1,000 lb
GPs, 3 x 500 lb GPs and 8 x 1,000 lb
TIs
No. 105 Sqn – 3 Mosquitoes:
*ML919* released; *ML964* and *ML986* no
release
No. 109 Sqn – 2 Mosquitoes:
*ML932-W* and *ML939-D* released

**Main Force**
No. 419 Sqn – 13 Lancasters:
*KB700-Z, KB704-Y, KB707-W, KB712-L,
KB716-D, KB719-T, KB727-H, KB728-
V, KB731-S, KB732-X, KB733-G,
KB734-F* and *KB736-M*
No. 427 Sqn – 17 Halifaxes:
*LV821-N, LV902-T, LV938-A, LV942-Q,
LV945-F, LV987-K, LV995-Y, LW130-L,
LW135-R, LW139-C, LW161-V, LW162-
D, LW163-U, LW165-M, LW166-S,
MZ295-O* and *MZ304-B*
No. 428 Sqn – 15 Halifaxes:

*HR857-K, HR925-I, HR988-C, HX183-E,
JN953-O, JN969-V, JP122-J, JP124-N,
JP127-T, JP191-B, JP197-Q, JP198-G,
JP201-S, JP203-U* and *LW325-A*
No. 429 Sqn – 19 Halifaxes:
*HX339, LV830, LV866, LV950, LV964,
LV965, LV969, LV973, LV993, LW127,
LW128, LW132, LW136, LW139,
MZ282, MZ285, MZ288, MZ302* and
*MZ303*
No. 431 Sqn – 18 Halifaxes:
*LK828-S, LK833-R, LK837-H, LK845-J,
LW572-Q, LW576-O, MZ509-C,
MZ517-D, MZ537-L, MZ602-U,
MZ628-Y, MZ655-T, MZ656-X, MZ658-
E, MZ681-V, MZ685-A, NA498-G* and
*NA499-W*
No. 434 Sqn – 17 Halifaxes:
*LK792-N, LK799-E, LW171-M, LW173-K,
LW174-R, LW176-J, LW389-F, LW433-
W, LW437-X, LW684-O, LW689-A,
LW713-P, MZ293-S, MZ297-Z, MZ626-
T* and two unknown

## 4. MAISY (49° 23'N/01° 04'W); by No. 4 Group
No. 8 Group: 5/5 Lancasters and 5/5
Mosquitoes marked from 03:14–03:23
hrs
No. 4 Group: 100/106 Halifaxes bombed
from 03:19–03:29 hrs

### SQUADRONS AND AIRCRAFT INVOLVED
**Marker Force**
No. 35 Sqn – 5 Lancasters:
*ND691-M, ND731-A, ND907-T, ND936-C*
and *ND933-S* released
No. 105 Sqn – 3 Mosquitoes:
*LR507, ML911* and *ML913* released
No. 109 Sqn – 2 Mosquitoes:
*LR513-V* and *ML907-B* released
**Main Force**
No. 77 Sqn – 15 Halifaxes:
*LL545-T, MZ673-B, MZ694-G, MZ697-L,
MZ698-J, MZ700-O, MZ702-R, MZ704-
P, MZ705-Q, MZ715-Z, NA508-A,
NA511-C, NA512-E, NA515-D* and
*NA524-F*
No. 102 Sqn – 26 Halifaxes:
*LW134-L, LW140-M, LW141-K, LW142-
N, LW143-O, LW158-P, LW159-Q,
LW160-A, LW168-D, LW191-G,
LW192-H, MZ289-J, MZ290-B, MZ292-
C, MZ298-F, MZ642-U, MZ644-V,
MZ646-W, MZ647-R, MZ648-X,
MZ651-Z, MZ652-S, MZ659-T, NA503-*

*A2, NA504-Y* and one unknown
No. 158 Sqn – 23 Halifaxes:
*HX329-Y, HX340-N, HX344-W, HX356-G,
LK760-E, LK808-V, LK839-S, LK863-
G, LK864-Z, LK876-O, LV771-R,
LV790-L, LV907-F, LV917-H, LV920-D,
LV940-J, LW658-U, LW719-Q, MZ286-
X, MZ567-B, MZ580-M, MZ582-T* and
*NA519-A*
No. 346 Sqn – 13 Halifaxes:
*LK728, LK744, LK955, LK999, LL126,
LL131, LL227, LL238, LL242, LL395,
LL396, LL397* and *LL398*
No. 466 Sqn – 13 Halifaxes:
*HX266, LK793, LV837, LV936, LV949,
LV955, LW116, LW178, MZ283,
MZ294, MZ299* and two unknown
No. 640 Sqn – 16 Halifaxes:
*LK757-M, LK866-L, LW446-C, LW463-A,
LW464-F, LW502-Y, LW554-K, LW641-
J, LW652-R, LW654-D, MZ544-Z,
MZ561-B, MZ640-S, MZ678-X, MZ707-
T* and *NA521-P*

**5. LA PERNELLE (49° 37'N/01°
18'W); by No. 5 Group**
No. 8 Group: 4/5 Mosquitoes marked
from 03:31–03:35 hrs
No. 5 Group: 108/122 Lancasters and 2/4
Mosquitoes bombed from 03:35–03:44
hrs

**SQUADRONS AND AIRCRAFT
INVOLVED**
**Marker Force**
No. 105 Sqn – 3 Mosquitoes:
*ML938* and *MM237* released; *ML981* no
release
No. 109 Sqn – 2 Mosquitoes:
*ML900-U* and *ML960-E* released
No. 627 Sqn – 4 Mosquitoes:
*DZ353-B* and *DZ421-C* remarked; *DZ418-
L* and *DZ462-N* not needed
**Main Force**
No. 44 Sqn – 16 Lancasters:
*LL938-S, LL965-C, LM434-F, ME628-V,
ME694-L, ME699-T, ME743-G,
ME791-K, ME804-O, ND552-X,
ND578-Y, ND751-J, ND869-M, ND973-
A, NE138-Z* and *NN697-R*
No. 49 Sqn – 20 Lancasters:
*JB178, JB399, JB701, JB714, LL900,
LL976, LM541, LM572, ME675,
ME808, ND383, ND473, ND512,
ND533, ND647, ND684, ND695,
ND787, ND957* and one uncertain
No. 57 Sqn – 16 Lancasters:

*JB318, LL940, LM114, LM115, LM517,
LM522, LM573, LM579, LM580,
LM582, ME626, ND471, ND954,
NN696* and two unknown
No. 83 Sqn – 20 Lancasters:
*JA705-M, JB309-N, ND333-W, ND442-O,
ND455-U, ND464-S, ND467-B,
ND529-D, ND551-B, ND840-A,
ND854-B, ND856-E, ND858-K,
ND922-J, ND930-Q, ND966-C,
ND974-H, ND979-G, NE165-Y* (Master
Bomber) and *?????-L*
No. 207 Sqn – 17 Lancasters:
*DV383, ED801, LL902, LL973, LM123
(?), LM578, ME667, ME683, ME805,
ME807, ME827, ND567, ND570,
ND866, ND872, NE168* and one
uncertain
No. 619 Sqn – 17 Lancasters:
*DV326-P, EE134-X, JB131-T, LL783-C,
LL808-D, LL969-G, LM420-R, LM484-
M, LM536-Q, ME568-F, ME745-L,
ND935-Z, ND728-N, ND932-U,
ND986-S, NE151-W* and one uncertain
No. 630 Sqn – 16 Lancasters:
*JB290, LL949, LL972, LM117, LM118,
LM537, ME650, ME739, ME782,
ME796, ND335, ND527, ND685,
PA992* and two uncertain

**6. HOULGATE (49° 18'N/00° 04'W);
by No. 6 Group**
No. 8 Group: 4/5 Mosquitoes and 5/5
Lancasters marked from 03:45–03:50
hrs
No. 6 Group: 102/106 Halifaxes bombed
from 03:50–03:59 hrs

**SQUADRONS AND AIRCRAFT
INVOLVED**
**Marker Force**
No. 105 Sqn – 2 Mosquitoes:
*LR497* and *ML973* released
No. 109 Sqn – 3 Mosquitoes:
*ML929-F* and *MM112-L* released; *LR510-
D* no release
No. 156 Sqn – 5 Lancasters:
*ND444, ND618, ND882, ND978* and
*NE119* released
**Main Force**
No. 420 Sqn – 18 Halifaxes:
*LW380-B, LW382-S, LW388-D, LW421-K,
LW575-F, LW645-T, LW674-E, LW676-
Y, MZ505-X, MZ569-R, MZ587-C,
MZ625-Q, MZ687-L, MZ713-U,
NA505-J, NA509-V, NA528-G* and one
uncertain

No. 424 Sqn – 19 Halifaxes:
*HX316-D, LV910-Y, LV951-A, LV953-V,*
*LV959-R, LV961-G, LV970-T, LV991-U,*
*LV997-E, LV998-H, LW113-F, LW117-*
*Q, LW119-O, LW121-X, LW131-J,*
*LW164-C, LW169-L, LW170-I* and
*LW194-W*
No. 425 Sqn – 18 Halifaxes:
*LW379-D, LW381-B, LW387-F, LW391-H,*
*LW394-L, LW467-W, LW672-N,*
*LW680-U, LW715-Q, MZ618-J,*
*MZ620-T, MZ621-O, MZ627-C,*
*MZ641-K, MZ683-A, MZ688-R,*
*MZ714-Y* and *NZ518-G*
No. 426 Sqn – 16 Halifaxes:
*LK796, LK871, LK878, LK879, LK886,*
*LW377, LW384, LW436, LW598,*
*MZ589, MZ597, MZ600, MZ674,*
*MZ690, NA510* and one uncertain
No. 432 Sqn – 17 Halifaxes:
*LK765-B, LK766-V, LW552-S, LW582-M,*
*LW595-Q, LW616-R, LW686-H,*
*MZ586-Y, MZ591-K, MZ603-E, MZ632-*
*W, MZ633-O, MZ660-J, MZ686-U,*
*NA516-F, NA527-N* and one uncertain
No. 433 Sqn – 18 Halifaxes:
*HX268-A, HX275-S, HX280-O, HX290-V,*
*HX353-X, LV839-C, LV842-D, LV911-I,*
*LV966-P, LV967-B, LV972-Q, LV992-N,*
*LW120-E, LW122-F, LW123-W, LW129-*
*G, LW370-T* and *MZ284-J*

**7. LONGUES (49° 21'N/00° 42'W); by
Nos. 6 and 8 Groups**
No. 8 Group: 4/5 Mosquitoes marking
No. 8 Group: 68/69 Lancasters bombing
  from 04:14–04:28 hrs;
1 FTR (156 Sqn) NB: 70 listed
No. 6 Group: 24/25 Lancasters bombing
  from 04:22–04:27 hrs

**SQUADRONS AND AIRCRAFT
INVOLVED**
**Marker Force**
No. 105 Sqn – 2 Mosquitoes:
*LR503* and *ML987* released
No. 109 Sqn – 3 Mosquitoes:
*ML933-T* and *ML967-S* released; *ML990-*
*J* no release
**Main Force**
No. 7 Sqn – 11 Lancasters:
*JA677-U, JA911-A, JB455-N, JB661-L,*
*ND387-L, ND387-O, ND460-W,*
*ND496-T, ND744-F, ND766-S, ND912-*
*P* and *NE122-V*
No. 35 Sqn – 11 Lancasters:
*ND653-N, ND690-O, ND692-P, ND694-*

*H, ND696-E, ND702-G, ND755-B,*
*ND846-J, ND916-F, ND928-Q* and
*NE175-R*
No. 156 Sqn – 11 Lancasters:
*JB186, JB228, JB230, ND340, ND348,*
*ND477, ND577, ND591, ND875,*
*NE120 and NE132*
No. 405, Sqn – 16 Lancasters:
*A, B, D, E, G, H, J, M O, P, Q, T, V, W, X*
*and Y* (serials uncertain)
No. 408 Sqn – 18 Lancasters (6 Group):
*DS688-R, DS692-S, DS700-H, DS707-C,*
*DS708-A, DS727-O, DS768-J, DS830-*
*W, DS848-X, LL617-P, LL636-G,*
*LL643-Q, LL675-K, LL722-N, LL725-Z*
and *LL730-V.* Only 16 correctly listed
on Form 541. Remaining two aircraft
possibly *DS729-D* and *LL675-M*
No. 419 Sqn – 7 Lancasters (6 Group):
*KB708-E, KB718-J, KB720-P, KB723-U,*
*KB724-K, KB726-A* and
*KB735-O*
No. 582 Sqn – 11 Lancasters:
*JA673-L, JB345-Q, ME623-C, ND502-N,*
*ND810-R, ND812-O, ND817-S,*
*ND931-H, ND980-E, NE166-D* (FTR)
and *NE169-J*
No. 635 Sqn – 9 Lancasters:
*JB728-B, ND359-H, ND453-R, ND709-J,*
*ND811-T, ND895-N, ND950-M,*
*ND965-K* and *NE131-D*

**8. MONT FLEURY (49° 20'N/00°
32'W); by No. 4 Group**
No. 8 Group: 5/5 Mosquitoes and 5/5
  Lancasters marked from 04:20–04:37
  hrs
No. 4 Group: 101/114 Halifaxes bombed
  from 04:37–04:49 hrs; 2 FTR

**SQUADRONS AND AIRCRAFT
INVOLVED**
**Marker Force**
No. 105 Sqn – 2 Mosquitoes:
*ML919* and *ML920* released
No. 109 Sqn – 3 Mosquitoes:
*ML907, ML927 and ML991* released
No. 582 Sqn – 5 Lancasters:
*ND750-M, ND899-B, NE130-G, NE140-A*
and *NE172-T* released
**Main Force**
No. 10 Sqn – 23 Halifaxes:
*HX286-R, HX323-M, HX327-N, HX332-P,*
*HX357-J, LK753-S, LK827-X, LV785-*
*C, LV818-K, LV825-G, LV870-H,*
*LV908-F, LV909-L, LV912-A, LW167-*
*O, LW545-Y, LW716-E, LW717-W,*

MZ532-Z, MZ576-T, MZ584-V, NA506-
Q and one uncertain
No. 51 Sqn – 23 Halifaxes:
HX321-H, LK751-T, LK844-M, LV782-I,
LV832-X, LV862-A, LV937-J, LV952-
F2, LW177-B, LW362-Y, LW364-B,
LW442-Q, LW461-D, LW546-R,
LW588-O, MZ535-K, MZ571-C,
MZ581-W, MZ624-E, MZ634-V,
MZ643-Z, MZ689-N and NA493-L
No. 76 Sqn – 24 Halifaxes:
LK747-L, LK785-T, LK831-N, LK832-H,
LK873-S, LW620-G, LW627-J, LW638-
W (FTR), LW644-O, LW646-E, LW648-
A, LW656-B, LW681-Y, MZ516-V,
MZ524-P, MZ528-K, MZ531-D,
MZ539-X, MZ599-U, MZ679-C,
MZ680-R, MZ691-Q, MZ693-F and one
uncertain
No. 78 Sqn – 24 Halifaxes:
LK829, LK838, LK840, LK848, LV796,
LV799, LV820, LV868, LV869, LV872,
LV874, LV915, LV957, LW511, MZ557,
MZ568, MZ577, MZ631, MZ636,
MZ639, MZ692, NA495, NA513 and
one unknown
No. 578 Sqn – 22 Halifaxes:
LK809-H, LK830-N, LK834-E, LK843-A,
LW346-Z, LW473-Q, LW587-V, LW675-
B, MZ511-M, MZ513-K, MZ515-T,
MZ519-U, MZ527-W, MZ543-X, MZ556-P, MZ558-S, MZ559-F, MZ560-
J, MZ572-C, MZ583-Y, MZ592-G and
MZ617-D

## 9. ST PIERRE DU MONT (49° 24'N/01° 00'W); by No. 5 Group

No. 8 Group: 3/5 Mosquitoes marked
from 04:46–04:47 hrs
No. 5 Group: 108/115 Lancasters and 4/4
Mosquitoes bombed from 04:48–05:03
hrs. Three aircraft FTR

### SQUADRONS AND AIRCRAFT INVOLVED

**Marker Force**
No. 105 Sqn – 2 Mosquitoes:
LR500 and ML914 no release
No. 109 Sqn – 3 Mosquitoes:
ML956-R, ML985-O and MM241-M
released
No. 627 Sqn – 4 Mosquitoes:
DZ415-Q, DZ477-K, DZ516-O and
DZ518-F
**Main Force**
No. 9 Sqn – 17 Lancasters:
W4964-J, DV396-G, JA690-M, LL785-F,

LL845-L, LL853-W, LL884-Q, LL901-V,
LL914-U, LL970, LM453-E, LM548-C,
ME579-A, ME704-B, ME757, ME809-X
and ND948-H
No. 50 Sqn – 17 Lancasters:
LL840, LL841, LL842, LL922, LM435,
LM591, ME700, ME798, ME813,
ND874 (FTR), ND991, PA968, PA994,
PA996 and three uncertain
No. 61 Sqn – 19 Lancasters:
JA872, JB138, LL777, LL911, LM452,
LM518, LM590, ME595, ME719,
ME725, ME732, ME783, ME987,
ND865, ND867, ND896, PA998 and
two uncertain
No. 97 Sqn – 19 Lancasters:
JB683-C, ME625-O, ND346-T, ND451-L,
ND452-S, ND495-M, ND501-Q,
ND589-D (Second Controller), ND739-
E (Deputy Controller, FTR; last heard
calling at 05:04 hrs), ND740-F, ND764-
B, ND807-P,
ND815-G (FTR), ND961-N, ND981-H,
NE121-E, NE124-J and PA973-A
No. 106 Sqn – 16 Lancasters:
JB641, JB663, JB664, LL953, LL955,
LL974, LL975, LM570, ME778,
ME789, ND331, ND339, ND680,
ND682, ND868 and NE150
No. 463 Sqn – 14 Lancasters:
DV229, DV280, DV374, HK536, LL847,
LM130, LM551, LM571, LM574,
LM587, ME614, ME615, ME701 and
NE133
No. 467 Sqn – 14 Lancasters:
R5868, DV277, DV372, LL789, LL843,
LL846, LL971, LM100, LM119, LM338,
LM440, LM552, LM583 and ND729

## 10. OUISTREHAM (49° 18'N/00° 15'W); by No. 3 Group

No. 8 Group: 3/5 Mosquitoes and 5/5
Lancasters marked from 05:02–05:07 hrs
No. 3 Group: 105/106 Lancasters bombed
from 05:07–05:15 hrs

### SQUADRONS AND AIRCRAFT INVOLVED

**Marker Force**
No. 105 Sqn – 2 Mosquitoes:
LR504 released; ML995 no release
No. 109 Sqn – 3 Mosquitoes:
ML898-P and ML980 released; MM123-O
no release
No. 635 Sqn – 5 Lancasters:
LM524-G, ND809-C, ND821-X, ND877-P
and ND898-S released

**Main Force**

No. XV Sqn – 20 Lancasters:
*L7566-Z, LL781-L, LL806-J, LL827-Q, LL889-B, LL854-S, LL890-T, LL923-O, LL945-M, LM109-E, LM110-G, LM111-C, LM465-U, LM468-F, LM473-P, LM575-H, LM576-D, LM588-W, ME695-R* and *NE145-K*

No. 75 Sqn – 26 Lancasters:
*HK553, HK554, HK557, LL866, LL921, LL942, LM104, LM544, ME691, ME702, ME751, ME752, ND752, ND756, ND782, ND801, ND904, ND911, ND915, ND917, ND918, ND920, NE148, NE181, PA967* and one uncertain

No. 115 Sqn – 24 Lancasters:
*HK541-P, HK545-E, HK548-W, HK55O-Y, HK551-E, HK552-U, HK555-F, HK556-F, LL864-H, LL943-C, LL944-Z, LM510-A, LM533-T, ME692-G, ME718-G, ME756-V, ME803-D, ND758-Y, ND760-K, ND761-C, ND790-H, ND900-S, ND913-N* and *ND927-B*

No. 514 Sqn – 21 Lancasters ('C' Flt identity: 'A2'):
*DS786-A2:F, DS795-A2:J, DS813-H, DS818-Q, DS822-T, DS842-F, LL620-N, LL635-M, LL670-A2:K, LL677-A2:E, LL678-A2:L, LL690-J, LL692-A, LL697-E, LL703-L, LL716-A2:G, LL726-A2:H, LL727-A2:C, LL728-B, LL733-S* and *LL734-G*

No. 622 Sqn – 15 Lancasters:
*L7576-K, R5625-B, ED430-A, ED474-S, LL802-M, LL803-G, LL812-Z, LL859-Q, LL885-J, LM443-T, LM466-P, LM477-L, LM491-E, ND765-O* and *NE146-F*

## WEAPON LOADS DELIVERED

| Target No. | | 1,000 lb HE (USA) | 1,000 lb HE MC | 1,000 lb GP | 500 lb HE (USA) | 500 lb MC | 500 lb GP | 250 lb TI | 250 lb RSF |
|---|---|---|---|---|---|---|---|---|---|
| 1 | | 1,008 | 902 | - | - | 112 | 256 | 8 | - |
| 2 | | 98 | 935 | - | - | 164 | 212 | 20 | - |
| 3 | H'fax | - | 30 | - | 88 | 508 | 496 | - | - |
| | Lanc (6 Gp) | - | 110 | - | - | 40 | - | - | - |
| | Lanc (8 Gp) | - | - | 53 | - | - | 3 | 1 | - |
| | Mosq (8 Gp) | - | - | - | - | - | - | 12 | - |
| 4 | H'fax (4 Gp) | - | 816 | 7 | - | 428 | 170 | - | - |
| | Lanc (8 Gp) | - | 53 | - | - | - | 3 | 8 | - |
| | Mosq (8 Gp) | - | - | - | - | - | - | 20 | - |
| 5 | Lanc (5 Gp) | 525 | 603 | - | - | - | 398 | 17 | - |
| | Mosq (5 Gp) | - | - | - | - | - | - | 2 | 2 |
| | Mosq (8 Gp) | - | - | - | - | - | - | 20 | - |
| 6 | H'fax (6 Gp) | - | 201 | - | 422 | - | 922 | - | - |
| | Lanc (8 Gp) | 53 | - | - | 3 | - | - | 1 and 4 x 1,000 lb TIs | - |
| | Mosq (8 Gp) | - | - | - | - | - | - | 16 | - |
| 7 | Lanc (6 Gp) | 196 | 66 | 72 | - | - | 24 | - | - |
| | Lanc (8 Gp) | - | 291 | 449 | - | 36 | 192 | 3 | - |
| | Mosq (8 Gp) | - | - | - | - | - | - | 16 | - |
| 8 | H'fax (4 Gp) | - | 804 | - | - | 238 | 373 | - | - |
| | Lanc (8 Gp) | - | 52 | - | - | - | 3 | 8 | - |
| | Mosq (8 Gp) | - | - | - | - | - | - | 20 | - |
| 9 | Lanc (5 Gp) | 697 | 480 | - | - | 64 | 365 | 2 | - |
| | Mosq (5 Gp) | - | - | - | - | - | - | 9 | - |
| | Mosq (8 Gp) | - | - | - | - | - | - | 12 | - |
| 10 | Lanc (3 Gp) | 8 | 1,000 | - | - | 307 | 136 | - | - |
| | Lanc (8 Gp) | - | 53 | - | - | 3 | - | 4 x 1,000 lb TIs | - |
| | Mosq (8 Gp) | - | - | - | - | - | - | 20 | - |

As a diversion early on 6 June, 31/31 Mosquitoes of No. 8 Group reputedly attacked Osnabruck, dropping, between 00:47 and 00:56 hrs, 23 x 4,000 lb MC, 6 x 500 lb MC, 15 x 500 lb GP and 11 x 250 lb TIs. Aircraft used:

139 Sqn: *DZ355-Q, DZ606-M, DZ609-D, DZ635-P, DZ644-V, DZ645-E, KB162-J, KB202-C, KB329, LR475, LR505* and *ML915-F*

571 Sqn: *ML942, ML970, ML976, ML984, MM116, MM118, MM120, MM121*

692 Sqn Mosquito IVs (each carrying 1 x 4,000 lb MC): *DZ599, DZ611, DZ630, DZ633, DZ636, DZ641, DZ642* and *DZ650*; Mosquito XVIs: *ML959* and *ML965*

## BOMBER SUPPORT OPERATIONS, 5/6 JUNE 1944

**No. 1 Group**:

No. 101 Sqn – 24 Lancasters flying Patrol 'D' over the English Channel:
*DV245-S, DV292-E, DV301-Y, DV302-H, LL756-Z, LL757-W, LL758-A, LL771-L, LL773-D, LL774-U, LL779-V, LL833-O* (FTR), *LL863-M, LM369-I, 'LM369-W', LM457-G, LM462-V2, LM472-T, LM474-N2* (?), *LM479-C, LM508-P* (?), *ME565-Q, ME613-M2* and *ME616-B*

**No. 100 Group**:

No. 199 Sqn – 16 Stirling IIIs flying at 18,000 ft operating *Mandrel* jammers until 04:50 hrs, flying outwards to Reading–Portland Bill. Patrol points as follows: 50° 42'N/00° 23'E, 50° 27'N/00° 03'E, 50° 23'N/00° 20'W, 50° 19'N/00° 43'W, 50° 23'N/01° 00'W, 50° 27'N/02° 17'W, 50° 25'N/02° 29'W and 50° 14'N/02° 23'W:
*LJ513-E, LJ518-K, LJ520-Z, LJ525-R, LJ531-N, LJ536-P, LJ538-T, LJ542-G, LJ543-J, LJ560-H, LJ562-V, LJ565-Q, LJ567-Y, LJ569-C, LJ578-S* and *LJ580-X*

No. 192 Sqn – 3 Halifax IIIs flew patrol line Yeovil–Tonbridge: *LW613-W, LW621-Q* and *LW624-T*

No. 214 Sqn – 5 Fortress IIs flew outwards to Reading and Portland Bill to operate Patrol 'D' SE–NW above No. 101 Squadron's altitude. Individual flight plans meant the aircraft operated from the following positions: 50° 15'N/02° 20'W, 50° 07'N/02° 35'W, 50° 00'N/02° 50'W and 49° 50'N/03° 00'N:
*SR377-M, SR381-F, SR382-B, SR386-N* and *SR388-H*

## NO. 100 GROUP MOSQUITO NIGHT-FIGHTER OPERATIONS

No. 141 Sqn – 6 Mosquitoes (plus 6 reserves) operated Patrol 'C':
*DD673-P, DD732-S, DD787-F, DZ240-H, DZ761-C* and *HJ710-T*

No. 169 Sqn – 10 Mosquitoes operated Patrol 'B': *W4076, DD753, DD790, DD799, DZ254, DZ296, DZ310, DZ741, DZ748* and *HJ923*

No. 239 Sqn – 2 Flights of 6+6 Mosquitoes held at advanced readiness; 5 operated Patrol 'A':
*W4074, W4097, DD722, DZ265* and *DZ256* (Flt Lt Welfare shot down a Bf

110 N of Aachen)

Nos. 85, 157 and 515 Squadrons operated *Intruder* patrols under the control of No. 11 (Fighter) Group

## NO. 3 GROUP SPECIALIZED OPERATIONS

No. 90 Sqn – 15 Stirling IIIs flew Operation *Titanic IV* dummy paratroop drops near Marigny:
*BK781-C, EF196-L, EF251-P, EH939-W, EH982-Y, EJ115-K, EJ122-U, LJ477-X, LJ506-V, LJ625-T, LK392-M, LK516-J, LK568-U, LK570-V* and *LK571-O*

No. 138 Sqn – 8 Halifax Vs flew Operation *Titanic I* dummy paratroop drops near Yvetot:
*A, D, E, H, L, M, O* and *R*

No. 149 Sqn – 7 Stirlings flew Operations *Titanic I* and *III* dummy paratroop drops: *EF140-A, EF161-R, EF193-T, EJ109-G, LJ621-M* (FTR), *LK388-L* and *LK385-C* (FTR)

No. 161 Sqn – 4 Halifaxes flew Operation *Titanic IV* dummy paratroop drops near Marigny: *U, W, X* and *Y*

## SPECIAL *WINDOW* DROPS BY NOS. 3 AND 5 GROUPS: ENGLISH CHANNEL

No. 218 Sqn (No. 3 Group) – 6 Stirling IIIs (and two reserves) – Operation *Glimmer*. Led by Sqn Ldr J. Overton (total crew 13) flying *EF133-A*, with *EF207-F, LJ472-K, LJ449-E* (reserve), *LJ517-U* (reserve), *LJ522-N, LJ632-G* and *LK401-J*

No. 617 Sqn (No. 5 Group) – 16 Lancasters – Operation *Taxable*:
*DV246-U, DV385-A, DV393-T, DV402-P, DV403-G, EE131-L, LM482-W, LM485-N, LM492-Q, ME554-F, ME555-C, ME557-S, ME559-Y, ME560-H, ME561-R* and *ME562-Z*

## SPECIAL DUTY OPERATIONS

No. 161 Sqn:

Halifax *T* operated 23:07 to 04:57 hrs – Operation *Politician* – drops in central France.

Hudson *M* – Operation *Westminster* – two agents dropped in Netherlands.

Hudson *A* – Operation *St Edmund* – agent taken to SW of Paris. Hudson *P* – Operation *Harlech* – unsuccessful operation to deliver agent to Roosendaal, Netherlands.

37

# The reaction

The Luftwaffe's response to Bomber Command's night activity is reckoned to have amounted to 54 defensive patrols, 53 of them over the St Omer–Rouen–Beauvais triangle and the Netherlands. Reaction commenced at 22:56 hrs when a German radio station announced that the 'gathering' enemy aircraft were thought likely to operate between Dieppe, Evreux and Chartres between 00:40 and 01:09 hrs, while others were over the Netherlands between 00:08 and 01:04 hrs. Thus, the enemy had somehow detected that British bomber support and intruder Mosquitoes would be operating.

Responding night-fighters of NJG4 and NJG5 were active until about 01:30 hrs. A second phase of Luftwaffe activity took place between about 03:00 hrs and 04:46 hrs to face British intruders expected during landing time. Nine single-engined and six twin-engined enemy fighters were, between 23:40 and 00:05 hrs, reported by bomber crews during the Crisbecq and St Martin operations. After bombing Merville, Halifax crews encountered activity by two single-engined fighters. One of three Ju 88s attacked a Halifax off Alderney, and German fighters followed other Halifaxes as far as Lyme Bay.

Throughout the night the enemy plotted Allied aircraft operating between Cherbourg and Dieppe, and Ju 88 night-fighters in the Paris–Evreux area were, at 23:57 hrs, vectored towards RAF bombers. From the second period of Luftwaffe activity six bombers failed to return, one of which was shot down near Mont Fleury by AA fire. Investigation suggested that of the total loss of 11 aircraft two fell to fighters, one more to AA fire and eight to uncertain causes, including two of the Mosquitoes operating over the Low Countries. One report spoke of two bombers colliding.

During the Maisy raid an Fw 190 was claimed as damaged and the previously mentioned Me 410 engaged by a Fortress II off Sidmouth may have been destroyed. Three fighters were met near La Pernelle, one of which attacked the bombers, and the Houlgate force encountered enemy fighters near Trouville. Aircraft raiding Longues and Mont Fleury reported fighters off Le Havre, and two west of Bayeux between 04:34 hrs and 04:52 hrs. Several Fw 190s from a formation of four attacked a bomber, and another fighter fired rockets. From all of the gun sites assorted slight AA fire was experienced, and rockets were fired from Ouistreham.

Precise combat results remain uncertain, but a Bf 110 was brought down over the Frisians and an Me 410 was also claimed in the Evreux area. The British loss of under one per cent is indicative of the level of surprise and confusion achieved.

## After the dawn

Soon after Bomber Command had completed its tasks, the US 8th AF swung into action, and not for the first time on D-Day. Six B-17s had, during the night, dropped propaganda leaflets over Normandy and 11 *Carpetbagger* B-24s had also operated. Shortly before Allied troops landed, over 900 USAAF 'heavies' bombarded German coastal defences, then gave them a second dose. As the following summary shows, 2,656 B-17 and B-24s operating in poor weather dropped 2,516 tons of HEs on beach areas, and on towns to prevent troop reinforcements getting through. Protecting the bombers generated 555 P-38, 287 P-51 and 505 P-47 sorties. Targets were:

### US 8TH AF OPERATIONS ON 6 JUNE 1944

| B-17 | B-24 | Target | Details |
|---|---|---|---|
| 419/458 | 354/448 | Assault beaches | Bombs on Pt du Hoc |
| 240/364 | 63/95 | Assault beaches | Follow-up raids |
| - /84 | 37/396 | Argentan | Road and railways bombed |
| - / - | 58/73 | Caen | Transport targets |
| 48/72 | - / - | Fleury Harcourt | Bombed by 24 PFF leaders & 24 bombers |
| - / - | 68/73 | Fleury Harcourt | Bombed visually by 19 PFF crews and 49 bombers |
| - / - | 8/12 | Coutances | Road and railways bombed |
| - / - | 26/28 | St Lô | Road and railways bombed |

Official analyses do not detail the targets for an

additional 190 B-17s and 263 B-24s.
Five aircraft failed to return, three from the first three operations. Additional attacks were made by aircraft of the US 9th AF.

## The second night

RAF Bomber Command's aircrews rested during daylight while their aircraft were feverishly prepared to attack enemy troop movements by road and rail. Nine likely movement areas were attacked, and marked in each case by No. 8 Group *Oboe* Mosquitoes with PFF Lancasters providing back-up. Additionally, Nos. 3, 4 and 5 Groups were ordered to mine approaches to French west coast ports and the Scheldt Estuary. A dozen USAAF B-17s dropped more leaflets designed to soothe French nerves. Light Night Striking Force Mosquitoes, 32 in number, bombed Ludwigshaven. The overall night's operations were thus:

| Target | Gp | Sorties FTR Effective/ Total | | TOT |
|---|---|---|---|---|
| Coutances (road, rail) 49° 03'N/00° 53'W (90 Halifaxes, 42 Lancasters) | 8 | 5/7 | - | 00:13-00:24 hrs |
| | 6 | 125/132 | - | 00:17-00:29 hrs |
| Vire (road, rail) 48° 50'N/00° 53'W | 8 | 4/5 | - | 00:31-00:34 hrs |
| | 1 | 105/107 | 3 | 00:34-00:48 hrs |
| St Lô (roads) 49° 07'N/01° 05'W | 8 | 5/7 | - | 00:48-00:59 hrs |
| | 4 | 103/108 | - | 00:50-00:58 hrs |
| Argentan (road) 48° 44'N/00° 01'W | 8 | 8/10 | - | 01:03-01:22 hrs |
| | 5 | 111/112 | - | 01:06-01:46 hrs |
| Lisieux (roads) 49° 08'N/00° 13'E | 8 | 5/7 | - | 01:32-01:43 hrs |
| | 3 | 93/97 | 1 | 01:35-01:50 hrs |
| Conde sur Noireau (roads) 48° 52'N/00° 33'W | 8 | 5/7 | - | 01:47-01:55 hrs |
| | 6 | 106/115 | - | 01:49-02:01 hrs |
| Châteaudun (rail centre) 48° 04'N/01° 20'E | 8 | 3/7 | - | 02:05-02:11 hrs |
| | 4 | 101/105 | 1 | 02:03-02:18 hrs |
| Achéres (rail centre) 48° 58'N/02° 06'E | 8 | 5/7 | - | 02:15-02:20 hrs |
| | 1 | 47/97 | 1 | 02:19-02:31 hrs |
| Caen (roads, etc) 49° 11'N/00° 21'W (No. 5 Group: low attack, 3,000 ft) | 8 | 4/5 | - | 02:31-02:34 hrs |
| | 5 | 121/124 | 6 | 02:32-02:59 hrs |
| Ludwigshafen | 8 | 32/32 | - | 01:08-01:24 hrs |
| Minelaying: (87 mines laid) | 3 | 9/10 | - | 00:14-02:02 hrs |
| | 5 | 2/2 | - | 00:59-01:08 hrs |
| | 4 | 6/6 | - | 01:14-01:20 hrs |

No. 3 Group Stirlings operated as follows:
1 La Pallice, 3 Ushant, 3 Scheldt, 3 off Frisians
No. 4 Group Halifaxes operated as follows:
3 Lorient, 3 St Nazaire
No. 5 Group Lancasters: area uncertain
Bomber Support – No. 100 Group:
18/18 effective sorties; no losses

**TOTAL EFFORT: 1,125 sorties; 1 Halifax and 10 Lancasters FTR**

## Subsequent operations

On 7/8 June 1944, RAF bombers again attacked road and rail targets. Such action, continued on 8/9 June, included the first use of 12,000 lb 'Tallboy' Deep Penetration or 'earthquake' weapons, dropped by No. 617 Squadron to block the Saumur tunnel 125 miles S of the battle area, thus preventing its use by Panzer reinforcements. Lancasters used were: *DV246-U, DV380-X, DV385-A, DV391-O, DV393-T, DV402-P, DV403-G, EE131-L, JB139-V, LM485-N, LM492-Q, ME554-F, ME555-C, ME557-S, ME559-Y, ME560-H, ME561-R* and *ME562-Z*

More communication centres were bombed before Bomber Command resumed the strategic offensive on 12/13 June with an attack on Gelsenkirchen's synthetic oil plant.

A new phase opened on the evening of 14 June when 221 Lancasters led by 13 PFF Mosquitoes raided E-boats in Le Havre, placed there to make night strikes upon Allied shipping in the English Channel. Enemy troop concentrations in the Caen area were bombed, then came a daylight raid on small warships in Boulogne.

Early on 13 June the first V-1 flying bombs were fired against southern England. Bomber Command responded on the night of 16/17 June by striking at four *Noball* main sites while over 400 other aircraft raided the Sterkrade Holten synthetic oil plant. Among those V-weapons attackers were a dozen Merlin-engined Halifax Vs of No. 346 (Free French) Squadron, operating against the V-weapons centre at Domleger. On 17/18 June rail targets and V-weapons storage areas were again targeted by Bomber

Command. Although 346 Squadron's Mk Vs set out for Domleger again, on 19 June, they were recalled. An era had come to an end, for the Merlin-engined Halifax had bowed out of Bomber Command's offensive in north-west Europe.

The fear was that the invasion period, 5 to 7 June 1944, would produce heavy losses. Instead, the strength of Bomber Command changed little, as the daily 18:00 hrs analysis of aircraft available compiled for the Joint Chiefs of Staff shows:

| Type | 5 June | 6 June | 7 June |
|---|---|---|---|
| **Lancaster** | | | |
| I/III | 813 | 819 | 815 |
| II | 54 | 54 | 54 |
| VI | 3 | 3 | 3 |
| X | 26 | 26 | 26 |
| **Total** | **896** | **902** | **898** |
| | | | |
| **Halifax** | | | |
| Bomber | 513 | 508 | 510 |
| Special duty | 26 | 27 | 27 |
| Bomber support | 10 | 10 | 10 |
| **Total** | **549** | **545** | **547** |

| | | | |
|---|---|---|---|
| **Mosquito** | | | |
| Bomber | 123 | 126 | 130 |
| VI | 1 | 1 | 1 |
| IV | 4(?) | 6 | 6 |
| NF II | 49 | 50 | 50 |
| FB VI (100 Group) | 35 | 35 | 35 |
| NF XVII | 4 | 4 | 2 |
| NF XIX | 40 | 36 | 36 |
| **Total** | **256** | **258** | **260** |
| | | | |
| **Stirling III** | | | |
| Bomber | 61 | 58 | 56 |
| Bomber Support | 20 | 20 | 20 |
| **Total** | **81** | **78** | **76** |
| | | | |
| **Fortress II** | | | |
| Bomber Support | 13 | 13 | 13 |
| | | | |
| **GRAND TOTAL** | **1,795** | **1,796** | **1,794** |

Wellingtons, Whitleys and Blenheims, once so familiar, had all gone from Bomber Command squadrons, although some still existed (*see Appendix 2*). Since the Battle of Britain, new types, advanced by the standard of those times had, as the following section shows, replaced them.

# The Avro Lancaster

Of the Lancaster, Air Chief Marshal Sir Arthur Harris wrote: '. . . this emergency design turned out to be, without exception, the finest bomber of the war. The Lancaster far surpassed all other types of heavy bomber . . .' A grand tribute, richly deserved. Astonishing, too, that a Service requirement approved by the Chief of the Air Staff on 24 August 1936 could result in such widely differing aeroplanes as the Halifax, Lancaster and, perhaps even more incredibly, the Mosquito! They certainly had one thing in common, for all had birth pains not of their own making, and in the Lancaster's case it emerged Phoenix-like from its disastrous origins.

All three types were born out of Rearmament Programme F, calling for a bomber force conceived around engines forecast to produce 2,000 hp – the Bristol Centaurus, Napier Sabre and Rolls-Royce Vulture. Government approval was for the total number of bombers, and although the Air Staff really wanted to arm the new Bomber Command with very long-range, four-engined heavy bombers, they decided on grounds of cost to order only 100 of those. Each of the supporting 'twins' was to be the equivalent in cost to three Fairey Battle light bombers and a multi-role aircraft suitable for bomber, general reconnaissance, torpedo bomber and general-purpose roles, for which reason it was strangely designated P.13/36 using the light bomber nomenclature. It would need a six-man crew, a top speed of 275 mph at 15,500 ft, and be able to carry an 8,000 lb bomb load for 2,000 miles or alternatively to accommodate 21 troops.

Companies tendering designs in November 1936 needed to ensure that the aircraft was suitable for catapult launch, a crazy notion that crippled the Avro submission. Official contention was thought to be that no engine would be powerful enough to enable such a heavily

*Long-service Lancaster III* DV326, *as* P-Peter *of No. 619 Squadron, took part in the La Pernelle raid of 5/6 June. (Avro)*

laden 'twin' to take off unassisted. Too late it transpired that concern really surrounded the belief that tyre pressures would be so high that metalled runways would be essential, and the cost of building these had brought concern. Runways, it was argued, were easy to bomb, readily halting operations.

At the P.13/36 Tender Conference in February 1937 two submissions were chosen. First preference was for Avro's scheme, the second for Handley Page's. Whereas the latter was continuing a successful bomber line, A.V. Roe faced a formidable task. With no bomber design background, Roy Chadwick and Roy Dobson had approached the task in a novel way by preparing a design around a large bomb bay which for strength was integral with the wing centre section forming the primary structural component. The 33-ft-long 5 ft 6-in-wide highly capacious bomb cavern was attached to a couple of strong longerons forming its roof and cabin floor. These bearers were attached to two wing spars and an extremely strong wing centre section with a 16 ft chord. As well as forming the heart of the aeroplane, the unit would assist full-scale production. A nose and cockpit section, centre fuselage, rear fuselage, outer mainplanes and wing-tips completed the basic structure. A twin-tail layout was possibly chosen in the belief that it conferred control advantages upon a large, powerful, twin-engined machine with engines attached to the ends of the 28 ft 6 in centre section – as close to the fuselage as the propeller discs permitted.

Avro had not previously tackled the design of an aircraft of over 10,000 lb all-up weight. Yet with no previous experience of stressed skin, all-metal construction, an impressive bomber had been devised featuring a light monocoque fuselage embracing formers and stringers. The daunting task, though, was to keep the all-up weight as low as possible – no higher than 38,000 lb – and to achieve a top speed of 330 mph and a service ceiling of about 24,000 ft. A well-conceived, advanced design, it was ruined by the catapult launch requirement which demanded an extremely strong aircraft which easily became too heavy.

Avro chose for the bomber the Rolls-Royce Vulture, virtually two famous Kestrel vee-cylinder engines married in an X-section powerplant. Handley Page also favoured that engine and a year later Hawker wanted it for their Hurricane fighter replacement, the Tornado. The pressure was on Rolls-Royce to make a

41

success of it – and, at the same time, to produce better and better Merlins and even another new engine, the Griffons.

In March 1937 the Air Ministry agreed to Air Staff plans for the new Bomber Command and replacement with P.13/36s of all medium bombers not delivered by 11 April 1939. The Treasury approved the scheme and on 30 April two prototypes of the Avro bomber were ordered. On 1 July 1937 200 production examples were ordered as specified in Specification 19/37, and the aircraft was soon named Manchester. Deliveries were to begin in January 1940 and Armstrong-Whitworth would help to build them after Whitley production ceased in April 1939, which did not happen.

Avro had designed a modern, 'up-market' Whitley with a wing spanning 72 ft. Rising weight brought a balancing span increase to 80 ft 2 in and compound taper. The Whitley-like tail unit was also modified, the tailplane span increased to 28 ft and the fins were positioned as endplates. All of that, reckoned to improve handling, further increased the all-up weight. Meanwhile, Handley Page had been busy fighting against the catapult idea, and 4 July 1937 brought its cancellation, for Handley Page had convinced the Air Ministry that the new bomber could operate from grass even when overloaded. Then on 26 August the torpedo bomber need was also withdrawn. Further confirmation of the catapult's demise came in September 1937 when the RAE stated that 'no suitable type has yet been designed'. It was at this stage – after much expense and effort – that the question of tyre pressure belief leaked! The change of mind had come too late for much weight-saving in early examples of the Avro bomber, so in May 1938 the company submitted their own plans for a catapult device. They were turned down in July 1938.

Was the over-strong, heavy structure all bad? In later years it permitted a higher, safe gross weight. When in December 1939 the Air Ministry asked for weight reductions, the company replied that replacement tools and jigs would cost some £50,000 and inflict a six- to nine-month delay – unacceptable to the Ministry.

The Avro bomber would carry all its bombs in the fuselage, in a bomb bay physically capable of holding a 12,000 lb load including large girth and long case bombs. For defence it would rely upon an FN 5 two-gun nose turret, FN 4 four-gun tail turret and a retractable FN 21A ventral turret in which the gunner sighted the guns periscopically while his feet were placed in two protruding wells.

Avro decided to keep faith with the Vulture, although it was in serious trouble and likely to suffer production delays. Voicing concern, the Air Ministry on 4 August 1937 told the firm that it should consider Bristol Hercules engines for the first aircraft, Vultures for the second. Formidable technical difficulties were facing Rolls-Royce – and their engine was proving to be heavier than expected, which could only bring more problems to the Manchester. Handley Page decided to abandon the Vulture and redesigned their bomber as a four-Merlin aircraft. Avro's design team in mid-1938 also produced four-motor layouts of their bomber, but these found no official favour because the firm had little bomber experience. Persevere with your twin design, they were told. That did not stop frequent official calls for equipment and detail design changes, and one most welcome came on 11 July 1938 when the dive-bombing idea was sensibly abandoned. Who would wish to have carried out steep dive-bombing in a Manchester? For Avro, bombardment with official ideas seemed endless. One of the most spectacular, of March 1939, was an order that the trio of new large bombers would each now need to feature 20 mm cannon in the dorsal and ventral turret; as exotic an idea as dive-bomber Manchesters.

In spite of so many tribulations, the Manchester prototype L7246 managed to fly first on 25 July 1939. Not surprisingly there was much to criticise, including poor directional and longitudinal stability and heavy controls. But the really big problem manifested itself spectacularly on 30 November 1939 when engine failure caused L7246 to force land on the way to official assessment at Boscombe Down. The aircraft proved that it could not maintain height on just one engine – even lightly loaded. By 10 December 1939, when L7246 eventually reached the A&AEE, it had also acquired a curious and curvaceous small central stabilizer, soon replaced by one of greater area. Without this third fin directional stability had been very poor.

Engine trouble struck again on 12 December and the aircraft ignominiously 'pancaked' on a cabbage patch. Brief handling also showed take-off performance to be exceptionally poor, even at the relatively low weight of 40,000 lb.

Not until January 1940 did the Director of Operational Requirements inform the two manufacturers that the general-purpose and general reconnaissance roles proposed for P.13/36 were no longer needed. It almost goes without saying that during their careers the three types eventually served in both roles!

After lengthy repairs, L7246 returned to Boscombe Down in May 1940, leaving Avro testing an equipped second example, L7247, first flown on 26 May and exhibiting familiar aerodynamic problems. The RAE reckoned that the overweight aircraft's inability to maintain height on one engine might be cured by increased wing area and a span increase. Roy Chadwick, the firm's chief designer, responded and also favoured thinner skinning. Modified elevators were designed and the wing span was increased from 80 ft to 90 ft 2 in. That was relatively straightforward because the wing-tips were detachable. It also made a 45,000 lb take-off satisfactory. But the full fuel load of 1,160 gal and a bomb load of 11,000 lb – which the bomb bay could readily accommodate – could not be carried simultaneously because that increased the all-up weight to 53,000 lb. Following more flight trials, the tailplane span was increased to 33 ft. Directional stability, though, still remained far from good. During test flying, with both prototypes variously modified, the Vulture engines quickly ran to excessive temperatures, and the ventral turret caused buffeting.

Full-scale Boscombe Down trials began on 5 August 1940 when L7276, the first production Manchester, reached the A&AEE. Six weeks later it was replaced by L7277 after another engine failure just after take-off overtook its predecessor. Testing showed the Manchester's maximum speed to be 261 mph at 17,000 ft, that it could climb to 20,000 ft in 30 minutes and had a service ceiling of 22,100 ft. Take-off to clear 50 ft using +9 lb boost took 1,175 ft and the cruise range was 1,220 miles when carrying 1,160 gal of fuel and a 6,000 lb bomb load. With structural strength sufficient to allow an 8,000 lb bomb load, it was such a pity that other factors prevented that.

Despite advantageous modifications, the production situation compelled the first 20 aircraft, L7276-L7295, to be delivered with the 28 ft inadequate span tailplanes. In June 1940 equipment deletion had been called for by Bomber Command, as much to hasten production as to reduce weight, and six of the early aircraft were also

*Avro Manchester L7277 featured the ingredients that made its successor a world-beater. (Avro)*

earmarked for the cannon turrets for which reason full equipment was not embodied in those. Delivery of the aircraft to Bomber Command began in November 1940. A feature of many a Manchester was a strange-looking FN 7 mid-upper turret, first installed in *L7246* during November 1940. Whereas it was many months before that became a standard fitting, early aircraft featured a large central fin which remained a common fixture long after the mid-1941 alternative fitting of 12-ft-tall fins and rudders. The all-up weight of fully-modified examples had risen to 50,000 lb, and the FN 7 turret's airflow effect brought alarming moments, for when the guns were swung full broadside the central stabilizer on several aircraft collapsed due to turbulence.

Operations began on 24 February 1941 and were beset by many problems. On 29/30 June 1941, four of six Manchesters participated in a raid on Hamburg, delivering 2 x 4,000 lb and 10 x 500 lb HE bombs. It was the last operation before engine problems became so serious that on 4 July 1941 Manchesters were grounded, and for a month the squadrons used Hampdens. A typical 45,000 lb Manchester of mid-1941 cruised at 245 mph at 19,000 ft and could carry an 8,000 lb bomb load for only 760 miles. One modified edition, its weight having risen to 50,000 lb, had a possible 1,700 mile range when carrying 8,000 lb. The potential bomb load, even of 12,000 lb, was never drawn upon operationally, with 10,350 lb being set as the highest permissible operational load, and only rarely carried. Manchester production ceased in December 1942, only 201 examples having been completed of the many ordered.

The end had really been brought about when Rolls-Royce independently decided to end Vulture development, and possibly prematurely because by 1942 the complex powerplant was performing fairly satisfactorily. The company, understandably, viewed the Merlin and Griffon as having more potential.

Abandonment of the Vulture could have been very serious, for Avro was to build Hawker Tornado fighters which were also cancelled. The Handley Page Halifax, easier to produce and performing much better than the Manchester, could so easily have fully replaced it. But as early as

March 1940 the DTD was well aware that Avro wanted, as a private venture, to raise the Manchester to four-engined status. The Air Ministry did not consider that a serious proposition, and gave the idea little support.

Like Handley Page, and as early as the autumn of 1937, Avro had considered a four-engined alternative bomber. Two Napier Sabres or Bristol Centaurus radials were other possibilities, both being engines in the 2,000+ hp category. But an alternative four-engine layout for the Avro 679 had more appeal when powered by four Hercules, Pegasus or Taurus radial engines – or even the Rolls-Royce Merlins, production of which was earmarked for fighters and to improve the Whitley.

The outbreak of war had concentrated emphasis on the Manchester, although forecasts suggested it to be both slow and costly to build. Yet necessity was such that by January 1940 the order had increased to 1,200 examples. But, as Vulture problems increased, February 1940 again brought about consideration of a four-Merlin-engined version. This time it was more seriously discussed with the Air Ministry, for Rolls-Royce was already developing the 1,280 hp Merlin XX as a 'power egg' so that an engine, complete with cowling, etc., could be easily attached to a nacelle.

Serious design work on the layout was initiated after encouraging performance calculations, and in May 1940 the newly-formed Ministry of Aircraft Production (MAP) asked that the work be speeded up. The initial scheme was completed during June 1940, the new wing layout to carry Merlin XX power eggs being completed on the basis that the Manchester-type centre section was retained and new outer mainplanes designed. Analysis showed that 70 per cent of Manchester parts could be utilized in a four-motor derivative. Then the Air Ministry expressed concern at any loss of Manchester production, and there were heated discussions in the DTD's office ranging over the whole topic. RAF favour in any case rested with the Halifax, especially since the Stirling was producing cause for concern. There was fear that transferred structural weight of the Manchester would disadvantage a four-motor version. Six times already it had been restressed in the search for better strength ratio, and in a twin-engined bomber weight problems were hard to absorb. While Handley Page had designed a wing 'economical on weight', the Ministry thought Avro would not be able to emulate it. The MAP thought the firm's performance forecasts too optimistic.

After prolonged consideration, the Air Ministry in July 1940 grudgingly gave approval for the four-engined version to go ahead and a contract followed, calling for two prototypes to be built over the next year. Some officials considered that 50,000 lb would be the greatest effective weight of such an aircraft, and that it would be much inferior to the Halifax which already was approaching a 57,000 lb all-up weight embracing increased war load. Roy Dobson strongly disputed such beliefs, claiming that Avro's bomber could also operate at that weight – and when carrying 1,160 gal of fuel. Others contended that the aircraft would just waste productive capacity.

The Avro scheme meanwhile won two good and powerful friends in AM Sir Arthur Tedder and AVM Sir Wilfrid Freeman. Furthermore, Bomber Command's belief was that only four-engined aircraft would by 1941 be capable of reliably delivering heavy loads to distant targets.

A plan had already been made to extend the Manchester's span to 95 ft, and now a further 5 ft was favoured to improve the newcomer's take-off. That meant fitting 7 ft wing-tips to what was now called the Type 683, disguised under the name 'Manchester

III'. 'Lancaster' replaced that in January 1941.

Prototype construction went ahead through autumn 1940 utilizing many Manchester parts and *BT308*, the 'Manchester III', first flew from Ringway on a cold, snowy 9 January 1941. It featured the 33-ft-span tailplane, four Merlin XXs and had new outer mainplanes able to carry additional fuel.

*BT308* hurried to the A&AEE in late January 1941, where the increased span was seen to have much improved the Avro bomber's take-off. General handling, too, was far better, and trials showed a cruising speed of around 240 mph at 4,000 ft. Avro replaced the triple fins with twin 12 ft types before further Boscombe Down tests based upon take-off at 38,000 lb, which showed the full supercharger top speed to be a creditable 310 mph at 22,800 ft. *DG595*, the second prototype, fully-equipped and stressed for an all-up weight of 60,000 lb, first flew on 13 May 1941.

Avro, working fast, 'tidied up' the aircraft for full-scale production, and by June 1941 contracts had been amended to call for 450 Lancasters, Manchester production being accordingly cut. A handful of early production Lancasters had, like *BT308*, a 100 ft wing span, but the advantages of greater span were such that Avro extended the 7 ft wing-tips by another 1 ft. Thereafter Lancasters had a span of 102 ft, and early examples were probably

*Lancaster prototype* BT308 *photographed in January 1941 and displaying its initial triple-fin configuration. (Avro)*

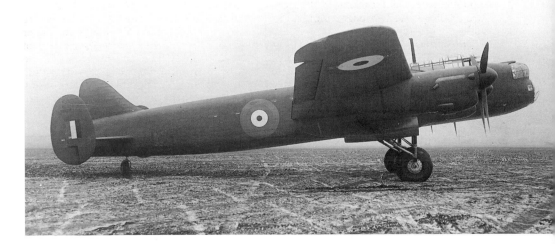

all modified to have the greater span. A further change to the basic fuselage of the Manchester was the fitting of an FN 50 dome-shaped dorsal turret, soon surrounded by combing shaped to prevent the gunner from firing at his own aircraft. A ventral turret was dispensed with, but the potential bomb load remained 12,750 lb. Production delivery started in November 1941, and in December 1941 No. 44 Squadron was first to receive Lancasters. Operations began with mine-laying, then on 11/12 March 1942 two Lancasters dropped bombs operationally for the first time. Expansion of the Lancaster force was phenomenal, production eventually reaching 36 aircraft a week. Had the Manchester I become the Mk III sooner . . . but hindsight is easy to exercise.

Most production Lancasters were remarkably similar to *DG595*, the greatest changes being featured by the Mk II, development of which was launched in February 1941. Belief being that air-cooled engines were better for bombers, Avro were instructed to go ahead with a Hercules VI-powered Lancaster. Although those radial engines were more powerful than the Merlin, the gain was nullified because of their greater weight and drag. Considerable modifications to the fuel supply and other services were needed, as well as different engine nacelles. Like the Merlin XXs, the Hercules engines were delivered as power eggs. Modifications to cowlings, intakes

and propeller spinners followed to reduce drag further. Armstrong Whitworth Aircraft, Coventry, did the design work on the Mk II, the prototype of which, *DT810*, first flew on 26 November 1941. Tests with the 63,000 lb loaded prototype showed its climb, range and cruising speed to be superior to the Mk I, but its ceiling was not as good. Mk IIs entered service with No. 61 Squadron, but first to be fully armed with them was No. 115 Squadron, equipped in March 1943 at East Wretham in No. 3 (Bomber) Group. By June 1943 all production Mk IIs were being initially fitted with dished bomb doors, allowing them to carry an 8,000 lb bomb, in effect two 4,000 lb 'cookies' fastened together, but their use was occasional.

Production Lancaster Mk Is at first had the 1,280 hp Rolls-Royce Merlin Mk XXII, later examples being fitted with 1,620 hp Merlin XXIVs. In theory, either engine could be fitted to a Mk I since they were similar but not identical as regards services.

When US-built Packard Merlin engines became available they powered the Lancaster III. First came the 1,300 hp Merlin 28, then the 1,390 hp Merlin 38, equivalent to the British-built Merlin XXIII and finally the Packard Merlin 224, equivalent to the Merlin XXIV. Although similar to the British Merlin – which made it again possible to produce hybrids – the US Merlins demanded different tools for

*DG585, the second prototype Lancaster, first flown on 13 May 1941 and photographed in November 1941 complete with FN 64 ventral turret. (Avro)*

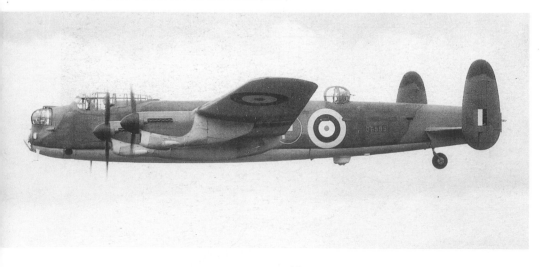

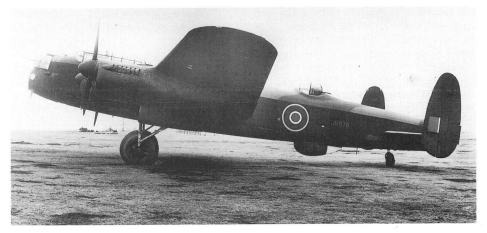

*A few Lancaster VIs with annular-cowled high-altitude rated Merlin engines were built and tried operationally in 1944. JB675 (illustrated) was the prototype. (IWM MH5958)*

differing maintenance procedures. Hybrids did most certainly exist.

Different engines slightly altered performance, but it was the fitting of paddle-bladed propellers that brought a more noticeable performance improvement, adding some 1,500 ft of ceiling and about 8 mph increase in speed, but at the cost of increased maintenance problems.

Available to Bomber Command by D-Day and held by Nos. 7 and 405 Squadrons, No. 8 Group, were examples of the Lancaster VI powered by Merlin 85/87 engines whose armour-plated coolant intakes were wrapped around the sides of the powerplant and which, being of semi-circular shape, reduced drag. Because of improved higher altitude performance, the Mk VIs were placed in the PFF and designed to make full use of radio and radar bombing aids. The Mks IV and Mk V, incidentally, featured a wing span increased to 120 ft and what was termed the 'Universal Nose', which a range of new bombers were to have. They were not available in 1944.

By D-Day, however, 57 examples of the Lancaster X built by Victory Aircraft of

*A 12,000 lb 'Tallboy', of the type first dropped on 8/9 June 1944 by No. 617 Squadron during their attack on the Saumur tunnel, being removed from Bardney's bomb dump. Alongside is a 25 lb practice bomb – somewhat smaller! (via Tim Mason)*

Canada had reached Britain. The newcomer, first flown on 3 August 1943 and recognizable by its *KB* serial range, was equivalent to the Mk III.

On 8/9 June, 18 Lancasters of No. 617 Squadron first dropped 12,000 lb 'Tallboy' Deep Penetration (DP) 'earthquake' bombs. Designed by Barnes Wallis, famous for devising the rotating mines dropped from Lancasters on the German dams in May 1943, 'Tallboy' high-velocity (Mach 3.0) spinning DP weapons were probably of more importance. A Lancaster could carry one of these streamlined bombs designed to collapse structures by shaking their foundations. Nearly half a century later a similar weapon was dropped on Baghdad in an attempt to collapse Saddam Hussein's hideaway.

By D-Day some 3,900 Lancasters had been delivered, production then issuing from five sources in Britain. They formed 53 per cent of Bomber Command's strength. When production terminated, 7,377 Lancasters had been built

The Lancaster was unquestionably the finest heavy bomber which the Allies operated during the European war. As its all-up weight rose from 45,000 lb to 60,000 lb, 63,000 lb, 65,000 lb and eventually 68,000 lb, its operational qualities became ever more superior. In simple terms it could convey a 14,000 lb bomb load for 1,650 miles, 10,000 lb for 2,250 miles. Only the American B-29 and British Lincoln bettered that – and they were later designs. Eventually the Lancaster was modified to

drop even a 22,000 lb 'Grand Slam' bomb. A truly remarkable achievement.

## Operations

The first Lancaster in RAF service was *BT308* which joined No. 44 Squadron at Waddington in mid-September 1941 to provide the squadron with Lancaster experience. But it was the delivery of *L7530*, *L7537* and *L7538* to the squadron on 24 December 1941 that really marked the Lancaster's squadron entry. Its first operational sorties, the laying of mines in Kiel Bay, took place on 3 March 1942.

By the start of March 1942, 61 crews were available to man a handful of Lancasters. On 10/11 March came their first bombing raid when *L7536* and *L7566* operated as part of a 150-aircraft force sent to Essen. There the two Lancasters unloaded 2,520 x 4 lb incendiary bombs.

On 17 April 1942 a dozen Lancasters drawn from Nos. 44 and 97 Squadrons set out in daylight to make a low-level dusk attack on the MAN engine works in Augsburg. Fighters intercepted them near Bernay and opposition at the target was fierce. Consequently only five aircraft returned, one of them, *R5508*, flown by Sqn Ldr J.D. Nettleton who was awarded the Victoria Cross for his gallant leadership. *R5508* lasted well, and between 21 February and May 1944, as *LS-C* of No. XV Squadron, Mildenhall, its home was on a dispersal approximately where the USAF AMC terminal now

*Lancaster* R5868-S *of No. 460 (RAAF) Squadron, a participant in Operation* Flashlamp *and seen at Binbrook, is now in Hendon's Bomber Command museum. (CH20145)*

stands. Build-up was so rapid that 73 Lancasters participated in the Cologne 1,000 bomber raid of 30 May 1942. Whereas in March 1942 Lancasters dropped only 18 tons of bombs, the May total was 361 tons and in July 1942 it rose to an amazing 1,477 tons, already eclipsing the Halifax total of 1,295 tons. By September 1942 the Lancaster bomb tonnage had, at some 2,287 tons, almost doubled itself.

The following month saw nine Lancaster squadrons mount two more dusk raids, 81 of 88 Lancasters drawn from nine squadrons flying a 1,719 mile track to deliver 256 x 1,000 lb HEs and 2,896 x 30 lb incendiaries to the Schneider arms works at Le Creusot. Then on 24 October 73 of 88 Lancasters made a dusk attack on distant Milan. This time the delivered load included a dozen 4,000 lb bombs as well as a large shower of incendiaries. By the end of the year Lancasters had dropped 11,367 tons of bombs, well exceeding the once-favoured Halifax's load of 7,274 tons.

The Lancasters' highest monthly bomb tonnage in 1943 was 14,063, dropped in August, and by the end of the year an amazing 100,517 tons had been dropped compared with 33,480 tons from Halifaxes.

The metamorphosis of the Manchester had been dramatic and quite astonishing. Yet it was not without sorrow, arising from the many losses, as on 15/16 September 1943 when eight Lancasters of No. 617 Squadron set out to breach the Dortmund–Ems Canal using 12,000 lb bombs for the first time. It was a costly failure for only two of the giant bombs fell at the canal and five Lancasters were shot down. Delivery of such large weapons was uniquely carried out by Lancasters, although Halifax II R9457-A of 76 Sqn was, on 10/11 April 1942, first to drop an 8,000 lb HC bomb. It was, in fact, the only one dropped by the Halifax, whereas Lancasters delivered 1,087 examples. Halifaxes released 467 x 4,000 HCs, Lancasters a horrendous 64,391 examples, and only the Lancaster was capable of unleashing the huge 22,000 lb 'Grand Slam' DP weapons, 41 of which had been dropped by the end of the war.

During June 1944 alone, Lancasters released 37,297 tons of bombs and Halifaxes 18,387 tons. That year the Lancaster tonnage totalled 361,004, the

Halifax's 146,113. By the end of the war Lancasters had released a staggering 38,653,351 standard 4 lb incendiary bombs, 2,536,368 explosive variants and over 7,000,000 more within five types of incendiary clusters.

Various yardsticks may be used to compare the effort and success of the RAF's principal bombers, including the following statistics compiled by the Operational Research Section of Bomber Command which showed:

| Type | Total night bombing sorties | Average load/lb per aircraft | Losses | % |
|---|---|---|---|---|
| Manchester | 957 | 5,106 | 62 | 5.6 |
| Stirling | 10,784 | 6,557 | 592 | 4.7 |
| Halifax | 52,024 | 7,849 | 1,733 | 3.3 |
| Lancaster | 108,264 | 9,525 | 3,081 | 2.9 |

### SUMMARY OF LANCASTER OPERATIONAL SORTIES AND LOSSES 1942 – MAY 1945

| | Day | Night |
|---|---|---|
| Sorties despatched | 40,139 | 108,264 |
| Failed to return | 263 | 2,818 |
| Written off | 73 | 401 |

What cannot be measured is the enormous wealth of courage shown by the crews of Bomber Command. It is easy at a distance to criticise wartime bombing policy, which those men carried out so bravely. But it should always be borne in mind that they were generally seen at the time to be retaliating for brutal attacks on our homeland and which so many of us had experienced. Bomber Command was good for our morale, and so was the Lancaster.

# Lancasters on squadron strength, 5/6 June 1944

Listing Lancasters held by squadrons on 5/6 June 1944 is difficult because some aircraft operated on 'loan' with other squadrons of their controlling base, and although official listings of Lancasters operating on the night of 5/6 June appear quite convincing there are many anomalies. Some aircraft are undoubtedly listed in error, with quoted examples having already been shot down, off charge and even yet to enter the squadron's service. Where aircraft individual letters are known to have been in use they have been slotted in against serial numbers. To produce this listing much cross-reference has been necessary. Early Lancasters were completed as Mk Is. *JA/JB*-numbered airframes were generally Mk IIIs, as were *ND*-numbered aircraft. Apart from Mk IIs as noted, *LL*- and *LM*-numbered airframes were Mk IIIs, except for Mk Is in the *LL740-LM310* range. There were, however, in-service engine changes invalidating original mark numbers. Recorded flying hours (where confirmed) are bracketed at the end of entries following 'FTR'. * indicates an aircraft likely to have operated on 5/6 June. The listing certainly provides a reminder of the enormous sacrifice made by the crews of Bomber Command.

## LANCASTERS EFFECTIVE ON SQUADRON STRENGTH, 5 JUNE 1944

### No. 7 Sqn, Oakington

| | |
|---|---|
| *U-JA677 | 25.3.44-6.9.44 |
| *A-JA911 | 22.7.43-28.9.44, 13.11.44-19.11.44 |
| *N-JB455 | 20.12.43-15/16.6.44 FTR (Lens) |
| *L-JB661 | 29.11.43-29.8.44 |
| *O-ND387 | 19.1.44 18.9.44 |
| *W-ND460 | 20.1.44-8.8.44 FTR (Normandy tactical op) (355.15) |
| *T-ND496 | 15.1.44-13.9.44 |
| *B-ND590 | 18.2.44-24.6.44 FTR (V-1 site) |
| *F-ND744 | 23.3.44-16.6.44 FTR (Stuttgart) |
| *S-ND766 | 24.3.44-24.6.44 FTR (V-1 site) |
| ND849 | 5.4.44-5.1.45 |
| *D-ND852 | 6.4.44-26.8.44 FTR (Russelheim) |
| *C-ND897 | 29.4.44-29.6.44 FTR (Siracourt) |
| *P-ND912 | 25.4.44-11.1.45 |
| *V-NE122 | 14.5.44-17.11.44 |
| NE123 | 14.5.44-26.8.44 FTR (Brest) |
| *R-NE126 | 20.5.44-13.9.44 FTR (Frankfurt) (210.40) |
| *G-NE129 | 22.5.44-10.6.44 FTR (Dreux) |
| PA964 | 24.5.44-6/7.10.44 FTR |
| PA974 | 2.6.44-10.6.44 |
| PA978 | 3.6.44-21/22.2.45 FTR |
| PA983 | 3/6/44-12/6/44 |

### No. 9 Sqn, Bardney

| | |
|---|---|
| W4380 | 14.4.44-29.3.44, 3.5.44-25.6.44, 3.7.44-5.9.44 |
| *J-W4964 | 21.4.43-22.6.43, 17.9.43-18.8.43, 18.9.43-?, ?-30.7.44, 4.8.44 – converted to instructional aircraft |
| *G-DV396 | 29.11.43-21.12.43-12.2.44-31.3.44, 29.4.44-14.10.44 |
| *M-JA690 | 19.9.43-4.12.43, 4.2.44-98.7.44 FTR (St Leu d'Esserent) |
| *F-LL785 | 27.1.44-5.7.44 FTR (Creil) |
| *L-LL845 | 1.6.44-8.6.44 |
| *W-LL853 | 4.3.44-24/25.6.44 FTR (Prouville) |
| *Q-LL884 | 18.3.44-12.9.44 EFB, crash-landed in USSR |
| *V-LL901 | 31.3.44-23.6.44, 8.7.44-24.9.44 FTR (257.35) |
| *U-LL914 | 10.4.44-23.9.44 FTR (372.40) |
| *LL970 | 10.5.44-24/25.6.44 FTR (Prouville) |
| *E-LM453 | 6.5.44-31.7/1.8.44 FTR (Rilly la Montagne V-1 site) |
| *C-LM548 | 23.4.44-22.6.44, 15.7.44-24.10.44 |
| *A-ME579 | 2.1.44-22.4.44, 26.4.44-7.6.44 EFB, crashed, Belvoir Castle, Leics |
| *B-ME704 | 25.3.44-22.6.44 FTR (Gelsenkirchen) |
| *O-ME757 | 23.4.44-24.6.44, 8.7.44-13.8.44 FTR (Brest) |
| *X-ME809 | 25.5.44-28.8.44, 23.9.44-11.6.45 |
| ME833 | 6.6.44-19.7.44 FTR (Revigny) |
| ND912 | 25.4.44-11.1.45 |
| *H-ND948 | 23.4.44-24/25.6.44 FTR (V-1 site) |

### No. 12 Sqn, Wickenby

| | |
|---|---|
| *S-JB462 | 12.10.43-24.11043, 15.1.44-30.6/1.7.44 FTR (Vierson) |
| *X-JB716 | 30.11.43-10/11.8.44 EFB |
| *Y-LL909 | 6.4.44-25.7.44, 26.8.44-14.10.44 FTR (Duisburg) (306.50) |
| *A-LL910 | 6.4.44-29.6.44 FTR (Siracourt) |
| *C-LL917 | 14.4.44-22.6.44 Cat E, burnt; crash-landed Wickenby |
| *H-LM106 | 16.5.44-21.7.44 FTR (Courtrai) |

*Lancaster III* U-Uncle *of No. 12 Squadron. (via Tim Mason)*

| | |
|---|---|
| *LM137 | 31.5.44-8.6.44 |
| *M-LM509 | 20.3.44-31.3.44, 6.5.44-3.11-44 |
| W-ME642 | 20.2.44-31.3.44, 12.5.44-24.6.44 FTR (crashed in English Channel) |
| *V-ME645 | 20.1.44-4.11.44 |
| O-ME742 | 10.4.44-7.5.44, 15.5.44-8.6.44 |
| *N-ME758 | 25.4.44-19.10.45, SOC |
| *R ME786 | 8.5.44 25.4.45 |
| *Q-ME788 | 21.5.44-14.10.44 FTR (ditched off Skegness) |
| G-ND424 | 4.1.44-27/28.6.44 FTR (Vaires) |
| *B-ND528 | 1.2.44-24.6.44 FTR (Saintes) |
| *U-ND627 | 20.2.44-5.7.44 FTR (Orleans) |
| *P-DN699 | 1.3.44-29.7.44 FTR (292.05) |
| *J-ND749 | 18.3.44-28.8.44 |
| *L-ND799 | 26.3.44-7.7.44 EFB |
| *K-ND842 | 31.3.44-1.7.44 FTR (Vierzon) |
| *PA986 | 28.5.44-12.6.44 FTR |

## No. XV Sqn, Mildenhall

| | |
|---|---|
| *Z-L7566 | 5.2.44-13.6.44 |
| *L-LL781 | 22.1.44-8.6.44 Cat E, crash-landed Friston |
| *J-LL806 | 22.4.44-6.12-45 SOC |
| *Q-LL827 | 15.2.44-16.6.44 FTR (Chalons-sur-Marne) (135.10) |
| *S-LL854 | 4.3.33-14/15.2.45 Cat AC FB |
| *B-LL889 | 29.3.44-15.6.44 FTR (Le Havre) (143.40) |
| *T-LL890 | 29.3.44-6.7.44 FTR (Wizernes) (197) |
| *O-LL923 | 7.5.44-5.1.45 FTR (Ludwigshafen) |
| *M-LL945 | 8.5.44-7/8.6.44 FTR (Massy-Palaiseau) |
| *E-LM109 | 21.5.44-22.8.44, 5.9.44-25.9.44 FTR (Calais) |
| *G-LM110 | 5.6.44-13.9.44 FTR (Frankfurt) |
| *C-LM111 | 90 Sqn aircraft, 8.8.44 FTR (Normandy) |
| LM142 | 3.6.44-25.7.44 FTR (Stuttgart) |
| LM156 | 4.6.44-13.6.44 FTR (Gelsenkirchen) |
| *U-LM465 | 16.2.44-13.6.44 FTR (Gelsenkirchen) |
| *F-LM468 | 20.2.44-11.6.44 FTR (Dreux) |
| *P-LM473 | 21.2.44-25.3.44, 15.4.44-29.11.44 |
| *A-LM534 | 7.5.44-8.6.44 FTR (Massy-Palaiseau) |
| *H-LM575 | 5.6.44-8.6.44 FTR (Massy-Palaiseau) |
| *D-LM576 | 5.6.44-21.6.44 EFA, burnt, crashed West Row, Mildenhall |
| *W-LM588 | 90 Sqn aircraft |
| *K-NE145/G | 90 Sqn aircraft |
| *R-ME695 | 18.3.44-7.6.44, 17.6.44-1.7.44 |
| ND958 | 24.4.44-25.5.44, 10.6.44-1.11.44 |
| PB112 | 30.5.44-29.11.44 |
| PB115 | 30.5.44-2.11.44 FTR |

## No. 35 Sqn, Graveley

| | |
|---|---|
| ME621 | 25.3.44-10.6.44 |
| ND555 | ?-27.9.44 |
| ND646 | 7.3.44-28.1.45 |
| *N-ND653 | 7.3.44-13.8.44 |
| *O-ND690 | 1.3.44-30.11.44 |
| *M-ND691 | 13.3.44-12.9.44 FTR (Wanne-Eickel) (334.55) |
| *P-ND692 | 7.3.44-7.8.44 |
| *H-ND694 | 6.3.44-7.8.44 |
| *E-ND696 | 8.3.44-25.4.44, 6.5.44-7.8.44 |
| *G-ND702 | 11.3.44-12.9.44 FTR (Gelsenkirchen) (280.55) |
| ND703 | 11.3.44-13.9.44 |
| *A-ND731 | 16.3.44-5.7.44 FTR (Villeneuve) (201.35) |

| | |
|---|---|
| ND734 | 12.3.44-24.6.44 FTR (V-1 site) (77) |
| *B-ND755 | 27.3.44-19/20.10.44 FTR (Stuttgart) |
| *J-ND846 | 4.44-5.7.44 (Villeneuve) |
| *T-ND907 | 29.4.44-28.11.44 |
| *F-ND916 | 29.4.44-5.1.45 |
| *Q-ND928 | 26.4.44-30.11.44 |
| ND929 | 30.4.44-9.5.44, 27.7.44-13.8.44 |
| *S ND933 | 25.1.44 30.11.44 |
| *C-ND936 | 30.4.44-30.11.44 |
| *R-NE175 | 30.5.44-25.7.44 FTR (Stuttgart) |
| PA966 | 31.5.44-10.6.44 |
| PA972 | 3.6.44-12.6.44 |

## No. 44 Sqn, Dunholme Lodge

| | |
|---|---|
| *S-LL938 | 22.4.44-22.6.44 FTR (Wesseling) |
| *B-LL939 | 57 Sqn aircraft |
| *C-LL965 | 6.5.44-12.9.44 FTR (Darmstadt) |
| *F-LM434 | 28.12.43-22.6.44 FTR (Wesseling) |
| *Q-LM592 | 31.5.44-22.6.44 FTR (Wesseling) |
| *V-ME628 | 1.2.44-25.6.44 FTR |
| ME634 | 2.2.44-8.5.44, 24.6.44-8.7.44 FTR (St Leu d'Esserent) |
| *L-ME694 | 18.3.44-26.7.44 FTR (Stuttgart) |
| *T-ME699 | 18.3.44-5.7.44 FTR (St Leu d'Esserent) |
| *G-ME743 | 10.4.44-28.7.44 FTR (Mimoyecques) |
| *K-ME791 | 5.44-11.6.44 |
| *O-ME804 | 27.5.44-22.6.44 FTR (Wesseling) |
| ND517 | 21.1.44-8.4.44, 3.6.44-18.7.44 FTR (Colombelles) (290.40) |
| *E-ND519 | 22.1.44-6/7.6.44 FTR (Caen) |
| *X-ND552 | 27.1.44-22.6.44 FTR (Wesseling) |
| *Y-ND578 | 27.1.44-21.7.45 |
| ND631 | 20.2.44-10/11.2.45 FTR (Leipzig) |
| *J-ND751 | 13.3.44-25.6.44 FTR (Pommerval) |
| *M ND869 | 11.4.44-16/17.3.44 FTR, crashed at sea |
| *A-ND973 | 11.5.44-22.6.44 FTR (Wesseling) |
| *Z-NE138 | 11.5.44-27.8.44 FTR, mining |
| *R-NN697 | 25.5.44-10.6.44 FTR (Etampes) |

## No. 49 Sqn, Fiskerton

| | |
|---|---|
| *JB174 | 97 Sqn aircraft |
| *JB178 | 4.9.43-19.7.44 FTR |
| *JB399 | 3.10.43-26.11.44 |
| JB473 | 17.10.43-19.7.44 FTR |
| *JB701 | 29.11.43-28/29.7.44 FTR (Stuttgart) |
| *JB714 | 29.11.43-10.6.44 FTR (Etampes) |
| *LL900 | 30.3.44-22.6.44 FTR (Wesseling) |
| *LL976 | 12.5.44-8.7.44 FTR (St Leu d'Esserent) |
| *LM541 | 1.5.44-8.7.44 FTR (St Leu d'Esserent) |
| *LM572 | 2.5.44-25.6.44 FTR (Pommerval) |
| *ME675 | 1.3.44-22.6.44 FTR (Wesseling) |
| ME787 | 7.5.44-29.8.44 |
| *ME808 | 29.5.44-22.6.44 FTR (Wesseling) |
| *ND383 | 21.12.43-25.3.44, 29.4.44-29.8.44 |
| *ND473 | 14.1.44-5.1.45 FTR (collision over France) |
| *ND512 | 21.1.44-27.11.45 |
| *ND533 | 21.1.44-9.6.44 FTR (Etampes) |
| *ND647 | 20.2.44-26.11.44 |
| ND683 | 29.2.44-22.6.44 FTR (Wesseling) (116.35) |
| *ND684 | 1.3.44-19.7.44 FTR (Revigny) (341.05) |
| *ND695 | 5.3.44-21/22.6.44 FTR (Wesseling) |
| *ND787 | 26.3.44-10.9.44 |
| ND792 | 30.3.44-12.5.44, 24.6.44-11.9.44 |

51

*ND957  27.4.44-2.9.44

## No. 50 Sqn, Skellingthorpe
*LL840  25.2.44-22.6.44 FTR (Gelsenkirchen)
*LL841  26.2.44-9.6.44 FTR (Rennes)
*LL842  26.2.44-25.7.44 FTR (Stuttgart)
*LL922  18.4.44-8.8.44 FTR (Secqueville)
        (321.40)
*LM435  31.12.43-10.8.44 FTR (Chatellerault)
*LM591  25.5.44-6.7.44, 2.9.44-24.9.44)
*ME700  18.3.44-24.9.44 FTR (Dortmund–Ems
        Canal)
*ME798  15.5.44-25.6.44 FTR (Prouville)
        (137.65)
*ME813  28.5.44-8.8.44 EFA, overshot, SOC
        22.8.44 (210.25)
*ND874  8.4.44-6.6.44 FTR (St Pierre du
        Mont) (176.15)
*ND991  2.5.44-6.10.44
NE135   11.5.44-1.6.44, 9.8.44-13.8.44 FTR
        (Russelheim)
*PA968  21.5.44-24/25.7.44 FTR (Donges)
*PA994  30.8.44 FTR (Königsberg)
*PA996  30.5.44-8.7.44 FTR (St Leu
        d'Esserent)

## No. 57 Sqn, East Kirkby
*JB318   21.9.43-7.6.44, 24.6.44-19.7.44 FTR
*F-JB486 21.10.43-24.3.44, 7.4.44-5.7.44 FTR
*LL939   22.4.44-27.4.44, 10.6.44-11.11.44
         FTR (Harburg) (344.50)
*LL940   23.4.44-7.1.46
*LM114   24.5.44-22.6.44, 19.8.44-26.11.45
*LM115   24.5.44-22.6.44 FTR (Wesseling)
*LM517   24.3.44-8.8.45
*LM522   24.3.44-10.4.44, 22.4.44-8.7.44 FTR
         (St Leu d'Esserent)
*LM573   14.5.44-22.6.44 FTR (Wesseling)
*LM579   24.5.44-20.7.44, 28.7.44-26.8.44 FTR
         (Darmstadt)
*LM580   10.5.44-22.6.44 FTR (Wesseling)
*LM582   24.5.44-10.8.44, 19.8.44-18.1.45,
         27.1.45-17.4.45, 29.6.45-7.10.45
*ME626   15.4.44-24.10.44, 29.10.44-20.11.44
*ND471   14.1.44-22.6.44 FTR, crashed in sea
ND472    14.1.44-17.4.45 EGA (ground
         accident)
ND509    21.1.44-2.6.44, 1.7.44-2.11.44
ND560    30.1.44-25.7.44 FTR (Stuttgart)
         (244.25)
*ND954   23.3.33-31.8/1.8.44 FTR (Joigny la
         Roche)
*NN696   24.5.44-22.6.44 FTR (Wesseling)

## No. 61 Sqn, Skellingthorpe
R5856    30.1.44-31.3.44, 10.6.44-8.7.44 FTR
         (St Leu d'Esserent)
*JA872   5.6.44-29.8.44
*JB138   22.8.43-2.2.45
*LL777   22.1.44-22.6.44, 26.7.44-6.12.44
         EFB, crash-landed in Belgium
*LL911   6.4.44-6.9.44, 20.9.44-9.2.45 FTR
         (Politz)
*LM452   31.1.44-29.7.44 FTR (Stuttgart)
LM481    3.3.44-8.5.44, 1.7.44-26.7.44,
         29.8.44-24.11.44
*LM518   7.4.44-25.6.44 FTR (Prouville)
*LM590   31.5.44-7.6.44
*ME595   5.5.44-31.6.44, 18.8.44-15.10.44 FTR
         (Brunswick)

ME596   14.1.44-5.4.44, 22.4.44-23.5.44,
        17.6.44-12/13.8.44 FTR (Russelheim)
*ME719  25.3.44-8.7.44
*ME725  31.3.44-6.12.44 FTR (Giessen)
*ME732  31.3.44-25.4.44, 19.4.44-3.8.44,
        1.9.44-24.9.44 FTR (Dortmund–Ems
        Canal)
*ME783  2.5.44-16.6.44 FTR (Chatellerault)
*ME987
*ND865  5.4.44-2.2.45
*ND867  5.4.44 FTR (St Leu d'Esserent)
        (226.10)
*ND896  4.4.44-18.12.44
ND902   14.4.44-20.5.44, 10.6.44-16.8.44,
        14.10.44-31.10.44 BFB
ND987   2.5.44-25.6.44 FTR (Prouville)
ND988   2.5.44-23.9.44 FTR (Dortmund–Ems
        Canal) (335)
*PA998  30.5.44-26.8.4 FTR

## No. 75 (New Zealand) Sqn, Mepal
*HK551  2.5.44-?
*HK553  24.5.44-?, to 115 Sqn
*HK554  24.5.44-?, to 115 Sqn
*HK557  5.44-?
LL865   15.3.44-22.5.44, RIW 5.6.44
*LL866  16.3.44-25/26.8.44 FTR (Russelheim)
        (251.40)
LL880   17.3.44-26.8.44 AC FB
LL888   26.3.44-16.6.44 FTR (Valenciennes)
*LL921  ?-19/20.7.44 FTR (Aulnoye)
*LL942  23.4.44-30.6.44 Cat E, blew up at
        Mepal
*LM104  19.5.44-7.10.44 FTR (Dortmund)
*LM544  5.44-14.6.45
LM593   2.6.44-25/26.8.44 FTR (Russelheim)
*ME691  4.3.44-20.7.44 FTR (Homberg)
*ME702  25.3.44-10.4.44, 29.4.44-10/11.6.44
        FTR (Dreux)
*ME751  115 Sqn aircraft
*ME752  115 Sqn aircraft
ME834   6.6.44-28.7.44, 23.9.44-?, to 115 Sqn
ME836   6.6.44-?, to 115 Sqn
ND747   13.3.44-14.5.44, 10.6.44-5.11.44
*ND752  13.3.44-21.7.44 FTR (Homberg)
        (198.45)
*ND756  13.3.44-29.7.44 FTR (Stuttgart)
*ND782  25.3.44-10.8.44, 16.9.44-7.10.44
*ND801  3.44-3/4.2.45 EFB
*ND904  115 Sqn aircraft
*ND911  ?-21.11.44 FTR (Homberg)
*ND915  ?-21.7.44 FTR (Homberg) (167.50)
*ND917  115 Sqn aircraft
*ND918  23.3.44-5.7.44
*ND920  115 Sqn aircraft
*NE148  5.44-9.7.44 FTR (Stuttgart)
*NE181  20.5.44-19.7.45
*PA967  6.44-21.7.44 FTR

## No. 83 Sqn, Coningsby
*M-JA705  7.7.43-7.7.45
*N-JB309  3.10.43-7.7.44
*W-ND333  3.1.44-2.9.44
*O-ND442  21.1.44-22.6.44
*L-?????  ?-?
*U-ND455  26.4.44-26.8.44 FTR (Darmstadt)
*S-ND464  21.2.44-16.7.44 EFA (Engine failure,
          crashed Lincs)
*B-ND467  1.2.44-13.5.44, 30.5.44-7.6.44 FTR
          (Caen)
*D-ND529  20.2.44-14.9.45

52

ND917 *of 'C' Flight, No. 75 Squadron, on 30 June 1944 became the first Lancaster to land on an airstrip in France. (IWM CL291)*

| | |
|---|---|
| *B-ND551 | 20.2.44-22.6.44 FTR (Wesseling) (267.40) |
| ND824 | 11.4.44-19.7.46 |
| *A-ND840 | 12.4.44-26.6.44 |
| *B-ND854 | 25.4.44-14.8.44 FTR (Brest) |
| *E-ND856 | 13.4.44-27.7.44 FTR (Givors) |
| *K-ND858 | 24.4.44-5.8.44 |
| *J-ND922 | 29.4.44-25.7.44 FTR (Stuttgart) |
| *Q-ND930 | 4.5.44-6.8.44 FTR (Bois de Cassan) |
| *C-ND966 | 7.5.44-8.7.44 FTR (St Leu d'Esserent) |
| *H-ND974 | 19.5.44-22.11.44 |
| *G-ND979 | 9.5.44-14.8.45 |
| *Y-NE165 | 20.5.44-28.9.44 |
| NE181 | 20.5.44-19.7.45 |

## No. 90 Sqn, Tuddenham

| | |
|---|---|
| LM111 | 20.5.44-8.8.44 FTR (Normandy) |
| LM157 | 5.6.44-13.8.44, 26.8.44-6.2.45 EFA |
| LM158 | 5.6.44-13.6.44 FTR (Gelsenkirchen) |
| LM159 | 5.6.44-29.5.45 FA AC, 7.8.45-2.5.46 |
| LM588 | 19.5.44-26.8.44 FTR (Russelheim) |
| NE145 | 19.5.44-28.6.44 EFB, shot down at Icklingham by Me 410 intruder when returning from Biennais |
| NE149 | 19.5.44-10.6.44 FTR (Dreux) |
| NE178 | 19.5.44-7.11-44 |

## No. 97 Sqn, Coningsby

| | |
|---|---|
| JB174 | 9.10.43-9.10.44 FTR |
| *C-JB683 | 11.12.43-19.8.44 |
| LM346 | 26.4.44-4.7.44 |
| *O-ME625 | 14.2.44-23.6.44 Cat E, burnt; crashed during training |
| *T-ND346 | 23.12.43-25.7.44 |
| *L-ND451 | 22.1.44-22.6.44 FTR (Scholven Buer) (270) |

| | |
|---|---|
| *S-ND452 | 12.1.44-9.9.44 |
| *M-ND495 | 9.1.44-17.8.45 |
| *Q-ND501 | 27.1.44-18.11.44 |
| *D-ND589 | 20.2.44-28.11.44 |
| *E-ND739 | 17.3.44-6.6.44 FTR (St Pierre du Mont) |
| *F-ND740 | 23.3.44-9.44 |
| ND746 | 23.3.44-18.5.44, 10.6.44-19.7.45 |
| *B-ND764 | 24.3.44-11.5.44, 27.5.44-9.6.44 FTR (Etampes) (125.20) |
| *P-ND807 | 29.3.44-23.8.44 FTR (Konigsberg) |
| *G-ND815 | 5.4.44-6.6.44 FTR (St Pierre du Mont) |
| *N-ND961 | 6.5.44-7/8/2/45 FTR (Dortmund–Ems Canal) |
| *H-ND981 | 20.5.44-23.6.44 EFA, mid-air collision |
| *E-NE121 | 13.5.44-30.7.44 FTR (V-site) (157.45) |
| *J-NE124 | 10.5.44-25.6.44 FTR (Prouville) (101.05) |
| NE167 | 20.5.44-17.8.44 FTR (120.05) |
| *A-PA973 | 5.6.44-21.3.45 FTR |

## No. 100 Sqn, Grimsby

| | |
|---|---|
| *B-ED749 | 22.4.43-15.6.44 |
| *T-JB289 | 9.11.43-23.6.44 FTR |
| *U-JB557 | 7.11.43-3.11.44 |
| *E-JB603 | 3.11.43-5.1.45 FTR |
| *L-LL898 | 30.3.44-27.4.44, 3.6.44-2.1.45 EFA, crashed at sea |
| *V-LL915 | 10.4.44-26.7.44 FTR (Stuttgart) |
| *H-LL958 | 6.5.44-1.7.44 FTR (Vierson) |
| *K-LM321 | 4.1.44-10.6.44 FTR |
| LM569 | 2.5.44-23.5.44, 24.6.44-19.7.44 FTR (Gelsenkirchen) |
| *Q-LM584 | 26.5.44-18.12.44, 20.7.44-28.8.44 |
| *S-LM585 | 26.5.44-1.8.44 FTR (Foret de Nieppes) |

*F-ME828  30.5.44-13.9.44 FTR (Frankfurt)
      (244)
*J-ND326  12.12.43-31.3.44, 22.7.44-25.10.44
*O-ND356  3.1.44-27.8.45
*G-ND388  26.12.43-31.12.44 FTR (Cologne)
*R-ND413  30.12.43-21.7.44 EFB, crashed on
      return (388.15)
*A-ND458  10.1.44-30.5.45
*P-ND594  2.44-10.11.44 FTR (Achères)
*N-ND644  20.2.44-16/17.3.45 FTR (Nuremberg)
*W-ND972  3.5.44-14.7.44
*N-PA969  23.5.44-13.6.44 FTR (Gelsenkirchen)

## No. 101 Sqn, Ludford Magna
*S-DV245  ?-23.3.45 FTR (Bremen)
*E-DV292  8.10.43-13.8.44 FTR (269.20)
*Y-DV301  11.43-1.7.44 FTR
*H-DV302  7.11.43-5.7.44, 15.7.44-30.4.45
  DV407  4.1.44-5.2.44, 19.4.44-2.5.44,
      20.5.44-5.6.44, 22.7.44-5.5.45
  LL755  8.4.44-1.6.44, 24.6.44-17.10.44,
      16.12.33-23.3.45 FTR (Bremen)
*Z-LL756  8.4.44-6.9.44 EFB crash-landed
*W-LL757  9.5.44-30.8.44 FTR (Stettin) (214.18)
*A-LL758  7.5.44-6.10.44 FTR (Saarbrucken)
      (310.55)
*L-LL771  7.5.44-22.6.44, 8.7.44-11.10.44 FTR
      (Breskens)
*D-LL772  21.5.44-29.12.44, 13.1.45-10.5.45
*LL773  4.2.44-12.2.44, 26.2.44-17.6.44 Cat
      E, force-landed at Woodbridge
*U-LL774  31.1.44-25.3.44, 15.4.44-14/15-10.44
      FTR (Duisburg)
*V-LL779  5.2.44-21.4.44, 13.5.44-21.7.44 FTR
      (Homberg)
  LL829  3.6.44-14.2.45
*O-LL833  2.3.44-6.6.44 FTR (in Channel)
  LL849  3.6.44-1.8.44 Cat E, burnt during
      night training
  LL862  20.3.44-4.5.44, 27.5.44-21.7.44 FTR
      (Cambrai)
*M-LL863  19.3.44-1.7.44 FTR (Vierson)
  LM161  6.6.44-13.9.44, 23.9.44-8.10.44,
      4.11.44-7.5.45
*I-LM369  27.10.43-31.3.44, 22.4.44-23.6.44,
      22.7.44-27.11.44
*G-LM457  16.2.44-22.7.44, 21.8.44-27.9.44,
      7.10.44-2.1.45
*V2-LM462  8.2.44-25.3.44, 7.4.44-29.7.44 FTR,
      (Nurnberg)
*T-LM472  22.5.44-28.9.44, 17.1.45-25.1.45 SOC
*N2-LM474  5.3.44-17.6.44 FTR (Sterkrade)
*C-LM479  3.3.44-13.6.44, 24.6.44-30.8.44 FTR
      (Stettin)
*P-LM508  25.3.44-22.6.44 FTR (Wesseling)
  LM596  25.3.44-6.44
  LM598  6.6.44-13.8.44 FTR (Brunswick)
*Q-ME565  4.1.44-11.5.44, 27.5.44-8.6.44 FTR
      (Foret de Cerisy)
  ME592  31.1.44-23.5.44, 17.6-44-25.6.44,
      8.7.44-30.8.44 FTR (Stettin)
*M2-ME613  3.2.44-22.6.44 FTR (Wesseling)
*B-ME616  31.1.44-1.7.44 FTR (Vierson)
  ME617  31.1.44-13.8.44 FTR (Russelheim)
  ND388  26.12.43-24.12.44 FTR (Cologne)

## No. 103 Sqn, Elsham Wolds
*JB655  13.11.43-10.11.44
*JB746  11.12.43/01.8.44 FTR
  LL941  24.4.44-9.5.44, 3.6.44-25.7.44 FTR

      (Stuttgart)
*LM116  27.5.44-30.8.44 (Stettin)
*LM124  28.5.44-8.7.44
*LM132  5.44-4.45
  LM538  26.4.44-29.5.44, 17.6.44-29.7.44 FTR
      (Stuttgart)
*ME674  2.3.44-13.7.44 FTR (Revigny)
*ME773  26.4.44-15.7.44 FTR (Revigny)
*ME799  16.5.44-29.7.44 FTR (Stuttgart)
      (166.30)
*ND381  27.12.43-4.11.44
*ND632  22.2.44-26.8.44 EFB, crashed on
      return
*ND990  6.5.44-13.7.44 EFB, crashed on return
*ND993  9.5.44-13.7.44 FTR (Revigny)
  NE117  6.5.44-29.7.44 FTR (Stuttgart)
      (107.10)
*NE136  11.5.44-15.7.44 FTR (Revigny)
  NE173  17.5.44-7.6.44 FTR (Vire)
*PA985  28.5.44-29.7.44 EFB
*PA999  29.5.44-13.7.44 FTR (Darmstadt)

## No. 106 Sqn, Metheringham
*JB641  18.11.43-8.7.44 FTR
*JB663  15.11.43-22.3.45
*JB664  15.11.43-28.6.44 FTR
*LL953  30.4.44-29.7.44, 17.8.44-6.11.44 FTR
      (Gravenhorst)
*LL955  30.4.44-22.6.44 FTR (Gelsenkirchen)
*LL974  12.5.44-28.6.44 FTR (Vitry le
      François)
*LL975  12.5.44-25.6.44 FTR (Pommerval)
*LM570  13.5.44-22.6.44 FTR (Gelsenkirchen)
  ME668  28.2.44-6.3.44, 1.4.44-8.7.44 FTR (St
      Leu d'Esserent)
  ME669  28.2.44-3.4.44-27.4.45 FTR
      (Schweinfurt)
*ME778  30.4.44-29.7.44 FTR (Stuttgart)
*ME789  9.5.44-8.7.44 FTR (St Leu
      d'Esserent)
  ME831  5.6.44-8.7.44 FTR (St Leu
      d'Esserent) (57.25)
*ND331  12.12.43-30.8.44 FTR (Konigsberg)
      (550.45)
*ND339  12.12.43-5.7.43-5.7.44 FTR (St Leu
      d'Esserent)
*ND680  3.3.44-7.6.44 FTR (Coutances)
      (140.50)
*ND682  3.3.44-16.12.44 FTR
  ND707  3.3.44-23.9.44
*ND868  5.4.44-23/24.9.44 (Dortmund)
*NE150  14.5.44-7.6.44 FTR (Coutances)
      (37.35)
  PB122  5.6.44-14.1.45 FTR

## No. 115 Sqn, Witchford
*P-HK541  4.44-3.10.44
*E-HK545  9.4.44-13.6.44 FTR (Gelsenkirchen)
*W-HK548  4.44-8.6.44 FTR (Massy-Palaiseau)
*Y-HK550  4.44-16.6.44 FTR (Valenciennes)
*E-HK551  75 Sqn aircraft
*U-HK552  4.44-8.6.44 FTR (Massy-Palaiseau)
*F-HK555  4.44-6.11.44
*F-HK556  4.44-27.8.44 FTR (Kiel)
  LL804  23.4.44-? (to 300 Sqn)
*H-LL864  28.3.44-14.5.44, 12.5.44-8.6.44 FTR
      (Massy-Palaiseau)
*N-LL935  20.4.44-1.9.44, 4.9.44-1.11.44
*C-LL943  25.4.44-19.7.44 FTR (Aulnoye)
*Z-LL944  25.4.44-28.8.44, 30.9.44-18.10.44,

1.12.44-16.12.44 FTR (Siegen)
*A-LM510 ?-13.6.44, 24.6.44-22.7.44 EFB,
crash-landed, Woodbridge
*T-LM533 19.4.44-7.6.44 FTR (Lisieux)
*G-ME692 26.3.44-15.10.44 FTR
(Wilhelmshaven)
*G-ME718 24.3.44-30.8.44 FTR (Stettin)
ME751 18.4.44-14.6.44, 24.6.44-7.44 FTR
21.7.44 on 75 Sqn
ME752 20.4.44-7.44
ME753 21.4.44-5.44
*V-ME756 20.4.44-14.11.44
*D-ME803 20.4.44-15.3.44
*Y-ND758 29.3.44-1.11.44
*K-ND760 27.3.44-8.6.44 FTR (Massy-
Palaiseau) (124.35)
*C-ND761 26.3.44-8.6.44 FTR (Massy-
Palaiseau) (102.35)
*H-ND790 24.3.44-8.6.44 FTR (Massy-
Palaiseau)
ND800 24.3.44-7.44
J-ND805 24.3.44-21.4.44, 10.6.44-14.10.44
FTR (Duisburg) (39.35)
*S-ND900 20.4.44-7.11.44
M-ND904 18.4.44-7.44 (to 75 Sqn)
*ND913 20.4.44-26.7.44 FTR (Homberg)
ND917 3.6.44-4.11.44 FTR (Solingen)
(257.50)
ND920 18.4.44-25.6.44 FTR (Rimeux)
(114.35)
*B-ND927 20.4.44-13.8.44 FTR (Brunswick)
(185.15)

## No. 156 Sqn, Warboys
*JB186 4.9.43-28.6.44
*JB228 9.43-7.8.44
*JB230 25.3.44-24.6.44 FTR
*ND340 4.1.44-29.10.44
ND345 3.1.44-2.12.44 FTR (Stuttgart)
*ND348 5.1.44-17.8.44
*ND444 21.1.44-12/13.8.44 FTR (Russelheim)
*ND477 23.2.44-5.10.44
ND534 20.2.44-11.9.44 FTR (Gelsenkirchen)
(317.40)
*ND577 21.2.44-8.6.44 FTR
(Versailles/Matelots)
*ND591 20.2.44-28.5.45
*ND618 20.2.44-9.9.44
ND808 31.3.44-28.12.44
*ND875 21.4.44-24.6.44
*ND882 22.4.44-7.8.44 RIW
*ND978 14.5.44-9.9.44 Cat E (228.50)
*NE119 22.5.44-14.1.45
*NE120 22.5.44-28.7.45
*NE132 15.5.44-20.11.44
PA982 3.6.44-7.6.44
PA984 6.6.44-15.7.44 FTR

## No. 166 Sqn, Kirmington
*W4994 3.11.43-29.11.32, 14.1.44-23.4.44,
27.5.44-22.6.44, 5.8.44-3.11.44
*DV367 3.11.43-8.6.44 FTR
*JB649 1.44-26.7.44 FTR
*LL896 26.3.44-13.7.44 FTR (Revigny)
(215.30)
*LM135 27.5.44-11.6.44 FTR (Achères)
(28.05)
*LM386 15.11.43-28.11.43, 11.12.43-26.7.44
FTR (Stuttgart)
*LM388 15.11.43-17.12.43, 15.1.44-13.7.44

FTR (Revigny)
*LM550 28.4.44-7.10.44
*LM581 26.5.44-13.6.44 FTR (Gelsenkirchen)
*LM586 17.5.44-28.6.44 FTR (Chateau
Bernapre)
*ME647 21.2.44-31.12.44 FTR (Osterfeld)
*ME746 18.4.44-3.9.45, 27.9.45-12.11.45 (?)
ME748 15.4.44-28.4.44, 1.7.44-14/15.10.44
FTR (Duisburg)
ME777 20.4.44-23.5.44, 3.6.44-13.6.44 FTR
(Gelsenkirchen)
ME779 30.4.44-11.12.44 FTR (Hasselt)
*ME806 29.5.44-5.8.44 EFB, collided with
PD227
*ME812 29.5.44-2.10.44
*ME829 30.5.44-24.9.44 FTR
(Cologne/Neuss)
*ND399 1.6.44-13.6.44 FTR (Gelsenkirchen)
*ND614 21.2.44-24.7.44 EFB, crashed on
return (304.20)
*ND621 22.2.44-6.7.44 FTR?
*ND626 2.2.44-26/27.10.44 FTR (mining)
*ND628 2.2.44-25.7.44 FTR (Stuttgart)
*ND635 21.2.44-2.1.45 FTR?
*ND678 2.3.44-6.7.44 FTR (Caen battle area)
(218.50)
*ND707 ?-?
*ND757 26.3.44-7.10.44
ND857 1.4.44-8.8.45
*NE112 6.5.44-30/31.8.44 FTR (Stettin)
*NE113 8.5.44-7.10.44
*NE170 21.5.44-3.8.44 FTR(?)
ND996 6.5.44-28.5.4 FTR (Aachen)

## No. 207 Sqn, Spilsby
*DV383 10.11.43-8.5.44, 27.5.44-26.11.44
*ED801 21.1.44-30.11.44
*LL902 1.4.44-9.7.44, 8.8.44-14/15.3.45
ERB, burnt; crashed Little Rissington
*LL968 9.5.44-20.5.44, 10.6.44-4.12.44 FTR
(Heilbronn)
*LL973 11.5.44-22.6.44 FTR (Wesseling)
*LM123 26.5.44-19.10.45, SOC 2.11.45
LM535 24.4.44-20.5.44, 17.6.44-2.11.44,
5.1.45-28.3.45
*LM578 9.5.44-22.6.44 FTR (Wesseling)
*ME667 28.2.44-6.10.44 FTR (Bremen)
ME678 5.3.44-9/10/44 FTR (Etampes)
ME681 5.3.44-23.5.44, 17.6.44-19.7.44 FTR
(Revigny)
*ME683 7.3.44-22.6.44 FTR (Wesseling)
*ME805 24.5.44-8.7.44 FTR (St Leu
d'Esserent)
*ME807 24.5.44-16.7.44 FTR (Nevers)
ME814 29.5.44-19.7.44 (Revigny) (86.05)
*ME827 29.5.44-22.6.44 FTR (Wesseling)
(42.03)
ME832 5.6.44-6.6.44 to 106 Sqn (FTR
5.7.44)
*ND567 30.1.44-8.7.44 FTR (St Leu
d'Esserent) (315.55)
*ND570 11.2.44-8.7.44 FTR (St Leu
d'Esserent)
*ND866 12.4.44-8.7.44 FTR (St Leu
d'Esserent)
*ND872 7.4.44-29.7.44 FTR (Stuttgart)
*NE168 23.5.44-5.1.45 FTR (Houffalize)

## No. 300 Sqn, Faldingworth
*M-EE124 13.5.44-24.6.44 FTR

| | |
|---|---|
| LL798 | 22.6.44-16-11.44 |
| *F-LL804 | 4.44-19.2.45 |
| *N-LL807 | 26.4.44-13.6.44 FTR (Gelsenkirchen) |
| *F-LL856 | 8.3.44-9.8.44 |
| LL959 | 9.5.44-1.7.44, 22.7.44-11.8.44 |
| *D-LM488 | 3.44-24.7.44 FTR (Kiel) |
| ME648 | 29.4.44-11.8.44 |
| ME671 | 29.4.44-12.8.44 |
| ME780 | 6.5.44-10.8.44, 23.9.44-6.9.44 |
| *C-??286 | ?-? |
| *C-?683 | ?-? |
| *O-??856 | ?-? |
| ND861 | 29.4.44-11.8.44 |
| ND863 | 29.4.44-13.8.44 |
| ND975 | 6.5.44-1.7.44 FTR(?) |
| ND982 | 8.5.44-7.8.44 |
| ND984 | 1.6.44-25.7.44 FTR (Stuttgart) |

## No. 405 (RCAF) Sqn, Gransden Lodge

| | |
|---|---|
| H-LM340 | 10.5.44-7.6.44, 17.6.44-12.8.44 |
| ND343 | 4.1.44-16.6.44 FTR (Lens) (298.15) |
| ND344 | 1.44-12.6.44 FTR (Tours) |
| ND352 | 1.1.44-10/11.6.44 FTR (Versailles) (390) |
| M-ND412 | 4.1.44-7.8.44 |
| G-ND524 | 10.2.44-9.12.44 |
| ND616 | 18.2.44-27.2.44 |
| V-ND855 | 23.4.44-10.12.44 |
| C-NE180 | 3.6.44-10.12.44 |
| B-PA965 | 2.6.44-14.7.45 |
| X-PA970 | 2.6.44-8.9.44 FTR |
| PA987 | 6.6.44-13.6.44 |
| | (Incomplete listing) |

## No. 408 Sqn, Linton-on-Ouse

| NB: | This squadron inherited many aircraft when 426 Sqn rearmed 4.5.44, although official records do not give precise details. |
|---|---|
| *R-DS688 | 2.44-12/13.6.44 FTR (Cambrai) |
| *S-DS692 | 9.43-24.7.44 EFB, burnt |
| *H-DS700 | 5.44-8.44 |
| *C-DS707 | 4.44-8.44 |
| *A-DS708 | 5.44-2.8.44 |
| Y-DS726 | 3.44-12/13.6.44 FTR (Cambrai) |
| *O-DS727 | 3.44-8.44 |

| | |
|---|---|
| *D-DS729 | ?-8.6.44 |
| DS730 | 3.3.44-1.9.44 |
| *J-DS768 | 24.8.43-7.6.44 |
| T-DS772 | 4.44-12/13.6.44 FTR (Cambrai) |
| *W-DS830 | 5.44-26.9.44 |
| I-DS838 | 5.44-? |
| *X-DS848 | 4.44-19.8.44 |
| *P-LL617 | 4.44-8.44 |
| F-LL634 | 5.44-8.44 |
| *G-LL636 | 3.44-8.44 |
| *Q-LL643 | 20.1.44-7/8.6.44 FTR (Achères) |
| *K-LL675 | 5.44-11.7.44 EFT, burnt out |
| *N-LL722 | 31.12.43-1.9.44 |
| *Z-LL725 | 2.1.44-28/29.7.44 FTR (Hamburg) |
| *V-LL730 | 3.44-8.44 |

## No. 419 Sqn, Middleton St George

| | |
|---|---|
| *Z-KB700 | 4.3.44-21.1.45 EFB, overshot landing |
| *Y-KB704 | 23.3.44-15.11.44 |
| *W-KB707 | 13.5.44-20.9.44 |
| *E-KB708 | 24.5.44-27.8.44 |
| *L-KB712 | 6.4.44-25.7.44 FTR |
| *D-KB716 | 21.4.44-? |
| *J-KB718 | 24.4.44-5.7.44 FTR (Villeneuve) |
| *T-KB719 | 21.4.44-24/25.7.44 (Stuttgart) |
| *P-KB720 | 5.5.44-24.8.44 |
| *U-KB723 | 1.5.44-4/5.7.44 FTR (Villeneuve) |
| *K-KB724 | 1.5.44-28.8.44 FTR |
| *A-KB726 | 27.5.44-12/13.6.44 FTR (Cambrai) |
| *H-KB727 | 4.5.44-5.7.55 FTR (Villeneuve) |
| *V-KB728 | 13.4.44-17.6.44 FTR |
| *S-KB731 | 30.4.44-13.6.44 FTR (117.45) |
| *X-KB732 | 16.5.44-6.45 |
| *G-KB733 | 7.5.44-1.6.45 |
| *F-KB734 | 23.5.44-17.6.44 FTR (crashed near Zeist) |
| *O-KB735 | 13.5.44-19.9.44 EFA, overshot |
| *M-KB736 | 14.5.44-7.6.44, 8.7.44-24.8.44 |

## No. 460 Sqn, Binbrook

| | |
|---|---|
| W5005 | 19.5.43-11.1.44, 5.2.44-25.2.44, 25.3.44-7.5.44? |
| *JB700 | 24.11.43-6/7.6.44 FTR (Vire) |
| *JB743 | 11.12.43-13.6.44 |
| *LL905 | ?-?, (29.7.44 FTR (Stuttgart) with 576 Sqn) |

*Lancaster III ME701-F of No. 463 (RAAF) Squadron attacked St Pierre du Mont on 5/6 June and Argentan the next night. (IWM MH6447)*

*LL907    6.4.44-8.7.44
*LL952    30.4.44-21.7.44, 16.8.44-18.8.44
*LL957    4.5.44-19.7.44 FTR (Gelsenkirchen)
*LL964    6.5.44-21.8.44
 LM141    2.6.44-?
*LM547    6.5.44-23.6.44 FTR (Rheims)
*ME649    20.2.44-28.9.44
 ME676    11.3.44 23.4.44, 3.6.44-11.6.44
*ME696    9.3.44-10.4.44, 6.5.44-10.6.44 FTR
          (Achères)
 ME697    21.3.44-26.6.44, 8.7.44-19.7.44
*ME698    3.44-15.7.44
 ME744    10.4.44-2/3.2.45 FTR (Wiesbaden)
*ME776    20.9.44-16.7.44
*ME784    4.5.44-29.6.44
*ME785    6.5.44-13.6.44 FTR (Gelsenkirchen)
*ME793    12.5.44-28.6.44 FTR (Vaires)
*ND392    30.12.43-22.11.44
 ND584    6.3.44-28.10.44
*ND615    5.3.44-4.12.44
 ND634    20.2.44-23.5.44, 10.6.44-15.7.44
 ND654    26.3.44-21.7.44 (Courtrai) (89.45)
*ND656    11.5.44-15.7.44
*ND864    10.4.44-22.8.45
 ND959    4.6.44-11.1.45
 ND968    3.6.44-4.45
 ND970    2.6.44-28/29.1.45 FTR (Stuttgart)
 ND971    3.6.44-6.12.44 FTR (Merseburg)
*NE116    1.5.44-23.6.44 FTR (Rheims)
 NE139    4.6.44-5.7.44
*NE163    15.5.44-22.7.44
*NE164    15.5.44-26.7.44
*NE174    19.5.44-5.7.44 FTR (Orleans)

## No. 463 Sqn, Waddington
*DV229    13.12.43-10/11.6.44 FTR (Orleans)
*DV280    29.1.44-21.6.44 FTR
*DV374    18.11.43-26.5.44, 31.5.44-19.7.44
          FTR
*ED611    4.2.44-7.5.44, 20.5.44-29.9.44,
          15.12.44-7/8.2.45 FTR(?)
*HK536    5.1.44-4/5.7.44 FTR (St Leu
          d'Esserent)
*LL790    28.1.44-28.5.44, 3.6.44-30.8.44 FTR
          (476.30) (Konigsberg)
 LL975    1.2.44-7.10.44 AC FB
 LL844    29.2.44-15.8.44, 19.8.44-28.9.44 RIW

*LL847    1.3.44-17/18.12.44 FTR (Munich)
*LM130    ?-11.3.45 EFA, collided with
          Hurricane PZ740
 LM309    3.5.44-15.5.44, 16.5.44-24.9.44, FTR
          (Dortmund–Ems Canal)
*LM551    9.5.44-19.7.44 FTR (Revigny)
*LM571    12.5.44-25.6.44 FTR (Prouville)
*LM574    15.5.44-24/25.6.44 FTR (Prouville)
*LM587    31.5.44-26.9.44 FTR (Cap Griz Nez)
 LM589    31.5.44-25.7.44 FTR (St Cyr)
 LM597    29.5.44-24.6.44 FTR (Prouville)
*ME614    21.1.44-5.7.44 FTR (St Leu
          d'Esserent)
*ME615    21.1.44-29.7.44 FTR (Stuttgart)
*ME701    9.3.44-2.7.44 EFB, flak damage
*NE133    10.5.44-4.11.44 FTR (Dortmund–Ems
          Canal)

## No. 467 Sqn, Waddington
*R5868    ?-?
*DV277    5.11.43-24.8.44
*DV372    5.11.43-2.3.44, 12.3.44-12.6.44 RIW
*DV373    5.11.43-2.11.43, 11.12.43-20.7.44,
          28.7.44-5.10.44 FTR
*LL789    28.1.43-15.8.44, 19.8.44-13.9.44 FTR
          (Stuttgart)
*LL843    29.2.44-25.7.44
*LL846    29.2.44-29.7.44 FTR (Stuttgart)
*LL971    14.5.44-22.6.44 FTR (Gelsenkirchen)
*LM100    13.5.44-2/3.2.45 FTR
*LM101    16.5.44-21.7.44 FTR (Courtrai)
*LM119    13.5.44-21.7.44 FTR (Courtrai)
*LM338    16.7.43-4.11.43, 11.12.43-8.7.44 FTR
          (St Leu d'Esserent)
*LM440    23.1.44-20.2.44, 4.3.44-9.6.44 EFB
 LM448
 LM450    27.1.44-25.6.44 FTR (Prouville)
*LM552    7.5.44-12.6.44 EFA, crashed during
          night training
*LM583    16.5.44-11.7.44
*ND729    13.3.44-25.6.44 FTR (Prouville)

## No. 514 Sqn, Waterbeach
*F-DS786   15.9.43-25.9.44
*J-DS795   ?-?
*D-DS787   16.9.43-11.9.44 FTR (Kamen)
*H-DS813   18.9.44-28/29.7.44 FTR (Stuttgart)

*Lancaster IIs LL728-B and DS813-H of No. 514 Squadron at Waterbeach.*

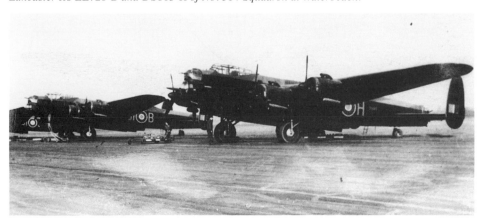

(376.30)
O-DS816  23.9.43-15.6.44 FTR (Valenciennes)
(282.05)
*Q-DS818  26.9.44-12/13.6.44 FTR
(Gelsenkirchen)
*T-DS822  28.9.44-8.6.44 FTR (Massy-
Palaiseau) (308.55)
*F-DS842  22.11.43-25.9.44
*N-LL620  3.11.43-30.6.44 FTR (Normandy)
(237.45)
LL624  4.44-26.8.44
*M-LL635  25.4.44-14.9.44 Cat E
LL666  4.44-10.10.44
*K-LL670  4.44-25.9.44
*E-LL677  2.12.43-8.9.44 SOC (315.20)
*L-LL678  12.43-12/13.6.444 FTR
(Gelsenkirchen)
*J-LL690  8.2.44-15/16.6.44 FTR
(Valenciennes)
*A-LL692  5.44-29.7.44 FTR (Stuttgart)
*E-LL697  11.3.44-12.8.44 Cat AC
*L-LL703  22.12.43-9.6.44 SOC
*G-LL716  4.44-3.8.44 FTR (Bois de Cassin)
*H-LL726  ?-?
*C-LL727  11.4.44-7/8.6.44 FTR (Massy-
Palaiseau)
*B-LL728  29.1.44-26.8.44 FTR (Kiel)
U-LL731  4.2.44-13.9.44 FTR (Frankfurt)
(302.30)
*S-LL733  24.5.44-30.7.44 FTR (Caen 'B')
(262.30)
*G-LL734  6.2.44-25.9.44

## No. 550 Sqn, Waltham (Grimsby)
*N-W5005  7.5.44-27.8.44
*M-DV279  13.1.44-6.3.44, 7.4.44-19.7.44 Cat E
*G-ED562  6.5.44-18.7.44
*C-EE193  10.4.44-10.8.44 FTR
*P-LL747  8.1.44-17.6.44 FTR (Sterkrade)
*D-LL748  22.4.44-26.7.44, 4.8.44-19.10.44, ?-
3.11.44(?)
*O-LL796  20.5.44-13.7.44 FTR (Revigny)
*A-LL800  29.5.44-29.7.44, 5.8.44-12.8.44 RIW
*J-LL811  4.5.44-5.11.44
*U-LL831  21.2.44-7.7.44, 15.7.44-3.11.44
*Q-LL837  24.2.44-15.7.44 FTR (Revigny)
*S-LL838  23.5.44-22.6.44 EFB, crashed, flak
damage
*L-LL850  3.3.44-7.7.44 EFB, burnt, Manston
*H-LM134  27.5.44-17.6.44 FTR (Sterkrade)
*T-LM455  3.2.44-29.7.44 FTR (Stuttgart)
*R-LM460  10.2.44-18.7.44
*F-ME556  22.4.44-6/7.6.44 FTR (Achères)
*E-PA991  29.5.44-29.8.44 FTR
*K-PA995  5.44-3.45 FTR (Dessau)

## No. 576 Sqn, Elsham Wolds
*M-ED888  27.11.43-31.10.44
*J-JA868  27.11.43-20.11.44
*V-JB460  18.3.44-25.6.44 FTR
*N-LL799  9.2.44-29.7.44 FTR (Stuttgart)
*X-LM122  22.5.44-2/3.11.44 FTR (Düsseldorf)
*I-LM439  8.1.44-19.8.44 FTR(?)
*A-LM532  16.4.44-3.7.44 FTR (Orléans)
*G-LM594  27.5.44-30.7.44, 4.8.44-14.2.45,
9.3.45-3.6.45
ME583  4.1.44-4.5.44, 3.6.44-29.6.44
*P-ME735  9.4.44-19.4.44, 20.5.44-25.10.44,
1.11.44-23.1.45, 10.2.45-21/22.2.45
FTR (Duisburg)

*Q-ME792  11.5.44-17.8.44 FTR (Gdynia)
(320.15)
*W-ME800  16.5.44-30.8.44 FTR (Stettin)
*C-ME801  18.5.44-16.10.45 Cat E
*K-ME810  27.5.44-17.6.44 FTR (Sterkrade)
(43.15)
ME811  26.5.44-7.6.44 FTR (Vire)
*L-ND859  10.4.44-5.7.44 FTR (Revigny)
(216.05)
*R-ND903  19.4.44-9.7.44
*F-ND994  9.5.44-15.7.44 FTR (Revigny)
*B-NE115  7.5.44-2.11.44 FTR (Düsseldorf)
(423.05)
NN696  24.5.44-22.6.44 FTR
*D-PA997  5.6.44-16/17.6.44 FTR (Sterkrade)
*S-PB128  6.44-28/29.7.44 FTR (Stuttgart)

## No. 582 Sqn, Little Staughton
*C-ME623  31.3.44-3.8.44, 18.9.44-30.11.44
*L-JA673  1.4.44-26.11.43
*Q-JB345  31.3.44-30.8.44
ND438  1.4.44-21.4.44, 10.66.44-8.12.44
*N-ND502  2.4.44-16.6.44 FTR (Lens) (274.20)
ND714  1.4.44-27.4.44, 9.6.44-10.6.44 FTR
(Etampes)
*M-ND750  31.3.44-28.6.44, 1.9.44-4.6.45
*R-ND810  3.4.44-29.7.44 FTR (Stuttgart) (192)
*O-ND812  5.4.44-1.7.44, 17.8.44-27.8.44
*S-ND817  3.4.44-7/8.8.44 FTR (Mare de
Magne)
ND862  14.4.44-25.11.44
ND880  22.4.44-12.10.44 EFB, crashed
Manston
*B-ND899  23.4.44-26.3.45
ND921  3.5.44-29.6.44 FTR (Blainville)
(75.15)
*H-ND931  4.5.44-24.7.44 FTR (Kiel) (158.10)
ND969  4.5.44-12/13.8.44 FTR (Russelheim)
(221.35)
*E-ND980  405 Sqn aircraft
*G-NE130  4.5.44-17.1.45 FTR (Zeitz)
*A-NE140  24.5.44-23.3.45
*D-NE166  27.5.44-6.6.44 FTR (Longues)
(20.25)
*J-NE169  27.5.44-6.7.44 FTR (Wizernes)
(75.20)
*T-NE172  29.5.44-15.6.44 FTR (Douai) (18.30)
PA981  1.6.44-7.6.44

## No. 617 Sqn, Woodhall Spa
*U-DV246  31.8.43-15.8.44
*X-DV380  11.11.43-7.4.44, 22.4.44-16.3.45,
7.4.45-24.5.45, 1.6.45-29.12.45
*A-DV385  11.11.43-6.4.45
O-DV391  25.11.43-6.4.45
*T-DV393  23.11.43-27.3.45
P-DV402  2.12.43-4.2.44, 1.3.44-6.8.44,
16.9.44-6.4.45
*G-DV403  10.12.43-23.4.44, 6.5.44-25.6.44 FTR
DV405  10.12.43-12.6.44, 16.7.44-6.4.45
*L-EE131  28.5.43-18.9.44 EFB, crashed in
USSR
V-JB139  15.9.43-5.8.44 FTR
*W-LM482  7.3.44-7.10.44 FTR (Kembs barrage)
*N-LM485  7.3.44-6.4.45
L-LM489  13.3.44-6.4.45
*Q-LM492  18.3.44-6.4.45
*F-ME554  16.12.43-12.2.44, 12.3.44-6.4.45
*C-ME555  16.12.43-35.7.44, 4.8.44-29.1.45
*S-ME557  12.12.43-1.8.44 FTR (Rill-la-

Montagne)
*Y-ME559  16.12.43-11.9.44 EFB, crash-landed
in USSR
*H-ME560  16.12.43-16.7.44 Cat E, burnt, crash-
landed
*R-ME561  20.12.43-22.12.44 EFB, hit ground in
fog
*Z-ME562  20.12.43-8.12.44, 16.2.45-6.1.45

## No. 619 Sqn, Dunholme Lodge
*P-DV326  5.10.43-21.9.44
*X-EE134  ?-?
*T-JB131  23.8.43-30.12.44
LL778  21.1.44-21.9.44
*C-LL783  23.1.44-7.6.44 FTR (Caen)
*D-LL808  28.4.44-22.6.44 FTR (Wesseling) (98)
*G-LL969  10.5.44-19.7.44 FTR (Revigny)
LL977  13.5.44-22.6.44 FTR (Wesseling)
LM378  18.10.43-19.7.44 FTR (Revigny)
*R-LM420  4.12.43-5.8.44, 28.9.44-11.12.44
*M-LM484  7.3.44-6.4.45
*Q-LM536  25.4.44-29.7.44 FTR (Stuttgart)
*F-ME568  23.12.43-4.8.44 FTR (Trossy St
Maximin)
*L-ME745  14.4.44-8.7.44 FTR (St Leu
d'Esserent)
*N-ND728  5.3.44-5.1.45 FTR (Royan)
*U-ND932  22.4.44-14.6.44, 22.7.44-44.12.44
FTR (Heilbronn)
*Z-ND935  22.4.44-26.7.44 FTR (Stuttgart) (168)
*S-ND986  2.5.44-21/22.6.44 FTR (Wesseling)
*W-ND151  15.5.44-21/22.6.44 FTR (Wesseling)
(77)
*V-?????  ?-?

## No. 622 Sqn, Mildenhall
*K-L7576  24.12.43-29.7.44 FTR (Stuttgart)
(538)
R5514  5.1.44-28.7.44
*B-R5625  17.3.44-9.7.44 FTR (V-1 site)

*A-ED430  18.2.44-21.7.44
*S-ED474  9.12.43-23.2.44, 4.3.33-27.7.44
*M-LL802  15.4.44-21.9.44 Cat E (329.25)
*M-LL803  20.4.44-2.11.44 FTR (Homberg)
*Z-LL812  11.2.44-13.6.44 FTR (Gelsenkirchen)
*Q-LL859  2.3.44-21.7.44 FTR (Homberg)
(225.20)
*J-LL885  23.3.44-29.7.44, 14.9.44-17.8.45
N-LM138  4.6.44-24.6.44 FTR (L'Hay V-site)
*T-LM443  14.1.44-5.3.44, 29.4.44-15.11.44
*P-LM466  16.2.44-12/13.8.44 FTR (Russelheim)
*L-LM477  29.2.44-25.7.44 FTR (Stuttgart)
*E-LM491  13.3.44-8.6.44 FTR (Massy-
Palaiseau)
C-LM511  18.3.44-12.9.44 FTR, mine-laying
E-LM577  4.6.44-31.10.44, 9.12.44-13.12.44
*O-ND765  24.3.44-8.6.44 FTR (Massy-
Palaiseau) (110.55)
*F-NE146  12.5.44-25.7.44 FTR (Stuttgart)

## No. 625 Sqn, Kelstern
*DV278  10.12.43-13.6.44
*ED814  4.12.43-1.7.44 FTR
*ED938  13.10.43-13.6.44 FTR (580)
*LL897  1.4.44-11.6.44 FTR (Achères) (142)
*LL956  1.5.44-14.10.44 EFB, crashed soon
after take-off (336)
*LL962  5.5.44-29.7.44 FTR (Stuttgart) (189)
*LM103  17.5.44-13.9.44 FTR (Frankfurt)
(276.01)
LM139  2.6.44-11.6.44 FTR (Achères)
*LM512  29.3.44-13.9.44 FTR (Frankfurt)
LM546  12.5.44-26.5.44, 17.6.44-29.7.44 FTR
(Stuttgart)
*ME594  10.1.44-2.5.44, 13.5.44-16.6.44
*ME682  15.3.44 ? to 75 Sqn
*ME733  8.4.44-13.8.44 FTR (Brunswick)
(268.32)
ME755  22.4.44-? to 460 Sqn in 7.44
*ND459  22.1.44-1.7.44 FTR (Vierzon) (371)
ND613  11.2.44-14.7.44

*Although a two-Flight squadron, No 626's Lancasters nevertheless had individual code letters squared, as evident on post-D-Day PD235-N.*

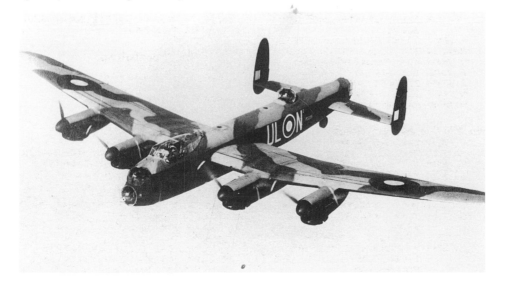

59

*ND619 11.2.44-3.11.44
*ND639 20.2.44-22.7.44
*ND742 11.3.44-10.6.44 FTR (Achères) (182)
*ND992 6.5.44-30.7.44, 9.9.44-15.10.44
*ND995 5.44-10.6.44, 1.7.44-22.7.44
*NE137 11.5.44-5.11.44
PB126 6.6.44-1.7.44 (46.00)

## No. 626 Sqn, Wickenby
*G-W4967 6.11.43-10.6.44
*V-W4990 26.5.44-7.6.44
LL798 9.2.44-27.4.44, 10.6.44-22.6.44
*Y-LL895 26.3.44- FTR 19.7.44 (Stuttgart)
(203.25)
LL918 16.4.44- RIW 30.8.44
*S-LL961 5.5.44-18.7.44, 7.1.45 FTR (air-to-air
collision)
*Z-LM102 19.5.44-23.6.44 FTR (Rheims)
*P-LM105 18.5.44-21/22.2.45 FTR (Duisburg)
*A-LM112 20.5.44-7.7.44 FTR (Caen, tactical)
(99.30)
*F-LM113 20.5.44-20.7.44, 9.8.44-1.10.45
*D-LM136 31.5.44-21.7.44 (Courtrai)
LM140 2.6.44-21.8.44 FTR (Russelheim)
LM530 26.7.44-18.12.44, 3.2.45-24.8.45
W-LM599 31.5.44-23.6.44, 8.7.44-17.8.44 FTR
(Brunswick)
*X-ME750 18.4.44-30.11.44
*L2-ME774 27.4.44-FTR 1.7.44 (Vierzon)
(118.50)
*K-ME830 31.5.44-29.7.44
*E-ND952 27.4.44-1.7.44 FTR (Vierzon)
*U-PA989 28.5.44-26.8.44 FTR
*R-PA990 28.5.44-7.8.45
*H-PA993 28.5.44-20.10.44 EFB
*L-????? ?-?
*Q-????? ?-?

## No. 630 Sqn, East Kirkby
*JB290 4.1.44-23.3.44, 29.4.44-18.9.45
*LL949 28.4.44-22/23.11.44 EFB, crashed in
sea on return
LL966 6.5.44-22.5.44, 10.6.44-14/15.2.45
FTR (Rositz)

*LL972 11.5.44-17.8.44 FTR (Stettin)
(178.25)
*LM117 5.44-18.7.44 FTR (Revigny)
*LM118 24.5.44-21/22.6.44 FTR (Wesseling)
(59.50)
*LM537 25.4.44-19.7.44 FTR (Revigny)
*ME650 24.2.44-27.8.44 FTR (Konigsberg)
ME729 30.3.44-19.7.44 Cat E (216.20)
*ME739 10.4.44-10/11.4.45 FTR (Leipzig)
*ME782 1.5.44/22/6/44 FTR (Wesseling)
(100.30)
*ME795 14.5.44-22.6.44 EFB, burnt (82.40)
*ME796 14.5.44-19.7.44 FTR (Revigny)
(127.25)
*ND335 12.12.43-26.8.44
*ND527 27.1.44-27.7.44 FTR, mine-laying
ND554 27.1.44-8/9.2.45 (Politz)
*ND685 29.2.44-7.6.44 FTR (Caen) (233.15)
ND688 4.2.44-23.4.44, 13.5.44-23.5.44,
24.6.44-8.7.44 FTR (St Leu
d'Esserent)
ND797 26.3.44-29.7.44 FTR
ND949 22.4.44-10.5.44, 17.6.44-9/10.4.45
EFB
*PA992 29.5.44-29.7.44 FTR
PB121 5.6.44-10.6.44 FTR (4.20)

## No. 635 Sqn, Downham Market
*B-JB728 20.3.44-16.6.44 FTR
*G-LM524 5.4.44-8.3.45, 8.6.45-3.8.45
W-ND355 30.3.44-26/27.8.44 FTR (Kiel)
*H-ND359 20.3.44-4.1.45
Y-ND450 20.3.44 22.5.44, 16.6.44-3.7.44
*R-ND453 20.3.44-6.10.44 EFB, crash-landed,
Woodbridge (338.25)
*J-ND709 20.3.44-9.3.45
F-ND735 25.3.44-18.5.44, 8.6.44-7/8.3.45 FTR
(Dessau)
*C-ND809 5.4.44-11.12.44
*T-ND811 30.3.44-4.8.44 FTR (Trossy St
Maximin)
*X-ND821 6.4.44-11.12.44
*P-ND877 21.4.44-1.4.45
*N-ND895 21.4.44-6.7.44 FTR (Wizernes)
*S-ND898 24.4.44-20.7.45

LL966-P, *a Lancaster of No.630 Squadron photographed at East Kirkby. (Ray Sturtivant)*

Additional to the above were six Lancaster B Mk VIs with annular cowled Merlin 85 engines. Some were undergoing operational trials, as the following outline histories indicate:

JB675: Rolls-Royce (RR) 25.11.43 – A&AEE 23.2.44 – Wyton 14.3.44 – 7 Sqn 14.4.44 – 405 Sqn 1.5.44 – 635 Sqn 24.7.44 – 7 Sqn 23.8.44 – RAE 17.12.44 – RR 20.1.45 – 58 MU 15.7.48 – SOC 31.7.48

JB713: RR 30.12.43 – Wyton 5.2.44 – 7 Sqn 21.3.44 – 405 Sqn 21.3.44 – 635 Sqn 25.7.55 – FTR 19.8.44

ND418: RR for Merlin 85 fitment 2.1.44 – Wyton 16.3.44 – 83 Sqn 20.3.44 – 7 Sqn 14.4.44 – 635 Sqn 24.7.44 – 582 Sqn 15.11.44 – RAE 17.12.44 – Bomb Ballistics Unit 28.2.46 – SOC 30.9.47

ND558: RR for Merlin 85 fitment 29.1.44 – A&AEE 21.5.44 – 635 Sqn 26.8.44 – RR 11.9.44 – Wyton 16.9.44, RR 28.2.46 – Bomb Ballistics Unit Woodbridge 12.11.46-1950.

ND673: RR for Merlin 85 fitting 8.3.44 – Wyton 21.6.44 – 7 Sqn 25.6.44 – 635 Sqn 24.7.44 – RAE 17.12.44 – SOC at Farnborough 31.1.47

ND784: Research and development aircraft, with Rolls-Royce 24.3.44 to 7.10 44. Used as Armstrong-Siddeley jet engine test-bed post-war.

# The de Havilland Mosquito bomber

The Mosquito remains the most ubiquitous military aircraft of all time. That this high-speed high-flier emerged from notions siring the Halifax, Lancaster and Manchester is surely incredible.

De Havilland, after seeing their DH 88 Comet racer win the 1934 Mildenhall to Australia McRobertson Air Race, applied its clean aerodynamics to their DH 91 Albatross, a fast, four-engined airliner. With war clouds gathering, the company next considered what contribution it could make to rearmament, gradually refining ideas for a high-speed, twin-engined, unarmed bomber of wooden construction which would draw most upon indigenous materials unlikely to be in short supply during a war.

Repeatedly the Air Ministry dismissed such ideas. Already a new fleet of hefty, turret-defended, heavy load-carrying large bombers had been commissioned. An unarmed small wooden bomber was regarded as a very misplaced notion from a firm with no recent bomber experience. But de Havilland persevered and in the first week of war again presented ideas for a small, unarmed bomber. Sceptical officials now requested more details and sought confirmation of the possible performance. Progress was being made!

At Salisbury Hall, near Hatfield, design work was revolving around a 54-ft-span twin Merlin-engined bomber able to carry a 1,000 lb load for 1,500 miles and have a top speed approaching 400 mph. Although its airframe skinning had twice the surface area of the Spitfire, the aircraft would have twice the power, with aerodynamic refinement and ducted radiators enhancing the performance and making it at least 20 mph faster than the Spitfire.

Having experienced the Blenheim, a bomber 'faster than the fighters', Bomber Command, unenamoured of the de Havilland scheme, suggested in December 1939 that maybe it could serve as a reconnaissance aircraft. After being heavily promoted by Sir Wilfred Freeman, an order for 50 such was agreed, giving de

Havilland a foot in the door.

Development went ahead on the basis of a photo-reconnaissance (PR) machine weighing about 17,000 lb, having a top speed of 397 mph at 23,700 ft and able to land in 637 yds. A bomber derivative would weigh about 18,850 lb, it was suggested. On 1 March 1940 the order for 50 DH 98 reconnaissance aircraft was confirmed. There was, behind the scenes, a hitherto unprinted aspect to the order. Who inspired the idea may never be known, but senior officers of the Fleet Air Arm suddenly expressed keen interest in having 50 DH 98s for use as high-speed target-towers! That almost instantly galvanized the RAF into having what had by now become the Mosquito. Not until long after the war did the RAF agree to the Navy having a few Mosquitoes – for target-towing!

The design was lucky to survive the 1940 drive for production of only current types. Ample room for nose guns had cleverly been built into the aircraft, and that feature, which helped to keep it alive, was seized upon at the end of 1940 when production was amended to call for 19 PR aircraft and 28 eight-gun fighters in addition to prototypes of both and a two-seat trainer. Foolishly it was summer 1941 before any order was placed for Mosquito bombers.

*W4050*, the Mosquito prototype, made its first flight on 25 November 1940. Very soon it was proving design forecasts to be accurate. By February 1941 *W4050* had been flown at 386 mph – 20 mph faster than the current Spitfire. Official trials at Boscombe Down confirmed the high performance before the tailwheel jammed on a rough surface and the Mosquito's fuselage fractured. De Havilland quickly brought along a replacement from *W4051*, and a gathering of carpenters armed with saws, glues and skill. What advantages wood displayed, for components could easily be made in any garden shed!

By May 1941 the 16,000 lb prototype had attained 392 mph at 22,000 ft, so a small order for bombers was placed. A replacement production fuselage fitted to *W4051* enabled that airframe to serve operationally, and an amendment to the first contract now asked that 10 examples be completed as 'PR/Bomber Conversion' aircraft. One of them, *W4064*, tested in October 1941, became on 15 November the first Mosquito bomber to join the RAF when it was handed over to No. 105 Squadron at Swanton Morley.

The true bomber prototype was *W4057*, sometimes called the Mosquito B Mk V. Bomb bay measurements showed it possible to increase the load and bombs with telescopic fins – very advanced for their time – were mooted before shortened vanes allowed the bomber to carry 4 x 500 lb HEs, double the initial load.

Further development surrounded high-altitude engines. *W4050*, grounded in October 1941, was fitted with two-stage Merlin 61s, but development took a

W4050, *the original Mosquito, was in 1942 fitted with Merlin 60-series engines for general Mosquito development work.*

considerable time to effect, partly because Mosquito versions were proliferating so fast. Operations, too, were well underway, for the PR aircraft began them in July 1941.

Not until 31 May 1942 did the bomber conversions go into action – as PR aircraft high-flying to assess the effectiveness of the 'Thousand Bomber' raid on Cologne. The last flight that day was undertaken by Sqn Ldr Channer who decided to fly *W4069* very low over Germany to escape detection. In so doing he virtually initiated a tactic which is now standard practice; further testimony to the Mosquito as a pacemaker. Meanwhile, high-level PR and light bombing sorties were in vogue, including an attempted daylight cloud cover Berlin raid on 19 September 1942. A week later came a headline-grabbing low-level attack on the Gestapo HQ in Oslo. So low did the 'Mossies' fly that some of their bombs went straight through the front then out of the back windows of the building. Only now was the British public permitted to know that the Mosquito existed – over a year after its introduction to service.

Comment surrounding the secrecy still suggests that some officials had decisions to disguise! Others, further away, had ample proof of the Mosquito's potential when twice on 30 January 1943 Nazi leaders speech-making in Berlin were rudely interrupted by the two Mosquito bomber squadrons. Between February and May 1943 Nos. 105 and 139 Squadrons went on to deliver highly spectacular low-level and shallow-dive attacks, often at dusk, and completed the series with a call on the Zeiss optics factory at Jena, deep in Germany. Such activity ended abruptly, when on 31 May 1943 No. 2 Group quit Bomber Command for Fighter Command. The Mosquito bomber squadrons left behind were given a very subsidiary role as night nuisance raiders, the value of which had yet to be appreciated.

There was another task in which the bomber version was already excelling. On 21 July 1942 Mosquito B Mk IV *DK300* landed at Stradishall and was at once subjected to extreme secrecy, for it was to join No. 109 Squadron and test special radio equipment codenamed *Oboe*. It entailed a 'cat' station to measure accurately the aircraft's range and direct its track towards a target. A 'mouse' station would signal to the crew the precise bomb release time. August 1942 saw the squadron move to Wyton and on 20 December 1942 it conducted a trial bombing raid relying upon *Oboe* to mark the Lutterade power station in the Netherlands. Very close by was a cemetery and when German radio proudly announced that bombs had fallen upon it, the RAF listeners, although disquieted by that news, also knew that *Oboe* was going to revolutionize the accuracy of RAF night raids. At first the *Oboe* stations could handle only one aircraft at a time, six per hour, and it was April 1944 before *Oboe Mk III* came into use, allowing four aircraft to operate simultaneously on the same wavelength.

To obtain maximum performance, both PR and *Oboe* Mosquitoes needed to fly as high as practicable, and summer 1942 brought a suitable Mosquito variant, the high flier with a 2 lb psi pressurized cabin. A specially modified bomber prototype, *MP469* was first flown on 8 August 1942, but within weeks it was carrying guns. It reached 38,500 ft in trials for use against high-flying German Ju 86 raiders. It was also the heaviest Mosquito yet, weighing 22,350 lb when fully laden. By this time 250 Mosquitoes had been produced.

Wedding the two-stage supercharger Merlin to the Mosquito meanwhile led to the Mk IX, produced as a PR aircraft or a bomber. The first example of the latter, *LR495*, flew in March 1943 and within weeks a Mk IX carrying a 500 lb bomb below each wing was also being tested. The 23,000 lb at which it was flying also proved that the Mosquito could lift a 4,000 lb bomb load – if there was room in the bomb bay. In April 1943 No. 109 Squadron received the first two production B Mk IXs, to enhance *Oboe* performance.

Load-carrying capability of the Mosquito was most amazingly explored when carriage of a 4,000 lb 'cookie' was tried using a Mk IV, *DZ594* which, with suitably deepened bomb bay, made its first flight in July 1943. Successful trials led to a decision on 9 October 1943 for more Mk IVs to be similarly modified. The first operational drops were made on Düsseldorf by Mk IVs of No. 692 Squadron on 23 February 1944.

Pressure cabin development had also proceeded, with its application to *DZ540* which in July 1943 first flew as the

*Mosquito B Mk IX* LR500, *reserve for the marking of St Pierre du Mont. (de Havilland)*

prototype Mk XVI. In October 1943 *ML926* was rolled out, the first production pressure cabin bomber B. Mk XVI, and in December No. 109 Squadron took delivery of two of the latest bombers. After the first 12 had been built, Mk XVIs came off the production lines fitted with dished doors, allowing 4,000 lb bombs to be carried.

From March 1943 *Oboe* Mosquitoes led Bomber Command's large-scale raids – when the equipment's range permitted. At distances greater than 278 miles that was impracticable – so far. The second half of 1943 saw the Mosquito bomber force enhanced by the addition of Oakington's No. 627 Squadron. The night nuisance role by then included follow-up raids after Main Force attacks, and the distraction of German defenders by Mosquito IVs and IXs wandering far and misleadingly over enemy territory. In January 1944 another Mk IV squadron formed, No. 692 at Graveley, by which time the first Canadian-built Mk IVs (designated B. Mk XXs) were being operated by No. 139 Squadron. The latter squadron soon had aircraft fitted with H2S radar which allowed them to act as pathfinders for what became the Light Night Striking Force.

On the night of the Normandy invasion Mosquitoes attacked Osnabruck, and on the following night they bombed Ludwigshafen. Over the Normandy coast Nos. 105 and 109 *Oboe* Squadrons and low-flying Mk IVs of No. 627 Squadron

marked for Bomber Command's 'heavies'.

It is always easy to be wise with hindsight, but had the Mosquito been in service by 1940 – which was quite feasible – and had Bomber Command opted for faster, higher-flying, larger-capacity, unarmed bombers . . . Certainly there would have been savings in training programmes, servicing and surely lives. Tactical flexibility would definitely have been enhanced and probably the accuracy of bombing too. A typical Mosquito Mk IX had a top speed of about 424 mph at 26,200 ft, making it compare most favourably with the Merlin 66-powered North American P-51 Mustang which, tested at Boscombe Down, reached 430 mph at 22,000 ft, after which its performance fell away. Little wonder the Mosquito loss rate was so very low. Even the best German jets had a tough task in catching the 'Mossies'. De Havilland even had an answer to such novelty items – the jet-engined Mosquito.

## Bomber Command Mosquitoes, 5 June 1944

| | |
|---|---|
| Mk IV — | serial number prefixes *DK* and *DZ* |
| Mk IX — | serial numbers within ranges *LR475-LR477, LR495-LR513, ML896-ML924* |
| Mk XVI — | serial numbers within ranges *ML925-MM226* and *PF* prefix |
| Mk XX — | serial number prefix *KB* |

64

Aircraft letter where given is that worn early June 1944

* operated 5/6 June 1944
+ operated 6/7 June 1944

### *No. 105 Sqn*, **Bourn**
|  |  |
|---|---|
| DZ429 | 26.11.43-28.6.44 |
| *+LR497 | 22.3.44-31.7.44 |
| *+LR500 | 22.3.44-24.5.45 |
| *+LR503 | 10.3.44-10.5.45 EFA during Canadian victory tour |
| *+LR504 | 14.3.44-6.12.44, 5.2.45-14.9.45 SOC |
| *+F-LR507 | 15.11.43-12.9.45 |
| *+G-LR508 | 5.7.43-24.1.44, 23.3.44-6.12.44 |
| *+S-ML902 | 22.8.43-14.1.45 EFA, crashed on take-off, Manston |
| *+U-ML911 | 17.9.43-22.12.44 BFB |
| *+E-ML913 | 24.9.43-5/6.7.44 FTR (Scholven/Buer) |
| *+B-ML914 | 24.9.43-10.4.45 |
| L-ML916 | 4.10.43-16.1.45, 10.3.45-24.7.45 EFA, undercarriage collapse, Melsbrock |
| *V-ML919 | 18.9.43-15.12.44 EFB, crashed on take-off |
| *+W-ML920 | 20.9.43 – history uncertain |
| Y-ML922 | 21.9.43-14.1.45 EFB written off – battle-damaged |
| *+Z-ML923 | 24.9.43-28.1.45 FTR (Stuttgart) |
| *+ML938 | 26.2.44-5.9.44, 25.9.44-20.9.45 |
| *+ML964 | 29.2.44-7.7.44 FTR, fighter damaged during Caen raid, disintegrated over Normandy |
| ML968 | 25.4.44-8.7.44 EFA overshot Waterbeach |
| *+ML973 | 5.44-? |
| +ML974 | 26.3.44-15.4.45, 15.6.45-19.9.45 |

|  |  |
|---|---|
| *+ML981 | 3.4.44-23.12.44 |
| *+ML982 | 3.4.44-2.12.44 |
| ML983 | 14.4.44-1.10.44, 10.11.44-7.12.44, 22.2.45-28.9.45 |
| *+ML986 | 17.4.44-4.10.44 EFB, undershot Bourn |
| *+ML987 | 17.4.44-14.7.44 Cat EFB, flak damage; crashed near North Walsham |
| ML991 | 4.44-3.8.45 |
| *+ML993 | 30.4.44-19.10.44 EFB, 'cookie' exploded soon after take-off, Little Staughton |
| *+ML995 | 30.5.44-11.12.44-28.3.45, 30.4.45-4.9.45 |
| ML996 | 10.3.44-6.10.44 FTR (Dortmund) |
| *+ML999 | 7.8.44-8.9.45 |
| *+Q-MM237 | 3.11.43-6/7.3.45 EFB, shot down in error over Norfolk |

### *No. 109 Sqn*, **Little Staughton**
|  |  |
|---|---|
| DZ433 | 13.1.44-12.6.44 RIW |
| *+D-LR510 | 17.12.43-4.4.45 |
| *+R-LR511 | 17.12.43-14.5.45 |
| *+V-LR513 | 16.11.43-15.10.44 |
| *+P-ML898 | 16.12.43-25.10.44, 26.12.44-31.12.44, 4.4.45-12.4.45, 23.5.45-11.9.45 |
| *+U-ML900 | 29.3.44-18.6.44 FA B |
| *+B-ML907 | 13.9.43-16.11.44 EFB, stalled on approach to Little Staughton |
| *+Y-ML927 | 21.12.43-17.2.45 |
| *+ML929 | 29.3.44-11.9.45 |
| +ML931 | 4.1.44-1.9.44 EFB, crash-landed, Woodbridge |
| *+W-ML932 | 4.1.44-1.9.44 FTR (Cologne) |
| *+ML933 | 21.1.44-2.11.44 |
| *+D-ML939 | 20.4.44-18.7.44 FB B, RIW |
| *+R-ML956 | 30.1.44-5.10.44 |
| *+E-ML960 | 19.2.44-29.6.44 EFB, burnt out at |

LR503-F *of 'C' Flight, No. 105 Squadron, the Mosquito bomber sortie record holder. Ultimately it flew an incredible 213 sorties.*

Manston
| | |
|---|---|
| ML961 | 16.3.44-27.12.44 FTR (Rheydt) |
| *+S-ML967 | 23.3.44-20.7.44 |
| ML976 | 27.3.44-21.9.44 |
| +ML979 | 3.4.44-27.11.44 FTR (Neuss) |
| *ML980 | 3.4.44-12.11.45 |
| *+O-ML985 | 30.4.44-FTR 31.8.44 (Leverkusen) |
| *+C-ML989 | 8.5.44-3.1.45 Cat E |
| *+J-ML990 | 15.5.44-4/5.12.44 FTR |
| *+S-ML991 | 5.44-3.8.45 FA B, crash-landing, undercarriage collapsed |
| *+ML992 | 30.5.44-27.12.44 |
| *+ML997 | 30.5.44-30.9.44 EFA, engine cut after take-off, Little Staughton |
| ML998 | 18.5.44-23.12.44 |
| *+L-MM112 | 30.5.44-23.11.44, 7.1.45-13.11.45 |
| MM114 | 11.5.44-8.9.45 |
| MM117 | 10.5.44-4.7.44, 1.9.44-6.2.45 |
| ML122 | 20.5.44-12.11.45 |
| *+O-MM123 | 21.5.44-22.12.45 |
| *+M-MM241 | 12.11.43-18.8.45 |

## No. 139 Sqn, Upwood
| | |
|---|---|
| DK291 | 8.5.44-1.12.44 |
| DK324 | 18.3.44-2.10.44 |
| *DZ355 | 9.5.44-18.12.44 |
| *DZ606 | 24.4.44-11.44 |
| *D-DZ609 | ?-11/12.6.44 FTR (Berlin) |
| DZ631 | 24.4.44-9.6.44 |
| DZ632 | 24.4.44-9.6.44 |
| *DZ633 | 26.3.44-11.7.44, 12.8.44-? |
| *DZ635 | 5.44-28.6.44 |
| *DZ644 | 24.4.44-30.6.44 FTR (Homberg) |
| DZ645 | 13.5.44-16.7.44 RIW |
| KB134 | 25.4.44-22.6.44 |
| *J-KB162 | 29.5.44-14.10.44 EFB |
| *KB202 | 5.5.44-7.8.44 EFB, crash-landed, from Cologne |
| *L-KB329 | 7.1.44-24.6.44 FTR |
| *W-LR475 | 4.11.43-29.7.44 EFB |
| *N-LR505 | 27.3.44-11/12.6.44 FTR (Berlin) |
| ML909 | 15.9.43-28.6.44 EFA |
| *ML915 | 19.3.44-2.9.44 |

## No. 571 Sqn, Oakington
| | |
|---|---|
| LR498 | 5.6.44-5.7.44 |
| L-ML941 | 27.5.44-4.10.45 |
| *ML942 | 19.4.44-6.1.45 FTR (Berlin) |
| K-ML963 | 19.4.44-9.7.44, 23.10.44-10/11.4.45 FTR (Berlin) |
| +ML968 | 25.4.44-8.7.44 EFA, overshot Waterbeach |
| *+ML970 | 19.4.44-26.8.44 |
| ML972 | 27.5.44-11.11.44 |
| *ML975 | 4.44-15/16.6.44 FTR (Gelsenkirchen) |
| *+ML976 | ?-? |
| *+ML984 | 4.44-20.7.44 FTR (Hamburg) |
| MM113 | 30.5.44-6/7.10.44 FTR (Berlin) |
| *+MM116 | 31.5.44-6.10.44, 21.12.44-20.5.45 |
| *+MM118 | 23.5.44-8.9.44 |
| +MM119 | 31.5.44-28.9.45 |
| *MM120 | 5.6.44-16.7.44 |
| *MM121 | 5.6.44-13.9.44 |
| +U-MM124 | 25.5.44-2.1.45 EFB (crashed near Newmarket) |
| +MM125 | 25.5.44-10/11.6.44 FTR (Berlin) |
| MM126 | 26.5.44-9.6.44 |
| MM127 | 25.5.44-9.6.44 |
| MM129 | 31.5.44-9.6.44 |
| MM130 | 3.6.44-17.6.44 |

| | |
|---|---|
| MM131 | 6.6.44-26.7.44 |
| *MM133 | 3.6.44-5.7.44 |
| PF380 | 26.5.44-25.6.44 RIW |

## No. 627 Sqn, Woodhall Spa
| | |
|---|---|
| *B-DZ353 | 24.11.43-8.6.44 FTR (Rennes) |
| *Q-DZ415 | 20.3.44-9.11.44, 12.3.45-6.9.45 |
| *L-DZ418 | 20.12.43-9.11.44, 23.3.45-15.6.45 |
| *C-DZ421 | 21.4.44-19.5.44 |
| *N-DZ462 | 20.12.43-24.7.45? |
| *+K-DZ477 | 13.12.43-14.8.44 EFA, night training |
| *O-DZ516 | 7.3.44-20.6.44 FTR (Siracourt – Master Bomber) |
| *F-DZ518 | 28.12.43-25.11.44 |
| E-DZ547 | 28.3.44-21.8.44(?) |
| DZ601 | 24.5.44-21.6.44 RIW |

## No. 692 Sqn, Graveley
| | |
|---|---|
| DZ534 | 24.4.44-22.6.44 |
| DZ599 | 4.4.44-26.8.44 |
| DZ608 | 16.4.44-4.5.44, 7.6.44-10.6.44- 10.6.44 FTR (Berlin) |
| *DZ611 | 5.5.44-11.7.44 |
| DZ630 | 28.4.44-7.44 |
| DZ633 | 26.3.44-8.44 |
| *DZ636 | 16.4.44-25.7.44 EFB |
| DZ637 | 17.2.44-5.7.44 |
| DZ640 | 26.3.44-4.5.44, 4.7.44-2.8.44 |
| *DZ641 | 6.4.44-7.44 |
| *DZ642 | 5.4.44-22.6.44 |
| DZ643 | 12.5.44-5.7.44 |
| *L-DZ650 | 15.5.44-27.7.44 |
| ML940 | 4.3.44-14.4.44, 25.7.44-4.8.44, 8.9.44-29.1.44 |
| *ML959 | 12.3.44-9.9.44, 22.11.44-17.12.44 EFB crash-landed, from Hanau |
| *ML965 | 15.3.44-14.4.44, 11.5.44-27/28.8.44 FTR (Mannheim) |
| P-ML966 | 3.44-6.44(?) |
| T-ML969 | 22.3.44-22.4.44, 8.6.44-21.8.44 |
| ML971 | 28.3.44-20.4.44, 19.5.44-4/5.6.44 EFB, crashed soon after take-off for Cologne |
| PF380 | 5.44-22.6.44 |

### SPECIAL DUTY MOSQUITO 'BOMBERS'
## No. 192 Sqn, Foulsham
| | |
|---|---|
| N-DK327 | 20.4.44-28.6.44 BFB |
| L-DK333 | 8.5.44-11.4.45 |
| I-DZ405 | 27.4.44-26.8.44 FTR |
| K-DZ410 | 17.3.43-11.4.45 |
| DZ491 | 30.3.33-3/4.3.45 BFB |
| J-DZ535 | 27.4.44-23.9.44 EFB |

# The weather-reporting Mosquitoes

High-flying, fast-penetrating Mosquito bombers were ideal for weather reconnaissance. As early as July 1942, when they were in very short supply, Bircham Newton's No. 1401 Meteorological Reconnaissance Flight (renamed No. 521 Squadron on 1 August 1942), began operating them ever further

66

*Mosquito* ML897 *used by No. 1409 (Met) Flight from July 1943 to November 1945.*

into Europe, gathering details of weather conditions over bomber target areas.

On 31 March 1943 the last Coastal Command Mosquito meteorological reconnaissance flight was undertaken. Next day the squadron's aircraft moved into No. 8 (PFF) Group, Bomber Command, which positioned its weather-seeking Mk IVs at Oakington. There they were reorganized as No. 1409 (Met) Flight whose strength was raised to 8 IE + 2 IR Mosquito IVs.

Rapid, high-altitude transit being essential for safety, the Flight received its first Mosquito B. Mk IX, *LR498* on 21 May 1943, followed by *LR502* which, on 27 May 1943, flew the first Mk IX operational sortie. Not until 13 October 1943, however, was the last Mk IV sortie flown.

As a result of No. 8 Group reorganization, and to position the Mosquitoes close to Group HQ, No. 1409 (Met) Flight on 8 January 1944 moved to Wyton. There, two days later, the unit received its first B. Mk XVI, the pressure cabin version, to use alongside the Mk IXs.

By now No. 1409 (Met) Flight's work had assumed great importance. As well as obtaining weather information for HQ Bomber Command, the Flight operated at night, dropping flares to ascertain cloud levels, thereby assisting the USAAF in planning its operations in the daylight ahead.

No. 1409 (Met) Flight will probably be best remembered for the sorties it flew in the days immediately preceding D-Day, when its Mosquitoes went in search of any coming improvement in the weather heading in from the Atlantic. It was partly upon the information obtained by crews of No. 1409 (Met) Flight that go-ahead for the invasion was finally given.

### No. 1409 (Met) Flight, Wyton

| | | |
|---|---|---|
| Mk IX | ML897 | 20.7.43-2.10.45 |
| Mk IX | ML906 | 1.9.43-18.4.44 AC FB, 6.6.44-10.12.44 |
| MK XVI | ML930 | 21.12.43-27.11.44 BFB |
| MK XVI | ML934 | 17.3.44-29.11.44 |
| Mk XVI | ML935 | 22.4.44-29.11.44 |
| Mk XVI | ML936 | 4.2.44-21.11.44 |

# The Handley Page Halifax

*'I will state categorically, one Lancaster is to be preferred to four Halifaxes. Halifaxes are an embarrassment now, and will be useless for the bomber offensive in six*

*months – if not before. The Halifax suffers about four times the casualties for a given bomb tonnage when compared with the Lancaster. Low ceiling and short range make it an embarrassment when planning attacks with Lancasters.'*

Thus wrote ACM Sir Arthur Harris, C-in-C Bomber Command, in December 1943. Clearly he was little enamoured of the Halifax, which usually operated at about 18,000 ft where heavy flak was lethal for the heavily laden bomber which could not easily get above 20,000 ft. There were many nights when Halifaxes were unable to operate above cloud cover. Sir Arthur Harris said that the Lancaster always carried '5,000 lb more than the Halifax III' over the same range, and could fly 500 miles further. In wanting Halifax production centres to switch to building Lancasters, he was somewhat unfairly comparing a second-generation bomber with an earlier design.

Since the First World War Handley Page had been synonymous with the heavy bomber, and by 1944 the company was producing a refined Halifax which originated from government approval given in 1935 for advanced twin-engined bombers with a top speed of 275 mph at 15,000 ft and able to carry a maximum bomb load of 8,000 lb. Like Avro's Manchester, the Handley Page design needed to be suitable for bombing, general reconnaissance, general purpose operations and troop-carrying. Ultimately it was the only accepted design which achieved all that, and did it well. P.13/16 designs were discussed in London on 10 February 1937, when favour settled upon the Avro 679. Since the requirement was of such great importance, the twin-engined Handley Page HP 56 was chosen as a back-up, and the company commenced detail design work on 9 April 1937, agreeing four days later to supply two prototypes within 21 months. On 30 April a contract was agreed to build them as *L7244* and *L7245*. Rolls-Royce Vultures would power the aircraft, although the even more powerful Napier Sabre was considered. During June 1937 the Air Council's supply committee decided to opt for quantity production of both the HP 56 and the Avro 679, with delivery to begin in April 1940.

Handley Page worked fast and on 8 July 1937 held the first mock-up conference with Ministry officials. They were already displaying a lack of confidence over the X-section Vulture engine with which technical difficulties were being experienced. Very high stresses upon the central crankshaft were calling for excellent compensatory lubrication and superbly efficient bearings. Since the Avro design also relied upon Vultures, other engines were being promoted for this alternative bomber, including the Bristol Hercules and the possible use of four lower-power Bristol Taurus radials. Because of the Vulture's problems the Air Staff, on 24 July 1937, decided that the HP 56 must be re-engined, and with four reliable powerplants. The only type likely to be available in sufficient numbers was the Rolls-Royce Merlin.

Handley Page were far from eager to undertake such a major redesign, but official pressure gave them little choice. Design work on the four-Merlin version, featuring modified mainplanes and a span increase from 88 ft to 98 ft 10 in, began on 18 August. Able to accommodate an 8,000 lb bomb load in a deep fuselage suitable for troop-carrying, the bomber's 1,980 gal fuel tankage should have enabled a 2,000-mile flight. All-up weight was forecast to be 47,000 lb. A mock-up of the four-engined version was completed for viewing in December 1937, by which time the idea of assisted take-off at least had been cancelled – thanks to Handley Page pressure but after causing three months' delay to the project. On 7 January 1938 100 examples were ordered of what was now the four-motor HP 57.

Prototype assembly began in May 1938, with the Merlin X engine being chosen. Although there were mainplane problems, the airframe of the first prototype was largely complete in December 1938. By then plans were calling for double the 250 Halifax Mk Is scheduled to be completed by April 1942. That meant finding new production centres, sub-contracting and relying upon a split-assembly system.

Construction of the second aircraft, the first to be fully-equipped, started in January 1939. Although assembly started in late April, wing assembly did not commence until 28 October 1939. May 1939 had seen the arrival at Handley Page of the first Merlin engines as complaints were voiced over slow delivery of materials. Those increased with the decision in September 1939 that the Halifax was now to become the RAF's standard heavy bomber. More were ordered before the prototype first flew.

Fearing a repetition of the disaster which overtook the Stirling prototype, the strong Messier undercarriage assembly of *L7244* was locked 'down' for its first flight, of 14 minutes' duration, on 25 October 1939. A suitably large and convenient airfield had been needed for that event, and Handley Page chose Bicester. The prototype was taken there by road and reassembled, as a result of which another two months had elapsed. Initial flights a success, the aircraft then flew to Radlett and by 19 November 1939 had flown 3½ hrs. It was then made ready for brief assessment at the A&AEE – 10 months later than expected and with the undercarriage still locked 'down'.

On 2 December retraction tests were satisfactorily undertaken, then the undercarriage fairing doors were installed. Full contractors' trials of the prototype began on 23 February 1940. On 7 May a Boulton Paul Type C two-gun nose turret was received and the prototype flew to Boscombe Down on 30 May 1940 for full assessment. Successively it was handled at weights of 46,000 lb and 48,000 lb and by July 1940 was flying at 50,000 lb. To cure fuselage shudder, wing root fillets were tried before reflex trailing edges were applied to the wing flaps.

The importance of the Halifax had been further emphasized on 5 December 1939, with a decision to order sufficient Halifaxes to back two years of operational service. This was to be achieved by Handley Page and de Havilland each building 300 Halifaxes, but on 27 February 1940 the DH order was cut to 200 aircraft and cancelled soon after. DH had better business in hand! Handley Page and the London Passenger Transport Board would instead each construct an extra 100 Halifaxes. English Electric at Preston, already building Hampdens, would also produce Halifaxes. Major components for the second prototype reached Radlett for assembly on 31 July 1940. Late delivery of nose and tail turrets delayed its first flight until 16 August 1940. Three days later the Boulton Paul Type R under-gun defence for the bomber was cancelled.

Delays evident in the Halifax programme were, in the Air Ministry's opinion, due to Handley Page trying to make the most of their Hampden. In reality the reasons were more complex. The May 1940 decision to concentrate upon production of the five main existing types was partly to blame and certainly delayed delivery of *L9465*, the first production aircraft to Specification 32/37, until 12 October 1940; an event which took place only two days after its first flight.

Boscombe Down had received *L7245* on 11 September and it was now joined by *L9465* for acceptance and service trials. Both prototypes and the first 50 Mk Is had wing leading-edge slats to help reduce the take-off run. These were soon locked closed in service, acceptable take-off performance being achieved by increased wing flap depression. Analysis undertaken

L7244, *the first Halifax, structurally complete but awaiting its nose turret.*

following testing of the second prototype showed a likely average all-up weight of 55,000 lb, maximum possible speed of 270 mph, and bomb loads varying from 11,366 lb for 880 miles to 5,880 lb for 1,860 miles. Maximum fuel load was 1,392 gal.

Only five Halifaxes had been delivered by 21 December 1940, 10 by 4 February 1941 and 20 by mid-March. Although many early aircraft needed extensive modifications, the Halifax was certainly the foremost RAF bomber at the time it entered service. The first 50 Mk Is were followed by 25 Mk I series ii Halifaxes, featuring pairs of Vickers K guns which could be poked through ports in the rear fuselage sides which more usually served as windows. All-up weight of this version had increased to 60,000 lb due to additional equipment.

Nine Mk I series iiis, with fuel capacity for up to 1,636 gal followed, then came the first major change. After *L9608*, delivered in September 1941, the superior 1,240 hp Merlin XX was introduced, improving the Halifax's performance but also necessitating bulky oil coolers. Fuel tankage was further increased to 1,882 gal. A bulbous Boulton Paul Type C turret, like that in the nose, was fitted in the dorsal position, replacing beam guns, after about a score of the latest variant had been built. The engine change led to the 85th (*L9609 et seq*) being designated HP 59 Halifax Mk II series i. Testing of modifications which led to the Mk II had started in July 1941 using *L9515*.

Worthwhile as the changes were, they did little to increase the aircraft's overall performance and operational usefulness because they increased considerably its all-up weight and wing loading. Although mass production was underway, the first 300 Halifaxes were virtually 'hand-made', partly due to the many modifications introduced which led to non-standardization, which in turn produced a variety of problems for the squadrons. As well as the parent firm, sub-contractors also built Mk IIs, English Electric flying their first example (*V9976*) on 15 August 1941.

An important Mk II improvement involved its undercarriage. Messier was unable to produce the original massive assemblies fast enough, and in any case, the bulky units took so long to retract they impaired take-off performance. Handley

Page therefore chose an alternative Dowty unit with hydraulics similar to those fitted to the Avro Lancaster, and a trial installation fitted to Mk I *L9250* was first flown from Staverton, Gloucestershire, in October 1941. To speed production Dowty employed castings instead of forgings, which unfortunately weakened the structure, as a result of which the aircraft's landing weight was restricted to 40,000 lb. Nevertheless, 904 examples of this variant, the HP 63 Halifax Mk V, were produced by Rootes Securities at Liverpool and by Fairey at their Stockport works between July 1943 and July 1944.

Further refinements involved engine nacelle contours. To further reduce fuselage in-flight oscillation, the inner nacelles of *L9515* were lengthened, and doors completely enclosing the retracted undercarriage were tried. Showing no appreciable advantages, these ideas were shelved for possible later Halifaxes.

Another, simpler, idea initiated in December 1941 led to the removal of the nose and dorsal turrets. Handley Page believed they afforded little protection to the bombers at night, and that their removal would save about 1,500 lb; and reducing drag must improve all-round performance. A metal fairing, Modification 398, called the 'Z' nose by the RAF, replaced the front turret and, in its standardized form, was flown in *W7744* during August 1942. Production quickly got underway, with fitment to squadron aircraft being undertaken at Handley Page's Rawcliffe depot. Aircraft with the new nose were designated Halifax Mk II series i (Special), and also had the distinctive triple fuel jettison pipes removed from beneath each mainplane because landing weight restrictions had been lifted.

In August 1942 Bomber Command complained about what they still considered to be the Halifax's unsatisfactory performance. Investigation into improving its aerodynamics led to the design and testing of a more elegant and transparent nose to supersede 'Mod 398'. Known as Modification 452, it was tested on *W7814* and *DG276* before being approved in December 1942 for the Halifax II and V. Both versions, when featuring Modification 462, were sub-designated 'series ia'. *HR679*, the first Halifax fully modified to Mk II series ia configuration, flew on 24 December 1942. Having a flat panel for the bomb aimer, the new fully-glazed nose was ideal for the navigator and included a .303 in Vickers K gas gun. Most Mk II series ias also featured a Boulton Paul four-gun dorsal turret. Early examples had it set higher and amid combing, allowing increased depression angles for the guns. That reduced performance and was soon abandoned in favour of a low-line turret installation.

The Mk II series ia, with an all-up weight of 60,000 lb, could carry a maximum bomb load of 13,000 lb for 650 miles, but a load of only about 2,000 lb to Berlin. Its top speed was 262 mph at 19,800 ft and service ceiling was 21,000 ft. Designed like the Short Stirling to carry bombs ranging in size up to the slender 2,000 lb type, the Halifax could not readily accommodate the 4,000 lb 'cookie' and its 8,000 lb twin derivative because of their girth. New bomb bay doors were designed and the Mk IIs and Vs had either modified original doors or the new type devised for later Halifaxes. A number of crashes during night landing approaches had resulted when both engines on one mainplane were out of use. Investigation showed the cause was rudder stalling which brought about spiral instability. Halifax rudders had already been the subject of considerable modification to cure overbalance and sideslip 'trailing'. An eventual cure was to fit D-shape fins and rudders of 50 per cent increased area, although only a limited

number of Mk II and V aircraft had this modification. They were in particular a feature of those in the Pathfinder Force fitted with H2S radomes.

Production of Merlin-powered Halifaxes at Handley Page Cricklewood totalled 1,965 aircraft. English Electric built 900 Mk IIs, the London Aircraft Production Group at Leavesden another 450 and Rootes at Speke a dozen – supplemented by 657 Mk Vs. The other 246 Mk Vs were produced by Fairey. Among the Mk Vs were special examples for the airborne forces squadrons and RAF Coastal Command.

By D-Day Bristol Hercules-powered Halifaxes armed all but two of the bomber squadrons. In September 1941 AM Linnell, Controller Research and Development, had requested Handley Page to switch as soon as possible to completing Halifax II series ias with Hercules VI or XVI engines. Although the idea was not new, and the firm still favoured the Merlin, it was clear that if the Halifax was to survive then application of the Hercules must come. Indeed the MAP, fearing inadequate Merlin XX production, ordered a Hercules XVI trial installation and designated the aircraft Halifax Mk III, surprisingly developed by Handley Page on low priority as the HP 61.

Structural modifications this time raised the all-up weight to 64,000 lb, but the top speed of the new version was estimated as 307 mph at 31,000 ft. *R9534*, which had served as a Mk II series i (Special)

*Most Halifax IIIs serving in June 1944 had 'square' wing-tips.*

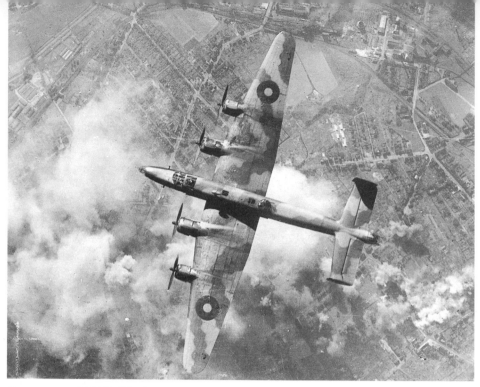

*From summer 1944 Halifax IIIs increasingly featured the increased wing span devised for a high-level bomber version. (IWM C4713)*

prototype was chosen as the Hercules VI trial installation aircraft and first flew in its new guise on 12 October 1942.

In February 1943 the MAP ordered the production of Hercules-engined Halifaxes and they began leaving the production line in August 1943, *HX226* being first off. Of over 2,000 Mk IIIs built, about 1,070 had been completed by 6 June 1944. Instead of the hitherto usual 98 ft 10 in wing span, area 1,200 sq ft, about a quarter of the Mk IIIs then in bomber squadron hands featured a 104 ft 2 in wing span, area 1,274 sq ft, originally intended for the high-level day bomber Merlin 60-powered Halifax IV, which never proceeded beyond the trials stage.

On 19 December 1943 *LV776* first flew powered by Hercules 100 'power egg' engines. A prototype for the Mk VI, it featured the extended wing-tips. A new fuel system coped with the 2,190 gal fuel load. Not until 10 October 1944 did a production example, *NP715*, make its first flight.

In two important respects the Halifax passed into history ahead of its main rival. One was its value to the airborne forces, the other was its service with RAF Coastal Command. As early as October 1941 its use as a paradropper was being considered, and two Mk IIs were soon modified for dropping trials for which exits were cut in the aft belly. Glider-towing was a relatively straightforward modification and in 1942 a Halifax II towed the Hamilcar glider during its trials. Halifaxes also towed those huge gliders into action on D-Day, to Arnhem and during the Rhine crossing.

In June 1944 an interim scheme came into play whereby production line conversions led to the A Mk III and later the A Mk VII, from which nose and mid-upper turret positions were deleted. A larger 'jump hole' was cut, but it was January 1945 before delivery of the 'Airborne' versions commenced. They were but a stepping stone to two schemes for special transport versions. Scheme A (Interim) resulted in the Halifax C Mk III, C Mk V and C Mk VII with seats for troops, stretcher-carrying facilities and no nose armament. Under Scheme B similar modifications were supplemented by the fitment of a large, fixed belly pannier, as featured by the C Mk VIII which entered production in February 1945.

Coastal Command's use of the Halifax

began with the Mk II adapted for long-range general reconnaissance. The nose turret was usually deleted and the mid-upper turret replaced by hand-operated .303 in machine-guns in beam or nose positions. Range was extended by the addition of two 80-gal tanks, and ASV radar was carried. Rocket projectile firing from under the outer wings was carried out successfully in March 1943, although Coastal Command did not rate it particularly successful. More value was obtained from the conversion of Mk Vs for meteorological reconnaissance, which commenced in July 1943 and which enabled probes to be flown far out over the Atlantic – very useful for 'long-range' weather forecasting in relation to D-Day.

## Operations

Personnel to man the first Halifax bomber squadron, No. 35, assembled at Boscombe Down in November 1940. There they trained using prototype *L7244*, specially fitted with dual controls. After No. 7 Squadron's Stirlings moved out of Leeming, No. 35 Squadron took their place in No. 4 (Bomber) Group. The squadron moved to Linton-on-Ouse from where, on 10/11 March 1941, six set out on the first Halifax bombing raid, target Le Havre. It was a luckless venture, for finding an unfamiliar aircraft in his sights over Surrey, an RAF night-fighter pilot engaged and shot down Halifax *L9489*. Undaunted, the bombers first ventured over Germany on 12/13 March 1941, target Hamburg.

On 1 May 1941 'C' Flight, No. 35 Squadron, became the basis for the second squadron, No. 76, which from Middleton-St George commenced operations on 12 June 1941. On 30 June 1941 Halifaxes carried out their first daylight operation, an event which emphasized the importance of beam guns and dorsal defence. This was made even clearer on 4 July when Kiel was raided in daylight, and more so on 24 July when five out of 15 which attacked the *Scharnhorst* failed to return. Not until October 1941 were sufficient Halifaxes available for the third squadron, No. 10, to equip. Thereafter build-up was steady, 131 Halifaxes taking part in the Cologne 'Thousand Bomber' raid on 30 May 1942.

On 5 August 1942 Nos. 35 and 405 (RCAF) Squadrons left No. 4 (Bomber) Group to join the Pathfinder Force with

whom Halifaxes operated until March 1944. Also operating in No. 3 Group in a specialized role were Halifax IIs of Nos. 138 and 161 (Special Duty) Squadrons. They flew mainly from Tempsford to drop SOE agents and supplies to Resistance forces. Their operations often involved low flying and target area loiter, making the Halifaxes vulnerable to ground fire. It was in part to afford them increased range that the turretless nose was developed, but nothing could have easily reduced their high loss rate.

Halifax IIIs were introduced in October 1943 and thereafter the bomber squadrons steadily converted, and by D-Day 21 were operating them. The only Victoria Cross won by a member of a Halifax crew went to Plt Off Cyril J. Barton flying *LK797* of No. 578 Squadron. As the bomber was approaching Nuremberg on 30 March 1944 it was repeatedly raked and seriously damaged by gunfire from night-fighters. Three of the crew misunderstood an intercom message and baled out. Out of contact with the others, Barton courageously pressed on and single-handedly released the bombs over the target. Then came an appalling journey home at the end of which, and with only one engine running, he crash-landed. Cyril Barton died in the crash, but the other three crew members survived.

## Halifaxes on squadron strength, 5 June 1944

(All Mk IIIs unless otherwise stated)

\* operated on 5/6 June 1944
+ operated on 6/7 June 1944

### *No. 10 Sqn,* **Melbourne**
   *HX232*  7.3.44-10.5.44, 20.6.44-5.10.44
\*+*R-HX286*  ?-9/10.4.45 FTR (Stade)
\*+*M-HX323*  16.3.44-5.10.44
\*+*N-HX327*  15.4.44-3.5.45
  \*P-*HX332*  10.3.44-4.3.45 shot down by intruder
      near Knaresborough
\*+*J-HX357*  12.3.44-17.8.44
\*+*S-LK753*  20.3.44-4.11.44, 15.12.44-8.4.45 FTR
      (Hamburg)
  +*U-LK812*  27.3.44-25.11.44
\*+*X-LK827*  20.3.44-15.10.44, 1.11.44-6.12.44
      FTR (Osnabruck)
\*+*C-LV785*  10.3.44-1.1.45 EFB, overshot on
      landing
\*+*K-LV818*  12.3.44-5.4.44, 10.11.44 ?-18.12.44
      FTR (Duisburg)
\*+*G-LV825*  7.3.44-17.6.44 EFB, crashed just after

| | take-off |
|---|---|
| *+H-LV870 | 12.3.44-28/29.6.44 FTR (Blainville sur l'eau) |
| U-LV878 | 12.3.44-23.3.44, 23.4.44-3.6.44, 22.6.44-15.10.44 FTR (Wilhelmshaven) |
| *F-LV908 | 2.3.44-6.9.44, 21.9.44-15.10.44 EFB, crash-landed |
| *+L-LV909 | 8.3.44-13.8.44, 26.8.44-6.1.45 FTR (Hanau) |
| *+A-LV912 | 12.3.44-24.3.44, 6.4.44-20/21.7.44 FTR (Bottrop) |
| *+O-LW167 | 5.44-17.1.45 (Magdeburg) |
| B-LW371 | 12.3.44-9.6.44 EFA, crash-landed at base |
| *+Y-LW545 | 27.3.44-24.6.44, 1.7.44-25.11.44, 20.1.45-15.2.45.6.3.45-29.4.45 |
| *+E-LW716 | 4.11.44 FTR (Bochum) |
| *+W-LW717 | 6.3.44-28/29.6.44 FTR (Blainville sur l'eau) |
| *Z-MZ532 | 26.3.44-9/10.6.44 FTR (Laval airfield) |
| W-MZ534 | 26.3.44-30.11.44 |
| +I-MZ574 | 14.4.44-23.24.9.44 FTR, Neuss |
| *+T-MZ576 | 13.4.44-28.10.44 EFB, ditched off Immingham |
| *+V-MZ584 | 18.4.44-1.7.44 ? FTR (St Martin le Hortier) |
| *+Z-MZ684 | 20.5.44-9/10.6.44 FTR (Laval) |
| NA502 | 6.5.44-29.6.44 |
| *+Q-NA506 | 14.5.44-27.6.44 |

### No. 51 Sqn, Snaith

| | |
|---|---|
| *H-HX321 | 7.4.44-19.7.44 |
| LK748 | 25.1.44-19.9.44 |
| *T-LK751 | 23.1.44-3.11.44 |
| *LK844 | 6.4.44-4.9.44, 21.9.44-14.11.44 EFA, crashed near Leeds during NFT |
| LK845 | 8.4.44-23.4.44, 16.5.44-? |
| LK846 | 6.4.44-6.8.44 Cat EFB, crashed near Beccles while returning from ops |
| *I-LV782 | 23.4.44-14.5.44, 20.5.44-1.7.44 FTR (Trappes) |
| *X-LV832 | 15.3.44-4.9.44, 21.9.44-4.5.45 |
| *A-LV862 | 22.3.44-6.7.44 Cat EFB, crashed on |

| | return from ops |
|---|---|
| LV865 | 15.3.44-28.5.44, 30.6.44-17.9.44 EFB, crashed taking off for Boulogne |
| *J-LV937 | 16.4.44-26.8.44, 15.9.44-9.7.45 FA AC |
| *XH:F-LV952 | 5.4.44-5/6.1.45 FTR (Hanover) |
| *B-LW177 | 23.5.44-1.7.44, 9.9.44-4.11.44 FTR (Bochum) |
| *Y-LW362 | 3.5.44-25.8.44 EFA, crash landed at Snaith |
| *B-LW364 | 6.1.44-9.6.44 EFB, crashed in Yorkshire on return from ops |
| *Q-LW442 | 30.12.43-7.1.44, 6.3.44-12.9.44, 1.11.44-27.2.45 |
| LW445 | 4.1.44-21.9.44 |
| *D-LW461 | 24.12.43-16.9.44, 18.10.44-16.1.45 FTR (Magdeburg) |
| LW480 | 26.4.44-4.12.44 |
| LW504 | 10.1.44-20.3.44, 6.5.44-12.7.44 |
| LW538 | 4.2.44-19.8.44 FTR (Sterkrade) |
| LW541 | 23.1.44-7.6.44, 5.7.44-12.7.44 |
| *R-LW546 | 24.1.44-7.8.44 FTR (Hazebrouck) |
| *O-LW588 | 8.2.44-12.8.44 FTR (Somain) |
| LW642 | 19.2.44-11.5.44, 19.6.44-15.7.44 |
| *K-MZ535 | 26.3.44-18.8.44, 29.9.44-21.11.44 |
| *C-MZ571 | 12.4.44-14.7.44 |
| *W-MZ581 | 16.4.44-21.7.44 EFB, battle damage, burnt out after crashing at Woodbridge ELG |
| *E-MZ624 | 1.5.44-12.9.44 EFB, battle damage, crashed at base |
| *V-MZ634 | 1.5.44-19.7.44, 2.9.44-5.10.44 |
| MZ635 | 1.5.44-15.7.44 |
| *Z-MZ643 | 5.5.44-13.6.44 EFB, written off – severe battle damage |
| *N-MZ689 | 20.5.44-24.6.44 |
| MZ708 | 27.5.44-22.6.44 |
| *L-NA493 | 28.4.44-27.6.44, 13.7.44-12.4.45 |
| NA496 | 30.4.44-27.2.45 |
| NA529 | 2.6.44-29.6.44 |

### No. 76 Sqn, Holme-on-Spalding Moor

| | |
|---|---|
| *L-MK747 | 12.3.44-6.12.44 |
| *T-LK785 | 20.2.44-15.10.44, 28.10.44-23.11.44 |
| LK788 | 20.1.44-25.5.44, 8.6.44-12.12.44, |

*Rectangular fins and rudders, a four-gun dorsal turret, H2S radome and, most important of all, Hercules radial engines were featured by the Halifax III, as typified by MZ359-G of No. 77 Squadron, and which entered service soon after D-Day.*

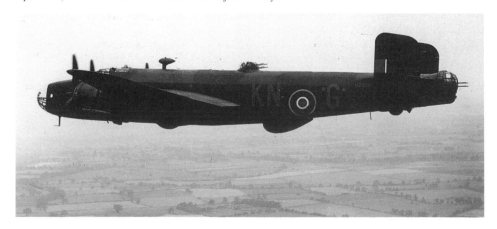

|  | 30.12.44-29.4.45 |
|---|---|
| *N-LK831 | 22.3.44-13.9.44, 26.9.44-5.1.45, 17.2.45-16.4.45 |
| *H-LK832 | 26.3.44-19.8.44, 10.9.44-29.12.44, 23.1.45-10.5.45 |
| *S-LK873 | 20.4.44-19.7.44 EFB, crashed returning from ops |
| LW363 | 9.2.44-21.7.44, 5.8.44-22.9.44 |
| *G-LW620 | 26.5.44-23.6.44 EFB, crashed returning from ops |
| *J-LW627 | 16.2.44-14.9.44, 5.10.44-13.4.45 |
| LW637 | 19.2.44-23.5.44, 20.6.44-13.8.44, 11.10.44-21.11.44 |
| *W-LW638 | 19.2.44-13.5.44, 26.5.44-6.6.44 FTR (Mont Fleury) |
| *O-LW644 | 19.2.44-13.6.44 FTR (Amiens) |
| *E-LW646 | 26.4.44-5.12.44 |
| *A-LW648 | 21.2.44-14.9.44, 18.10.44-14.11.44 FTR (Bochum) |
| *B-LW656 | 24.2.44-24.6.44 FTR (Laon) |
| *Y-LW681 | 29.2.44-13.6.44 EFB, crash-landed Woodbridge |
| LW695 | 3.3.44-7.6.44, 3.7.44-12.8.44 FTR (Russelheim) |
| *V-MZ516 | 23.3.44-10.9.44, ?-1/2.2.45 EFB, engine problems caused crash |
| *P-MZ524 | 22.3.44-FTR 16.7.44 (aborted on 6.6.44) (Nucourt, crashed in France) |
| *K-MZ528 | 28.3.44-29.10.44, 21.12.44-13.4.45 |
| *D-MZ531 | 28.3.44-23.4.44, 19.5.44-8.6.44 FTR (Juvisy) |
| *X-MZ539 | 30.3.44-29.6.44 FTR (Blainville sur l'eau) |
| *U-MZ599 | 24.4.44-28.10.44 FTR (Westkapelle) |
| *C-MZ679 | 14.5.44-29.6.44 FTR (Blainville sur l'eau) |
| *R-MZ680 | 17.5.44-14.9.44, 12.10.44- EFB 3/4.3.45, returning from Kamen, shot down by intruder near Cadney Brigg, Lincs |
| *Q-MZ691 | 20.5.44-23.10.44 EFB (aborted on 6.6.44), crashed near Old Buckenham |
| *F-MZ693 | 23.5.44-5.1.45, 17.2.45-4.5.45 |
| NA522 | 31.5.44-5.6.44 BFA, SOC 9.6.44 |

## No. 77 Sqn, Full Sutton

| JB911 | (Mk II) 31.3.43-16.9.43, 7.10.43-19.11.43, 24.12.43-24.6.44 |
|---|---|
| LK725 | 3.6.44-6.44 |
| *N-LL544 | 25.5.44-6.6.44, 20.6.44-9.8.44, 26.8.44-22.9.44 |
| *T-LL545 | 25.5.44-4.8.44, 10.8.44-9.12.44 |
| *B-MZ673 | 21.5.44-17.6.44 RIW |
| *G-MZ694 | 25.5.44-8.7.44 |
| MZ695 | 25.5.44-13.10.44, 8.11.44-10.4.45 |
| *L-MZ697 | 24.5.44-14.7.44 |
| *J-MZ698 | 24.5.44-17.6.44 FTR (Sterkrade) (35.50) |
| *K-MZ699 | 26.5.44-8.7.44 |
| O-MZ700 | 25.5.44-9.8.44, 27.8.44-25.12.44, 17.2.44-15.4.45 |
| MZ701 | 24.5.44-8.6.44 EFB, engine trouble caused crash near Elvington (6.55) |
| *R-MZ702 | 25.5.44-FTR 23.6.44 (Laon) (33.55) |
| MZ703 | 5.44-18.6.44 FTR (Caen, crashed in France) (82.20) |
| *P-MZ704 | 25.5.44-25.8.44, 11.9.44-5.10.44 |
| *Q-MZ705 | 26.5.44-17.6.44 FTR (Sterkrade) (38.55) |
| *Z-MZ715 | 3.6.44-17.6.44 FTR (Sterkrade) (32.05) |

| *A-NA508 | 31.5.44-17.6.44 FTR (Sterkrade) (42.35) |
|---|---|
| *C-NA511 | 21.5.44-6.6.44 EFB, crashed on take-off, all killed (19.55) |
| *E-NA512 | 22.5.44-12.7.44 |
| *D-NA515 | 21.5.44-3.6.44, 24.6.44-14.7.44 |
| *S-NA520 | 26.5.44-14.7.44 |
| *F-NA524 | 29.5.44-17.6.44 FTR (Sterkrade) (32.00) |
| NA525 | 29.5.44-28.9.44, 18.10.44-7.3.45 |
| NA531 | 2.6.44-13.7.44, 24.7.44-13.10.44 |

## No. 78 Sqn, Breighton

| *+LK829 | 8.4.44-23.6.44, 14.7.44-9.10.44 |
|---|---|
| *+LK838 | 14.4.44-13.9.44, 26.9.44-4.11.44 FTR (Bochum) |
| *+LK840 | 8.4.44-23.6.44 FTR (Laon) |
| LK847 | 8.4.44-3.6.44, 10.6.44-10.5.45 |
| *+LK848 | 23.4.44-8.6.44, 26.6.44-? |
| LL546 | 28.5.44-13.8.44 |
| LV788 | 14.1.44-28.4.44, 17.6.44-18.9.44 Cat B |
| *+LV796 | 21.1.44-7/8.10.44 FTR (Kleve) |
| *+LV799 | 14.1.44-16.3.44, 24.4.44-9.7.44 FTR, crashed at sea |
| LV815 | 23.1.44-3.8.44, 14.8.44-17.8.44, 11.9.44-7.12.44 |
| *+LV820 | 23.1.44-13.6.44 FTR (Amiens) |
| *+LV868 | 19.2.44-6/7.6.44 EFB, serious night-fighter damage |
| *+LV869 | 22.3.44-16.9.44 FTR (Kiel) |
| *+LV872 | 25.2.44-3.8.44, 8.8.44-23.10.44 EFB, burnt; crashed near Woodhall Spa |
| *+LV874 | 28.3.44-15.6.44 FTR (Douai) |
| LV876 | 24.4.44-28.5.44, 10.6.44-30.8.44 |
| *+LV915 | 22.3.44-13.6.44 FTR (Amiens) |
| *+LV957 | 31.3.44-17.6.44, 8.8.44-12.89.44 FTR (Brunswick) |
| LW178 | 24.5.44-4.6.44 |
| *+LW511 | 14.1.44-6.10.44 FTR (Gelsenkirchen) |
| *+MZ557 | 30.3.44-26.8.44, 30.9.44-1.12.44 |
| *+MZ568 | 12.4.44-8.6.44 FTR (Juvisy) |
| *+MZ577 | 12.4.44-18.6.44 FTR (Juvisy) |
| *MZ631 | 30.4.44-13.6.44 FTR (Amiens) |
| *+MZ636 | 1.5.44-8.6.44 FTR (Juvisy) (29.10) |
| *+MZ639 | 8.5.44-5/6.3.45 |
| *+MZ692 | 21.5.44-23.6.44 FTR (Laon) |
| *+NA495 | 29.4.44-6.5.45 |
| *+NA513 | 16.5.44-19.7.44 FTR (Wesseling) (93.15) |
| *NA526 | 2.6.44-16.9.44, 2.10.44-19.2.44, 16.3.44-3.5.45 |

## No. 102 Sqn, Pocklington

| JD304 | (Mk II) 7.3.44-2.5.44 FBA (SOC 18.7.44) |
|---|---|
| *+L-LW134 | 5.5.44-4.8.44 |
| *M-LW140 | 6.5.44-7/8.6.44 EFB, crashed near Carnaby returning from Alencon |
| *K-LW141 | 7.5.44-23.6.44, 17.7.44-12.9.44, 28.9.44-2.11.44 FTR (Düsseldorf) (171.55) |
| *N-LW142 | 8.5.44-7/8.2.45 EFB burnt out |
| *+O-LW143 | 8.5.44-28/29.6.44 FTR Granville-sur-Lo (79.35) |
| *+P-LW158 | 10.5.44-1.1.45 EFB, burnt out |
| *+Q-LW159 | 10.5.44-29.6.44 FTR Granville-sur-Lo (74,00) |
| *+A-LW160 | 11.5.44-25.11.44 |
| *+D-LW168 | 15.5.44-24.12.44 FTR (Mulheim) |

*+E-LW179  23.5.44-16.1.45 FTR (Magdeburg)
*+G-LW191  25.5.44-28.10.44, 7.11.44-9.11.44
           (Sterkrade)
*H-LW192   25.5.44-17.6.44 FTR
*T-LW195   25.5.44-13.8.44 FTR (Brunswick)
*+J-MZ289  7.5.44-18.9.44 EFA, crashed in sea
           during 'bombex'
*+C-MZ292  12.5.44-16/17.6.44 FTR (Sterkrade)
*+F-MZ298  23.5.44-23/24.7.44 FTR (Les Hauts
           Boissons)
   MZ300   25.5.44-6.10.44, 31.10.33-27.2.45
 M-MZ301   25.5.44-16/17.6.44 FTR (Sterkrade)
'*U-MZ642  6.5.44-16/17.6.44 FTR (Sterkrade)
           (56.15)
*+V-MZ644  6.5.44-28/29.6.44 FTR (Granville-
           sur-Lo) (87.55)
*+W-MZ646  6.5.44-28/29.6.44 FTR (Granville-
           sur-Lo) (97.50)
*+R-MZ647  6.5.44-12.8.44 FTR (Russelheim)
           (147)
*+X-MZ648  7.5.44-25.6.44, 13.8.44-3.11.44
*+Z-MZ651  9.5.44-12.6.44 FTR ((Massy-
           Palaiseau)
*+S-MZ652  ?-?
*+T-MZ659  12.5.44-8/9.6.44 FTR (Alençon,
           probably crashed in North Sea)
   MZ676   13.5.44-29.2.45
   MZ710   28.5.44-8.6.44
   MZ711   27.5.44-8.6.44
 *S-NA502  6.5.44-28/29.6.44 FTR (Granville-
           sur-Lo) (89.05)
 *A2-NA503 11.5.44-30.7.44 EFB, burnt out,
           crashed on return from Normandy
 *Y-NA504  12.5.44-17.8.44 FTR

## No. 158 Sqn, Lissett
*+Y-HX329  20.12.43-12.9.44 FTR
           (Gelsenkirchen)
*N-HX340   27.12.43-29.11.44
*+W-HX344  29.12.43-19.8.44
*+G-HX356  24.1.44-8.1.44 EFA
*+E-LK760  3.2.44-8.6.44 Cat E
*+V-LK808  19.3.44-14.10.44, 4.11.44-25.11.44
*+S-LK839  31.1.44-17.8.44 E, burnt out; crashed
           approaching Lissett
   LK850   11.4.44-7.6.44, 4.8.44-11.8.44,
           2.9.44-15.10.44 EFB, burnt out;
           crashed taking off from Lissett
*+G-LK863  10.4.44-8.6.44 FTR (Versailles)
*+Z-LK864  11.4.44-13.8.44
*+O-LK876  22.4.44-8.6.44, 2.9.44-24.11.44
*+R-LV711  2.1.44-8.3.44, 29.4.44-18.7.44,
           12.8.44-FTR 4.11.44 (Bochum)
*+L-LV790  27.1.44-12/13.6.44 FTR (Amiens)
           (195.25)
*+F-LV907  10.3.44-SOC 18.5.44
*+H-LV917  7.3.44-26.7.44, 10.8.44-14.10.44,
           9.11.44 – SOC 18.5.45
*+D-LV920  7.3.44-20/21.2.45 FTR
           (Düsseldorf/Reisholz)
*+J-LV940  15.2.44-8.11.44 EFA, ground
           accident, Lissett
*+U-LW658  26.2.44-18.7.44, 16.8.44-14.10.44
*+Q-LW719  9.3.44-25.3.44, 5.5.44-8.6.44, 3.8.44-
           18.11.44 FAB
*+X-MZ286  31.5.44-8.7.44 Cat EFB, in the sea
           north of Bridlington
*+B-MZ567  26.5.44-12/13.6.44 FTR (Amiens)
           (34.00)
*+M-MZ580  14.4.44-26.7.44, 25.8.44-16.9.44
*+T-MZ582  15.4.44-17.12.44, 6.1.45-22.2.45

+K-MZ703   26.5.44-?.6.44
   MZ730   4.6.44-18.7.44 FTR (Caen for
           Operation *Goodwood*)
   MZ734   6.6.44-5.9.44, 15.9.44-25.10.44 FTR
           (Essen) (221.40)
*+A-NA519  24.5.44-14.7.44
   NA523   27.5.44-28.8.44

## No. 346 (Free French) Sqn, Elvington (formed 10 May 1944, equipped with Halifax V)
   LK660   15.5.44-20.6.44
*+R-LK728  30.5.44-24.6.44
 E-LK731   15.5.44-24.6.44
*+F-LK737  26.5.44-24.6.44
*+M-LK744  15.5.44-20.6.44
*+H-LK955  15.5.44-13.6.44 Cat B, SOC 27.6.44
*+S-LK999  13.5.44-20.6.44
   LL124   27.5.44-20.6.44
*+J-LL126  15.5.44-24.6.44
*+D-LL131  15.5.44-20.6.44
*+K-LL227  15.5.44-20.6.44
   LL237   15.5.44-20.6.44
*+B-LL238  15.5.44-6.6.44 BFB
*+C-LL242  13.5.44-24.6.44
   LL246   30.5.44-20.6.44
+L-LL253   26.5.44-20.6.44
   LL270   6.4.44-5.10.44
*+A-LL395  26.5.44-24.6.44
*+Q-LL396  26.5.44-20.6.44
*G-LL397   15.5.44-24.6.44
*O-LL398   15.5.44-24.6.44
*T-LL462   31.5.44-24.6.44
*U-LL463   31.5.44-24.6.44
   MZ709   24.5.44-3.8.44, 18.8.44-27.4.45

## No. 419 (RCAF) Sqn, Middleton St George
Still holding *JP131* 11.2.44-9.6.44

## No. 420 (RCAF) Sqn, Tholthorpe
*+B-LW380  16.12.43-12.5.44, 31.5.44-29.10.44
           AC FB
*+S-LW382  16.12.43-6.6.44 EFB, exploded over
           Norfolk (160.15)
*+D-LW388  21.12.43-8.6.44, 18.6.44-30.10.44
           EFB, stall landing, Manston
*+K-LW421  23.12.43-16.6.44, 30.6.44-2.7.44
           EFB, burnt out; crashed on take-off,
           Linton-on-Ouse
 P-LW393   23.12.43-26.8.44, 18.9.44-15.11.44
   LW416   23.4.44-23.5.44, ?-17.9.44
   LW423   23.3.44-16.6.44 RIW
*+F-LW575  4.5.44-11.11.44
*+T-LW645  21.2.44-16.10.44
*+E-LW674  29.2.44-11.6.44 FTR (Versailles)
*+Y-LW676  29.2.44-16.10.44
*+X-MZ505  13.3.44-28.5.44, ?-24.10.44
 H-MZ540   30.3.44-26.5.44, 20.6.44-12.12.44
*+R-MZ569  13.4.44-8.6.44 RIW
*+C-MZ587  18.4.44-8.8.44, 26.8.44-31.10.44
*+W-MZ594  22.4.44-29.8.44 EFB, battle damage;
           crashed at Woodbridge (275.55)
   MZ595   22.4.44-28.5.44, 8.8.44-14.10.44,
           31.10.44-15.11.44
*+Q-MZ625  28.4.44-17.9.44
*+L-MZ687  18.5.44-12.7.44, 31.7.44-17.8.44 FTR
           (Kiel)

```
 *+U-MZ713   ?-15.7.44 FTR (Ferfay V-1 site)          31.7.44-14/15.10.44 FTR (Duisburg)
             (119.25)                       *+L-LW394   27.12.43-3.2.44, 5.3.44 ROS, 1.7.44-
 *+J-NA505   ?-8.6.44 FTR (Achères) (37.35)            8/9.2.45 FTR (Wanne Eickel)
 *+V-NA209   ?-23.10.44 BFA, overshot        +S-LW397   13.12.43-20.6.44 EFB
             Wellesbourne Mountford, re- Cat E  *+W-LW467   4.1.44-12.5.44, 22.5.44-28.6.44 AC,
             31.10.44                                   RIW 8.7.44
 *+G-NA528   ?-?                            *+N-LW672   29.2.44-18/19.7.44 FTR (Wesseling)
                                             *+U-LW680   29.2.44-20.6.44 EFB (see MZ683
No. 424 (RCAF) Sqn, Skipton-on-Swale                    below)
  *D-HX316   26.11.43-1.10.44               *+Q-LW715   10.3.44-16.6.44 FTR (Boulogne)
  +P-HX319   30.11.43-21.1.45                 MZ538    30.3.44-12.6.44, 12.6.44-18.12.44
 *+Y-LV910   2.3.44-29.6.44 FTR (Metz)                  EFB, crashed on take-off, Tholthorpe
    LV947    22.3.44-7.5.44, 17.6.44-28.10.44, *+J-MZ618   26.4.44-28.6.44, SOC 4.7.44 (137.45)
             25.11.44-1.1.45                *+T-MZ620   27.4.44-12.6.44, 18.6.44-4.3.45
 *+A-LV951   30.3.44-13.8.44 FTR (Brunswick) *+O-MZ621   28.4.44-4.11.44 BFB, Cat E 25.11.44
 *+V-LV953   11.4.44-16.3.45                *+C-MZ627   29.4.44-13.9.44, 1.11.44-9.12.44,
 *+R-LV959   27.3.44-5.8.44 FTR (V-1 site)             21.12.44-27.2.45 (506M)
 *+G-LV961   13.3.44-29.6.44 FTR (Metz)     *+K-MZ641   4.5.44-10.6.44, 1.7.44-20.7.44 FTR
 *+T-LV970   4.4.44-4/5.7.44 FTR (Villeneuve)           (Hamburg)
 *+H-LV988   6.4.44-28.4.44, 1.6.44-10.6.44  *+A-MZ683   5.44-28.6.44 EFB, burnt out in crash-
 *+U-LV991   7.4.44-8.9.44 Cat B                        landing; collided with LW680
 *+E-LV997   20.4.44-17.5.44, 26.5.44-29.7.44 FTR  *+R-MZ688   19.5.44-7.8.44
             (Hamburg)                       *Y-MZ714   27.5.44-24.2.45
 *+H-LV998   20.4.44-13.1.44 FTR            *+G-NA518   5.44-17.6.44, ?-26.2.45
 *+F-LW113   20.4.44-26.8.44 RIW
 *+Q-LW117   20.4.44-13.8.44, 10.9.44-17.9.44 EFB  No. 426 (RCAF) Sqn, Linton-on-Ouse
             crashed on take-off, base        *LK796    ?-?
 *+O-LW119   25.4.44-18.6.44, 28.6.44-5.3.45  *LK871    23.4.44-20.6.44
 *+X-LW121   5.44-14/15.6.44 FTR (Cambrai)    *LK878    23.4.44-20.6.44
 *+J-LW131   1.5.44-2/3.11.44 FTR (Düsseldorf)  *LK879    26.4.44-17.6.44 FTR (Sterkrade)
 *+C-LW164   13.5.44-18.1.45 EFB, exploded on   LK880    23.4.44-1.6.44 Cat B, SOC 9.6.44
             take-off                         *LK886    22.4.44-20.6.44
 *+L-LW169   16.5.44-6.7.44 FTR (Siracourt)    LK887    23.5.44-20.6.44
 *+I-LW170   16.5.44-4.9.44 AC               *LW377    3.44-30.4.44, 19.5.44-7.6.44 EFB,
 *+W-LW194   28.5.44-29.9.44, 11.11.44-21.1.45           damaged by falling bombs; ditched
    LW392    16.12.43 31.10.44                           off Slapton Sands, Devon
                                             *LW384    11.4.44-17.9.44
No. 425 (RCAF) Sqn, Tholthorpe              *LW436    22.4.44-20.6.44
    LK796    2.3.44-13.5.44, 20.6.44-19.8.44 Cat E  *MZ589    18.4.44-20.6.44
    LW375    10.12.43-1.6.44 Cat B, 18.6.44 RIW  *MZ597    22.4.44-20.6.44
 *+D-LW379   16.12.43-1.11.44 FTR (Oberhausen)  *MZ600    22.4.44-20.6.44
  *B-LW381   2.12.43 18.6.44, 28.6.44 11.11.44   MZ645    6.5.44-?
 *+F-LW387   1.6.44-11.6.44, 22.6.44-31.10.44  *MZ674    ?-?
 *+H-LW391   3.12.43-21.3.44, 15.4.46.7.44,    *MZ690    19.5.44-8.6.44, 18.7.44-13.10.44
                                              *NA510    ?-113.6.44 FTR (Cambrai)
```

*Halifaxes of No. 425 (RCAF) Squadron.*

## No. 427 (RCAF) Sqn, Leeming

*+N-LV821 ?-13.8.44 FTR (Brunswick)
*T-LV902 29.2.44-12.9.44 AC RIW
*+A-LV938 18.3.44-29.6.44 FTR (Metz)
*+Q-LV942 26.3.44-?, to 429 Sqn
*+F-LV945 22.3.44-28.11.44 AC FA
*+E-LV966 ?-?
LV985 7.4.44-19.4.44, 2.5.44-16.5.44,
8.6.44-18.7.44 FTR (Caen)
*+K-LV987 13.4.44-7/8.6.44 FTR (Achères)
LV994 14.4.44-28.5.44, 23.6.44-1.7.44
*+Y-LV995 14.4.44-12/13.6.44 FTR (Arras)
*+L-LW130 29.4.44-13.9.44, 27.10.44 SOC
18.4.45
+C-LW133 3.5.44-12.10.44, 19.12.44-SOC
24.3.45 (5073M)
*+R-LW135 3.5.44-12/13.6.44 FTR (Arras)
(75.20)
*C-LW139 borrowed from 429 Sqn
*+V-LW161 borrowed from 429 Sqn
*+D-LW162 borrowed from 429 Sqn
*+U-LW163 5.44-4.8.44
*+M-LW165 13.5.44-12/13.6.44 FTR (Arras)
*+S-LW166 14.5.44-4/5.7.44 FTR (Villeneuve St
Georges)
MZ288 3.5.44-30.11.44 FTR (Duisburg)
+O-MZ291 20.5.44-27.12.44 EFB crashed taking
off from Leeming
*O-MZ295 ?-?
*+B-MZ304 29.5.44-20.10.44, 4.1.44-25.11.44
FTR, mining

## No. 428 (RCAF) Sqn, Middleton St George (flying Mk II)

*+K-HR857 21.2.44-20.6.44
*+I-HR925 22.4.44-5.7.44
*+C-HR988 21.2.44-5.7.44
*+E-HX183 (Mk III), ?-?
*+O-JN953 29.4.44-12.6.44 EFB
JN967 6.11.43-2.6.44, 26.6.44-11.7.44
JN968 13.3.44-1.6.44, 11.7.44-13.7.44
*+V-JN969 24.12.43-16.6.44
+H-JN976 10.11.43-6.7.44
*J-JP122 10.3.44-15.6.44
*+N-JP124 12.3.44-11.7.44
*+T-JP127 22.11.43-6.7.44
+Y-JP130 20.4.44-11.7.44
JP132 26.11.43-11.7.44
*+B-JP191 9.1.44-1.2.44, 7.3.44-12.7.44
*+Q-JP197 21.1.44-15.6.44
*+G-JP198 21.1.44-20.6.44
*+S-JP201 29.4.44-? to 1666 CU 29.5.44?
JP202 6.5.44-20.6.44
*+U-JP203 6.5.44-20.6.44
JP204 28.5.44-11.7.44
*+A-LW325 19.4.44-20.6.44

## No. 429 (RCAF) Sqn, Leeming

*+HX339 9.5.44-30.9.44
LK803 20.5.44-20.8.44
K-LL547 26.5.44-12.7.44
*+Q-LV830 9.5.44-14.2.45
*+LV866 9.5.44-22.6.44 RIW
*N-LV913 4.3.44-10.4.44, 3.6.44-14.7.44 EFB,
burnt out; crashed taking off from
Leeming
*+G-LV950 23.3.44-31.7/1.8.44 FTR (Coquereaux
V-1 store)
*+T-LV964 31.3.44-5/6.1.45 FTR (Hanover)
*+J-LV965 1.4.44-9.10.44 EFB crash-landed, Old

Buckenham
*+LV969 4.4.44-25.4.44, 20.5.44-9.6.44 RIW
*+W-LV973 4.4.44-23.4.44, 23.5.44-10.6.44 FTR
(Versailles)
*+M-LV993 13.4.44-18.3.45
LV996 17.4.44-13.6.44, 29.7.44-14.10.44
*+F-LW127 28.4.44-18.7.44 FTR, hit by bombs,
Caen area
*+LW128 28.4.44-8.6.44 EFB, crashed near
Benson
*+H-LW132 20.4.44-9.8.44 EFB, engine fire;
crashed near Littlehampton
*+Z-LW136 3.5.44-25.9.44 FTR (Calais)
*+P-LW139 6.5.44-30.9.44, 28.9.44-28.10.44,
17.11.44-23.2.45 EFB, burnt out;
overshot Leeming (480.20)
LW161 11.5.44-24.3.45 became 5075M
LW162 12.5.44-14.2.45
LW163 12.5.44-?
*+A-MZ282 6.5.44-1.3.45
*+U-MZ285 1.5.44-12.10.44, 7.12.44-1.3.45
*+O-MZ288 borrowed from 427 Sqn
*MZ302 26.5.44-29.6.44 FTR (Metz)
*+R-MZ303 26.5.44-1.3.45
W-MZ314 ?-30.1.44 FTR (Duisburg)

## No. 431 (RCAF) Sqn, Croft

*+S-LK828 19.3.44-15.6.44, 20.6.44-3.10.44
*+R-LK833 26.3.44-29.7.FTR (Hamburg)
*+H-LK837 26.3.44-16/17.6.44 FTR (Sterkrade)
*+J-LK845 5.44-29.7.44 FTR
LK989 5.5.44-20.7.44
LV998 17.4.44-20.11.44
*+Q-LV572 3.5.44-19.7.44 FTR (Vaires)
*P-LW432 11.4.44-17.7.44 EFA, ground
accident, Croft
*+O-LW576 3.5.44-13.9.44
LW962 11.4.44-20.8.44 RIW
*+C-MZ509 19.3.44-14.6.44, 17.6.44-26.8.44 Cat
E, crashed taking off
*+D-MZ517 19.3.44-9.8.44, 4.9.44-2.10.44
*+L-MZ537 8.4.44-16/17.6.44 FTR (Sterkrade)
*+U-MZ602 ?-8.6.44 FTR (Versailles/Matelot)
*+Y-MZ628 30.4.44-19.7.44 FTR (Vaires)
*+T-MA655 11.5.44-16.9.44, 27.9.44-7.10,44
*+X-MZ656 12.5.44-9.10.44
+K-MZ657 12.5.44-6.7.44 Cat E, burnt out in
take-off crash
*+E-MZ658 11.5.44-26.8.44 EFA (276.50)
*+V-MZ681 19.5.44-3.10.44
*+A-MZ685 19.5.44-17.7.44
*+G-NA498 15.4.44-9.10.44
*+W-NA499 1.5.44-29.7.44, 4.8.44-16.9.44,
5.10.44-15.10.44
+B-NA514 16.5.44-16/17.6.44 FTR (Sterkrade)
(71.05)
NA517 20.5.44-2.8.44

## No. 432 (RCAF) Sqn, East Moor

+X-LL547 31.5.44-26.6.44
*+B-LK765 15.3.44-9.8.44, 18.8.44-20.8.44
*+V-LK766 16.2.44-12.6.44, 27.6.44-29.6.44,
18.7.44-8.44
LW412 28.5.44-8.11.44
*S-LW552 22.4.44-17.6.44, 23.6.44-7.44 (to 415
Sqn)
*M-LW582 14.2.44-8.6.44 FTR (Achères)
*+Q-LW595 ?-7.44 (to 415 Sqn)
+S-LW592 ?-7.44 (to 415 Sqn)
+D-LW596 8.2.44-30.6.44

LW598 6.2.44-9.6.44 EFB, flak damaged; crashed and burnt, Newton-on-Ouse, Yorkshire
*+R-LW616 5.44-13.6.44 FTR (Cambrai)
*+H-LW686 ?-7.44 (to 415 Sqn)
MZ585 16.4.44-20.5.44, 10.6.44-27.10.44
*+Y-MZ586 20.4.44-7.44 (to 415 Sqn)
*+K-MZ591 20.4.44-28/29.6.44 FTR (Metz)
*+A-MZ601 3.5.44-13.6.44 FTR (Cambrai)
*+E-MZ603 ?-7.44 (to 415 Sqn)
*+W-MZ632 4.5.44-22.2.45
*+O-MZ633 1.5.44-7.7.44, 31.7.44-31.8.44 EFA (183.05)
MZ653 10.5.44-? fate uncertain
+L-MZ654 10.5.44-29.6.44, 18.7.44-3.11.44
MZ674 15.5.44-4.10.44
*+J-MZ660 11.5.44-15.11.44
*+U-MZ686 5.44-7.44 (to 415 Sqn)
*+F-NA516 28.5.44-17.6.44 FTR (Sterkrade)
*+N-NA527 31.5.44-26.2.45

## No. 433 (RCAF) Sqn, Skipton-on-Swale

*+A-HX268 3.11.43-3.10.44
*+S-HX275 18.11.43-8.8.44 EFB
*+O-HX280 12.11.43-29.9.44
*+V-HX290 24.11.43-6.10.44
HX292 23.11.43-18.6.44
*+X-HX353 30.12.43-4/5.7.44 FTR (Villeneuve St Georges)
*+C-LV839 4.2.44-17.3.44, 28.4.44-29.6.44, 22.7.44-11.8.44
*+D-LV842 1.2.44-21.7.44 RIW
*+I-LV911 3.3.44-17.6.44, 5.7.44-26.7.44 EFB, burnt out; crashed on take-off
*K-LV941 5.3.44-25.4.44, 30.5.44-4.2.45
*+P-LV966 31.3.44-14/15.6.44 FTR (Cambrai)
*+B-LV967 31.3.44-2.2.45
*+Q-LV972 7.4.44-24.11.44
*+N-LV992 13.4.44-29.7.44 RIW
LW115 20.4.44-25.5.44, 19.6.44-14.7.44, EFB, burnt out
*+E-LW120 26.4.44-4/5.7.44 FTR (Villeneuve St Georges)
*+F-LW122 26.3.44-21.7.44, 30.7.44-3.3.45
*+W-LW123 26.4.44-4/5.7.44 FTR (Villeneuve St Georges)
*+G-LW129 29.4.44-30.6.44, 31.7.44-6.10.44 FTR (Dortmund)
LW361 24.1.44-3.10.44
*L-LW368 2.2.44-25.9.44
*+T-LW370 24.1.44-27.9.44, 2.12.44-19.1.45
LW374 14.1.44-21.12.44
*+J-MZ284 25.4.44-1.8.44, 25.8.44-2.11.44 FTR (Castrup Rauxel)
MZ285 25.4.44-? (to 429 Sqn)

## No. 434 (RCAF) Sqn, Croft

*+N-LK792 9.5.44-16/17.6.44 FTR (Sterkrade)
*+E-LK799 10.5.44-7.8.44 EFB, swung on take-off, hit LW176
+D-LK801 10.5.44-17.6.44 FTR (Sterkrade)
*+M-LW173 18.5.44-27.9.44
*+K-LW173 19.5.44-12/13.6.44 FTR (Arras)
*R-LW174 19.5.44-1.6.44, 9.6.44-24.10.44, 25.11.44-4.2.45
+Q-LW175 20.5.44-13.6.44, 24.6.44-13.8.44 FTR (Brunswick)
*+J-LW176 20.5.44-7.8.44 EFB, hit by LK799
*+F-LW389 10.5.44-25.8.44 RIW
*+W-LW433 9.5.44-17.6.44 FTR (Sterkrade)

*+X-LW437 9.5.44-29.7.44 FTR (Hamburg)
*+O-LW684 10.5.44-10.6.44 FTR (Versailles)
*+A-LW689 10.5.44-13.9.44, 23.9.44-29.9.44, 7.10.44-23.10.44
*+P-LW713 9.5.44-12/13.6.44 FTR (Arras)
+R-LW714 9.5.44-20.6.44, 18.7.44-30.9.44
*+S-MZ293 18.5.44-12/13.6.44 FTR (Arras)
*+Z-MZ297 19.5.44-16/17.6.44 FTR (Sterkrade)
MZ520 21.3.44-25.4.44-18.5.44-17.6.44 FTR (68.05)
*+T-MZ537 8.4.44-17.6.44 FTR (with 431 Sqn?)
*+T-MZ626 10.5.44-30.8.44 EFA, crashed during NFT
MZ681 18.5.44-3.10.44
MZ716 4.6.44-6.7.44, 26.7.44-9.10.44
*+B-NA494 8.5.44-7.10.44
*+C-NA497 10.5.44-14.8.44, 8.9.44-30.9.44
NA528 31.5.44-30.7.44 Cat E, burnt out; overshot White Waltham

## No. 466 (RAAF) Sqn, Leconfield

HX243 5.11.43-25.7.44 FTR
*+HX266 3.11.43-3.10.44
HX343 19.12.43-28.6.44
*LK793 3.44-7.10.44
LV823 21.3.44-15.7.44
LV833 1.2.44-25.7.44 FTR (Stuttgart)
*+LV837 30.1.44-13.9.44 AC FB
+LV904 29.2.44-29.3.44, 19.4.44-6.10.44, 22.10.44-23.11.44
*+LV936 14.3.44-8.5.44, 1.6.44-28.6.44, 8.7.44-4/5.11.44 FTR (Bochum)
*+LV949 19.3.44-23.6.44, 29.6.44-7.11.44, 9.12.44-9.3.45
*+LV955 24.3.44-16.6.44, 24.6.44-23.8.44
*+LW116 21.4.44-22.6.44 FTR (Siracourt)
+LW172 18.5.44-8.4.45 FTR
*LW178 ?-?
LW372 30.1.44-11.8.44, 25.8.44-6.10.44 FTR
*+MZ283 ?-7/8.6.44 FTR (Juvisy)
MZ287 30.4.44-6.6.44, 17.6.44-8.8.44
*+MZ294 14.5.44-10.8.44, 11.9.44-28.11.44
*+MZ296 14.5.44-23.8.44
*+MZ299 21.5.44-25.7.44, 1.8.44-19.8.44, 17.9.44-15.10.44 FTR (Wilhelmshaven)
MZ306 3.6.44-23.8.44?
MZ307 4.6.44-20.8.44, 30.8.44-17.9.44 EFA, crashed taking off from Driffield
MZ308 4.6.44-23.8.44, 28.8.44-?

## No. 578 Sqn, Burn

+O-LK794 29.2.44-18.7.44 EFB, blown apart; crashed Bisham, Berkshire
*+H-LK809 25.1.44-15.11.44
*+N-LK830 25.3.44-24.6.44, 22.7.44-5.8.44, 27.9.44-15.3.45
*+E-LK834 25.3.44-21.7.44 Cat E, burnt out; collided with MZ696
*+A-LK843 1.5.44-25.9.44, 26.10.44-5.1.45, 18.1.45-15.3.45
+R-LK846 16.4.44-6.8.44 EFB
*+Z-LW346 4.3.44-25.4.44, 13.5.44-12.1.45
A-LW469 16.1.44-3.8.44, 9.9.44-7.1.45
D-LW471 16.1.44-1.5.44 Cat B FA
*+Q-LW473 16.1.44-9.4.44
Z-LW474 16.1.44-28.5.44, 28.6.44-8.11.44
+Q-LW475 16.1.44-16.2.44, 1.4.44-10.10.44, 18.11.44-2.12.44
+T-LW543 20.1.44-10.5.44, 23.5.44-4.4.45

| | |
|---|---|
| *+V-LW587 | 5.2.44-18.4.45 |
| *+B-LW675 | 29.2.44-12.6.44 FTR (Amiens) |
| L-LW678 | 29.2.44-30.5.44, 10.6.44-22.8.44, ?-6.10.44, 17.11.44-14.1.45 |
| *+M-MZ511 | 18.3.44-19.4.44, 2.5.44-21.7.44 FTR (Bottrop) |
| *K-MZ513 | 15.3.44-6.6.44 FTR (Mont Fleury) |
| *T-MZ515 | 18.3.44-28.10.44, 25.11.44-4.1.45, 17.1.45-9.4.45 |
| *U-MZ519 | 9.3.44-7.7.44 EFB, crashed near Farnsfield, Notts |
| *+W-MZ527 | 21.3.44-22.4.45 |
| *+X-MZ543 | 30.3.44-25.9.44 |
| *+P-MZ556 | ?-21.7.44 FTR (Bottrop) |
| *S-MZ558 | 31.3.44-27.6.44 |
| *+F-MZ559 | 1.4.44-4.9.44, 28.9.44-18.11.44 EFB, collided in circuit with NR241; crashed near Camblesforth, Yorkshire |
| *+J-MZ560 | 31.3.44-14.8.44, 2.9.44-9.4.45 |
| *C-MZ572 | 14.4.44-22.7.44 FTR (Bottrop) |
| *+Y-MZ583 | 15.4.44-28.6.44, ?-14/15.1.45 FTR (Dulmen) |
| *+G-MZ592 | 22.4.44-13.6.44 FTR (Amiens) (51.20) |
| +Z-NA501 | 6.5.44-19.7.44, 5.8.44-22.12.44 FTR (Bingen) |
| +K-MZ696 | 21.5.44-21.7.44 EFB, crashed into LK834 near Balkholme, Yorkshire (89.00) |
| *+D-MZ617 | 24.4.44-21.7.44 FTR (Bottrop) |

(142.00)

+H-MZ619  26.4.44-7.6.44 FTR (Châteaudun)

### No. 640 Sqn, Leconfield

| | |
|---|---|
| *+M-LK757 | 28.1.44-8.8.44 EFB, crashed approaching Boscombe Down |
| LK786 | 15.4.44-22.5.44, 6.6.44-28.8.44 |
| *+L-LK866 | 11.4.44-8.6.44 FTR (Versailles) (81.30) |
| LL543 | 6.6.44-6.7.44 AC |
| *C-LW446 | 16.1.44-21.4.44, held. RIW 1.8.44 |
| *+A-LW463 | 16.1.44-31.3.44, 23.5.44-17.6.44 FTR (Sterkrade) |
| *+F-LW464 | 16.1.44-25.7.44 FTR (Stuttgart) |
| *+Y-LW502 | ?-27.6.44 EFA |
| *K-LW554 | 21.4.44-22.2.45 |
| *+J-LW641 | 9.2.44-25.3.44, 1.4.44-7.12.44 |
| *+R-LW652 | 24.4.44-26.9.44 |
| *+D-LW654 | 24.2.44-11.8.44 FTR (Dijon) |
| *+N-MZ500 | 19.4.44-3.8.44, 8.8.44-12.10.44 |
| *+Z-MZ544 | 31.3.44-30.9.44 |
| *+B-MZ561 | 1.4.44-13.9.44, 26.9.44-10.44 |
| *+S-MZ640 | 4.5.44-1.7.44, 8.7.44-21.7.44, 29.7.44-13.9.44 EFA, crashed taking off from Leconfield |
| *+X-MZ678 | 14.5.44-18.9.44 |
| *+T-MZ707 | 26.5.44-6.11.44 |
| MZ731 | 4.6.44-21.8.44, 30.8.44-30.9.44 |
| *+P-NA521 | 26.5.44-28.8.44 |

# The Short Stirling

In the mid-1930s the Air Staff made plans for a powerful strategic bomber force. Medium bombers would form its main strength, supported by 100 specialized long-range, four-engined bombers. For the latter role the Short Stirling was chosen.

Short Bros seemed a natural choice for the contract, having designed advanced long-range, four-engined seaplanes, including the Sunderland. An offshoot of the company in Belfast, Short & Harland, also obtained a bomber contract – for the Handley Page Hereford based on the Hampden.

When the company tendered to Specification B.12/36 it did so with a 115-ft wing span landplane 'Night Bomber' loosely based upon the Sunderland but powered by four Napier Dagger in-line sleeve valve engines. The proposed exceptionally strong structure, very heavy and durable, originated from such needs for seaplanes; likewise the Exactor throttle control system which hydraulically translated commands instead of using a conventional wire style. A maximum bomb load of 14,000 lb meant using wing bomb cells, which in turn necessitated a deep aerofoil section and a 42-ft-long fuselage belly bomb bay; so long that it needed longitudinal stiffeners, which inhibited the girth of the weapons it could accommodate.

The proposed wing span was too great to permit six of the aircraft to be accommodated in a 'C' Type hangar, as intended. Therefore Shorts had to reduce the span to 99 ft 2 in. While that gave the aircraft a rapid rate of roll – useful in combat – the considerable amount of lift lost drastically increased the take-off run. Then serious troubles with the Dagger engine led to its early replacement by the Bristol Hercules radial. Nose, tail and a retractable ventral turret were chosen for defence and a domed canopy to provide the pilots with a superb view; useful, too, for the fire controller.

So important was the costly, new four-engined bomber that Shorts built a half-scale replica and test flew it to gain some idea of the likely handling of the full-sized machine. It proved beyond doubt that the large bomber would need a very long take-off run, but it was too late for the aircraft to be radically redesigned by increasing the angle of attack of the mainplanes.

Instead the undercarriage was redesigned. The result resembled tall and complicated scaffolding containing a crate into which the lower oleo assembly folded, and which was then swung forward to be neatly tucked away. It was a clever feature, but take-off swing inherent in the design, a bumpy surface and maybe battle damage all showed it to be the Stirling's Achilles' heel.

The prototype, L7600, first flew on 14 May 1939, and as it was completing its landing run a binding brake grabbed a wheel and an undercarriage assembly collapsed, leading to the complete write-off of the aircraft. Not until December 1939 did the second prototype fly, and it was June 1940 before the first production example of what had become the Stirling was first flown.

By then it was only too apparent that the Stirling was fast becoming very heavy as more and more operational equipment was added. Whereas a loaded weight of 45,000 lb had been envisaged for the first examples joining Bomber Command at Leeming, with No. 7 Squadron in September 1940, the normal loaded weight had by then risen to 57,400 lb. Worse still, the Hercules II engines installed peaked in their output at a mere 10,300 ft, which limited the bomber's operational ceiling to under 12,000 ft. Its very deep wing would have allowed the high-powered and unconventional Armstrong Siddeley Deerhound to have been installed as a buried engine, but the Deerhound was never developed sufficiently. Only a better Hercules could improve the Stirling.

At the beginning of 1942 the handful of Stirlings in Bomber Command, by then at RAF Oakington, were producing a wide range of irritating troubles. Pressure was applied for operations to commence – for both propaganda and political reasons – with Sir Winston Churchill demanding that these new 'super-bombers' should start bombing Berlin. Boulogne was a more realistic option, but on 10 February 1941 Stirlings quite successfully dropped bombs on a Rotterdam oil target. On their return they faced an airfield whose surface had been churned into mud which, on 26 March, forced the squadron to move temporarily to Newmarket Heath, six days after they had first bombed Germany.

Being virtually hand-made, production of the Stirling was so slow that not until April 1941 did a second squadron, No. XV at Wyton, begin equipping with them. Although they were fast and amazingly manoeuvrable, the Stirlings were poorly defended amidships, for the ventral turret was useless. Hand-held guns were poked through side windows until the FN 7A dorsal turret, designed for the Blackburn Botha, found a new home atop many a Stirling's fuselage. Thus armed, there were a number of occasions in 1941 when Stirlings very effectively took on German fighters, even in daylight. But by the end of 1941 only 150 Stirlings had been delivered and although some performance improvement had come from fitting 1,185 hp Hercules XI engines peaking at 12,750 ft, it looked increasingly unlikely that the aircraft could remain effective for very long. Yet it was so strong, and although it could not carry bombs greater in size than long, slender 2,000-pounders, it could accommodate vast incendiary loads because its lifting ability was very good. Reliability in general increased, and by 1942 three squadrons in No. 3 Group were operating Stirlings. But to reach Italy they had to fly between the high alpine peaks. For many months they proved the most effective bombers when judged by loads delivered, and they could still put up a good fight in daylight. One returned from a night raid with a crew who made three confirmed fighter 'kills'. Perhaps best of all, the Stirling was favoured among its crews, who still recall a feeling of safety produced by the sheer strength of the aircraft and its ability to take enormous punishment – unless a night-fighter poured fire into the clearly marked wing fuel tanks, which caused many losses.

In December 1942 the Hercules VI version, the Mk III fitted with wire throttle controls, entered service with No. XV Squadron at Bourn. First flown in June 1942, its prototype (R9309) – which in September 1942 spectacularly crashed on

Porton Down due to an engine fire – raised hopes that were soon dashed, for even the latest and most successful Hercules wartime variant could raise the operating ceiling to just 16,700 ft, 2,300 ft above that of the latest Mk I and well below the Lancaster's 22,000 ft level. The Mk III's top speed was 262 mph attained at 13,000 ft in FS gear, with a weak cruise maximum of 215 mph at 18,500 ft attainable only when carrying a reduced load. Nevertheless, Mk IIIs replaced Mk Is in the squadrons in 1943 and first operated on 7 February 1943. Loss rates steadily increased, for like the Stirling, German defences improved.

The crunch came in July 1943 with the decision to fade out Mk III production and at the end of the year commence re-equipping No. 3 Group squadrons with Lancasters. Stirling production did not cease for in December 1943 a switch was made to building Mk IV transports. Some Mk IIIs were also modified into Mk IVs.

By D-Day only Nos. 90, 149 and 218 Squadrons were still operating Mk III bombers and No. 199 was about to produce nightly a *Mandrel* screen with the aid of Stirling IIIs. Sea mining, in which Stirlings had long played a prominent part, continued after D-Day, along with many supply drops to Resistance forces. Stirlings of No. 90 Squadron last operated on 7 June 1944, they left No. 218 in August, and re-equipment of No. 149 with Lancasters was completed on 29 August 1944. Four remaining Stirlings of No. 149 Squadron operating from Methwold against Le Havre soon after daylight on 8 September 1944 brought the Stirling's bombing career in Bomber Command to a close.

## Stirling IIIs on squadron strength, 5 June 1944

### No. 90 Sqn, Tuddenham
*C-BK781  9.4.43-13.7.44
 B-BD816  5.5.44-12.6.44
 Q-EE896  13.6.43-24.6.44
 R-EF188  29.9.43-12.6.44
*L-EF196  18.10.43-24.6.44
*P-EF251  21.3.44-24.6.44
*W-EH939  21.3.44-14.6.44
*Y-EH982  22.10.43-14.6.44
*K-EJ115  5.5.44-8.6.44
*U-EJ122  6.10.43-14.6.44
*X-LJ477  24.1.44-14.6.44
*V-LJ506  30.3.44-24.6.44
*T-LJ625  25.4.44-24.6.44
 A-LK383  13.10.43-14.6.44
*M-LK392  17.10.43-14.6.44
*J-LK516  11.3.44-24.6.44
 U-LK568  18.4.44-27.4.44, 20.5.44-14.6.44
 S-LK569  19.4.44-17.5.44 AC FB, 6.44-24.6.44
*V-LK570  19.4.44-24.6.44
*O-LK571  20.4.44-24.6.44

### No. 149 Sqn, Methwold
 V-EE953  5.5.44-8.6.44 EFB overshot
          Methwold
*A-EF140  8.9.43-25.6.44 FTR (Rousseauville)
*R-EF161  5.5.44-29.8.44
 S-EF192  5.5.44-17.8.44
*T-EF193  31.5.44-17.8.44
 F-EF207  14.10.43-29.8.44
 B-EF262  26.4.44-17.8.44
 K-EF411  21.6.43-29.8.44
*G-EJ109  8.9.43-23.9.44

*Stirling III EF411-K of No. 149 Squadron, pictured at Methwold in July 1944, sowed mines off Brest on 6/7 June and flew a total of 69 assorted sorties. (via A.J. Wright)*

| | | | |
|---|---|---|---|
| Q-LJ511 | 13.4.44-7.7.44 FA, swung on take-off | J-EF181 | 25.3.44-12.6.44 EFA, tyre burst, base |
| E-LJ577 | 21.2.44-23.8.44 | L-EF185 | 27.9.43-17.8.44 |
| *M-LJ621 | 19.4.44-5/6.6.44 FTR – special operation | *F-EF207 | 4.5.44-17.8.44 |
| | | D-EF233 | 29.4.44-17.8.44 |
| P-LJ623 | 27.4.44-25.8.44 | P-EF251 | 21.3.44-24.6.44 |
| *C-LK385 | 5.5.44-5/6.6.44 FTR – special operation | C-EF291 | 7.4.44-28.8.44 |
| J-LK386 | 27.11.43-24.6.44 EFB, crashed, Hartfordbridge Flats, from Brest | Z-EF299 | 14.1.44-13.6.44 EFA, undercarriage collapse, base |
| *L-LK388 | 9.10.43-17.7.44 EFA, heavy landing, Methwold, overturned | Q-EJ112 | 12.9.43-28.7.44 |
| | | LJ447 | 29.9.43-17.8.44 |
| D-LK394 | 22.10.43-25.6.44 FTR (Rousseauville) | *E-LJ449 | 1.10.43-17.8.44 |
| | | *K-LJ472 | 28.11.43-17.8.44 |
| K-LK397 | 26.4.44-23.6.44 EFA, belly-landed, Methwold | B-LJ481 | 1.12.43-17.8.44 |
| | | *U-LJ517 | 6.2.44-28.7.44 |
| U-LK568 | 20.5.44-14.6.44 | W-LJ521 | 16.2.44-28.7.44 |
| | | *N-LJ522 | 3.4.44-27.7.44 |
| | | *G-LJ632 | 9.5.44-26.7.44 |
| | | M-LK396 | 30.4.44-17.8.44 |
| **No. 218 Sqn, Woolfox Lodge** | | *J-LK401 | 10.5.44-17.8.44 |
| *A-EF133 | 23.12.43-17.8.44 | LJ568 | 5.44-28.7.44 |

# The supporting Mosquitoes

On 8 November 1943 No. 100 (Bomber Support) Group formed within Bomber Command to provide night-fighter support and promote radio countermeasures (RCM) for the bomber offensive. Mosquitoes became the backbone of the force.

In 1942 ACM Sir Arthur Harris, C-in-C Bomber Command, had first suggested using Mosquito night-fighters in a long-range fighter support role. That inevitably meant British radar being risked over enemy territory, and its loss would be serious. Although none of the few available intruder Mosquitoes had radar, the idea temporarily faded.

By 1943, mounting bomber losses brought renewed interest in giving bombers some level of fighter support, and on 14 June Beaufighter VIfs of No. 141 Squadron, Wittering, started to explore the possibilities operationally. Fitted with aged wide-band AI Mk IV radar, they also had *Serrate* equipment. This could detect enemy fighter transmissions from up to 100 miles away, providing their bearing but not the enemy's range.

After 233 sorties the trials ended on 7 September 1943, by which time 13 enemy aircraft had been claimed as destroyed in combat, despite the Beaufighter being slow for the task and its radar subject to various forms of enemy interference.

Other, quite different support was also being provided by Mosquitoes of No. 605 Squadron. They operated on the flanks of the bomber stream, seeking enemy night-fighters, or flew to their known assembly points to engage them during what were called *Mahmoud* patrols. To be effective the Mosquitoes needed rearward-looking radar, something developed at the Fighter Interception Unit.

Additional support had been introduced in May 1943 when Mosquito IIs of No. 25 Squadron began *Flowers*: night intruder attacks directed at specific night-fighter airfields. The effectiveness of such operations increased in August 1943 when the Mosquito Mk VI fighter-bomber was introduced.

Although it was conceived as a bomber, de Havilland made sure that cannon could be accommodated in the floor of the forward part of the Mosquito's fuselage. A prototype Mosquito eight-gun fighter, *W4052*, was ordered on 18 May 1940 from within the original 50-aircraft order. Three months later the Air Ministry issued a long-range maritime fighter requirement for a fighter to deal with Focke-Wulf Fw 200 Condors attacking shipping around the British Isles. That role the Mosquito could obviously fulfil, so, on 16 November 1940, the first production order for 50

Mosquitoes was further amended to include fighters which, because of their ample endurance, were earmarked for convoy escort duties. There was some consideration over the merit of installing a gun turret at the cabin rear, giving increased operational flexibility, but the fixed gun arrangement eventually won through.

Prototype construction took place at Salisbury Hall near where, on 13 May 1941, the German spy Karel Richter baled out of a Heinkel He 111 only to be soon captured and eventually executed. Had he landed on 15 May he might have seen W4052 take off from a field adjacent to its birthplace as young Geoffrey de Havilland somewhat boldly flew the prototype to Hatfield 'to save time' and avoid dismantling. By then the newcomer had been given a home-based night-fighter role.

Trials showed it to be about 6 mph slower than the standard Mosquito bomber, for it notched up a creditable 378 mph at 22,000 ft. Application of a thick coat of matt black paint radically changed that, cutting the speed by 26 mph. Little wonder it was soon discarded in favour of a smoother grey and green finish.

For all their speed and superb operational capabilities, Mosquitoes were quite demanding to fly, and to ease pilot training 20 fighters were ordered to be modified into dual-control trainers called T Mk IIIs. Mosquito development was remarkably straightforward although the rear of the engine nacelles needed lengthening to smooth the airflow, and a larger tailplane was required. One of the most intransigent problems concerned the exhaust shrouds which generated excessive heat, particularly on the Mk IIs, and which burnt through engine cowlings. It took some time to clear that problem.

The NF Mk II, which No. 100 (Bomber Support) Group was to inherit, joined Fighter Command in January 1942 and two squadrons, Nos. 157 at Castle Camps and then No. 151 at Wittering, were operational in time for the Luftwaffe's April 1942 *Baedeker* raids on British cultural centres.

By that time further Mosquito potential was being exploited. Aft of the cannon there was room to carry internally two 250 lb bombs. Utilizing this space, the Mosquito intruder was born and supplied to No. 23 Squadron which specialized in intruder activity. The strength of the Mosquito airframe was such that a 250 lb bomb could also be hung beneath each mainplane. Airframe *DZ434* (renumbered *HJ662*) was selected to test the idea and first flew on 1 June 1942. The highly successful FB Mk VI had been born. It also led to the development of a new 'basic' wing with points either for bomb racks or long-range tanks and suitable for all Mosquitoes. It was, however, the NF Mk II which first equipped the bomber support squadrons.

October 1943 found Nos. 169 and 239 Squadrons – both ex-Army co-operation squadrons based at Ayr – starting to work up on Mosquitoes. No. 141 Squadron, too, had recently converted to Mosquito Mk IIs with which, after they were fitted with long-range tanks, the squadron resumed operations on 3 November 1943. In November it became part of No. 100 (BS) Group, under whose control it began operations on 17 December 1943. No. 169 Squadron moved to Little Snoring on 8 December 1943 and No. 239 Squadron to West Raynham on 9 December. Both were then fully-equipped with Mk IIs which they introduced to operations in the last week of January 1944.

Their tasks were threefold: 1) to engage enemy night-fighters in the target area and patrol there to give rear support; 2) to tackle enemy fighters in their airborne assembly areas; and 3) to provide protection for the bombers by flying about 40 miles away from the bomber stream. Although the tactics were mixed, the Mosquitoes were soon destroying German fighters.

Within a few weeks the aged Mk IIs, distinctive like so many 100 Group Mosquitoes because of their grey and green camouflage and black sides and undersurfaces, were showing many signs of wear, and their radar quickly became troublesome. Badly worn engines were eventually replaced with Merlin XXIIs. Some improvement in 100 Group's situation came in February 1944 when No. 515 Squadron, which had operated the *Mandrel* radar jamming screen, logically moved from Fighter Command to Bomber Command, but to perform in yet another role: low-level intruding on enemy airfields. When on 5 May No. 515 Squadron began operating with Mosquito

FB Mk VIs – then in short supply – they were examples borrowed from No. 605 Squadron, with whom No. 515 trained. By D-Day it held its own quota.

During May 1944 the 100 or so Mosquitoes in 100 Group flew 212 sorties and claimed to destroy 18 enemy aircraft. Such success strengthened belief in bomber support operations, and the go-ahead was given to fit *Serrate* in FB Mk VIs which would replace Mk IIs, some of which by this time had rearward-looking radar. Replacement was underway by D-Day, No. 169 Squadron on 18 June 1944 being the first to operate the modified Mk VIs, which had fully replaced Mk IIs by July 1944.

Despite the fighter cover, bomber losses were mounting, so two more Mosquito squadrons, Nos. 85 and 157, left ADGB and moved to Swannington and into No. 100 Group early in May 1944. No. 85 Squadron was flying the latest Mosquito night-fighter, the Mk XIX fitted with AI VIII radar. As soon as the even more advanced, five-mile-range narrow beam AI Mk X-equipped Mosquito Mk XIXs became available, No. 85 re-equipped and passed on its older Mk XIXs to No. 157 Squadron. Both squadrons were, by 21 May 1944, ready to operate.

Design work on the Mosquito Mk XIX fighter – originally intended to have two-stage Merlins and proposed as a Coastal Command variant – had begun in November 1943. Powered by Merlin XXVs tuned for high-speed, low-level duty, and initially fitted with AI Mk VIII in the 'thimble' nose and later the 'bull' or Universal nose, the Mk XIX first flew in April 1944 and on 21 April was released for service, being the latest fighter variant. Although weighing 20,421 lb fully loaded, and thus being heavier than previous Mosquito fighters, it could still attain 378 mph – but at 13,200 ft, which was why two-stage engines had initially been intended for this mark. On 5/6 June low-level operations commenced, No. 85 Squadron taking the NF Mk XIX on operations for the first time by flying a dozen patrols over Normandy, while four of '157's examples operated over Deelen, Eindhoven, Gilze-Rijen and Soesterberg. Standard tactics involved low-level intruding while carrying two bombs, low-level patrolling before climbing ahead of the bomber stream, and loitering in the target area for 30 minutes after an attack. Finally, more low-flying Mosquitoes carrying two bombs would provide an unwelcome homecoming for German fighters. Mosquito *MM630-E* of No. 157 Squadron was the first Mk XIX to register a 'kill', a Ju 188 destroyed on 12/13 June 1944 near Compiegne.

Additional to Mosquito fighters and fighter-bombers in No. 100 Group were half a dozen Mk IV bombers. In November 1942 three Mk IVs had been placed in a special operations unit, No. 1474 Flight of No. 3 (Bomber) Group, and on 4 January 1943 the Flight became part of No. 192 Squadron. In great secrecy the Mosquitoes were fitted with equipment to detect enemy radio and radar transmission frequencies, a task begun off the enemy coast on 11 June 1943 and still taking place during the D-Day period, by which time the squadron

*Bomber support Mosquito VIs usually carried 'invasion stripes' to the end of hostilities. PZ459-O of No. 515 Squadron was one such example.*

generally held six Mosquito Mk IVs.

# Mosquitoes of No. 100 (Bomber Support) Group, 5 June 1944

*operated one mission
** two missions on 5/6.6.44

## MOSQUITO NF Mk II

### No. 141 Sqn, West Raynham
### 4.12.43–3.7.44

| | | |
|---|---|---|
| *P-DD673 | 24.3.44-9.6.44 EFB | |
| G-DD725 | 17.10.43-23.8.44 | |
| *S-DD732 | 30.3.44-22.6.44 EFB | |
| DD736 | 1.4.44-21.7.44 | |
| DD735 | 30.12.43-16.11.44 | |
| *DD753 | 30.12.43-8.2.44, 25.3.44-16.11.44 | |
| DD758 | 18.9.43-8.6.44 EFB, belly-landed, West Raynham; hit two Spitfires | |
| *F-DD787 | 7.4.44-28.6.44 FTR | |
| *H-DZ240 | 6.4.66-25.7.44 | |
| DZ300 | 27.5.44-17.6.44 EFB | |
| DZ303 | 25.9.43-22.8.44 | |
| *C-DZ761 | 25.9.43-22.8.44 | |
| B-HJ659 | 7.10.43-?.44 | |
| T-HJ710 | 1.44-? | |
| A-HJ911 | 11.3.44-13.2.45 | |
| J-HJ937 | 2.6.44-21.7.44 | |
| X-HJ941 | 13.11.43-28.6.44 FTR | |

### No. 169 Sqn, Little Snoring 8.12.43; Great Massingham 14.6.44–10.8.45

| | |
|---|---|
| *W4076 | 19.2.44-7.7.44 |
| *A-W4085 | 2.3.44-10.7.44 AC FA |
| DD605 | 6.12.43-4.7.44 |
| **DD779 | 13.3.44-? |
| *DD790 | 19.3.44-28.6.44 |
| DD799 | 20.1.44-7.7.44 |
| *DZ254 | 5.2.44-30.8.44 |
| *DZ296 | 17.2.44-18.7.44 |
| **DZ310 | 9.2.44-24.6.44 |
| **DZ741 | 8.3.44-28.6.44 |
| *DZ748 | 4.5.44-28.6.44 |
| N-HJ917 | 3.2.44-17.6.44, 12.8.44-7.9.44 |
| HJ922 | 3.2.44-28.4.44, major inspection, 18.7.44-11.9.44 |
| *HJ923 | 239 Sqn aircraft |
| *DD753 | 141 Sqn aircraft |

### No. 239 Sqn, West Raynham 10.12.43–10.7.45

| | |
|---|---|
| *W4074 | 2.5.44-8.6.44 EFA, overshot runway, base |
| W4078 | 20.3.44-28.8.44 BFA |
| B-W4092 | 27.3.44-21.6.44 |
| *W4097 | 22.3.44-10.10.44 |
| *DD622 | 7.4.44-6.8.44, 4.10.44-6.10.44 |
| DD720 | 21.1.44-7.7.44 |
| *DD722 | 27.3.44-25.9.44 |
| DD749 | 25.4.44-3.8.44 EFA, burnt out, stalled during overshoot |
| DD756 | 22.4.44-21.6.44 |
| DD759 | 17.2.44-3.8.44 |
| *DD789 | 17.3.44-9.10.44 |
| *DZ256 | 7.4.44-27.10.44 EFA, spun in Stapleford Woods, near Newark, during fighter affiliation with |

| Lancaster | |
|---|---|
| *DZ265 | 11.3.44-7.10.44 |
| DZ271 | 4.2.44-6.4.44, 6.44-10.44 |
| DZ290 | 8.2.44-6.10.44 |
| DZ297 | 9.2.44-9.9.44 |
| DZ298 | 6.4.44-4.11.44 |
| *DZ309 | 17.4.44-24.8.44 BFA |
| DZ654 | 28.1.44-17.3.44, 17.6.44-29.8.44 FTR |
| DZ661 | 14.2.44-1.4.44, 17.6.44-16.9.44 |
| HJ649 | 4.2.44-9.4.44, 4.7.44-14.10.44 |
| HJ916 | 18.5.44-28.6.44 |
| HJ923 | 22.4.44-17.8.44 |
| HJ934 | 8.3.44-15.2.45 |

## MOSQUITO FB Mk VI

No. 23 Sqn arrived in Britain from MAC on 1 June 1944 and moved into Little Snoring. Resumed flying 19 June 1944. Commenced operations 5/6 July 1944

### No. 23 Sqn, Little Snoring

| | |
|---|---|
| PZ176 | 26.5.44-1.10.45 |
| PZ177 | 24.5.44-18.9.44 FTR |
| PZ178 | 25.5.44-22.3.45 |
| PZ180 | 25.5.44-18.9.44 EFA, tyre burst, undercarriage collapsed |
| PZ181 | 26.5.44-3.4.45 |
| PZ182 | 31.5.44-17.4.45 FBB |
| PZ183 | 26.5.44-3.4.45 |
| PZ187 | 1.6.44-21.11.44 |

### No. 141 Sqn, West Raynham, equipping

| | |
|---|---|
| LR531 | 20.4.44-28.6.44 |

### No. 169 Sqn, Little Snoring 8.12.43; Great Massingham 4.6.44–10.8.45

| | |
|---|---|
| NS995 | 31.3.44-3.7.44 BFA |
| C-NS997 | 28.3.44-9.3.45 |
| NS998 | 20.3.44-14.1.45 |
| NT112 | 31.3.44-9.44 |
| NT113 | 31.3.44-14.1.45 |
| NT116 | 4.44-5.1.45 FTR |
| NT118 | 12.4.44-13.1.45 |
| NT121 | 4.44-25.3.45 |
| NT148 | 13.4.44-20.8.44 EFA, crashed on Square Farm, Syderstone, Norfolk |
| NT150 | 17.4.44-14.1.45 BFB |
| NT156 | 21.4.44-21.9.44 |
| NT169 | 19.4.44-9.3.45 |
| NT172 | 20.4.44-6.12.44 FTR |
| NT173 | 21.4.44-12.8.44 FTR |
| NT178 | 21.4.44-14.1.45 |

### No. 239 Sqn, West Raynham, equipping

| | |
|---|---|
| PZ174 | 24.5.44-21.7.44 FTR |

### No. 515 Sqn, Little Snoring 3.44–10.6.45

| | |
|---|---|
| DD666 | (Mk II) 3.44-18.3.44, 13.6.44-25.7.44 |
| MM420 | 15.3.44-14/15.9.44 FTR |
| NS932 | 19.3.44-19.7.44 |
| NS933 | 19.3.44-19.7.45 |
| NS944 | 19.3.44-27/28.8.44 FTR |
| *NS950 | 14.3.44-6.6.44 FTR |
| *NS951 | 14.3.44-13.8.44 BFA, re-Cat E |
| *NS953 | 19.3.44-29.10.44 FTR |
| NS954 | 20.3.44-18.6.44 BFA |

NS955 20.3.44-?
NS957 22.3.44-19/20.3.45 FTR
NS961 21.3.44-?
NS962 20.3.44-18.9.44 FTR
S-NS992 4.5.44-5.3.45 ground accident, Cat E
26.5.45; (ex-617 Sqn)
*NS993 14.5.44-FTR 30.9.44, forced landing,
Dubendorf, Switzerland
*NT132 13.4.44-10.9.44 AC FB
*PZ161 18.5.44-27.8.44 FTR
*PZ163 16.5.44-4.9.44 EFB
PZ184 3.6.44-16.9.44 FTR
PZ188 1.6.44-3.4.45
*PZ189 31.5.44-FTR 5.6.44

## MOSQUITO NF Mk XIX
### *No. 85 Sqn,* **Swannington**
**1.5.44–14.7.44, 19.8.44–27.6.45**
MM624 18.5.44-7.11.44 FTR
MM625 11.5.44-2.7.44 EFA overshot base
MM626 9.5.44-8.12.44
MM627 9.5.44-4.12.44
MM628 9.5.44-30.10.44 FTR
MM629 9.5.44-22.11.44 EFB, shot down in
error
MM632 11.5.44-14.8.44 FTR
MM633 16.5.44-16.4.45 FTR
MM634 11.5.44-8.12.44
MM635 16.5.44-12.8.44
MM636 16.5.44-12.8.44
MM640 25.5.44-13.10.44
MM641 18.5.44-8.12.44
MM642 20.5.44-8.12.44
MM644 20.5.44-8.12.44

MM645 20.5.44-26.10.4
MM646 18.5.44-12.8.44
MM648 23.5.44-26.9.44 EFA, crashed at East
Barton, Norfolk

### *No. 157 Sqn,* **Swannington**
**7.5.44–21.7.44, 29.8.44–6.45**
DZ291 (Mk II) 9.11.43-16.3.45(?)
*E-MM630 2.6.44-9.12.44
P-MM637 27.5.44-28.7.44, 2.9.44-15.10.44,
31.1.45-21.2.45
Q-MM639 27.5.44-15.7.44, 7.9.44-7.10.44
F-MM643 27.5.44-29.9.44 FTR
J-MM650 23.5.44-14/15.3.45 FTR
MM652 27.5.44-18.11.44 FA
MM653 21.7.44-21.2.45
MM654 23.5.44-22.7.44 EFB, crashed on
take-off, West Malling
MM655 23.5.44-23.7.44 EFA, undercarriage
collapsed on take-off, West Malling
MM656 27.5.44-29.7.44 BFA
H-MM670 30.5.44-25.8.44
C-MM671 27.5.44-25.10.44 EFA, power loss on
take-off, abandoned run
MM672 2.6.44-1.9.44 EFA, night collision
with Mosquito *MM676,* Lime Kiln
Farm, Hayden, Norfolk
MM673 2.6.44-8.7.44 FA
*T-MM674 2.6.44-16.9.44 BFB overshot,
Swannington
MM675 2.6.44-25.6.44
W-MM676 6.6.44-25.6.44 BFA
A-MM678 6.6.44-6/7.10.44 FTR

# The supporting 'heavies'

## Boeing Fortress II

Bomber Command's 1941 experiences of the vaunted B-17C 'Flying Fortress' were unforgettable. Its range was ample, it could fly high, but opening the gun ports let in penetrating intense cold giving the crew frostbite, while bold vapour trails revealed the aircraft's position to the defenders. By the time the Americans joined the war, superior B-17Es and B-17Fs were flying and available in sufficient numbers to operate in formation to obtain protection.

Although production rates made these B-17s available under Lend Lease, previous experiences and the small bomb bay rendered the Fortress unattractive to RAF Bomber Command, equipped with the superb Lancaster and Mosquito. Those Fortresses that found their way to the RAF were employed by Coastal Command as long-range maritime bombers armed with depth charges, with which some notable attacks were made upon U-boats.

Nevertheless, the high-flying performance of the B-17 retained British interest, and this increased when No. 100 (BS) Group formed. Fortresses, it was suggested, could participate in specialized operations, flying above the main stream bomber force, jamming, receiving, intercepting and transmitting radio signals over greater distances than Lancasters or Halifaxes, and with greater safety.

The US 8th AF was approached and readily agreed to spare a few B-17Fs from its 1st Air Division for radio countermeasures (RCM) operations. To work up the force Sculthorpe airfield was taken over from No. 2 Group on 1 January 1944, and on 10 January 1944 three

USAAF B-17Fs arrived with their crews to train RAF personnel how to handle the aircraft. A new RAF squadron, No. 586, was to operate RCM B-17Fs.

Two B-17Fs reached TFU Defford in early January 1944 to be fitted with special signals equipment. The three USAAF B-17s and crews at Sculthorpe soon formed the basis of an equivalent American squadron, the 803rd (Photographic) Squadron. For British B-17Fs aircrew were drawn partly from No. 214 Squadron, then flying Stirlings and awaiting conversion to Lancasters under the No. 3 Group Ladder Plan. The association of '214' soon led to that number being given to the new Fortress II squadron instead of the intended No. 586.

Three B-17Fs joined No. 214 Squadron during January 1944, the first arriving from Rougham on the 28th and two more the next day, one coming from Thurleigh. By the first week of February 1944 13 B-17Fs, mainly withdrawn from a variety of front-line 8th AF bases, were in No. 100 Group hands. They had been released by the 8th AF after it received 13 replacement B-17Gs. Although the first eight B-17G Fortress IIIs for the RAF arrived in February 1944 and another 14 in March, none was operated by No. 100 Group prior to D-Day. The Fortress IIIs were to have their chin turrets replaced by a large radome. To cope with expected wastage another 16 B-17Fs were earmarked under Lend Lease.

By 1 March No. 214 Squadron had 10 operational Fortress IIs and a B-17G navigational trainer. The other four B-17Fs were at Hinton-in-the-Hedges having RCM equipment installed by No. 26 Group. Six of the others were flown there for modification during March, their places being taken, for training purposes, by another B-17F and seven loaned B-17Gs which almost certainly retained their USAAF fin serial numbers. Also at Sculthorpe between 19 March and 24 May was *AN537*, one of the aged Fortress Is, assigned for flying training before being passed to No. 1699 Flight which formed to train Fortress aircrew and which, on 10 May, took on charge Fortress III *HB778*, the first to join Bomber Command.

By the end of March 1944 five B-17Fs fitted with interim *Airborne Cigar*, *Monica Mk IIA* and *Gee* were on squadron strength.

Another five B-17s equipped with *Mandrel* and *Carpet* jammers were on the strength of the 803rd (P) Squadron, USAAF by mid-April, making Sculthorpe a jointly-operated and quite unique B-17 base.

No. 214 Squadron began operating on 20/21 April 1944, despatching *SR386-N* and *SR388-H* to support a bombing raid on La Chapelle while *SR377-N* and *SR382-B* worked with other bombers attacking Ottiglas, SE of Brussels. Carrying an eight-man crew (a pilot, two navigators, a flight engineer, wireless operator, special equipment operator and two air-gunners), the Fortress IIs, often operating around 23,000 ft were fitted with *Gee* for navigation, equipment to jam German airborne radar and VHF voice communications – for which tall radio masts atop the fuselage were eye-catching features – and *Monica* tail warning radar. *H2S* was later added, in the chin radome.

By the third week of April the USAAF was modifying a B-17G as an RCM prototype. Seven modified B-17Fs at this time returned to No. 214 Squadron from Prestwick, where Scottish Aviation had been working on them, and the squadron operated seven times in April. A month later, after much modification work, No. 214 Squadron held its full complement of 12 Fortress IIs and two in reserve. After operating on 12/13 May the squadron stood down and on 16 May 1944 moved to Oulton. Sculthorpe closed for upgrading to very heavy bomber base status. Operations by No. 214 Squadron were resumed on 19/20 May 1944.

For No. 214 Squadron, the night of 5/6 June 1944 was ill-starred. Two of the five Fortresses operated had to return early and a third was damaged by a night-fighter attack. Not until 11/12 June 1944 did the Fortresses resume operations, flying a patrol over St Valery-en-Caux. Equipment then included two Fortress IIIs, *HB763* and *HB774*, which were posted in on 7 June 1944.

## FORTRESS IIs ON THE STRENGTH OF NO. 214 SQUADRON, 5 JUNE 1944

| Serial | US identity | Base supplying | Dates used, etc |
|---|---|---|---|
| SR376 | 42-3177 | Ridgewell | 2.2.44-21.12.44 |
| *M-SR377 | ? | ? | 29.1.44-9.2.45 |
| D-SR378 | 42-30241 | Knettishall | 2.2.44-4.1.45 |
| O-SR379 | ? | Snetterton | 3.2.44-31.12.44 |

| | | | |
|---|---|---|---|
| S-SR380 | 42-30639 | Framlingham | 2.2.44-19.10.44 |
| *F-SR381 | 42-30773 | Bassingbourn | 2.2.44-21.7.44 RIW |
| *B-SR382 | 42-30809 | Chelveston | 2.2.44-22.6.44 EFB |
| SR383 | 42-30812 | Thurleigh | 29.1.44-8.12.44 |
| A-SR384 | 42-30970 | Gt Ashfield | 2.2.44-22.5.44 EFB |
| SR385 | 42-30986 | Knettishall | 2.2.44-30.8.45 |
| *N-SR386 | ? | Rougham | 28.1.44-8.12.44 |
| SR387 | 42-30127 | Framlingham | 2.8.44-14.2.45 |
| *H-SR388 | ? | Burtonwood | 2.2.44-27.12.44 BFB |
| P-SR389 | ? | Thurleigh | 5.2.44-7.1.45 |

For flying training No. 214 Squadron operated Fortress Is *AN520* (19.2.44-5.44) and *AN537* (19.3.44-24.5.44) until these passed to No. 1699 Flight.

## Handley Page Halifax

When RCM Flights formed they were part of No. 3 (Bomber) Group, which had for many months operated modified Wellingtons. Initially they were operated by No. 1474 Flight which on 4 January 1943 became No. 192 Squadron whose 'A' Flight, using Wellington Ics, IIIs and Xs, concentrated upon ELINT duties and the development of *Mandrel*. During December 1943 the squadron moved from Feltwell to Foulsham to join No. 100 Group. There one of its tasks was to carry out radar 'mapping' and electronic searches.

The roomy Halifax was better for such tasks but had been out of place in No. 3 Group, for Halifaxes were concentrated in No. 4 (Bomber) Group. Two Mk IIs (*DT735* and *DT737*) had nevertheless been acquired in January 1943 and were soon supplemented by another two (*DK244* and *DK246*). The Mk IIs served in an RCM role until February 1944 when Mk IIIs replaced

them and the unit's Halifax establishment was increased.

### HALIFAX IIIs ON SQUADRON STRENGTH, 5 JUNE 1944
### No. 192 Sqn, Foulsham

| | |
|---|---|
| Y-LK781 | 20.2.44-26.9.44 |
| Z-LK782 | 20.2.44-13.8.44, 17.10.44-26.10.44 |
| LK874 | 18.4.44-25.9.44 |
| *W-LW613 | 15.2.44-26.10.44 |
| *Q-LW621 | 30.4.44-5.7.44 FTR |
| S-LW623 | 15.2.44-26.10.44 |
| *T-LW624 | 24.3.44-27.9.44 |
| U-LW625 | 12.2.44-23.3.44, 13.4.44-23.5.44, 15.7.44-2.6.45 |
| Y-MZ564 | 12.2.44-28.4.44, 10.7.44-11.8.44, 5.9.44-2.10.44 |
| R-MA638 | 1.5.44-12/13.7.44 EFB, overshot Foulsham on landing (34.05) |
| P-MZ706 | 27.5.44-15.3.45 |
| MZ717 | 4.6.44-30.11.44 AC FB |

## Short Stirling III

Bomber Command transferred No. 199 Squadron (16 + 4 Stirling IIIs) from No. 3 to No. 100 (BS) Group on 1 May 1944, and to North Creake, a station just opening. The aircraft were fitted with 'a selection of *Mandrels* to form a screen against early warning radars', to quote Bomber Command. The squadron was also to carry out 'spoofs' employing new types of *Window*. At TFU Defford *Mandrel* jamming equipment was installed in 12 Stirlings, the remaining eight being modified at Foulsham. The intention was to start operating on 20 May 1944. By then four Stirlings still needed the application of TFU skill and not until 5/6 June 1944 did the first operation commence. That involved pairs of Stirlings orbiting in formation over eight fixed positions in the

*Although No. 214 Squadron operated ex-8th AF Fortress IIs on D-Day, Mk IIIs including B-17G-BO HB773 were already being prepared for No. 100 Group.*

English Channel throughout the night.

Despite the fact that this was the squadron's first *Mandrel* operation, and the equipment new, seven of the most important jamming stations were manned successfully throughout the night, with the jamming covering bands between 70 and 200 megacycles. A similar task was undertaken off the American beach areas by four B-17s of the 803rd (P) Squadron, USAAF *Mandrel* operations rapidly increased in complexity and by mid-June the jammers would orbit some 80 miles off the enemy coast and at points about 28 miles apart to jam *Freya* radar. Single USAAF B-17s would operate between the paired Stirlings. Other Stirlings were placed at 40-mile intervals to stop these narrow-beam stations looking between jamming centres. TR1657 *Mandrel* was also soon in use for spot frequency jamming in the band between 150 and 200 megacycles. The *Mandrel* screen, behind which RAF night bombers could assemble proved very effective and later, by advancing it, even greater protection from enemy early warning radar was obtained.

### STIRLING IIIs ON SQUADRON STRENGTH, 5 JUNE 1944
#### No. 199 Sqn, North Creake
```
EF270     23.1.44-3.8.44
X-EF459   20.1.44-28.7.44
A-LJ510   21.4.44-24.10.44 RIW
*E-LJ513  5.5.44-10.11.44
B-LJ514   5.5.44-24.2.45
H-LJ516   28.7.45-17.4.45
```

```
*K-LJ518  29.4.44-25.9.44 EFB, crashed at
                     Saxthorpe, Norfolk
*Z-LJ520  2.5.44-24.2.45
*R-LJ525  30.4.44-31.1.45
*N-LJ531  29.4.44-17.6.44 FTR
*P-LJ536  26.4.44-16.9.44 FTR
*T-LJ538  22.5.44-21.2.45
*G-LJ542  30.4.44-31.1.45
*J-LJ543  29.4.44-6.12.44
 D-LJ544  29.4.44-6.12.44
*X-LJ557  4.44-?
*H-LJ560  30.4.44-29.8.44 EFA, undercarriage
                     collapsed on take-off
*V-LJ562  5.5.44-10.11.44
*Q-LJ565  14.5.44-10.11.44
*C-LJ569  22.5.44-16.9.44 EFB, crashed on
                     take-off, North Creake
*S-LJ578  29.2.44-10.9.44 EFB, undercarriage
                     collapsed
*X-LJ580  11.3.44-31.1.45
 L-LJ582  11.3.44-10.11.44
 N-LJ595  6.7.44-22.2.45
```

## The Special Duty squadrons

For Nos. 138 and 161 (Special Duty) Squadrons, D-Day certainly marked the beginning of their end. Their operations had demanded great courage, whether during lonely, low-level supply drops involving large and vulnerable aircraft or touchdowns for brief stays in enemy territory. While both squadrons carried out supply drops and delivered agents – particularly to France and the Low Countries – it was No. 161 Squadron which mainly undertook agent retrieval using Westland Lysanders. By June 1944, although Lysanders still equipped part of No. 161 Squadron, pick-ups were fewer

Mandrel *Stirling LJ514-B, amply supplied with aerials and operated by No. 199 Squadron on 5/6 June. (Frank Smith)*

and increasingly involved the use of a handful of the longer-ranged Lockheed Hudsons, better known for their part in Coastal Command's operations. The Hudson's origins are discussed in *Aircraft For The Few*.

No. 138 Squadron originated from No. 1419 Flight, born as No. 419 Flight at North Weald/Stapleford Tawney in 1940. After moving to Stradishall to equip with Whitleys, No. 1419 Flight, on 25 August 1941, became No. 138 Squadron and made use of Newmarket Heath, Stradishall's satellite. Not until 4/5 September 1941 did a Lysander make the first pick-up sortie.

In November 1941 the Whitley Mk Vs congregated at Stradishall from where during the next three months they flew 50 sorties. Two aircraft, Malta-based, operated over Yugoslavia. Too slow for daylight operations and exceptionally cold at night, the Whitley was replaced by the Halifax II.

In March 1942 No. 138 Squadron moved to Tempsford from where it supported Resistance workers throughout Europe. Lysanders were by then in No. 161 Squadron which formed at Newmarket Heath on 15 February 1942. The squadron's first Lysander operation, involving *V9428-C*, took place on 27/28 February; then on 1 March it moved to Graveley, and to Tempsford in April, by which time it held 12 Whitleys, six Lysanders, two Halifaxes, a Hudson and a Wellington. During November 1942 'A' Flight converted from Whitleys to Halifax IIs, while the two other Flights used Lysanders and Hudsons.

October 1943 saw Lockheed Hudsons replace Douglas Havocs for *Ascension* flights. Steadily climbing outward and with oxygen 'on' above 10,000 ft, they flew patrol lines high off the Dutch coast at around 20,000 ft, establishing radio contact with Resistance workers. Useful contact was achieved during 67 out of 125 Havoc sorties and 178 out of 296 flown by Hudsons.

Hudsons had other uses, too. During 72 out of 100 sorties they homed successfully on to marked drop zones, delivering from between 500 and 700 ft various supplies to the Resistance. Such operations cost 10 of 161 Squadron's Hudsons. More spectacular were Hudson landings and pick-ups in enemy territory, for they needed a minimum 1,600 ft run, which restricted site availability. Between November 1942 and September 1944, 46 Hudson landings were attempted, 36 resulting in successful pick-ups. On 18 October 1943 a double Hudson pick-up was attempted and, far from easy, it was made worse when both aircraft became temporarily bogged down. Before any landings took place PR aircraft photographed the area, looking for obstructions as well as recording the terrain.

By mid-1944 Hudsons were particularly useful because of their longer range when compared with the Lysanders. Spacious and quiet on the approach, they also had strong undercarriage legs. Post D-Day, they increasingly performed as conventional transports flying to France and Belgium

Tales of Lysander pick-ups are legendary. Ten landings had been made by the end of 1941 – nine in France, one in Belgium. Of 38 attempted in 1942, half were successful. During 1943 11 out of 157 tries were fruitful, the usual procedure being for a red triangle of makeshift lights and a white letter indicating the area, and a white light showing downwind of the apex. The short-field performance of the Lysander meant that a strip 250 yds by 50 yds was sufficient for operations, but night landings were far from simple. On 16/17 December 1943 two Lysanders crashed, landing blind. Until spring 1944 the undefended Lysanders – lightened and having a fixed external ladder and as large a belly fuel tank as practicable – operated from Tangmere. Use was certainly made of such Lysanders as were available, with a Newmarket-based target-towing Mk III being borrowed for one sortie. Total loses amounted to four pilots killed and one made PoW. Four others escaped home. In 1944 50 out of 63 pick-ups proved effective, operations ending in August 1944. February of that year saw the first 'letter snatch' when a Lysander, in the manner by which it was initially promoted, hooked a package strung between two poles.

In May 1944 161 Squadron's 'A' Flight Lysanders flew seven sorties, Halifaxes 67 and Hudsons of 'C' Flight 19 *Ascensions*. On the night of 5/6 June Halifax *MA-T* flown by P/O Tattershall flew Operation *Politician* (23:07–04:57 hrs). The mission involved the dropping of 10 containers, five agents and, in the Le Blaine area,

*Z-Zulu, one of the remaining operational Lysander IIIs of No. 161 Squadron in June 1944. ('Lucky' Newhouse, via R.L. Ward)*

leaflets. Four other Halifax Vs – *MA-U, W, X and Y* (23:34–02:37 hrs) – participated in Operation *Titanic IV*, dropping mixed loads and *Window*. Meanwhile, F/O Menzies flying Hudson *MA-M* on a *Westminster* to the Netherlands (23:30–03:44 hrs), only partially completed, including the dropping of two agents and releasing of 15 pigeons. F/O Ferris in Hudson *MA-A* flying Operation *St Edmund* (23:42–03:40 hrs), dropped one agent in France and released 15 pigeons SW of Paris. Flt Sgt Morris in *MA-P* flying Operation *Harlech* was unable to locate Roosendaal, his drop zone, so abandoned his sortie. In June No. 161 Squadron's Halifaxes flew 64 sorties and undertook 74 operations, Hudsons 12 sorties and 13 operations in addition to 10 mainly new-contact *Ascension* operations.

On 6/7 June, Halifaxes flew a *Darwin* and a *Stationer*, while *MA-U* flew a *Stationer* and a *Charitaitie* (23:25–04:25 hrs). Flying two operations within one sortie was quite common, the former involving the dropping of five agents, four containers and two packages and the latter more packages. Hudson *MA-R* flew a *Gondolier* and dropped one agent and three packages one mile from Ruovray after torches were seen flashing. The closest Lysander operation to

D-Day came on 3 June when *B, D* and *P* operated. The latter, carrying them in Operation *Japonica* (22:45–04:15 hrs), landed two agents at 01:15 hrs; *B* flying Operation *Camaraderie* (22:30–05:05 hrs) landed three agents at 01:15 hrs and brought one back; and *D* flying Operation *Forsythia* in a first-rate sortie, landed an agent and brought three back.

Between 23:24–03:00 hrs on 5/6 June, eight Halifax Vs of No. 138 Squadron took part in Operation *Titanic I*, one dropping fake paratroopers. On 6/7 June nine Halifaxes operated between 23:09–04:06 hrs in more customary style, dropping packages or agents during Operations *Beaune, Daviston, Donald VI, Hermit II* and *III, Historian* and *Orange*.

The final Hudson SOE sortie, an unsuccessful radio-listening *Westminster*, was carried out by *MA-L* between 12:30–15:35 hrs on 31 October 1944. As for the Lysanders, they were phased out of front-line use in October 1944. Plt Off Cruickshank flew *T1707* to Brussels on 18 October 1944 and on the way back crashed at Chorley Wood. His passengers were safe, but he suffered spinal injuries during what was the last day of Lysander operational flying.

On 28 August 1944 No. 138 Squadron was declared completely rearmed with Stirling IVs and on 9 March 1945 became a Main Force Lancaster bomber squadron based at Tuddenham. From Tempsford it had despatched 2,562 drop sorties and delivered 995 agents. No. 161 Squadron made 1,198 drops before disbanding on 2 June 1945, and for a loss of 29 aircraft.

## HALIFAX Vs (SPECIAL DUTIES) ON SQUADRON STRENGTH, 5 JUNE 1944

### *No. 138 Sqn*, Tempsford
```
LL118   29.12.43-3.9.44
LL187   29.12.43-3.9.44
LL250   12.5.44-25.8.44
LL251   8.2.44-12.7.44 FTR
LL254   8.2.44-29.8.44
LL282   16.2.44-26.8.44
LL290   20.2.44-28.8.44
LL306   25.5.44-8.6.44 FTR
LL308   25.3.44-5.6.44, 22.6.44-9.8.44
LL354   25.5.44-26.8.44
LL364   9.5.44-8.6.44, 15.6.44-9.7.44 FTR
LL385   5.6.44-12.8.44
LL387   4.6.44-19.7.44 FTR
LL390   30.4.44-6.6.44, BFB, SOC 28.6.44
LL409   ?-10.6.44
LL416   11.5.44-8.6.44 FTR ((38.20))
LL465   4.6.44-20.8.44
LL466   4.6.44-8.6.44 FTR
LL467   5.6.44-12.8.44
LL468   6.6.44-25.8.44
```

### *No. 161 Sqn*, Tempsford
```
LK695   16.11.43-8.6.44 RIW
LL248   27.1.44-5.8.44 FTR
LL249   27.1.44-12.8.44
LL358   26.5.44-9.8.44 FTR
LL367   5.6.44-4.9.44
LL381   19.4.44-12.8.44
LL388   3.6.44-22.6.44
```

```
LL392   1.5.44-12.8.44
LL453   26.5.44-12.8.44
```

## HUDSON I/IIIAs ON SQUADRON STRENGTH 5 JUNE 1944

### *No. 161 Sqn*, Tempsford
```
N7263   22.6.42-2.8.44 BFA
FH406   ?-?
FK763   ?-?
O-?????  ?-?
```

## LYSANDER III/IIIAs ON SQUADRON STRENGTH, 5 JUNE 1944

### 'A' Flight, *No. 161 Sqn*, Tempsford
```
H-P9129   4.6.44-7.8.44 EFB
T1445     ?-?
T1446     11.4.44-2.12.44
T1707     6.6.44-10.10.44 Cat E
A-T1770   18.2.42-16.8.44 EFA, crashed,
          Chorley Wood (1419 Flt 15.5.41 –
          138 Sqn – 18.2.42)
F-V9283   20.3.42-22.7.44
V9287     7.1.44-2.12.44
V9326     29.12.43-2.12.44
G-V9353   16.3.42-27.8.43, 8.44 – 38 Group HQ
          9.3.45-19.3.45
V9737     31.3.44-28.7.44 E MR
V9738     28.3.44-5.12.44
V9748     1.12.43-5.8.44 EFA
V9749     6.4.44-14.10.44
```

NB: Although this squadron flew Lysander III/IIIAs, it also used some early Lysanders re-engined. There was never a shortage of aircraft suitable for conversion. *JR* identity letters are thought to have been introduced mid-1944 because the squadron held a large number of aircraft. The Lysanders moved to Winkleigh in August 1944 after the operations ceased and were used as light cross-Channel transports. Some were retained until May 1945.

*Lockheed Hudson MA:K of No 161 Squadron.*

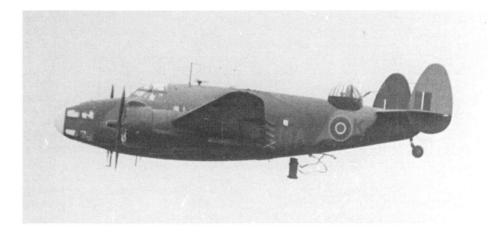

# Part Two
# The Lifters

Operation *Neptune's* airborne forces component proved successful for it enabled the Orne bridges to be seized intact, and the dangerous Merville battery to be silenced. After difficult fighting, high ground in the Boise de Bavent–Breville area was captured and the east flank of the bridgehead secured. Although some drops went astray, the extremely courageous airborne troops acquitted themselves well enough for each venture to succeed.

Airborne troops arriving by parachute or glider were a small but very important proportion of the landing force, and performed vital tasks on both flanks of the lodgement area. It demanded an incredible amount of specialized training, rarely undertaken before or since, to obtain full value from the equipment and aircraft specially provided for the purpose. For the first time the RAF was involved in a massive combined 'triple Services' venture and deploying transports on a scale it had hitherto not known. Reaching that high-point had meant traversing a long road.

## The Origins of the transport force

Despite a need to sustain worldwide influence, pre-war British governments disgracefully neglected air transport. Absence of aerodromes, devised flight routes, relatively short-range transport aircraft of limited capacity, all were prominent aspects of a sorry tale. Most available aircraft were slow, among them low-flying elegant seaplanes with restricted tactical value. The British Empire had little choice but to depend almost entirely upon shipping to maintain its world status.

Such aerial movement of troops and supplies as took place in the Middle East and India during the 1920s and 1930s involved the use of a few 'bomber-transports'; lumbering Vickers Victoria and Valentia 'wire and string' biplanes often deployed to cope with restless inhabitants. Although the Bristol Bombay joined in by 1940, it never entirely replaced these faithful, long-serving old warriors.

At home, where the nationwide railway steamed supremely, RAF transports were even more sparse. The one transport squadron, No. 24, gave VIPs during the 1930s and indeed through the 1940s a taste of a cleaner, faster means of conveyance. De Havilland airliners, Percival light transports and Miles communicators all found a niche in No. 24, and when Prince Edward became His Majesty a special King's Flight was formed to convey 'the people's favourite'.

At the start of hostilities a handful of large airliners were pressed into service to convey urgent supplies to France. Handley Page 42s, Short *Scyllas*, de Havilland Albatrosses, Armstrong Whitworth Ensigns, Bristol Bombays – all were involved and mostly wore civil registrations to make them acceptable to non-belligerent countries during government-inspired activities. On 1 May 1940 No. 1680 Flight, Doncaster, which had been formed to administer the activity, was renamed No. 271 Squadron – just in time to rescue Britons and their possessions before our closest ally fell apart.

Within hours the inquest into how that event came about was underway. Certainly the German airborne forces had played a useful part in each *Blitzkrieg*, so in autumn 1940 Churchill demanded that a British paratroop force be formed. Training the troops was straightforward, but which type of aircraft could carry them into action – and in sufficient numbers? The answer to both questions was a resounding 'none'. It was then that a novel notion emerged: place the paratroopers in large wooden gliders, tow those in train – two, three, behind a four-engined bomber. Unfortunately only minuscule numbers of such tugs could be built even by late 1942, and being required by Bomber Command they would need to have two roles. Then came the suggestion that weapons and vehicles could also be carried in gliders released to slide almost silently onto landing zones (LZs). Detailed requirements were soon listed, the first calling for a small, sailplane-like glider carrying eight men and which, after release, could travel 50 or so miles, quietly conveying a special sabotage force. A larger glider, the X27/40, came next. Able to deliver its own weight – troops or equipment – it would be cast off close to the landing ground. A third idea involved fitting lifting surfaces enveloping a tank. Since the gliders and operating techniques would take many months to perfect and their employment remained distant, a search for interim paratroop aircraft was undertaken in autumn 1940 and narrowed to aged Tiger-engined Armstrong Whitworth Whitley bombers. By cutting an aft-floor exit, a useful trainer – even an operational transport – was produced. Whitley IIIs soon gathered at the Central Landing Establishment, Ringway, to provide the backbone transports for a paratroop training school.

Whereas Nos. 24 and 271 Squadrons were administered by Fighter Command the new organization – with close Army ties – joined Army Co-operation Command. On 31 January 1941 a special No. 38 Wing was established to hold two new squadrons, No. 296 Glider Experience Squadron and No. 297 Parachute Exercise Squadron. Feeding these would be the paratroop school and Thame's glider pilot training school initially employing light pre-war civilian sailplanes towed by Avro 504s little changed from those employed in the First World War. From these humble beginnings came the extensive British Airborne Forces and two Groups of RAF Transport Command so important on D-Day.

## Learning the lessons

Overseas the importance of transport aircraft was ever increasing – and particularly during the North African desert fighting. Bombays, Valentias, Hudsons – all shuffled to and fro lifting supplies and men, and quickly evacuating the wounded to base hospitals. That would be a major task during any invasion of north-west Europe. In 1941 a handful of Douglas DC-3s were introduced. Faster, reliable, easier to load, they were ideal aircraft for the desert war, and as soon as America was attacked by Japan the British told their new fighting ally that they would like some more.

When General Montgomery's El Alamein assault came underway, No. 216 Group – born out of the 1916 roots of military air transport and now part of the Desert Air Force, with increasing numbers of modern transport aircraft, supplied many of the needs of the advancing 8th Army. Its Bombays, Hudsons and DC-3s used hastily prepared, simple landing grounds, leapfrogging them when the Army raced across the desert as lengthening lines of communication increasingly posed problems for the Army, especially for casualty evacuation – 'casevac' in modern parlance. To the rescue came the air transport backing which performed extremely well. This was something that had to be incorporated into planning for the forthcoming invasion of north-west Europe.

Until Operation *Colossus*, undertaken over southern Italy tested the techniques, paradropping had been sidelined. Although far from successful the operation taught useful lessons. Many more were learnt when Albemarles towed Horsa gliders during the July 1943 invasion of Sicily.

## Transferring the learning

It was not only in the transport field that the RAF learned much during the desert war. Another lesson was that to be really effective, tactical fighter squadrons needed mobility, taking them as close to the front-line as possible. By early 1943 a scheme was being prepared around self-contained mobile 'airfields' comprising squadrons and essential backing. It was tested in south-east England during the joint Army/RAF exercise, *Spartan*, of

March/April 1943. As Army units moved, RAF 'airfields' followed them, while No. 2 Group and some fighter squadrons made harassing attacks and fighter reconnaissance squadrons assisted the soldiers in one of the most important of any RAF exercises. Once the Allies had secured a foothold across the Channel, tactical transports would move the 'airfields' to landing grounds; rapidly prepared sites built by the Airfield Construction Branch following pre-invasion search and photographic reconnaissance.

## Expansion and preparation

The first major stage in the build-up of the transport force came on 13 October 1943 when No. 38 Wing was raised to Group status and its expansion began. No longer would it have Whitley-equipped split paratrooping and glider squadrons, but would use Albemarles, Halifaxes and Stirling Mk IVs for glider towing, paratrooping and resupply. Paratroops and gliders would be released *en masse*, and that required extensive day and night training.

Phase One of expansion, to be completed by 15 November 1943, called for three squadrons (Nos. 296, 297 and 298) each equipped initially with 20 Albemarles. Additionally, No. 295 Squadron – formed at Tarrant Rushton with 20 Halifaxes and manned by existing '295' crews supplemented by 'C' Flight of the old No. 297 Squadron – was to tow tank-carrying gliders. A half-squadron (No. 299) would be formed by renaming 'B' Flight, No. 297 Squadron, temporarily flying Lockheed Venturas at Stoney Cross until Stirling GT Mk IVs became available in mid-January 1944. No. 296 Squadron was already at Hurn when No. 570 Albemarle Squadron formed at the opening of Phase II on 15 November 1943. More reinforcement came on 7 January 1944 with the arrival at Tarrant Rushton of No. 196 Stirling Squadron from Leicester East, where No. 620 Squadron also was flying Stirlings.

The first task for all squadrons was to practise accurate night flying, which included supply drops to Resistance forces. Next, they had to become proficient at glider towing before undertaking rapid stream take-offs, assembly, formation flying and glider release at precise pinpoints – by day and then at night. No. 295 Squadron's Halifax crews learnt the art of towing the 110-ft wing span tank-carrying Hamilcar while the others familiarized themselves with Horsa towing.

The size of the airborne assault required for Operation *Overlord* meant that a second Airborne Forces Group would be needed. As No. 46 Group, it would later deliver supplies to advanced landing grounds and undertake extensive casevac operations.

When it formed, few of its crews had any experience of Airborne Forces activities, none had operated in north-west Europe or undertaken glider towing – and they all had a mere four months to become fully proficient. That was achieved by very careful planning, ample improvisation and the realization that operations would be spectacular. The biggest problem for No. 46 Group was obtaining sufficient suitable transports. Stirlings and Halifaxes could tow gliders but they could not land on improvised strips. Harrows might have been ideal for that, but the choice narrowed to the Douglas C-47, increasingly numerous in the USAAF. A substantial number were made available under Lend-Lease and early in 1944 150 were flown to Britain to become Unit Equipment for the new European Transport Support Group (alias No. 46 Group) formed on 1 January 1944, the first to form in Transport Command, and soon commanded by Air Commodore A.R. Fiddament.

The Group's first two squadrons (No. 271 at Doncaster and No. 512 at Hendon) had few crews with C-47/Dakota qualifications. Both bases, blighted by industrial haze, were unsatisfactory for night-flying training and Hendon was close to a balloon barrage. By the end of January 1944 permission had been given for both squadrons to move, to Broadwell and Down Ampney respectively, where more would later join them.

For the planned five squadrons No. 46 Group was being given three incomplete airfields – Blakehill, Broadwell and Down Ampney. Within range of France for Dakotas towing Horsas, reasonably close to main roads and the railway network needed to bring troops for operations, the airfields required major modifications. Each had been built to accommodate two US 8th AF medium bomber squadrons and had dispersed hardstandings for 60 aircraft. Now they needed glider marshalling areas at either end of the main runway, special lead-in tracks, glider parking space and aprons for loading and unloading aircraft. These additions were built by the Army Pioneer Corps. Perforated steel planking – secured by the AEAF on a high priority – was laid very quickly. Much additional personnel accommodation was built, along with facilities for handling casualties and wide roads allowing ambulances to pass other vehicles easily.

No. 38 Group did not face as many basic problems as No. 46 Group, although its airfields at Keevil and Fairford needed modifications suiting them for glider operations. Albemarle squadrons moved to the Permanent RAF Stations at Brize Norton and Harwell. In both Groups RAF crews would tow gliders flown by RAF-trained Army Glider Pilot Regiment men who, after landing, would fight as conventional soldiers. RAF Transport Command, formed on 3 March 1943, would have overall control of British airborne operations, carrying out orders from C-in-C AEAF.

As Dakotas became available from the Dakota Modification Centre, Doncaster, glider-towing was briefly practised before concentration passed to paratroop training in March and April, with the Dress Rehearsal for the Normandy airborne landing, controlled from the Eastcote Command Post, taking place at the end of April. Although the intention to launch an invasion of France was obvious to all, its place and the details were most heavily guarded secrets. Not until 17 February 1944 was Maj Gen R.N. Gale OBE DSO MD, Cdr 6th Airborne Division, warned of the need to train to seize bridges over the River Orne and the Caen Canal near Ranville (Map Ref. T1174), with this task to form part of the *coup de main*. Then on 24 February the 6th Airborne Division was placed under No. 1 (Assault) Corps and full details of the planned invasion were revealed to him. Few who took part in the Dress Rehearsal had much idea of what was to follow in June.

For the purpose of the exercise the Corps area extended from the River Severn estuary to the eastern borders of Wiltshire and Oxfordshire, with the Cotswolds representing the high ground east of the River Orne. All the Airborne Forces were committed, along with the US 9th AF Troop Carrier Command. In daylight, this huge armada headed southerly across the Channel before turning for their inland mock assault. Guarding the massed transports was a vast fighter screen which no enemy dare approach. The speed with which No. 46 Group had taken its place so well in the front line was quite astonishing. Lessons learnt in the rehearsal were, again, placed within *Overlord* plans as the airborne troops assembled for the two big shows.

## Preparations

Prime Airborne Forces participants in Operation *Neptune* were the 3rd and 5th Parachute Brigades and 6th Airlanding (Gliderborne) Brigade of the 6th Airborne Division. Although some 1,040 Horsas and 50 Hamilcars were available the RAF's No. 38 Group, commanded by AVM L.N. Hollinghurst CB OBE DFC and No. 46 Group under AC A.R. Fiddament, held only about 400 paratroop glider tug aircraft, which meant that two lifts were needed. The first, Operation *Tonga*, began late on 5 June; the second followed during the evening of D-Day.

General Gale's orders called firstly for the seizure of two bridges and the silencing of the Merville/Franceville gun battery. Secondly, he was to prevent the enemy from moving into the area between the Rivers Dives and Orne. Thirdly, his troops must deny enemy reinforcements crossing the Trearn–Sommerville–Colombel road.

War Office Intelligence rated the likely initial German defenders as none too impressive. The British coastal assault area contained elements of two infantry divisions: the 711th (to the west) and 716th (to the east) totalling some 26,000 men, and probably able to operate at only about 40 per cent of their capability. Reinforcements were reckoned likely to prove far superior, including the 352nd Infantry Division (line infantry) and the 12th SS Panzer (*Hitler Jügend*) Division – some 21,000 troops with Panzer tanks and likely to arrive on the scene within 24 hrs. That made it imperative that the British forces advance inland as fast and as far as possible.

Reality proved different, for the 352nd Infantry Division was quickly sent to engage the American landing to the west and to bolster two inadequate infantry divisions in the Cherbourg Peninsula. The 21st Panzer Division, dispersed during early May in woods north of Rennes, had recently started an exercise in the Caen area. Its presence was to prevent the British from seizing Caen and its Carpiquet airfield.

Likely enemy response was carefully considered during invasion planning, and so was the need for high security. Yet without revealing some details training would suffer, so in April 1944 planning was extended to take place at Group and Divisional levels. In secure headquarters it went ahead – at Milston, Wiltshire, near the Airborne HQ at Bulford, and at Netheravon where HQ No. 38 Group was situated along with No. 46 Group's advanced HQ. Final planning for the airborne operations took place in the Officers' Mess, Netheravon.

In February 1944 the terrain of the Caen area, much of it consisting of large flat fields ideal for glider landing, began to be closely studied. Army needs were paramount and, apart from one zone close to the coast, the selected areas were thought easy to locate even at night.

Extensive photo coverage on 17 April generated a major shock by revealing anti-glider landing posts being erected throughout the chosen landing area, which called for radical changes. No longer would it be practical for the main glider assault to take place in darkness, so the second paratroop landings were substituted in place of gliders of the 6th Airlanding Brigade. The paratroops could remove obstacles to allow the gliders to land in cleared lanes during the evening of D-Day. Gen Gale understandably saw all this as a significant setback, for his glider force was the stronger of the two and carried essential artillery and powered vehicles. Daylight operation also raised the question of the possibility of German fighters attacking tugs and gliders. But glider landings at night, on obstructed areas, were also fraught with danger.

The overall plan was amended and soon finalized. At the start, six Horsas towed by Halifaxes would be released from 6,000 ft to land as silently as possible, three each on LZs 'X' and 'Y' – by the Bénouville Bridge (later called Pegasus Bridge) and a bridge over the River Orne. The glider pilots would brake as quietly as possible, glider wheels having been well-oiled, allowing almost silent landings for maximum surprise. After glider release each tug would soon aim 6 x 500 lb bombs at a factory near Caen to create a diversion Both the 3rd and 5th Parachute Brigades would form the main force and at 03:30 hrs the HQ Staff, 6th Airborne Division, more troops and an anti-tank gun battery would be landed on LZ 'N', to establish HQ at Le Bas de Ranville.

Thirty minutes before the main paratroop assault, 60 men of the 22nd Independent Parachute Company, dropped from Albemarles as pathfinders, would establish ground aids, coded identity lights and beacons and prepare for gliders bringing troops and light transport.

Three main drop zones/landing zones were eventually selected: LZ 'V' near Varaville would receive the forces intending to demolish Dives bridges, seize high ground and silence the Merville Battery; LZ 'K' (Touffreville) would be used by the troops preventing the enemy from crossing the Troan–Sannerville road; and LZ 'N' (Ranville) would be the main glider LZ. Here most of the Horsas and paratroops would land, and resupply take place. South of Ouistreham, LZ 'W' was the stand-by in case problems occurred at LZ 'N'. Operations would span a very compact timetable. The 5th Paras would drop before 01:00 hrs on DZ 'N' to hold the area Bénouville–Ranville–Le Base de Ranville, capture the medium-gun battery one mile south of Ouistreham, then clear and protect LZ 'N' for 68 gliders scheduled to land there two hrs before dawn. Another 146 gliders would follow in the evening.

The 3rd Paras would drop on LZs 'N' and 'V' simultaneously as the 5th Paras landed to operate on the nearby ground rising to 200 ft, also along the southern road. Canadian squadrons of No. 6 Group would bomb the Merville/Franceville gun battery (Map Ref. T155776) from -20 to -10 minutes before 9th Parachute Battalion attacked, either to capture or destroy it by 30 minutes before dawn. They would be assisted by a special party delivered nearby in three Horsas 2½ hrs before first light and 1½ hrs before the first landing craft reached the Normandy beaches at high tide. Bridges at Troarn, Bures, Robehomme and Varaville would have to be destroyed to prevent enemy reinforcements reaching the lodgement area's eastern flank, and no later than two hrs after dawn. Inland, SAS groups would be dropped to conduct sabotage activities.

The main airborne landing, Operation *Mallard*, involving the 6th Airlanding Brigade and the Airborne Armed Reconnaissance Regiment, would take place at 21:00 hrs DBST on D-Day. Some 220 Horsas would land the main force on LZs 'N' and 'W', and 30 Hamilcars would carry the reconnaissance element to LZ 'N' where another four Hamilcars would land heavy divisional equipment. Reinforcements would arrive in containers dropped from Stirling GT Mk IVs.

Flight planning to achieve all this was extremely complex. Assembling the huge formations would take some time, after which course changes needed to be kept to the minimum. The longest possible straight run-in to the release points at necessary heights was essential for glider release, and could only be prescribed shortly before the operations. To aid accuracy, chosen tracks lay along whole number *Gee* lattice lines where possible, with operating frequencies being changed at the last moment. Accurate map reading and ground marking by the pathfinders remained vital to success. All the No. 46 Group Dakotas carried *Gee*, also *Rebecca II* navigation equipment responding to *Eureka* ground beacons to be established by the paratroop pathfinders.

Between 23:45 hrs and 04:30 hrs, night-fighters would constantly patrol over German night-fighter bases. Fortunately, anti-aircraft gun defences were relatively sparse.

# THE OPERATIONS

## The Opening Assault and Operation *Tonga*

*Tonga* was originally timed for the night of 4/5 June, when tidal conditions were ideal for the seaborne forces. Three days before its launch all transport bases were sealed and crews were fully briefed. Medmenham's Central Photographic Unit had built a model of the assault area and used it to make a colour film affording aircrew a realistic image of their run-in routes. All participants were shown both items, displayed in great secrecy at Netheravon.

Battle orders embracing both airborne Groups called for the following:

| | |
|---|---|
| No. 46 Group | Five squadrons each of 30 Dakotas |
| No. 38 Group | Four squadrons each of 22 Albemarles |
| | Four squadrons each of 22 Stirling IVs |
| | Two squadrons each of 18 Halifaxes |
| Reserve | 36 aircraft |
| Glider force | 300 aircraft |

Operation *Tonga*, Phase I began with sub-Operation *Deadstick* in which, at 00:20 hrs

*A 'vertical' showing the landing positions of the three Pegasus Bridge Horsas. The 'famous' circular gun post is visible near the bridge, with Horsa PF800 closest. (Museum of Army Flying)*

*The three most famous Horsas, which landed by Pegasus Bridge, with* PF800 *on the right and possibly* PF812 *much shattered. (Museum of Army Flying)*

DBST, three Horsas landed almost in silence on tiny LZ 'X' at the eastern end of the Bénouville swing bridge over the Caen Canal. Another three landed on LZ 'Y' close to the nearby bridge over the River Orne on the road to Ranville. From the six gliders scrambled 168 men of the 2nd Battalion, Oxford & Buckinghamshire Light Infantry and the Royal Engineers. With a mixture of speed, stealth and vigour they swiftly overcame the defenders. A bridgehead was formed at the western end of the Bénouville Bridge and the eastern end of the Orne Bridge was soon further secured by 40 men of 7 Parachute Battalion who had dropped on DZ 'N' as an advance party when the gliders landed. The main body of 7 Battalion, 5th Parachute Brigade followed to give support, and helped hold the bridge during 23 hrs of heavy fighting, including counter-attacks by armour, until seaborne forces relieved them.

Success of the main landings hinged upon the next part of Phase I, the pathfinder drop by men of the 22nd Independent Parachute Company carried in six Albemarles operating from Brize Norton (*1* and *2*) Harwell (*46* and *47*) and Hampstead Norris (*48* and *49*). Their orders were to drop at 00:40 hrs and establish illumination and radio beacons to guide the main forces to the three DZs. All six pathfinder aircraft reached Normandy, but exit from the belly of the Albemarle was difficult. In three cases two or more drop runs were needed,

men dropping from one aircraft 14 minutes late. At DZ 'V' all radar and visual beacons carried by the first stick of paratroops were lost or damaged. The second group had a 20 minute walk to the site, arriving as the main drop commenced. From another aircraft troops dropped at DZ 'N' instead of DZ 'K', and established the 'K' beacon on DZ 'N'. As a result, 14 sticks of paratroops landed on the wrong DZ and before the second group of 20 pathfinders arrived – again, after the main force dropped. However, by scattering, the vanguard provoked confusion among German forces.

Altogether, 142 Dakotas (13 towing gliders and the rest carrying around 20 paratroops per aircraft) set out within Phase II late on 5 June with orders to drop at 00:50 hrs and complete their drops by 01:00 hrs DBST. As well as No. 575 Squadron's drop at DZ 'N', No. 46 Group's Dakotas carried the 3rd Parachute Brigade, chosen to attack the Merville battery and the Dives bridges, and to take the high ground. No. 38 Group's main lift involved the 5th Parachute Brigade who were to seize the base area around Ranville and drop the troops who would clear LZ 'N' for the gliders bringing Divisional HQ, more troops and much equipment.

The first Dakotas to set forth were seven towing Horsas which started take-off from Down Ampney at 22:48 hrs DBST. Two minutes later six more, of No. 233

Squadron, commenced take-off from Blakehill Farm carrying Royal Engineers with bridge demolition equipment to be landed on LZ 'K' in the south of the trans-Orne salient. That was to allow the companies to blow two bridges, those at Bures and Dives. Dark was the night, with cloud layers between 4,000 and 6,000 ft and the wind up to 20 mph from the west.

Although map reading was difficult and crews relied upon radar for navigation, all combinations reached the LZ. Two of the No. 233 Squadron group, seeing the 'K' lights erroneously flashing from LZ 'N', cast off there, and a third glider landed nearby. Two more landed at the correct place but the sixth, in which the occupants died, landed some way off.

From around 23:10 hrs a further 31 Dakotas drawn from Nos. 233, 271 and 575 Squadrons set forth from Blakehill Farm carrying 615 men of the 8th Parachute Battalion and 163 containers. On the dark night the lead aircraft homed on to the *Eureka* beacon 'K', still transmitting in error from DZ 'N' where there were also lights. Luckily, 10 aircraft dropped on the right LZ and several sticks fell within a one-mile radius of it. Despite the problems, sufficient troops mustered as intended in a nearby copse to enable them to carry out their tasks. Groups of Royal Engineers made their ways independently to carry out their tasks. Near Bures, one squad lined up with the 8th Parachute Battalion to blow a bridge without hindrance, whereas at Troarn the paratroops met resistance in the northern outskirts. A group of Royal Engineers, hearing the shooting while approaching on the Sannerville road in a Jeep and trailer brought over in a Horsa, rushed the defences, reached the bridge and blew a gap – later widened by the 8th Parachute Battalion – then made a detour to reach the high ground just south of the Bois de Bavent, by which time it was daylight. During the day many of the scattered groups united around the woods behind Bures. Not until late on 6 June was the extent of the drops in error realized.

Apart from the seizure of the bridges it was the capture of the heavy gun battery at Merville that was the other most important task. It involved a drop on LZ 'V', the hardest for the main force to locate. Both pathfinder aircraft reached the correct spot but all their equipment was lost or fell in marshy ground, and one man in the first drop received a broken leg. The second group landed 1,000 yd away and, after gathering their equipment from around them, found that the main party was already landing. The half-hour gap between the drops clearly gave insufficient time for the pathfinders to organize themselves and establish markers. From one Albemarle six men jumped too soon, just after it crossed the coast. Another aircraft – fired upon – had to make two runs over its DZ and dropped late. Two others reported *Gee* failures, and one Albemarle crew lost time trying to find the right coastal entry point. The sixth aborted after being hit by flak and seven attempts to find the DZ. As a result, only two green lights were flashing for the Dakota force, and few crews saw them.

Lift for the Phase III main body which landed at 03:20 hrs was supplied from Broadwell and Down Ampney – 39 Dakotas of Nos. 48 and 271 Squadrons carrying 725 troops of the 1st (Canadian) Parachute Battalion, Brigade HQ and smaller units, and 32 Dakotas of No. 512 Squadron carrying 540 men of 9 Parachute Battalion which had also supplied the advance party. Down Ampney also contributed seven out of 11 tugs for Horsas laden with demolition charges, Jeeps and guns. Tugs for the other four were Albemarles.

As they arrived, clouds of dust and smoke were rising from the attack by No. 6 Group, Bomber Command on the gun battery two miles away. The north-westerly wind had blown a huge pall of smoke right across the run-in and DZ and ample flak added to the confusion, which led to scattered landings. From 17 Dakotas the paratroops were dropped within the DZ, 14 more within a one-mile radius and another 11 some half-a-mile away to the east. The Canadians suffered most, nine sticks landing on the banks of the River Dives, five around Breville and two far off in the suburbs of Ouistreham. Three gliders parted from their tugs over the French coast, and the other eight were released north of the LZ. Three glider pilots, seeing the lights at LZ 'N', landed there while others emerging from the smoke finished in a semi-circle about 1 1/2 miles to the south-east of the intended LZ.

Problems were further increased because

the chosen DZ was within a maximum radius of two miles from the gun battery, which meant dropping either in woodland or on drained fen. Unfortunately the Dives had flooded, making the chosen fen area a morass, so that those who landed in the right spot had to cross bog and ditch. Lt Col T.B. Otway DSO was aghast to see the leader of the stick behind him disappear into the bog with only his collapsing parachute marking the spot. Calling to others nearby, Otway grabbed the lines, but they were unable to save him. Container loads similarly vanished. Muster was a lengthy business. Although the drop began at 00:50 hrs, by 02:50 hrs only 150 men of 9 Parachute Battalion had reached the rendezvous, in addition to the advance party. Between them they held only one machine-gun, no mortars and no mine detectors, and there were no REs or field medical personnel.

Despite these daunting handicaps 9 Parachute Battalion penetrated the outer wire and battery minefield defences while facing heavy fire and with only the darkness for protection. They eventually overran the position, putting the guns out of action, but for the loss of 80 men. The remainder retired to high ground in front of Sallenelles. They held the northern part of the salient until relieved late in the afternoon, by which time stragglers had joined them raising the contingent's strength to 360 men. As for the Merville gun battery, it was finally captured and held by Royal Marine Commandos.

The Canadians had met almost no opposition and demolished bridges at Varaville and Robehomme before they occupied a sector in the Bois de Bavent near 8 Parachute Battalion.

All the foregoing drops had an element of the special about them. In another, involving 131 aircraft (all but the 21 of No. 575 Squadron, Broadwell, being supplied by No. 38 Group), the 5th Parachute Brigade was airlifted to DZ 'N'. There, the correct signals were being displayed, and action already taking place at the Orne bridges helped in locating the DZ.

From No. 575 Squadron Dakotas 360 men of 13 Parachute Battalion had dropped to clear and hold DZ 'N' for both mass-

*Horsas and a solitary Hamilcar seen at LZ 'N' during the morning of 6 June from Spitfire PA925 of No. 16 squadron, flown by Wg Cdr C.F. Webb. (Museum of Army Flying)*

glider landings, the first at 03:20 hrs DBST and the second in the evening of D-Day. Simultaneously, 7 and 12 Parachute Battalions as well as Brigade HQ troops were dropped by No. 38 Group. Of the 131 aircraft detailed to make the airlift, two went unserviceable before take-off and six failed to reach Normandy, including five Stirlings reported missing. Most sticks fell at the DZ. The main body consisted of 2,125 troops of whom a total of 2,026 dropped, along with 702 out of the 755 containers being carried.

One-and-a-half hrs later, Divisional HQ troops including most of an anti-tank battery and heavy equipment arrived in 48 Horsas and three Hamilcars on the cleared, lit lanes. More had been expected for 68 Horsas and four Hamilcars had taken off. But the weather had deteriorated since the paratroop operations. Rain reduced the visibility, and there was much low cloud. Four gliders had cast off over England and three more in cloud. Another seven parted from their tugs when tow-ropes broke, or flak hit them, between the French coast and Ranville. In all, 25 gliders were hit by flak, but no passengers were injured aboard any that landed on the LZ until the crash-landings and collisions on landing. To provide intentional confusion four Albemarles, in pairs, operated to the east of the dropping area in an attempt to mislead the enemy.

Despite the wastage the effort was worthwhile, for the enemy was fast recovering from his surprise. Within four hrs of the *coup de main* attack, the 21st Panzer Division moved into action in the general area north of Caen, its commander sending the formidable 125th Panzer Grenadier Regiment against the Ranville bridgehead.

The first counter-attack came with the dawn, but it was repulsed. A full-scale counter-attack, including self-propelled guns, began at 11:00 hrs and it entered the village.

The gliderborne anti-tank battery claimed three of the self-propelled guns and a tank, but by 13:00 hrs the position was critical, with the two Battalions which bore the brunt of the fighting having had 50 men killed and 420 wounded additional to any lost during the landings. Luckily the 1st Special Service (Commando) Brigade, among the first seaborne troops ashore, crossed the Orne bridge to turn the tide of battle and then was diverted to Le Bas de Ranville, which it held until the evening landing of the 6th Airlanding Brigade. In helping out, though, the 1st Special Service Brigade delayed their entry to Franceville Plage. Before the evening of D-Day the east Orne salient was secured.

# Operation *Mallard*

Of the British D-Day airborne ventures *Mallard*, the mass-landing from 21:00 hrs DBST of 247 gliders on the evening of 6 June, was so successful that it set the operational patterns for Arnhem and the Rhine crossing. Tug pilots could, in daylight, easily identify landmarks. That enabled the accurate landing on cleared strips of Horsas (and at 21:20 hrs Hamilcars *221* to *254*) of both groups on to LZ 'N', and 39 Horsas towed by No. 38 Group on to LZ 'W' close to Ouistreham and the converging waterways. Although night operations included an important surprise element, they were far more difficult to mount effectively. Daylight operations nevertheless raised considerable risks, for a stream of slow, low-flying gliders, well spaced for over 100 miles, made for ideal flak targets. The alternative – glider operations at night – and a disturbing memory of the 1943 assault on Sicily raised consideration of the risks inherent in either venture. In retrospect success was judged overwhelmingly to favour daylight lifts, especially after the forecast problems which *Mallard* faced were largely absent.

*Mallard* completed the air movement to France of the 6th Airborne Division; the 12th Devons arrived in ships. Airlifted in the Horsas were the 6th Airlanding Brigade

*Albemarles towing Horsas across the English Channel during the evening of Operation* Mallard *and passing over HMS* Ramillies *and HMS* Warspite *(centre). (F. Holland)*

consisting of the 1st Ulster Rifles, 2nd Oxford and Bucks Light Infantry, Brigade HQ and troops; the Airborne Armoured Regiment and the 211th Light Battery, Royal Artillery. Within the Horsas were men with their light equipment, Jeeps, field guns and ammunition trailers. The larger Hamilcars supplied 75 mm guns and armoured vehicles. Stirlings and Albemarles towed off 110 Horsas leaving Halifaxes to haul the Hamilcars. All but six Horsas operated with success.

Four squadrons of Dakotas – Nos. 48, 271, 512 and 575 – were detailed to tow Horsas, 34 from each of the two bases operating. At Broadwell and Down Ampney, where equipment loading had taken place the previous day, gliders were marshalled to a complex plan while aircrew rested after Operation *Tonga*.

Gathering the long train was spectacular and involved the airborne sorting of 257 combinations (247 of which proved effective) in order to correctly position them on the headings for designated LZs. From their bases the combinations headed at 145 mph for Old Sarum then flew northerly, next fitting into the rendezvous

*Stirling IVs towing Horsas during the evening of Operation* Mallard. *(IWM CL23)*

area before swinging straight towards the landing areas near which release was ordered to take place at 1,000 ft. Then they turned for Bognor, leaving the French coast at 180 mph. On the right flank, the US 9th AF, was simultaneously organizing its airlift. RAF Spitfires and Mustangs swarming around the British contingent added a lively touch to a supremely magnificent portrayal of Allied might homing towards *Eureka* beacons set in place the previous night. Not surprisingly, all except a few brave Luftwaffe pilots viewed the spectacle from the safety of the ground. In excellent weather, visibility 10 to 15 miles, patchy high cloud enhanced what in peacetime would have been a superb summer's eve, for there was a temporary break in D-Day's bad weather. Along the route, and at the LZs, radar beacons assisted in navigation.

Two tow ropes broke over England among the No. 46 Group contingent. One glider ditched in the Channel and another was lost to uncertain causes. Otherwise, 142 of the 146 Horsas landed in the intended place, a highly impressive performance. Anti-aircraft fire from a small wood south of the Orne bridges, although less than forecast, set fire to the port engine of a No. 48 Squadron Dakota. Two of the crew baled out from 500 ft and the others raced from the aircraft after it crashed behind enemy lines. Four other Dakotas sustained flak damage.

By the time the gliders arrived the ground situation had improved. The 1st Special Service (Commando) Brigade had entered the Sallonelles area, all of which was captured the next day. Then they advanced to Franceville Plage. Forward elements of the 3rd British Infantry Division fought their way from the beachhead to the bridges, and by 03:00 hrs on 7 June were defending the Orne road viaduct in the Danville district where the 6th Airborne Division had been fighting hard throughout D-Day. Stirlings, after releasing their gliders, had dropped supply containers to troops west of the Orne, but lack of transport prevented any of their contents from being spread among the 6th Airborne force for some time.

## Resupply

Rapid containerized resupply following

*Mallard* was a vital ingredient of Operation *Neptune*. Four *Rob Roy* operations were flown, followed by three *Sunflowers* and Operation *Coney*. The largest of them, *Rob Roy I*, involving a drop on DZ 'N' where *Eureka* beacons were functioning, was ordered for 23:50 hrs on 6 June. AA gunners, with clues to run-in routeing, had more success and disturbed the Dakota stream sufficiently for its supplies to fall away to the 3rd Division. The whole of No. 233 Squadron, 30 Dakotas along with 10 each from Broadwell and Down Ampney, were detailed to drop 116 tons of supplies consisting of food, ammunition, radios, explosives, bedding, stretchers, barbed wire, medical stores and petrol, all packed into a total of 18 containers, 609 panniers and 88 bundles. The Dakota force approached the LZs in vics of three spaced at half-minute intervals. All went well until the leaders, flying at under 1,000 ft, came within range of Allied ships at anchor off the mouth of the Orne. Their guns opened up, hitting two of Broadwell's aircraft which were forced to turn about. One soon crashed in the sea.

The formation had been effectively forced apart, and early reports spoke of seven Dakotas shot down although the loss was not as bad as first thought. Trouble had arisen through ships drifting under the entry area and their gunners not being warned of the likelihood of formations of aircraft overhead. They had nevertheless failed to identify the Dakotas, whose aircrews had fired insufficient colours of the day. German aircraft had been attempting to attack the ships, making for trigger-happy fingers.

## The Effort

On 7 June (D+1) the airborne forces reviewed their efforts, summarizing them as follows:

1. Dropping on D -1/D-Day of reconnaissance parties of SAS troops (Operation *Sunflower I*).
2. Dropping of task forces in Brittany on D+1/2 (Operation *Coney*).
3. Dropping and landing of the 3rd and 5th Parachute Brigade Groups and a proportion of Division troops on the night of D -1/D-Day (Operation *Tonga*).
4. Landing of the 6th Airlanding Brigade

on the evening of D-Day (Operation *Mallard*).
5. Resupply of the 3rd and 5th Parachute Brigade Groups on the night of D-Day/D+1 (Operation *Rob Roy I*).

Subsequent operations during this period involved dropping base parties to reinforce those dropped in *Sunflower I* and code-named *Sunflower II* and *III*. Back-up drops to the 6th British Airborne Division were undertaken during *Rob Roy II*. Total losses during these operations amounted to 3.5 per cent of the British and 2.5 per cent of the USAAF effort. Considering the scope of *Tonga* and *Mallard*, which constituted the greatest airlift of assault forces attempted to that time, they were low. Only the immense airborne undertaking involving the 1st Allied Airborne Army at Arnhem and Nijmegen in September 1944 ever exceeded those for D-Day.

All daylight airborne forces, also resupply missions flown in daylight, had fighter cover. Squadrons covering seaborne assault areas, and home reserves, were all held at readiness should assistance have been required in protecting the transports. In the event none of those fell to enemy aircraft. In the period D-Day to D+4, 1,839 sorties were flown by dedicated fighter escort to airborne forces. Another 419 sorties escorted further resupply missions. Additionally, intruders silenced AA batteries on run-in routes, and others attacked AA gun positions near DZs and LZs.

During the 24 hrs of intense activity from late 5 June to the end of *Rob Roy*, No. 46 Group had despatched 266 sorties for seven separate tasks. The diversity of loads carried may be seen from this listing:

2,727 paratroops
1,081 gliderborne troops and crews
609 panniers
500 containers
86 packages (bedding, etc)
66 motor cycles
58 Jeeps
48 loaded trailers
19 handcarts
10 Bangalore torpedoes
8 six-pounder guns
4 dogs

As the Dakotas crossed the Normandy coast during *Tonga* on 5/6 June they unloaded 1,400 20 lb anti-personnel bombs on gun emplacements to discourage small arms fire.

Losses totalling 10 aircraft occurred only during the two major missions and *Rob Roy I*. Hardest hit were Nos. 233 and 512 Squadrons, each of which lost four aircraft. Another 47 were variously damaged. Of the aircrew two had been killed, two wounded and 26 were missing at the time. A number were subsequently picked up or found to be safe. Sqn Ldr Rae's No. 512 Squadron crew had an eventful time. After releasing their glider during *Mallard* his aircraft was hit by AA fire which shot away the controls and seriously wounded both the navigator and radio operator. Luckily the Channel was calm when the Dakota ditched, and the crew took to their dinghy. Although an ASR launch picked them up within minutes, they spent an uneasy night off Normandy because German bombers attacked nearby shipping. One bomber was shot down on land, another exploded above their launch and rained down upon it in fragments.

The big question for many crews was 'What has happened to the troops we delivered?' Luckily, they did not at the time know how scattered the drops had been, particularly of the essential pathfinders. The No. 46 Group crews had come to know well many of the 9th Paras during repeated practices using a mock-up of the Merville battery built near Newbury. Despite heavy losses the left flank held during D-Day until seaborne forces reinforced it. The salient was never in danger of being overrun. Although vast quantities of stores quickly arrived on shore, and bulldozing of airstrips had begun by 7 June, the possibility of transport aircraft landing in Normandy with supplies was at least a week away.

Whereas everything in the 'British' areas had sorted itself out quite well by the end of 6 June, things were far from well in the American area. Although they fielded three times as many aircraft in the initial assault as the RAF – 925 C-47s and 104 gliders – they had not achieved the essential concentration in the Cherbourg Peninsula. Opposition they met was slight, even including foreign mercenaries commanded by German officers. Luck was against the Americans, for they were also going to lose their *Mulberry* harbour during a storm at

*Bénouville bridge photographed by Wg Cdr C.F. Webb on 9 June 1944 from Spitfire PR Mk XI PA947-P of No. 16 Squadron.*

sea on the second night. American troops landing on *Omaha* beach faced a rocky shore which, although it provided some cover, made its storming more difficult. Then came the daunting prospect of ascending the cliffs. The huge cemetery above *Omaha* beach bears testimony to the extent of the American sacrifice. Luckily, their landings at Grandcamp-les-Bains met with success, which soon allowed them to take the terrain south to Carentan.

What was immediately clear by 7 June

was the advantage of daylight airborne forces operations. Airdrops certainly reduced seaborne landing losses, for their flanks were protected from the start. Another clear lesson was that all attacks should be afforded equal support; none should be suddenly given additional importance in time or space. Ground aids proved no substitute for good navigation in which map-reading played an essential part.

## OPERATION *NEPTUNE* – AIRLIFTS BY NOS. 38 AND 46 GROUPS

| Mission | AIRCRAFT | | | | | | GLIDERS | | |
|---|---|---|---|---|---|---|---|---|---|
| | Des-patched | Effective | Aborted | Missing | Des-troyed | Damaged | Des-patched | Released pre LZ | Lost post LZ |
| *Tonga* | 373 | 359 | 14 | 9 | - | 7 | 98 | 80 | 18 |
| *Mallard* | 257 | 247 | 10 | 2 | 6 | 21 | 257 | 247 | 10 |
| *Rob Roy I* | 50 | 47 | 3 | 9 | - | 19 | - | - | - |
| *Rob Roy II* | 6 | 6 | - | - | - | - | - | - | - |
| *Rob Rob III* | 12 | 5 | 7 | - | - | - | - | - | - |
| *Rob Rob IV* | 15 | 15 | - | - | - | - | - | - | - |
| *Sunflower I* | 3 | 3 | - | - | - | - | - | - | - |
| *Sunflower II* | 2 | 1 | 1 | - | - | - | - | - | - |
| *Sunflower III* | 6 | 6 | - | - | - | - | - | - | - |
| *Coney* | 9 | 9 | - | - | - | - | - | - | - |
| **Totals** | **733** | **698** | **35** | **20** | **6** | **47** | **355** | **327** | **28** |

**Analysis of loads carried**

| | | | | | |
|---|---|---|---|---|---|
| Troops | 7,162 | Tanks | 18 | Bombs | 2,000 lb |
| M/T | 286 | Bicycles | 35 | Panniers | 731 |
| Artillery weapons | 29 | Signals items | 12 | Containers | 622 |

# AIRLIFTS BY THE US 9TH TROOP CARRIER COMMAND DURING 5/6 JUNE 1944

| Mission | AIRCRAFT | | | | Des-troyed | Damaged | GLIDERS | | |
|---|---|---|---|---|---|---|---|---|---|
| | Des-patched | Effective | Aborted | Missing | | | Des-patched | Released pre LZ | Lost post LZ |
| Albany | 443 | 433 | 10 | - | 13 | 83 | - | - | - |
| Boston | 378 | 372 | 6 | 8 | - | 115 | - | - | - |
| Chicago | 52 | 51 | 1 | 1 | 1 | 3 | 52 | 51 | 1 |
| Detroit | 52 | 52 | - | 1 | 1 | 6 | 52 | 46 | 6 |
| Elmira | 177 | 177 | - | 5 | - | 92 | 176 | 176 | - |
| Freeport | 208 | 148 | 55 | 5 | 3 | 94 | - | - | - |
| Galveston | 100 | 98 | 2 | - | - | 24 | 100 | 98 | 2 |
| Hackensack | 101 | 101 | - | - | - | - | 100 | 100 | - |
| Keokuk | 32 | 32 | - | - | - | - | 32 | 32 | - |
| Memphis | 119 | 117 | 2 | - | 3 | 35 | - | - | - |
| **Totals** | **1,662** | **1,581** | **76** | **20** | **21** | **452** | **512** | **503** | **9** |

**Analysis of loads carried**

| | | | | | |
|---|---|---|---|---|---|
| Troops | 17,262 | Equipment | 1,141,217 lb | Bombs | 26,652 lb |
| M/T | 281 | Ammunition | 798,683 lb | Petrol | 1,947 gal |
| Artillery weapons | 333 | Rations | 87,373 lb | | |

## SUMMARY OF US OPERATIONS

| Operation | Outline |
|---|---|
| Albany | Paratroop drop, 101st Airborne Division, St Mere Eglise area shortly after midnight, D -1/D-Day |
| Chicago | 51 gliders, landed at dawn, same area, D-Day |
| Boston | Paratroop drop, 82nd Airborne Division, St Sauveur le Vicomte shortly after midnight, D-1/D-Day |
| Detroit | 46 gliders, landed at dawn, same area, D-Day |
| Elmira | 176 gliders, landed at dusk, D-Day |
| Galveston | 98 gliders, landed at dawn, D+1 |
| Hackensack | 100 gliders, landed at dusk, D+1 |
| Freeport & Memphis Keokuk | Resupply missions for 82nd Airborne Division, 432 tons supplies, D+1/D+2 Resupply missions for 101st Airborne Division, night, D+1. Needed because no contact yet between paratroops and the seaborne force |

Equipment, operational strength and serviceability returns for 18:00 hrs on 5 June 1944 showed this pattern:

## RAF TRANSPORT COMMAND

| Type | Sqn | Estab | | Service-able | Unser-viceable |
|---|---|---|---|---|---|
| **No. 38 Group** | | | | | |
| Halifax V | | | | | |
| | 298 | 20 | | 37 | 1 |
| | 644 | 20 | | 35 | 1 |
| **Totals** | **2** | **40** | | **72** | **2** |
| Albemarle I, II, V | | | | | |
| | 295 | 26 | I/II | 21 | ? |
| | | | V | 11 | |
| | 296 | 26 | I/II | 20 | ? |
| | | | V | 10 | |
| | 297 | 26 | I/II | 16 | ? |
| | | | V | 13 | |
| | 570 | 26 | I/II | 24 | ? |
| | | | V | 8 | |
| **Totals** | **4** | **104** | | **123** | **3** |
| Stirling IV | | | | | |
| | 190 | 26 | | 38 | ? |
| | 196 | 26 | | 35 | ? |
| | 299 | 26 | | 39 | ? |
| | 620 | 26 | | 34 | ? |
| **Totals** | **4** | **104** | | **146** | **4** |
| Horsa | 1 HGSU | 1,040 | | 959 | - |
| Hamilcar | 1 HGSU | 80 | | 66 | - |
| **Totals** | **1** | **1,120** | | **1,025** | **-** |
| **OVERALL** | **11** | **1,368** | | **1,366** | **9** |
| **No. 44 Group** | | | | | |
| Albemarle | 511 | | | - | |
| Dakota | 511 | | | 11 | 9 |
| | | 25 | | | |
| Liberator II | 511 | | | 3 | 1 |
| York | 511 | | | 2 | 6 |
| **Totals** | **1** | **25** | | **6** | **16** |

| Type | Sqn | Estab | Service-able | Unser-viceable |
|---|---|---|---|---|
| Stirling III | 525 | | 1 | - |
| Warwick C.I | 525 | 25 | - | 12 |
| Wellington C Mk IA | 525 | | - | - |
| **Totals** | **1** | **25** | **1** | **12** |
| **OVERALL** | **2** | **50** | **7** | **28** |

**No. 46 Group**

| Type | Sqn | Estab | Service-able | Unser-viceable |
|---|---|---|---|---|
| Anson | | | | |
| | 48 | 5 | 2 | 1 |
| | 233 | 5 | 1 | - |
| | 512 | 5 | 1 | - |
| | 575 | 5 | - | 1 |
| **Totals** | **4** | **20** | **4** | **2** |
| Dakota | 48 | 30 | 34 | 1 |
| | 233 | 30 | 35 | 1 |
| | 271 | 30 | 35 | 1 |
| | 512 | 30 | 34 | 1 |
| | 575 | 30 | 37 | 1 |
| **Totals** | **5** | **150** | **175** | **5** |
| Oxford | 233 | - | 1 | 1 |
| | 512 | - | 1 | - |
| **Totals** | **2** | **-** | **2** | **1** |
| Sparrow | 271 | 6 | - | - |
| **OVERALL** | **5** | **176** | **181** | **8** |

## NON-OPERATIONAL SUPPORT

**No. 24 Squadron**

| Hudson III | 1 | 1 |
|---|---|---|

| Hudson IIIA | 3 | 1 | |
|---|---|---|---|
| Hudson V | 11 | - | 1 |
| Hudson VI | - | 1 | |
| Wellington | - | - | |
| Flamingo | 3 | - | |
| Lockheed 12A | 6 | 3 | 1 |
| DH 89A | 5 | 6 | - |
| York | 5 | 2 | 1 |
| Oxford Ambulance | 3 | 1 | 1 |
| Dakota | 2 | 3 | - |
| Reliant | 2 | - | - |
| Goose | 1 | 1 | - |
| Oxford I | - | 1 | - |
| **Totals** | **35** | **24** | **7** |

**Metropolitan Communications Squadron**

| Proctor | 21 | 17 | 6 |
|---|---|---|---|
| Oxford | 4 | 5 | 1 |
| Spitfire I | 4 | 3 | 1 |
| Tiger Moth | 3 | 3 | - |
| Vega Gull | 3 | 2 | 1 |
| Percival Q.6 | 2 | 1 | - |
| Beechcraft 17 | 1 | 1 | - |
| Hudson I | 1 | 1 | - |
| Lockheed 12A | 1 | 1 | - |
| Anson | 1 | - | 1 |
| Koolhoven FK43 | 1 | - | 1 |
| Mohawk | 1 | - | 1 |
| Miles M.38 | 1 | - | - |
| **Totals** | **44** | **34** | **12** |

**Dakota Modification Section, Doncaster**

| Dakota | - | 24 | 8 |
|---|---|---|---|
| **OVERALL** | **79** | **82** | **27** |

# The Armstrong Whitworth Albemarle

Tapping a large labour market to build aircraft, even those new to the task such as furniture makers and volume car builders using indigenous materials, seemed a smart idea. When in 1937 the Air Ministry suggested testing it by building an experimental machine made of steel and wood composite drawing upon design capability already stretched, the Air Staff was aghast. They saw no need for the aircraft, adding that the international situation allowed no time for experimentation. Such positive rejection undoubtedly caused the civilians and politicians to pursue their ideas forcefully, and in 1938 the Air Ministry issued

Specification B.9/38 outlining a twin-engined bomber, top speed 300 mph and range 1,500 miles when carrying a 1,000 lb bomb load. They had perchance hit upon a formula later exploited by the Mosquito – which they repeatedly rejected! As for the Air Staff, they vehemently opposed the idea, having no role for any such aircraft.

Bristol and Armstrong Whitworth proposed attractive projects. The former outlined an aeroplane with a nosewheel undercarriage – very avant-garde. The latter proposed a twin-Merlin bomber built of tubular steel and compressed wood to be operated as a high-speed 'hedge-hopper'. Again, advanced thinking. The RAF now

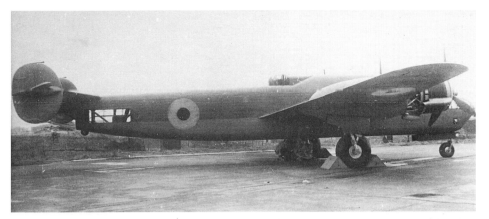

*P1360, the first prototype Albemarle, in original 1940 configuration.*

faced having two unwanted yet novel designs being foisted upon it. To avoid having two aircraft, the Bristol Type 155 was in July 1938 amalgamated with the Armstrong Whitworth design, the latter a five-man general reconnaissance project which was the larger and more ambitious of the pair. Armstrong Whitworth laid out their AW 41 for two Merlins, forecasting a 3,500 lb offensive load over 2,500 miles and a top speed of 320 mph. A first flight was promised for May 1939.

To reduce wing loading the span was increased from 61 to 67 ft. A switch to heavier Bristol Hercules engines came because the RAF preferred air-cooled engines in long-range aircraft. Armstrong Whitworth wanted to use the Armstrong Siddeley Deerhound engine, buried in the thick wing, but its development was too slow.

To free the company's main design office at Baginton to concentrate upon the Whitley and newer bomber designs based upon the AW 41 configuration, work was passed to Hamble. Two prototypes, *P1360* and *P1361*, were ordered on 18 August 1938 and a 200-aircraft production order was raised to 1,000 in November 1939, with delivery to commence a year later. All would come as envisaged from the furniture and car industries. Main components would be taken to the Gloster Aircraft Works at Brockworth for assembly and testing. That meant training a large workforce able to ensure strength and stiffness in their products, use new resin adhesives, and to maintain high quality inspection skills.

In autumn 1939 the Blackburn Botha torpedo-bomber was in trouble, so Armstrong Whitworth was ordered to prepare the AW 41 as an alternative. With no experience of designing for the specialized maritime role, the company suggested carrying one torpedo beneath each mainplane. That would have fouled flying controls. In any case, it was too late for radical alterations. In January 1940 all existing orders were confirmed. The first 250 examples would now be built as bombers – for which no niche existed.

On 20 March 1940, 10 months late, the prototype first lifted off, but only after an incredibly long take-off run. To reduce that a further 10 ft was added to the wing span, both prototypes being taken to Baginton for modifications. As a result, some parts already built were scrapped. It was obvious that the new aircraft builders would find difficulty in carrying out the sort of modification schemes so common in the aircraft industry.

*P1360* flew again on 28 September 1940. Two days later it was again in trouble following a wheels-up landing, and much heavier now it was fitted with revised stabilizers. It was an ill-fated aeroplane for on 4 February 1941 a large section of wing skinning came adrift. The parachute lines of a test crew member, upon baling out, wrapped around the tail, yet miraculously he survived the crash-landing.

The second prototype, wing span 77 ft, flew on 20 April 1941, and this time it proved to be impossible to fly the aircraft off at the maximum loaded weight. Indeed, it could not be operated above 32,000 lb –

111

3,000 lb below the scheduled loaded weight. Named Albemarle, 1,000 examples were on order.

Boscombe Down's trials soon showed that it was possible to get airborne at 36,500 lb – but only by taking a 1,240 yd take-off run and carrying a reduced operational load. Once airborne the Albemarle handled like a Wellington III, the novel nosewheel gear making it pleasant to land. Yet its top speed was only 250 mph TAS at 11,500 ft, service ceiling 17,500 ft, range with 3,500 lb a mere 1,300 miles; some 2,060 miles in the general reconnaissance configuration. A four-gun dorsal turret was its only effective defence for its ventral turret proved useless. Large glazed areas needed a lot of blinds to ensure blackout. Overall, the Albemarle was inferior to the Wellington which it was now intended to replace.

Separating designers from the production teams generated problems, particularly with aircraft weight, so on 1 April 1941 a new firm named A.W. Hawkesley Ltd, using an amalgamation of the manufacturers' names, was established at Brockworth. By mid-1941, and with only one prototype flying, the programme had, in the money of the time, cost a staggering £6 million – maybe £200 million in present-day money – bringing Ministerial suggestions for cancellation. Maybe as a face-saver production was, in September 1941, cut by half. There was a useful spin-off because Albemarle builders also constructed Horsa gliders and Mosquitoes.

Looming was the problem of what to do with 500 Albemarles. Use them to train Liberator crews or air-gunners? As air-sea rescue aircraft, for which the wide turning circle made them unsuitable? On 20 August 1941 the conclusion was reached that the Albemarle had 'no future'. Then, once more, face-saving rescued it, and orders were given for the formation of six new bomber squadrons to operate Albemarles. As for the rest, selling them to Brazil was mooted – or converting them into freighter/transports. Then, quite suddenly, the Albemarle found a future, for by cutting a hole in its floor it could be used to drop paratroops. With only 13 Albemarles flying the suggestion was made to install Bristol Hercules VI engines in the 201st and subsequent aircraft, producing a superior 'Mk II'. Instead, Hercules VIs were fitted to other types and the Albemarle II and subsequent versions relied upon the Hercules XI. The first Mk II, V1606, entered service on 3 April 1943. Fitting Merlins in a Mk III was still on the cards, and the Mk IV fitted with American Wright Cyclones was test-flown. All would be for paratroop-dropping or freight-carrying. Surplus Albemarles were to be generously presented to the USSR!

Autumn 1942 saw the Albemarle confirmed as a transport aircraft serving as a 10-seat troop carrier, glider tug, long-

*Albemarle I V1599, an AWA development aircraft used by the RAE from May 1944 to February 1946. Ample nose and rear fuselage glazing dated from reconnaissance-bomber requirements. (AWA)*

range transport and passenger-cum-freight machine. It would replace the Whitley in No. 38 Wing squadrons.

## Operations

Events moved fast. No. 511 Squadron, Lyneham, on 1 December 1942 commenced night runs carrying 3,000 lb freight loads to Gibraltar in Albemarle special transports in which the dorsal turret was replaced by manhandled twin guns. 11 February 1943 saw the sanctioning of Albemarles to tow Horsas, with No. 297 Squadron being chosen for the task. No. 296 was earmarked for Albemarle troop carriers, the first of which joined the squadron on 30 January 1943. Leaflet dropping over Rouen on 9/10 February 1943 marked the start of the Albemarle's offensive career, and on 17 April two Albemarles actually dropped bombs on France.

Tests at the AFEE suggested that the Albemarle/Horsa combination was unable to get above 700 ft, but No. 38 Wing, disbelieving that, cut the fuel load, making the aircraft suitable for operations to the near European mainland. But there were other plans for Albemarles – the towing of Waco CG-4As and Horsas transporting airborne troops during the invasion of Sicily in July 1943.

For the first assault, on 9 June, 25 Albemarle/CG-4A combinations operated, 17 gliders landing on Sicily. For the second operation, on 13/14 July, 10 troop-carrying Albemarles and 12 glider tugs carried troops to the Primosole Bridge area. By then the aircraft engines were repeatedly overheating, and the airframes generally suffered badly in the high temperatures of North Africa. Meanwhile in Britain, an even more important role had been found for the Albemarle. Incredible as it must seem, it was chosen to spearhead the invasion of northern Europe.

No. 42 OTU trained enough Albemarle crews to man four squadrons – No. 296, No. 297 which began equipping in June 1943, and No 295 in October 1943 whose Halifaxes were transferred to No. 298 Squadron; and a new squadron, No. 570, which formed on 15 November 1943 and received Albemarle IIs.

Early in 1944 *V1761*, the first Mk V, appeared. This was a Mk II variant fitted with fuel jettison gear. *V1766*, the first Mk V for the RAF, was delivered on 17 March 1944. The final variant was the Mk VI, similar to its predecessor apart from facilities for side-loading and the first of which reached the RAF on D-Day.

Brize Norton and Harwell each accommodated two squadrons for the Normandy landings holding between them 93 Albemarles supplemented by four drawn from No. 42 OTU, Hampstead Norris. An hour before midnight on 5 June 1944, three aircraft of No. 295 Squadron (*P1656, V1740* and *V1764*) and three of No. 570 Squadron (*V1617, V1694* and

*Albemarles towing Horsas to Normandy on the evening of 6 June. (F. Holland)*

113

*V1814*) set off, each carrying 10 paratroopers whose tasks were to place guiding beacons at the three drop zones (DZs) where the main paratroop force would land. At DZ 'L' only one team was accurately dropped; at DZ 'N' the sticks were not well positioned; and at DZ 'V' the drops were successful but equipment would not work, which resulted in a scattered Main Force drop.

Another 35 Albemarles, mostly carrying 10 men but some only nine and more equipment, set forth with part of the main party of the paratroop drop. Aircraft known to have been involved are:

295 Squadron:
*P1430, V1751, V1753* and *V1784*
296 Squadron:
*V1501, V1605* (FTR), *V1630, V1696, V1698, V1699, V1701, V1744, V1765* and *V1774*
297 Squadron:
*P1367, P1378, P1383, P1384, P1395, P1400, P1471, V1700, V1716, V1742, V1743, V1772* and *V1812*
570 Squadron:
*P1379, P1441, V1645, V1704, V1842*, two from No. 42 OTU including *P1442* (FTR) and possibly *V1642/'75'*, and another Albemarle identity uncertain

The third operation involved 45 Albemarles, each towing a Horsa glider carrying a variety of equipment. Five gliders cast off prematurely, leaving the remainder to drop on landing zones reasonably close to the earlier paratroop dropping zones. The tugs used in this operation were:

295 Squadron:
*P1396, P1436* (glider aborted), *P1397* (paratroop lift), possibly *P1404, P1445, V1607, V1647* (glider aborted), *V1723, V1749* (carrying Gen Gale and Divisional HQ staff) and one uncertain
296 Squadron:
*P1435, V1632, V1646, V1748, V1750, V1757, V1763, V1766, V1775, V1777, V1810, V1813* and one uncertain
297 Squadron:
*P1395, P1409, P1651, V1769, V1771, V1778* (glider aborted), *V1781, V1823* and *V1825*
570 Squadron:
*V1602, V1620* (glider aborted), *V1623,*

*V1624, V1626, V1703, V1746* (glider aborted), *V1752, V1754, V1767* and two uncertain

Evening on D-Day saw 73 Albemarles set off for Normandy, each towing a Horsa as they participated in Operation *Mallard*. Two gliders failed to complete the journey and one Albemarle was shot down by AA fire. Known participants for this occasion are:

295 Squadron:
*P1396, P1430, P1436, P1656, V1601, V1723, V1751, V1753, V1764, V1766, V1777, V1780, V1787, V1809, V1819, V1820* (glider aborted) and three uncertain
296 Squadron:
*P1387, P1388, P1391, V1501, V1605, V1616, V1630, V1646, V1696, V1699, V1701, V1774, V1785, V1810, V1815, V1818, V1821* and one uncertain
297 Squadron:
*P1378, P1395* (glider aborted), *P1409, P1460, P1471, V1716, V1769, V1772, V1773* (FTR), *V1776, V1781, V1782, V1823, V1825* and one uncertain
570 Squadron:
*P1441, P1557, V1617, V1627, V1643, V1645, V1694, V1704, V1746, V1756, V1761, V1783, V1811, V1814, V1816, V1842* with *V1642* (of 42 OTU) and two others uncertain.

Operations were resumed on 7/8 June when, within Operation *Coney,* French paratroops were airlifted to assist Resistance forces attacking bridges and other tactical targets behind enemy lines. Further night support sorties were undertaken before the Albemarles force was halved in July when Nos. 295 and 570 Squadrons converted to Stirling GT Mk IVs.

## Albemarles on squadron strength, 5 June 1944

### No. 295 Sqn, Harwell

| | |
|---|---|
| P1370 | 15.5.44-7.9.44 |
| P1374 | 5.5.44-6.6.44 EFB, force-landed 1¹/₂ miles W of Harwell |
| P1377 | 5.5.44-1.10.44 |
| P1390 | 12.5.44-26.8.44 |
| P-P1396 | 10.11.43-26.8.44 |
| M-P1397 | 19.3.44-7.9.44 |
| P1404 | ?-? |
| P1430 | 12.11.43-6.10.44 |

| | |
|---|---|
| *P1436* 9.11.43-30.9.44 | *V1629* 31.12.43-25.10.44 |
| *P1445* 24.1.43-26.8.44 | *V1630* 31.12.43-10.11.44 |
| *P1461* 25.2.44-24.9.44 | *V1632* 23.12.43-25.10.44 |
| *P1656* 17.3.44-24.9.44 | *V1646* 3.1.44-23.11.44 |
| *V1601* 26.11.43-26.8.44 | *V1695* 23.12.43-8.8.44 |
| *V1607* 24.12.43-10.9.44 | *V1696* 3.44-6.11.44 |
| *U-V1647* 6.4.44-6.8.44 | *V1698* 31.12.44-2.11.44 |
| *V1723* 12.11.43-10.9.44 | *V1699* 13.12.43-8.8.44 named *Aphelia VI* |
| *V1740* 26.11.43-27.9.44 | *V1701* 3.1.44-22.10.44 |
| *V1748* 12.11.43-13.8.44 | *V1744* 3.1.44-11.7.44 FTR |
| *V1749* 12.11.43-10.9.44 | *V1755* 3.1.44-22.10.44 |
| *V1750* 12.11.43-10.9.44 | *V1765* 31.3.44-6.11.44 |
| *V1751* 18.11.43-10.9.44 | *V1774* 31.3.44-20.11.44 |
| *V1753* 24.11.43-13.8.44 | *V1775* 7.4.44-6.11.44 |
| *V1757* 15.1.44-31.8.44 | *V1779* 26.4.44-7.12.44 |
| *V1759* 15.1.44-19.9.44 | *V1785* 26.4.44-15.11.44 |
| *V1763* 22.3.44-31.8.44 | *V1810* 1.5.44-7.6.44 |
| *V1764* 21.3.44-31.8.44 | *V1813* 1.5.44-22.11.44 |
| *V1766* 22.3.44-27.9.44 | *V1815* 8.5.44-20.11.44 |
| *V1777* 14.4.44-5.7.44 RIW | *V1818* 13.5.44-15.11.44 |
| *V1780* 30.4.44-10.9.44 | *V1821* 20.5.44-6.11.44 |
| *V1784* 29.4.44-6.6.44 RIW Portsmouth Aviation | *V1822* 15.5.44-20.11.44 |
| *V1786* 29.4.44-27.9.44 | |
| *V1787* 29.4.44-10.9.44 | |

## No. 297 Sqn, Brize Norton

| | |
|---|---|
| *V1809* 30.4.44-19.9.44 | *P1367* ?-7.7.44, 22.7.44-8.8.44 |
| *V1819* 18.5.44-31.8.44 | *P1378* 7.5.44-24.8.44 |
| *V1820* 18.5.44-10.8.44 | *P1381* 20.12.43-6.5.44, 10.6.44-24.9.44 EFA |
| | *P1383* 14.11.43-24.7.44 |
| | *P1384* 12.11.43-24.8.44 |

## No. 296 Sqn, Brize Norton

| | |
|---|---|
| *P1365* 5.12.43-16.10.44 | *P1394* 31.8.43-17.10.44 |
| *S-P1373* 25.5.43-25.8.44 | *P1395* 30.3.44-16.10.44 |
| *P1387* 19.8.43-25.10.44 | *P1399* 1.7.43-8.8.44 |
| *P1388* 14.12.43-25.10.44 | *P1400* 14.1.44-28.7.44 FTR from SOE flight |
| *P1391* 9.9.43-21.11.44 | *P1409* 18.7.43-4.12.44 |
| *P1432* 27.5.43-25.10.44 | *P1460* 7.11.43-16.10.44 |
| *P1435* 21.5.43-23.9.44 EFA, overshot, Long Marston | *P1470* 14.11.43-23.8.44 |
| | *N-P1471* 14.11.43-8.8.44 named *NERTZ* |
| *P1501* 25.5.43- FTR 9.8.44 | *P1651* 20.5.44-6.6.44 AC FB, ?-13.11.44 |
| *P1510* 5.5.44-25.10.44 | *V1700* 6.1.44-11.12.44 |
| *P1525* 21.5.43-2.10.44 | *V1710* 21.10.43-11.12.44 |
| *V1605* 31.12.43-6.6.44 FTR, shot down by AA fire | *V1716* 28.10.43-11.12.44 |
| | *V1722* 31.10.43-22.10.44 |
| *V1616* 29.12.43-18.9.44, 28.10.44-? | *V1738* 31.10.43-31.10.44 |
| | *V1742* 7.11.43-8.8.44 |

*Transport aircraft on D-Day generally wore a full array of 'invasion markings', as displayed here on Albemarle GT Mk V V1823-S of No. 297 Squadron. It crashed and was destroyed near Bretton, Wiltshire, on 22 December 1944 during glider-towing practice.*

| | | | |
|---|---|---|---|
| *V1743* | 11.11.43-9.9.44 | *V1620* | 1.12.43-14.7.44 |
| *V1769* | 31.3.44-29.9.44 | *V1623* | 30.11.43-10.10.44 |
| *V1771* | 29.3.44-22.10.44 | *V1624* | 18.3.43-5.10.44 |
| *V1772* | 24.3.44-? | *V1626* | 22.3.44-19.7.44 |
| *V1773* | 31.3.44-6/7.6.44 FTR | *V1631* | 31.3.44-7.10.44 |
| *V1776* | 7.4.44-26.11.44 | *V1643* | 20.12.43-28.8.44 |
| *V1778* | 18.4.44-3.11.44 | *V1645* | 2.12.43-14.7.44 |
| *V1781* | 19.4.44-16.9.44 | *V1694* | 24.12.43-10.10.44 |
| *V1782* | 1.5.44-27.8.44 EFB, overshot, Brize | *V1697* | ?-? |
| | Norton | *X-V1703* | 23.12.43-2.10.44 |
| *V1812* | 10.5.44-31.10.44 | *V1704* | 24.12.43-19.7.44 |
| *S-V1823* | 16.5.44-3.11.44 | *V1746* | 2.12.43-4.10.44 |
| *V1825* | 29.5.44-16.11.44 | *V1752* | 30.11.43-19.7.44 |
| *V1828* | 6.6.44-31.10.44 | *V1754* | 30.11.43-3.10.44 |
| *V1841* | 6.6.44-23.11.44 | *V1756* | 23.12.43-4.10.44 |
| | | *V1761* | 9.5.44-1.10.44 |
| | | *V1767* | 22.3.44-4.10.44 |
| **No. 570 Sqn, Harwell** | | *V1768* | 21.3.44-17.9.44 |
| *P1371* | 12.4.44-13.8.44 | *V1783* | 25.4.44-28.8.44 |
| *P1379* | 21.1.44-4.8.44 | *V1811* | 15.5.44-2.10.44 |
| *V-P1441* | 20.12.43-7.10.44 | *V1814* | 10.5.44-28.8.44 |
| *P1557* | 14.5.43-7.10.44 | *V1816* | 18.5.44-3.10.44 |
| *V1602* | 24.3.44-10.10.44 | *V1842* | 29.5.44-7.8.44 |
| *V1617* | 29.11.43-1.10.44 | | |

# The Douglas Dakota III

In assessing America's aircraft, historians may well rate the DC-3 Dakota as the best. After its major war-winning contribution it conquered the post-war airline world, remaining for decades the most dependable transport. Vast numbers of airline passengers unknowingly flew in D-Day veterans, and there are active, still, Dakotas which delivered paratroops to Normandy on D-Day. A progressive development of the Douglas Commercial 1 (DC-1), first flown on 1 July 1933, the RAF's D-Day Dakotas were Mk IIIs equivalent to the USAAF's C-47A. Following the DC-1 had come the production version, the 1934 DC-2, and to make that even more useful a night sleeper variant was developed. Passengers could then cross the North American continent in style, and so much faster than by train. This, the DC-3DST (Douglas Sleeper Transport), first flew on 12 December 1935. A troop carrier conversion for the US Army, the C-53 Skytrooper, entered service in October 1941. Three months later its cargo-carrying equivalent, the C-47 Skytrain, also joined the forces.

Whereas the DC-3 and C-53 had a small port-side exit door aft, the C-47 featured a large cargo door with a smaller one within it. The RAF acquired, by various means, a handful of DC-2s and DC-3s for overseas use, particularly appreciating their value when a number were used during the El Alamein campaign. Experience from the desert war (applied during *Overlord* planning) led to the C-47 being the RAF's choice for its tactical mobility and transport support organisation. Transport Command, given six months to form a five-squadron Dakota-equipped paradrop and glider tug force, decided to concentrate them in a new Group, No. 46, which began functioning on 4 February 1944.

Although rare in Britain before 1944, RAF 'Dakotas' – by which name the entire class came to be known in Britain and many other countries – were not entirely absent. The first Dakota I, *FD769*, made landfall here on 11 February 1943 and, like its follower, *FD770* which arrived on 18 February, it was bound for BOAC where they became *G-AGFX* and *G-AGFY* respectively. The first British-based RAF example was *FD772* which also arrived on 11 February and joined No. 24 Squadron at Hendon a week later, where it was soon joined by *FD782*. Eight Dakota Is had

*No. 46 Group in June 1944 relied upon the Dakota III. FD903, depicted here as* NQ:I, *served with No. 24 Squadron.*

reached Britain by the end of May 1943. In June 1943 a new transport squadron, No. 512, formed at Hendon to operate most of the Dakota Is and began using them in August.

Whereas the RAF's Dakota IIs bypassed the UK, the first Mk III, *FD819*, arrived on 30 April 1943. Bound for BOAC at Whitchurch it became *G-AGHF*. *FD826* joined No. 24 Squadron on 4 May, and served with No. 512 Squadron from 23 August 1943 to 12 June 1944.

Acquisition of Dakota IIIs was far from easy, for the USAAF wanted all that were built. A strong case was argued for 150 to be available for the five RAF squadrons in time for the D-Day assault, and the Americans eventually agreed to supply them – and indeed many more – under Lend-Lease. The first of these to reach Britain, *FZ560*, arrived on 30 December 1943. So desperate was the need that No. 512 Squadron were flying it the next day. *FZ548* which arrived via the Azores on 31 December 1943 joined No. 512 Squadron before heading for SEAC. Next to come was *FZ549* which arrived on 18 January 1944 and on 25 January became the first Dakota to join No. 271 Squadron. Mid-May 1944 saw it transferred to No. 24 Squadron. On 30 November 1946 it was sold to KLM, Royal Dutch Airlines.

Many early Dakota IIIs were shuffled around, *FZ560* joining the Air Transport Tactical Development Unit (ATTDU) on 6 February 1944 and later the Parachute Training School (PTS) at Ringway. *FZ564* was used for load-dropping and glider tug tests at Farnborough and later by Airspeed Ltd – after radio and radar communications trials at TRE Defford. Another early arrival was *FZ592* used by No. 271 Squadron and damaged in September 1944 during an Arnhem resupply sortie.

Since they already existed the first squadrons to equip fully with Dakotas were Nos. 271 and 512. Although both received examples in January 1944, main delivery began in February 1944, of Dakotas with serial numbers in the *FZ* and *KG* ranges. Delivery did not proceed in numerical order, and there were diversions overseas. By the end of January 15 Dakota IIIs had arrived for No. 46 Group, another 68 by the end of February with the first from the second batch, *KG373*, reaching Britain on 13 February 1944. Deliveries continued to D-Day and well beyond, with 40 Dakotas arriving during May 1944 and six (*KG606*, *KG609*, *KG615*, *KG618*, *KG622* and *KG631*) touching down in Britain on 5 June 1944, during the evening of which the five squadrons held 174 Dakotas against their intended establishment of 180 – sufficient for the prescribed operations.

Although Nos. 271 and 512 Squadrons were equipping with Dakota IIIs at the start of 1944, very few crews were at that time qualified to fly them, so intense training courses were ordered providing 50 hours' flying prior to operations. Fortunately the aircraft were easy to fly, for learning the techniques required for airborne operations was not so easy. Trials were first needed to ensure that the Dakota could safely tow a fully-laden Horsa – a test it readily passed. All crews involved first underwent ground school training at No. 21 Heavy Glider Conversion Unit, Brize Norton, from mid-February 1944 before towing was practised.

Nothing is perfect. Poor downward forward view from the Dakota meant that map reading and general navigation for tactical purposes were difficult. A fourth crew member to assist in those tasks was therefore added. All Dakotas arrived without night-towing station-keeping lights – essential for safety. Existing light circuits, although wired, were unconnected. That was not important since the RAF was unhappy with existing fuselage mountings which would make Dakotas easy prey for night-fighters. Instead, station-keeping lights were fitted to wing-tip trailing edges, and triple-colour navigation lights were installed above and below the fuselage in place of customary wing-tip lights. During the spectacular large-scale night practices the mass of lights visible provoked reference to 'flying Christmas trees'. All of the aircraft also had *Gee* and *Rebecca II* navigation aids. These modifications – beyond squadron level to carry out – meant that Dakotas needed to pass through the Dakota Modification Centre, Doncaster, which played an unsung, essential part in the invasion preparations.

Expansion of No. 46 Group first involved No. 575 Squadron which formed at Hendon on 1 January 1944 from elements of No. 512 Squadron and which, along with '575', moved out of the London smog and balloon barrage to the operational base at Broadwell, Oxfordshire, on Valentine's Day 1944, from where in March and April 1944 it concentrated on paratroop dropping. First, it dropped containers, then switched to dropping two, five, then 10 troops for whom exit from the Dakota's side door was a new technique to master. By mid-March most troops were Dakota-drop proficient.

There were some tragic accidents. One paratrooper's feet became entangled in parachute static strops as he stepped from a Dakota, and he became suspended from the aircraft. Concluding that his best chance of survival might come from cutting the strops when the aircraft was flying as low as 20 ft above water, the captain arranged for such a try over Poole Harbour where a launch was positioned to retrieve him. The run was made, release achieved, but tragically the soldier was picked up dead. Modified strops were then ordered to be fitted to all aircraft.

As training intensified, parachute packing proved no mean problem. Repacking so many parachutes after major exercises was such a task that Dakotas began ferrying replacements from the PTS at Ringway to No. 46 Group squadrons.

Having so many aircraft taking part in night exercises in the confined space of non-operational areas was also worrying because the Dakotas needed to drop glider tow ropes before landing, then return singly to bases. Only by staggering the exercises, between Nos. 38 and 46 Groups and the C-47-equipped US 9th Troop Carrier Command, could safety be achieved. During night cross-country flying over south-west England aircraft tracks were plotted by the ROC, and the Dakota squadrons participated in *Bullseye* searchlight co-operation exercises. Night-fighter evasion tactics for the Dakotas were worked out by the ATTDU and Air Fighting Development Unit. To give crews a taste of operational flying, each flew a leaflet-dropping mission over Normandy, relying upon *Gee* for navigation. No aircraft were lost. Training also involved stream take-offs, No. 271 Squadron once getting 18 aircraft airborne in 56 seconds. One departure every six seconds became quite normal.

Expansion of No. 46 Group became complete after two Coastal Command squadrons were transferred to Transport Command. Most Dakotas were delivered to Britain along the southern route, which took them via Bermuda to the Azores where some of them picked up ground personnel and equipment belonging to the two new squadrons, Nos. 48 and 233. Their aircrew brought their Hudsons home, the whole movement being completed in a fortnight, and for the loss of only two Hudsons in Biscay. No. 233 Squadron went to Blakehill; No. 48 to Down Ampney, there joining veteran No. 271 Squadron.

The expectation was that the invasion would incur heavy losses, so each squadron – established at 48 crews – always had 30

*Dakota KWICHERBICHEN UK, possibly FZ592 of No. 271 Squadron. (Ray Sturtivant collection)*

fully operational crews with five more in reserve. Another 18 crews passed out from No. 107 OTU every three weeks, pilots taking a six-week course.

## Operations

Dakota D-Day operations have already been described. The aircraft involved in them were as follows:

## Operation *Tonga*

No. 48 Squadron:
*FZ620, FZ624, FZ671, KG321, KG331, KG337, KG338, KG346, KG350, KG364, KG370, KG391, KG394, KG397, KG401, KG404, KG406, KG408, KG409, KG414, KG416, KG417, KG419, KG423, KG426, KG428, KG429, KG436, KG439, KG452* and one other uncertain
No. 233 Squadron:
*FZ672, FZ678, FZ679, FZ681, FZ685, FZ686, FZ688, FZ692, KG313, KG315, KG329, KG341, KG356* (FTR), *KG399, KG400, KG403, KG410, KG412, KG413, KG420, KG424, KG427, KG429*(?)(FTR), *KG430, KG433, KG437, KG440, KG447, KG448* and *KG455*
No. 271 Squadron:
a) towing Horsas: *KG387, KG444, KG500, KG512, KG516, KG545* and *KG564*
b) carrying paratroops: *FZ613, FZ618, FZ639, KG345, KG357, KG362,*

*KG367, KG376* and *KG515*
c) 'A' Flt paradropping from Blakehill Farm: *FZ601, FZ668, KG340, KG358, KG365, KG372, KG374, KG378, KG514* and *KG562*
No. 512 Squadron:
*FZ610, FZ647, FZ648, FZ649, FZ651, FZ656, FZ694, FZ696, KG314, KG322, KG323, KG324, KG330, KG333, KG344, KG347, KG348, KG354, KG361, KG369, KG371, KG373, KG377, KG379, KG390, KG392, KG407, KG418, KG422, KG480, KG486* and one uncertain
No. 575 Squadron:
*FZ593, FZ640, FZ662, FZ695, KG310, KG311, KG312, KG326, KG328, KG332, KG334, KG345, KG355, KG359, KG363, KG388*(?), *KG425, KG431, KG434, KG442* and *KG449*

## Operation *Mallard*

No. 48 Squadron:
*KG317, KG321* (damaged), *KG331, KG346* (damaged), *KG350, KG364, KG370* (glider aborted), *KG406, KG408, KG409, KG411* (damaged), *KG416, KG417* (or *KG418*), *KG419, KG423* (FTR), *KG426* (FTR) and *KG428*
No. 271 Squadron:
*FZ607, FZ615, FZ628, FZ639, FZ660, KG318, KG345, KG362, KG367, KG376, KG387, KG389, KG500, KG512, KG515, KG516* and two uncertain

119

No. 512 Squadron:
FZ647, FZ649, FZ651, FZ658, FZ690, FZ694, FZ696, KG314, KG322, KG323, KG348, KG354, KG368, KG371, KG373, KG377, KG379 and KG407

No. 575 Squadron:
FZ623, FZ640, FZ674, FZ695, KG310, KG311, KG312, KG325, KG326, KG328, KG334, KG349, KG355, KG363, KG388, KG425, KG442 and one uncertain

## Operation *Rob Roy*

No. 48 Squadron:
KG337, KG404, KG419, KG421, KG423 and KG439

No. 233 Squadron:
FZ666, FZ669, FZ680, FZ681, FZ688, FZ692, KG315, KG329 (FTR), KG341, KF412, KG424 (FTR), KG433, KG437, KG441, KG448, KG455 and KG566.

No. 271 Squadron:
FZ613, FZ655, KG489 and KG545; and operated from Blakehill Farm: FZ622, KG318 (crashed at Friston 01:21 hrs), KG365, KG378 (FTR), KG488 and KG514

No. 512 Squadron:
FZ610, KG324, KG327, KG344, KG347 (FTR) and KG480 (FTR)

No. 575 Squadron:
KG320, KG332, KG359, KG402 and KG431

## Dakotas during the aftermath

Dakotas played a major role by transporting squadron personnel to France and bringing home wounded within a week of the initial assault. Dakota squadrons involved in the early activities were:

*No. 48 Squadron:*
On 18 June 1944 personnel ferried from Tangmere to 'B4' by KG364-AF, KG404-AN, KG411-UF, KG421-UW and KG423-AZ.

*No. 233 Squadron:*
On 13 June participated in the first casevac flight to France, when at 05:05 hrs FZ686 and KG427 set off for 'B2' and returned in the evening with casualties. At 13:00 hrs on 13 June FZ678 and KG440 left Thorney Island transporting HQ No. 83 Group personnel to 'B2'. KG440 returned carrying three stretcher cases. On 15 June KG559 carried HQ No. 144 Wing to 'B3', and around 05:40 hrs FZ669, FZ678, FZ686, KG341, KG430 and KG437 set out for 'B3' carrying 169 personnel, kit, 54 bomb racks and equipment. They returned mid-afternoon with 114 casualties (75 stretcher cases). At 06:50 hrs on 15 June KG351 set out from Northolt for 'B2' carrying two VIPs and six passengers. Next day FZ669 took the glider recovery party, a Jeep and baggage to 'B4'. At 10:15 hrs six

Dakotas moved RAF personnel to Advanced Landing Grounds in France, sometimes arriving under shellfire. (IWM CL515)

Dakotas (including *FZ666*, *KG412*, *KG427* and *KG566*) carried 104 personnel from Tangmere to 'B2' and returned with 111 casualties (82 stretcher cases). At 14:05 hrs *KG437* conveyed ammunition and supplies to 'B5'.

*No. 271 Squadron:*

On 13 June Sqn Ldr Pearson, flying *KG562*, set off to make the first Dakota landing in France when he carried, among others, four press representatives to 'B2'. He brought back 14 stretcher cases and six walking wounded.

*No. 512 Squadron:*

On 17 June seven Dakotas moved 76 personnel and kit of No. 124 Typhoon Wing to France, landing on the 1,700 yd runway of B5 some three miles from enemy lines. As wounded were being put aboard the Dakotas enemy shelling began, so the aircraft flew to B2 to where ambulances conveyed the wounded. In all, 138 casualties were brought home. Designated Operation *E.1* and led by Sqn Ldr Coventry, the Dakotas involved were *FZ696-Q*, *KG314-C1*, *KG379-W*, *KG392-V*, *KG558-X*, *KG560-F* and one uncertain. On 20 June 15 Dakotas during Operation *E.2* moved No. 121 Wing from Hurn to 'B6'.

*No. 575 Squadron:*

Assisted on 17 June in the lift from 'B5' to Holmsley South using *FL518*, *FZ593*,

*One of the first wounded soldiers is lifted aboard a Dakota in France prior to being flown to Gloucestershire. (IWM CL423)*

*KG320*, *KG326*, *KG343*, *KG349*, *KG363* and one other. On 27 June nine aircraft moved No. 129 Wing to 'B5'.

*Unloading from a Dakota (probably* FZ607*) at Blakehill Farm. (IWM CL420)*

These were the main early lifts carried by Dakotas.

## Dakotas on squadron strength, 5 June 1944 (Mk IIIs unless otherwise stated)

\* Operated on 5/6 June 1944
\+ Used in Operation *Mallard*, 6 June 1944
\# Used in Operation *Rob Roy*, 6/7 June 1944

NB: 1) September 1944 losses arose mainly from the Arnhem operation; 2) Information in parentheses at the end of entries lists a selection of Dakotas in post-war use, mainly with civilian organizations.

### No. 24 Sqn, Hendon (using three Dakota Is)

| | |
|---|---|
| A-FD772 | 14.4.44-16.6.44 (named *Windsor Castle*) |
| AQ-FD795 | 21.2.44-10.9.45 (*G-AIJD*) |
| FD797 | 22.1.44-10.9.45 MI MFS (*G-AJZX*) |

### No. 48 Sqn, Down Ampney

| | |
|---|---|
| FZ617 | 28.2.44-? (*G-AGJT – PH-AZT – PH-TBA – OO-TBA – PH-TFB – N94530 – N3BA* a freighter with Academy Airlines in 1993) |
| \*+AQ-FZ620 | 28.2.44-22.9.44 EFB |
| \*+UO-FZ624 | 26.2.44- ? (*G-AGZB*, Channel Airways, crashed on Isle of Wight 6.5.62) |
| \*AU-FZ671 | 27.2.44-9.9.45 |
| \*+AJ-KG321 | 28.2.44-? (*OO-AWM* – Nigerian Air Force) |
| \*+UZ-KG331 | 13.3.44-EA A 1.1.45 |
| \*#VL-KG337 | 13.3.44-15.9.45 (RCAF – CAF – CF-NTF – C-FNTF) |
| \*AB-KG338 | 29.2.44-24.9.44 |
| \*+AY-KG346 | 26.2.44-29.9.44 FTR (ROS 8-24.6.44) |
| \*+UL-KG350 | 13.3.44-22.9.44 (RCAF – C-GWMX – N29958 May 1982 and since) |
| \*+AF-KG364 | 28.2.44-29.4.45 (*G-AIOE – LX-LAC – SX-BBA – 12373* of Hellenic Air Force, May 1957) |
| \*+UN-KG370 | 26.2.44-24.9.44 FTR |
| UK-KG386 | 28.2.44-13.2.45 (*G-AGZE – F-BEFS*) |
| \*+AD-KG391 | 5.3.44-23.9.44 FB RIW (*G-AJHZ – EC-ASQ*) |
| KG393 | 29.8.3.44-24.9.44 FB RIW |
| \*AM-KG394 | 28.2.44-6.6.44 FB RIW |
| +AB-KG395 | 28.2.44-24.9.44 |
| \*AC-KG397 | 26.2.44-? |
| \*+AF-KG401 | 8.3.44-20.9.44 EFA |
| \*#AN-KG404 | 5.3.44-23.9.44 Cat E, burnt out |
| \*+UD-KG406 | 27.3.44-10.1.45 |
| \*AK-KG408 | 26.2.44-10.1.45 (*G-AHCV*, broken up January 1970) |
| \*+AH-KG409 | 29.2.44-24.9.44 |
| \*UF-KG411 | ?-? |
| \*UG-KG414 | 29.2.44-15.9.45 (*BJ764* of Indian Air Force) |
| \*+UM-KG416 | 22.4.44-9.9.45 |
| \*AR-KG417 | 22.4.44-22.9.44 FTR |
| +#AV-KG419 | 29.2.44-25.8.44 FA (*OO-CBO*, crashed in the Congo, January 1947) |
| #UW-KG421 | 29.3.44-22.8.44, written off 2.10.44 |
| \*+#AZ-KG423 | 29.2.44-5.9.45 |
| \*+UV-KG426 | 29.2.44-7.6.44 FTR |
| \*+UX-KG428 | 19.3.44-20.9.44 FTR |
| \*AS-KG436 | 29.2.44-29.8.45 (*EI-ACT*) |
| \*#UY-KG439 | 19.3.44-9.9.45 |
| \*AL-KG452 | 29.2.44-24.9.44 (*CF-TED*) |

### No. 233 Sqn, Blakehill Farm

| | |
|---|---|
| #J-FZ666 | 22.4.44-6.10.44 |
| #FZ699 | 29.2.44-28.9.44 (RCAF – C-GCXE – HI-502 – N688EA in 1993) |
| \*FZ672 | (107 OTU aircraft) |
| \*FZ678 | 18.3.44-7.9.45 |
| \*FZ679 | 24.4.44-28.9.44 |
| #FZ680 | 12.3.44-26.7.45 |
| \*#F-FZ681 | 15.3.44-? (*G-AGYZ – ET-AGQ*) |
| \*FZ685 | 15.3.44-24.4.45 BFB |
| \*FZ686 | 15.3.44-5.45 |
| +#FZ688 | 18.3.44-14.6.44 |
| \*#FZ692 | 15.3.44-28.9.44 |
| \*UM-KG313 | 4.3.44-16.9.45 (*G-AHCT* – withdrawn in August 1972, with Fairey Air Surveys) |
| \*#KG315 | 29.2.44-28.9.44 |
| \*#KG329 | 29.2.44- FTR 7.6.44, shot down by Allied AA gunfire |
| \*#KG341 | 3.44-? |
| KG342 | 8.3.44-17.9.45 |
| KG351 | 4.3.44-9.2.45 |
| \*KG356 | 6.3.44-5/6.6.44 FTR |
| KG398 | 12.3.44-27.12.44 (*G-AJAV – VR-SCP*) |
| \*KG399 | 15.3.44-23.9.44 FTR |
| \*UT-KG400 | 12.3.44-30.9.44 |
| \*UQ-KG403 | 29.2.44-17.9.45 |
| \*KG410 | 8.3.44-5.45 (*G-AIRH – ZS-DDC – CR-LDK*) |
| \*#KG412 | 4.3.44-28.9.44 |
| \*KG415 | 12.3.44-13.9.45 (*G-AGZD – VP-BCC – HR-LAG*) |
| \*U-KG420 | 29.2.44-5.9.45 (*G-AGZA* – crashed at Ruislip December 1946) |
| \*#KG424 | 30.3.44-6/7.6.44 FTR, shot down by Allied AA gunfire |
| \*D-KG427 | 29.2.44-28.9.44 |
| \*KG429 | 8.3.44-5/6.6.44 FTR |
| \*KG430 | 3.44-4.1.45 |
| \*#KG433 | 29.2.44-9.9.45 |
| \*#B-KG437 | 29.2.44-5.9.45 (*G-AGYX – PH-MAG – 5N-ATA*; later in USA) |
| \*KG440 | 8.3.44-29.8.44 (*CF-GHL – C-FGHL*; with Buffalo Airways in 1993) |
| #KG441 | 29.2.44-18.9.45 |
| \*KG447 | 12.3.44-10.6.44 (*G-AIOG – TG-ISG*; crashed in Iceland, January 1961) |
| \*#KG448 | 4.3.44-19.3.34 |
| \*#G-KG455 | 24.3.44-16.9.45 |
| \*#KG566 | 2.6.44-23.9.44 EFB |

### No. 271 Sqn, Blakehill Farm

| | |
|---|---|
| FZ592 | 14.2.44-21.10.44 |
| \*L-FZ601 | 26.2.44-1.3.45 (ROS 7.6-13.7.44) (*OO-SBA – SE-CBZ*) |
| +O-FZ607 | 12.2.44-7.10.45 (*G-AJGX – SX-BAI*) |
| \*#FZ613 | 11.2.44-3.10.45 |
| +FZ615 | 14.2.44-17.10.45 |
| #DQ-FZ622 | 26.2.44-29.8.45 (ROS 12.4-12.6.44) ? |
| \*+FZ628 | 14.2.44-13.2.45 (*TF-ISA*) |

*+FZ639  14.2.44-18.9.44
#FZ655  12.2.44- ?
+FZ660  26.2.44-31.8.44
FZ667  26.2.44-7.6.44 FTR
*J-FZ668  26.2.44-26.9.44
+#H-KG318  8.5.44-25.11.44 EFA, burnt
KG327  8.3.44-15.11.45 (LN-NAB – SE-CFM – OE-LBC – G-ATZF; destroyed in Vientiane)
*KG340  26.2.44-22.9.44 FTR
*+KG345  26.4.44-19.9.44 (RCAF post-war)
*KG357  8.5.44-22.9.44 RIW MFS (YU-ABA June 1947-1970)
*A-KG358  26.4.44-25.6.44 (battle damage 7.6.44)
*+B-KG362  19.3.44-13.8.44
*#ND-KG365  19.3.44-10.2.45 (HC-SBR – HC-SJB – HP-212 – HK-862; crashed March 1964, Bogata)
*+KG367  14.2.44-16.4.45
*K-KG372  19.2.44-15.6.44 (YU-ABE; crashed June 1951)
KG374  6.44-20.9.44 FTR
KG375  18.2.44-5/6.6.44 EFB
*+KG376  14.2.44-18.9.44
*#H-KG378  26.2.44-19.11.45
*+KG387  22.4.44-18.9.44
+KG389  26.2.44-18.9.44
*KG444  22.4.44-22.9.44 FTR (flown at that time by Jimmy Edwards)
#KG488  26.4.44-20.9.44
#KG489  10.5.44-6.6.44 (ROS 20.5-6.6.44)
*+KG500  25.4.44-24.5.45 FTR (RIW 9.6-23.6.44)
*+KG512  8.5.44-25.9.44 EFA
*#KG514  8.5.44-29.8.45 (FB ROS 21.9.44-21.11.44)
*+KG515  8.5.44-22.4.46
*+KG516  8.5.44-22.9.44 FTR
*#NS-KG545  31.5.44-18.11.45
*KG562  6.44-17.10.45, first transport aircraft flight to land in France, at 'B2' 13.6.44 (RCAF – N6678 – CF-NAR – C-FNAR; crashed in Quebec,

February 1977)
*KG564  31.5.44-17.11.45 (LV-ACI – PP-XEU – PP-CDN – PT-LBK in 1980)

## No. 512 Sqn, Broadwell

FZ609  23.2.44-12.12.44 (G-AJGX)
*#O FZ610  ? 27.7.44 Cat E
*+H-FZ647  9.2.44-10.10.45 (TC-EKE – ET-ABY)
*M-FZ648  ?-?
*+K-FZ649  23.2.44-24.3.45 FTR
*+J-FZ651  14.2.44-3.45 (OO-SBA – SE-CBZ – OE-FDA – crashed Majorca, May 1959)
*K-FZ656  12.2.44-22.9.44
+FZ658  12.2.44-25.10.44 (RCAF)
+E-FZ690  ?-7.6.44 FTR
*+R-FZ694  24.2.44-24.9.44
*+Q-FZ696  24.4.44-3.10.45
*P-FZ699  ?-?
*+C1-KG314  22.4.44-3.45 (PH-TVC, crashed in Netherlands, December 1947)
*+C-KG322  23.2.44-22.9.44 RIW
*+U-KG323  22.4.44-21.4.45
*#A-KG324  23.2.44-21.9.44 FTR
*T-KG330  23.2.44-11.9.45
*N-KG333  23.2.44-7.44
*#L-KG344  22.4.44-8.10.45 (SX-BAE – 12351 Hellenic Air Force)
*#S1-KG347  22.4.44-7.6.44 FTR
*+K-KG348  22.2.44-2.10.45 (G-AHCY)
*+Z-KG354  22.4.44-24.9.44
*U-KG361  23.2.44-15.10.45
*+Y-KG368  19.3.44-116.4.45 (NC1388N – CF-GEI; crashed, 1952)
*+X-KG371  14.2.44-8.10.45 (F-BAXV – TS-AXV – 7T-VAV)
*+B-KG373  23.2.44- ? (PH-TDR – VT-CNC – Indian Air Force)
*+S-KG377  14.2.44-9.10.45 (G-AJAV)
*+W-KG379  14.2.44-26.7.45
*E-KG390  8.3.44-15.10.44 (OO-CBL; crashed in Belgian Congo, 1948)
*V-KG392  10.4.44-? (OY-AAB – OY-KLA – F-

KG562 *NORMANDY EXPRESS, which, early on 13 June, became the first Allied transport aircraft to land in Normandy. It returned from 'B2' with stretcher casualties. (IWM)*

123

```
                OAID – F-BIID – TR-LML to Canada     *+P-KG328  23.2.44-23.9.44
                  in 1969)                            *#KG332   23.2.44-26.4.45
   *+D-KG407   10.4.44-25.10.44 (CF-TEI)            *+N-KG334   23.2.44-15.12.45 (G-AJZD – F-
    *T-KG418   22.4.44-21.9.44 FTR                              BFGU)
   *B1-KG422   18.4.44-24.9.44                        Z-KG339   24.4.44-21.6.44
    *G-KG480   10.4.44-7.6.44 FTR                       KG343   23.2.44-17.6.44 EFA
   *A1-KG486   11.4.44-15.10.44                         KG345   (271 Sqn aircraft)
    Z-KG544    3.6.44-3.10.45 (LV-ACH; crashed,       +KG349   29.2.44-5.3.45
                  July 1959)                          *+KG355   24.4.44-1.1.45 E EA – destroyed on
   X1-KG558    3.6.44-11.9.45 (LV-ADJ – T-09                    the ground
                  Argentine Air Force, 1950)         *#KG359   29.2.44-21.9.44 AC FB
    F-KG560    3.6.44-25.8.44                        *+KG363   23.2.44-2.1.45
                                                        KG380   23.2.44-?
                                                     *+KG388   24.4.44-20.9.44 FTR
No. 575 Sqn, Broadwell                                  KG402   13.4.44-3.10.44
   *U1-FZ593   29.2.44-19.9.44 (LN-NAD)             *+KG425   8.3.44-24.9.44
    +FZ623     2.44-?                                *#KG431   25.4.44-31.1.46
   *+FZ640     28.2.44-31.12.44                     UG-KG432   3.6.44-31.1.46 (FB ROS 20.9.44-
    FZ646      26.2.44-22.6.45                                  2.10.44)
   *X-FZ662    26.2.44-16.11.45                       *KG434   25.4.44-6.6.44 EFB, crashed on take-
    +FZ674     23.2.44-6.8.44 EFB, crashed in                  off, Broadwell
                  France                               KG438   ?-17.6.44 (OY-AZB; crashed in
   *+B-FZ695   18.4.44-15.12.45                                Sweden, February 1947)
   *+KG310     12.4.44-6.9.44                      *+DH-KG442   8.3.44-31.8.46
   *+KG311     23.2.44-17.7.44                       *KG449    18.4.44-26.9.44 EFB
   *+KG312     8.3.44-24.9.44                         KG501    25.4.44-24.9.44 (YU-ABJ)
   #C-KG320    23.2.44-15.12.45                     NN-KG550   3.6.44-10.1.45 (OO-SBB; crashed in
    +S-KG325   8.3.44-24.9.44                                  Libya, July 1971)
   *+Y-KG326   23.2.44-21.9.44 FTR
```

# The Handley Page Halifax GT Mk V

Although Halifaxes had in 1942 been selected as transport aircraft, and had towed Horsas to North Africa for the airborne assault on Sicily, only two squadrons participated in the Normandy invasion, both using standard Halifax Mk Vs (designated GT – Glider Tug – Mk V). They were modified to carry containers in the bomb bay and had their dorsal turrets removed to lighten the aircraft. It was their

*Halifax GT Mk V N-November of No. 644 Squadron about to tow a Hamilcar out of Tarrant Rushton. (IWM CH18846)*

configuration that led to them being selected as Hamilcar tugs. Operating from Tarrant Rushton they also towed Horsas to Normandy, including the six that carried the troops for the *coup de main* on the two bridges, and the three that landed near the Merville gun battery.

## Halifax GT Mk Vs on squadron strength, 5 June 1944

* operated during Operation *Tonga*, 5/6 June 1944
+ Hamilcar tug, Operation *Mallard*, 6 June 1944

### No. 298 Sqn, Tarrant Rushton

| | |
|---|---|
| LK651 | 4.11.43-9.2.44, 1.6.44-16.11.44 |
| *+G-KG654 | 24.11.43-8.3.44, 1.4.44-26.7.44, 10.9.44-? |
| *C-LK988 | 8.4.44-1.2.45 |
| LL129 | 20.1.44-6.7.44 FTR |
| *+O-LL147 | 28.1.44-10.12.44, 17.12.44-21.12.44 |
| *+J-LL148 | 28.1.44-14.8.44 (towed Hamilcar in *Tonga*) |
| LL149 | 29.1.44-5.10.44 |
| LL224 | 30.3.44-23.11.44 |
| +S-LL256 | 8.4.44-20.29.44 Cat E |
| *B-LL271 | 4.4.44-9.11.44 |
| *+Y-LL273 | 12.4.44-11.9.44 FTR |
| LL274 | 19.4.44-16.11.44 |
| *T-LL278 | 4.4.44-9.11.44 |
| LL291 | 15.4.44-24.8.44 |
| LL293 | 24.4.44-15.10.44 FTR |
| LL302 | 6.4.44-16.11.44 |
| *R-LL303 | 5.4.44-13.11.44 |
| LL304 | 5.4.44-16.11.44 |
| LL311 | 15.4.44-16.11.44 |
| LL325 | 6.4.44-5.10.44 |
| LL330 | 23.4.44-23.11.44 |
| LL332 | 14.4.44-5.10.44 |
| LL333 | 19.4.44-22.9.44 FTR (possibly used on D-Day by 644 Sqn) |
| LL334 | 26.4.44-6.8.44 FTR |
| *+K-LL335 | 26.4.44 16.11.44 (towed Horsa 92) |
| *+V-LL336 | 9.5.44-19.2.45 |
| LL337 | 26.4.44-11.11.44 |
| *L-LL343 | 23.4.44-30.8.44 FTR |
| *+J-LL347 | 5.5.44-16.11.44 |

| | |
|---|---|
| *+H-LL348 | 6.5.44-7.6.44 FTR |
| *+W-LL349 | 30.4.44-28.11.44 |
| *L-LL353 | 28.4.44-5.10.44 |
| LL354 | 8.5.44-23.11.44 |
| *+G-LL355 | 8.5.44-23.11.44 (towed Horsa 91) |
| *+F-LL361 | 8.5.44-22.2.45 |
| *+O-LL382 | 5.5.44-16.11.44 |
| |S-LL384 | 8.5.44-5.10.44 |
| +F-LL401 | 8.5.44-25.8.44 FTR |
| LL404 | 13.5.44-16.11.44 |
| *T-LL406 | 13.5.44-16.10.44 (towed Horsa 93) |
| *K-LL407 | 1.8.5.44-6.6.44 FTR |

### No. 644 Sqn, Tarrant Rushton

| | |
|---|---|
| LK641 | 28.3.44-27.8.44 EFA |
| LK655 | 28.3.44-14.8.44 |
| *D-LL198 | 15.3.44-9.11.44 |
| LL217 | 28.3.44-16.11.44 |
| *N-LL218 | 20.4.44-5.10.44 (towed Horsa 96) |
| *G-LL219 | 26.3.44-23.11.44 (towed Hamilcar in *Tonga*) |
| LL270 | 6.4.44-5.10.44 |
| LL275 | 4.4.44-16.11.44 |
| LL277 | 4.4.44-5.10.44 |
| +Q-LL281 | 26.4.44-5.10.44 |
| +O-LL292 | 16.5.44-16.8.44 AC FB |
| LL301 | 30.3.44-14.8.44 |
| *A-LL305 | 6.4.44-23.11.44 |
| +H-LL309 | 8.4.44-30.11.44 |
| *C-LL310 | 10.4.44-15.10.44 Cat E |
| *T-LL312 | 14.4.44-9.11.44 |
| *N-LL326 | 15.4.44-16.11.44 |
| LL327 | 8.4.44-5.10.44 |
| *+Y-LL328 | 19.4.44-27.10.44 |
| LL329 | 16.4.44-27.10.44 |
| *+K-LL331 | 27.4.44-9.11.44 |
| *J-LL338 | 6.5.44-9.11.44 |
| *R-LL340 | 5.5.44-17.12.44 |
| LL342 | 25.4.44-27.10.44 |
| *P-LL344 | 23.4.44-9.11.44 (towed Horsa 95) |
| *+F-LL345 | 29.4.44-23.11.44 |
| *+Z-LL350 | 23.4.44-23.11.44 (towed Horsa 94) |
| *+L-LL351 | 3.5.44-16.11.44 |
| *+Q-LL352 | 3.5.44-30.11.44 |
| *P-LL357 | 5.5.44-2.11.44 |
| *+L-LL399 | 8.5.44-9.11.44 |
| *T-LL400 | 6.5.44-31.8.44 FTR |
| *+F-LL402 | 11.5.44-1.10.44 EFB (towed Horsa in *Mallard*, dropped nine containers) |
| *G-LL403 | 11.5.44-5.10.44 FTR (towed Hamilcar in *Tonga*) |
| +M-LL405 | 16.5.44-27.10.44 |

# The Short Stirling GT Mk IV

With the 1941 idea of dropping paratroopers from large gliders came the need for suitable tug aircraft. Both the Halifax and Stirling were obvious candidates, but in short supply. Bomber Command demanded them all. Nevertheless, a Stirling was tested at the AFEE in September 1941. Although rated unsuitable for paradropping due to exit problems, it could carry 26 troops.

Ideas had also changed. A large airborne force of paratroops was easier to produce than a glider-borne force. Nevertheless, in January 1942 the AFEE Stirling *N3702* was to be seen towing a train of three small Hotspur gliders before being tried as a tug for the Airspeed Horsa. The feasibility of that led to the March 1942 introduction of basic towing gear in production Stirlings and renewed interest in gliders.

By mid-May 1942, 2,345 Horsa gliders and 104 large Hamilcar troop-carrying gliders were on order – and the Army was pressing for 3,500 Horsas and 360 Hamilcars, the towing needs of which could never have been met. Even if the paratroopers jumped from tugs *and* Horsas, 500 tugs and 500 gliders would certainly be needed for each operation.

In August 1942 a surprising twist led to the Armstrong Whitworth Albemarle being cleared to become the main glider tug for No. 38 Wing, although towing caused its two engines to rapidly overheat. There being few Albemarles, attention soon switched to the Halifax and Lancaster. Bomber Command wanted all it could acquire of those, so it was back to the Stirling.

*N3702* was still undertaking various tests at the AFEE, Sherburn-in-Elmet, and in April 1943 it was joined by Stirling *BK645*, used for towing trials in which, loaded to 59,300 lb, the aircraft (still fully turreted) showed itself able to tow off a 15,250 lb Horsa. The combination needed a 2,040 yd run to clear 50 ft and took 26 minutes to attain 8,000 ft, which amounted to its operational ceiling. All was achieved without over-heating.

On 30 July, with glider tug needs for the invasion now being planned increasingly causing concern, agreement was reached to take Stirlings off bombing operations and switch them to transport duties. Stirling 'A' would be the Mk III converted into a transport, Stirling 'B' would be Mk III production aircraft completed for glider towing without gun turrets and having a paradropping exit in the rear floor of the aircraft. Both were designated Stirling GT Mk IV.

A prototype was rapidly devised in August 1943, and by 31 October 1943 six more Mk III conversions to Mk IV configuration had been undertaken at 23 MU, Aldergrove. Production switched from the Mk III to Mk IV at Belfast in December

*Some Stirling IVs had, like* EF503 *(an early conversion), all turrets removed. Others had their tail turrets and many had nose glazing.*

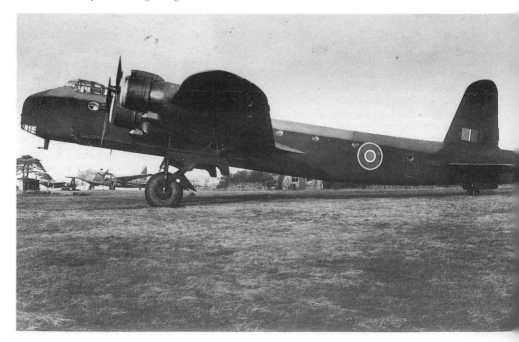

*Stirling IVs of No. 196 Squadron subsequent to Operation* Neptune.

1943, with *EF317* to *EF323* the first to be completed. Eventually 120 Mk IIIs were converted after delivery, and 201 Mk IIIs under construction were completed as Mk IVs.

Removing all turrets increased the ceiling by 1,100 ft and added 12 to 15 mph speed, but many Mk IVs retained a rear turret. In MS gear at 11,800 ft the top speed was 235 mph TAS. Whereas the bomber had operated at a take-off weight of 70,000 lb the Mk IV glider tug weighed 60,000 lb and the troop carrier 58,000 lb.

First to join a squadron was *EF318* which arrived at Stoney Cross on 23 January 1944 for No. 299 Squadron. That same month No. 190 Squadron commenced conversion at Leicester East. To fulfil the plan for four Stirling IV squadrons, Nos. 196 and 620 left Bomber Command in November 1943, and moved to Tarrant Rushton in January 1944.

Stirling GT Mk IV operations began in January with night drops of supplies to the Resistance forces. Far from easy operations, they entailed flying low while facing intense AA fire. March 1944 was largely devoted to working up in glider towing, often involving the removal of a Horsa from its storage site to its operational base. April and May brought large-scale towing exercises. For their part in the D-Day landings, the transportation from Fairford and Keevil of the 5th Paratroop Brigade in Phase II of Operation *Tonga*,

each Stirling would convey 20 troops and their equipment.

## Operations

At 14.00 hrs on 5 June the crews were briefed. Despite the clouds and strong winds the operation was going ahead. From Keevil troops of the 12th Battalion, 6th Airborne Division, would drop on a 2½-mile-square patch east of the River Orne, near Ouistreham, their task being to ensure capture of bridges over the river and the Orne Canal. The 46 Stirlings stood in two lines diagonally facing each other and tightly packed on the marshalling area at the end of the active runway. By late evening swarms of troops were busy fitting their parachutes, aided by an army of RAF and WAAF personnel.

At 23:00 hrs the 184 Hercules engines of the Stirlings burst into life before the first aircraft rolled at 23:19 hrs, with the others following at 30-second intervals. They made straight for the DZ, facing light flak on the run-in. A number of Stirlings were hit and Flt Sgt T. Gilbert's aircraft was shot down.

Close behind came Fairford's contingent whose take-offs began at 23:30 hrs. Approaching the DZ low, in loose formation and good visibility, they delivered their troops during a 3½-hr round-trip. Both Fairford squadrons, No. 620 leading, encountered quite heavy flak.

Three of their Stirlings were brought down. Losses – far less than forecast – were heavy enough.

Once home the crews snatched a rest, for in the evening they would have to undertake a potentially more hazardous daylight glider-towing venture.

By late afternoon 71 Horsas had been positioned near their tugs, and soon after 18:00 hrs troops of the 6th Airlanding Brigade emplaned in the gliders which were to land on LZ 'W' and reinforce the night drop paratroop force. Fairford's squadrons would tow 35 gliders, and another 36 would be taken from Keevil. Plentiful fighters would protect Operation *Mallard*.

As the gliders and tugs chugged across the Channel there was an amazing lack of enemy response. It was almost as if the Germans were watching the spectacle in disbelief. But it was to prove far from easy for the glider pilots, many of whom found it impossible when landing to avoid obstructions around the landing zone. Pilots of the Stirlings also had some alarming moments because balloons already protecting the assault area were not close-hauled and had to be shot down. There was also intense light AA fire – some from Allied ships – which damaged many Stirlings. One, Flt Lt Thoing's aircraft, was forced down in a French field. The crew escaped and were soon back at Fairford. The next task was resupply within Operation *Rob Roy*.

## Stirlings known to have participated in Operation *Tonga*, 5/6 June 1944

No. 190 Squadron:
*EF214, EF242, EF263, EF316, LJ818, LJ820, LJ823, LJ825, LJ829, LJ832, LJ833, LJ939, LK433, LK498* and nine uncertain.
No. 196 Squadron:
*EF234, EF276, EF309, LJ564, LJ810, LJ835, LJ837, LJ841* (FTR), *LJ843, LJ845, LJ846, LJ848, LJ851, LJ924, LJ925, LJ944, LJ945, LK505, LK510* and one uncertain
No. 299 Squadron:
identities of the participants uncertain
No. 620 Squadron:
*EF237, EF256, EF268, EF275, EF293, EF295* (FTR), *EF296, EJ116* (FTR),

*LJ588, LJ847, LJ849* (FTR?), *LJ850, LJ865, LJ866, LJ869, LJ872, LJ875, LJ887, LJ892, LJ917, LJ921, LK432* and one uncertain

## Stirlings known to have participated in Operation *Mallard*, 6 June 1944

No. 190 Squadron:
*EF214, EF260, EF263, EF264, LJ816, LJ818, LJ823, LJ825, LJ827, LJ829, LJ831, LJ832, LJ927, LJ939, LK405, LK431, LK513* and one uncertain
No. 196 Squadron:
*EF248, EF261, EF276, LJ461, LJ564, LJ836, LJ837, LJ843, LJ846, LJ848, LJ923, LJ924, LJ928, LJ937, LJ945, LJ954* and *LK505*
No. 299 Squadron:
identities of the 18 participants uncertain
No. 620 Squadron:
*EF237, EF256, EF268* (crashed in France), *EF293, EF296, EF303, LJ847, LJ850, LJ866, LJ872, LJ873, LJ875, LJ892, LJ914, LJ917, LJ970, LK432* and one uncertain

## Stirling IVs on squadron strength, 5 June 1944

\* participated in Operation *Tonga*, 5/6 June 1944
\+ participated in Operation *Mallard*, 6 June 1944

### *No. 190 Sqn*, Fairford

| | | |
|---|---|---|
| *\*+EF214* | 29.1.44-19.12.44 | |
| *\*EF242* | 11.5.44-17.5.45 | |
| *+EF260* | 10.2.44-21.9.44 FTR | |
| *\*+EF263* | 8.5.44-19.9.44 FTR | |
| *+EF264* | 27.4.44-20.4.45 | |
| *EF270* | 6.10.44-1.2.45 | |
| *EF298* | 24.2.44-23.7.44 | |
| *\*EF316* | 23.4.44-20.4.45 | |
| *LJ563* | 18.5.44-20.2.46 | |
| *LJ564* | 14.5.44-7.7.44 EFA, overshot, Keevil | |
| *+LJ816* | 21.1.44-11.12.44 | |
| *\*+LJ818* | 28.1.44-24.2.45 | |
| *\*LJ820* | 21.1.44-24.2.45 | |
| *\*+LJ823* | 24.1.44-22.9.44 FTR | |
| *LJ824* | 26.1.44-31.5.45 | |
| *\*+LJ825* | 26.1.44-20.4.45 | |
| *LJ826* | 27.1.44-17.5.45 | |
| *+LJ827* | 24.1.44-26.8.44 FTR, SOE sortie | |
| *LJ828* | 28.1.44-14.6.44 EFA, crashed into *LJ829* on dispersal | |
| *\*+LJ829* | 26.1.44-21.9.44 EFB, hit by *LJ828* on dispersal | |
| *LJ830* | 31.1.44-23.6.44 | |
| *+LJ831* | 26.1.44-21.9.44 EFB | |
| *\*+LJ832* | 27.1.44-20.4.45 | |

| | |
|---|---|
| *LJ833 | 2.2.44-21.9.44 FTR |
| LJ869 | ?-31.3.45 |
| LJ881 | 17.5.44-21.9.44 FTR |
| LJ889 | 19.5.44-31.5.45 |
| LJ895 | 17.5.44-24.5.45 |
| LJ898 | 4.5.44-25.5.45 |
| LJ916 | 24.5.44-21.9.44 FTR |
| +LJ927 | 27.4.44 22.7.44 |
| LJ934 | 5.44-31.5.45 |
| LJ936 | 21.5.44-25.4.45 |
| LJ937 | 18.4.44-12.3.46 |
| *+LJ939 | 17.5.44-19.9.44 FTR |
| LJ943 | 27.4.44-21.9.44 FTR |
| +LK405 | 25.3.44-31.5.45 |
| +LK431 | 28.1.44-31.5.45 |
| LK433 | 25.3.44-17.5.45 |
| LK498 | 23.4.44-21.9.44 FTR |
| +LK513 | 2.5.44-7.44 |

## No. 196 Sqn, Keevil

| | |
|---|---|
| *EF234 | 19.4.44-9.11.44 FTR, SOE sortie |
| +EF248 | 7.2.44-20.9.44 FTR |
| +EF261 | 27.4.44-4.1.45 |
| EF272 | 31.1.44-1.45 |
| *+EF276 | 27.4.44-4.1.45 |
| *EF309 | 25.4.44-19.7.44 EFA, belly-landed, Keevil |
| EF429 | 19.5.44-9.2.46 |
| +LJ461 | 12.5.44-21.8.44 |
| LJ502 | 12.3.44-1.2.45 |
| *+LJ564 | 14.5.44-7.7.44 EFB |
| *LJ810 | 20.4.44-21.9.44 FTR |
| LJ813 | ?-? |
| *LJ835 | 28.1.44-9.44 |
| +LJ836 | 2.2.44-22.2.45 |
| +LJ837 | 30.1.44-22.2.45 |
| LJ838 | 5.2.44-6.6.44 BFB |
| LJ840 | 31.1.44-21.9.44 EFB |
| LJ841 | 31.1.44-5/6.6.44 FTR |
| *+LJ843 | 31.1.44-21.9.44 FTR |
| *LJ845 | 31.1.44-4.1.45 |
| *+LJ846 | 2.2.44-2.7.45 |
| *+LJ848 | 31.1.44-4.1.45 |
| *LJ851 | 3.2.44-20.9.44 FTR, crashed, Eindhoven |
| LJ870 | 29.1.44-19.2.34 EFA, swung on landing |
| LJ888 | 14.5.44-30.3.45 FTR, SOE operation |
| LJ894 | 17.5.44-21.2.45 FTR, SOE operation |
| +LJ923 | 7.5.44-21.4.45 EFA at B108 |
| *+LJ924 | 25.4.44-10.6.44 |
| *LJ925 | 19.5.44-8.3.45 FTR |
| +LJ928 | 29.4.44-21.9.44 FTR |
| +LJ937 | 18.4.44-11.1.45 |
| *LJ944 | 25.4.44-6.44 |
| *+LJ945 | 18.4.44-21.9.44 FTR |
| LJ947 | 9.5.44-20.9.44 EFB, crashed near Brussels |
| LJ949 | 19.5.44-23.9.44 FTR, crashed, Leende, Netherlands |
| +LJ954 | 17.5.44-20.9.44 FTR |
| LJ988 | 28.5.44-20.9.44 FTR |
| LK440 | 25.4.44-6.6.44 |
| *+LK505 | 5.5.44-22.2.45 |
| *LK510 | 23.4.44-6.1.45 |

## No. 299 Sqn, Keevil (D-Day participants uncertain)

| | |
|---|---|
| EF243 | 30.4.44-28.6.44 |
| EF267 | 22.1.44-19.9.44 FTR |

| | |
|---|---|
| EF305 | 24.2.44-8.7.44 EFA |
| EF319 | 7.1.44-19.9.44? |
| EF321 | 7.1.44-20.7.45 |
| EF323 | 6.5.44-14.2.45 |
| EH950 | 19.5.44-23.7.45 |
| LJ572 | 17.5.44-21.6.45 |
| LJ811 | 18.1.44-8.8.44 |
| LJ813 | 18.1.44 1.2.44 |
| LJ815 | 12.1.44-24.2.45 |
| LJ819 | 21.1.44-6.6.44 FTR |
| LJ821 | 24.1.44-17.4.45 |
| LJ844 | 9.5.44-23.6.44 |
| LJ877 | 24.2.44-17.11.44 |
| LJ878 | 1.5.44-6.8.44 FTR, SOE operation |
| LJ879 | 25.2.44-23.2.45 |
| LJ884 | 2.3.44-21.9.44 |
| LJ885 | 25.2.44-6.6.44 FTR |
| LJ891 | 25.2.44-24.9.44 |
| LJ893 | 9.5.44-25.5.45 |
| LJ896 | 1.5.44-21.2.45 FTR |
| LJ897 | 1.3.44-4.7.44 EFA, overshot, Tarrant Rushton |
| LJ915 | 25.2.44-24.9.44 |
| LJ919 | 17.5.44-11.1.45 |
| LJ940 | 14.5.44-14/15.8.44 FTR, SOE operation |
| LJ942 | 14.5.44-2/3.4.45 FTR, SOE operation |
| LJ948 | 7.5.44-3.12.44 |
| LJ955 | 14.5.44-20.7.45 |
| LJ956 | 17.5.44-24.5.45 |
| LJ971 | 19.5.44-29.1.46 |
| LK439 | 30.4.44-20.1.45 |

## No. 620 Sqn, Fairford

| | |
|---|---|
| EF203 | 21.10.43-26.6.44 |
| *+EF237 | 7.2.44-13.12.44 |
| *+EF256 | 7.2.44-10.8.44 FTR, SOE operation |
| *+EF268 | 30.4.44-6.6.44 FTR |
| EF275 | 27.2.44-21.8.44 |
| *+EF293 | 4.2.44-9.7.44 |
| *EF295 | 7.2.44-5/6.6.44 FTR |
| *+EF296 | 8.2.44-6.9.44 EFA, crash-landed, Fairford |
| +EF303 | 10.2.44-9.7.44 |
| *EJ116 | 13.5.44-5/6.6.44 FTR |
| LJ566 | 18.5.44-2.6.45 |
| *LJ588 | 18.5.44-19.4.45 |
| LJ827 | 7.2.44-20.4.45 |
| *+LJ847 | 7.2.44 20.4.45 |
| *LJ849 | 8.2.44-6.6.44 FTR? |
| *+LJ850 | 11.2.44-17.6.44 FTR, SOE operation |
| *LJ865 | 10.2.44-9.7.45 |
| *+LJ866 | 7.2.44-20.4.45 |
| *LJ869 | 7.2.44-9.6.44 FA, collided with Horsa LH562, belly-landed |
| *+LJ872 | 8.2.44-20.4.45 |
| +LJ873 | 10.2.44-24.9.44 FTR(?) |
| *+LJ875 | 8.2.44-13.3.45 |
| *LJ887 | 21.5.44-9.7.45 |
| *+LJ892 | 24.4.44-7.12.44 |
| +LJ914 | 11.5.44-1.12.44 FTR, SOE operation |
| *+LJ917 | 2.5.44-7.12.44 |
| LJ918 | 21.5.44-16.11.44 |
| LJ920 | 21.5.44-4.8.44 FTR |
| *LJ921 | 9.5.44-7.6.44 |
| LJ930 | 21.5.44-21.12.44 |
| LJ935 | 9.5.44-9.7.44 |
| LJ948 | 8.2.44-9.7.44 |
| LJ952 | 17.5.44-26.4.45 |
| +LJ970 | 18.5.44-28.12.44 FTR, SOE operation |
| *+LK432 | 10.2.44-7.6.45 |

# Gliders: the Horsa and the Hamilcar

## Airspeed Horsa

'Glider' – a delicate, shapely, small wooden form, designed to dance around the sky in June's sunshine. The 88 ft span wooden high-wing Horsa weighing almost 17 tons fully loaded, production of which was agreed to by the Army Council on 1 October 1940, was as far removed from the popular image as is possible. Airspeed worked so fast that a mock-up of the glider was officially viewed at Salisbury Hall, Hertfordshire, on 15 January 1941.

The concept which produced the glider was also far removed from the manner by which it performed in Normandy. A tug towing a glider was thereby lifting a far greater load than it could itself carry since it was, in effect, increasing its wing area. The most suitable tugs matched in size/weight the gliders they towed. Initially the glider was viewed as a means of increasing the number of paratroops that could participate in an airdrop. Over Europe, Whitleys carrying 10 to 15 troops would tow the 25-seater X.26/40 glider; any used in India would rely upon Vickers Valentias as tugs! By early 1941 a policy change was being mooted – the gliders would land with their cargo which could be either men or other loads. Various other notions were considered, among them a rear gunner to protect the glider's tail, the dropping of container loads from gliders, even using them as supplementary towed bombers and also releasing them, packed with explosives, against specially chosen targets. To lift two Brigade Groups the 800 gliders thought necessary were ordered. By late August 1941, when *DG597*, the prototype, was ready to fly from Hounslow, that contract had been amended to call for 600, leaving the other 200 Horsas to become towed bombers. This scheme soon faded, leaving plans for 600 Horsas for European airborne operations. Another 400 for use in India would be built there in railway carriage works. Instead, American Waco CG-4As were ultimately supplied.

Gliders being of wooden construction, the furniture industry was enlisted as the main Horsa-building community, Harris Lebus being approached to start in March 1942 by constructing components for half of the gliders. Output reached a peak rate of 50 per month by January 1943.

During the prototype's trial flying a major problem was being tackled: the storage of gliders for operations unlikely before mid-1943. From the furniture factories the components were taken by

*Rare illustration showing the Horsa glider prototype,* DG597.

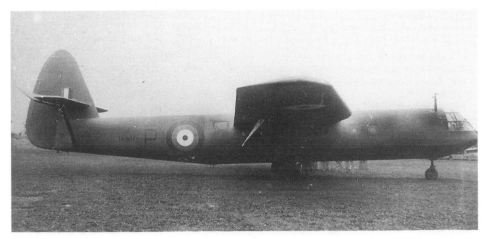

road to Maintenance Units where, because of their size, the Horsas often had to be erected outside hangars. Then came the problem of where to store these highly combustible, gale damage-prone structures. The adopted solution was to place them on RAF bomber stations, control surfaces removed, in groups of about 30. Various ideas for hiding them were considered, but unless they were completely hidden such activity might arouse too much enemy interest.

By May 1942 the Horsa production order called for 2,345 to be built. Army reckoning was that it needed 1,975 for one operation and 600 for a back-up. That also meant operating in repeat waves both times because of the limited number of tugs available. All Bomber Command's aircraft would have been needed for one major airborne operation, which would have meant halting the bombing campaign for four to five weeks.

A curb had to be placed on such activity, but Brigadier Gale on 23 September 1942 asked for 2,800 Horsas and 200 tank-carrying Hamilcars. The MAP pointed out to the War Office that timber supplies were not inexhaustible, and that there was also the question of how to train so many glider pilots.

*DP279*, the first production Horsa, came on MAP charge on 22 April 1942. It was, on 12 July 1942, the first to join a unit, the Heavy Glider OTU at Shrewton. Two days later the Heavy Glider Training Unit, Brize Norton (later the Heavy Glider Conversion Unit), received is first example, *DP281*. Thereafter, these and No. 296 Glider Exercise Squadron received a stream of Horsas. Then came delivery of Horsas to Glider Maintenance Squadrons which, as part of No. 1 Heavy Glider Support Unit, cared for them on-site. Some were even ferried as far as Scotland for dispersal, where from October 1943 71 were stored on 18 airfields.

Development of the Horsa continued throughout 1942 and 1943. After the idea of paratroops jumping from gliders was replaced by the plan to land the gliders with the troops aboard, the Army, in November 1942, asked that the Horsa's rear fuselage section be made easily and quickly detachable, that a stronger floor be fitted and loading troughs be made available for the rear fuselage as well as for the side

door. A few days later came the proposal for a hinged rear fuselage. That never came about, but after D-Day a hinged nose was featured by the Horsa Mk II; but it was a complicated modification. More feasible was the 'get out gear' which allowed troops to break out of a glider damaged in landing. Another useful modification, No. 122 (the fitting of *Rebecca*), allowed gliders to home in on beacons set up on LZs.

Although Winston Churchill had as early as June 1940 been most enthusiastic about building up airborne forces, he was shaken to learn of the enormous effort being expended and ordered that production be curbed to about 1,250 gliders, and stated that means must be found to retrieve them after action.

There was constant tactical, production and general improvement of the Horsas. Early examples featured bifurcated towing in which the rope divided into a yoke for attachment at twin towing points on the wings. In August 1943 single-point nose-towing was chosen for future aircraft. But what the Army most keenly desired was faster exit from the glider. A swinging tail was too difficult to engineer, but unloading a field gun or a Jeep through the side door was very difficult. So, in November 1943, the Army pressed again for a nose-swinging modification in time for use in *Overlord*. The MAP immediately replied that none could become available because it entailed so much redesign, development and production retooling. Delay in unloading, the Army retorted, could jeopardise the whole operation. Then the MAP ordered development of quick-release nuts joining the main fuselage to the rear section, allowing it to be detached in two or three minutes after touchdown. Simple ramps, vertically stowed during flight after incorporation of Modification No. 307, would bridge the 3 ft gap to the ground. By D-Day, after a hectic modification programme, all Horsas were intended to be of the 'Red Horsa' type incorporating the rear unloading Modification No. 306. In a further attempt to ease landing problems, RAE Farnborough tested a braking parachute on a Horsa, but it was never used operationally. A scheme whereby small General Aircraft Hotspur gliders might be used to carry urgently needed items to the beachhead was also abandoned. The census of 1 June 1944 showed that while 1,727

*Two of the Horsas which landed by the Bénouville bridge at the start of the airborne assault. (IWM B5233)*

Horsas were in service, a considerable number were of the 'White Horsa' type with side-opening doors and fixed rear fuselages.

With rapidly increasing numbers of erected Horsas in hand, a plan of November 1943 called for 22 RAF stations each to store 32 gliders. Nos. 295, 296 and 297 Squadrons would each have 40, which by early 1944, when production amounted to 140 Horsa Is per month, would account for 704. Another 628 were in various stages of completion or assembly.

Loaded, carrying 25 troops and two pilots, and with the undercarriage fitted, a Horsa I weighed 38,000 lb. The varying load could include a 6-pounder anti-tank gun, 20 mm cannon, 40 mm Bofors gun, 5 cwt car, 75 mm US pack Howitzer, 10 cwt trailer or Signmund trailer, motor cycles, bicycles, Summerfelt tracking, Bailey Bridge units and many smaller items.

During February 1944 work began on the dispersed gliders to prepare them for action. Seating was installed, control surfaces refitted, belly skids attached; and

*A plaque now marks the position of each Horsa's landing point by the Caen canal. PF800's plaque is nearest and that for the Horsa which partly landed in the pond is in the distance.*

*The Cafe Gondree, the first building to be liberated in Normandy.*

*Troops crossing the Bénouville (Pegasus) bridge in June 1944, with Horsas in the background. (Museum of Army Flying)*

as soon as each was ready for flight a tug aircraft – usually an Albemarle – would tow it to its operational base.

It was in six Horsas participating in sub-Operation *Deadstick*, wearing the chalked identities *91* to *96* (and including *PF800*) and towed out of Tarrant Rushton by Halifaxes of Nos. 298 and 644 Squadrons, that troops were conveyed to LZ 'X', by the side of the Caen Canal, to seize the Bénouville bridge (better known as Pegasus Bridge) and LZ 'Y' to capture the Orne bridge at the start of Operation *Tonga*, the British airborne assault. They crossed the French coast at 00:07 hrs, cast off over Cabourg and when at 1,500 ft on descent the glider doors were opened to enable a rapid exit. Horsas *95* and *96* headed west then almost due south, which course took them to the Orne bridge whereas *94* landed in error to the south-east of Cabourg near two Dives bridges.

By then gliders *91*, *92* and *93* had quietly passed their LZ, and then turned on to a reciprocal track having made sure of their LZ. It was *PF800* (*91*) flown by Staff Sgt J. Wallwork that touched down at 00:16 hrs, conveying the first fighting troops to land on D-Day. In swerving to avoid *91*, Horsa *92* skidded to a halt and broke its back by a pond in which the nose of *93* came to rest. Six of those aboard were trapped in this

Horsa and most tragically the only casualty at LZ 'X' was brought about by one man drowning in the pond. The German sentry on the canal bridge was uncertain of what had happened, but not for long. Lt Brotheridge gathered his platoon and they rushed across the bridge, guns firing. As they reached the far side the enemy was opening up too, and Brotheridge, hit in the neck by machine-gun fire, died an hour later. By then 'Pegasus Bridge', and indeed

*The real 'Pegasus Bridge' and commemorative panel in June 1987, from near the Cafe Gondree.*

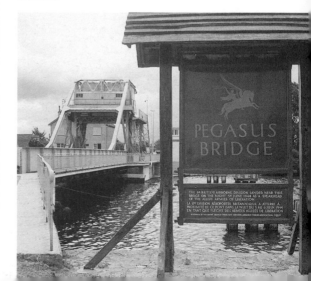

*Courcelles-sur-Mer airfield, as built by 12 June 1944 and seen from Mosquito DZ414. (IWM)*

the little cafe alongside, had been elevated to become great names in history.

Phase II of *Tonga* included release on LZ 'K' of another six Horsas (*218* to *223*) towed by Dakotas from Blakehill Farm and which touched down at 00:45 to 00:50 hrs. A further six, *261* to *267*, were towed out of Down Ampney by Dakotas and *66* to *69* by Albemarles operating from Harwell for release at LZ 'V'. The task for their

*A view of Horsas on LZ 'N' near Ranvile, taken by Spitfire PA947 flown by Wg Cdr C.F. Webb of No. 16 Squadron, No. 34 Wing HQ, during an afternoon sortie on 9 June 1944. (Museum of Army Flying)*

occupants was to lay six 15 ft x 3 ft special identity strips, light smoke candles and establish Fane lights to enable 68 Horsas (*29* to *45* from Brize Norton; *97* to *116* from Tarrant Rushton; and *70* to *90* from Harwell) to land on LZ 'N' at 03:20 hrs. Another three Horsas (possibly including *27* and *28*) brought in the troops to help the assault on the Merville gun battery. The numbers mentioned enabled troops to identify glider loadings.

During D-Day, three LZs were prepared for the main British glider landings. These were LZ 'N' (6½ miles NE of Caen by the Orne), LZ 'K' (5½ miles E of Caen and two miles E of Troarn) and LZ 'W' (9½ miles NE/four miles E of Cabourg).

In Operation *Mallard* some 220 Horsas towed by Albemarles, Dakotas and Stirlings set off, conveying the 6th Airlanding Brigade to LZs 'N' and 'W'. Composition of the force is officially listed as comprising the following:

Dakotas, Broadwell: 37 Horsas to LZ 'N' (*1* to *37*); Dakotas, Down Ampney: 37 Horsas to LZ 'N' (*38* to *74*); Albemarles, Brize Norton: 38 Horsas to LZ 'N' (*75* to *112*); Albemarles, Harwell: 39 Horsas to LZ 'W' (*113* to *151*); Stirlings, Keevil: 34 Horsas to LZ 'W' (*152* to *185*); Stirlings, Fairford: 35 Horsas to LZ 'W' (*186* to *220*)

The long train, which rendezvoused at

2,500 ft, released its Horsas from 1,000 ft.

No full list of the airframe serial number/chalk number tie-ups for gliders used seems to have survived, but Horsas known to have been written off as a result of the two main assaults are as follows:

## Operation *Tonga*
LF918
LG916, LG917
LH133, LH175, LH179, LH189, LH224, LH234, LH236, LH243, LH269, LH271, LH273, LH276, LH301, LH321, LH324, LH329, LH379, LH431, LH434, LH466, LH469, LH478, LH497, LH495, LH507, LH513, LH515, LH518 and LH521
LJ264, LJ267, LJ310, LJ311 and LJ326
PF768, PF791, PF793 and PF800
PW706, PW709, PW716, PW721, PW732, PW735 and PW758

## Operation *Mallard*
DP416, DP427, DP438, DP519, DP539, DP601, DP628, DP695, DP704, DP706, DP744, DP770, DP811 and DP828
HG748, HG858, HG869, HG912, HG968, HG971 and HG977
HS111 and HS126
LF906, LF909, LF912, LF916, LF953 and LF957
LG675, LG679, LG694, LG715, LG716, LG725, LG736, LG747, LG774, LG787,

LG790, LG831, LG849, LG853, LG868, LG870, LG879, LG880, LG883, LG915, LG939, LG948, LG951, LG985, LG986, LG992 and LG995
LH120, LH132, LH145, LH146, LH170, LH173, LH185, LH203, LH206, LH213, LH217, LH230, LH239, LH242, LH264, LH281, LH295, LH316, LH317, LH328, LH336, LH339, LH344, LH353, LH373, LH375, LH378, LH380, LH381, LH388, LH402, LH405, LH406, LH410, LH429, LH432, LH436, LH437, LH442, LH444, LH451, LH453, LH457, LH465, LH470, LH491, LH492, LH499, LH500, LH508, LH516, LH519, LH525, LH528, LH532, LH533, LH534, LH553, LH554, LH566, LH567, LH568, LH570, LH571, LH572, LH575, LH578, LH579, LH580, LH582, LH600, LH601, LH942, LH943 and LH966
LJ111, LJ116, LJ124, LJ187, LJ266, LJ270, LJ285 and LJ314
PF690, PF693, PF694, PF695, PF700, PF703, PF705, PF707, PF709, PF710, PF715, PF716, PF720, PF722, PF723, PF724, PF725, PF744, PF758, PF760, PF769, PF787, PF790, PF803, PF810 and PF816
PW637, PW646, PW647, PW649, PW652, PW653, PW658, PW659, PW662, PW663, PW664, PW665, PW666, PW671, PW675, PW676, PW695, PW705, PW712, PW713, PW714, PW717, PW720, PW722, PW726, PW733, PW734, PW748, PW759,

*Some of the Horsas which landed on LZ 'N', with that which brought Maj Gates in the foreground (IWM B5600).*

*Celebrations marking the 50th anniversary on 6 June 1994 of the landing taking place by Pegasus Bridge.*

PW760, PW761, PW770, PW773, PW774, PW783, PW785, PW786, PW819, PW828, PW847, PW871, PW879, PW884, PW889 and PW897

Losses on D-Day were considerable. When 236 gliders delivered by No. 38 Group were inspected in Normandy, 168 were found to be repairable in 214 days; but even then only 24 would be in good enough condition to be towed out by Dakota. Tests had been carried out in May 1944 in which the glider's tow rope was positioned between two posts. A hook fitted beneath a Dakota would snatch the tow rope and a drum would absorb the enormous induced strain until the tension was sufficient to allow the glider to be safely towed aloft. In the event only 40 Horsas were retrieved from Normandy, by more conventional methods. None of these appears to have been used operationally again.

## General Aircraft Hamilcar

Autumn 1940 saw preliminary discussions open between the MAP and General Aircraft Ltd (GAL) about the possibility of devising some means of airlifting a 7$\frac{1}{2}$ ton Tetrarch tank, the tug for which would have to be one of the new four-motor bombers. Novel schemes were suggested, one being for a simple wing and tail unit attached to

the tank from which flying controls would be operated. This was dismissed because it would complicate, and probably compromise, tank design. Track gear would also pose major problems.

Another idea was for a more simple, low-wing layout involving a tail section leading to a fuselage which enveloped the tank. That meant ensuring sufficient ground clearance for the essential large flaps while keeping the loading platform close to the ground.

The Army then weighed in with an additional requirement, the carrying of two Universal Bren Gun Carriers. That pointed to the wisdom of having greater load flexibility embodied in Specification X.27/40, which resulted in General Aircraft proposing a large high-wing glider carrying mixed heavy loads.

Detailed design work began in February 1941 on the favoured project, a 110 ft wing span wooden glider with nose cargo entry. For operational landings the wheeled undercarriage would be discarded and the glider would land on skids, enabling vehicles, via ramps, to exit more easily from the glider whose loaded weight was limited to 35,500 lb, the maximum haul load the chosen Halifax and Stirling tugs could reasonably cope with. When in March 1942 *DP206*, the Hamilcar prototype, was completed, it was found to weigh, in tare state, a mere 800 lb below the stipulated level, which meant that everything possible would need to be done to ensure that weight limitations were not exceeded.

Although the glider's angular design and box-like structure were conventional, its size and large surface areas were far beyond the company's previous experience. In length it measured 68 ft 1 in and its maximum height was 27 ft. Therefore, a half-scale model was built to explore loads on controls and the likely cg range. Meticulous attention was taken in building its flying controls to ensure that control circuit friction would not obscure the results obtained in flight testing. One special design feature was the pneumatic flap operation with infinite selectivity and which was to prove very popular with Hamilcar glider pilots.

Although DP206, the full-scale Hamilcar prototype, first flew from Snaith, much early flying was undertaken from Chelveston where it joined the half-scale model, T-0227. The former, during trials, was towed by a Halifax II, the latter by a Whitley. Towing off the lightly loaded Hamilcar was one thing; testing it fully loaded needed a very long 'runway' for safety reasons. It was therefore moved to Newmarket Heath from where, between July and September 1942, the huge glider was test-flown from the long grass runway at increasingly heavier weights. Eventually came tests in which its wheeled undercarriage was released after take-off, leaving the glider to land on its under fuselage skids.

Only parts for the two prototypes (DP206 and DP210), 10 pre-production trials/trainers in the DR serial range and 10 production examples (HH921 to HH930) were built at the Feltham works of GAL. The remainder were constructed as sub-assembly parts by the Birmingham Railway Carriage and Wagon Co Ltd, the Co-operative Wholesale Society and by AC Motors Ltd. Completed components were then taken by road mainly to Lyneham and some to North Luffenham, at which stations they were assembled then flight tested. Such technique was quite sound, but the mechanics of the scheme brought concern to the War Office, for by 1 January 1944 only 27 Hamilcars against the MAP plan for 100 had been erected. Six more were being used for trials, two damaged examples had become instructional airframes, one had been taken to India and DR852 had been struck off charge. By mid-January only 15 of those intended for use during the Normandy landings had been assembled, and six of these were at No. 1 Heavy Glider Maintenance Unit, Netheravon. Tarrant Rushton, the base from which Hamilcars would operate, was being used by GAL as their test centre. There was soon insufficient room for GAL because the gliders were so large, cumbersome to manoeuvre and consumed so much hangar space. Therefore, work on them was also undertaken at Cottesmore – until the USAAF said it needed all the space available. The company than had to use its Dunholme Lodge outpost for incorporating

*With a 110 ft wing span the Hamilcar seemed huge when it first appeared in 1942. Illustrated is DR853, one of 10 in the development batch.*

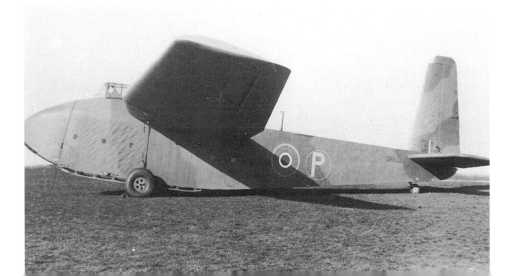

modifications, including the fitting of *Rebecca*. Slow delivery of the gliders prompted the Americans to forego the score promised to them, despite the fact that they had nothing remotely similar. Their teams helping to assemble the gliders were at once withdrawn, which meant that the 30 required by the Army/RAF would not now be ready by 1 March 1944.

This lack of Hamilcars caused considerable alarm, particularly when it was pointed out that some were likely to be lost during the essential training programme. The production version weighed 18,592 lb and its all-up weight was 37,500 lb. That provided a maximum disposable load of 18,908 lb. A dozen standard loading combinations had been devised. From those a load schedule for each of 30 Hamilcars to be used on D-Day was established in December 1943. No. 38 Group, playing safe, stressed that it needed at least eight more gliders in reserve, particularly as operational exercises called for the use of 20. The total lost during training was an alarming six.

By 1 March 1944 the War Office had programmed Hamilcar D-Day loads as follows:

Class 'A': 17 gliders (plus six reserves) – one T9 tank and three men – including *HH930*, *HH935*, *HH937*, *HH960*, *HH963*, *HH964*, *HH970*, *LA638*, *LA650*, *LA651*, *LA652*, *LA653*, *LA655* and *LA669*

Class 'B': four gliders (plus two reserves) – three Rotatrailers each – including *LA636*, *LA637* and *LA640*

Class 'C': three gliders – Tetrarch tank, three 3 in Howitzers, three men – *LA641*, *LA644* and *LA645*

Class 'D': three gliders – two Universal Carrier Mk IIs, six men – *HH925*, *HH972* and *LA642*

Class 'E': two gliders – one Universal Carrier Mk II, 3 in mortar carrier, 10 motor cycles, 10 men – including *HH926*

Class 'F': one glider – slave battery carrier, 5 cwt car, six men – *HH928*

Not all airframes had by that time been allocated loadings. Although 30 and eight reserves were listed, the Army really wanted 50 gliders for the first operation, but there was no way so many could be generated. Six of the Class 'A' gliders were to be used for training – and to all involved it was stressed that no mistakes in their use were acceptable.

On 1 April a request for another 15 Hamilcars was made, to convey airfield construction equipment to Normandy. Although desirable, it was a need that could not be met. Rapid exit for wheeled loads, however, received much attention. The most favoured idea was for wheels to be jettisoned after take-off, leaving the gliders to land on skids. The Hamilcar had been designed so that a tank's engine could run in-flight, allowing it to be driven out immediately after the glider slid to a halt, which required the fuselage to be close to the ground. But only 18 sets of parachutes to deposit jettisoned wheels safely had been produced by January 1944. Barely had supply eased in mid-February when radical

*LA722, a production Hamilcar. (BAe)*

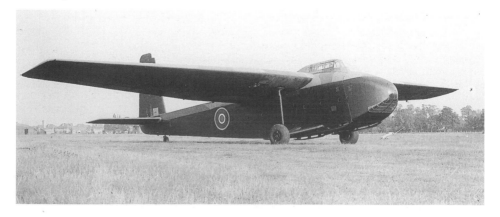

*Horsas and Hamilcars assemble on Tarrant Rushton's runway, with Halifaxes of No. 298 Squadron alongside. (Ray Sturtivant collection)*

change came about – the gliders would, after all, land on a wheeled undercarriage because that allowed them to be manoeuvred after touchdown. Difficulties with exit height were overcome by making modifications to the shock absorbers and the undercarriage chassis, enabling it to be speedily collapsed after landing. The remaining problem concerned erecting sufficient gliders.

By 30 March 1944 No. 33 MU, Lyneham, had put together 50 and despatched 37 to North Luffenham for fitting out. General Aircraft had already assembled there the quota of 12 allocated to them. By 20 April sufficient gliders had been fitted out to meet the D-Day commitment, and by mid-May, with 81 put together at Lyneham and four more ready to fly, the situation was much improved.

The next task was to assemble at Tarrant Rushton 34 Hamilcars for D-Day use, along with as many as eight reserves. On an airfield already housing 40 or so Horsas and two squadrons of Halifax tugs, there were clearly problems. Nevertheless, assembly proceeded as planned.

## Operations

The first three Hamilcars to operate did so near the end of Operation *Tonga*. Halifax V *LL148* of No. 298 Squadron took off at

02:10 hrs on 6 June and towed one glider, and was soon followed by *LL219-G* and *LL403-G*, both of No. 644 Squadron, each having a Hamilcar on tow.

A fully-loaded Hamilcar was a hefty load for a Halifax V and when 31 tug-and-glider combinations set forth around 19:30 hrs on 6 June for their part in *Mallard*, they did so under no mean strain, and it took them some time even to form up at the low height set for the operation. Halifaxes of No. 298 Squadron were towing 16 gliders and No. 644 Squadron another 15. All landed successfully at around 21:30 hrs on LZ 'N'. One which landed heavily on rough ground was at once set on fire by enemy gunners. Its operation was nevertheless successful for the tank was driven out and into battle! Hamilcars used on D-Day were:

*HH923, HH924, HH926, HH927, HH928,
HH929, HH930, HH932, HH934,
HH935, HH957, HH959, HH960,
HH962, HH963, HH964 and HH970
LA636, LA637, LA638, LA639, LA640,
LA641, LA642, LA644, LA645, LA650,
LA651, LA652, LA653, LA655, LA669,
LA670 and LA671*

None was retrieved for further use although as in the case of the Horsas, spare parts were taken from them.

# The Hawker Hurricanes: Transport Command's postmen

Aptly, and probably surprisingly, it was a Hawker Hurricane (*MW340*), flown by Sqn Ldr J. Storrar DFC, CO No. 1697 Flight alias the Air Despatch Letter Service that, by landing on strip 'B3' (Ste Croix-sur-Mer) shortly after noon on Saturday 10 June, became the first Allied aircraft to land in France after D-Day and then return. Wg Cdr Beytagh in *MW339* accompanied him, both pilots being told to turn about if the landing ground could not be identified. Their greater concern was that light-fingered soldiers and sailors might fire upon them!

Orders for the flights were issued by HQ 2nd TAF at 09:30 hrs, and at 11:30 hrs both Hurricanes took off from Northolt. Ten minutes later a signal was received from MLO ordering cancellation of the sorties. It had come too late and shortly after noon the two aircraft landed safely on 'B3'. Each carrying a bag of dispatches, the aircraft returned with similar loads and landed back safely at 13:40 hrs. The Hurricanes, flying one behind the other across the Channel at 3,000 ft, had each lowered their undercarriage at the coast. Both pilots soon picked out the ALG. Nearer completion than others, it was a bulldozed strip only 80 ft wide and 1,200 yds long. Difficult to recognize, 'B3' lay roughly half-way between Caen and Bayeux. To reach it meant avoiding kite balloons flying from ship and shore so both pilots maintained 3,000 ft until over 'B3' before slowly spiralling down.

Two other Hurricanes, *MW338* flown by Belgian Flt Lt Piercot and *MW359* piloted by Flt Lt Dewhurst, set out for 'B3' 10 minutes before the first two landed. Theirs was a more adventurous escapade after the leader lost his maps. Finding themselves off track, and unexpectedly over the US beach area, they quickly decided to seek a landing ground and chose 'AFT3898', incomplete with only a 400 yd runway and surrounded by balloons. Nevertheless, they landed safely and were soon off again in their unarmed Hurricanes. After a wide sweep over German lines, they found themselves exciting questioning defences by arriving out of hostile airspace before landing on 'B3'. Before the day ended *MW339* and *MW340* flown respectively by Flt Sgt Cunnison and Flt Lt Steward had again sampled Normandy's terrain.

On 12 June another two Hurricane flights were made, by Sqn Ldr Storrar (*MW340*) and Flt Lt Melbourne (*MW359*), a New Zealander. This time documents were carried under each fuselage in a 100 lb container dropped from 300 ft. To reach the DZ the Hurricanes again passed between balloons, undercarriage down and wings 'waggling'.

The belief that rapidly established secure radio links between SHAEF and Advanced SHAEF, 21st Army Group and 2nd TAF might not be possible had generated, on 2 March 1944, approval for the formation at Hendon of No. 1697 Flight (Air Despatch Letter Service). Jointly serving the Allies, the ADLS would bridge the gap between teleprinter line concentration points in Britain and in the field. Since fluid battle situations seemed likely to mean crossing enemy positions when conveying messages, fighter aircraft were needed, and the choice fell upon the Hurricane IIc/IV because of its tough construction and wide track undercart. Although retaining guns but carrying no ammunition, the aircraft were thought able to survive most situations.

On 22 April 1944, as No. 1697 Flight formed, 22 personnel reported to Hendon and the first three Hurricanes arrived a week later. At 09:30 hrs on 9 May the 11 Hurricanes on strength left for their operational station, Northolt. From there on 16 May internal schedule mail flights began, to Thorney Island (an important forward air base during *Neptune* and *Overlord* and where No. 1697 Flight had a detachment from 20 May) and to Harrowbeer.

External 90-gal overload tanks were now fitted beneath each Hurricane's mainplane. Mail, inserted via the detachable nose, would be carried in the starboard tank and

*Hurricane IIc* MW367-B Jessie *of the ADLS arrives at 'B2'. (IWM)*

45 gal of fuel in the other to balance the aircraft. Although speed and manoeuvrability were much reduced, the Hurricane proving its strength on 26 May when Flg Off W.S.H. Roberts in *MW335*, flying in low cloud, collided with and snapped a barrage balloon cable near Plymouth, then flew on to a safe landing at Thorney Island.

Various combinations of external tanks to carry mail/fuel as well as fuselage cells were considered, and partly to extend range. With an 11 cu ft fuselage cell and two 45-gal drop tanks the Hurricane's range would be 1,000 miles. After tank jettison the aircraft would be fully manoeuvrable. With 90-gal tanks and 31 cu ft of mail provision, range would be only 350 miles, and it was this loading that was approved for Normandy runs. On occasions when aircraft could be refuelled mail could be carried internally.

Each aircraft carried a special identity number until 1 June when *DR* unit identity letters began to be applied and, on 5 June, AEAF black and white stripes were added. It was 8 June before No. 46 Group instructed the ADLS to have two aircraft at

*The reception committee meets* F-Freddie *at 'B2'. (IWM)*

*Unloading a Hurricane in France. (IWM)*

readiness and next day gave orders for Normandy flights to start on 10 June. The state of 'B3' and the narrowness of the beachhead brought a halt to flights after 10 June, front-line container drops being substituted on 12 June. Next day landings were again ordered to be made on 'B2', more complete than 'B3'. On 17 June Sqn Ldr Storrar and Flg Off D.L. Milner flew to 'B2' in an Anson to view the handling and reception area to where all flights were now made. By 18 June Hurricanes had made 31 landings in France, and all the aircraft had been modified to carry mail in the fuselage. They had visited French soil a further 37 times by the end of the month.

A second ADLS phase began with the attachment on 2 July of two Dakota IIIs (*KG337* and *KG428*) in which No. 1697 Flight conveyed VIPs and Press parties to 'B8'. During the first week of July the Hurricanes too started using 'B8', and soon 'B14' became their turnround ALG. Flights to France were common, daily events by August, 18 being made by Hurricanes on the 1st alone and one by an Anson. All along it had been envisaged that Ansons, able to carry a 1,000 lb mail load, would take over, leaving Hurricanes to operate to forward sites. During August Hurricanes flew 214 sorties carrying 8,654 lb of documents across the Channel, the 45 Anson sorties allowing 15,838 lb of mail and freight to be taken in and 18,243 lb to

be brought back – along with 11 passengers. To Flt Lt Barclay on 27 August had fallen the distinction of being the first to land an aircraft in Paris (Issy-les-Mollineaux), from where he returned with material for Press use.

Courier services continued throughout September, then on 11 October No. 1697 Flight's role and future came under review. Winter flying would best be carried out by Ansons (which had served the Continental Rear Area) and as a result their activity became concentrated in a new Northolt-based Flight, No. 1322, which commenced Continental runs on 24 October and thus before it was officially formed on 30 October. No. 1697 Flight's Hurricanes left for Brussels on 8 January 1945, the organization eventually disbanding at Northolt on 7 March.

### No. 1697 Flight (ADLS), Northolt (4.44–8.44)

| | |
|---|---|
| *LF770* | 29.4.44-28.9.44 AC FB |
| *LF773* | 29.4.44-2.7.44 BFB |
| *LF774* | 28.4.44-30.6.44 BFB, 3.8.44-26.3.45 |
| *MW335* | 29.4.44-26.5.44 AC FA RIW |
| *MW336* | 28.4.44-13.9.44 EFA |
| *MW338* | 1.5.44-3.2.45 |
| *MW339* | 29.4.44-14.2.45 |
| *MW340* | 28.4.44-18.12.44 BFB |
| *MS359* | 28.4.44-ADLS 2TAF 8.1.45-10.7.45 |
| *MW360* | 30.4.44-ADLS 2TAF 8.1.45-10.7.45 |
| *MW361* | 28.4.44-ADLS 2TAF 8.1.45- BAFO Comm Wg 30.8.45-20.4.46 |
| *MW367* | 29.4.44-13.9.44 Cat B |
| *PG546* | 13.6.44-28.1.45 |

# Ansons and 'Sparrows': The flying ambulances

The success of 'casevac' operations in the Western Desert led to consideration of how they could be undertaken during the invasion of France. Although casualties were expected to be high, 'Sparrows' and Dakotas would obviously be unable to operate from beachhead strips. After due consideration the decision was made to form a fleet of Avro Anson trainers converted into air ambulances. Upwards of 100 were therefore taken into No. 46 Group along with aircrew and maintenance personnel, all of whom moved to Hendon. There a selection of the Ansons (Mks I and X) were fitted out to accommodate three stretcher cases, two sitting casualties and a nursing orderly, or six ordinary passengers. A panel door through which a stretcher could pass was to be fitted by the starboard wing fillet. VHF radio equipment for operations was also added, these interim measures leading later to development of the Anson Mks XI and XII and later civil and military transport derivatives.

The ambulances were then to be placed in four flights, each with five aircraft and attached to four of the Dakota squadrons. No. 271 Squadron was to have three flights, each of six Ansons, to supplement its existing 'Sparrows' and which would be operated as special 2nd TAF Group Support Units. Remaining Transport Command Ansons formed an emergency reserve pool at Watchfield, part of which later became part of the Air Despatch Letter Service.

Instead, only two Group Support Flights each with six Ansons eventually developed, and were stationed at the aircraft parks from which replacement machines for 2nd TAF were supplied. From them the modified Ansons largely forsook their primary role and took essential spares to landing strips, and returned with pilots who had ferried out replacement aircraft. Because the Anson transport crews drawn from training organizations needed operational navigation and signals briefing before entering battle zones, they had been placed in No. 46 Group. A constant stream of aircraft headed for France to replace those battle worn, lost or damaged, once the fighter squadrons began operating from strips across the Channel. Overseas Aircraft Despatch Units supplying 2nd TAF – No. 4 OADU at Redhill working with No. 83 Group's 'pool' and No. 5 OADU with No. 84 Group at Aston Down – also used Ansons as ferry aircraft.

Slow extension of the beachhead restricted the Ansons to making few sorties, and about a month after D-Day the Watchfield air ambulance reserve began to be run-down. Emergency calls ceased and a second projected airborne assault – to help a breakout from the beachhead – had to be abandoned when 2nd TAF asked for 87 Dakota loads to be flown to France to enable squadrons to operate from advanced landing grounds. To bolster the transport force additional aircraft – mainly taken from trunk route flying – were instead brought in from No. 44 Group, leaving the Ansons to shift small freight items to France.

Whereas Ansons played only a limited part as air ambulances, making a total of 124 sorties, the faithful ex-No. 44 Group Handley Page 'Sparrows' later performed outstandingly well. Gathered in the independent Sparrow Ambulance Flight, the 12 examples (six UE and six reserves, one of which provided spares) remained only for administration purposes under the parent No. 271 Squadron and waited at Doncaster for the call to mercy flying.

The story of the 'Sparrow's' introduction is an unusual one. No. 271 Squadron was flying a motley selection of ex-civil transports when in summer 1940 it was called upon to assist fighter squadron deployment within the British Isles. All the aircraft were quite unsuitable so No. 271's CO, Wg Cdr Glover, and his engineering officer, toured maintenance units to seek suitable substitutes. They came across a Handley Page Harrow bomber still in fair condition and, considering it of possible use, had it flown to Doncaster where the bombing gear was removed and gun turrets were replaced with shapely wooden fairings. Most pleased with the new transport, they eventually gathered another 12 Harrows for their club! All soon had nose and tail fairings, reinforced floors and modified side doors. Trials showed them able to lift two-ton loads easily, in service often more. Within days they were 'hopping around like sparrows', moving personnel and the equipment of entire squadrons, and answering Air Chief Marshal Dowding's requests as he skilfully rotated his force during the Battle of Britain. So successfully did the modified Harrows perform that their 'innovators' asked the Air Ministry and also MAP whether they could have 40 newly-built ones to bolster the force, but their call came far too late. Popularly called 'Sparrows', they were officially designated 'Harrow (Transport Conversion)'; by 1944 'Sparrow' had become the officially accepted name.

The Sparrow Ambulance Flight at Doncaster had to await action until 12 August, when the six front-line aircraft were ordered to 'B14' (Amblie). No refuelling facilities existed there so they were ordered to 'B15' (Ryes). First to leave Doncaster was K6994 (Flt Lt H. Quartermann) followed at 10-minute intervals by K6993 (Plt Off F.C. Wilkinson), K6986 (Flt Lt A. Speak), K7000 (Flt Lt W.G.E. Buchanan), K7024 (Flt Lt N. Evans) and K6973 (Flt Lt F.L. Ferguson).

Primary task for the 'Sparrows' was to shuttle casualties and essential loads between the most forward landing strips and the rear landing groups into which Dakotas since mid-June were operating. On 9 September the Flight moved to 'B6' (Coulombs), and to 'B48' (Amiens/Glisy) on 14 September. As many as 30 casualties were now being carried by each aircraft.

On 26 September K6973 carrying 25 casualties was being flown from 'B78' (Eindhoven) to 'B56' when, 10 miles north of Diest, it was fired upon by enemy anti-aircraft guns. Shrapnel seriously injured the pilot's leg and Flt Sgt Want, the radio operator, received serious injuries to his left hand. Some casualties also received further wounds. As for K6973, its starboard flap was hanging off and it sported many battle scars when it touched down at Evérè.

During September the Sparrow Ambulance Flight flew 5,226.5 operational hours, the forward shuttle ultimately

handling 40,000 casualties without aircraft loss – until its tragic end. Operational control of the Flight passed to 2nd TAF in October 1944, although crews and maintenance personnel were still provided by No. 46 Group. Their base remained Evérè where, at 09:00 hrs on 1 January 1945, 30 to 40 mixed Bf 109 and Fw 190 fighter-bombers suddenly struck, destroying all seven 'Sparrows' present. While the spectacular strike did little to alter the course of hostilities, it brought a sad end to a group of aeroplanes always a thrill to see in wartime and which had contributed to victory in a manner quite out of proportion to their numbers.

## Ansons with D-Day associations

**Flown to Hendon for preparation (subsequent squadron number in parentheses):**
On 30.4: *NK446, NK447, NK448, NK533* (possibly the first Ambulance Transport, to 512 Sqn 21.5.44)
On 3.5: *NK489* (512), *NK490* (575)
In mid-May: *MG471*, NK262, NK451, *NK506, NK693, NK710* (24 Sqn)
On 21.5: *NK493* (575), *NK528* (512), *NK664* (48), *NK665* (233)
On 23.5: *NK492* (575), *NK498* (512) *NK532, NK674, NK695* (575)
On 25.5: *MG533, MG557, MG558, MG564, MG569, MG574, MG579, MG581, MG588, MG594, NK261, NK500, NK507, NK674*
On 31.5: *NK675* (512), *NK692, NK702, NK707* (48), *NK716* (MCS)
*NK446* was posted out on 21.5, *NK532* on 3.7. The others moved out between 11-19.7.

**Blakehill Farm – posted in for casevac service, most being held between 30.5–31.7.44:**
*NK320, NK531, NK657, NK658, NK659, NK660, NK661, NK666, NK668* (definite conversion to 'Ambulance Transport'), *NK695, NK699, NK700, NK705* (30.5.44 – AC FB 20.6.44), *NK708, NK722, NK725* (BFA 26.6.44), *NK728, NK731*

**Watchfield Store 10–31.5:**
*MG533, MG865, NK261, NK693, NK701, NK702, NK704*

**No. 1310 Flight, Bognor, 11.7.44–7.8.44 unless noted:**
*NK261, NK451, NK500, NK660* (to 26.7),

NK674 (to 26.7), NK693

**No. 1311 Flight, Aston Down, absorbed by No. 84 GSU on 31.8.44:**
*MG469* (11.5.44-10.8.44), *MG471* (11.7.44-31.8.44), *MG533* (11.7.44-31.8.44), *MG580* (6.5.44-10.8.44), *MG583* (6.5.44-10.8.44), *MG585* (6.5.44-11.8.44), *NK506* (11.7.44-31.8.44), *NK507* (11.7.44-21.8.44), *NK658* (10.7.44-7.8.44)

**No. 1312 Flight, Llandow:**
*NK666* (10.7.44-25.7.44, Ambulance), *NK668* (10.7.44- ?, Ambulance), *NK692* (10.7.44-1.1.45 EFA), *NK696* (10.6.44-5.12.44 burnt, enemy action), *NK699* (12.7.44- ?), *NK700* (10.7.44- ?), *NK702* (10.7.44-7.44)

**ADGB, Redhill (24.5.44–17.8.44; transferred to 83 GSU):**
*MK382, MK384, NK662, NK663* ADGB also used *MG555* (24.5.44-11.8.44) based at Aston Down

**HQ SHAEF, Heston:**
*NK706* (13.5.44-16.7.45)

**AEAF Communications Squadron:**
*NK221* (22.5.44-15.2.45), *NK225* (19.5.44-1.2.45), *NK229* (22.5.44-21.11.44)

**HQ 2nd TAF Communications Squadron:**
*MH187* (22.2.44-29.10.44), *MH192* (19.2.44-15.11.44), *MH231* (20.2.44-15.11.44), *MH233* (23.2.44-23.11.44), *MH234* (22.2.44-17.11.44), *NK175* (20.2.44-23.11.44), *NK183* (24.2.44-23.11.44), *NK202* (20.2.44-11.44)

**No. 83 Group Communications Flight, Redhill:**
*MH189* (24.2.44-2.11.44), *MH230* (1.3.44-29.10.44), *MH236* (1.3.44-16.11.44), *NK179* (24.2.44-2.11.44), *NK439* (23.3.44-9.11.44)

**No. 84 Group Communications Flight, Aston Down:**
*MH190* (20.2.44-10.11.44), *MH191* (24.2.44-18.12.44), *MH232* (28.2.44-10.11.44), *MH235* (14.3.44-8.11.44), *NK186* (23.2.44-14.12.44), *NK443* (22.3.44-4.2.45)

A number of Ansons were also held on stand-by at Shoreham for possible use as

*Avro Ansons variously supported the forces in France. NK670 of No. 83 Group Communications Flight, Redhill, is seen delivering bread to a French airfield on 17 August 1944. (Bruce Robertson collection)*

radio relay stations operating over the English Channel.

NB: Anson deliveries to D-Day had reached *NK824*

## 'Sparrows' on squadron strength, 5 June 1944
### *No. 271 Sqn,* Doncaster (6.44)
K6937 18.6.42-23.3.44, ?-15.10.44 SOC
K6941 21.2.42-23.3.44, 5.2.45-15.3.45 SOC
K6943 23.4.40-1.1.45, destroyed
K6949 31.12.42-26.3.45, ground accident

K6973 2.7.41-1.1.45, destroyed
K6975 8.2.42-31.8.43, 14.8.43-8.11.44 SOC
K6978 31.12.41-27.7.43, 23.3.44-25.5.45 SOC
K6987 23.6.41-2.45
K6994 11.6.41-8.9.42, 27.1.43-1.1.45, destroyed
K6998 28.6.40-20.2.45 SOC
K7000 22.7.40-29.11.40, 11.2.42-21.9.43, 1.2.44-10.2.45 FA
K7005 18.5.41-23.5.41, 2.8.41-14.12.44 Cat E
K7010 29.5.40-12.4.43, 14.8.43-25.5.45 SOC
K7014 24.10.40-12.6.41, ?-31.8.44 SOC
K7024 3.5.40-21.5.43, 23.9.43-1.1.45, destroyed
K7032 16.9.40-28.12.42, 16.7.43-17.8.44

# Part Three
# The Fighters

The main share of the RAF's D-Day activity was undertaken by the squadrons of 2nd TAF and ADGB, part of the AEAF which, between 23:00 hrs on 5 June and 21:00 hrs on 6 June, flew 5,276 sorties. During the following 24 hrs another 7,455 sorties flown amounted to half the total effort by the Allied air forces. Little wonder that their activity was complex, their organization vast.

On 1 June 1943 HQ 2nd Tactical Air Force (2nd TAF) formed and No. 2 (Bomber) Group joined Fighter Command preparatory to becoming part of 2nd TAF. Then on 15 November 1943, a major reorganization of RAF Fighter Command came with the formation of the Allied Expeditionary Air Force (AEAF) under ACM Sir Trafford L. Leigh-Mallory KCB DSO. Many of Fighter Command's squadrons were switched to 2nd TAF, commanded by AM Sir Arthur Coningham GCB DSO MC DFC AFC. Fighters and fighter-bombers including Mustangs, Spitfires and Typhoons were placed in two new Groups, Nos. 83 and 84. Four Spitfire squadrons, two intended Tempest squadrons and six Mosquito night defence squadrons were switched to No. 85 Group whose eventual job was to defend the lodgement area. No. 2 Group also passed to 2nd TAF. Switching some rocket-firing Beaufighter Mk X squadrons and some Wellington squadrons from Coastal Command to No. 2 Group for a night strike role was considered in March 1944. Instead, one new Wellington Mk XIII night reconnaissance squadron, No. 69, joined No. 34 (PR) Wing.

The remaining 39 fighter and fighter-bomber squadrons were shared among Nos. 10, 11, 12 and 13 Groups controlled by AM Sir Roderic Hill's Air Defence of Great Britain (ADGB). That also held four inshore air-sea rescue squadrons and the partially operational Fighter Interception Unit. During the assault phase No. 11 Group was responsible for fighter cover over the beachhead and was operationally answerable to HQ 2nd TAF. ADGB controlled night operations.

ADGB's task was primarily protection of the home base from bombers, intruders and particularly from reconnaissance aircraft spying upon invasion preparations, the latter task being undertaken mainly using Spitfire HF Mk VIIs and the then very new Griffon-engined Mk XIVs. In conjunction with the USAAF, and reinforced by 2nd TAF squadrons, ADGB provided extensive cover to shipping during sea passage and while gathered in south coast ports. Then it provided cover as the invasion fleet sailed to Normandy. A third and vitally important task was to prevent the Luftwaffe from attacking ground forces during Operation *Neptune*, especially on D-Day and then within the lodgement area. Beachhead cover by day (and night), maintained until 3 July 1944, was gradually scaled down by then from six- to two-squadron strength.

Tactical forces practised their part during combined forces Exercise *Prank* over and around Studland Bay during March 1944. Bostons and Mitchells giving close support dropped 60 lb practice bombs, and Typhoon cannon fire represented rocket firing while overhead four Spitfire Wings rehearsed protecting the landing. Eight airborne 'Bomphoons' were constantly available to answer Army needs.

A major question mark hovered over the likely German response to the build-up and execution of *Neptune*. Intelligence assessments suggested the maximum available strength (feasible reinforcements in parentheses) to comprise a force of 550 long-range bombers (LRBs), 70 fighter-bombers, 400 (200) single-engined fighters (SEFs), 220 (100) twin-engined fighters (TEFs) and 110 reconnaissance aircraft. That left 375 SEFs and 550 TEFs defending the Reich. Between them all they might mount around 1,750 sorties on D-Day, fewer if pre-invasion raids on embarkation ports were attempted. Yet a mere two LRBs and 10 long-range reconnaissance aircraft operated directly against Britain in daylight on 3 June, and around 50 fighters responded to wide-scale Allied operations over France. Intelligence breakdown of available Luftwaffe forces suggested this layout:

### South of France:
135 LRBs including 85 Ju 88 potential torpedo-bombers; 30 Do 217s equipped with radio-controlled bombs; nine Ju 88/188 reconnaissance aircraft; nine fighters and nine Ar 196s.
### Western/south-west France:
18 Ju 290s (Mont de Marsan); nine Bv 222s (Lake Biscarosse); 35 He 177s equipped with radio-controlled bombs (Bordeaux/Merignac); and 30 Fw 200s (Cognac/Château Bernard).
### North-west France:
30 Ju 88s and 15 Do 217s (Vannes and Kerlin Bastard); nine Ju 88/188 and nine Me 410/Ju 88 reconnaissance aircraft (Rennes); 20 SEFs (Morlaix and Dinard); 20 Ju 88s and nine SEFs (Bernay and Evreux); six Ju 88/188s and nine Me 410s (Buc); 30 Ju 188s (Bretigny); 20 Ju 88/188s (Avord); 20 He 177s (Orléans/Bricy); 10 He 177s (Châteaudun); and 35 Me 410s (St André and Dreux). A total of 180 bombers, 45 long-range reconnaissance aircraft and 12 tactical fighters.
### France east of the Seine, and in Belgium:
30 Ju 88s (Melun/Villaroche and Le Culot); 10 Ju 88/188s (Montdidier); 30 Fw 190s (Roye/Amie); nine SEFs (Monchy Breton); 25 Ju 88/188s and 20 Fw 190s, precise locations unknown.
### Netherlands:
30 Me 410s (shared between Eindhoven, Gilze Rijen and Soesterberg); six Ju 88/188s (Soesterberg).

### North-west Germany:
20 Ju 188s (Munster/Handorf); 10 He 177s (Rheine); 15 Ju 188/Do 217s (Heseppe); 36 Ju 88s (Zwisschenahn); 30 Ju 88s (Varel); 25 Ju 88s (Marx); and 20 Ju 88s (Wittmundhafen).

Final instructions for protective fighter cover during Operation *Neptune* were issued on 1 June 1944. They called first for high-flying Spitfire patrols to increase from 4 June over the No. 10 and 11 Group areas as seaborne invasion forces prepared to sail. Fighters were to prepare to deal with raids on bases of the airborne forces, then at 04:00 hrs on 5 June Spitfires would commence flying constant shipping cover, the extent apparent from the accompanying listing.

From 16:00 hrs on D-1, when many ships set sail, USAAF P-38s of seven fighter groups would commence 90-minute high cover patrols. All this foregoing activity would continue until 23:30 hrs, by which time the leading element of the assault force should have reached 49° 50'N. RAF Mosquitoes would then give cover until daybreak. All the aircraft would by then be wearing bold, distinctive black and white wing and fuselage markings as prescribed by *Overlord* 'Instruction 19' of 13 May.

Night protection of shipping outside Home Waters, in the Main Shipping Route and seaward, and subsequently over the lodgement area was an entirely British commitment shared among four ADGB and six No. 85 Group, 2nd TAF Mosquito Mk XIII squadrons able to operate 30 to 40 aircraft simultaneously. The former defended the UK and land bases, and protected shipping within cover of land-based radar stations. No. 85 Group defended the 'overseas base' as well as shipping beyond static radar cover. Both Nos. 418 and 605 Squadrons had special interdictor tasks on 5/6 June, and six Mosquitoes of No. 29 Squadron stood by to assist them. Eight aircraft of No. 604 Squadron were held ready to counter enemy minelaying aircraft and any delivering low-level night attacks on the main shipping route. Radar stations at Worth Matravers, Blackgang and Foreness controlled operations below 5,000 ft, leaving Sopley and Blackgang radars to mastermind higher level activity. All night-fighters were ordered to clear the assault area by 04:30 hrs on D-Day, allowing day fighters to take over.

On 6 June (and subsequent days) from Civil A.M. Twilight -30 minutes to Civil P.M. Twilight +30 minutes, fighters gave cover to Operation *Neptune* totalling 1,547 sorties, 880 of them by RAF Spitfires. They fielded continuously six low and three high cover squadrons with six RAF squadrons always standing by in reserve. Hour-long top- cover patrols were provided by the following five USAAF P-47 fighter groups (squadrons in parentheses):

36th Fighter Group, Kingsnorth (22nd, 23rd, 53rd)

50th Fighter Group, Lymington (10th, 31st, 313th)

373rd Fighter Group, Woodchurch (410th, 411th, 412th)

404th Fighter Group, Winkton (506th, 507th, 508th)

406th Fighter Group, Ashford (512th, 513th, 514th)

They provided protection in depth, each of the three squadrons in one patrol placing four aircraft between 8,000 and 9,000 ft, eight between 10,000 and 12,000 ft and four more between 14,0000 and 15,000 ft.

RAF Spitfires continuously patrolled below cloud, or between 3,000 and 5,000 ft, over all five British and American landing beaches and inland to a depth of five miles. They also protected the vast number of assault craft and naval vessels south of a line 49° 35' N, and extended their watch eastwards and westwards for 50 miles from the flanks of the assault area. Throughout the day, and to the same schedule repeated over many days, a dozen Wings of Spitfire LF Mk Vs and LF Mk IXs operated, two Wings (each comprising three squadrons) at anyone time. One Wing covered the western beaches, the other the eastern area. Wing Leaders allocated patrol areas to be flown during each 50-minute patrol, this activity commencing at 04:30 hrs on D-Day. Over the western landing areas one squadron covered *Utah* beach, one *Omaha* beach, leaving the third to patrol to the north and west. Over the eastern assault area two squadrons patrolled the entire length of the three British Commonwealth and Allied beaches while the third squadron gave low cover over the eastern area and to the east and north of *Sword* beach.

Essential local radar control of the patrols was provided from three Fighter Direction Tenders: No. 216 situated off the American beaches, No. 217 off the British beaches and No. 13 placed in the main shipping route.

Assuming heavy fighting to be a certainty and possibly forcing squadrons to withdraw from the line, 15 RAF and 15 USAAF fighter squadrons were designated 'Readiness Squadrons'. For this purpose the USAAF earmarked the 354th, 358th, 362nd, 363rd and 371st Fighter Groups and the British chose Spitfires of Detling's Nos. 80, 229 and 274 Squadrons along with Lympne's Nos. 33, 74 and 127 Squadrons and No. 150 Wing (Nos. 3 and 486 Squadrons flying Tempest Vs plus Spitfire IXs of No. 56 Squadron).

No. 122 Wing (83 Group) stood by with Mustang IIIs, likewise No. 133 Wing (84 Group) whose three squadrons (Nos. 129, 306 and 315) also flying Mustang IIIs were to operate from Coltishall under No. 12 Group to provide any long-range cover needed by Coastal Command Beaufighters should they have to attack naval forces in daylight. Mustangs also searched for enemy shipping coming in from the North Sea which Typhoons of No. 137 Squadron stood by to attack.

Only a basic outline of policy for the tactical Fighter-Bomber Air Support Force could be agreed by the joint Anglo-US planning committee. Action would have to be in response to need on the day. In all, 33 squadrons were allotted to the strike fighter force, including 18 RAF squadrons (seven operating 'Bomphoons') placed in seven Wings. Four of the remainder were USAAF P-47s squadrons, the other being Warmwell's 474th Fighter Group using P-38s.

One other specialized task given to the single-seat fighter force was the observation of the accuracy of fire from warships. The RAF contribution for the task comprised Nos. 26 and 63 Squadrons flying Spitfire Mk Vs and Nos. 168, 268, 414 and 430 Squadrons using Mustangs, which from noon on D-Day were expected to be released to revert to their normal fighter-reconnaissance role. For that purpose they were placed in No. 35 Wing (Gatwick) or No. 39 Wing (Odiham), and operated along with Mustangs of the 67th Tactical Reconnaissance Group, USAAF (Middle Wallop).

In the following listing squadrons appear

under their controlling organization AFTER the foothold in Normandy was achieved. ADGB squadrons – except those flying Hurricanes – were established at 18 aircraft each. Some squadrons held more than their listed effective, reserve and unserviceable strength, for although taken off-charge the aircraft awaited removal for servicing, etc. Similarly, any detailed listing of individual aircraft, although later attempted, is all the more difficult due to the reverse of the procedure.

Equipment, operational strength and serviceability returns to HQ AEAF for 18:00 hrs on 5 June 1944 showed this pattern: return for 6 June 18:00 hrs in parentheses:

# AIR DEFENCE OF GREAT BRITAIN
## FIGHTERS

| Aircraft type FIGHTERS: | Sqn | Serviceable | Unserviceable |
|---|---|---|---|
| **Spitfire V** | | | |
| | 64 | 14(14) | 8(8) |
| | 118 | 19(18) | 6(7) |
| | 130 | 18(18) | 2(4) |
| | 234 | 21(21) | 1(1) |
| | 303 | 20(19) | 3(4) |
| | 345 | 17(17) | 4(3) |
| | 350 | 18(17) | 3(3) |
| | 402 | 19(17) | 3(5) |
| | 501 | 20(20) | 1(1) |
| | 504 | 18(18) | 2(2) |
| | 611 | 15(15) | 7(7) |
| **Totals** | **11** | **199(194)** | **40(45)** |
| (Established: 198) | | | |
| **Spitfire HF VII** | | | |
| | 124 | 17(19) | 4(2) |
| | 131 | 19(17) | 1(4) |
| | 616 | 18(17) | 2(4) |
| **Totals** | **3** | **54(53)** | **7(10)** |
| (Established: 54) | | | |
| **Spitfire F IX** | | | |
| | 33 | 18(20) | 3(2) |
| | 80 | 19(19) | 3(3) |
| | 229 | 14(16) | 7(5) |
| | 274 | 16(17) | 5(3) |
| **Totals** | **4** | **67(72)** | **18(13)** |
| (Established: 72) | | | |
| **Spitfire LF IX** | | | |
| | 1 | 15(18) | 4(3) |
| | 56 | 18(21) | 2(-) |
| | 126 | 15(17) | 5(4) |
| | 165 | 16(16) | 4(4) |
| **Totals** | **4** | **64(72)** | **15(11)** |
| (Established: 72) | | | |
| **Spitfire HF IX** | | | |
| | 74 | 19(19) | 4(4) |
| | 127 | 21(20) | -(1) |
| **Totals** | **2** | **40(39)** | **4(5)** |
| (Established: 36) | | | |
| **Spitfire F XII** | | | |
| | 41 | 17(17) | 4(3) |
| **Spitfire XIV** | | | |
| | 91 | 14(16) | 7(5) |
| | 322 | 14(16) | 7(5) |
| | 610 | 8(13) | 11(8) |
| **Totals** | **3** | **36(45)** | **25(18)** |
| (Established: 54) | | | |
| **OVERALL** | **28** | **501** | **107** |
| (Established: 513) | | | |

NB: RAF Peterhead and RAF Skeabrae each operated three Spitfire HF Mk VIs and the latter also had three HF Mk VIIs, none of which was on AEAF strength.

| | Sqn | Serviceable | Unserviceable |
|---|---|---|---|
| **Mustang III** | | | |
| | 316 | 18(18) | 2(2) |
| **Tempest V** | | | |
| | 3 | 15(18) | 4(1) |
| | 486 | 9(16) | 9(2) |
| **Totals** | **2** | **24(34)** | **13(3)** |
| **Hurricane I** | | | |
| | 1449 Flt | 1(1) | -(-) |
| **Hurricane II** | | | |
| | 1449 Flt | 9(8) | 1(2) |
| **Totals** | **1** | **10(9)** | **1(2)** |
| (Established: 6) | | | |
| **Beaufighter VI(f)** | | | |
| | 68+ | 14(14) | 2(3) |
| | 406* | 15(15) | 2(2) |
| **Totals** | **2*** | **29(29)** | **4(5)** |

+ rearming; no longer established with Beaufighters yet still employing them operationally
* Rearming with Mosquitoes, but still holding and operating Beaufighters

| | Sqn | Serviceable | Unserviceable |
|---|---|---|---|
| **Mosquito FB VI** | | | |
| | 418 | 18(18) | 2(1) |
| | 605 | 20(19) | 1(2) |
| **Totals** | **2** | **38(37)** | **3(3)** |
| **Mosquito NF XII/XIII** | | | |
| | 29 | 17(16) | 1(3) |
| | 96 | 17(16) | 1(3) |
| | 151 | 18(17) | 3(3) |
| | 264 | 16(16) | 3(3) |
| | 307 | 14(14) | -(1) |
| | *406 | 3(4) | 3(2) |
| | 409 | 16(14) | 3(5) |
| | 410 | 19(15) | 3(7) |
| | 488 | 17(17) | 2(3) |
| | 604 | 15(16) | 3(2) |
| **Totals** | **9** | **152(145)** | **23(30)** |
| (Established: 162) | | | |

* rearming, but still established at 18 Beaufighters

| | Sqn | Serviceable | Unserviceable |
|---|---|---|---|
| **Mosquito NF XVII** | | | |
| | 25 | 15(15) | 4(4) |
| | *68 | 5(6) | -(1) |

| | | |
|---|---|---|
| 125 | 15(17) | 4(2) |
| *219 | 12(14) | 3(1) |
| *456 | 13(18) | 5(-) |

| Totals | 3(+2*) | 60(70) | 16(8) |
|---|---|---|---|

* rearming with Mosquito NF XXX

| OVERALL | 16 | 250(252) | 42(41) |
|---|---|---|---|

(Established = 288)

## FIGHTER/GROUND ATTACK:
**Typhoon 1B**

| | | |
|---|---|---|
| *3 | 1(1) | 1(1) |
| 137 | 19(19) | 2(2) |
| 263 | 18(20) | 2(-) |
| *486 | 1(1) | -(-) |
| 1320 Flt | 4(4) | -(-) |

| Totals | 2(+2*) | 43(45) | 6(4) |
|---|---|---|---|

(Established: 42)
* no Typhoons on establishment

## FIGHTER RECONNAISSANCE:
**Hurricane II**

| 309 | 20(19) | 2(3) |
|---|---|---|

**Spitfire V**

| | | |
|---|---|---|
| 26 | 20(20) | 1(1) |
| 63 | 19(19) | 2(2) |

| Totals | 3 | 59(58) | 5(6) |
|---|---|---|---|

Squadrons assigned to 2nd TAF all had an Establishment of 18 aircraft, apart from AOP Auster squadrons established at 16 aircraft each.

# 2nd TACTICAL AIR FORCE

| Aircraft type | Sqn | Serviceable | Unserviceable |
|---|---|---|---|

**FIGHTERS:**
**Spitfire LF IXc**

| | | |
|---|---|---|
| 66 | 17(17) | 2(2) |
| 132 | 19(20) | 1(-) |
| 302 | 17(16) | 1(5) |
| 308 | 18(15) | -(6) |
| 310 | 16(18) | 3(1) |
| 312 | 19(18) | -(1) |
| 313 | 18(18) | 3(3) |
| 317 | 17(18) | 1(3) |
| 329 | 15(15) | 6(6) |
| 331 | 17(18) | 3(1) |
| 332 | 15(16) | 4(3) |
| 340 | 15(15) | 6(6) |
| 341 | 15(15) | 5(6) |
| 349 | 20(19) | -(1) |
| 401 | 20(20) | 1(1) |
| 403 | 18(18) | 2(2) |
| 411 | 20(19) | 1(2) |
| 412 | 20(19) | 1(3) |
| 416 | 20(21) | 2(1) |
| 421 | 19(19) | 2(2) |
| 441 | 16(18) | 6(2) |
| 442 | 13(19) | 7(1) |
| 443 | 14(19) | 6(2) |
| 453 | 20(20) | -(-) |
| 602 | 22(20) | 1(1) |

| Totals | 25 | 440(450) | 64(60) |
|---|---|---|---|

(Established: 450)

**Spitfire LF IXe**

| | | |
|---|---|---|
| 222 | 22(19) | 1(2) |
| 485 | 18(18) | 1(1) |

| Totals | 2 | 40(37) | 2(3) |
|---|---|---|---|

## SPITFIRE

| GRAND TOTAL | 27 | 48(487) | 66(63) |
|---|---|---|---|

(Established: 486)

**Mustang III**

| | | |
|---|---|---|
| 19 | 16(17) | 2(1) |
| 65 | 15(17) | 3(3) |
| 122 | 18(18) | 1(1) |
| 129 | 13(15) | 5(4) |
| 306 | 17(17) | 1(1) |
| 315 | 17(18) | 3(3) |

| Totals | 6 | 96(102) | 15(13) |
|---|---|---|---|

(Established: 108)

## FIGHTER RECONNAISSANCE:
**Mustang I**

| | | |
|---|---|---|
| 168 | 15(14) | 3(4) |
| 414 | 18(17) | 1(2) |
| 430 | 17(20) | 4(1) |

| Totals | 3 | 50(51) | 8(7) |
|---|---|---|---|

**Mustang IA**

| | | |
|---|---|---|
| *2 | 8(4) | 3(5) |
| 268 | 15(16) | 4(4) |

| Totals | 1(+1*) | 23(20) | 7(9) |
|---|---|---|---|

* rearming with Mustang II

**Mustang II**

| *2 | 8(8) | 3(3) |
|---|---|---|

* rearming with Mustang II

## MUSTANG

| GRAND TOTALS | 5 | 81(79) | 18(19) |
|---|---|---|---|

## FIGHTER/GROUND ATTACK:
**TYPHOON 1B:**

| | | |
|---|---|---|
| 164 | 16(15) | 1(2) |
| 174 | 18(20) | -(1) |
| 175 | 15(17) | 2(5) |
| 181 | 18(18) | 3(4) |
| 182 | 14(18) | 6(2) |
| 183 | 17(14) | 2(2) |
| 184 | 19(19) | 2(2) |
| 193 | 11(11) | 13(13) |
| 197 | 12(17) | 5(5) |
| 198 | 16(15) | 2(4) |
| 245 | 9(19) | 7(2) |
| 247 | 14(15) | 7(6) |
| 257 | 14(16) | 1(4) |
| 266 | 10(13) | 8(11) |
| 438 | 17(18) | 4(3) |
| 439 | 16(17) | 5(4) |
| 440 | 18(18) | 4(4) |
| 609 | 17(18) | 2(1) |

| Totals | 18 | 271(298) | 68(75) |
|---|---|---|---|

(Established: 324)

## PHOTOGRAPHIC RECONNAISSANCE:
**Spitfire PR XI**

| | | |
|---|---|---|
| 4 | 15(17) | 5(1) |
| 16 | 17(18) | 2(1) |
| 400 | 18(18) | -(1) |

| Totals | 3 | 53(53) | 7(3) |
|---|---|---|---|

**Mosquito PR IX/XVI**

| 140 | 9(10) | 9(7) |
|---|---|---|

## NIGHT RECONNAISSANCE:

| Wellington XIII | 69 | 5(6) | 13(7) |
|---|---|---|---|

**AIR OBSERVATION POST:**
Auster IV

| | | | |
|---|---|---|---|
| | 652 | 16(15) | -(-) |
| | 653 | 14(14) | 1(1) |
| | 658 | 15(7) | -(-) |
| | 659 | 15(15) | 1(1) |
| | 660 | 13(13) | 3(3) |
| | 661 | 14(14) | 3(3) |
| | 662 | 16(16) | -(-) |
| **Totals** | **7** | **103(94)** | **8(8)** |

(Established: 112)

Several months prior to *Overlord*, a major 'paper' reorganization of 2nd TAF took place. Aircraft within 2nd TAF were, from 14 April 1944, taken on charge by support units within Nos. 83 or 84 Groups. Although assigned to them, they were nevertheless placed in squadron hands. The belief was that they could easily be switched from one squadron to another should losses become unduly high. Thus, individual aircraft records of Typhoons, for example, show many operating with squadrons as being assigned to 'reserve' units until 8 June 1944 when, with losses far lower than expected, they were posted on to squadron strength. To facilitate rapid modifications and repairs a special 'No 3501 Servicing Unit' had been established at Cranfield. Its holding on 5 June was:

*No. 3501 Servicing Unit*, **Cranfield**
Mustang III 2+1
Spitfire II (2); Vb (35+36); Vc (4+6); VII (5+1); F.IX (14+9); HF.IX (6+4); LF.IX (8+6); XII ((3+0); XIV (4+7)
Typhoon 3+2

Other units giving immediate backing to 2nd TAF and their 5 June strengths, were:

*No. 83 Group Support Unit*, **Redhill**
Mustang I 2+13
Mustang III 4+4
Spitfire LF.IX 14+22
Typhoon 16+15

*No. 84 Group Support Unit*, **Aston Down**
Auster IV 1+0
Mosquito PR Mk IX/XVI 1+1
Mustang IA 0+1
Mustang III 3+7
Spitfire Vb (1+0); F.IX (2+1); LF.IX (4+69); LF.IXe (0+35); PR.XI (3+2)
Typhoon 0+27

NB: 2+1, etc, translates as serviceable + unserviceable.

For operations on D-Day the operational layout by Wings and bases was thus:

## CONTROLLED BY No. 11 (FIGHTER) GROUP
**Day-fighter Wings:**
**Spitfire IX (Tangmere Sector):**
No. 125, Ford: Nos. 132, 453, 602 Sqns
No. 126, Tangmere: Nos. 401, 411, 412 Sqns
No. 127, Tangmere: Nos. 403, 416, 421 Sqns
No. 131, Chaily: Nos. 302, 308, 317 Sqns
No. 132, Bognor: Nos. 66, 331, 332 Sqns
No. 134, Appledram: Nos. 310, 312, 313 Sqns
No. 135, Selsey: Nos. 222, 349, 485 Sqns
No. 144, Ford: Nos. 441, 442, 443 Sqns
No. 145, Merston: Nos. 329, 340 341 Sqns

**Spitfire V (Tangmere Sector):**
Horne: Nos. 130, 303, 402 Sqns
Deanland: Nos. 64, 234, 611 Sqns
Friston: Nos. 350, 351 Sqns
Shoreham: No. 345 Sqn
Spitfire XIV (Biggin Hill Sector):
No. 148 Wing, West Malling: No. 91 Sqn
Mustang III (Tangmere Sector):
No. 122, Funtington: Nos. 19, 65, 122 Sqns
No. 133, Coolham: Nos. 129, 306, 315 Sqns

**Day-fighter Wings (Readiness Force), Biggin Hill Sector:**
Spitfire IX (unless otherwise stated):
Lympne: Nos. 33, 74, 127 Sqns
Detling: Nos. 80, 229, 274 Sqns
Under re-equipment:
No. 150 Wing, Newchurch No. 56 Sqn with Nos. 3 and 486 Sqns (Tempest V)

**Mixed:**
No. 141 Wing, Hartford Bridge (Tangmere Sector): No. 322 Sqn (Spitfire XIV)
No. 150 Wing, Bradwell Bay (North Weald Sector): No. 124 Sqn (Spitfire HF VII)

### TYPHOON FIGHTER-BOMBER WINGS
**(providing immediate air support as required)**
**Middle Wallop Sector:**
No. 121 Wing, Holmsley South: Nos. 174, 175, 245 Sqns

No. 123 Wing, Thorney Island: Nos. 198, 609 Sqns
No. 124 Wing, Hurn: Nos. 181, 182, 247 Sqns
No. 136 Wing, Thorney Island: Nos. 164, 183 Sqns
No. 143 Wing, Hurn*: Nos. 438, 439, 440 Sqns
No. 146* Wing, Need's Oar Point: Nos. 193, 197, 257, 266 Sqns
* Typhoon bomber squadrons, others rocket-firing squadrons

## Others:
No. 129 Wing, Westhampnett: No. 184 Sqn Channel Stop Squadron, Manston: No. 137 Sqn under North Weald Sector control

## FIGHTER-RECONNAISSANCE WINGS
### Tangmere Sector:
No. 34 Wing, Northolt: Nos. 16 (Spitfire XI), 69 (Wellington XIII), 140 (Mosquito IX/XVI) Sqns
No. 39 Wing, Odiham: Nos. 168, 414*, 430 (Mustang I) and No. 400 (Spitfire XI) Sqns
Lee-on-Solent: Nos. 26 and 63 Sqns (Spitfire V)
No. 3 Naval Wing, Lee-on-Solent: Nos. 808, 885, 886, 897 Sqns

### Biggin Hill Sector:
No. 35 Wing, Gatwick: Nos. 2* and 268* (Mustang I/II) and No. 4 (Spitfire XI) Sqns
* These squadrons operated from Lee-on-Solent during the morning of 6 June 1944

## MOSQUITO NIGHT-FIGHTER SQUADRONS
### Assigned No. 11 (Fighter) Group:
No. 96 Sqn: Mk XII/XIII (AI Mk VIII radar), West Malling (Biggin Hill)
No. 125 Sqn: Mk XVII (AI Mk X radar), Hurn (Middle Wallop Sector)
No. 219 Sqn: Mk XXX(AI Mk X radar), Bradwell Bay (North Weald)
No. 456 Sqn: Mk XXX (AI Mk X radar) Ford (Tangmere)

### Intruder Force:
No. 418 Sqn: Mk VI, Holmsley South (Middle Wallop)
No. 605 Sqn: Mk VI, Manston (North Weald)

## Assigned to No. 85 Group, 2nd TAF (under operational control of No. 11 (Fighter) Group):
All operating Mk XIIIs fitted with AI Mk VIII radar
No. 29 Sqn, West Malling (Biggin Hill)
No. 264 Sqn, Hartford Bridge (Tangmere)
No. 409 Sqn, West Malling (Biggin Hill)
No. 410 Sqn, Hunsdon using Ford as operating base (North Weald)
No. 488 Sqn, Zeals (Middle Wallop)
No. 604 Sqn, Hurn (Middle Wallop)

## SQUADRONS of No. 10 GROUP, ADGB
### Day-fighter:
No. 1 Sqn, Predannack: Spitfire IX
No. 41 Sqn, Bolthead: Spitfire XII
No. 126 Sqn, Culmhead: Spitfire IX
No. 610 Sqn, Culmhead: Spitfire XIV
No. 131 Sqn, Harrowbeer: Spitfire VII
No. 263 Sqn, Harrowbeer: Typhoon (West Channel stop)
No. 616 Sqn, Fairwood Common: Spitfire VII
No. 1449 Flight, St Mary's: Hurricane I/II

### Night-fighter:
No. 68 Sqn Fairwood Common: Mosquito XVII/XIX
No. 151 Sqn, Predannack: Mosquito XII/XIII
No. 406 Sqn, Winkleigh: Beaufighter VIf

## SQUADRONS of No. 12 (FIGHTER) GROUP
### Day-fighter:
No. 309 (Flight), Hutton Cranwick: Hurricane II (Sqn HQ Drem)
No. 316 Sqn, Coltishall: Mustang III
No. 504 (Flight), Acklington: Spitfire V
No. 504 (Flight), Digby: Spitfire V

### Night-fighter:
No. 25 Sqn, Coltishall: Mosquito XVII/XIX
No. 307 Sqn, Church Fenton: Mosquito XII/XVII

Such, then, was the strength and the layout of the defensive, protective fighters and the strike fighters.

## NO. 2 GROUP, 2nd TAF
Still with a very different role from any other part of 2nd TAF, the strength of No. 2 Group at 18:00 hrs on 5 June was thus:

| Aircraft type | Sqn | Serviceable | Unserviceable |
|---|---|---|---|
| **Boston IIIA/IV** | | | |
| 88 { IIIA | | 16(18) | 3(1) |
|      IV | | -(2) | -(-) |
| 342 { IIIA | | 17(14) | 1(3) |
|       IV | | -(1) | -(-) |
| **Totals** | **2** | **33(35)** | **4(4)** |
| | | | |
| **Mitchell II** | | | |
| | 98 | 16(14) | 5(7) |
| | 180 | 17(18) | 5(3) |
| | 226 | 16(17) | 4(3) |
| | 320 | 17(17) | 2(3) |
| **Totals** | **4** | **66(66)** | **16(16)** |
| | | | |
| **Mosquito FB VI** | | | |
| | 21 | 17(17) | 3(3) |
| | 107 | 17(18) | 2(1) |
| | 305 | 20(21) | 2(1) |
| | 464 | 18(19) | 2(1) |
| | 487 | 18(18) | 2(2) |
| | 613 | 20(21) | 2(-) |
| **Totals** | **6** | **110(114)** | **13(8)** |
| **TOTAL NO. 2 GROUP STRENGTH** | **12** | **209(215)** | **33(28)** |

**Aircraft Reception Flights**

| | | | |
|---|---|---|---|
| Boston IIIA | 416 ARF | -(3) | -(2) |
| Mitchell II | 416 ARF | -(4) | -(4) |
| Mosquito VI | 417 ARF | 1(7) | 26(22) |

**No. 2 Group Repair & Salvage Unit (Consolidated)**

| | | |
|---|---|---|
| Boston IIIA | 1(-) | 3(-) |
| Mitchell II | -(-) | 2(10) |
| Mosquito VI | 2(2) | 10(10) |

Each of the aircraft types had its own designated role as hitherto mentioned. After their early smoke-laying sorties the Bostons stood by in case the Royal Navy requested more. At midday they were released and prepared for a day and night bombing role not unlike that ordered for the Mitchells. Although the Mosquitoes were quite able to operate effectively by day they were given a specialized night task. Because of these variations the work of No. 2 Group is later described by considering each type of aircraft.

# Fighter operations: Protecting the gathering

Preventing the Germans from knowing where the invasion would take place was paramount, and equally essential was the protection from air attack of the assembling invasion fleet. Firing of the wooden gliders and sinking the landing craft would have been catastrophic, yet amazingly the Germans never seriously attempted either.

To protect the vast number of ships assembled in south coast ports, British and American fighters began dedicated patrols on 3 June 1944. These continued throughout 4 June in ever increasing strength, and from 05:30 to 22:30 hrs on 5 June 20 squadrons of No. 11 Group Spitfires flew 75 patrols, in relays, between the Thames Estuary and Portsmouth area. Between 05:15 and 22:30 hrs Spitfires of Nos. 1, 41, 131, 126 and 610 Squadrons flew 42 patrols over coastal areas west of Portsmouth. At 16:00 hrs on 5 June the full-cover plan began with the USAAF providing top cover.

Over the Solent, the main shipping assembly area, the latest Spitfires – Mk XIVs of Nos. 91 and 322 Squadrons – between 11:30 and 18:55 hrs flew 18 patrols looking for enemy reconnaissance aircraft, while Spitfire HF Mk VIIs of No. 124 Squadron similarly watched off the south-east coast. RAF fighters were five times scrambled for possible 'bogeys', all proving negative. Low cloud and rain, which was to make the invasion a difficult task, also helped to shield its 4,000 ships from prying eyes.

Some other patrols are particularly worth mentioning, for they were flown by Hawker Hurricanes based on the Scilly Isles. From there they played a part out of all proportion to their small number, by searching for enemy anti-shipping aircraft slipping into British waters from the west. On 5 June they flew five patrols in areas where attacks were forecast.

The following listing includes as many protective patrols as official records reveal.

# PROTECTION OF SHIPPING DURING SEA PASSAGE AND FIGHTER OPERATIONS, 5 JUNE 1944 BY SPITFIRES

## No. 10 Group Area

| Time | Sqn | Type | Notes and aircraft used |
|---|---|---|---|
| 05:15-06:00 | 616 | VII | F, G, P, R |
| 05:15-06:50 | 131 | VII | MD111, MD144, MD146, MD173 |
| 05:20-07:00 | 41 | XII | MD801, MD803, MD841, MD847 |
| 06:30-08:00 | 616 | VII | E, K, V, X |
| 06:45-08:10 | 610 | XIV | three aircraft |
| 07:30-09:00 | 131 | VII | MB884, MD110, MD120, MD129 |
| 07:55-09:05 | 41 | XII | MB837, MB841, MB847, MB881 |
| 08:10-09:20 | 165 | IX | MK514-Z, MK564-Y, MK752-W |
| 08:30-10:00 | 616 | VII | B, W, Y, one unknown |
| 09:15-10:20 | 165 | IX | MK480-F, MK589-G, MK838-K, MK855-E |
| 09:30-11:05 | 131 | VII | MB884, MD132, MD169, MD183 |
| 10:00-11:30 | 616 | VII | D, E, G, K |
| 10:10-11:25 | 165 | IX | MK564-Y, MK751, MK752-W, ML199-X |
| 10:10-11:40 | 610 | XIV | three aircraft |
| 10:20-11:40 | 41 | XII | EN224, MB845, MB862, MB882 |
| 10:30-12:25 | 616 | VII | N, Q, R, W |
| 11:00-12:30 | 131 | VII | MD111, MD144, MD146, MD171 |
| 11:15-12:35 | 41 | XII | ??620, MB845, MB882, one unknown |
| 11:15-12:35 | 165 | IX | MK480-F, MK589-G, MK838-K, MK855-E |
| 11:40-13:00 | 131 | VII | MD110, MD120, MD129, MD169 |
| 12:00-13:30 | 126 | IX | B, D, F, G, M, P, S, Y |
| 12:00-13:35 | 610 | XIV | one aircraft |
| 12:15-13:35 | 610 | XIV | two aircraft |
| 12:15-13:40 | 615 | IX | MK514-Z, MK564-Y, MK811-S, ML199-X |
| 13:00-14:40 | 131 | VII | MD134, MD168, MD170, MD173 |
| 13:15-14:35 | 141 | XII | MB798, MB804, MB837, MB842 |
| 13:15-14:40 | 1 | IX | MK726, MK733, MK867, ML122 |
| 13:30-15:20 | 131 | VII | MD110, MD117, MD132, MD165 |
| 14:00-15:00 | 1 | IX | MK659, MK901, ML313, NH255 |
| 14:05-15:40 | 126 | IX | MK126-G, MK989-L, ML366-J, NH397-B |
| 14:20-15:50 | 610 | XIV | two aircraft |
| 14:30-16:00 | 126 | IX | MK673-M, MK893-P, MK993-O, MK995-N |
| 15:00-16:35 | 1 | IX | MK733, MK744, MK926, ML122 |
| 15:23-16:20 | 41 | XII | EN221, MB803, MB841, one unknown |
| 15:30-16:35 | 131 | VII | MB884, MD117, MD171, MD173 |
| 15:35-17:00 | 131 | VII | MD110, MD129, MD165, MD169 |
| 15:50-17:10 | 1 | IX | MK901, MK986, MK987, ML270 |
| 16:36-17:55 | 126 | IX | ?????-S, MK923-Z, NH397-B, NH402-Y |
| 16:40-18:00 | 610 | XIV | one aircraft |
| 17:30-19:00 | 131 | VII | MD120, MD132 |
| 17:35-19:05 | 131 | VII | MD119, MD134, MD144, MD146 |
| 17:40-19:00 | 41 | XII | EN221, MB803, MB841, one unknown |
| 18:30-19:45 | 126 | IX | MK893-P, MK993-O, ML214-K, ML397-D |
| 18:45-20:00 | 610 | XIV | one aircraft |
| 19:35-21:00 | 131 | VII | MB884, MD111, MD117, MD120, MD129 |
| ??:??-??:?? | 131 | VII | MD168, MD170, MD171 |
| 19:45-21:00 | 1 | IX | MK926, MK986, MK997, NH253 |
| 19:45-23:01 | 41 | XII | EN224, EN620, MB794, MB881 |
| 20:30-22:00 | 1 | IX | MK744, ML270, NH255, one unknown |
| 20:32-22:05 | 126 | IX | MK673-M, MK893-P, MK923-Z, MK989-L, MK995-N(?), ML366-J, ML398-F, NH402-Y |
| 20:32-20:27 | 1 | IX | MK388, MK741, ML270, NH255 |
| 20:53-22:10 | 610 | XIV | one aircraft |
| 21:25-22:20 | 1 | IX | MK659, NH246 |
| 21:25-22:55 | 41 | VII | EN221, EN620, MB795, MB881 |
| 21:30-23:00 | 131 | VII | MD111, MD119, MD134, MD173 |
| 21:35-23:10 | 131 | VII | MB884, MD110, MD132, MD165 |
| 22:40-23:15 | 165 | IX | MK471-N, MK752-W |

No. 1449 Flight, Hurricane IIc
Shipping/Sector patrols area eight miles west of Trevose Head and 10 miles west of Land's End:

| | | |
|---|---|---|
| 19:00-19:50 | | Z2985, JS340 |
| 21:10-22:45 | | Z2985, JS340 |
| 22:25-22:50 | | BE173, JS383 |

## No. 11 Group Area

| Time | Sqn | Type | Notes and aircraft used |
|------|-----|------|-------------------------|
| 04:00-06:00 | 402 | V | *P8788, AB897, AB910, BL969* |
| 05:00-06:55 | 402 | V | *AA738, BM645, EE715*, one unknown |
| 05:20-06:30 | 274 | IX | *MA585, MH876, MH935* |
| 06:15-08.00 | 274 | IX | *MA579, MA810, MH349, MH853* |
| 07:20-08:40 | 402 | V | Standing patrol off Beachy Head; *W3129, EE680* |
| 07:20-09:15 | 274 | IX | *BS128, BS284, BS474, MA818* |
| 07:50-09:30 | 312 | IX | S of Bournemouth; *MH474, MJ792, MK775, MK895* |
| 08:15-09:55 | 312 | IX | S of Bournemouth; *MJ553, MJ840, MJ940, MK180* |
| 08:20-10:15 | 402 | V | *W3250, AA738* |
| 08:30-10:20 | 274 | IX | *MA585, NH349, MH603* |
| 09:20-10:50 | 402 | V | *EE686, EE715* |
| 09:30-10:55 | 312 | IX | S of Bournemouth; *MH499* or *MJ499, MJ572, MK244, MK805* |
| 09:35-10:20 | 274 | IX | N Foreland–Beachy Head; *BS395, LZ919* |
| 09:45-11:30 | 274 | IX | *MA579, MH876, MH935* |
| 10:20-12:15 | 402 | V | *W3129, BN645* |
| 10:25-11:25 | 453 | IX | S of St Catherine's Point; E and S |
| 10:30-11:55 | 127 | IX | Patrol Convoy *Effective*, S of Dover; *ML235, ML243* |
| 10:50-11:45 | 33 | IX | 24 ships, Isle of Sheppey; *MJ120, BS286* |
| 10:50-11:30 | 313 | IX | Isle of Wight–Studland Bay, over LCTs; *MH496, MK189, MK320, MK361* |
| 10:50-11:50 | 33 | IX | *BS534, MH606* |
| 10:50-12:10 | 308 | IX | *MJ503, MK720* |
| 11:00-13:00 | 274 | IX | *BS284, BS395, MA818, MH853* |
| 11:00-12:30 | 313 | IX | Isle of Wight–Studland Bay, over LCTs; *JK620, JK840, MJ900, MJ963* |
| 11:20-12:30 | 402 | V | *W3250, BM233* |
| 11:20-12:50 | 80 | IX | Clacton–Dungeness; *JL227, MH873* |
| 12:00-13:30 | 313 | IX | Isle of Wight–Studland Bay, over LCTs; *MJ292, MJ293, MK211, MK606* |
| 12:15-13:50 | 274 | IX | *BS128, BS474, MA585, MH603* |
| 12:20-13:35 | 402 | V | *W3454, AB897* |
| 12:20-14:50 | 80 | IX | Clacton–Dungeness; *MH319, MH878* |
| 12:35-14:10 | 127 | IX | S of Dover; *ML185, ML238, ML251, ML343* |
| 13:00-14:00 | 402 | V | *AB897, AB910* |
| 13:00-14:40 | 80 | IX | Clacton–Dungeness; *MA806*, one unknown |
| 13:25-14:55 | 274 | IX | *BS395, MA585, MA810, MH853* |
| 13:50-15:35 | 80 | IX | Clacton–Dungeness; *BS512, EN127, JL227, MH671* |
| 14:00-15:05 | 402 | V | *P8788, BL969* |
| 14:30-16:00 | 127 | IX | Cover Convoy *Talbot*; *ML196, ML210, ML211, ML343* |
| 14:35-16:16 | 329 | IX | *MJ524-G, MJ912, MK132-S, MK301-L, MK319-X, MK322-J, MK347-V, MK359-H, MK374-Y, MK418-N, NH151-T, ?????-P* |
| 15:15-17:00 | 302 | IX | SE of Isle of Wight; *MK563, MK723, MK745, MK786, MK688, MK839, MK841, MK905, MK915, MK924, MK983, MK999* |
| 15:25-17:30 | 340 | IX | W of Isle of Wight; *MJ351-J, MJ744-O, MJ746-H, MJ795-K, MJ822-U, MK896-Z, MJ896-Z, MK123-C, MK183-T, MK196-E, MK234-X, MK290-D* (Lt Blisot crash-landed, Bognor), *NH249-N* |
| 15:30-16:50 | 127 | IX | Patrol Convoy *Talbot*; *MK675, MK680, ML145, ML210, ML238, ML348, NH194, NH313* |
| 16:00-17:40 | 229 | IX | North Foreland–South Goodwins area |
| 16:20-18:00 | 308 | IX | *MH183, MH374, MH423, MJ294, MJ503, MK529, MK578, MK679, MK720, ML113, ML362, ML578, PL269* |
| 16:20-18:00 | 402 | V | *AB910, BL969* |
| 16:30-18:00 | 127 | IX | Patrol Convoy *Talbot*; *ML196, ML210, ML235, ML255, NH417*, one unknown |
| 16:55-18:15 | 341 | IX | Patrol W of Isle of Wight; *MJ363, MJ564, MJ617, MJ662, MJ671, MJ723, MJ780, MJ815, MJ890, MK238, MK561, NH270* |
| 17:00-??:?? | 402 | V | *W3454, BM233* |
| 17:20-18:45 | 453 | IX | S of St Catherine's Point, 12 aircraft; *B, D, F, G, H, K, M, S, T* included |
| 17:20-19:00 | 127 | IX | Patrol Convoy *Shark*; *ML182, ML210, ML251, NH417* |
| 17:45-19:15 | 401 | IX | *MH413, MH724, MJ131, MJ138, MJ180, MJ231, MJ289, MK263, MK780, MK845, MK902, ML129* |
| 17:55-??:?? | 229 | IX | Details unknown |
| 18:00-19:15 | 402 | V | *P8788, AD180* |

156

| | | | |
|---|---|---|---|
| 18:10-19:45 | 441 | IX | *MJ139, MK177, MK350, MK375, MK399, MK415, MK420, MK460, MK465, ML205*, one unknown |
| 18:25-18:50 | 127 | IX | Patrol Convoy *Shark*; *ML243, ML255* |
| 18:35-20:00 | 274 | IX | *LZ919, MA585, MA818, MH853* |
| 18:45-20:15 | 421 | IX | *MJ793, MJ880*, MJ994, *MK199, MK235, MK573, MK920, NH183, NH344*, two unknown |
| 19:00-20:15 | 402 | V | *AB910, BL969* |
| 19:00 20:10 | 80 | IX | Clacton–Dungeness. *EN172, MA228, MH319, JL227* |
| 19:20-??:?? | 229 | IX | Details uncertain |
| 19:30-20:45 | 127 | IX | Convoy *Talbot* |
| 20:00-20:40 | 80 | IX | *AB196, BS556, MH873, MH881* |
| 20:03-20:55 | 234 | V | Hastings–Beachy Head, 15 miles S of Dungeness; |
| 20:20-21:25 | 402 | V | *W3529, BM233* |
| 20:30-22:20 | 127 | IX | Convoy *Shark* |
| 20:45-221:5 | 416 | IX | St Catherine's Point–Osamage; *MJ575, MJ770, MJ787, MJ828, MJ874, MJ882, MJ929, MK117, MK559, MK835, MK837, ML292* |
| 20:55-22:35 | 402 | V | North Foreland; *AA738, EE686, EE715*, one unknown |
| 21:00-22:15 | 402 | V | *P8788, W3454* |
| 21:15-22:35 | 453 | IX | S of Catherine's Point; *B, D, G, H, J, L, M, N, P, Y* |
| 21:30-22:35 | 74 | IX | North Foreland–Hastings; two aircraft |
| 21:45-23:20 | 401 | IX | *MH413, MH724, MJ138, MJ246, MJ289, MK195, MK263, MK780, MK845, MK902, ML129, ML305* |
| 21:45-23:50 | 402 | V | North Foreland; *W3454, BL969* |
| ??:??-22:30 | 229 | IX | North Foreland–South Goodwins; last of four patrols |
| 22:10-23:00 | 441 | IX | *MJ139, MK177, MK350, MK415, MK417, MK420, MK460, MK465, MK466, MK515, MK630, MK633* (MK465, Brochu: crashed in sea, 22:40 hrs; pilot rescued 42 hrs later) |
| 22:20-23:15 | 303 | V | E and 10 miles S of Beachy Head; *W3262, BL617* |
| ??:??-23:10 | 234 | V | Hastings–Beachy Head, 15 miles S of Dungeness |

## Nos. 11 & 85 Groups

**Anti-reconnaissance patrols (No enemy aircraft encountered)**

| | | | |
|---|---|---|---|
| 05:25-07:55 | 91 | XIV | Solent; *NH697, NH705* |
| 05:35-07:35 | 322 | XIV | Solent area; *B, H* |
| 05:40-??:?? | 124 | VII | *EN509, MB916* |
| 06:55-??:?? | 124 | VII | *MD139, MD167* |
| 07:20-07:40 | 322 | XIV | Solent area; *A* |
| 07:20-08:25 | 322 | XIV | Solent area; *F* |
| 07:45-09:20 | 322 | XIV | Solent area; *X, Q* |
| 08:05-??:?? | 124 | VII | *MB766, MD164* |
| 08:55-10:10 | 91 | XIV | *NH654, RB182* |
| 09:05-??:?? | 124 | VII | *MD113, MD126* |
| 09:30-11:05 | 322 | XIV | Solent area; *H, F* |
| 10:30-??:?? | 124 | VII | *MB766, MD162* |
| 10:30-12:00 | 91 | XIV | Solent; *RB161, RB183* |
| 11:00-??:?? | 124 | VII | *MB825, MD145* |
| 11:30-12:55 | 322 | XIV | Defensive patrol, Isle of Wight; *X, Q* |
| 11:50-??:?? | 124 | VII | *MD112, MD145* |
| 12:30-14:05 | 91 | XIV | Solent; *RB174, RB182* |
| 12:30-??:?? | 124 | VII | *MD113, MD126* |
| 13:10-??:?? | 124 | VII | *MD163, MD164* |
| 13:30-??:?? | 124 | VII | *MB766, MB825* |
| 13:30-15:10 | 322 | XIV | Solent area; *U, Y* |
| 14:15-??:?? | 124 | VII | *EN509, MD139* |
| 14:30-15:05 | 91 | XIV | Solent; *RB183, RM617* |
| 15:15-??:?? | 124 | VII | *MB866*, one unknown |
| 15:30-17:00 | 322 | XIV | Solent area; *M, B* |
| 16:20-??:?? | 124 | VII | *MD163, MD164* |
| 16:30-17:20 | 91 | XIV | Solent; *RB165, RB186* |
| 16:45-18:10 | 91 | XIV | Solent; *RB180, RB188* |
| 17:20-??:?? | 124 | VII | *EN506, MD113* |
| 17:30-18:55 | 322 | XIV | Solent area; *V, M* |
| 18:20-19:50 | 124 | VII | Details unknown |
| 18:40-20:15 | 91 | XIV | Solent; *RB183, RM617* |
| 19:05-??:?? | 124 | VII | *MD126, MD145* |
| 19:35-21:10 | 322 | XIV | Defensive patrol, Isle of Wight; *Q, F* |
| 19:50-20:50 | 124 | VII | Details unknown |
| 20:20-21:45 | 124 | VII | Details unknown |
| 20:30-22:00 | 91 | XIV | Solent; *NH697, RB185* (abortive) |

| Time | Sqn | Type | Notes and aircraft used |
|---|---|---|---|
| 20:30-22:35 | 91 | XIV | Solent area; four aircraft |
| 21:20-22:30 | 124 | VII | Details unknown |
| 21:25-22:35 | 91 | SIV | Solent; *RB160, RB188* |

**Offensive operation**

| | | | |
|---|---|---|---|
| 18:00-19:45 | 165 | IX | *Rodeo* W of Ushant–Penmatch Point–Ile de Groix – return; photos taken of 'fishing' boats; *MK589-G, MK831-K, MK855-E* |

**Interception patrols/investigations**

| | | | |
|---|---|---|---|
| 10:55-12:05 | 403 | IX | Scramble, cover MTBs out of Portsmouth; *MJ752, ML411* |
| 12:55-??:?? | 126 | | X-raid, friendly; *MK993-O, ML214-K* |
| 16:30-18:36 | 616 | VII | X-raids, Start Point–Lizard |
| 17:45-17:50 | 616 | VII | X-raids, Start Point–Lizard |
| 18:30-18:57 | 41 | XII | X-raids, Start Point–Lizard; two aircraft |
| 18:30-19:00 | 616 | VII | Scramble; *G, F* |
| 18:32-19:01 | 165 | IX | X-raids, Start Point–Lizard; *MK426-D, MK854-H* |

**Shipping reconnaissance**

| | | | |
|---|---|---|---|
| 04.45-05.42 | 403 | | Also weather recce Cherbourg area; *MJ951, NH196* |
| 10:50-11:45 | 33 | | *BS286, MJ120* |
| 10:50-11:50 | 33 | | *MA524, MH606* |
| 11:50-??:?? | 33 | | Off Dieppe; *BS129, BS408* |
| 12:50-13:50 | 33 | | Off Ostend; *MA326(?), MK694* |
| 18:00-19:15 | 165 | | To St Mathieu; *MK514-Z, ML199-X* |
| 20:15-21:10 | 56 | | Calais–Ostend; two aircraft |
| 21:30-22:26 | 56 | | Boulogne–Dieppe; two aircraft |
| 21:49-22:56 | 611 | Vb | Off Le Havre |

The above data are based upon Squadron, Wing and Group records. An HQ Fighter Command report of operations 16:00 to 21:00 hrs 5 June 1944 summarised the activity as follows:

**General:**
12 shipping reconnaissance patrols
22 interception standing patrols
71 shipping protection patrols (and two by Hurricanes)
**Offensive:**
3 Spitfires 165 Sqn: offensive patrol over Britanny 18:00-19:45
8 Spitfires 56 Sqn: shipping reconnaissance Dieppe-Zebrugge 16:15-19:05
2 Spitfires 165 Sqn: shipping reconnaissance Channel Islands 15:30-16:40
2 Spitfires 165 Sqn: shipping reconnaissance off Brest 18:00-19:00
**Defensive:**
8 patrols by 322 Sqn Spitfires, Isle of Wight period 11:30-18.55
8 patrols by 92 Sqn Spitfires, Solent period 14:32-20:15
**Interceptions:**
2 616 Sqn Spitfires: X-raids Start Point–Lizard 16:30-18:36
2 41 Sqn Spitfires: X-raids Start Point–Lizard 18:30-18:57
2 165 Sqn Spitfires: X-raids Start Point–Lizard 18:32-19:01

# Fighter Activity

## Phase One

Twilight came early on that stormy, dreary evening of 5 June. Very rough seas made the Channel passage extremely unpleasant for those aboard the large, small and very small ships. Included were personnel aboard the three Fighter Direction Tenders, each with a vital role to play.

Spitfires and USAAF fighters ended shipping protection patrols at 22:30 hrs, then the night force took over to prevent the Luftwaffe attacking convoys and to assist Bomber Command by strafing gun sites. Thus, it operated in a night intruder role rather than just as a night defence interceptor force.

Almost first away was, surely surprisingly, one of the last front-line

Beaufighter VIfs, operating from Winkleigh in Devon. Along with a Mosquito, identity unknown and also of No. 406 (RCAF) Squadron, it was sent to patrol over the airfields at Lannion and Morlaix.

Fielding their total Mosquito FB Mk VI strength, Nos. 418 and 605 Squadrons operated between 23:45 and 04:30 hrs. They positioned their 24 aircraft close to prescribed airfields. Six AI Mk VIII radar-equipped Mosquitoes of 29 Squadron, also Mosquitoes of No. 515 Squadron, No. 100 Group, assisted them in their airfield neighbourhood watch. Additionally '418' and '605' each despatched another six aircraft. Their task was ground strafing synchronized with Bomber Command raids in three zones of the airborne forces' landing area, viz: Rontenay-Saillerie, St Martin de Varreville, and Sallanelles some 10 miles west of Le Havre. More precisely, four of 418 Squadron's aircraft patrolled the area 49° 20'N–49° 30'N–01° 30'W to the west coast of the Cherbourg Peninsula from 23:50 hrs until 04:45 hrs, and two more in the area 49° 20'N–49° 30'N–01° 30' W. No. 605 Squadron had two aircraft patrolling Cherbourg Peninsula's east coast between 23:50 and 04:45 hrs and another four simultaneously in the area 49° 10'N–French coast–00° 05'W to 00° 20'W from five minutes before Civil Twilight.

These twelve special intruders, as intended, forced searchlights and light anti-aircraft guns into action thus exposing their positions which were promptly set upon, those around Caen by No. 605 Squadron and in the west by No. 418 Squadron's Mosquito FB Mk VIs, thereby helping to clear the way for the transport force. Sims and Sharples of No. 418 Squadron were reckoned to be the first crew to penetrate into enemy airspace during the first-night phase of *Neptune*. The dozen Mosquitoes of No. 418 Squadron managed 20 attacks on airfields. Operating over the Cherbourg Peninsula the squadron claimed to destroy five AA guns and a railway bridge, and also fired at a number of trains. All intruders made way, in ample time, for the airborne forces.

Freelance standing patrols were carried out be 12 crews of No. 85 Squadron (No. 100 Group), three of No. 29 Squadron (No. 85 Group) and three of No. 151 Squadron (No. 10 Group). Their operations took place in these specified areas:

49° 30'N/03° 00'W–49° N/02° 20'W–49° 00'N/02° 10'W–49° 00'N–01° 10' W, then Vire–Argentan, Argentan–Bernay, Bernay–Pavilly, Pavilly–50° 05'N/01° 00'E, patrols being permitted between 5,000 and 8.000 ft. Patrols took place in three phases, times and respective squadrons being:

23:45–01:15 hrs: One of 29 Sqn (callsign *Love*), one of 151 Sqn (*Mike*), and four of 85 Squadron (*Nan, Oboe, Peter, Queenie*). That pattern was repeated by identical forces operating between 01:00 and 02:40 hrs and 02:35 and 04:05 hrs. Away from the assault area more Mosquitoes were active, as shown in the following summary.

Luftwaffe response to the night effort was very limited, the only claims by RAF night-fighters being an Me 410 shot down near Evreux by Flg Off LeLong and Sgt McClaren of 605 Squadron, and a 'probable' Ju 88 or Ju 188 claimed by Flg Off Pearce flying *MM504* of 409 Squadron. Guided by Wartling GCI station, he caught the raider over the Somme Estuary. No enemy night activity took place over the British Isles. All known night-fighter sorties are listed in the following summary.

### PHASE ONE: NIGHT ACTIVITY
### 21:00 hrs 5 June to Sunrise 6 June 1944

#### OFFENSIVE OPERATIONS:

(22:45–01:20 hrs) No. 264 Squadron: One Mosquito XII, first offensive patrol, Flt Lt Fox: *HK480*

(22:56–02:40 hrs) No. 406 Squadron: Beaufighter VIf *KW109* and Mosquito *W; Night Ranger*, Morlaix–Lannion area

(22:59–03:29 hrs) No. 29 Squadron: Five Mosquito XIIIs; patrols over northern France, Belgium, north-west Germany, Belgium; all uneventful: *HK416, HK513, MM463, MM516, MM548*

(23:00–02:25 hrs) No. 264 Squadron: Six Mosquito XIIIs patrol St Pierre–St Martin de Varreville: *HK477, HK502, HK516, HK519, MM493, MM549*

(23:05–01:45 hrs) No. 307 Squadron: Mosquito XII *HK141-P* patrols Leuuwarden

(23:08–05:45 hrs) No. 418 Squadron: All 18 Mosquito VIs operated. 12 attacked 20 airfields in France. Trains and five AA guns in Cherbourg Peninsula attacked. Dropped 8 x 250 lb and 10 x 500 lb HEs. One crash-landing at base. Individual aircraft identities – see Mosquito listing. (23:10–04:41 hrs) No. 605 Squadron: All 18 Mosquito VIs operated. Attacked ground targets around Caen pre-troop landings. Florennes, Laon and St Andre airfields bombed. Dropped 6 x 250 lb and 11 x 500 lb HEs. Me 410 shot down near Evreux.

| Time | Sqn | Aircraft type | serial(s) | Notes |
|------|-----|---------------|-----------|-------|
| 23:10-01:40 | 307 | Mosquito XIII | HK119-D | Patrol Leeuwarden |
| 23:23-02:30 | 25 | Mosquito XVII | HK293 | Neatishead patrol |
| 23:25-02:05 | 25 | Mosquito XVII | HK283 | Neatishead patrol |
| 23:30-02:10 | 25 | Mosquito XVII | HK280 | Happisburgh patrol |
| 23:30-02:25 | 25 | Mosquito XVII | HK304 | Neatishead patrol |
| 23:50-02:51 | 25 | Mosquito XVII | HK322 | Patrol Leeuwarden;shot down a Bf 110 off Ameland (Flg Off Bent/Flt Lt Davis) |
| 01:20-04:20 | 151 | Mosquito XIII | MM437 | *Ranger*, Vannes |
| 01:30-??:?? | 151 | Mosquito XIII | MM450 | *Ranger*, Kerlin Bastard; FTR |
| 03:20-05:25 | 25 | Mosquito XVII | HK293 | Patrol |
| 03:25-05:20 | 25 | Mosquito XVII | HK257, HK357 | Patrol |

**OPERATION *OUTMATCH*: Standing night patrols over English Channel shipping and where indicated (#) over the intended beachhead area. Two scrambles (+) called**

**No. 10 Group Area:**

| Time | Sqn | Aircraft type | serial(s) |
|------|-----|---------------|-----------|
| 22:30-01:45 | 68 | Beaufighter VIf | MM850 |
| 22:30-01:50 | 68 | Beaufighter VIf | V8613 |
| 22:40-01:45 | 406 | Beaufighter VIf | ND225 |
| 22:45-01:50 | 406 | Beaufighter VIf | ND221 |
| 22:45-05:45 | 151 | Mosquito XIII | MM438 |
| 22:45-05:45 | 151 | Mosquito XIII | MM479# |
| 22:50-01:10 | 151 | Mosquito XIII | MM572 |
| 22:50-02:20 | 151 | Mosquito XIII | MM494# |
| 23:40-??:?? | 29 | Mosquito XIII | HK515+ |
| 00:30-01:55 | 488 | Mosquito XIII | HK420 |
| 00:30-02:45 | 488 | Mosquito XIII | MM556 |
| 00:30-04:10 | 151 | Mosquito XIII | MM448# |
| ??:??-01:50 | 410 | Mosquito XIII | HK462 |
| ??:??-01:55 | 410 | Mosquito XIII | HK432 |
| 01:25-??:?? | 29 | Mosquito XIII | HK422+ |
| 01:55-??:?? | 604 | Mosquito XII | ? |
| 02:10-04:15 | 151 | Mosquito XIII | MM447 |
| 02:30-05:10 | 264 | Mosquito XIII | HK473, HK479-F, HK480-P, HK506-K, HK519, MM467 Flew six Dorrington patrols |
| 02:30-05:45 | 151 | Mosquito XIII | MM520 |
| 02:45-05:35 | 406 | Beaufighter VIf | KW102(?) |
| 02:45-05:45 | 151 | Mosquito XIII | MM479# |
| 03:00-06:00 | 406 | Beaufighter VIf | KW119 |
| 03:20-05:40 | 151 | Mosquito XIII | MM524 |

**No. 11 Group Area:**

| Time | Sqn | Aircraft type | serial(s) |
|------|-----|---------------|-----------|
| 22:25-01:05 | 409 | Mosquito XIII | MM619 |
| 22:25-01:20 | 409 | Mosquito XIII | MM491 |
| 22:29-01:15 | 409 | Mosquito XIII | MM510 |
| 22:30-00:45 | 409 | Mosquito XIII | MM589 |
| 22:30-00:55 | 96 | Mosquito XIII | MM577 |
| 22:30-01:00 | 96 | Mosquito XIII | MM451 |
| 22:40-01:25 | 125 | Mosquito XVII | HK252 |
| 22:45-01:15 | 125 | Mosquito XVII | HK318 |
| 22:45-01:20 | 125 | Mosquito XVII | HK346 |
| 22:45-01:30 | 125 | Mosquito XVII | HK262 |
| 23:00-01:15 | 604 | Mosquito XIII | MM567 |
| 23:00-01:35 | 604 | Mosquito XIII | MM569 |
| 23:00-01:45 | 604 | Mosquito XIII | MM496 |
| 00:20-02:25 | 96 | Mosquito XIII | MM499 |
| 00:20-03:45 | 409 | Mosquito XIII | MM518 |
| 00:25-02:25 | 409 | Mosquito XIII | MM523 |
| 00:25-02:35 | 409 | Mosquito XIII | MM555 |
| 00:25-03:50 | 96 | Mosquito XIII | HK499 |
| 00:30-03:45 | 96 | Mosquito XIII | MM495 |
| 00:45-03:05 | 125 | Mosquito XVII | HK284 |
| 00:45-03:15 | 125 | Mosquito XVII | HK299 |
| 00:50-01:10 | 125 | Mosquito XVII | HK245 |
| 00:50-03:30 | 125 | Mosquito XVII | HK247 |
| 01:00-01:35 | 125 | Mosquito XVII | HK238 |
| 01:00-03:15 | 604 | Mosquito XIII | MM529 |
| 01:00-03:15 | 604 | Mosquito XIII | HK457 |
| 01:00-03:30 | 604 | Mosquito XIII | MM517 |
| 01:25-01:55 | 96 | Mosquito XIII | MM492 |
| 01:25-04:05 | 409 | Mosquito XIII | MM504 (probably destroyed a Ju 88, Somme Estuary) |
| 01:25-04:10 | 96 | Mosquito XIII | HK417 |
| 01:50-03:50 | 125 | Mosquito XVII | HK309 |
| 02:00-05:45 | 604 | Mosquito XIII | MM500 |
| 02:45-04:50 | 125 | Mosquito XVII | HK316 |
| 02:45-04:50 | 125 | Mosquito XVII | HK355 |
| 02:45-04:55 | 125 | Mosquito XVII | HK291 |
| 02:45-05:00 | 96 | Mosquito XIII | HK370 |
| 02:50-04:55 | 409 | Mosquito XIII | MM573 |
| 02:55-05:00 | 604 | Mosquito XIII | MM509 |
| 03:00-05:00 | 604 | Mosquito XIII | MM552 |
| 03:00-05:00 | 604 | Mosquito XIII | HK522 |
| 03:40-05:05 | 96 | Mosquito XIII | HK406 |
| 03:50-05:05 | 125 | Mosquito XVII | HK346 |

**No. 12 Group Area: Patrols under Neatishead and Happisburgh Radar in defence of East Anglian bases:**

| Time | Sqn | Aircraft type | serial(s) |
|------|-----|---------------|-----------|
| 03:20-05:25 | 25 | Mosquito XVII | HK293 |
| 03:25-05:20 | 25 | Mosquito XVII | HK257 |
| 03:25-05:20 | 25 | Mosquito XVII | HK357 |
| 23:05-01:45 | 307 | Mosquito XII | HK141-K |
| 23:10-01:40 | 307 | Mosquito XII | HK119-D |

| | | | |
|---|---|---|---|
| 00:55-03:10 | 307 | Mosquito XII | *HK176-W* |
| 00:55-03:15 | 307 | Mosquito XII | *HK159-S* |

**No. 13 Group Area: Standing defensive patrol Dunbar–Fifeness–Arbroath:**

| | | | |
|---|---|---|---|
| 23:14-00:20 | 309 | Hurricane IIc | *LF658-H*, *LF705-K* (Flt Lt Jarram and Flt Lt Sawickis) |
| 22:45-23:53 | 899 | Seafires | Two Seafires patrolled Peterhead– Kinnaird Head– Collieston |

## Phase Two

Surprise, surprise! By an astonishing twist of fate one of the first Spitfires to protect the seaborne forces bound for Normandy was a Battle of Britain veteran, *X4272*, which in September 1940 served very briefly with No. 19 Squadron at Duxford before being withdrawn for armament modifications. In late spring 1941 it went to Rolls-Royce, Hucknall, where fitment with a Merlin XLV engine changed it into a Mk V. It had also been modified to carry two cannon. On D-Day it was with No. 501 Squadron and during the early morning overture *J-Johnnie* was being flown by Flt Lt J.R. Davies. For company it had another old-timer, *W3702*, in the hands of Sqn Ldr M.G. Barnett. These were but two of a number of long-serving Spitfires protecting the initial landings.

At Deanland, Friston and Horne, Spitfire air and ground crews had begun at 03:00 hrs the final preparations for the launch of their Spitfires. Mk Vs of No. 130 Squadron were first away at 03:42 hrs, followed at 03:48 hrs by those of No. 611 Squadron and at 04:00 hrs by No. 501 Squadron's contingent, all of which, at 04:30 hrs, began providing fighter cover as the landing forces closed in on France. No. 130 Squadron operated off Barfleur, No. 611 off *Omaha* Beach and No. 501 provided general support and rear support.

Throughout the ADGB, all the day fighter squadrons were brought to Readiness at 04:00 hrs, and at 04:40 hrs a section of Hurricanes belonging to No. 309 Squadron on detachment to Hutton Cranswick joined in. They stood by until 23:00 hrs without being called upon to operate.

Six more Spitfire Mk V squadrons took off at around 04:30 hrs and at 05:20 hrs relieved the opening team. These were on station when the troops began landing in force at 06:00 hrs. This time No. 234 Squadron was fielding a veteran Spitfire, *P8709*, flown by Flt Sgt S.T. Famrilon. With him was Flt Sgt Sims, and during their patrol at 4,000 ft they encountered light AA fire which possibly damaged *AA936*. Sims was unable to make it home and was last seen flying at 500 ft, south of St Catherine's Point. He and his Spitfire were the first to go missing during daylight on 6 June. No. 402 (RCAF) Squadron also fielded two old-timers, *W3129* and *W3250*, both of which faced heavy flak from Le Havre. To No. 350 (Belgian) Squadron went the distinction of being first to have a genuine Mk Vc, *AR492*, operating on D-Day.

Other early operators were two rocket-firing and two conventional fighter Typhoons of No. 137 Squadron which took off at 04:50 hrs to scour the eastern end of the Channel between Nieuport and Berck-sur-Mer at sea level and 1/2 mile off the coast. Their search for 'trade' led them to six enemy motor torpedo boats off Cap Griz Nez which would need watching.

An update of the weather conditions was undertaken by Sqn Ldr A.R. Hall DFC (*MK572-B*) and Plt Off R.A.N. McLaren (*MK475-A*) who took off at 05:15 hrs for the Le Havre–Cherbourg area. On their return they described the weather as 'shocking' with 'low cloud and heavy rain' from 10/10 cloud between 500 and 1,000 ft, with a second layer 10/10 between 4,000 and 10,000 ft. Three other No. 56 Squadron pairs returned from other Channel areas with similarly dismal weather reports.

Nevertheless, pairs of Spitfire HF Mk VIIs of Nos. 124 and 131 Squadrons were despatched hourly from 05:15 hrs to make high-level patrols; no chances were being taken. At the opposite end of the height scale and between Start Point and Portland Bill, sections of Spitfire Mk IXs of No. 126 Squadron operating at 3,000 ft commenced shipping protection patrols.

To make certain enemy aircraft could not attack the landing forces, eight Spitfire IXs of No.1 Squadron set off from Predannack at 05:30 hrs to deal with any likely offenders found at Kerlin Bastard and Vannes airfields.

Although the ADGB Mustang IIIs played a very limited part during the first day's operations, their initial participation also began early, at around 05:40 hrs, when a pair of No. 316 Squadron's aircraft were ordered to fly a brief defensive patrol. At 08:40 hrs another two flew the usual *Jim Crow* shipping reconnaissances off Den Helder and returned to report three large motor vessels.

The most difficult and demanding part of Operation *Neptune* began at 06:00 hrs when the vanguard of the vast army stormed ashore on the Normandy beaches. At the east end Commonwealth forces at around 07:30 hrs crossed flat, open beaches to reach sand dunes and buildings along promenades, while in the west the Americans confronted shoreline rocks and cliffs. As the actual landings began, Spitfire LF Mk IX squadrons replaced the old Mk Vs and were to mount the succeeding four patrols on this and indeed subsequent days, providing the troops with continuous protection by flying low- to medium-level patrols. As planned, each six-squadron 50 min patrol embraced eastern and western regions with one squadron guarding each end of the total patrol area. Returning from the fourth patrol, pilots of Nos. 403, 416 and 421 Squadrons gave graphic descriptions of the sinking of a 'cruiser' in the western area by shore batteries, and of small ships being sunk too, some by rocket fire.

At the western end of the English Channel, No. 263 Squadron had, despite appalling weather, eight Typhoons searching for shipping around Ile de Batz and Ushant between 07.00 and 07.30 hrs. While they searched, more Typhoons went into action for the first time on D-Day in support of troops landing in the eastern beach area, thereby carrying out the first close support action during the invasion. Expectation that the Luftwaffe must soon intervene was reaching fever pitch, but a combination of poor weather and the enormity of the Allied air force undoubtedly discouraged the defenders. What were not similarly daunted were more aged Spitfires, found in particular among the ranks of No. 402 (RCAF) Squadron. Among them, when they took off at 09:45 hrs carrying 45 gal drop tanks, were *P8788, W3250* yet again, *W3454* and, in the hands of Plt Off. G.W. Lawson one of the best known, perhaps best loved of all Spitfires, *AB910*. Still such an active,

hallowed member of the Battle of Britain Memorial Flight today, *AB910* was particularly busy, and flew many sorties during the early weeks of the invasion. It would be pleasing to report that her lifelong partner *P7350* was there. Sadly, no such luck!

Phase Two of the fighter protection officially ended at 11:00 hrs – and still the vaunted Luftwaffe had not shown up. More importantly, the RAF squadrons could gaze down upon a sea covered by ships and see the Allied soldiers swarming ashore. There had been some very fierce fighting, but the very bad weather which gave them a fearsome crossing ironically helped them – once they were ashore. This time they could not, as they did at Dunkirk, ask 'Where is the RAF?' It was so obvious, for all to hear, or see; and perhaps most amazingly of all, only one Spitfire was so far missing.

### PHASE TWO: FIGHTER ACTIVITY
### Sunrise to 11:00 hrs 6 June 1944

ASSAULT AREA COVER:
50-minute low cover patrols, each squadron theoretically flying 12 Spitfires.
Eastern assault area:
Nos. 64, 130, 234, 303, 345, 350, 402, 501 and 611 Squadrons flying Spitfire Vs, remainder flying Spitfire IXs.
TOBA = Time Over Beach Area

**PATROL 1: 03:42–06:17 hrs (TOBA: 04:30 hrs)**
No. 130 Squadron: Individual aircraft identities unknown
No. 611 Squadron: *AR364, AR427, AR467, AR608, BL263, BL472, BL541, BM368, EE665, EE680*
No. 501 Squadron: *W3702-M, X4272-J, AA945-E, AB989-C, BL409-L, BL632-S, BM256-V, BM304-T, BM593-Q, EP395-A, EP757-O*
**PATROL 2: 04:30–07:10 hrs (TOBA: 05:20 hrs)**
*Western assault area:*
No. 234 Squadron: *P8709, AB279, AR343, BL235, BL563, BL646, BM200, EN858, EN903, EP766, EP768, AB976* (Flt Sgt Sims crashed in sea 10 miles S of St Catherine's Point)
No. 345 Squadron: *AD227, AD386, AR328, AR405, BL496, BL673, BL927,*

BM178, BM312, BM366, BM413, EP284
No. 64 Squadron: W3656, AA756, AA972, AB143, AB194, AB403, BL370, BL374, BM129, BM327, BM414, EP601
*Eastern assault area:*
No. 303 Squadron: AB271, BL292, BL385, BL464, BL697, BL730, BM207, BM348, EE753, EP411, EP509
No. 402 Squadron: W3129, W3250, AA738, AD180, BL547, BL969, BM205, BM233, BM490, EE680, EE715
No. 350 Squadron: W3759, W3970, AB276, AR492 (Mk Vc), BL780, BM343, BM344, EE613, EE723, EN950 (Flt Lt Benesoen baled out 25 miles SW of Friston)

**PATROL 3: 05:20–07:50 hrs (TOBA: 06:10 hrs)**
*Western assault area:*
No. 302 Squadron: MK309, MK370, MK520, MK723, MK688, MK745, MK905, MK915, MK924, MK958, MK999
No. 308 Squadron: MH374, MH750, MK578, MK679, MK720, MK981, ML113, ML183, ML231 and two unknown
No. 317 Squadron: 12 Spitfire IXs; individual aircraft identities unknown
*Eastern assault area:*
No. 222 Squadron: MH416, MK663, MK774, MK784, MK797, MK804, MK829, MK896, MK906, ML193
No. 349 Squadron: MJ253, MJ353, MJ502, MJ748, MJ879, MJ964, MK148, MK153, MK178, MK252, MK302, MK354
No. 485 Squadron: MK677, MK849, MK886, MK897, MK904, MK914, MK950, ML176, ML355, ML377, ML412

**PATROL 4: 06:20–08:25 hrs (TOBA: 07:00 hrs)**
*Western assault area:*
No. 403 Squadron: 'LVC' (Wg Cdr Chadburn), MJ238, MJ348, MJ570, MJ886, MJ951, MK570, MK808, ML415, ML420, NH235 and one unknown
No. 416 Squadron: MJ575, MJ611, MJ770, MJ828, MJ872, MJ874, MJ929 (spare only), MJ953, MK139, MK207, MK559, ML292
No. 421 Squadron: MH415, MJ820,

MJ855, MJ870, MJ880, MJ994, MK199, MK472, MK573, MK920, NH183, NH344 and one unknown
*Eastern assault area:*
No. 441 Squadron: MJ139, MK177, MK350, MK399, MK415, MK417, MK420, MK460, MK515, MK633, MK737, ML205
No. 442 Squadron: Individual aircraft identities unknown
No. 443 Squadron: Individual aircraft identities unknown, but included *MH850-H*

**PATROL 5: 07:20–09:20 hrs (TOBA: 07:50 hrs)**
*Western assault area:*
No. 66 Squadron: MH715, MH723, MJ150, MJ559, MJ581, MK228, MK297, MK449, MK474, MK586, ML123, MH254, NH173
No. 331 Squadron: Individual aircraft identities unknown
No. 332 Squadron: Individual aircraft identities unknown
*Eastern assault area:*
No. 310 Squadron: MJ291, MJ477, MJ509, MJ605/9(?), MK198, MK242, MK280, MK304, MK964, NH174, NH179
No. 312 Squadron: MH474, MJ499, MJ751, MJ792, MJ799, MJ840, MJ881, MK483, MK580, MK775, MK895 and one unknown
No. 313 Squadron: JK840, MJ201, MJ293, MJ361, MJ668, MJ900, MK180, MK208, MK211, MK291, MK320

**PATROL 6: 07:55–10:15 hrs (TOBA: 08:40 hrs)**
*Western assault area:*
No. 132 Squadron: Individual aircraft identities unknown
No. 453 Squadron: Individual aircraft identities unknown
No. 602 Squadron: MH512, MH709, MH716, MJ239, MJ252, MJ276, MJ981, MK232, MK235, MK612, MK624, ML307, NH203
*Eastern assault area:*
No. 401 Squadron: MH413, MJ131, MJ128, MJ180, MJ246, MJ289, MJ313, MK263, MK300, MK902, ML129, ML305,
No. 411 Squadron: 'GCK' (Wg Cdr G.C. Keefer), MH754, MJ125, MJ313, MJ454, MJ468, MK776, MK832, MK885, NH195, NH243

No. 412 Squadron: *MH450, MH826,
MJ148, MJ193, MJ334, MJ384, MJ485,
MJ959, MK237, MK253, MK622,
MJ633* and one unknown
**PATROL 7: 08:45–11:10 hrs (TOBA:
09:30 hrs)**
*Eastern assault area:*
No. 234 Squadron: *AA973, AB183,
AR343, BL235, BL415, BL563, BL981,
BM200, EN768, EN858, EN903* and
one unknown
No. 303 Squadron: *AA929, AB271,
AD204, BL292, BL385, BL464, BL617,
BL630, BL697, BM207, BM348, EE753*
No. 345 Squadron: *W3310, W3843,
AA847, AB986, AD238, AD386, AR328,
AR405, BL496, BL673, BM312, EP284*
*Western assault area:*
No. 329 Squadron: *NJ912-Z, MK265-B,
MK293-I, MK301-L, MK319-X,
MK347-V, MK359-H, MK416-A,
MK418-N, MK453-K, NH151-T*
No. 340 Squadron: *MJ351-J, MJ744-O,
MJ746-H, MJ822-U, MJ896-Z, MJ960-
F, MJ966-B, MK115-P, MK127-G,
MK183-T, MK290-D, MK294-R*
No. 341 Squadron: *MJ363, MJ564,
MJ617, MJ662, MJ671, MJ723, MJ772,
MJ780, MJ815, MJ890, MK201, MK365*
**PATROL 8: 09:25–11:35 hrs (TOBA:
10:20 hrs)**
*Western assault area:*
No. 64 Squadron: *W3656, AA756, AA972,
AB143, AB194, AB403, AD132, BL370,
BL734, BM129, BM327, EP601*
(09:35-11:20 hrs) No. 130 Squadron:
Individual aircraft identities unknown
(09:26-11:57 hrs) No. 611 Squadron :
*P8038, AR364, AR427, AR467, AR608,
BL263, BL472, BL692, BM368, EE660,
EE665, EP300*
*Eastern assault area:*
(09:35-10:30 hrs) No. 350 Squadron:
*W3759, W3970, AA720, AB180, AB276,
AR492, BL780, BM343, BM344,
BM583, EE613* (Mk Vc), *EE723,
EP242*
(09:45-12:15 hrs) No. 402 Squadron :
*P8788, W3250, W3454, W3529, AA920,
AB910* (Plt Off G.W. Lawson), *BL547,
BM205, EE680, EE686, EP548* and one
unknown
(09:50-12:05 hrs) No. 501 Squadron:
*W3702-M, X4272-J, AA945-E, AB989-
C, AR519-H, BL468-K, BL632-S,
BM256-V, BM593-Q, EE465-N, EP109-
R, EP707-B*

**Offensive operations**
(04:53-06:10 hrs) No. 137 Squadron: Four
Typhoons, eastern *Channel Stop* (*see
under* Typhoon operations)
(05:30-06:45 hrs) No. 1 Squadron: Eight
Spitfire IXs, *Roadsted 154*, Kerlin
Bastard–Vannes airfields; no enemy
activity: *MK659, MK744, MK901,
MK926, ML122, ML313, NH246* (Sqn
Ldr H.P. Lardner-Burk), *NH255*
(05:35-06:05 hrs) No. 501 Squadron: Two
Spitfire Vbs, E/R-Boat search, Cap de
la Hague to Barfleur (three E/R-Boats
in Cherbourg and three coasters):
*AD324-G, EP281-F*
(06:25-07:43 hrs) No. 263 Squadron: *see
under* Typhoon operations
(07:00-07:50 hrs) No. 486 Squadron: Two
Tempest Mk Vs search off Boulogne;
see under Tempest
(08:25-09:40 hrs) No. 91 Squadron: Four
Spitfire XIVs sweep to Boulogne:
*NH654, RB165, RB180, RB183*

**Defensive standing patrols**
(03:26-05:25 hrs) No. 25 Squadron: Three
Mosquito NF XVIIs patrol off East
Anglia; *HK257, HK293, HK357*
(04:25-06:00 hrs) No. 91 Squadron: Two
Spitfire XIVs patrol of Thames Estuary:
*NH701, RB188*
(05:20-11:45 hrs) No. 124 Squadron: 12
Spitfire HF VIIs, in pairs, patrol 50
miles S of Brighton: *EN506-MD113,
MD112-MD145, MB766-MB825,
EN509-MD167, MD139-MD886,
MD130-MB916* (10:15-11:45 hrs)
(05:40-05:55 hrs) No. 316 Squadron: two
Mustang IIIs patrol off East Anglia:
*FB135-M, FX903-R*
(08:40-09:30 hrs) No. 316 Squadron: two
Mustang IIIs patrol off Great Yarmouth:
*FB276-N, FX864-Q*
(09:35-10:30 hrs) No. 350 Squadron: Two
Spitfire Vs patrol 50 miles S of
Brighton

**Shipping reconnaissance patrols**
(05:00-05:48 hrs) No. 316 Squadron: Four
Mustang IIIs, shipping search to Betten;
seven stationary ships seen
(08:40-09:35 hrs) No. 56 Squadron:
Channel search, Boulogne–Dieppe:
*MK715-T, ML115-S*

**Shipping protection patrols**
(04:50-09:30 hrs) No. 74 Squadron: 12

Spitfire IXs (paired) patrol Isle of Wight–Dover. Individual identities unknown

(05:15-08:27 hrs) No. 126 Squadron: 12 Spitfire IXs (paired) patrol S of Plymouth to S of Portland: *MK993-O, MK995-N, ML214-K, NH340-A, MK893-P, MK923-Z, MK126-G, ML397-D, MK923-Z, MK989-L, ML398-F* and one unknown

(05:15-12:05 hrs) No. 131 Squadron: Eight Spitfire HF VIIs (paired) patrol S of Plymouth to S of Portsmouth: *MD110, MD119, MD132, MD165, MD168, MD169, MD170, MD171*

(09:15-10:55 hrs) No. 127 Squadron: Two Spitfire IXs patrol Convoy *Shark*, No. 11 Group area: *ML247, ML348*

(09:28-11:05 hrs) No. 126 Squadron: Two Spitfire IXs patrol S of Portland

(09:30-10:45 hrs) No. 610 Squadron: Two Spitfire XIVs patrol S of Plymouth

**Meteorological reconnaissance**

(05:16 -06:55 hrs) No. 56 Squadron: Two Spitfire IXs, Le Havre area: *MK475-A, MK572-B*

(05:55-06:10 hrs) No. 56 Squadron: Four Spitfire IXs, Abbeville–Gravelines: *MK378-H, MK633-O, MK794-?, MK955-M*

**Enemy response**

(09:47-10:05 hrs) 15 fighters operating 60 miles S of Le Havre

(09:54-10:05 hrs) One enemy aircraft operating 35 miles SSE of Le Havre

# Phases Three to Five

By mid-morning all the Allied air forces were asking 'Where *is* the Luftwaffe?' Tackling the protecting fighters would have been suicidal for the enemy, and it is little wonder that his reaction in daylight was so limited. During mid-morning there had been groups of German fighters milling around far to the south of the battle area. No. 443 Squadron caught sight of two Fw 190s but was unable to close on them. Enemy response was almost negligible. At 12:10 hrs Flg Off Anderson of No. 80 Squadron glimpsed a Ju 88 at 3,500 ft well south of Dover and possibly intent upon attacking shipping. He closed on the raider which, he reported, promptly jettisoned its load and fled. Heavy German guns firing from the Pas de Calais may have been responsible for the splashes seen.

There were half-hearted attempts by Ju 88s to bomb ships, using cloud cover. They were hotly engaged by anti-aircraft gunners who bagged an Fw 190 just after it had dropped a bomb which caused casualties and damage on HMS *Bulolo*, the HQ ship which controlled fighter-bomber ground attacks. Very soon after landing, ground forces had balloons flying to prevent fighter-bomber attacks on assault beaches. Updated intelligence indicated that Luftflotte 3 had some 500 serviceable aircraft – 160 day and 50 night-fighters, and some 185 bombers for certain.

In its diary No. 64 Squadron recorded seeing no enemy aircraft, and that 6 June was 'not eventful as imagined'. But during its afternoon patrol the Selsey Wing comprising Nos. 222, 349 and 485 Squadrons patrolling the Eastern Sector was directed to a group of Ju 88s. Blue Section, 222 Squadron, led by Plt Off R.H. Reid (*MK863*) chased four of them, fired at one, but made no claim. Not so No. 485 Squadron whose Blue Section, led by Flg Off J. Houlton destroyed two. One, the first enemy aircraft shot down by fighters in daylight on D-Day, fell to Houlton (*ML407*) and the other three pilots – Flt Lt K.J. Macdonald (*MK732(?)*), Flg Off Mayston (*MK897*) and Flt Sgt E.G. Atkins (*ML377*) – shared the other. No. 349 Squadron also shot down two and damaged three more.

Small formations of German fighters were also airborne during the afternoon and Flt Lt H. Russel and Flg Off G.F. Ockenden between them picked off a Bf 109. Less fortunate were three reconnoitring Mustangs which, flying low and displaying their prominent invasion markings, were bounced by four Fw 190s which soon shot down one.

The main event of the evening phase was Operation *Mallard*, the movement in gliders of the 6th Air Landing Brigade, strongly escorted by fighters. It proved very memorable to the participants. 'The whole operation was like an H.G. Wells episode in *Things To Come*,' wrote No. 56 Squadron's diarist. 'Masses of ships off the Orne Estuary, hundreds of military aircraft over the beachhead, fires and smoke from the ground. Through all this arrived a train of tugs and gliders and their fighter escort, screaming over the beachhead at 200 to 300 ft. It all baffles description, must be left to the imagination. Never, as long as the pilots who took part in it live, will they ever forget that great operation, the greatest day in history.' The tugs were so slow that the fighters had to 'zig-zag' to keep pace with them.

With such tempting targets it was assumed the Luftwaffe would have a go, and Mustang pilots of No. 306 Squadron, also some flying top cover, caught brief glimpses of German fighters. But the enemy kept its distance.

Halfway through its evening patrol over *Sword* area, No. 401 Squadron saw 20 enemy aircraft approaching from the south. As the Spitfires climbed to attack, a Ju 88 sneaked in and placed bombs on the beach. The German fighters then turned back and the Ju 88 escaped into cloud.

As soon as darkness fell German bombers at last reacted. Assorted Ju 88s (including torpedo-bombers), Do 217s and He 177s – about 150 in all – released Hs 293 glider-bombs, dropped guided FX1400s, laid 'oyster' mines in Seine Bay and operated at low levels against shipping. This time there were casualties and ships were damaged, but Mosquito night-fighters were also in the area. Among them was *HK286*, second-highest scoring Mosquito night-fighter and being flown by Wg Cdr K. M. Hampshire, CO No. 456 Squadron, who shot down a KG40 He 177 off Cherbourg. Two more fell to *HK290* and one to *HK303*, all of No. 456 Squadron. *HK248* of No. 219 Squadron destroyed a Ju 188 and an Me 410 fell to *HK319*. No. 604 Squadron was also very active, an Me 410 falling to *MM500* and four other enemy aircraft being claimed.

Although throughout 7 June the Luftwaffe made no sustained effort to reach the lodgement area, several Fw 190s and Me 410s penetrated Allied shipping lanes, and managed to sink an American destroyer and a landing ship. Inland, enemy fighters attempted to protect the Wehrmacht in the Flers–Romilly area. In total, it was a pathetic response to such a portentous event, but the wide-ranging pre-invasion onslaught by the Allied air forces – which most surely made the invasion practicable – had taken an enormous toll of the Luftwaffe's ability to fight.

## PHASE THREE: FIGHTER ACTIVITY
### 11:00 to 16:00 hrs 6 June 1944

ASSAULT AREA COVER
**PATROL 9: 11:15–13:25 hrs (TOBA: 12:00 hrs)**
*Western assault area:*
No. 403 Squadron: *MJ238, MJ348, MJ570, MJ664, MJ572, MJ951, MJ988, MK570, MK808, ML415, NH196, NH235*
No. 416 Squadron: *MJ575, MJ770, MJ787, MJ824, MJ929, MK117(?), MK139, MK207, MK835, MK837, ML292*
No. 421 Squadron: *MJ820, MJ870, MJ880, MJ891, MJ987, MJ994, MK199, MK472, MK573, MK891, MK920, NH344*
*Eastern assault area:*
No. 441 Squadron: *MJ139, MK350, MK399, MK415, MK420* (flak- damaged, crash-landed base; Plt Off F.A.W.K. Wilson), *MK460, MK504, MK515, MK630, MK633, MK737, ML205*
No. 442 Squadron: Individual aircraft identities unknown
No. 443 Squadron: Individual aircraft identities unknown

**PATROL 10: 12:15–14:25 hrs (TOBA: 12:50 hrs)**
*Western assault area:*
No. 331 Squadron: Individual aircraft identities unknown
No. 332 Squadron: Individual aircraft identities unknown
No. 66 Squadron: *MH715, MH723, MJ150, MJ559, MK228, MK449, MK569, MK586, ML123, NH150, NH173, NH254*
*Eastern assault area:*
No. 310 Squadron: *MJ291, MJ477, MJ509, MJ530, MJ605, MJ722, MJ825, MK198, MK242, ML343, NH174* and leader's aircraft
No. 312 Squadron: *MH499, MJ499, MJ572, MJ840, MJ900, MK180, MK244, MK580, MK775, MK805, MK895, MK983* and one uncertain
No. 313 Squadron: *JK840, MJ201, MJ361, MJ668, MJ900, MK188, MK189, MK205, MK211*
**PATROL 11: 13:05–15:15 hrs (TOBA: 13:40 hrs)**
*Western assault area:*
No. 132 Squadron: Individual aircraft

identities unknown

No. 453 Squadron: 11 aircraft; individual identities unknown

No. 602 Squadron: *MH508, MH512, MH709, MH736, MJ239, MJ305, MJ339, MJ981, MK232, MK255, MK612, MK624, ML307* and one uncertain

*Eastern assault area:*

No. 401 Squadron: *MH724, MJ131, MJ138, MJ246, MJ289, MK195, MK300, MK780, MK845, MK902, ML305, NH403*

No. 411 Squadron ('GCK' leading): *MH498, MJ454, MJ468, MJ985, MK776, MK832, MK843, MK885, NH195, NH243* and two uncertain

No. 412 Squadron: *MH826, MJ144, MJ148, MJ193, MJ334, MJ386, MJ392, MJ959, MK622, MK633* and two uncertain

**PATROL 12: 13:40–16:05 hrs (TOBA: 14:30 hrs)**

*Western assault area:*

No. 303 Squadron: *W3373, AA860, AA929, AB271, AD204, BL292, BL385, BL464, BL630, BL697, EE753, EP509*

No. 234 Squadron: *P8709* (Flg Off J. Metcalf), *AA973, AB183, AB279, AR343, BL233, BL415, BL981, BM200, EN858, EN861, EP766*

No. 345 Squadron: *W3310, AA847, AB986, AD386, AR405, BL496, BL673, BL927, BM312, BM413, EP284* and one uncertain

*Eastern assault area:*

No. 329 Squadron: *MJ524-C, MK132-S, MK293-I, MK301-L, MK319-X, MK359-H, MK374-Y, MK416-A, MK418-N, MK453-E, MK839-R, NH151-T*

No. 340 Squadron: *MJ177-S, MJ744-O, MJ518-W, MJ822-U, MJ960-F, MJ966-B, MK123-C, MK183-T, MK196-E, MK204-N, MK290-D, NH249-M*

No. 341 Squadron: *MJ363, MJ564, MJ617, MJ662, MJ671, MJ780, MJ910, MK238, MK844, NH270*

**PATROL 13: 14:40–17:00 hrs (TOBA: 15:20 hrs)**

*Western assault area:*

No. 302 Squadron: *MK309, MK520, MK568, MK688, MK716, MK719, MK745, MK786, MK905, MK924, MK958, MK999*

No. 308 Squadron: *MH374, MH423, MH750, MJ294, MJ503, MK578,*

*MK679, MK720, MK918, ML183, ML231* and one uncertain

No. 317 Squadron: Individual aircraft identities unknown

*Eastern assault area:*

No. 222 Squadron: *MK663, MK774, MK787, MK797, MK799, MK804, MK863, MK889, MK892, MK906, ML193*

No. 349 Squadron: Individual aircraft identities unknown

No. 485 Squadron: *MK677, MK722, MK732, MK849, MK886, MK897, MK904, MK914, ML361, ML368, ML377, ML407*

**Offensive operations**

(10:55–12:10 hrs) No. 1 Squadron: Seven Spitfire IXs, *Roadsted 155*, sweep over Kerlin Bastard–Plouescat–Landenau–Vannes: *MK659, MK726, MK926, ML122, ML313, NH246, NH255*

(11:55–13:35 hrs) No. 41 Squadron: Two Spitfire XIIs, *Rodeo*, St Malo: *MB798, MB842*

(14:00–15:45 hrs) No.1 Squadron: Four Spitfire IXs (*MK744, MK986, ML270, NH253*); No. 165 Squadron: Three Spitfire IXs (*MK480-F, MK838-K, MK855-E*) and Wg Cdr D. Smallwood; *Roadsted*, Gael–Vannes–Kerlin Bastard and attacking ground targets

**Defensive standing patrols**

(11:15–12:35 hrs) No. 91 Squadron: Solent patrol, two Spitfire XIVs: *RB161, RB174*

(10:15–16:45 hrs) No. 124 Squadron: Channel patrols by pairs of Spitfire HF VIIs: *MB916-MD130, MD163-MD164, MD139-MB886, MD113- EN506, MB766-MB827, MD145-MD127*

(11:00–16:35 hrs) No. 131 Squadron: Channel patrols by quartets of Spitfire HF VIIs: (11:00–12:30 hrs) *MD111, MD144, MD146, MD171*; (11:40–13:00 hrs) *MD110, MD120, MD129, MD169*; (13:00–14:40 hrs) *MD134, MD168, MD170, MD173*; (13:30–15:00 hrs) *MD110, MD117, MD132, MD165*; (15:30–16:35 hrs) *MD110, MD165, MD171, MD173*

(12:10–13:20 hrs) No. 91 Squadron: Solent patrol, two Spitfire XIV *NH697, RB182*

12:25–13:50 hrs. No. 610 Squadron. Solent patrol, two Spitfire XIVs;

individual aircraft identities unknown

(12:30–12:50 hrs) No. 616 Squadron: Two
Spitfire VIIs: *P, Q*

(13:05–14:30 hrs) No. 91 Squadron:
Solent patrol, two Spitfire XIVs:
*RB161, RM617*

(13:05–14:50 hrs) No. 616 Squadron: Two
Spitfire VIIs: *W, Y*

(14:10–15:45 hrs) No. 91 Squadron:
Solent patrol, two Spitfire XIVs:
*NH654, NH720*

(14:40–16:25 hrs) No. 274 Squadron:
Four Spitfire IXs: *BS128, BS395,
MA585, MH603*

(14:40–16:00 hrs) No. 610 Squadron:
Solent patrol, two Spitfire XIVs:
individual aircraft identities unknown

(15:00–16:35 hrs) No. 616 Squadron: Two
Spitfire VIIs: *Y, P*

(15:38–16:09 hrs) No. 309 Squadron: Bell
Rock patrol, two Hurricane IIcs:
*LF658-E, LF705-K*; plot was 'friendly'

(15:50–17:30 hrs) No. 274 Squadron:
Four Spitfire IXs: *BS284, BS474,
LZ919, MH853*

## Shipping reconnaissance patrols

(12:34–14:35 hrs) No. 316 Squadron: Two
Mustang IIIs, Hook-Terschelling

(12:15–13:20 hrs) No. 41 Squadron:
Spitfire XII *MB881*

## Shipping protection patrols

(10:15–11.40 hrs) No. 1 Squadron: Two
Spitfire IXs patrol S of Dartmouth;
individual aircraft identities unknown

(10:25–11:45) hrs No. 41 Squadron: Three
Spitfire XIIs: *MB803, MB804, MB837*

(10:27–14:56 hrs) No. 41 Squadron: Four
Spitfire XIIs, two patrols S of Lizard;
individual aircraft identities unknown

(12:40–??:?? hrs) No. 80 Squadron: Four
Spitfire IXs patrol Foreland–Dover:
*EN127, MA301, MA806, MA842*

(10:30–11:55 hrs) No. 127 Squadron: Two
Spitfire IXs, Channel; individual
aircraft identities unknown

(10:30–13:00 hrs) No. 131 Squadron: Two
Spitfire VIIs patrol S of
Portland–Plymouth; individual aircraft
identities unknown

(11:27–13:34 hrs) No. 126 Squadron: Two
Spitfire IXs patrol S of Portland;
individual aircraft identities unknown

(11:29–16:00 hrs) No. 610 Squadron:
Four Spitfire XIVs patrol S of Lizard;
individual aircraft identities unknown

(11:30–14:19 hrs) No. 1449 Flight: Four
Hurricane IIcs patrol S of Dartmouth;
individual aircraft identities unknown

(11:35–13:00 hrs) No. 127 Squadron: Two
Spitfire IXs patrol eight miles off
Dover: *ML209, NH190*

(11:35–15:20 hrs) No. 616 Squadron:
Four Spitfire VIIs patrol
Portland–Plymouth; individual aircraft
identities unknown

(12:05–13:14 hrs) No. 80 Squadron: Four
Spitfire IXs patrol area S of
Dover–Folkestone: *AB196, EN172,
JL227, MH878*

(12:28–13:50 hrs) No. 610 Squadron: Two
Spitfire XIVs patrol S of Lizard;
individual aircraft identities unknown

(12:35–14:10 hrs) No. 127 Squadron:
Four Spitfire IXs patrol Solent–Dover;
individual aircraft identities unknown

(13:05–14:45 hrs) No. 610 Squadron: Two
Spitfire XIVs patrol S of Portland;
individual aircraft identities unknown

(13:55–15:25 hrs) No. 33 Squadron: Four
Spitfire IXs cover 26-ship convoy in
Channel: *BS286, MA326, MA814,
MH606*

(13:25–15:10 hrs) No. 229 Squadron:
Three Spitfire IXs patrol Channel;
individual aircraft identities unknown

(14:00–15:15 hrs) No. 165 Squadron: Two
Spitfire IXs patrol S of Dartmouth:
*MK881-S, ML119-X*

(15:10–16:50 hrs) No. 33 Squadron: Four
Spitfire IXs continue convoy cover:
*MA524, MH666, MJ120, MJ216*

## Scrambles

(14:17–14:54 hrs) No. 41 Squadron: Two
Spitfire XIIs protect returning B-24, N
of Sept Ile: *MB481, MB843*

(13:05–15:41 hrs) No. 1449 Flight: Four
Hurricane IIcs investigate plot SW of
Scilly Isles; individual aircraft identities
unknown

(15:35–16:10 hrs) No. 309 Squadron:
Hurricane scrambled, recalled: *LF658-
E*

## Enemy activity

(11:17–11:26 hrs): One enemy defensive
patrol 30 miles S of Le Havre

(11:27–12:00 hrs): One enemy
reconnaissance aircraft NE of Shetland
Isles

(11:35–12:15 hrs): One enemy aircraft
plotted S of Boulogne

168

(12:00–12:35 hrs): One enemy reconnaissance aircraft NE of Shetland Isles
(14:48–15:11 hrs): Two patrols each of two aircraft over Netherlands

**PHASE FOUR: FIGHTER ACTIVITY 16:00 hrs to 21:00 hrs 6 June 1944**

ASSAULT AREA COVER:
**PATROL 14: 15:30–17:35 hrs (TOBA: 16:10 hrs)**
*Western assault area:*
No. 403 Squadron: *MJ238, MJ752, MJ886, MJ951, MJ988, MK808, ML411, ML415, ML420, NH196, NH235* and one unknown
No. 416 Squadron: *MJ575, MJ611, MJ770, MJ787, MJ824, MJ882, MJ953, MK117, MK835, MK837, ML292*
No. 421 Squadron: *MJ235, MJ820, MJ855, MJ870, MJ880, MJ891, MK199, MK994, NH183, NH344, NH415*
*Eastern assault area:*
No. 441 Squadron: Individual aircraft identities unknown
No. 442 Squadron: Individual aircraft identities unknown
No. 443 Squadron: Individual aircraft identities unknown
**PATROL 15: 16:20–18:25 hrs (TOBA: 17:00 hrs)**
*Western assault area:*
No. 331 Squadron: Individual aircraft identities unknown
No. 332 Squadron: Individual aircraft identities unknown
No. 66 Squadron: Individual aircraft identities unknown
*Eastern assault area:*
No. 310 Squadron: *MJ477, MJ509, MJ530, MJ605, MJ722, MJ825, MK242, MK964, ML343, NH174, NH179*
No. 312 Squadron: *MH474, MH499, MJ553, MJ572, MJ799, MJ881, MJ940, MK180, MK244, MK449, MK483, MK895, MK912*
No. 313 Squadron: *MJ201, MJ291, MJ293, MJ361, MJ668, MJ900, MJ963, MK189, MK205, MK208, MK211*
**PATROL 16: 17:05–19:05 hrs (TOBA: 17:50 hrs)**
*Western assault area:*
No. 132 Squadron: Individual aircraft identities unknown
No. 453 Squadron: Individual aircraft

identities unknown
No. 602 Squadron: *MH508, MH526, MH708, MH709, MJ239, MJ252, MJ276, MJ305, MK232, MK614, MK624, ML307, NH203*
*Eastern assault area:*
No. 329 Squadron: Individual aircraft identities unknown
No. 340 Squadron: *MJ177-S, MJ746-H, MJ834-Z, MJ896-X, MJ960-F, MJ966-B, MK115-P, MK123-C, MK127-G, MK202-L, MK204-N, MK290-D, MK294-R*
No. 341 Squadron: *MJ363, MJ564, MJ617, MJ662, MJ723, MJ815, MJ890, MJ910, MK201, MK365, MK844, NH270*
**PATROL 17: 18:15–20:15 hrs (TOBA: 18:40 hrs)**
*Western assault area:*
No. 130 Squadron: Individual aircraft identities unknown
No. 501 Squadron: *W3378-Y, W3702-M, AA945-E, AB989-C, AD465-N, BL468-K, BL632-S, BM304-T, EP109-R, EP395-A, EP398-P, EP707-B*
No. 611 Squadron: *P8038, AA839, AR427, AR608, BL263, BL692, BM203, BM203, BM258, BM641, EE665, BM131, EP300*
*Eastern assault area:*
No. 401 Squadron: *MJ131, MJ180, MJ231, MJ246, MK185, MK780, MK845, MK885(?), ML135, ML305, NH403*
No. 411 Squadron: 'GCK' (Wg Cdr G.C. Keefer), *EN566, MH498, MH754, MJ287, MJ454, MJ468, MJ905, MK776, MK832, MK885* and one unknown
No. 412 Squadron: *MJ136, MJ144, MJ148, MJ193, MJ255, MJ384, MJ392, MJ485, MJ959, MK237, MK622, MK633*
**PATROL 18: 18:45–21:00 hrs (TOBA: 19:30 hrs)**
*Western assault area:*
No. 302 Squadron: *MK723* (Wg Cdr Kowalski), *MK520, MK563, MK688, MK716, MK719, MK745, MK786, MK905, MK924, MK958, MK999* and two unknown
No. 308 Squadron: *MH374, MJ294, MJ503, MK578, MK679, MK720, MK918, ML113, ML117, ML183, ML231, PL269*
No. 317 Squadron: Individual aircraft identities unknown
*Eastern assault area:*
No. 222 Squadron: *MH416, MK784,*

MK787, MK799, MK804, MK863,
MK883, MK896, MK906, ML193,
ML414
No. 349 Squadron: Individual aircraft
identities unknown
No. 485 Squadron: MK677, MK754,
MK722, MK849, MK867, MK914,
MK950, ML368, ML377, ML407, ML412

**PATROL 19: 19:40–21:40 hrs (TOBA: 20:20 hrs)**
*Western assault area:*
No. 403 Squadron: 'LVC' (Wg Cdr
Chadburn), MJ238, MJ348, MJ664,
MJ988, MK808, MK881, MK951,
ML411, ML420, NH196, NH235
No. 416 Squadron: MJ611, MJ770, MJ787,
MJ824, MJ872, MJ874, MJ929, MK117,
MK139, MK559, MK837, ML292
No. 421 Squadron: MJ793, MJ820,
MJ880, MJ987, MK199, MK472,
MK920, MK993, MK994, NH344 and
two unknown
*Eastern assault area:*
No. 441 Squadron: Individual aircraft
identities unknown
No. 442 Squadron: Individual aircraft
identities unknown
No. 443 Squadron: Individual aircraft
identities unknown

**Offensive operations**
(16:00–17:40 hrs) No. 165 Squadron:
Eight Spitfire IXs, *Rodeo*, Grand
Champs–Mauron area; uneventful:
MJ221-T, MK242-A, MK426-D,
MK471-N, MK589-G, MK752-W,
MK811-S, ML119-X
(17:30–19:00 hrs) No. 131 Squadron:
Eight Spitfire VIIs repeat above
operation: MD119, MD120, MD132,
MD134, MD144, MD146 and two
unknown
(17:35–19:20 hrs) No. 91 Squadron: 12
Spitfire XIVs sweep to Rouen: NH654,
NH698, NH701, NH705, NH707,
NH710, NH714, NH720, RB169,
RB185, RB188, RM617
(19:35–21:00 hrs) No. 131 Squadron:
Eight Spitfire VIIs patrol Lyme Bay:
MB884, MD111, MD117, MK120,
MD129, MD146, MD170, MD171
(20:00–22:05 hrs) No. 165 Squadron: 11
Spitfire IXs, *Rodeo*, north-west France:
MJ221-T (FTR, Flt Lt A.D. May),
MK199-X, MK242-A, MK471-N,
MK480-F, MK514-Z, MK564-Y,
MK589-G (FTR, Flt Lt G. Clouston),

MK749-L, MK811-S, MK855-E

**Defensive standing patrols**
(15:10–20:35 hrs) No. 124 Squadron: 10
Spitfire VIIs, Channel patrols;
individual aircraft identities unknown
(15:15–18:15 hrs) No. 322 Squadron: Six
Spitfire XIVs, Isle of Wight area;
individual aircraft identities unknown
(15:38–16:09 hrs) No. 309 Squadron: Two
Hurricane IIcs, Bell Rock: LF658-E,
LF705-K
(16:35–18:00 hrs) No. 610 Squadron: Two
Spitfire XIVs, Solent patrol; individual
aircraft identities unknown
(18:00–21:08 hrs) No. 322 Squadron: Six
Spitfire XIVs, Isle of Wight area;
individual aircraft identities unknown

**Shipping patrols**
(15:00–17:59 hrs) No. 1 Squadron: Six
Spitfires, paired patrols S of
Dartmouth: MK659-MK926, MK901-
ML313, MK726-ML122
(15:38–19:55 hrs) No. 41 Squadron: 12
Spitfire XIIs, shipping/ASR, paired
patrols S of Lizard: MB620-MB881,
MB845-MB862, MN795-MB882,
MB620-MB881, MB795-MB862,
MB803-MB837
(15:50–17:30 hrs) No. 274 Squadron:
Four Spitfire IXs patrol North Foreland
to Dover: BS284, BS474, LZ919,
MH853)
(15:58–17:25 hrs) No. 126 Squadron: Two
Spitfire IXs patrol of Portland–
Plymouth: MH381-S, MK893-P
(16:25–17:50 hrs) No. 127 Squadron:
Four Spitfire IXs patrol S of Beachy
Head: ML185, ML238, NH194, NH313
(16:44–17:55 hrs) No. 610 Squadron: Two
Spitfire XIVs patrol south of Lizard;
individual aircraft identities unknown
(16:20–17:50 hrs) No. 274 Squadron:
Four Spitfire IXs, Dungeness patrol:
MA579, MA810, MH349, MH379
(17:40–20:10 hrs) No. 1449 Flight: Four
Hurricane IIcs patrol S of Dartmouth:
BE173, BN114 17:40–19:15 hrs; Z2985,
JS340 18:40–20:10 hrs
(18:03–19:25 hrs) No. 131 Squadron:
Four Spitfire VIIs patrol S of
Portland–Plymouth: MD117, MD129,
MD169, MD186
(18:15–20:00 hrs) No. 486 Squadron: Two
Tempest Vs patrol 20 miles E of
Beachy Head; individual aircraft

identities unknown
(18:35–20:00 hrs) No. 3 Squadron: Four
Tempest Vs patrol S of Beachy Head;
individual aircraft identities unknown
(19:30–20:15 hrs) No. 127 Squadron: Four
Spitfire IXs patrol S of Beachy Head:
*MK680, ML238, ML247, ML348*

**Interception patrols**
(16:00–16:38 hrs) No. 1449 Flight: Two
Hurricane IIcs investigate plot off
Scilly Isles; friendly: returning
Liberators: *BE173, JS340*

**Enemy activity**
(17:30–18:05 hrs): Enemy reconnaissance
aircraft 70 miles SW of Scilly Isles
(18:41–19:35 hrs): Defensive response by
20 enemy aircraft, first plotted 20 miles
SE of Evreux
(19:21–19:35 hrs): Defensive response by
30 enemy aircraft, 50 miles SE of Le
Havre

**PHASE FIVE: FIGHTER ACTIVITY
21:00 hrs 6 June 1944 to Sunrise 7 June
1944**

ASSAULT AREA COVER:
**PATROL 20: 20:35–22:50 hrs (TOBA:
21:10 hrs)**
*Western assault area:*
No. 331 Squadron: Individual aircraft
identities unknown
No. 332 Squadron: Individual aircraft
identities unknown
No. 66 Squadron: *MH715, MJ143,
MJ150, MJ559, MK297, MK449,
MK474, MK569, MK586, NH150,
NH173, NH254*
*Eastern assault area:*
No. 310 Squadron: *MJ291, MJ509,
MJ722, MJ906, MK198, MK280,
MK304, MK605, MK964, ML343,
NH174, NH179*
No. 312 Squadron: *NH474, NH499, NJ553,
MJ572, MJ881, MK180, MK244,
MK449, MK483, MK580, MK895* and
one unknown (possibly *NH546*)
No. 313 Squadron: *MJ118 MJ668, MJ900,
MJ963, MK189, MK201, MK205,
MK208, MK291, MK320, MK606* and
one unknown
**PATROL 21: 21:30–23:15 hrs (TOBA:
22:00 hrs)**
*Western assault area:*
No. 132 Squadron: Individual aircraft

identities unknown
No. 453 Squadron: Individual aircraft
identities unknown
No. 602 Squadron: *MH512, MH526* (ASP
P.H. Clostermann, FF), *MH709, MH716,
MH736, MJ276, MJ305, MJ981,
MK232, MK255, MK624, NH203*
*Eastern assault area:*
No. 401 Squadron: *MJ131, MJ138(?),
MJ180, MJ231, MJ246, MJ289,
MK195, MK300, MK780, ML129,
ML135, NH403*
No. 411 Squadron: 'GCK', *EN566,
MH498, MJ125, MJ287, MJ454,
MJ468, MJ905, MK754, MK776,
MK885* and one unknown
No. 412 Squadron: *MJ136, MJ144,
MJ148, MJ193, MJ334, MJ384, MJ392,
MJ485, MJ959, MK253, MK622*
**PATROL 22: 22:00/6th–00:20 hrs/7th
(TOBA: 22:50–23:40 hrs)**
*Western assault area:*
No. 130 Squadron: Individual aircraft
identities unknown
No. 64 Squadron: *W3234, W3656, AA756,
AA972, AB143, AB403, AD132, BL370,
BL374, BM129, BM327.* Last aircraft
back landed 00:10 hrs
No. 611 Squadron: *P8038, AA839, AR427,
BL692,* BM131, *BM200, BM345,
BM368, BM641, EE660, EE665.* Last
aircraft back landed 00:20 hrs
*Eastern assault area:*
No. 402 Squadron: *P8788, W3250,
W3454, W3529, AA738, AA920 AB910*
(Plt Off H.C. Nicholson), *BL969,
BM490, BM645, EE686, EP548* and
one unknown
No. 501 Squadron: *W3378-Y, AB989-C,
AD324-G, AD465-N, AR392-D, AR519-
H, BL409-L, BL632-S, BM304-T,
EP109-R, EP281-F, EP757-O*
No. 350 Squadron: *W3759, W3970,
AA720, AB180, BL780, BM343,
BM344, BM583, EE613* (Sqn Ldr
Donnet), *EE723, EP242, EP667*

**Offensive operations
Operation *Mallard* – No. 11 Group
*Ramrod 976*: 19:50–22:30 hrs**

**Fighters providing escort cover to tugs
and gliders**
(20:30–22:35) No. 19 Squadron: 11
Mustang IIIs escort Halifax/Hamilcar:
*FB113, FB116, FB122, FB153,
FB201, FB227, FX882, FZ141,*

171

FZ166, FZ186, FZ195

(20:15–22:25) No. 33 Squadron: 11 Spitfire IXs fly top cover to glider release: *BS286, BS348, BS408, MA807, MA814, MH666, MH692, MH777, MH823, MJ120, MK694*

(19:50–22:25) No. 56 Squadron: 12 Spitfire IXs escort Albemarles: *MK475-A, MK517-P, MK572-B, MK585-F, MK633-O, MK715-T, MK909-E, MK955-M, ML115-S, ML266-L, ML341-G, ML351-C*

(20:25–22:15) No. 65 Squadron: 13 Mustang IIIs escort Halifaxes/Hamilcars: *FB102, FB160, FB173, FX884, FX905, FX944, FX967, FX988, FZ112, FZ129, FZ151, FZ166, FZ173*

(19:50–22:25) No. 80 Squadron: 11 Spitfire IXs escort Albemarles: *AB196, BS556, EN127, JL227, MA228, MA301, MA842, MH671* and two unknown

No. 129 Squadron: 11 Mustang IIIs: *FB108-G, FB125-F, FB165-T, FB169-H, FB171-S, FB212-J, FX941-X, FX959-M, FZ121-V, FZ130-D, FZ184-Z*

(19:40–22:50 hrs) No. 229 Squadron: Spitfire IXs escort Dakotas; individual aircraft identities unknown

(19:52–22:00 hrs) No. 234 Squadron: 12 Spitfire Vbs escort Dakotas: *P8709, AB279, AR343, BL235, BL415, BL981, BL992, BM200, EN768, EN858, EN903, EP766*

(19:40–22:50 hrs) No. 274 Squadron: Five Spitfire IXs escort Dakotas: *BS227, MA818, MH349, MH603* and one unknown

(20:00–22:35 hrs) No. 302 Squadron: Eight Spitfire IXs escort Stirlings: *MK372* (Wg Cdr Kowalski), *MK688, MK716, MK745, MK786, MK924, MK958, MK999*

(20:15–22:10 hrs) No. 306 Squadron: 12 Mustang IIIs escort Halifaxes/Hamilcars; individual aircraft identities unknown

(20:20–22:15 hrs) No. 315 Squadron: Mustang IIIs escort Halifaxes/Hamilcars; individual aircraft identities unknown

(20:00–22:00 hrs) No. 329 Squadron: Spitfire IXs *MJ524-C, MK132-S, MK301-L, MK319-X, MK322-J, MK347-V, MK359-H, MK416-A, MK418-N, MK453-E, MK839-R*

(20:00–22:00 hrs) No. 340 Squadron: 13 Spitfire IXs escort Stirlings: 'AGM' (Grp. Capt. Malan), *MJ177-S, MJ351-J, MJ518-W, MJ744-O, MJ822-U, MK123-C, MK127-G, MK183-T, MK196-E, MK202-L, MK290-D, NH249-M*

(20:15–22:15 hrs) No. 341 Squadron: 12 Spitfire IXs escort Stirlings: *MJ363, MJ498, MJ564, MJ617, MJ662, MJ671, MJ723, MJ815, MJ890, MJ910, NH270* and one unknown

(19:52–22:00 hrs) No. 345 Squadron: 12 Spitfire Vbs escort Dakotas: *W3310, AB986, AD386, AR328, AR405, BL496, BL673, BL927, BM178, BM366, BM635, EP284*

**Daylight fighter offensive operations**

(20:00–22:05 hrs) No. 165 Squadron: 12 Spitfire IXs sweep over Brittany; Ju 88 destroyed near Landevant, goods train attacked nearby. *MK589-G* (Flt Lt Clouston) shot down; *MJ221-T* (Flt Lt May) crashed in sea, five miles S of base

(20:15–21:50 hrs) No. 610 Squadron: Eight Spitfire XIVs fly close escort to Typhoon attack off Gravelines

(20:30–22:50 hrs) No. 616 Squadron: Four Spitfire VIIs (*A, B, C, E*) sweep Gael–Vannes–Kerlin Bastard, attack trains at Baud, Bleomal and Vannes and radar station NE of Monchontour

**Protective night beach cover patrols**

(22:30–05:30 hrs) No. 264 Squadron: 11 Mosquito XIIIs fly patrols over western area: *HK473, HK475, HK477, HK480, HK502, HK516, HK518, HK519, MM455, MM549* and one unknown

**Night *Intruder* operations**

(22:18–05:26 hrs) No. 418 Squadron: 15 Mosquitoes operate over northern France and Brittany. Four Ju 52 and one Ju 88 destroyed, one aircraft damaged

**Transport targets attacked**

(22:40–23:46 hrs) No. 29 Squadron: Four Mosquitoes (*HK428, HK516, HK517, HK524*) patrol Coulommiers, Evreux, Melun and St Andre. Ju 88 destroyed by *HK524*; *HK516* shoots down an enemy aircraft and claims a 'probable' near Bretigny

(22:49–23:04 hrs) No. 151 Squadron: Two Mosquitoes (*MM447, MM479*) fly *Ranger* patrols to Vannes, Kerlin Bastard

(23:03–02:33 hrs) No. 406 Squadron: Two

Mosquito XIIIs patrol Lannion and Morlaix; *?????-D* claims a Do 217
(23:34–04:33 hrs) No. 605 Squadron: 10 Mosquito VIs operate patrols over Chartres*, Creil, Evreux, Florennes*, Juvincourt, Laon/Athies*, Orléans/Bricy*, St Andre* and St Trond*. (* Bombs dropped on these airfields)

**Defensive standing patrols**
*No. 10 Group area:*
(23:40–01:40 hrs) No. 151 Squadron: Mosquito XIIIs *HK503, MM511*
*No. 11 Group area:*
(20:15–22:05 hrs) No. 124 Squadron: Two pairs of Spitfire VIIs, eastern Channel: *MB916-MD163, MD164-EN509*
(20:15–22:40 hrs) No. 322 Squadron: Two pairs of Spitfire XIVs, Isle of Wight; individual aircraft identities unknown
(22:25–05:04 hrs) No. 410 Squadron: 10 Mosquito XIIIs, Channel: *HK458, HK459, HK467, HK532, MM457, MM462, MM477, MM501* and two unknown
(22:30–05:10 hrs) No. 96 Squadron: 15 Mosquito XIIIs (one FTR), Channel: *HK406, HK417, MM451, MM461, MM492, MM495, MM524* and eight unknown. All airborne before 23:59 hrs
(22:44–04:00 hrs) No. 29 Squadron: Two Mosquito XIIIs, Channel; individual aircraft identities unknown
(22:45–05:04 hrs) No. 125 Squadron: 14 Mosquito XVIIs, Channel: *HK287, HK299, HK309, HK316, HK325* and nine unknown. All airborne before 23:59 hrs
(22:45–05:15 hrs) No. 219 Squadron: 10 Mosquito XVIIs: *HK260, HK320, HK344, HK362* and six unknown
(22:45–05:15 hrs) No. 456 Squadron: 10 Mosquito XVIIs, Cherbourg area. Shot down four He 177s: Flg Off Stevens (*HK290*) two, Wg Cdr Hampshire (*HK286*) one, Flg Off Pratt (*HK303*) one.
(23:00–??:?? hrs) No. 604 Squadron: Two Mosquito XIIIs, Channel
(00:03–02:55 hrs) No. 488 Squadron. One Mosquito XII, Channel
(02:35–05:25 hrs) No. 409 Squadron. Nine Mosquito XIIIs, Channel: *MM453, MM504, MM510, MM512, MM547, MM555, MM574, MM587, MM619*

*No. 12 Group area:*
(22:14–22:35 hrs) No. 316 Squadron: Two Mustang IIIs patrol off Great Yarmouth; individual aircraft identities unknown
(23:04–03:10 hrs) No. 307 Squadron: Two Mosquito XIIIs patrol Humber–Scarborough area, two patrol over Netherlands: *HK129, HK194, HK200, HK234*
*No. 13 Group area:*
(21:50–22:52 hrs) No. 899 Squadron, FAA: Four Seafires patrol Peterhead–Collieston
(23:00–00:48 hrs) No. 118 Squadron: Two Spitfire Vbs patrol E of Shetland Isles
(23:14–00:08 hrs) No. 309 Squadron: Two Hurricane IIcs patrol Fifeness–Aberdeen: *LF658-E, LF705-K*
(23:45–01:06 hrs) No. 118 Squadron: Two Spitfire Vbs patrol E of Orkney
(23:45–01:14 hrs) No. 118 Squadron: Two Spitfire Vbs patrol Pentland Firth

**Shipping protection patrols (English Channel)**
(19:15–20:15 hrs) No. 127 Squadron: Spitfire IXs *MK680, ML238, ML247, ML348*
(19:45–20:37 hrs) No. 41 Squadron: Four Spitfire XIIs, individual aircraft identities unknown
(22:00–22:55 hrs) No. 131 Squadron: Four Spitfire VIIs, individual aircraft identities unknown
(20:10–21:20 hrs) No. 1449 Flight: Hurricane IIcs *BE173, BN114*
(21:50–05:54 hrs) No. 68 Squadron: Beaufighter VIfs *V8613, MM850, ND268* and one unknown
(22:40–04:46 hrs) No. 406 Squadron: Four Beaufighter VIfs, Operation *Bigot*–Channel patrol: *KW105, KW110, ND223, ND225*
(00:31–05:37 hrs) No. 151 Squadron: Four Mosquito XIIs, individual aircraft identities unknown

**Enemy night activity**
Over United Kingdom: nil
(00:30–01:00 hrs): One reconnaissance aircraft passed Shetland Isles
(03:28–03:38 hrs): One reconnaissance aircraft NE of Shetland Isles
(23:25–04:15 hrs): Defensive patrols – 162 enemy aircraft known to have operated over northern France, Belgium and Netherlands (mostly in area

Brussels–Ostend–St Omer–Beauvais–Laon). A few flew north to operate over or off the Dutch Isles and the Hook of Holland. Most headed for Evreux area, some operated over Seine Estuary and beachhead to attack shipping, and 51 sorties were recorded as operating off Cherbourg. Included were He 177s using Hs 293 glider bombs. No. 456 Squadron claimed to destroy four He 177s. Luftwaffe units thought to have operated included III/KG3, III/KG6, III/KG26, I/KG27, KG40 and I/KG66.

# De Havilland Mosquito fighters

The eight-gun Mosquito Mk II formed the basis for the whole range of Mosquito fighters, and by 1944 they were to be found in No. 100 (Bomber Support) Group and at training and research units and no longer in Fighter Command. Its derivatives, still powered by the Merlin XXI, played a major part in the night defence role.

First to evolve was the NF Mk XII, a modification of the Mk II fitted with a 'thimble' nose containing the scanner for AI MK VIII interception radar which replaced the four machine-guns. Prototype conversion using *DD715* began in July 1942, 100 airframes were selected for change, and on 2 January 1943 the first of 97 Mk IIs for production conversion flew into Marshall's at Cambridge. Modification was rapid and No. 85 Squadron, Hunsdon, which received the first example on 28 February, flew the first Mk XII patrol on 28 March 1943. AI Mk VIII represented a great advance over the long-used Mk IV, the first 'kill' by a Mosquito NF Mk XII

taking place on 14/15 April 1943. On D-Day only 27 Mk XIIs remained in the front line, being flown by Nos. 307 and 406 Squadrons.

The most common Mosquito night-fighter then was the NF Mk XIII, which equipped eight squadrons holding 155 examples. The Mk XIII represented the start of a second development phase from which also came the fighter-bomber Mk VI fitted either with Merlin 21 or 23 engines wedded to the 'basic' wing. The latter, also fitted to later bombers as well as fighters, enabled the carrying of external bombs or long-range fuel tanks, petrol load rising from 547 gal to 716 gal which converted into a most creditable 5½ hrs endurance and greater diversity, allowing the NF Mk XIII to operate as a fighter-bomber, in which role it operated in Italy.

Early Mk XIIIs had AI Mk VIII radar in the same type of 'thimble' nose as the Mk XII. Deliveries began in October 1943, the first Mk XIII patrol taking place on 8

*Mosquito NF Mk XIII* HK428-K *of No. 29 Squadron had the variant's early 'thimble' nose radome for its AI Mk VIII radar. (de Havilland)*

*Standard Mosquito NF Mk XIII MM560, seen at Le Culot on 5 October 1944.*

October with the first 'kill', by *HK367* of No. 488 Squadron, being made on 8 November 1943. A 264 Squadron Mosquito XIII, *HK480* flown by Flt Lt Fox, was probably the first night-fighter over the beachhead area on 5 June 1944.

The Mk XIII was the RAF's principal night-fighter in 1944, but others were being designed to accommodate superior radar by then available. To accommodate it a 'universal' nose was designed, primarily for the next mainstream 'upmarket' development, the NF Mk XIX. This had Merlin 25s for which boost pressure of up to +18 lb could be applied to improve low- and medium-level performance. In late 1943 the first new American SCR 720 AI radar, known to the British as AI Mk X, reached Hatfield. There it was installed in Mosquito *DZ659* for trials and proved to be the best AI yet devised.

Mosquito production was at a peak by then and because existing Mosquitoes were performing so well introduction of the NF XIX was delayed until March 1944 with *MM624*, the first production example, appearing the following month. Consequently, few Mk XIXs were in service by D-Day, and they were introduced to operations on 5/6 June 1944 by two Bomber Command No. 100 (Bomber Support) Group squadrons, Nos. 85 and 157.

The difference in performance between the Mosquito Mk II and later fighters lay more in their superior radar than anything else, and since a pool of Mk IIs remained, 100 were selected for fitment of the new SCR 720 radar. Marshall's Flying School converted 98 of what were designated NF Mk XVIIs which carried the radar in the older 'thimble' nose. First to equip were Nos. 25 and 85 Squadrons, the former flying the first operational patrol on 4 January 1944. At the time of D-Day five squadrons (two rearming) held 78 Mk XVIIs between them.

Mk XIXs became increasingly more common in the squadrons, particularly those of No. 100 Group. From mid-1944 their excellent low-level performance made them particularly useful when engaging V-1 flying-bombs and for strikes upon German airfields. At the other end of the performance envelope came the AI Mk X-equipped NF Mk 30, a Mk VI airframe powered by Merlin two-stage supercharger Merlin 72s. Its development was far from easy, burning through of exhaust shrouds being particularly difficult to eradicate before late 1944. The Mosquito fighter story had in the process come full circle; exhaust gases were just as keen to burn through the cowlings of the first of the breed.

# De Havilland Mosquito night-fighters on squadron strength, 5 June 1944

* operated on 5/6 June 1944

**AIR DEFENCE OF GREAT BRITAIN**
No. 10 Group
*No. 68 Sqn,* **Fairwood Common (rearming)**
   *HK307* 2.6.44-22.2.45

### No. 151 Sqn, Predannack
NF Mk XIII
| | |
|---|---|
| HK377 | 3.11.44-2.3.44, 19.5.44-30.11.44 |
| HK503 | 2.1.44-21.9.44 |
| *HK505 | 2.1.44-10.6.44 FTR |
| *MM437 | 12.2.44-14.12.44 |
| *MM438 | 20.2.44-? |
| MM446 | 22.2.44-11.8.44 |
| *MM447 | 11.2.44-? |
| *MM448 | 18.2.44-29.7.44? |
| *MM450 | 20.2.44-6.6.44 FTR |
| MM452 | 10.2.44-29.7.44 |
| MM459 | 18.2.44-18.8.44 |
| MM468 | 28.2.44-8.7.44 |
| MM469 | 29.2.44-29.7.44 |
| *MM479 | 1.3.44-8.9.44 |
| *MM494 | 6.3.44-? |
| *MM511 | 23.4.44-8.7.44 |
| *MM520 | 15.5.44-13.7.44 RIW |
| *MM524 | 22.4.44-29.7.44 |
| MM525 | 16.4.44-2.5.44, 19.7.44-21.9.44 |
| MM559 | 15.5.44-18.6.44 RIW |
| MM561 | 15.5.44-21.6.44, 16.8.44-28.9.44 |
| MM562 | 15.5.44-1.8.44 EFA |
| MM568 | 16.4.44-7.12.44 |
| *MM572 | 30.4.44-11.8.44 |
| HJ970 | T Mk III 20.4.44-24.6.44 |
| HJ980 | T Mk III 16.4.44-24.6.44 |

### No. 406 Sqn, Winkleigh (re-equipping with Mosquito NF Mk XII)
| | |
|---|---|
| HK138 | 23.4.44-14.6.44 Cat E |
| N-HK164 | 23.4.44-28.12.44 |
| HK179 | 23.4.44-? |
| HK223 | 31.3.44-7.44 |
| HK228 | 27.4.44-18.9.44 EFA |
| HK231 | 16.4.44-10.44 |

No. 11 Group
### No. 96 Sqn, West Malling
NF Mk XII
| | |
|---|---|
| *HK370 | 4.44-? |
| HK372 | 13.10.43-20.8.44 |

| | |
|---|---|
| HK376 | 17.10.43-3.7.44 |
| HK379 | 13.2.44-21.6.44 RIW |
| HK396 | 6.11.43-15.7.44 |
| *HK406 | 10.11.43-8.7.44 |
| *HK417 | 15.11.43-11.44 |
| HK419 | 22.11.43-26.8.44 EFA |
| HK421 | 1.12.43-8.7.44 |
| HK425 | 29.11.43-9.11.44 |
| HK433 | 22.3.44-22.2.45 |
| HK469 | 23.1.44-1.3.45 |
| HK499 | 5.44-6.10.44 FTR |
| *MM451 | 28.2.44-? |
| MM461 | 6.3.44-4.1.45 |
| *MM492 | 16.3.44-12.44 |
| *U-MM495 | 30.3.44-30.12.44 |
| *V-MM499 | 7.3.44- EFA 25.6.44 |
| *MM524 | ?-7.12.44 |
| *MM577 | 5.5.44-4.12.44 |

### No. 125 Sqn, Hurn
NF Mk XVII
| | |
|---|---|
| *HK238 | 31.5.44-10.1.45 |
| *HK245 | 30.5.44-1.2.45 |
| *HK247 | 8.2.44-22.2.45 |
| *HK252 | 7.2.44-11.6.44 BFA |
| HK256 | 30.5.44-7.10.44 FTR |
| HK262 | 7.2.44-22/23.2.45 FTR |
| HK263 | 7.2.44-29.3.45 |
| *HK284 | 8.2.44-9.9.44 |
| *HK287 | 3.2.44-5.3.45 |
| *HK291 | 7.2.44-21.8.44 FTR |
| *HK299 | 7.2.44-3.10.44 |
| *HK309 | 3.2.44-22.3.45 |
| HK310 | 10.2.44-25.6.45 |
| *HK316 | 10.3.44-22.3.45 |
| *HK318 | 10.2.44-1.3.45 |
| *HK325 | 12.2.44-5.4.45 |
| *HK346 | 5.2.44-1.3.45 |
| *T-HK355 | 5.2.44-22.3.45 |

### No. 219 Sqn, Bradwell Bay
NF Mk XVII
| | |
|---|---|
| HK248 | 16.2.44-28.10.44 |
| HK250 | 24.2.44-3.9.44 |

*Mosquito NF Mk XII HK425 served with No. 96 Squadron before joining No. 409 Squadron in November 1944. It was photographed at Twenthe.*

*HK254  26.2.44-14.2.45
*HK260  18.2.44-18.8.44
HK279  26.2.44-21.6.44 RIW
HK289  25.2.44-?
HK292  23.2.44-?
**HK308  7.4.44-27.8.44
HK315  2.3.44-11.7.44 EFB
*IIK319  24.2.44-2.8.44
**HK320  26.2.44-30.7.44 EFA
*HK344  16.2.44-2.8.44
*HK345  30.3.44-2.8.44
HK348  1.3.44-8.44
*HK358  26.2.44-10.6.44 EFB
*HK362  16.2.44-2.10.44

## No. 456 Sqn, Ford
NF Mk XVII
HK246  31.1.44-15.2.45
*HK249  31.1.44-30.8.44
HK253  29.1.44-8.2.45
HK264  29.1.44-8.3.45
**HK282  10.2.44-18.1.45
*HK286  29.1.44-4.1.45
*HK290  8.2.44-18.1.45
HK297  3.2.44-21.6.44
HK302  4.3.44-8.2.45
*HK303  6.2.44-18.1.45
*HK312  31.1.44-12.7.44 FTR
HK313  31.1.44-4.1.45
**HK317  6.2.44-9.6.44
HK323  10.2.44-4.1.45
*HK353  2.44-1.45
*HK356  29.1.44-4.1.45
*HK359  3.2.44-11.1.45
HJ899  (T Mk III) 7.4.44-7.7.44

## No. 11 Group – Intruders
## No. 418 (RCAF) Sqn, Holmsley South
FB Mk VI
HJ719  30.5.43-4.7.44
HJ821  8.7.43-16.2.45
HR137  12.5.44-4.1.45
HR149  12.5.44-23.7.44 EFA
HR183  29.5.44-17.7.44 EFB
K-HX811  18.7.43-8.9.44 FTR
MM426  14.2.44-14.2.45
G-NS830  14.2.44-5.1.45 FTR
NS839  19.2.44-6.1.45
NS857  21.2.44-1.2.45
NS858  19.2.44-6.6.44 BFB
W-NS856  24.4.44-30.9.44 FTR
U-NS930  4.4.44-27.2.45
T-NS991  6.6.44-17.5.45
NT137  2.6.44-19.6.44
NT152  2.5.44-11.1.45
NT155  2.6.44-23.11.44
C-NT195  29.5.44-19.7.44 EFA

## No. 605 Sqn, Manston
FB Mk VI
HJ729  ?-?
L-HJ779  19.6.43-3.10.44 FTR
HJ780  19.6.43-7.6.44
HR152  19.5.44-9? 10-2.45 FTR
HR155  19.5.44-10.44
LR379  31.5.44-1.11.44
NS838  9.3.44-11.12.44
NS842  9.3.44-1.11.44
NH878  9.3.44-31.8.44 FTR
NS880  31.3.44-26.6.44 EFA
NS892  12.3.44-13.6.44 EFB

NS914  8.3.44-23.9.44 AC FB
NS936  8.3.44-28.5.44
NS941  11.3.44-8.6.44 FTR
NS960  24.4.44-18.7.44 BFB
NT119  29.6.44-26.9.44 FTR
NT122  31.5.44-6.6.44 FTR
NT139  27.5.44-17.7.44
NT186  12.5.44-9.7.44 EFB

## No. 12 Group
## No. 25 Sqn, Coltishall
NF Mk XVII
HK237  22.12.43-28.9.44
HK243  3.5.44-16.10.44
HK244  21.1.44-28.9.44
*HK257  27.12.43-4.11.44
HK278  20.1.44-11.1.45
*HK280  15.2.44-23.10.44
HK283  6.1.44-25.10.44
HK285  22.12.43-4.11.44
HK288  21.1.44-13.6.44 FTR crashed at Empe, Netherlands
*HK293  29.1.44-12.7.44 BFA
HK298  2.3.44-4.11.44
HK300  23.1.44-24.9.44 FTR
HK301  23.1.44-16.10.44
*HK304  23.1.44-4.11.44
HK305  23.1.44-26.7.44 EFA
*HK322  25.1.44-20.2.45
HK354  28.1.44-9.6.44 FTR
*HK357  23.1.44-27.10.44

## No. 307 Sqn, Church Fenton
NF Mk XII
HK107  28.1.44-8.44
N-HK108  4.2.44-9.8.44 EFA
V-HK109  21.4.44-26.6.44
K-HK110  30.1.44-4.1.45
H-HK111  13.2.44-16.11.44
F-HK115  10.2.44-2.12.44 EFA
D-HK119  22.1.44-29.7.44 RIW
Z-HK129  10.4.44-4.1.45
P-HK141  6.2.44-28.12.44
*S-HK159  8.2.44-7.11.44 BFA
N-HK165  10.4.44-28.12.44
*W-HK176  10.4.44-23.6.44 Cat E
HK180  21.5.44-21.9.44
HK193  5.6.44-27.11.44
L-HK194  21.5.44-18.9.44 EFA
HK199  5.6.44-11.44
G-HK200  13.5.44-29.6.45
Q-HK201  21.2.44-28.12.44
J-HK206  13.5.44-26.6.44
HK230  21.2.44-7.8.44 FTR

## Fighter Interception Unit, Wittering
D-HJ702  (Mk II) 23.7.43-21.7.44
P-HJ705  (Mk II) 8.10.43-24.5.44
HK197  (Mk XII) 25.4.44-26.3.45
HK415  (Mk XIII) 22.11.43-29.7.44
HK427  (Mk XIII) 19.10.43-26.11.44
HK236  (Mk XVII) 30.11.43-8.3.45
A-HK360  (Mk XVII) 17.4.44-30.8.45

## De Havilland Mosquito night-fighters
No. 85 Group, 2nd TAF
## No. 29 Sqn, West Malling
NF Mk XIII
*HK403  11.11.43-1.3.45

177

*HK413 29.11.43-7.6.44 FTR
HK416 ?-?
HK422 22.11.43-8.3.45
*HK428 28.1.44-22.10.44
*HK513 10.4.44-4.2.45 EFA
C-HK515 28.1.44-22.7.44 AC FB
*HK516 detached from 264 Sqn 4.44-7.44
*HK517 10.4.44-23.9.44 FTR
L-HK522 10.4.44-27.8.44
*F-HK524 10.4.44-2.11.44
V-HK529 ?-?
HK530 10.4.44-2.12.44 FTR
*J-MM463 28.2.44-19.9.44 FTR
MM516 11.4.44-1.7.44 EFA
*B-MM548 13.5.44-16.7.44 EFA
Y-MM553 10.4.44-6.7.44 EFB
MM567 10.4.44-15.2.45

## No. 264 Sqn, Hartford Bridge
NF Mk XIII
HK471 31.12.43-18.7.44 EFB
HK472 27.12.43-27.8.44 BFA
*HK473 28.12.43-18.1.45
HK475 30.12.43-2.11.44
*HK477 27.12.43-23.1.45 BFA
*HK479 4.1.44-1.45
*HK480 30.12.43-24.6.44 FTR
*HK502 31.12.43-19.4.45 BFA
*HK506 7.1.44-9.11.44
HK512 7.1.44-15.10.44
HK514 14.1.44-28.9.44
*HK516 14.1.44-12.8.44 Cat E, burnt
*HK518 14.1.44-22.8.44 RIW
*A-HK519 14.1.44-16.11.44
HK531 3.5.44-30.8.44
MM455 1.3.44-22.8.45
*J-MM467 18.3.44-20.7.44 EFB
T-MM493 18.3.44-28.3.45
MM549 18.5.44-2.11.44
LR561 (T Mk III) 2.6.44-14.8.44

## No. 409 Sqn, Hunsdon/West Malling
NF Mk XIII
HK460 26.3.44-30.6.44 EFB
*MM453 19.3.44-20.9.44 FTR
MM491 21.3.44-5.10.44
*MM504 21.3.44-13.9.44
MM508 22.3.44-21.11.44
*MM510 25.4.44-27.7.44 EFB
*MM512 5.5.44-7.10.44 FTR
*MM518 1.5.44-15.7.44 EFA
*MM523 11.5.44-16.3.44, 11.5.44-10.3.45
*MM547 7.5.44-10/11.7.44 FTR
MM554 26.4.44-12.4.45 AC FA
*MM555 26.4.44-23.11.44
F-MM560 23.6.44-20.2.45 FA B
*P-MM573 25.4.44-28.6.44 EFA
*MM574 25.4.44-6.10.44 FTR
MM576 23.4.44-16.6.44 FTR
*MM587 5.5.44-7.8.44 EFB
*MM589 7.5.44-20.9.44 FTR
MM590 15.5.44-11.12.44
*MM619 24.5.44-29.10.44
LR540 (T Mk III) 30.5.44-19.6.44

## No. 410 Sqn, Hunsdon
NF Mk XIII
HK366 15.3.44-21.9.44
HK430 12.12.43-21.9.44
*HK432 2.12.43-2.7.44 RIW
HK456 12.43-?

*HK458 12.43-?
*HK459 15.12.43-13.6.44 EFB
*HK462 21.12.43-12.6.44
HK463 22.12.43-24.6.44 EFB
HK466 24.12.43-13.8.44
*HK467 12.43-?
HK470 22.12.43-21.9.44
HK501 7.1.44-10.7.44 EFB
HK521 8.2.44-12.6.44
HK523 23.1.44-29.7.44 BFB
MM447 15.3.44-23.6.44 FTR
MM449 28.2.44-21.9.44
D-MM456 1.3.44-3.9.44
*Z-MM457 18.3.44-21.6.44 EFB
MM458 2.3.44-28.4.44, 27.6.44-21.9.44
*K-MM462 28.2.44-3.7.44
*U-MM477 15.3.44-7.9.44
MM499 7.3.44-25.6.44 EFA
MM501 17.3.44-22.2.45
MM570 9.5.44-8.7.44 FTR
MM571 27.4.44-9.44?
MM620 21.6.44-19.10.44 FTR

## No. 488 Sqn, Zeals
NF Mk XIII
HK380 24.10.43-25.7.44
HK381 11.11.43-19.6.44
*HK420 29.11.43-19.4.45
*HK427 12.12.43-19.10.44
*HK504 4.1.44-6.10.44 FTR
HK532 30.3.44-4.1.45
*HK534 8.2.44-19.8.44
*MM439 29.2.44-8.9.44
E-MM466 25.2.44-9.11.44
MM476 25.2.44-17.6.44
MM498 18.4.44-21.9.44
MM502 30.4.44-20.9.44
*D-MM513 4.4.44-20.9.44
MM515 5.4.44-4.1.45
*MM519 31.3.44-30.9.44
*MM551 2.4.44-15.7.44 EFB
*B-MM556 11.4.44-5.8.44 AC FA
*MM558 9.4.44-25.6.44 BFA
MM588 11.5.44-7.7.44
LR562 (T Mk III) 31.5.44-3.9.44

## No. 604 Sqn, Hurn
HK170 Mk XII 2.3.44-7.10.44
HK232 Mk XII 16.4.44-28.12.44
*HK457 2.44-?
HK525 8.2.44-1.3.45
V-HK526 3.2.44-7.4.44, 14.6.44-27.8.44
HK527 2.2.44-2.11.44
MM460 5.3.44-6.44
MM465 1.3.44-11.1.45
N-MM478 5.3.44-2.11.44
A-MM488 5.3.44-2.11.44
*T-MM496 5.3.44-12.8.44 BFA
*MM500 4.3.44-15.11.44
*MM507 3.44-11.44
*MM509 10.5.44-19.10.44
*R-MM514 24.4.44-8.8.44
*MM517 11.4.44-22.2.45
*X-MM522 1.5.44-12.10.44
M-MM526 15.5.44-2.8.44 EFB, crashed at A8
MM528 10.5.44-28.8.44 EFA
*MM529 9.5.44-22.5.45
*S-MM552 11.4.44-26.4.45
MM563 5.5.44-26.8.44, 10.8.44-28.4.45
*J-MM569 27.4.44-12.10.44
MM621 4.7.44-7.8.44 FTR

# The Hawker Hurricane

It is not generally realized that the Hurricane was still a home-based front-line RAF fighter in June 1944. Perhaps even more astonishing, the first RAF aircraft to land and take off from an advanced landing ground in Normandy was a Transport Command Hurricane. The number of AEAF Hurricanes was nevertheless small, a mere 33 out of 2,723 in RAF hands of which 1,597 were in use overseas. Of the total, 22 (basically Mk IIcs) were serving at Drem in No. 309 (Polish) Squadron as tactical fighter-reconnaissance aircraft.

Another 10 of the tough Hurricanes, ideal for the purpose, were available on D-Day to No. 1449 Flight based at St Mary's for the defence of the Scilly Isles and vital nearby sea lanes. No. 1449 Flight's operational strength included two Mk IIbs, two Canadian-built Mk XIIbs, and one of the remaining 352 RAF Hurricane Mk Is of which 223 were still active with the RAF in Britain. Another 16 Mk Is, incidentally, were in MAP hands and the remaining 113 were overseas. The FAA held a further 47 Mk Is and 102 Mk IIs. Hurricane production was still underway in June 1944 and on D-Day two Mk IIs, *PZ746* and *PZ747*, were delivered to the RAF at No. 22 MU, Silloth.

No. 1449 Flight had formed with Hurricane Is in No. 10 Group on 10 April 1942 (to replace a detachment of No. 87 Squadron, based on the Scilly Isles), and received Mk IIs in March 1943. The Flight's final operation, flown on 29 August 1944 between 16:00 and 17:30 hrs, terminated the Hurricanes outstanding home defence career and involved *Z2985*, *HV839* and *JS383*. No. 1449 Flight disbanded on 17 September 1944.

## Operations carried out by No. 1449 Flight, 6 June 1944

11:25-12:55 hrs: *BE173* (Flt Sgt A.R.A. Day) and *JS340* (W. Off H.D. Stone) (Aus)

12:30-14:25 hrs: *Z2985* (Flg Off E.L.R. Poole) and *Z5307* (W. Off Goldsbrough)

13:55-14:20 hrs: *BE173* (Flt Lt C.E.O. Hamilton-Williams) and *JS340* (Flg Off D.J. Turner); scramble – intercepted friendly aircraft

14:30-15:25 hrs: *BE173* (as above) and *JS340* (as above); again scrambled – another friendly aircraft

16:30-16:45 *hrs: JS340* (Flt Sgt A.W. Anderson) and *BE173* (W. Off H.D. Stone); scrambled – friendly aircraft

17:40-19:15 hrs: *BE173* (Flt Lt C.E.O. Hamilton-Williams) and *BN114* (Flg Off D.J. Turner)

18:40-20:10 hrs: *Z2985* (Flt Sgt A.R.A. Day) and *JS340* (W. Off H.D. Stone)

20:10-21:10 hrs: *BE173* (Flt Lt C.E.O. Hamilton-Williams) and *BN114* (Flg Off D.J. Turner)

Sortie notes: Patrol 'Line C' by sections of two aircraft; 17:40–19:15 hrs escorted six destroyers

## Hawker Hurricanes on front-line squadron strength, 6 June 1944

### No. 309 Sqn, Drem (detachment Hutton Cranswick)

Mk IIc:

| | |
|---|---|
| G-LF331 | 23.5.44-4.10.44 |
| Z-LF335 | 7.5.44-25.10.44 |
| Y-LF342 | 7.5.44-17.10.44 |
| F-LF363 | (not flown operationally by No. 309 Sqn during June, but flown on ship protection patrols during July 1944) |
| A-LF620 | 1.4.44-6.11.44 |
| T-LF633 | 21.5.44-28.9.44 EFA, shot down in error, off Peterhead |
| LF647 | 23.5.44-13.10.44 |
| J-LF650 | 7.4.44-12.44 |
| E LF658 | 1.4.44-15.10.44 |
| O-LF685 | 11.4.44-25.10.44 |
| B-LF695 | 23.5.44-1.11.44 |
| L-LF699 | 10.4.44-25.10.44 |
| K-LF705 | 8.4.44-18.10.44 |
| W-????? | 5.44-10.44 |

### No. 1449 Flight, St Mary's, Isles of Scilly

Active aircraft June 1944 – full histories

Mk II:

| | |
|---|---|
| *Z2985 | 15 MU 16.4.41, 71 Sqn 28.4.41, 18 MU 21.5.41, 43 Sqn 18.6.41, Taylorcraft overhaul 1.4.42, 29 MU 4.6.42, 3 Sqn 12.6.42, B FA 2.2.43, RIW 11.2.43, 22 MU 28.5.43, 1449 Flt 25.8.43, flying accident during operations 19 June 1944, Cat E 29.9.44 |
| Z5307 | 48 MU 30.7.41, 79 Sqn 3.8.42, 615 Sqn 12.1.42, 79 Sqn 26.1.42, major overhaul at Field Consolidated 9.3.42, |

179

44 MU 29.4.42, 257 Sqn 26.5.42, 32 Sqn 29.6.42, 247 Sqn 22.9.42, Field Consolidated repair 8.3.43, 10 MU 3.4.43, 1449 Flt 18.8.43 to David Rosenfield for reduction to spares 2.11.44

*BE173  Hawker (Controller R & D) 11.9.41, A & AEE 11.4.43, B  FA 16.5.43 – Field Consolidated RIW, 5MU 17.9.43, 1449 Flt 13.4.44, 527 Sqn 28.9.44, SOC 31.2.45

*BN114  (Mk IIb) Hawker (Controller, R&D) 30.11.41, A&AEE 9.2.42, 87 Sqn 18.5.42, 174 Sqn 23.5.42, chosen for overseas 7.42 but allocation cancelled, retained by 174 Sqn, declared Cat B/RIW 18.4.43, ready 22.5.43, 20 MU 31.5.43, 1472 Flt 25.6.43, held by

1449 Flt 20.1.44-11.44

HV839  (Mk IIb) 22 MU 21.8.42, 175 Sqn 27.8.42, 56 OTU 5.5.43, 1449 Flt 24.4.44, 527 Sqn 28.9.44, 22 MU 7.11.44, SOC  30.11.45

Mk XII (designated Mk II on 1944 Census):

*JS340  Sailed from Halifax, NS, on SS *Demitrios Chandris* 18.6.42, arr UK 9.7.42, 13 MU 4.8.42, 48 MU 27.8.42, 247 Sqn 23.9.42, major inspection at Morrisons, Whittlesey 11.3.43, 48 MU 23.5.43, 1449 Flt 4.7.43, AC FA 20.9.44, Cat E 11.10.44

JS383  Late Canadian introduction – erected at 13 MU Henlow 8.4.43, 48 MU 11.5.43, 1449 Flt 21.5.43, Cat E 29.9.44

# The Hawker Tempest

Hawker launched the Typhoon II in July 1941 as a faster, longer duration Typhoon powered by the superior Sabre Mk IV. Most radical feature was its thin, elliptical planform wing designed to accommodate four cannon. Performance estimates of September 1941 encouraged the MAP to agree that production changeover to the Typhoon II should come quickly, and especially when the company announced plans for an even better version.

Although the Napier Sabre was in deep trouble, faith in the Mk IV was strong. Hawker forecast for the Typhoon Mk II

(Typhoon I bracketed) at top speed of 445 mph at 26,000 ft (409 mph at 20,000 ft), service ceiling of 37,900 ft (33,950 ft) and duration of 1.73 hours (1.54 hours), the latter achieved by moving the engine forward and making space for 180 gallons of fuel. Two radiators would be tucked beneath the new 295 sq ft area wing. On 17 September decision was made to order two prototypes. Unexpectedly, three weeks later, Fighter Command asked that the aircraft feature a 'Universal Wing' for either four cannon, or two cannon and four machine-guns with .50 in guns to attract

*The Tempest V prototype* HM595 *during development.*

USAAF interest. Redesign seriously delayed the fighter.

Two prototypes (*HM595* and *HM599*) were eventually ordered on 18 November 1941, Hawker promising the first would fly in March 1942 and production commence in spring 1943. Although the Sabre IV was forecast to pass type trials before 1942, Hawker's private belief was that the Typhoon II would initially have a refined Sabre II and that proved to be so when aircraft began leaving production lines in November 1943, six months' delay arising from wing redesign, radiator repositioning and Sabre problems.

Specification F.10/41 outlining the Typhoon II (Sabre IV) was drafted in December 1941. With a forecast diving speed of 550 mph at 10,000 ft the basic Typhoon airframe called for strengthening. The current chin radiator reckoned as unsuitable for the more powerful Sabre IV, RAE Farnbrough investigated (i) an enlarged version, (ii) the possibility of one, Mustang-like, under the aft fuselage, and (iii) wing leading edge radiators. Favoured were the drag-cutting latter. Hawker ideas for under-wing radiators *à la* Bf 109, complex to engineer, were abandoned in December 1941.

January 1942 brought a completely new approach for, with the Sabre IV distant and Sabre II still troublesome, Sir Henry Tizard suggested fitting the new very powerful Bristol Centaurus radial engine. On 24 January 1942 design of this variant was sanctioned and plans initiated for six development examples.

As Hawkers were being pressurized to hasten design work another challenge engulfed them; the Air Ministry had decided all new fighters must carry six cannon despite the obvious impracticality of the suggestion. Emphasis was also being directed towards installing .50 in guns needing large leading edge gun ports and having to be set well back on strong take-up points. Extensive gun heating arrangements were also necessary. Not until October 1942 did Fighter Command agree to forego the 'Universal Wing' concept and the Air Ministry forget six cannon in favour of a four cannon layout, all of which had seriously delayed development.

April 1942 saw the initiation of yet another version, the Hawker P.1061

Typhoon II with a Rolls-Royce Griffon II engine and ordered into production to replace the Napier Sabre. With the complex under-wing radiators it was now to enter service early in 1944 replacing all the Sabre examples! A further Typhoon II layout with a Griffon 61 two-stage supercharged engine would replace Griffon Spitfires. On 10 April 1942 Sydney Camm, Hawker's Chief Designer, presented likely performance details to the MAP showing the Griffon II aircraft attaining 400 mph at 20,000 ft and the Mk 61 machine reaching 430 mph at 31,500 ft. He was, incredibly, then told that all Griffon production was now earmarked for Spitfires! To review potential, CRD on 12 May 1942 told Hawker to fit a Griffon II into only the second Typhoon II. Contract amendments were clarified on 17 June 1942 calling for two each of the Sabre, Griffon and Centaurus versions. That the aircraft successfully operated is surely amazing.

Not surprisingly, the War Cabinet was deeply worried about the whole situation and particularly concerned about the Sabre saga. Only 1,400 engines were likely to be available by the time 3,260 Typhoon I/II airframes were completed thus forcing about half of them into pugatory store. Increased emphasis, therefore, became directed towards the Centaurus Typhoon despite a forecast low ceiling and poor rate of climb. Without the Sabre IV version the RAF would have to be satisfied with Griffon and Merlin Spitfires supplemented by Merlin Mustangs.

So different from the Mk I was the Typhoon II that on 6 August 1942 it was renamed Hawker Tempest of which four marks were then prescribed, *viz*, Mk I (Sabre IV), Mk II (Centaurus), Mk III (Griffon II) and Mk IV (Griffon 61). On 25 August 1942 agreement was reached that the radiator in the Mk I aircraft would be moved from under wing to mainplane root leading edges, not only to reduce drag but also to have additional protection from enemy fire. The change unfortunately reduced the fuel load to 123 gallons. Additional importance was given to the survivability aspect because the new fighter was not to have a low-level strike fighter role.

Increasing concern was being expressed over the high loaded weight of the new fighter – around 12,000 lb, and thus about twice that of early Spitfires. Mid-August 1942 saw the formulation of plans for a light fighter, Sydney Camm quickly proposing a scaled down Typhoon II with a 36 ft wing span and powered by any of the three engines already in vogue.

On 2 September 1942 Tempest *HM595* (Sabre II powered and fitted with a nose radiator just as Hawkers had forecast) was the first of the breed to fly and served as the Mk V prototype. In manner so utterly 'British Official' MAP pointed out on 5 September 1942 that no contract existed for any 'Hawker Tempest'! Nobody had suitably amended the contract so one was rapidly drawn up calling for a 'Special Typhoon I/P1 Sabre IV'. There had been inadequate compensation for moving the mainplanes further back than on the Typhoon, and flight trials showed needs for additional fin and rudder areas. After assorted configurations were tested a large dorsal fin fillet soon became standard. English Electric took control of Napier in December 1942 injecting differing management skills, inspection and production, into the Acton firm. They also abandoned the Sabre IV, the 50 built being re-designated Sabre Mk IIE. The change also brought the demise of any production prospect for the Tempest I although its prototype began flight tests on 29 January 1943. Production of 90 Tempests was scheduled for 1943 and all of a Mk V (Sabre II) version whose prototype testing showed a disappointing top speed of 420 mph at 15,000 ft and climb to 20,000 ft taking 6.35 minutes. Not surprisingly, there was a desire to forge ahead with the lightened version (which eventually became the sprightly post-war Fury – and delayed the Tempest II).

Trials revealed that the Tempest I handled better than the Mk V, although its engine required larger radiators. Without operational load it attained 458 mph at 25,600 ft.

By May 1943 the Tempest V was in production, the first example, *JN729*, making its initial flight on 21 June 1943. Fitted with long-barrelled Mk II 20 mm Hispano cannon this early version designated Mk V srs i carried 132 gallons of fuel which gave it a 2.8 hour duration when fully loaded, alternatively producing a range of 675 miles when cruising at 220 mph. Fully loaded it could reach 20,000 ft in 6.85 minutes, had a service ceiling of 34,800 ft and reached 411 mph at 6,600 ft (MS gear) or 432 mph at 18,400 ft (FS gear and +9 lb boost). Full load tests of the Mk I showed that to have a top speed of 439 mph. A week after *JN729* flew the Centaurus engined Mk II prototype *LA602* also first flew. The Mk II played no operational part in the European war and it was the Mk V which came into service early in 1944. Although on D-Day its task was home defence, within the reserve force, the Tempest V soon played a most active and valuable part intercepting flying-bombs and engaging Me 262s and flying ground attack operations.

## Operations

On 14 January 1944 No. 486 Squadron became the first to receive a Tempest V. Five were at Beaulieu for familiarization by the end of the month. Then on 28 February

*Tempest V Z-Zulu of No. 3 Squadron at Newchurch. (IWM CH14095)*

1944 two of them, soon followed by the rest, were passed to No. 3 Squadron at Manston which, on 6 March, moved to Bradwell Bay to begin conversion there and at Ayr. Next came the turn of No. 486 Squadron, which moved from Beaulieu to Drem on 28 February there to convert fully. Tempests began operations unspectacularly on 23 April 1944 when *JN734* and *JN736* of No. 3 Squadron flew an air/sea rescue sweep east of Orfordness. On 28 April the Squadron moved to its operational base, ALG Newchurch, where next day Tempests of 486 Squadron arrived with No. 56 Squadron, later the third Tempest squadron, to form No. 150 Wing, 85 Group. The first offensive operation came on 3 May when nine Tempests of No. 3 Squadron and eight from No. 486 made a sweep over Dunkirk Armentieres–Berck-sur-Mer–Dungeness as

part of Ramrod 826. No enemy fighters were encountered. Day rangers, dusk intruders against airfields, patrols and shipping reconnaissances followed, generally carried out by pairs of aircraft. The sorties flown by Tempests on D-Day brought little enemy reaction. That came on 8 June when, during a beachhead cover patrol by No. 3 Squadron led by Wg ,Cdr R.P. Beamont in *JN751* – the aircraft that became his usual mount – and flying with *JN739*, *JN743*, *JN745* and *JN797*, four German fighters were destroyed between them by the leader, Flt Lt Warne and Plt Off G.A. Witman. Such combats were relatively rare, and victories too – until the enemy unleashed his 'Doodlebugs'. First to score was 3 Squadron's Plt Off R. Dryland and by the end of that day the squadron had destroyed 11 V-1s.

## SUMMARY OF OPERATIONS BY TEMPEST Vs OF NO. 150 WING, NEWCHURCH, 6 JUNE 1944

| Time | No. | Sqn | Task and aircraft |
|---|---|---|---|
| 07:00-07:56 hrs | 2 | 486 | Search off Boulogne: *JN806*, *JN811* |
| 13:15-14:05 hrs | 2 | 3 | Escorting Beaufighters off Hardelot: *JN735*, *JN745* |
| 18:05-20:00 hrs | 2 | 486 | Ship protection 20 miles E of Beachy Head: *JN797*, *J809* |
| 18.35-20.00 hrs | 3 | 3 | Ship protection S of Beachy Head: *JN751*, *JN743*, *JN752* |
| 18:35-20:00 hrs | 4 | 3 | Ship protection: *JN738*, *JN755*, *JN769*, *JN796* |
| 21:41-23:17 hrs | 3 | 3 | Channel shipping protection: *JN753*, *JN759*, *JN812* |
| 21:45-23:10 hrs | 4 | 486 | Channel shipping protection: *JN793*, *JN818*, *?????* (3 Sqn aircraft) |
| 22:30-00:05 hrs | 6 | 3 | Patrol western assault area: *JN751*, *JN735*, *JN755*, *JN768*, *JN769*, *JN796* |
| | 8 | 486 | Patrol western assault area: *JN736*, *JN758*, *JN767*, *JN770*, *JN794*, *JN801*, *JN803*, *JN811* |
| 22:45-22:55 hrs | 6 | 486 | Patrol western assault area: *JN770*, *JN794*, *JN804*, *JN811*, *JN866*, *JN894* and one uncertain |

## Tempest Vs on squadron strength, 5 June 1944

\* flew one sortie
\*\* two sorties on 6 June 1944

Both Tempest squadrons were based at ALG Newchurch. With No. 56 Squadron (Spitfire IX) and No. 124 Squadron (Spitfire HF VII Bradwell Bay), they formed No. 150 Wing.

### No. 3 Sqn, Newchurch

| | | |
|---|---|---|
| \*\**JN735* | 28.2.44-6.7.44 EFA | |
| *JN736* | 26.3.44-? | |
| \**JN738* | 28.2.44-11.8.44 RIW | |
| *JN739* | 25.2.44-20.6.44 BFB | |
| \**JN743* | 25.2.44-26.7.44 | |
| *JN748* | 24.5.44-? | |
| *JN749* | 24.5.44-? | |
| \*\**JN751* | 16.3.44-2.9.44 RIW | |
| \*\**JN752* | 13.3.44-3.7.44 EFB | |
| \**JN745* | 18.4.44-? | |
| \**JN753* | 21.3.44-22.6.44 RIW | |

| | |
|---|---|
| \*\**JN755* | 17.3.44-26.9.44 RIW |
| \**JN759* | ?-? |
| \**JN760* | 13.4.44-18.10.44 AC FA |
| *JN761* | 28.3.44-6.10.44 |
| *JN765* | ?-? |
| \**JN768* | 26.3.44-6.10.44 |
| \*\**JN769* | ?-? |
| \**JN793* | 5.6.44-? |
| \*\**JN796* | (486 Sqn aircraft used on 6.6.44) |
| \**JN812* | ?-1.10.44 FTR |
| \**JN818* | ?-13.9.44 FTR |

### No. 486 Sqn, Newchurch

| | |
|---|---|
| \**JN736* | (3 Sqn aircraft used on 6.6.44) |
| \**JN754* | 2.4.44-6.10.44 |
| \**JN758* | 27.4.44-23.7.44 EFB |
| *JN763* | 11.4.44-21.2.45 |
| *JN765* | 10.4.44-9.6.44 |
| S-*JN766* | 4.4.44-16.66.44 BFB |
| \**JN767* | 4.4.44-6.10.44 |
| \*\**JN770* | 21.4.44-30.8.44, ROS, 18.9.44-6.10.44 |
| *JN772* | 10.4.44-10.6.44 EFB |
| *JN773* | 6.4.44-2.7.44 EFB |
| \*\**JN794* | 16.4.44-27.7.44 |
| *JN795* | 10.4.44-1.5.44 AC FA |
| *JN796* | 16.4.44-15.7.44 RIW |

# The North American Mustang III

In April 1942 – even before Mustang Mk I operations began, on 5 May – Rolls-Royce was looking into the possibility of fitting a two-stage Merlin 61 to the Mustang and forecast a top speed of 441 mph at 25,500 ft. RAE figures were less optimistic, suggesting 427 mph at 25,500 ft, but still indicating a fast, high-ceiling, long-range fighter. Mustang I *AL975* was, on 30 April 1942, set aside to be converted. Since the American Packard company was to build Merlins this seemed a good idea, and on 9 June 1942 AM F.J. Linnell told the Americans about the idea. VCAS wanted six airframes for test installations, but that also meant losing six precious Spitfire Mk IXs.

Events moved fast. Instead, on 15 June three airframes were ordered for conversion and trials. With the Napier Sabre engine in deep trouble Britain's need for fighters was getting desperate, however good the Spitfire Mk IX was. On 20 July,

even before the Merlin Mustang was a reality, an Anglo-American agreement was signed for 1,200 Packard Merlin V-1650-3 (i.e. Merlin 61 equivalent) Mustangs (half for Britain), to be built between January and October 1943. Adjustments eventually led to Mustang airframes being traded for Spitfire Mk Vs which the US 9th AF in the UK used for fighter-reconnaissance operations before D-Day. Britain ultimately requested 3,000 Merlin-engined Mustangs!

Shipments of the Packard Merlin 61-powered Mustang Mk III finally commenced in late 1943, with the course of the war making the long-range P-51 very attractive to the USAAF. A&AEE tests showed the typical Mk III, 9,200 lb in weight at take-off, to have a top speed of 424 mph at 15,500 ft with medium supercharger running, and a highly creditable 450 mph at 28,000 ft using full supercharger. Some Mk IIIs had engines equivalent to the RM14SM/Merlin 100,

FX901, *a typical Mustang III – but without the essential cockpit hood modifications produced by Malcolm Ltd and fitted, at No. 3501 SU, Cranfield, to many Mk IIIs. (Rolls-Royce)*

AM203, *the second Mustang X, flew for the first time in late 1942. (Rolls-Royce)*

providing a maximum speed of 455 mph at 17,800 ft. Eventually the RAF received 930 P-51B/C Mustang Mk III variants, the first examples filtering into No. 65 Squadron in December 1943 and flying their first operational sorties on 15 February 1944. Strong criticism of the Mustang pilot's view aft led to the British Malcolm company designing a domed sliding canopy which was fitted at No. 3501 SU, Cranfield, to Fighter Command's Mustang IIIs.

By D-Day 218 Mustang Mk IIIs were operationally available to the RAF, another 148 were in MAP hands and 81 were in shipment. No. 316 Squadron, ADGB, held 20 and the six squadrons of 2nd TAF had some 115 examples.

On D-Day the Mustang Mk IIIs were held in reserve until the evening when they provided escort to transports and gliders participating in Operation *Mallard*. Next day they undertook fighter-bomber operations against tactical targets, in which role they became very active. By autumn 1944 RAF Mustang IIIs were generally used as long-range escort fighters.

## Mustang IIIs on squadron strength, 5 June 1944

\* operated on 6 June 1944

NB: As with other 2nd TAF aircraft, some Mustangs in squadron use remained assigned to support units until 8 June 1944.

Examples are included in this listing. Note too that aircraft were shared between squadrons within their Wing.

### *No. 19 Sqn,* Funtington
```
 FB104    27.3.44-19.6.44 BFB
 FB109    3.44-15.9.44
*FB113    4.44-13.7.44 BFB
*FB116    83 GSU 8.6-19 Sqn 22.6-12.8.44 FTR
*FB122    ?-?
 FB152    8.6.44-17.7.44 AC FB
*FB153    8.6.44-17.7.44 FB AC
 FB154    8.6.44-22.6.44 Cat B
*FB201    22.3.44-26.8.44 FTR
 FB217    23.3.44-22.6.44
*FB227    ?-?
*FX882    ?-14.6.44 FTR
 FX944    21.3.44-22.6.44
 FX975    5.44-7.6.44 FBB
 FX990    22.3.44-30.9.44 FTR
 FX997    23.3.44-24.6.44
 FZ139    23.3.44-6.7.44
*FZ141    ?-8.6.44 FTR
*FZ166    ?-?
 FZ173    26.1.44-22.6.44
*FZ186    21.3.44-19.9.44
*FZ195    5.44-?
```

### *No. 65 Sqn,* Funtington
First operation 15.2.44, with No. 19 Sqn
```
*FB102    14.2.44-11.6.44 FTR EFA
*FB103    20.3.44-22.6.44
 FB119    14.2.44-12.8.44 FTR
 FB122    14.2.44-8.6.44 FBB
*FB160    8.6.44-10.8.44 FTR
*FB173    83 GSU 4.5 – 65 Sqn 22.6.44-28.6.44
          FTR
*FX884    ?-11.6.44 FTR
*FX905    ?-?
 FX926    ?-22.6.44
*FX938    4.1.44-22.6.44
*FX967    ?-?
*FX988    10.1.44-26.6.44 FTR
 FZ102    4.1.44-8.12.44 FTR
```

185

*Servicing underway in France on Mustang III FZ190 of No. 19 Squadron. (IWM Cl571)*

| | |
|---|---|
| *FZ112 | 20.4.44-13.7.44 |
| FZ123 | 20.3.44-26.6.44 FTR (ROS 26.5-8.6.44) |
| FZ125 | 10.3.44-20.9.44 FTR |
| *FZ129 | ?-? |
| *FZ151 | ?-? |
| FZ179 | 10.1.44-6.7.44 EFB burnt |
| FZ193 | ?-26.7.44 FTR |

| | |
|---|---|
| *FX986 | ?-18.6.44 FTR |
| *FZ106 | 20.3.44-26.9.44 RIW |
| *FZ114 | 28.3.44-27.7.44 |
| *FZ118 | 20.3.44-8.6.44 FTR |
| *FZ167 | 83 GSU 2.5-122 Sqn 8.6.44-28.7.44 FTR |
| *FZ177 | 7.3.44-1.3.45 EFB |

### No. 129 Sqn, Coolham

(Last Spitfire operation 8.1.44, first Mustang operation 26.3.44. One operation on 6.6.44: *Ramrod 976* 20:15–22:05 hrs)

| | |
|---|---|
| *G-FB108 | 6.4.44-11.6.44 FTR |
| FB112 | 31.3.44-14.9.44 |
| *F-FB125 | 13.4.44-7.5.45 EFA |
| FB143 | 8.4.44-6.6.44 RIW |
| *T-FB165 | 13.4.44-4.7.44 |
| *H-FB169 | 13.4.44-15.6.44 FTR |
| *S-FB171 | ?-? |
| FB182 | ?-11.6.44 FA |
| *J-FB212 | 14.5.44-8.6.44, 22.6-23.8.44 |
| *X-FZ941 | 4.4.44-24.7.44 |

### No. 122 Sqn, to Funtington 28.5.44

| | |
|---|---|
| *FB107 | 3.44-26.7.44 FTR (ROS 12.6-22.6.44) |
| *FB110 | 4.3.44-16.9.44 FTR |
| *FB122 | 20.3.44-8.6.44 BFB |
| FB208 | 23.2.44-22.6.44 |
| *FB209 | ?-? |
| FX889 | 8.6.44-7.44 |
| FX935 | 83 GSU 24.5 – 122 Sqn 8.6 – 9.7.44 |
| *FX938 | 83 GSU – 8.6.44-22.6.44 |
| FX939 | 20.3.44-6.7.44 |
| FX940 | 27.3.44-10.12.44 EFB |
| *FX982 | 3.44-12.6.44 BFB |
| *FX984 | 5.44-19.6.44 BFB |

*A Mustang III of No. 122 Squadron setting out on a fighter-bomber sortie. (IWM CL735)*

*Mustang IIIs of No. 315 Squadron. (IWM MH6845)*

FX949  ?-?
FX952  8.4.44-6.7.44
*M-FX959  10.4.44-8.6.44 FTR
*V-FZ121  1.4.44-23.6.44 EFB
*D-FZ130  4.4.44-22.6.44 BFB
FZ143  19.4.44-15.6, 29.6-23.7.44
FZ172  1.4.44-22.6.44
FZ176  8.4.44-17.6.44 FTR
*Z-FZ184  7.4.44-6.7.44

## No. 306 Sqn, Coolham

FB111  18.4.44-5.8.44 BFB
FB139  8.4.44-7.6.44 FTR
FB157  8.4.44-26.7.44
FB168  12.4.44-24.6.44
FB196  8.6.44-28.6.44 FTR
FX973  13.4.44-24.6.44 FTR
FX986  15.5.44-6.7.44
FX970  19.4.44-24.6.44 FTR
FX983  ?-23.7.44
FX987  12.4.44-22.7.44, 10.8-12.9.44
FX994  ?-10.6.44 FTR
FZ104  1.4.44-8.6.44
FX163  10.4.44-13.6.44 FTR
FZ180  8.4.44-?
FZ189  1.4.44-7.6.44 FTR
FZ192  1.4.44-24.7.44
FZ196  4.4.44-4.8.44 AC FB
FZ197  5.44-8.6.44 FTR

## No. 315 Sqn, Coolham

(first Mustang operation 26.4.44)
FB145  13.4.44-22.7.44 FA AC
FB166  13.4.44-4.7.44 RIW
FB170  4.4.44-15.6.44
FB188  8.4.44-9.6.44 FTR
FX855  13.4.44-10.8.44
FX865  20.5.44-6.7.44

FX895  10.4.44-18.4.44 EFA
FX917  15.5.44-6.7.44
FX942  20.5.44-6.7.44
FX960  20.5.44-11.6.44 FTR
FX974  31.4.44-6.7.44
FX985  2.6.44-13.8.44
FX995  5.44-13.9.44
FZ135  11.4.44-27.6.44
FZ147  8.4.44-23.6.44 EFB
FZ154  1.4.44-24.7.44
FZ155  1.4.44-6.44
FZ160  8.4.44-17.7.44 EFB
FZ169  20.4.44-13.8.44
FZ171  1.4.44-12.6.44
FZ175  1.4.44-7.44

## No. 316 Sqn, Coltishall (ADGB)

*M-FB135  1.4.44-4.7.44
FB136  20.4.44-4.7.44
K-FB161  20.4.44-4.7.44
FB172  1.4.44-14.8.44
I-FB181  20.4.44-4.7.44
FB197  14.4.44-1.7.44
F-FB220  19.4.44-11.6.44 FBB
V-FB232  20.4.44-27.6.44
B-FB233  18.4.44-?
N-FB276  ?-?
Q-FX864  20.4.44-28.6.44
U-FX876  18.4.44-9.7.44
J-FX888  20.4.44-19.6.44 EFB
R-FX903  16.5.44-12.9.44
FX904  14.4.44-22.6.44
FX912  20.4.44-9.7.44
A-FX945  16.5.44-28.6.44
FX956  1.6.44-9.7, 14.7-23.11.44
X-FX958  3.6.44-28.6.44
Y-FX966  19.4.44-9.7.44
FX980  5.6.44-4.7.44
D-FZ113  15.4.44-14.6.44 FB AC

# The Vickers-Supermarine Spitfire

A main element of the Allied victory, the Spitfire and its famous Merlin engine remain one of the most successful marriages of all time. *Aircraft for the Few* outlines the early days of the Spitfire, and by the end of the Battle of Britain Rolls-Royce was investigating a low-altitude blower version of their latest Merlin, the Mk XX, which eventually became the RM5S or Merlin 45; output 1,205 bhp at 15,500 ft applying +9 lb boost. Forecasts of the likely performance of a Spitfire so powered suggested a speed increase of 18 mph above 17,000 ft, improved climb of 350 ft/min and a higher ceiling. With the Typhoon much delayed, and the Bf 109 becoming ever better, any improvement of the Spitfire was worthwhile.

On Christmas Eve 1940, during a conference at Boscombe Down, the decision was made to put the Merlin 45 Spitfire into production by April 1941, the Ministry of Aircraft Production suggesting an initial batch of 600. C-in-C Fighter Command called the Merlin 45 'a priceless asset', adding 'Put it into earlier Spitfires when they need major repair.' Within days that idea was applied to *K9788*, then Merlin 45s were fitted to the 25 remaining of No. 19 Squadron's troublesome cannon-armed Spitfire Is to be operationally tried by No. 92 Squadron.

On 15 January 1941 a contract was agreed for 500 of these new Spitfires designated 'Mk II (Merlin 45)' and, from early February 1941, known as Mk V. They were to be Castle Bromwich-built for delivery by September 1941. So urgent was the need that by the end of February 1941 five production Mk Vs were already in being, and Rolls-Royce had converted another four Mk Is. That involved changing the radiator, header tank, air intake, cowling, engine cooling control and fitting a revised fuel system. In achieving a top speed of around 378 mph and an all-up weight of 6,460 lb the Mk Vs engine ran 'hot' and the propellers needed pitch setters. Otherwise, all went so well that the favoured Spitfire III was cancelled.

Converting Spitfire Mk IIs (introduced during the Battle of Britain) to take Merlin 45s proved too difficult, whereas fitting all-metal ailerons to all Spitfires was easy and made them lighter to handle. With sufficient engines available and eight-gun wings, Supermarine produced an eight-gun variant which was called the Mk Va, while the production build-up of dedicated Mk Vs was soon rapid. All those were fitted with two 20 mm Hispano cannon and four .303 in Browning machine-guns and designated Mk Vb. The 'universal' wing for the Spitfire Mk III allowing for eight machine-guns, two cannon and four guns, or four cannon was now favoured for the Mk V of which 3,003 were ultimately to be Castle Bromwich-built and another 780 by Vickers-Supermarine. A stronger Spitfire airframe, the 'Type B', became the basis of the four-cannon Spitfire Vc.

On 5 June 1944 326 Spitfire Mk Vs (nearly all Vbs) were in the hands of AEAF squadrons out of a total of about 1,200 in Britain. Many featured clipped wing-tips, the development of which produced stormy moments. With the Fw 190 posing a very serious threat staff at the Air Fighting Development Unit, Duxford, decided in September 1942 to remove the wing-tips from Spitfire Vb *AA937*, in the belief that it would lighten it and increase its rate of roll. First flown on 2 October 1942 the 'clipped' Spitfire was capable of faster directional change linked to better manoeuvrability to 30,000 ft, above which performance deteriorated. Some 8 mph faster at 10,000 ft and 5 mph at 20,000 ft than a 'normal' Spitfire V, *AA937* had a turning circle of 1,025 yds compared with the 1,450 yds at 20,000 ft of the Fw 190. For low-level operations the new version was fine, and remained in operational use until late summer 1944.

One might assume that RAF senior management would have applauded Duxford's initiative. Not at all! AM Ralph Sorley, ACAST, was very angry – publicly at least – at the making of such a potentially 'dangerous' modification without permission. Privately he expressed the opinion that it was a 'very good idea'! He pondered upon its application to other Spitfire variants, and in under a week 20 sets of parts for No. 91 Squadron's Mk Vs were ordered. In December HQ Fighter Command admitted that they had ordered trials of clipped wings on a Mk IX. Promptly, another 19 sets of wing-tip blocks were ordered.

Spitfire and Merlin engine development were probably the British aircraft industry's most remarkable wartime achievements. Modifying the Merlin 45 to accept a four-bladed propeller enabled the Spitfire to reach 40,000 ft, June 1941 seeing this and other advances as the subjects of another important Spitfire conference. The prototype high-flying Mk VI was to fly in September 1941, and two other prototypes were to be powered by the slowly developing Rolls-Royce Griffon. 'Universal' wings would be fitted to Mk Vs, but not before the 520th example was built. Two 60-round belt-fed cannon would be usual, and better fed. Main interest, though, surrounded another new Merlin.

Rolls-Royce had, since 1940, been developing a two-stage blower version for very high-altitude operation. Called Merlin RM6 or Merlin 60 series, the new engines wedded to a Spitfire 'Type B' airframe suitably modified led to the best of all Spitfires, the Mk IX. So superb was the new engine that the Controller R&D wanted it fitted for flight trials even before it had completed a 100-hr type bench test.

An early Merlin 61 was installed in Spitfire Mk III *N3297* and the combination was first flown, from Hucknall, on 20 September 1941. Production of this new version, the Mk VIII (so named because the high-altitude Merlin 46/47 versions would be Mks VI and VII) was scheduled for May 1942.

Boscombe Down trials showed the 7,600 lb Merlin 61 Spitfire, with a power-weight ratio lower than that of the Mk V, able to reach 42,500 ft. While in the 17,000 to 25,000 ft band its climb was none too good and needed boost pressure of +12 lb at 27,500 ft, *N3297* attained 421 mph – very fast at this time – and not surprisingly there were calls for the cancellation of all but Merlin 61 Spitfires. In December 1941 production of 100 Mk VIIIs was called for by October 1942.

Rolls-Royce was next asked to develop their Griffon III or IV for trials in a Spitfire Vc airframe specially for low-level operations. The combination first flew as *DP845* on 27 November 1941, and eventually 100 were produced as the Mk XII, one squadron of which (No. 41) was operational on D-Day and employed particularly around the Channel Islands protecting air-sea rescue operations.

Developing the refined Mk VIII took quite a long time, its first flight taking place in November 1942. An interim Merlin 61 Spitfire was meanwhile evolved, based upon the Mk V's earlier airframe. This was the Mk IX, so successful that to the end of the war many ADGB and 2nd TAF

*Pointed wing-tips, broad-chord pointed rudder and a high-altitude grey/blue finish identify* MD124 *as a Spitfire HF Mk VII, but Spitfire marks were more reliably identifiable by their engine type. Some Mk VIIs retained the conventional wing plan. (Supermarine)*

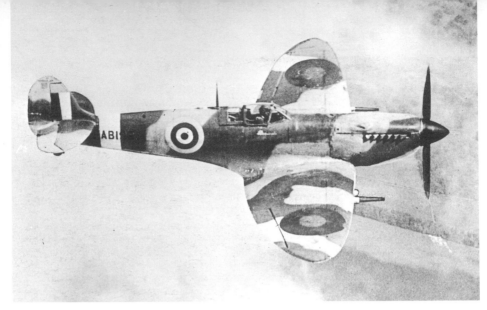

AB196, *an early Spitfire Mk IX seen here during Merlin 60-series development flying, was in the hands of No. 308 Squadron on D-Day. (Rolls-Royce)*

squadrons operated this mark while Mk VIIIs were sent mainly overseas. Superior to the Fw 190 at high levels, the Mk IX entered service with No. 64 Squadron, Hornchurch, in June 1942 and first operated on 28 July 1942. Two days later the squadron claimed four Fw 190s, by which time Nos 72 and 402 Squadrons also had Mk IXs.

Next came adjustments to the Merlin 61 involving a cropped impeller, making power output peak at between 10,000 ft and 20,000 ft. This resulted in the production of the Merlin 66 of 1943, fitted to the Spitfire LF Mk IX with which 17 squadrons were equipped for D-Day operations. Engine modifications and clipped wing-tips added 20 mph to the top speed of the IXs. Most

Mk IXs featured two cannon/four machine-gun 'B' armament because of inadequate gun heating arrangements for four cannon and their weight.

The single-stage Griffon III/IV Spitfire F Mk XII with a top speed of 396 mph at 18,600 ft, and which entered service in April 1943, proved disappointing. By then the Air Staff were wanting a two-stage 'Griffon 61' Spitfire. An interim example, converted Mk VIII *JF316*, first flew in January 1843, flight testing revealing it able to attain 445 mph at 25,000 ft although weight limitations reduced its potential. Nevertheless, 50 production examples were ordered additional to six Mk VIII prototype conversions. The surprisingly successful 'no frills' Spitfire with a Griffon 65 driving

*Spitfire LF Mk IXcs of No. 66 Squadron during a beach cover patrol, photographed on 12 June 1944 from famous Mosquito DZ414 crewed by Sqn Ldr Patterson and Flg Off Howard. (IWM)*

*Three squadrons were operating the latest 1944 Spitfire variant, the Mk XIV, including No. 610 whose RB158 is depicted. (IWM CH13815)*

a curious-looking five-bladed propeller was labelled Spitfire Mk XIV. Service release came on 17 September 1943, by which time the 8,500 lb fighter – about one-third heavier than a Mk I – featured an enlarged fin and rudder to compensate for the considerable torque from an engine driving a propeller in the opposite direction from that of a Merlin.

Delivery began on 28 October 1943. No. 610 Squadron in January 1944 became the first to receive them, and by D-Day, with 114 delivered 51 were in squadron hands, Nos. 91 and 322 Squadrons were also using Mk XIVs, particularly against expected yet absent intruder and reconnaissance aircraft in the Solent area. Heavy but powerful, the new Spitfires were challenging to introduce, for engine exhaust stacks quickly burnt away and tyres soon needed changing because of the heavy operating weight. Most Mk XIVs needed special modifications, rapidly undertaken in particular by de Havilland at Witney during the 'Gem' programme.

Renowned as a fighter, 42 Spitfire Vs also performed in another very useful role on D-Day when two squadrons, Nos. 26 and 63, each flew 76 sorties spanning 108 hrs 25 mins while advising ships' gunners on their aim.

A census of aircraft in service on 1 June 1944 – the closest one to D-Day – showed 5,681 Spitfires in service, 2,185 of them overseas. The Metropolitan Air Force held 2,350, 619 were in maintenance units, 318 within the Civilian Repair Organization and 80 being used for research and

*Spitfire LF Mk IXc MK264-R of No. 308 (Polish) Squadron. (Ray Sturtivant collection)*

development. Of the Mk I and IIs 478 still existed. ADGB and the AEAF held between 1,077 serviceable Spitfires and another 190 unserviceable. In 2nd TAF there were 40 LF Mk IXes featuring .50 in guns in place of the trusted .303s of Battle of Britain fame. A distant link with those times lurked within the Metropolitan Communications Squadron at Hendon, still using four aged Spitfire Is.

## Meritorious Spitfires

Of the long-life Spitfires protecting the Allied armies and navies on D-Day the most meritorious must be *X4272*, a Battle of Britain Spitfire which twice patrolled over Normandy on 6 June. Between 04:00 and 05:45 hrs it was flown by Flg Off J.R. Davies, and between 06:50 and 12:05 hrs by Plt Off R.H. Bennet. Briefly, in September 1940 No. 19 Squadron used it before its withdrawal for cannon fitment. At Hucknall a Merlin XLV was fitted converting *X4272* into a Mk V. After storage in MUs, in October 1943 it joined No. 501 Squadron at Hawkinge. As *J-Johnny*, it first operated on 22 October 1943. The squadron was flying *Jim Crows*: ASR searches and weather reporting sorties over the Channel. On 4 January *X4272* flew its first close escort during *Ramrod 416*, a B-26 raid on a V-1 site. Thereafter, *Ramrods* and *Sweeps* interspersed normal activities with an unusual operation – a

Beaufighter escort to the Channel Islands – coming on 13 April. More *Ramrods* and escorts followed.

Operating from Friston between 7 and 30 June 1944, *X4272* managed 23 beachhead patrols before on 2 July moving with the squadron to Westhampnett. *X4272*'s fate is uncertain. According to its Form 78, it was written off on 12 July Category EFB, yet it appears to have taken part in the squadron's final Mk V operation on 27 July, in the hands of Flt Sgt L.S. Clarke.

The other special 'D-Day Spitfire' is *AB910*, well-known as a member of the Battle of Britain Memorial Flight. In summer 1943 *AB910* joined No. 402 Squadron, Digby, then participated in No. 12 Group *Rodeos* and *Ramrods*. During May 1944 alone it flew nine offensive sorties, and four times on 5 June flew shipping protection sorties, piloted consecutively by Flg Off D.R. Drummond, Flg Off K.M. Collins, then twice by Flg Off G.B. Lawson who, between 09:45 and 12:15 hrs, took it over the British beach area on D-Day. Its second sortie came between 22:00 and 23:59 hrs when Plt Off H.C. Nicholson was the pilot. A companion on the day was aged *P8788* which flew two D-Day patrols and more thereafter. On 7 June Lawson took *AB910* back to Normandy (04:30 to 07:10 hrs) and Plt Off K.A. Heggie flew it from 09:40 to 10:45 hrs. Although on 8 June Lawson was flying *AB910* and 18 Fw 190s were distantly seen,

*One of the best-known remaining Spitfires,* AB910 *was Horne-based on D-Day and very active during the invasion period. In 1994, flying with the Battle of Britain Memorial Flight, AB910 wore commemorative markings of No. 402 (RCAF) Squadron.*

at no time during the period was it involved in combat. Over the period 7 June to 13 July 1944, *AB910* flew 23 patrols. Mk IXbs then replaced the squadron's Mk Vs and *AB910* moved to 53 OTU. After serving with No. 527 Squadron and the Radio Warfare Establishment, Watton, *AB910* became *G-AISU*, then Vickers received it. On 15 September 1965 they gave it to the RAF.

*R6888* was a second Battle of Britain Spitfire active during the D-Day period. From 11 July to 28 October 1940 it served with No. 19 Squadron, was used by AFDU Northolt from 28 November 1940 and subsequently saw service with Nos. 92, 302, 308, 130 and 222 Squadrons. Circa May 1944 it joined No. 611 Squadron with whom it served until written off, probably on 15 June 1944 and apparently due to battle damage.

Another aged example in use was *P8038*, delivered initially as a Mk II to No. 38 MU on 23 February 1941. It joined No. 303 Squadron on 13 March, 412 Squadron on 18 May and served with 313 Squadron in August 1941. It was then converted into a Mk Vb operated by No. 322 Squadron between January and mid-May 1942, and by No 2 (USA) Squadron from 28 August 1942 to April 1943. From 1 July 1943 to 21 July 1944 it was used by No. 611 Squadron, and by No. 53 OTU between March and June 1945. Eventually it was sold to Portsmouth Aviation on 27 September 1945 for breakdown.

Among the Mk IXs was *AB196*, a very early example. Delivered in December 1941 as a Mk Vc, Rolls-Royce soon fitted a Merlin 61, converting it into a Mk IX used by Supermarine for development work at Worthy Down from April to August 1942. Then it moved to Heston where it was stationed until May 1943. No. 303 Squadron operated *AB196* between July and November 1943 when No. 308 Squadron received the aircraft. Accidentally damaged on 29 May 1944 it was removed for works attention on 9 June, but instead was written off on 12 July 1944. *AB279*, also delivered in December 1941, had a more active life serving with Nos. 222, 91, 332, 65 and 308 Squadrons almost without any break. The Poles then passed it to No. 501 Squadron on 27 August 1943. After overhaul from 26 October 1943 it again served briefly with No. 501 Squadron and with No. 234 Squadron from 30 April to 5 October 1944.

Of well-known survivors to this day *MH434* was with No. 222 Squadron from 13 August 1943 to 15 June 1944; *MJ772* (alias *159* of the Irish Air Corps) served with No. 341 Squadron from 20 January to 18 June 1944 and with No. 340 Squadron between 22 June and 3 August 1944;

*Spitfire LF Mk IX ML407, the first Spitfire to destroy in combat a German aircraft on D-Day, but not the first RAF aircraft to make a 'kill'. That distinction went to a Mosquito. ML407 was being flown at the time by a New Zealander, Flg Off John Houlton, seated in the rear cockpit when this photograph of the modified aircraft, owned and flown by Caroline Grace, was taken at Duxford 50 years later.*

*With* ML407 *when the first Spitfire 'kill' was made,* MK732 *– now in Dutch hands – remains active.*

*MK297* of the Confederate Air Force was used by No. 66 Squadron from 17 February to 21 September 1944; and MK732, maintained airworthy in the Netherlands, was with No. 485 Squadron in summer 1944, precise dates being uncertain. It was flying at the same time as *ML407*, flown by Flg Off J. Houlton, and was the first to shoot down a German aircraft on D-Day. Officially it joined No. 485 Squadron on 30 April 1944, staying with the squadron until late 1944. Later it flew with Nos. 341, 308, 349, 345 and 322 Squadrons. *ML417*, which for some years has flown as *21-T,* did not operate on D-Day.

Listing all Spitfires available on 6 June 1944 is fraught with difficulties. RAF Form 78 Aircraft cards show many Spitfires known to have operated as unassigned to squadrons. A considerable number came off Group Support Unit strength on 8 June and were allocated to squadrons. Other similar major movement dates were 15 June and 22 June, possibly arising from the RAF's usual regular Thursday accounting day. Correlating Form 78s with Form 540/541s Squadron Operational Records Books reveals a very large number of certain errors, particularly in the recording of serial number prefix letters where *MA, MH, MJ, MK* and *ML* produced confusion. The inclusion of erroneous order of digits, too, injects more confusion. There are instances where aircraft certainly shot down are shown as operating well into June

1944; and more problems arise as a result of squadrons 'borrowing' for operations aircraft from other squadrons within the same Wing. Although returns to controlling organizations listed squadron strength, these appear often not to have taken account of aircraft briefly out of line for servicing by non-squadron personnel or manufacturers' teams, and not necessarily removed from squadron base. Personal observation of the aircraft provided very limited information because so many had their serials over-painted by 'invasion markings', and pilots' log entries have often proved to be of limited help in placing aircraft within squadrons. Although pitfalls in producing any listing are many, the following attempt has nevertheless been made.

## Spitfires on squadron strength, 5 June 1944

\* operated on 6 June 1944

### No. 1 Sqn, Predannack
Spitfire LF.IXb/LR

|  |  |
|---|---|
| MK583 | 11.4.44-11.6.44 ROS |
| MK644 | 11.4.44-22.5.44 ROS, 9.6.44- EFA 2.3.45, crash-landed Manston |
| *MK659 | 14.4.44-3.12.44 ROS |
| *MK726 | 27.4.44-23.7.44 ROS, 11.8.44-16.4.45 |
| *MK733 | 14.4.44-FA 20.4.44, 2.5.44- SAL MI 18.4.45 |
| *MK744 | 14.4.44- FTR 17.8.44 |
| MK846 | 14.4.44-5.6.44 ROS, 9.6.44-12.10.44 |
| *MK867 | 14.4.44- FTR 27.9.44 |
| *MK901 | 13.4.44-13.12.44 |
| MK919 | 10.4.44-22.5.44 ROS, 7.7.44- EFA |

|  | 12.9.44, crashed Detling |
| *MK926 | 16.4.44-12.10.44 |
| *MK986 | 18.4.44-9.8.44 ROS, 18.9.44-16.4.45 |
| *MK987 | 16.4.44-15.6.44 |
| *MK988 | 16.4.44-15.7.44 ROS, 25.7.44-16.4.45 |
|  | MI |
| MK997 | 16.4.44-5.7.44 ROS, 25.7.44 – FA |
|  | 19.2.45 (later sold to Norway) |
| ML117 | 28.5.44-2.6.44 ROS, 16.6.44-3.3.45 |
|  | FA |
| ML119 | 16.4.44-18.6.44 (later to Czech AF) |
| *ML122 | 28.5.44-6.7.44 |
| *ML270 | 6.6.44-22.6.44 RIW (later to French |
|  | Air Force) |
| *ML313 | 26.5.44-18.6.44, 28.7.44-1.9.44 |
| ML423 | ?-9.6.44 ROS, 30.6.44-14.8.45 |
| *NH246 | 28.5.44-22.3.45 FA |
| *NH253 | 28.5.44-21.7.45 |
| *NH255 | 28.5.44-31.8.44, 15.9.44-17.4.45 |

## No. 33 Sqn, Lympne
Spitfire IX (many assigned to 310 Sqn 8.7.44)

| BS129 | 1.6.44-16.6.44 FA, 1.7.44-19.9.44 |
| BS239 | 5.44-22.6.44 ROS, 14.7.44-28.8.44 |
| BS281 | 25.5.44-3.7.44 |
| *BS286 | 5.44-26.5.44 ROS, 15.6.44-8.7.44 |
| *BS348 | 28.5.44-8.7.44 |
| *BS408 | 1.6.44-8.7.44 |
| BS534 | 23.5.44-8.7.44 |
| EN527 | 28.5.44-4.6.44 ROS, 30.6.44-8.7.44 |
| *MA326(?) | 16.5.44-14.6.44 ROS, 28.6.44-1.7.44 |
| *MA524 | 20.5.44-28.9.44 |
| *MA807 | 16.5.44-19.6.44 EFB |
| MA813 | 16.5.44-16.6.44 |
| *MA814 | 28.5.44-3.7.44 |
| MH326 | 16.5.44-19.6.44 BFB |
| *MH606 | 26.5.44-28.6.44 |
| *MH666 | 16.5.44-8.7.44 |
| *MH692 | 16.5.44-8.7.44 |
| *MH777 | 16.5.44-17.8.44 AC FB |
| MH790 | 16.5.44-14.6.44 FA, ROS, 15.7.44- |
|  | 20.8.44 EFB |
| *MH823 | 16.5.44-8.7.44 |
| MH830 | 16.5.44-5.6.44 ROS, 9.7.44-10.8.44 |
| *MJ120 | 16.5.44-8.7.44 |
| *MJ216 | 16.5.44-8.7.44 |
| MJ623 | 16.5.44-17.6.44 |
| *MK694 | 74 Sqn aircraft on loan |

## No. 41 Sqn, Bolt Head
Spitfire XII

| *EN221 | 30.5.44-27.6.44 |
| EN224 | 15.5.44-27.6.44 |
| EN227 | 8.6.44-20.9.44 |
| EN231 | 9.3.43-18.6.44 FTR, ditched in |
|  | English Channel |
| EN605 | 22.3.44-23.9.44 |
| EN619 | 27.4.44-28.9.44 |
| *EN620 | 14.3.44-?.6.44 |
| *MB794 | 29.9.43-9.6.44 FTR |
| *MB795 | 29.9.43-15.9.44 |
| *MB803 | 15.5.44-21.6.44 |
| *MB804 | 22.8.43-16.7.44 |
| MB830 | 2.10.43-23.6.44 |
| *MB837 | 1.9.43-8.7.44 |
| MB840 | 19.10.43-20.9.44 |
| *MB841 | 15.5.44-18.7.44 |
| *MB842 | 7.3.44-12.6.44 FTR, crashed in |
|  | English Channel |
| *MB845 | 20.7.43-?.6.44 |

| *MB847 | 20.7.43-21.6.44 |
| MB858 | 7.9.43-15.12.44 |
| *MB862 | 7.8.43-20.9.44 |
| *MB876 | 15.5.44-18.6.44 FTR |
| MB877 | 28.5.44-17.7.44 collided on take-off |
|  | with Tiger Moth DE575 |
| MB880 | 14.12.43-17.8.44 FTR |
| *MB881 | 21.12.43-7.6.44 damaged during a |
|  | Rhubarb |
| *MB882 | 21.12.43-20.9.44 |

## No. 56 Sqn, Newchurch

| MJ790 | ?-17.6.44 |
| *T-MK115 | 9.5.44-8.6.44 (to 340 Sqn) |
| *H-MK378 | 20.5.44-30.6.44 BFB (later to French |
|  | Navy) |
| *A-MK475 | 9.5.44-3.8.44 |
| *P-MK517 | 9.5.44-17.7.44 |
| *B-MK572 | 9.5.44-17.7.44 |
| *F-MK585 | 4.5.44-18.7.44 RIW |
| *O-MK633 | ?-8.6.44 (to 331 Sqn) |
| MK666 | 27.5.44-17.7.44 |
| *T-MK715 | 9.5.44-17.7.44 |
| MK724 | 9.5.44-21.5.44 BFB, ROS, 9.6.44- |
|  | 17.7.44 |
| MK790 | 9.5.44-29.6.44 EFB (with 416 Sqn – |
|  | crashed Bazenville) |
| *MK794 | 27.5.44-17.7.44 |
| *E-MK909 | 4.5.44-17.7.44 |
| *M-MK955 | 9.5.44-22.5.44 AC FB, ROS, 1.6.44- |
|  | 17.7.44 |
| MK991 | 23.4.44-4.5.44 BFB, RIW 13.6.44 |
| *S-ML115 | 6.5.44-17.7.44 |
| *L-ML266 | 9.5.44-13.6.44, 28.7.44-17.9.44, |
|  | 29.9.44-16.1.45 |
| ML276 | 9.5.44-20.6.44 |
| ML277 | 9.5.44-11.6.44 FA |
| D-ML293 | 10.5.44-4.7.44 |
| *G-ML341 | 10.5.44-17.7.44 |
| *C-ML351 | 9.5.44-18.5.44, 30.5.44-18.7.44 |
| ML421 | 10.5.44-6.6.44 to AST |
| Z-NH155 | 17.5.44-17.7.44 |

## No. 64 Sqn, Deanland
Spitfire Vb

| W3234 | 3.5.44-12.7.44 |
| W3320 | 25.9.43-10.7.44 |
| *W3656 | 25.9.43-12.6.44 AST |
| X4257 | 25.9.43-3.7.44 BFB |
| *AA756 | 27.4.44-? |
| *AA972 | 25.9.43-10.7.44 |
| *AB143 | 24.9.43-26.9.44 |
| *AB194 | 26.10.43-6.7.44 RIW |
| *AB403 | 25.9.43-28.6.44 RIW |
| *AD132 | 7.3.43-12.7.44 |
| AD419 | 5.44-16.6.44 EFA |
| AR292 | 6.4.44-12.7.44 |
| *BL370 | 25.9.43-12.7.44 |
| *BL374 | 25.9.43-21.6.44 |
| *BL734 | 25.9.43-18.7.44 |
| BL763 | 27.4.44-12.7.44 |
| *BM129 | 30.4.44-10.6.44 BFB |
| *BM327 | 22.5.44-13.7.44 RIW |
| *BM414 | 25.9.43-12.7.44 |
| BM514 | 25.9.43-20.6.44 RIW |
| *EP601 | 27.4.44-12.7.44 |

## No. 66 Sqn, Bognor
Spitfire IX

| EN563 | 15.4.44-6.8.44 |

EN565  2.12.43-24.4.44 BFA, RIW 12.6.44
EN568  20.1.44-17.6.44 BFA
*MH715  485 Sqn aircraft to 66 Sqn 8.6.44-18.7.44 RIW
*MH723  17.2.44-15.6.44, 27.7.44-15.8.44
*MJ143  ?-31.7.44 AC FB
*MJ150  ?-21.7.44, 25.7.44-26.8.44 EFB, flak damaged, crashed in Normandy
*MJ559  24.5.44-? (AC FB on 416 Sqn 18.7.44)
*MJ581  7.3.44-14.6.44 FA
*MK228  310 Sqn aircraft to 66 Sqn 8.6.44-20.7.44
*MK297  17.2.44-31.8.44, 7.9.44-21.9.44
*MK449  7.3.44-15.7.44 FTR (Lancaster escort Pas de Calais)
*MK474  7.3.44-27.8.44, 7.9.44-28.9.44
*MK569  ?-24.9.44
*MK586  ?-20.6.44, 29.6.44-28.9.44
MK686  ?-16.6.44 BFB
*ML123  ?-6.7.44 FTR when used by another squadron
*NH150  ?-28.9.44
*NH173  ?-16.6.44 FA, 27.7.44-28.9.44
*NH254  ?-28.9.44

NB: *MJ150, MJ559, MK569, MK586, ML123, NH150, NH173, NH254* although with No. 66 Squadron by D-Day are typical examples of the many not officially assigned away from No. 84 GSU until 8.6.44.

## No. 74 Sqn, Lympne
Spitfire HF IX unless otherwise stated, mostly to 312 Sqn 8.3.44 (Examples used on D-Day unknown)
MK670  (F Mk IX) 16.5.44-8.7.44
MK672  (F Mk IX) 16.5.44-?
MK681  16.5.44-8.7.44
MK682  16.5.44-8.7.44
MK691  (F Mk IX) 16.5.44-27.5.44 AC FB, 9.6.44-8.7.44
MK694  (F Mk IX) 16.5.44-8.7.44
ML154  26.5.44-8.7.44
ML171  16.5.44-8.7.44
ML195  (LF Mk IX) 19.5.44-8.7.44
ML200  4.5.44-10.6.44 FTR, fuel short, crashed in Normandy
ML207  (LF Mk IX) 4.5.44-20.6.44 ROS, to 312 Sqn 28.9.44
ML212  4.5.44-8.7.44
ML230  4.5.44-8.7.44
ML232  26.5.44-8.7.44
ML233  20.5.44-8.7.44
ML236  (F Mk IX) 4.5.44-8.7.44
ML240  (F Mk IX) 20.5.44-8.7.44
ML241  4.5.44-9.6.44 (FA, with 442 Sqn), 4.8.44-9.44
ML245  4.5.44-8.6.44 to 312 Sqn
ML259  20.5.44-8.7.44
ML261  4.5.44-8.7.44
Ml296  4.5.44-8.7.44
ML364  4.5.44-8.7.44

## No. 80 Sqn, Detling
Spitfire IX
*AB196  29.5.44-9.6.44 RIW
BS409  29.5.44-5.9.44
BS462  29.5.44-10.6.44 BFB
BS512  2.6.44-5.9.44
BS556  20.5.44-4.7.44

*EN127  29.5.44-31.8.44 FTR
*BS642  ?-?
EN172  29.5.44-5.7.44, 8.9.44-19.9.44 RIW
*JL227  29.5.44-23.9.44
*MA228  6.44-5.9.44
MA301  29.5.44-5.9.44
MA378  29.5.44-31.8.44 RIW
*MA806  29.5.44-31.8.44 FTR
MA832  ?-20.5.44 ROS, 23.6.44-16.9.44 BFB on 33 Sqn
*MA841  ?-18.5.44 FA, to AST 6.6.44
MA842  29.5.44-10.6.44 EFB
*MH319  29.5.44-22.6.44 FA (crashed on take-off), re-cat E 14.7.44
MH378  29.5.44- RIW 31.8.44
*MH671  29.5.44-23.6.44 RIW
MH828  29.5.44-16.8.44 RIW
MH873  29.5.44-8.8.44 EFA undercarriage collapsed, Filton
*MH878  29.5.44-22.6.44, 14.7.44-4.9.44
*MH880  29.5.44-10.6.44
*MH881  29.5.44-5.9.44
MJ311  29.5.44-18.6.44, 25.6.44-3.9.44

## No. 91 Sqn, West Malling
Spitfire F XIV (most withdrawn from squadron for a few days for modifications)
NH654  27.3.44-13.7.44
NH697  8.3.44-29.8.44
NH698  7.3.44-8.9.44
NH701  14.3.44-8.44
NH705  21.3.44-14.5.44, 31.5.44-19.8.44
NH707  20.3.44-18.8.44
NH710  20.3.44-29.8.44
NH720  6.44-22.6.44
RB161  21.2.44-13.4.44, 3.5.44-29.8.44
RB165  8.3.44-29.8.44
RB169  29.2.44-26.4.44, 17.5.44-29.8.44
RB174  ?-?
RB177  27.2.44-22.4.44, 5.5.44-10.5.45
RB180  7.3.44-17.6.44, 12.7.44-8.44
RB181  25.2.44-30.5.44, 16.6.44-29.8.44
RB182  26.2.44-12.4.44, 27.4.44-11.7.44
RB183  4.3.44-19.4.44, 5.44-29.8.44
RB185  ?-?
RB186  ?-?
RB188  29.2.44-29.8.44
RM617  1.5.44-28.6.44 EFB

## No. 118 Sqn, Castletown
Spitfire Vb
W3309  2.6.44-17.6.44
W3375  13.3.44-11.6.44
W3428  30.5.44-14.6.44 FA
W3624  13.3.44-?
W3957  13.3.44-3.10.44
AA744  13.3.44-21.7.44
AA979  13.3.44-26.9.44
AD266  13.3.44-16.7.44 RIW
AD374  13.3.44-22.6.44 ROS, 11.8.44-21.9.44
BL255  22.5.44-3.10.44
BL304  13.3.44-7.44
BL416  28.4.44-7.44
BL525  13.3.44-21.7.44
BL600  24.5.44-7.44
BL641  21.5.44-16.6.44 AST
BL696  13.3.44-7.44
BL718  13.3.44-7.44
BL787  13.3.44-9.7.44
BL850  27.4.44-21.7.44

BM132 25.5.44-21.7.44
BM147 31.5.44-12.6.44
BM423 31.3.44-7.44
BM493 28.4.44-23.7.44
BM509 31.3.44-7.44?
EP515 13.3.44-24.5.44, ROS, 13.6.44-
21.7.44

## No. 124 Sqn, Bradwell Bay
Spitfire HF VII
*EN506 ?-? (use remains uncertain)
*EN509 9.11.43-3.8.44
EN511 31.8.43-19.8.44
*MB766 28.8.43-27.6.44
*MB825 ?-?
*MB886 24.5.44-23.8.44
*MB916 9.11.43-19.8.44
MD112 10.1.44-3.8.44
MD113 12.1.44-19.8.44
MD126 20.3.44-3.8.44
MD127 30.4.44-3.8.44
MD130 8.3.44-3.8.44
MD135 12.3.44-3.8.44
MD139 24.2.44-3.8.44
MD145 30.4.44-3.8.44
MD161 29.3.44-12.4.44, ROS, 16.6.44-3.8.44
MD162 25.3.44-3.8.44
MD163 19.5.44-3.8.44
MD164 27.3.44-3.8.44
MD167 30.4.44-3.8.44

## No. 126 Sqn, Culmhead
Spitfire IX
MH437 ?- FTR 6.6.44
*X-MH438 29.5.44- FTR 6.6.44, crashed in the
English Channel
*G-MK126 30.5.44-17.6.44 (AC FA on 56 Sqn),
ROS, used to 4.1.45
MK361 7.5.44-8.6.44
M-MK673 10.5.44-21.10.44, 12.11.44-2.1.45
*P-MK893 10.5.44-8.1.45
*Z-MK923 10.5.44-29.12.44
*L-MK989 10.5.44-15.6.44 AC FA
*O-MK993 10.5.44-2.1.45
MK994 10.5.44-11.7.44 FA
*N-MK995 10.5.44-5.9.44 ROS, 16.9.44-29.9.44
AC FB
*K-ML214 (LF IX) 7.5.44-10.10.44, ROS,
14.11.44-15.12.44
J-ML366 7.5.44-8.7.44 FTR
*D-ML397 30.5.44-8.8.44 ROS, 15.9.44-12.10.44
*F-ML398 8.5.44-7.8.44 ROS, 27.8.44-11.9.44
*A-NH340 8.5.44-20.7.44 EFB
B-NH397 10.5.44-1.8.44 EFB
Y-NH402 10.5.44-26.7.44 EFB
NH403 10.5.44-28.12.44 RIW AST
NH406 10.5.44-14.9.44 EFB

## No. 127 Sqn, Lympne
Using mixed LF and HF IX mostly passed to 313 Sqn
8.7.44
W3445 (Mk V) 3.3.44-25.9.44
*MK675 16.5.44-8.7.44
*MK680 16.5.44-8.7.44
MK965 6.5.44-31.5.44 ROS, 10.6.44-8.7.44
ML145 (HF IX) 5.44-23.5.44 ROS, 10.6.44-
8.7.44
ML172 (HF IX) 16.5.44-?
ML174 (HF IX) 16.5.44-20.6.44 ROS, 7.7.44-
5.10.44 (to 313 Sqn)

ML182 15.5.44-8.7.44
*ML185 (HF IX) 16.5.44-8.7.44
ML187 (HF IX) ?-27.5.44 BFB, RIW, 8.8.44
ML196 (LF IX) 22.5.44-8.7.44
*ML209 1.6.44-8.7.44
ML210 (LF IX) 6.5.44-8.7.44
ML211 (LF IX) 2.6.44-8.7.44
ML235 (HF IX) 6.5.44 ?
*ML238 (HF IX) 6.5.44-8.7.44
ML243 (HF IX) 6.5.44-30.5.44 ROS, 8.7.44
to 313 Sqn
*ML247 (HF IX) 6.5.44-8.7.44
ML251 (HF IX) 5.6.44-8.7.44
ML255 (HF IX) 5.5.44-8.7.44
ML343 (HF IX) 5.5.44-8.7.44
*ML348 (HF IX) 22.5.44-8.7.44
ML406 (HF IX) ?-27.5.44 ROS, 21.7.44-?
ML413 (HF IX) 30.5.44-29.6.44
*NH190 30.5.44?-8.7.44
*NH194 6.44-8.7.44
NH303 2.6.44-8.7.44
*NH313 2.6.44-8.7.44
NH417 2.6.44-8.7.44

## No. 130 Sqn, Horne
Spitfire V (D-Day participants unknown)
W3436 30.4.44-8.6.44 RIW
W3574 18.4.44-12.5.44, 23.6.44-?
W3946 18.4.44-22.6.44 Cat E
AB208 (Vc) 22.5.44-17.6.44 B FA
AB487 18.4.44-26.5.44 AC FA, RIW 19.6.44
AB794 9.5.44-12.6.44 E FA
AB849 16.5.44-25.6.44 EFB
AD348 9.5.44-27.6.44 RIW (named *Alas de
Uruguay*)
AR283 18.4.44-26.7.44
AR323 24.5.44-12.6.44 FA, RIW
AR500 18.4.44-25.6.44 EFB
BL925 22.4.44-16.8.44
BM157 18.4.44-23.11.44
BM190 15.8.44-16.2.44 RIW
BM252 27.4.44-17.5.44, 10.6.44-27.10.44
BM515 24.5.44-13.6.44, ROS, 23.6.44
15.7.44 AC FB
BM528 18.4.44-13.8.44
BM633 30.4.44-28.7.44
EE685 18.4.44-10.6.44 B FA, Cat E 17.6.44

## No. 131 Sqn, Culmhead
Spitfire HF VII
BR138 (Mk X) 19.3.44-22.2.45
MA809 (Mk X) 24.3.44-23.2.45 RIW
MB883 24.2.44-7.6.44 FTR
MB884 6.44-?
MB932 ?-?
MD110 26.2.44-12.10.44, 20.10.44-3.11.44
MD111 7.2.44-18.6.44 ROS, 23.6.44-9.11.44
MD117 22.5.44-4.7.44 ROS, 3.8.44-7.10.44
MD119 26.2.44-8.6.44 RIW
MD120 26.2.44-12.6.44 ROS, 23.6.44-
23.11.44
MD123 29.2.44-12.6.44 FTR
MD125 12.3.44-19.6.44 RIW
MD128 22.5.44-12.6.44 RIW
MD129 26.2.44-23.11.44
MD131 7.3.44-1.6.44, 16.6.44-21.6.44 RIW
MD132 13.3.44-2.10.44 RIW
MD134 3.3.44-12.7.44 RIW
MD136 3.44-14.6.44 RIW
MD143 3.3.44-23.11.44
MD144 5.3.44-23.11.44

197

| MD146 | 8.3.44-23.11.44 |
| MD160 | 2.3.44-12.6.44 RIW |
| MD165 | ?-23.11.44 (to 154 Sqn) |
| MD168 | 27.3.44-23.11.44 |
| MD169 | ?-23.11.44 |
| MD170 | ?-23.11.44 |
| MD171 | ?-4.8.44 RIW |
| MD173 | 27.3.44-23.11.44 |
| MD183 | ?-23.11.44 |
| MD186 | 6.44-23.11.44 |

## No. 132 Sqn, Ford
Spitfire IX

| MH431 | 22.9.43-15.6.44 |
| MH486 | 26.9.43-15.6.44 |
| MH718 | 6.10.43-15.6.44 |
| MJ398 | 20.11.43-15.6.44 |
| MJ639 | ?-6.6.44 |
| MK610 | 3.4.44-11.6.44, 2.6.44-7.8.44 RIW |
| MK631 | ?-12.6.44 BFA |
| MK695 | 26.5.44?-20.7.44 |
| MK736 | 18.5.44?-6.7.44 |
| MK737 | 3.5.44-? (30.6.44 EFB, by then with 442 Sqn) |
| MK810 | 8.5.44?-21.5.44 AC FB, 6.7.44 to 602 Sqn |

## No. 165 Sqn, Predannack
Spitfire IXb

| *T-MJ221 | ?-6.6.44 FTR from *Rodeo*, crashed in sea |
| *D-MK426 | 30.3.44-17.10.44 |
| *N-MK471 | 30.3.44-12.6.44 FTR, shot down in France by flak |
| *F-MK480 | 11.4.44-19.5.44 FA |
| *Z-MK514 | 28.2.44-12.2.45 |
| Q-MK567 | 28.3.44-12.6.44 EFA, crashed in English Channel |
| *G-MK589 | 30.5.44-6.6.44 FTR, in sea 2 miles west of Tregastel |
| I-MK637 | 28.3.44-2.2.45 RIW |
| B-MK638 | 30.3.44-26.7.44 EFB, crash-landed Lympne |
| *L-MK749 | 28.3.44-23.6.44 Cat E |

| MK751 | 30.3.44-6.6.44 FTR, in sea off Predannack |
| W-MK752 | 30.3.44-13.7.44 EFB |
| MK788 | 29.4.44-22.5.44 AC FB, RIW, 12.6.44 |
| A-MK801 | 28.3.44-19.5.44 ROS, 16.6.44-1.9.44 |
| *S-MK811 | 29.3.44-1.7.44 BFB |
| *K-MK831 | 29.3.44-18.5.44 ROS, 16.6.44-5.9.44 FTR from Netherlands |
| MK838 | 30.5.44-26.7.44, 8.9.44-28.12.44 |
| H-MK854 | 29.3.44-25.2.45 |
| *E-MK855 | 11.4.44-7.6.44 FTR, crash-landed SW of Carhaix |
| P-ML175 | 5.6.44-2.8.44 ROS, 15.9.44-28.12.44 |
| X-ML199 | ?-28.6.44 RIW, belly-landed 14.6.44 at base |
| ML242 | 30.5.44-3.2.45 MI CRO |

## No. 222 Sqn, Selsey
Spitfire Mk IXb

| MA371 | 30.8.43-8.6.44 (to 349 Sqn) |
| MH371 | 13.8.43-8.6.44 (to 349 Sqn) |
| *MH416 | 14.8.43-22.6.44 to 84 GSU |
| MH424 | 14.8.43-15.6.44 |
| MH430 | 15.8.43-15.6.44 |
| MH434 | 13.8.43-15.6.44 |
| MH439 | 13.8.43-15.6.44 |
| MH499 | 6.9.43-8.6.44 |
| MH753 | 6.10.43-8.6.44 |
| MJ118 | 18.10.43-8.6.44 |
| MJ201 | 6.11.43-8.6.44 |
| MJ232 | 28.10.43-8.6.44 |
| MJ253 | 6.11.43-15.6.44 |
| MK511 | 14.4.44-19.5.44 AC FB, 27.7.44 to 135 Wing and FTR on 222 Sqn 1.12.44 (Mitchell escort, Wesel), crashed near Tholen |
| *MK663 | 27.3.44-7.9.44 |
| MK669 | 2.4.44-24.8.44 |
| MK717 | 2.4.44-1.5.44, 21.5.44-? |
| *MK774 | 20.4.44-29.9.44 EFB, force-landed near Gouda, on armed recce |
| *MK784 | 16.4.44-7.9.44 |
| *MK787 | 12.4.44-22.7.44 |
| *MK797 | 30.3.44-29.6.44 FTR, shot down by |

MD111-Q, *a pointed wing-tip Spitfire HF Mk VII of No. 131 Squadron, had a high-altitude fighter finish and Type B roundels.* (A.S. Thomas collection)

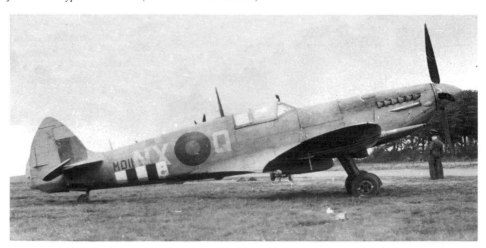

*Bombing-up J-Johnny, a Spitfire LF Mk IXe of No. 132 Squadron, at 'B14' (Amblie) in July 1944. (IWM CL723)*

| | Fw 190 during beachhead patrol |
|---|---|
| *MK799 | 21.4.44-14.12.44 |
| *MK804 | 2.4.44-16.12.44 |
| *MK829 | 14.4.44-15.6.44 |
| MK833 | 2.4.44-8.1.45 |
| *MK863 | 5.44-19.10.44 BFG |
| *MK883 | 12.4.44-7.8.44 Cat E |
| *MK889 | 4.4.44-8.6.44 |
| *MK892 | 4.4.44-10.6.44 EFB |
| *MK896 | 14.4.44-14.12.44 |
| *MK906 | 21.4.44-5.10.44, 9.11.44-14.11.44 |
| *ML193 | 5.44-8.6.44 |
| *ML414 | 5.44-13.6.44 BFB |
| NH290 | 4.6.44-? |

## *No. 229 Sqn*, **Detling**
Spitfire IXb

| | |
|---|---|
| BS137 | 5.44-3.8.44 |
| BS167 | 29.5.44-11.6.44 FTR |
| BS340 | 29.5.44-21.12.44 |
| BS393 | 29.5.44-5.1.45 |
| BS466 | 24.5.44-? |
| MA369 | 4.6.44-25.7.44 BFB, re-cat E |
| MA372 | ?-29.5.44 ROS, 28.7.44-5.10.44 |
| MA381 | 11.5.44-12.12.44 |
| MA639 | 6.6.44-11.6.44 |
| MA817 | 29.5.44-23.6.44 FTR, shot down over Normandy by Fw 190 |
| MA849 | 20.5.44-24.8.44 Cat AC |
| EN174 | 6.6.44-28.12.44 |
| MH314 | 29.5.44-3.10.44 |
| MH333 | 29.5.44-14.9.44 BFA |
| MH369 | 4.6.44-25.7.44 BFB, 4.8.44 re-cat E; flak damage caused crash-landing at Ludham |
| MH372 | ?-4.6.44 ROS, 28.7.44-5.10.44? |
| MH381 | 11.5.44-12.12.44 |
| MH388? | ?-29.6.44 FA |
| MH825 | 15.5.44-18.10.44 |
| MH829 | 29.5.44-17.6.44 BFB, RIW |
| MH835 | 29.5.44-5.1.45 |
| MH852 | 29.5.44-17.6.44 FTR, from anti-*Diver* patrol |
| MH855 | 29.5.44-16.12.44 |
| MH871 | 29.5.44-23.6.44, 15.7.44-16.8.44 |

| | EFA, later repaired |
|---|---|
| MH909 | 29.5.44-5.12.44 |
| MH910 | 29.5.44-4.7.44 |
| MJ192 | 29.5.44-3.6.44 (AC FA on 274 Sqn), 28.7.44-6.11.44 (AC FB on 303 Sqn) |
| MJ220 | 15.10.43-11.5.44, 4.6.44-6.7.44 |
| MJ222 | 29.5.44-30.7.44 ROS, 24.8.44-28.12.44 |
| MJ310 | 29.5.44-6.6.44 ROS, 16.6.44-28.9.44 |
| *MJ388 | 29.5.44-29.6.44 AC FA |

## *No. 234 Sqn*, **Deanland**
Spitfire LF Vb

| | |
|---|---|
| *P8709 | 10.1.44-4.8.44, 29.9.44-7.6.45 |
| W3426 | 13.2.44-28.7.44, 19.1.45-28.2.45 |
| AA936 | 8.1.44-6.6.44 EFA |
| *AA973 | 30.4.44-5.7.44 SOC |
| *AB183 | 30.4.44-14.6.44 BFA, 28.6.44 RIW |
| *AB279 | 30.4.44-18.9.44 AC FA, ROS, 29.9.44-5.10.44 |
| AD470 | 5.5.44-12.10.44 |
| AD515 | 5.1.44-24.5.44 ROS, 11.6.44 and retained until 17.5.45 |
| *AR343 | 31.5.44-27.7.44 SOC |
| *BL233 | ?-4.7.44 EFB |
| *BL235 | ?-12.10.44 |
| *BL415 | 20.5.44-14.6.44 AC, 14.7.44 RIW |
| *BL563 | 9.1.44-26.9.44 |
| *BL646 | ?-? |
| BL720 | 31.5.44-? |
| BL788 | 11.5.44-3.6.44 |
| *BL981 | 6.44-9.10.44 |
| *BL992 | 24.1.44-5.10.44 |
| *BM200 | 28.4.44-14.6.44, 19.6.44-27.7.44 SOC |
| *EN768 | 24.1.44-19.6.44 FTR |
| *EN858 | 6.1.44-5.10.44 |
| *EN861 | 22.12.43-11.8.44 |
| *EN903 | 11.1.44-5.10.44 |
| *EP766 | 6.1.44-21.7.44 |

## *No. 274 Sqn*, **Detling**
Spitfire F IX

| | |
|---|---|
| *BS128 | 15.5.44-7.8.44 ROS, 19.8.44-3.9.44 |
| *BS227 | 15.5.44-29.8.44 |
| *BS284 | 29.5.44-28.7.44 BFB, 16.8.44 RIW |

199

| | |
|---|---|
| *BS395 | 29.5.44-21.7.44 BFB |
| *BS474 | 29.5.44-21.8.44 |
| EN123 | 26.5.44-11.9.44 |
| *LZ919 | 20.5.44-29.8.44 |
| MA331 | 29.5.44-24.7.44 AC FB |
| MA349 | 29.5.44-25.7.44 ROS, 8.8.44-29.8.44 |
| MA362 | 29.5.44-17.6.44 EFA (missing) |
| *MA579 | 15.5.44-11.7.44 |
| *MA585 | 29.5.44-21.8.44 |
| MA747 | 29.5.44-15.8.44 RIW |
| *MA810 | 29.5.44-23.6.44 RIW |
| MA818 | 5.44-13.6.44 ROS, ?-8.9.44 RIW |
| MH331 | 29.5.44-24.7.44 AC FB |
| *MH349 | 29.5.44-25.7.44 ROS, 8.8.44-20.8.44 |
| MH362 | 29.5.44-19.6.44 FTR |
| *MH379 | 10.6.44-21.8.44 |
| *MH603 | 2.6.44-21.8.44 |
| MH824 | 5.44-19.5.44 AC FB, ROS, 10.6.44-21.8.44 |
| MH826 | 29.5.44-5.6.44 ROS, 12.6.44-9.7.44 EFA, collided with balloon cable, crashed at Ightam, Kent |
| *MH853 | 29.5.44-15.8.44 |
| MH876 | 29.5.44-15.8.44 |
| MH881 | 29.5.44-?, to 80 Sqn |
| MH933 | 28.5.44-13.6.44, 21.6.44-2.10.44 (EFB crash-landing with 229 Sqn) |
| MH935 | 29.5.44-17.6.44 FTR from bomber escort to Alençon |
| MH939 | 29.5.44-21.8.44 |
| MJ314 | 4.44-15.5.44 (AC on 274 Sqn ) ROS, 12.6.44-21.8.44 |

## No. 302 (Polish) Sqn, Chailey

Spitfire IX

| | |
|---|---|
| AR513 | (Mk Vc) 19.5.44-1.6.44 AC FA, ROS; to 9 MU 21.9.44 |
| MA374 | 30.4.44-15.6.44 |
| MA742 | 28.9.43-22.6.44 |
| MH712 | 31.5.44-18.6.44 |
| MH739 | 30.4.44-15.6.44 |
| MJ138 | ?-? |
| MJ219 | 27.10.43-5.11.44 AC FB |
| MK370 | 3.5.44-15.6.44 |
| *MK520 | 1.5.44-15.6.44 |
| *MK563 | 3.5.44-15.6.44 |

| | |
|---|---|
| *MK568 | 3.5.44-22.6.44 |
| *MK688 | 3.5.44-17.6.44 |
| *MK716 | 3.5.44-24.6.44, 21.7.44-27.7.44 |
| *MK719 | 5.5.44-15.6.44 |
| *MK723 | 3.5.44-15.6.44 |
| *MK745 | 5.44-15.6.44 |
| *MK786 | 3.5.44-15.6.44 |
| *MK839 | 3.5.44-15.6.44 |
| MK841 | 5.5.44-27.6.44 |
| *MK905 | 3.5.44-7.6.44 AC FB (no details) |
| *MK915 | 3.5.44-15.6.44 |
| *MK924 | 3.5.44-15.6.44 |
| *MK958 | 3.5.44-15.6.44 |
| MK959 | 3.5.44-15.6.44 |
| MK983 | 3.5.44-22.6.44 |
| *MK999 | 3.5.44-15.6.44 |

## No. 303 (Polish) Sqn, Horne

Spitfire Vb; final Mk V operation 18.7.44, last flying 19.17.44

| | |
|---|---|
| W3262 | (Mk V LF LR) 6.3.44-19.7.44 RIW SAL |
| W3373 | (Mk Vb LF LR) 6.3.44-20.5.44 ROS,. 5.6.44-18.7.44 RIW SAL |
| W3380 | 25.3.44-27.3.44 ROS, 24.8.44 -8.9.44 |
| AA751 | 17.4.44-19.7.44 RIW |
| AA860 | 16.4.44-2.8.44 |
| AA929 | 19.5.44-13.7.44 |
| AB271 | 17.4.44-23.6.44 EFB |
| AB921 | 24.5.44-2.8.44 |
| AD204 | (named *Andoverian*) 19.5.44-23.7.44 (AC FA on 130 Sqn), ROS, 27.8.44-15.9.44 |
| AD247 | 25.3.44-26.7.44 (EFB on 130 Sqn) |
| BL292 | 24.5.44-29.6.44 ROS, 3.7.44-31.7.44 |
| BL385 | 6.3.44-28.6.44 RIW |
| BL464 | 25.5.44-3.8.44 |
| BL617 | 9.4.44-22.6.44 EFB, crashed in Channel, engine trouble |
| BL630 | 9.4.44-13.5.44 ROS, 10.6.44-27.7.44 |
| BL697 | 28.5.44-2.8.44 |
| BL730 | No details known |
| BM156 | 25.3.44-2.8.44, ROS, 30.8.44-3.9.44 |
| BM207 | 17.4.44-29.9.44 |
| BM348 | 25.3.44-17.7.44 AC FB |
| BM407 | 30.4.44-15.6.44 EFB – no evidence of damage in ORB |

*A Spitfire LF Mk IX of No. 310 (Czech) Squadron. Diverse individual markings followed the application of 'invasion stripes', including lettering and numbering on fins. (via John Sigmund)*

*Spitfire* BS126-Z *of No. 310 (Czech) Squadron after overshooting North Weald on 29 June 1944. (via John Sigmund)*

| | | | | |
|---|---|---|---|---|
| EE753 | 22.5.44-12.7.44 | | *MK679 | 3.5.44-22.6.44 |
| EP411 | 22.5.44-2.8.44? | | *MK720 | 3.5.44-15.6.44 |
| EP509 | 6.3.44-11.5.44 AC FA, ROS, 10.6.44- | | MK747 | 15.6.44-2.8.44 |
| | 15.8.44 | | MK918 | 6.44-22.6.44 |
| EP651 | 30.4.44-6.7.44 FB AC | | *MK981 | 3.5.44-29.5.44, ROS, 12.8.44-26.8.44 |

### No. 308 (Polish) Sqn, Chailey
Spitfire LF IX

| | | | |
|---|---|---|---|
| | | *ML113 | 3.5.44-22.6.44 |
| BS451 | 16.11.43-19.8.44 ROS, 22.9.44- | *ML177 | 3.5.44-22.6.44 |
| | 26.10.44 | *ML183 | 3.5.44-29.6.44 |
| MA683 | 16.11.43-9.7.44 | *ML231 | 5.5.44-22.6.44 |
| *MH374 | 30.4.44-15.6.44 | *ML362 | 3.5.44-22.6.44 |
| *MH423 | ?-15.6.44 | *PL269 | ?-? |
| *MH750 | ?-? | | |
| *MJ294 | ?-15.6.44 | | |

### No. 310 (Czech) Sqn, Appledram
Spitfire LF IX

| | |
|---|---|
| *MJ503 | 3.5.44-22.6.44 |
| MK529 | 3.5.44-22.6.44 |
| *MK578 | 5.44-16.6.44 |

| | |
|---|---|
| MJ201 | 8.6.44-(ex 222 Sqn) – 15.6.44 |
| *MJ291 | 4.1.44-22.6.44 |
| *MJ477 | 8.6.44-22.6.44 |
| *MJ509 | ?-15.5.44 ROS re-cat B 20.7.44 |

*Spitfire LF Mk IX* J-Johnny *of No. 312 (Czech) Squadron, Appledram, wearing full invasion markings. (via John Sigmund)*

*Carrying a 90-gal drop tank, a Spitfire LF Mk IX of No. 312 (Czech) Squadron sets off on a protection patrol. (via John Sigmund)*

| | |
|---|---|
| *MJ605 | 27.1.44-22.6.44 |
| *MJ714 | 31.12.43-19.5.44 ROS, 8.6.44-22.6.44 |
| *MJ722 | 31.1.44-22.6.44 |
| *MJ825 | 20.1.44-15.6.44 |
| MJ829 | 24.1.44-22.6.44 |
| *MJ906 | 23.1.44-7.6.44 |
| *MK198 | 8.6.44-15.6.44 |
| MK228 | 5.2.44-22.5.44 AC FB, to 66 Sqn 8.6.44 |
| *MK242 | 8.2.44-? |
| *MK280 | 8.6.44-15.6.44 |
| *MK304 | 7.2.44-22.6.44 |
| *MK964 | Cat B on 349 Sqn 14.6.44, joined 310 Sqn, 84 GSU 22.6.44 |
| *NH174 | 5.44-22.6.44 |
| *NH179 | 5.44-22.6.44 |

### No. 312 (Czech) Sqn, Appledram
Spitfire LF IX

| | |
|---|---|
| BM322 | (Mk V) 21.5.44-4.7.44 |
| MH474 | 4.44-3.7.44 |
| MH499 | 6.44-5.7.44 |
| *MJ499 | 4.44-11.6.44 EFB (on 312 Sqn) |
| *MJ553 | 4.2.44-10.8.44 |
| *MJ572 | 3.44-22.6.44 |
| *MJ751 | 4.2.44-21.5.44 AC FB? |
| *MJ792 | 21.1.44-22.6.44 |
| *MJ799 | 13.2.44-22.6.44 |
| *MJ840 | 18.2.44-11.6.44 EFB, crashed at Washington, Sussex |
| *MJ881 | 7.4.44-8.6.44 RIW |
| *MJ940 | 20.4.44-10.6.44 FTR, collided in combat off beachhead |
| *MK180 | 6.44-22.6.44 |
| *MK244 | Used by squadron, 412 Squadron aircraft |
| *MK483 | 6.44-22.6.44, 12.8.44-6.9.44 |
| *MK580 | 5.44-11.6.44 EFB, crashed in Sussex, fuel shortage |
| *MK775 | 5.44-22.6.44 |
| *MK805 | 5.44-29.6.44 |

| | |
|---|---|
| *MK895 | 5.44-22.6.44 |
| *MK912 | 5.44-22.6.44 |
| NH546 | 6.44-31.8.44 |

### No. 313 (Czech) Sqn, Appledram
Spitfire LF IX

| | |
|---|---|
| *JK620 | 5.44-8.6.44 |
| *JK840 | ?-22.6.44 (Mk Vc converted to LF Mk IX) |
| MH328 | 30.3.44-8.10.44 |
| MH496 | 6.44-22.6.44 |
| *MJ201 | 6.44-15.6.44 |
| *MJ292 | 6.44-6.7.44 |
| *MJ293 | 8.6.44-15.6.44 |
| *MJ361 | 16.2.44-29.6.44 |
| *MJ530 | 18.3.44-6.44 (used by 310 Sqn) |
| *MJ668 | 6.44-27.6.44 |
| *MJ900 | 8.6.44-29.6.44 |
| *MJ963 | 16.2.44-29.5.44 AC FB, 29.6.44 to 84 GSU |
| *MK180 | 5.44-22.6.44 |
| *MK188 | 15.2.44-29.6.44 |
| *MK189 | 6.44-22.6.44 |
| *MK205 | 17.2.44-21.4.44, 22.6.44 to 420 RSU |
| *MK208 | 16.2.44-29.6.44 |
| *MK211 | 16.2.44-29.6.44 |
| *MK291 | 16.2.44-22.6.44 |
| *MK320 | 2.44-29.6.44 |
| MK532 | 5.44-22.6.44 |
| MK606 | 17.2.44-29.6.44 |
| MK678 | 10.5.44-22.6.44 |
| MK827 | 8.6.44-22.6.44 |

### No. 317 (Polish) Sqn, Chailey
Spitfire LV IX – aircraft operated on D-Day unknown

| | |
|---|---|
| MH713 | 15.10.43-11.6.44 EFB (on 332 Sqn) |
| MH717 | 24.9.43-15.6.44 |
| MH728 | 24.9.43-8.6.44 |
| MH731 | 7.10.43-8.6.44 |
| MH840 | ?-7.6.44 |

*Fair waves the corn by Spitfire LF Mk IX '320', possibly* ML320 *of No. 317 Squadron. (IWM CL538)*

| | |
|---|---|
| MH846 | 9.10.43-8.6.44 |
| MH847 | 12.10.43-15.6.44 |
| MJ174 | 11.1.44-8.6.44 |
| MJ235 | 11.1.44-12.6.44 FTR (on 332 Sqn) |
| MJ391 | 25.1.44-8.6.44 |
| MK661 | 3.5.44-28.5.44 AC FB, 3.5.44, to 131 Airfield 8.6.44, 317 Sqn 15.6.44-22.6.44 |
| MK684 | 1.5.44-27.6.44 |
| MK690 | 3.5.44-6.7.44 |
| MK698 | 3.5.44-18.7.44 RIW |
| MK898 | 1.5.44-31.8.44 |
| ML130 | 1.5.44-12.6.44, 13.7.44-20.7.44 |
| ML178 | 1.5.44-22.6.44 |
| ML191 | 3.5.44-22.6.44 |
| ML198 | 1.5.44-20.6.44 FTR |
| ML250 | 1.5.44-22.6.44 |
| ML268 | 3.5.44-13.7.44 |
| ML310 | ?-7.6.44 FTR from assault area patrol |
| ML350 | 3.5.44-20.6.44 AC FB |
| ML372 | 3.5.44-22.6.44 |
| ML374 | 3.5.44-6.7.44 |
| NH400 | 3.5.44-29.6.44 |

### No. 322 (Dutch) Sqn, Hartfordbridge Flats
Spitfire Mk XIV – aircraft operated on D-Day unknown

| | |
|---|---|
| NH653 | 29.3.44-3.10.44 |
| NH655 | ?-? |
| NH658 | 6.4.44-10.7.44 |
| NH659 | 7.4.44-28.8.44 |
| NH661 | 16.5.44-19.6.44 BFA |
| NH699 | 13.3.44-4.8.44, 2.9.44-1.11.44 |
| NH702 | 12.3.44-5.9.44 |
| NH704 | ?-? |
| NH709 | 20.3.44-7.7.44, 26.8.44-8.9.44 |
| NH714 | ?-? |
| NH716 | 7.5.44-29.8.44 |
| RB147 | 22.3.44-11.6.44 |
| RB158 | 20.3.44-29.8.44 |
| RB160 | 14.3.44-31.5.44, 1.7.44-20.8.44 |
| RB168 | 3.4.44-20.6.44, 26.8.44-6.9.44 AC FB |

| | |
|---|---|
| RB171 | 27.3.44-10.6.44 |
| RB189 | 28.4.44-11.7.44, 12.9.44-29.12.44 |
| RM672 | 6.44-3.7.44, 5.8.44-4.10.44 |

### No. 329 (Free French) Sqn, Merston
Spitfire LF IX

| | |
|---|---|
| *C-MJ524 | 28.2.44-15.6.44, 22.6.44-6.7.44 |
| *S-MK132 | 5.44-20.6.44 |
| B-MK265 | 28.2.44-29.6.44 |
| MK283 | 18.2.44-13.7.44 |
| I-MK293 | 5.44-6.7.44 |
| W-MK298 | 29.2.44-7.6.44 AC FB |
| *L-MK301 | 6.44-29.6.44 |
| P-MK305 | 7.3.44-29.5.44 BFA, 8.6.44 RIW |
| MK318 | 3.3.44-22.6.44 |
| *X-MK319 | 3.3.44-15.6.44 |
| *J-MK322 | 3.3.44-12.5.44 BFB, 6.7.44 84 GSU |
| *V-MK347 | 6.44-29.6.44 |
| *H-MK359 | 29.2.44-13.7.44 |
| MK370 | ?-? |
| *Y-MK374 | 28.2.44-15.6.44 |
| *A-MK416 | 28.2.44-6.7.44 |
| *N-MK418 | 28.2.44-29.6.44 |
| E-MK453 | 22.2.44-29.6.44 |
| *R-MK839 | 6.44-29.6.44 |
| *T-NH151 | 6.44-6.7.44 |

### No. 331 (Norwegian) Sqn, Bognor
Spitfire LF IX – aircraft operated on D-Day unknown

| | |
|---|---|
| MJ197 | 4.44-25.7.44 |
| MJ217 | 9.2.44-3.8.44 |
| MJ224 | 9.11.43-7.44 |
| MJ476 | 6.44-21.9.44 |
| MJ583 | 23.1.44-25.7.44 |
| MJ633 | 31.1.44-26.10.44 |
| MJ712 | 26.1.44-10.8.44 |
| MJ728 | 31.1.44-15.6.44 FTR, crashed near Evreux, flak damage |
| MJK732 | 23.1.44-22.6.44 |
| MJ774 | 10.2.44-5.10.44 |
| MJ827 | 31.1.44-9.6.44 (EFB on 403 Sqn) |

MJ834  26.1.44-11.6.44 FTR
MJ908  22.1.44-5.10.44
MJ930  4.3.44-3.8.44
MK633  6.44-29.6.44

## No. 332 (Norwegian) Sqn, Bognor

Spitfire LF IX – aircraft operated on D-Day unknown
MH713  ?-11.6.44 AC FB (ex-317 Sqn)
MH720  26.3.44-15.6.44
MJ218  ?-7.6.44 EFB, crash-landed in France
       during patrol
MK251  4.3.44-5.10.44
MK341  ?- FTR 19.6.44, in the sea off
       Hastings
MK588  ?-6.7.44, 27.7.44-17.9.44 FTR, fell to
       flak, Terneuzen
MK667  ?-10.8.44
MK731  ?-5.11.44
MK793  ?-29.6.44
MK812  8.6.44-21.9.44
MK966  ?-9.6.44 EFB
NH304  ?-4.7.44 FTR
NH312  ?-17.9.44 AC FB

## No. 340 (Free French) Sqn, Merston

Spitfire LF IX
*S-MJ177  23.1.44-8.6.44
*J-MJ351  13.2.44-9.6.44 FTR, fell to flak near
          Isigny
*W-MJ518  7.2.44-13.7.44
*O-MJ744  7.2.44-6.7.44
*H-MJ746  9.2.44-20.4.44 AC FA
*K-MJ795  23.1.44-28.2.44, ROS, 3.3.44-5.6.44
          BFA, 16.6.44 RIW
*U-MJ822  9.2.44-6.7.44
   MJ873  11.2.44-27.4.44, 20.5.44 FB, 15.6.44
          BFB
*Z-MJ896  9.2.44-6.7.44
*F-MJ960  9.2.44-6.7.44
*B-MJ966  6.44-13.7.44
*F-MK115  6.44-6.7.44
*C-MK123  31.1.44-29.6.44
*G-MK127  9.2.44-7.6.44 AC FA, 15.6.44-13.7.44
*T-MK183  11.2.44-20.6.44 FB
*E-MK196  3.3.44-17.6.44 AC FB
*L-MK202  6.44-6.7.44

*N-MK204  6.44-20.6.44 FTR, crashed in France
 X-MK234  31.1.44-6.7.44
*D-MK290  3.3.44-5.6.44 AC FB, 15.6.44-10.8.44
*R-MK294  13.2.44-4.5.44, 21.5.44-17.6.44 BFB
   MK308  18.2.44-21.7.44
*M-NH249  6.44-13.7.44

## No. 341 (Free French) Sqn, Merston

Spitfire LF IX
 EN576  31.1.44-15.6.44
 EN635  17.10.43-15.6.44
*MJ363  6.44-29.6.44
 MJ498  9.2.44-22.6.44 FBB
 MJ522  23.2.44-22.6.44
*MJ564  29.1.44-24.7.44
*MJ617  31.1.44-10.6.44 AC FA
*MJ662  9.2.44-10.6.44 force-landed in France
*MJ671  18.2.44-13.7.44
*MJ723  29.1.44-3.8.44
 MJ752  31.1.44-27.7.44
*MJ772  20.1.44-18.6.44 AC FB
*MJ780  29.1.44-15.6.44, 22.6.44-3.8.44
*MJ815  6.44-1.7.44
 MJ871  9.2.44-8.6.44, 15.6.44-29.6.44
*MJ890  9.2.44-29.6.44
 MJ910  31.1.44-15.6.44 FTR force-landed in
        France?
 MJ912  31.1.44-8.6.44
*MK201  12.2.44-22.6.44 AC FB
*MK238  23.1.44-10.6.44 EFB, hit by flak,
        force-landed in France
*MK365  18.2.44-8.6.44
 MK484  6.4.44-21.7.44
 MK561  6.4.44-16.6.44 AC FA
 MK564  25.4.44-15.6.44 (AC FB on 403 Sqn)
*MK844  8.6.44-28.9.44
*NH270  8.6.44-3.8.44

## No. 345 (Free French) Sqn, Shoreham

Spitfire Vb LR/LF
*W3310  31.5.44-29.7.44 AC, 26.8.44-15.9.44
 W3765  3.4.44-31.5.44 ROS, 25.6.44-17.6.44?
 W3771  10.4.44-10.7.44 FTR
*W3843  7.4.44-6.6.44 EFB
 AA833  3.4.44-2.6.44 AC
*AA847  3.4.44-10.7.44 FTR

*Red and blue spinner bands and 'AH-Z' beneath the cockpit identify this as a Bognor-based No. 332 (Norwegian) Squadron Spitfire. (via A.S. Thomas)*

|  |  |
|---|---|
| AB970 | 6.6.44-8.6.44 EFB, SOC |
| *AB986 | 3.4.44-11.8.44 |
| *AD227 | 25.4.44-16.8.44 BFA |
| *AD238 | 13.4.44-8.7.44 |
| *AD386 | 3.4.44-11.8.44 |
| *AR328 | 25.4.44-19.7.44 RIW |
| *AR405 | 7.4.44-17.7.44 BFB, RIW |
| BL369 | 30.5.44-28.9.44 |
| *BL496 | 7.4.44-22.6.44 ROS, 6.7.44-17.8.44 |
| BL673 | 22.5.44-17.8.44 |
| *BL927 | 31.3.44-17.8.44 |
| *BM178 | 3.4.44-14.6.44, 29.6.44-2.11.44 |
| *BM312 | 12.4.44-7.6.44 EFB |
| *BM366 | 13.4.44-30.11.44 RIW |
| *BM413 | 6.44-4.8.44 |
| BM535 | 13.4.44-8.6.44 BFB |
| BM556 | 12.4.44-21.5.44 ROS, 16.6.44-17.8.44 |
| *BM635 | ?-28.9.44 |
| *EP284 | 14.4.44-28.9.44 |

## No. 349 (Belgian) Sqn, Selsey
Spitfire IX – not all aircraft operated on D-Day known

|  |  |
|---|---|
| EN332 | 19.1.44-3.12.45 |
| EN348 | 6.5.44-29.8.44 |
| MJ230 | 8.6.44-22.6.44 |
| MJ253 | 16.2.44-11.6.44 |
| MJ353 | ?-? |
| MJ369 | 16.2.44-16.4.44, 5.5.44-22.9.44 |
| MJ502 | 5.44-15.6.44 |
| *MJ748 | 16.2.44-7.6.44 FTR, shot down by AA near Caen |
| *MJ879 | 16.2.44-15.6.44 |
| MJ889 | 16.2.44-21.3.44 AC FA, held until 15.6.44 |
| MJ955 | 16.2.44-12.6.44 AC FB |
| MJ960 | 9.2.44-6.7.44 |
| *MJ964 | 5.44-15.6.44 |
| *MK148 | 16.2.44-25.4.44 ROS, ?-11.6.44 FB |
| *MK153 | 1.3.44-15.6.44 |
| MK175 | 16.2.44-12.6.44 EFB, hit by MJ955 after landing at Selsey |
| *MK178 | 2.44-15.7.44 |
| MK233 | 16.2.44-13.4.44 ROS, ?-28.9.44 |
| *MK252 | ?-8.6.44 FTR, from operation over Normandy |
| *MK302 | 5.44-15.6.44 |
| *MK354 | 16.2.44-22.6.44 |
| MK362 | 16.2.44-8.6.44 |
| MK363 | 16.2.44-6.6.44 FTR, from operation over France |

## No. 350 (Belgian) Sqn, Friston
Spitfire Mk V LF/LR (last operational use 4.7.44, first operational use of Mk IX 6.7.44)

|  |  |
|---|---|
| W3209 | 11.5.44-12.6.44 BFB |
| *W3759 | 26.3.44-16.8.44 |
| *W3970 | 13.3.44-23.7.44 |
| *AA720 | 22.5.44-10.6.44 FTR, crashed in sea |
| *AA910 | 13.3.44-22.3.44 ROS, 6.5.44-23.7.44 |
| AB141 | 18.4.44-10.6.44 |
| *AB180 | 13.3.44-14.7.44 |
| *AB276 | 10.4.44-24.6.44 ROS, 7.7.44-15.7.44 |
| *AR492 | (Vc) 13.3.44-14.7.44 |
| *BL780 | 3.4.44-11.6.44 ROS, 15.7.44-13.8.44 |
| *BM343 | 13.3.44-7.6.44 AC FB, flak damage |
| *BM344 | 13.3.44-20.6.44 RIW AST |
| *BM363 | 19.5.44-8.6.44 EFB, crashed 5 miles from base |
| *BM422 | 13.3.44-21.3.44 ROS, 12.5.44-10.6.44 |

|  |  |
|---|---|
|  | FTR |
| BM543 | 31.5.44-22.6.44 RIW |
| *BM583 | 19.5.44-7.8.44 BFB (on 345 Sqn) |
| *EE613 | (Vc) 13.3.44-14.7.44 |
| *EE723 | 13.3.44-14.6.44 EFB, crashed in Channel, pilot rescued by RN |
| *EN950 | ?-6.6.44 FTR, pilot baled out |
| *EP242 | 29.3.44-13.7.44 RIW |
| EP387 | 13.3.44-7.6.44 ROS, 29.6.44-23.7.44 |
| EP664 | 13.3.44-26.3.44, 1.6.44-14.7.44 |
| EP667 | 6.4.44-23.7.44 |

## No. 401 (Canadian) Sqn, Tangmere
Spitfire LF IX

|  |  |
|---|---|
| *MH413 | ?-22.6.44 EFB, shot down by friendly AA, Bayeux |
| *MH724 | ?-29.5.44 ROS, 6.44-1.10.44 |
| MH725 | 24.3.44-1.10.44 BFB |
| MJ127 | 8.11.43-5.10.44 |
| *MJ131 | 22.6.44-3.7.44 FTR |
| *MJ138 | 8.11.43-? |
| MJ152 | ?.44-17.6.44 |
| *MJ180 | 22.6.44-29.6.44 |
| *MJ231 | 22.6.44-25.7.44 FTR, hit by AA fire, Lisieux |
| *MJ246 | 22.6.44-28.6.44 FTR, pilot baled out near Caen |
| *MJ289 | 21.11.43-6.7.44 |
| *MJ313 | 21.11.43-22.6.44 Cat B |
| MJ428 | ?-28.6.44 shot down by Fw 190s south of Caen |
| *MK195 | 22.4.44-29.6.44, 27.7.44-16.9.44 (AC FB on 412 Sqn) |
| *MK263 | ?-22.6.44 BFB |
| *MK300 | 22.6.44-4.8.44, 24.8.44-31.8.44, 12.10.44-29.12.44 EFB |
| *MK780 | ?-23.6.44 AC FB |
| *MK845 | 22.6.44-28.9.44 |
| MK882 | ?-30.6.44 AC FB, crash-landed |
| *MK902 | ?-7.6.44 FTR, possible AA casualty |
| *ML129 | 22.6.44-25.6.44, 6.7.44-24.8.44 |
| *ML135 | 22.6.44-1.7.44 EFB, flak damage, south of Carentan |
| *ML305 | 27.6.44-24.8.44 |
| NH260 | 22.6.44-18.8.44 EFB |

## No. 402 (Canadian) Sqn, Horne
Spitfire V

|  |  |
|---|---|
| *P8788 | 27.4.44-25.7.44 |
| *W3129 | 13.5.44-15.7.44 |
| *W3250 | 30.5.44-8.6.44 ROS, 1.7.44-17.5.45 |
| *W3454 | 30.9.43-25.7.44 RIW |
| *W3529 | 4.12.43-13.6.44 RIW |
| *AA738 | 30.3.44-20.7.44 |
| *AA920 | 5.6.44-20.7.44 |
| AB509 | (Vc) 22.5.44-14.6.44 to Station Flight, Redhill |
| AB897 | 14.4.44-10.6.44 EFB |
| *AB910 | ?-? |
| *AD180 | 27.3.44-22.6.44 EFB |
| *BL547 | 5.9.43-19.7.44 RIW |
| *BL969 | 5.6.44-22.6.44 EFB |
| *BM205 | 13.3.44-20.7.44 |
| *BM233 | 27.4.44-22.6.44, 27.8.44-30.9.44 |
| BM490 | 24.5.44-8.6.44 ROS, 18.7.44-3.8.44 |
| *BM645 | 27.3.44-20.7.44 |
| EE680 | 13.4.44-15.8.44? |
| *EE686 | 27.9.43-14.7.44 |
| EE715 | 28.5.44-2.8.44 |
| EP548 | 25.4.44-10.5.44, 6.6.44-6.7.44 |

205

## No. 403 (Canadian) Sqn, Tangmere
Spitfire LF IX

| | |
|---|---|
| *MJ238 | 5.44-7.44 |
| *MJ348 | 5.44-17.8.44 |
| *MJ570 | 5.2.44-14.7.44 FTR, from Flers area |
| *MJ664 | 5.2.44-17.8.44 AC FB |
| MJ789 | 31.1.44-11.6.44 FTR (on 453 Sqn), shot down by AA |
| MJ793 | 31.1.44-27.7.44 |
| MJ827 | ?-9.6.44 (331 Sqn aircraft, FTR on 403 Sqn, shot down off *Omaha* beach) |
| MJ870 | 27.1.44-25.6.44 EFB, collided with *PL275* on take-off from Bazenville |
| *MJ886 | ?-9.6.44 |
| MJ891 | 30.1.44-27.7.44 |
| *MJ951 | ?-9.6.44 BFB (421 Sqn aircraft) |
| MJ954 | 24.1.44-10.6.44 BFB |
| MJ983 | 22.1.44-29.6.44 |
| *MJ988 | 11.2.44-28.6.44 EFA, crashed near Falaise, engine trouble |
| MK120 | 23.1.44-10.6.44 EFB (on 421 Sqn), undercarriage collapsed, Tangmere |
| MK194 | ?-10.6.44 AC FB, ROS, to HQ 127 Wing 29.6.44 |
| *MK570 | ?-18.6.44 FTR |
| *MK808 | ?-22.6.44 AC FA |
| MK859 | 5.44-14.6.44 FTR |
| MK881 | ?-14.7.44 FTR |
| ML248 | 5.44-28.6.44 FTR |
| ML411 | 5.44-24.8.44 FB |
| ML415 | 5.44-16.7.44 FB |
| ML420 | 5.44 17.7.44 BFB |
| NH196 | (411 Sqn a/c used on loan 5.6.44-6.6.44) |
| NH235 | 5.44-17.6.44 BFA |

## No. 411 (Canadian) Sqn, Tangmere
Spitfire LF IX

| | |
|---|---|
| *EN566 | Details uncertain |
| EN579 | 17.10.43-7.6.44 RIW |
| EN633 | 23.10.43-9.7.44 |
| EN636 | 17.10.43-15.6.44 |
| MA366 | 11.10.43-14.10.44 RIW |
| MH366 | 11.10.43-14.10.44 |
| *MH498 | 23.10.43-5.7.44 |

| | |
|---|---|
| *MH754 | ?-29.6.44 EFB, engine trouble, crashed south-east of Caen |
| *MJ125 | 6.11.43-6.7.44 |
| MJ133 | 21.11.43-23.8.44 |
| *MJ287 | ?-21.12.44 EFA |
| *MJ313 | 21.11.43-22.6.44 |
| *MJ454 | 2.12.43-29.6.44 |
| *MJ468 | 4.44-25.6.44 AC FA, 13.7.44-22.9.44 |
| MJ486 | 2.44?-25.6.44, 13.7.44-22.9.44 |
| *MJ905 | 5.44-20.6.44 EFB, engine failure, crashed in Channel |
| *MJ985 | Details uncertain |
| MK254 | 16.2.44-29.5.44 AC FB (on 313 Sqn) |
| MK446 | 13.3.44-12.6.44 EFB |
| *MK776 | ?-EFB 27.6.44 |
| *MK832 | 5.44-28.9.44 |
| *MK843 | 3.44-10.7.44 AC FA |
| *MK885 | ?-7.9.44 BFB |
| *NH195 | 5.44-11.6.44 EFB |
| *NH243 | 6.44-29.6.44 |

## No. 412 (Canadian) Sqn, Tangmere
Spitfire LF IX

| | |
|---|---|
| *MH450 | Details uncertain |
| *MJ136 | Details uncertain; frequently mentioned in ORB of 6.44 |
| *MJ144 | 21.11.43-30.5.44, BFA, 8.6.44 RIW |
| *MJ148 | 21.11.43-18.6.44 BFB |
| *MJ193 | 21.11.43-14.6.44 AC FB |
| *MJ255 | 11.11.43-11.6.44 AC FB |
| MJ304 | 23.11.43-2.8.44 FTR, shot down near Argentan |
| *MJ334 | 11.43-22.6.44 |
| *MJ384 | ?-17.6.44 FTR |
| *MJ392 | ?-? |
| *MJ485 | 4.44-12.8.44 FTR |
| *MJ959 | ?-28.9.44 |
| MK199 | 4.44-2.7.44 EFB |
| *MK237 | 5.44-27.9.44 FTR |
| MK244 | 8.2.44-22.6.44 |
| *MK253 | ?-18.7.44 |
| MK576 | 6.44-29.6.44 |
| *MK622 | 4.44-7.7.44 FTR, shot down by AA, west of Falcone |
| *MK633 | 5.44-6.44, supposedly also used by 331 Sqn in 6.44 |
| MK916 | 6.44-20.7.44 AC FB |

*Repairing a No. 403 (RCAF) Squadron Spitfire after a misfortune in Normandy on 11 June 1944. (IWM CL186)*

*Spitfire* S-Sugar, *its port mainplane torn away, was being flown by Flg Off H.G. Southwood when it was shot down on 11 June and crashed by a road near Tilly-sur-Seulles. (IWM B5661)*

## No. 416 (Canadian) Sqn, Tangmere

Spitfire LF IX

| | |
|---|---|
| *MJ575 | Details uncertain |
| *MJ611 | Details uncertain |
| *MJ770 | 30.1.44-4.10.44 RIW |
| *MJ787 | 31.1.44-17.6.44 BFB, 10.7.44 RIW |
| *MJ824 | 2.44-13.6.44 EFB, collided with NH415 near Caen |
| *MJ828 | 31.1.44-25.9.44 AC FB |
| MJ855 | 10.2.44-27.7.44 |
| *MJ872 | ?-17.8.44 |
| *MJ874 | 26.1.44-29.9.44 EFB, crash-landed |
| *MJ882 | 23.1.44-28.6.44 AC FA |
| *MJ929 | ?-8.6.44 EFB, crashed in Channel |
| *MJ953 | 18.2.44-18.7.44 AC FB |
| *MK117 | 22.1.44-10.7.44 FTR, shot down west of Fleury Harcourt |
| *MK139 | 1.2.44-5.8.44 AC FA |
| MK147 | 5.5.44-10.8.44 |
| *MK207 | 13.2.44-26.7.44 AC FB |
| MK472 | 4.44-15.6.44 (BFB on 421 Sqn, damaged by enemy fighters, Cat E 21.6.44 |
| *MK559 | Details uncertain, but AC FB on 341 Sqn 19.6.44 |
| *MK835 | 5.44-14.7.44 FB, force-landed in Normandy |
| *MK837 | 5.44-12.10.44 |
| *ML292 | 5.44-14.6.44 BFB |
| NH408 | 4.6.44-28.6.44 |

## No. 421 (Canadian) Sqn, Tangmere

Spitfire LF IX

| | |
|---|---|
| *MH415 | Details uncertain |
| MJ554 | 26.1.44-7.6.44 EFB |
| *MJ793 | 27.7.44-31.8.44 |
| *MJ820 | 27.7.44-18.8.44 EFB, flak damage, crashed south-west of Mezidon |
| *MJ855 | 27.7.44-12.10.44 |
| *MJ870 | (403 Sqn aircraft, used on loan) |
| *MJ880 | 23.1.44-12.7.44 AC FB, 27.7.44-23.8.44 FTR, shot down by fighters |
| *MJ891 | ?-7.9.44 |
| MJ951 | 22.1.44-9.6.44 BFB (on 403 Sqn) |

*Two Spitfires of No. 421 Squadron. (IWM CL782)*

| *MJ987 | (403 Sqn aircraft, used on loan) |
| *MJ994 | 31.1.44-29.6.44 |
| MK120 | (403 Sqn aircraft, used on loan, 10.6.44 EFB, undercarriage collapsed on landing, Tangmere) |
| *MK199 | (412 Sqn aircraft, used on loan) |
| *MK235 | ?-13.6.44 EFB, collided with *NH415*, crashed in Normandy |
| MK300 | 4.44-22.6.44, to 401 Sqn |
| MK468 | 4.44-6.7.44 |
| *MK472 | 4.44-15.6.44 FTR |
| *MK573 | 6.44-30.6.44 AC FB, 13.7.44-3.11.44, 23.11.44-30.11.44 |
| *MK920 | ?-12.11.44 |
| MK941 | ?-26.6.44 BFB |
| *NH183 | 5.44-7.6.44 EFA |
| *NH344 | 5.44-17.6.44 BFB |
| *NH415 | 17.5.44-19.8.44 EFB |

### No. 441 (Canadian) Sqn, Ford
Spitfire LF IX

| MH447 | 5.44-12.6.44 FTR |
| MH756 | 12.3.44-3.7.44 FTR, engine trouble, crashed in Channel |
| *MJ139 | 5.44-17.8.44 |
| *MK177 | 12.3.44-15.6.44 EFB, overshot on landing, re-Cat B 22.6.44 |
| *MK350 | 11.3.44-22.6.44 |
| *MK375 | 11.3.44-10.7.44 RIW |
| MK392 | 13.3.44-27.7.44 |
| *MK399 | 13.3.44-15.6.44 EFA, crash-landed Ste Croix-sur-Mer |
| *MK415 | 11.3.44-1.7.44 AC FB, to 144 Wing 13.7.44 |
| *MK417 | 12.3.44-10.8.44 |
| *MK420 | 11.3.44-6.6.44 EFB, re-cat B, serious flak damage |
| *MK460 | 24.3.44-2.6.44, re-cat E 28.6.44 |
| MK465 | 13.3.44-5.6.44 EFB (crashed at 22:40 hrs) |
| MK503 | 13.3.44-18.4.44 AC FA, ROS, 9-10.6.44 |
| *MK504 | 11.3.44-18.4.44 AC FA, to 83 GSU 17.8.44 |
| *MK515 | 11.3.44-15.6.44 AC FA |
| *MK630 | Dates uncertain |
| *MK633 | Use uncertain; assigned to 331 Sqn, flown by 441 Sqn |

| *MK907 | 5.44-10.8.44 |
| *ML205 | Use uncertain |

### No. 442 (Canadian) Sqn, Ford
Spitfire LF IX – aircraft operated on D-Day unknown

| MJ286 | 13.3.44-22.6.44 |
| MJ364 | 11.3.44-20.7.44 Cat B |
| MJ471 | 13.3.44-28.9.44 |
| MJ515 | 13.3.44-14.10.44 RIW |
| MJ528 | 13.3.44-28.6.44 AC FB |
| MJ608 | 13.3.44-7.6.44 EFB, fuel shortage, crashed in Channel |
| MK141 | 13.3.44-13.8.44 EFB, engine trouble, crashed near Camilly |
| MK157 | 13.3.44-12.5.44 AC FA, 8.6.44 EFB, crashed in Normandy |
| MK193 | 13.3.44-3.7.44 BFB |
| MK206 | ?-13.4.44 AC FB, 9.6.44 EFA, damaged at Ford by *DD758* |
| MK250 | 13.3.44-24.8.44 RIW |
| MK295 | 13.3.44-23.4.44 AC FA, 13.7.44-28.9.44 |
| MK309 | 13.3.44-22.6.44 to 453 Sqn |
| MK397 | 11.3.44-16.6.44 FTR |
| MK777 | 5.44-7.7.44 AC FB, 13.7.44-24.8.44 |
| MK826 | 24.3.44- EFB 1.8.44, hit by flak, crashed near Caen |

### No. 443 (Canadian) Sqn, Ford
Spitfire LF IX – aircraft operated on D-Day unknown

| MA370 | 13.3.44-1.7.44 |
| MH370 | 13.3.44-1.7.44 |
| H-MH850 | ?-7.6.44 FTR, engine trouble, crashed west of Cabourg |
| J-MJ366 | 11.3.44-27.6.44 AC FB |
| MJ451 | 13.3.44-15.6.44? |
| R-MJ455 | 13.3.44-8.6.44 FB and crash-landed |
| MJ741 | 13.3.44-10.7.44 BRB |
| MJ779 | 13.3.44-25.7.44 |
| MJ957 | Use uncertain |
| MK200 | 11.3.44-26.4.44 ROS, 9.6.44 – RIW 30.6.44 |
| MK261 | 11.3.44-19.10.44 |
| MK315 | 11.3.44-28.9.44 |
| G-MK343 | 11.3.44-12.6.44 BFB, flak damage, north-east of Caen |
| MK356 | 11.3.44-6.8.44 |
| MK367 | 11.3.44-22.6.44 |

*A gathering of No. 443 Squadron Spitfires at 'B3' (Ste. Croix-sur-Mer) in June 1944. (IWM CL87)*

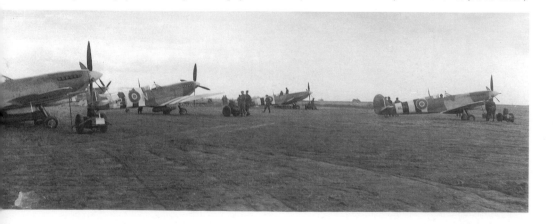

*Filmed from Mosquito DZ414, Spitfires using 'B3', where the first examples – Canadian-manned – touched down at 13:30 hrs on 10 June 1944. (IWM CL111)*

| | |
|---|---|
| T-MK397 | 11.3.44-16.6.44 FTR, shot down near Caen |
| W-MK605 | ?-16.6.44 FTR, shot down near Caen |
| S-MK607 | ?-16.6.44 FTR, shot down? |

### No. 453 (Australian) Sqn, Ford

Spitfire LF IX (aircraft operated on D-Day unknown; aircraft listing incomplete)

| | |
|---|---|
| MH443 | 15.3.44-15.6.44 |
| MH449 | ?-15.3.44 AC FA, ROS, 26.6.44-29.6.44 |
| MK260 | 15.3.44-? |
| MK284 | 15.3.44-? |
| MK288 | 15.3.44-? |
| MK299 | 15.3.44-? |
| MK325 | ?-23.4.44 BFB, 12.6.44 RIW |
| MK355 | 15.3.44-? |
| MK547 | 3.44-15.4.44 AC FA, ROS, 9.6.44-12.8.44 |
| MK575 | 5.44-26.7.44 |
| MK618 | 3.44-14.7.44 EFB |

### No. 485 (New Zealand) Sqn, Selsey

Spitfire LF IX

| | |
|---|---|
| MH501 | 24.8.43-15.6.44 |
| MJ154 | 25.10.43-9.44? |
| MK114 | 11.2.44-31.6.44 |
| MK198 | 11.2.44-23.4.44 AC FA, 8.6.44 to 310 Sqn |
| MK245 | 6.2.44-27.7.45 |
| MK246 | 6.2.44-25.3.44 ROS, 23.4.44-10.6.44 |
| *MK677 | 3.5.44-20.8.44 AC FB, ROS, 9.10.44-11.10.44 |
| *MK722 | 21.4.44-8.6.44 |
| *MK732 | Details uncertain |
| *MK754 | ?-8.6.44 |
| *MK849 | 21.4.44-13.7.44 |
| *MK862 | 22.5.44-8.6.44 AC |
| *MK886 | 21.4.44-16.11.44 |
| *MK897 | 25.4.44-15.11.44 |
| *MK904 | 1.5.44-22.6.44 |
| *MK914 | 23.4.44-6.7.44 |
| *MK950 | 30.4.44-29.6.44 |

*Differing positions for squadron identity letters are visible on these Spitfire IXs of No. 453 (RAAF) Squadron at 'B11' (Longues). (IWM MH6847)*

| | |
|---|---|
| *ML176 | 6.5.44-3.9.44 BFA |
| *ML355 | 30.4.44-14.6.44 RIW |
| *ML361 | 1.5.44-22.7.44 |
| *ML368 | ?-8.6.44 (EA B 1.1.45) |
| *ML377 | 30.4.44-10.8.44 |
| ML400 | 30.4.44-22.5.44 AC FA, ROS, 24.6.44-17.9.44 |
| *ML407 | 30.4.44-12.10.44 AC FB re-Cat B 19.10.44 |
| *ML412 | 3.5.44-8.7.44, 20.7.44-10.9.44 |

## No. 501 Sqn, Friston
Spitfire LF V

| | |
|---|---|
| Y-W3378 | 29.4.44-15.8.44 |
| W3606 | 29.4.44-27.6.44 |
| *M-W3702 | 24.10.43-12.7.44 EFB |
| *J-X4272 | Dates uncertain |
| *E-AA945 | 27.4.44-15.8.44 |
| *C-AB989 | 5.44-2.8.44 |
| *G-AD324 | 29.4.44-27.6.44 BFB, ROS, 11.8.44-3.11.44 RIW |
| *N-AD465 | 27.4.44-2.8.44 |
| *D-AR392 | 5.44-7.8.44 |
| *H-AR519 | 19.5.44-15.8.44 |
| *L-BL409 | 13.4.44-15.8.44 |
| *K-BL468 | 29.4.44-2.8.44 |
| *S-BL632 | 18.5.44-2.8.44 |
| *V-BM256 | 3.3.44-23.6.44 AC |
| *T-BM304 | 22.10.43-5.8.44 BFB (on 345 Sqn) |
| W-BM385 | 5.11.43-27.5.44, ROS, 12.6.44-14.7.44 BFB |
| *Q-BM593 | 31.5.44-13.8.44 RIW |
| *R-EP109 | 3.3.44-27.6.44 ROS, 13.8.44-3.9.44 |
| *F-EP281 | 30.5.44-15.8.44 |
| *A-EP395 | 27.3.44-12.8.44 |
| *P-EP398 | 29.4.44-14.7.44 EFB |
| *B-EP707 | 13.4.44-15.8.44 |
| *O-EP757 | 8.11.43-15.8.44 |

## No. 504 Sqn, Castletown (detachments at Acklington and Digby)
Spitfire Vb LF/LR mainly disposed of to 310 Sqn 15.7.44

| | |
|---|---|
| W3207 | 15.3.44-15.7.44 |
| AB203 | 15.3.44-5.7.44 |
| AB364 | 15.3.44-15.7.44 |
| AD557 | 27.4.44-15.7.44 |
| AR331 | 15.3.44-13.6.44 AC FB |
| AR396 | 15.3.44-15.7.44 BFB |
| AR424 | 15.3.44-15.7.44 |
| AR441 | 15.3.44-15.7.44 |
| BL329 | 15.3.44-25.4.44 ROS, 26.6.44-3.7.44 to 118 Sqn |
| BL486 | 15.3.44-15.7.44 |
| BL851 | 15.3.44-15.7.44 |
| BL907 | 15.3.44-15.7.44 |
| BM381 | 15.3.44-15.7.44 |
| BM428 | 15.3.44-15.7.44 |
| BM578 | 15.3.44-15.7.44 |
| BM636 | 15.3.44-15.7.44 |
| EP125 | 14.3.44-15.7.44 |
| EP169 | 15.3.44-6.4.44 AC FA, ROS, 15.7.44 to 310 Sqn |
| EP485 | 15.3.44-15.7.44 |

## No. 602 Sqn, Ford
Spitfire LF V

| | |
|---|---|
| BL686 | 25.1.44-7.3.44 ROS, 1.7.44-7.12.44 |

Spitfire LF IX

| | |
|---|---|
| *MH508 | 6.44-20.7.44 |

| | |
|---|---|
| *MH512 | ?-1.7.44 FTR, shot down by AA |
| *MH526 | 6.10.43-6.7.44 |
| *MH708 | 6.10.43-6.7.44 |
| *MH709 | Dates uncertain |
| *MH716 | 25.9.43-15.6.44 |
| *MH736 | 6.44-6.7.44 |
| *MJ239 | 6.44-16.6.44 |
| *MJ252 | Dates uncertain |
| *MJ276 | 5.44-15.6.44 FTR, force-landed in France, BBOC |
| *MJ305 | 5.44-7.7.44 FTR, shot down by AA |
| *MJ339 | 5.44-7.6.44 FB, force-landed in France, engine trouble |
| *MJ981 | 5.44-23.6.44 AC FA, crashed on take-off |
| *MK232 | 6.44-10.8.44 |
| *MK255 | 6.44-24.8.44 |
| MK611 | 5.44-11.6.44 serious battle damage |
| *MK612 | 4.44-? |
| *MK614 | 4.44-1.8.44 FTR |
| *MK624 | 4.44-10.7.44 RIW |
| ML252 | 4.44-4.7.44 FTR |
| ML307 | 5.44-7.8.44 |
| *NH203 | 5.44-10.6.44 FTR |

## No. 610 Sqn, Harrowbeer
Spitfire F XIV (aircraft operated on D-Day unknown)

| | |
|---|---|
| NH688 | 12.4.44-13.7.44, 18.8.44-4.45 |
| NH695 | 26.5.44-4.7.44 RIW |
| NH719 | 26.5.44-25.8.44, 9.44-10.12.44 FTR |
| RB140 | 25.4.44-30.10.44 EFB |
| RB142 | 2.1.44-12.7.44 EFB |
| RB145 | 3.1.44-4.7.44, 16.9.44-20.10.44 |
| RB148 | 1.1.44-7.6.44 RIW |
| RB150 | 4.44-30.8.44 EFB |
| RB151 | ?-? |
| RB153 | 6.1.44-9.7.44 EFB |
| RB154 | 6.1.44-5.44, 5.44-25.12.44 |
| RB156 | 5.44-26.3.45 |
| RB157 | 5.44-4.1.45 |
| RB163 | 23.2.44-23.6.44 |
| RB164 | 20.2.44-23.6.44, 14.7.44-23.1.45 AC FB |
| RB166 | 23.2.44-25.4.44, 10.5.44-29.8.44 |
| RB170 | 11.4.44-14.4.44, 2.6.44-10.8.44 |
| RB176 | 22.2.44-29.3.45 |

## No. 611 Sqn, Deanland
Spitfire LF Vb

| | |
|---|---|
| *P8038 | 1.7.43-21.7.44 |
| R6888 | 4.44?-15.6.44 EFB |
| *AA839 | 26.5.44-6.8.44 |
| *AR364 | 17.11.43-6.8.44 |
| AR373 | 9.11.43-23.7.44 |
| *AR427 | 27.4.44-6.8.44 |
| *AR467 | 28.5.44-15.6.44 RIW |
| AR517 | 22.3.44-10.7.44 |
| *AR608 | 26.7.43-10.7.44 |
| *BL263 | 31.8.43-6.8.44 |
| *BL472 | 14.4.44-6.7.44 AC FA |
| *BL541 | 27.4.44-6.8.44 |
| *BL692 | 23.12.43-6.8.44 |
| *BM131 | 5.44-6.8.44 |
| *BM200 | Used on loan from 234 Sqn |
| *BM203 | 12.11.43-14.7.44, 21.7.44-10.4.45, 4.5.45-2.6.45 |
| *BM258 | 6.44-? |
| *BM345 | 24.8.43-12.6.44 AC FA, hit by flak, landed safely |
| *BM368 | 14.4.44-6.8.44 |

BM572  27.4.44-18.5.44 AC FA, ROS,
       16.6.44-24.5.45
*BM641  27.4.44-23.7.44
*EE660  27.5.44-6.8.44
*EE665  25.9.43-6.7.44
*EP300  8.10.43-19.10.44

## No. 616 Sqn, Fairwood Common
Spitfire VII
EN417  9.11.43-24.8.44
EN477  9.11.43-31.8.44
EN808  3.4.44-22.6.44
MB762  26.2.44-?
MB769  28.9.43-8.9.44
MB822  17.4.44-19.6.44 RIW
MB824  8.1.44-19.8.44
MB885  15.5.44-20.8.44
MB915  7.11.43-8.11.44
MB934  9.7.44-19.8.44
MD101  25.11.43-2.5.44, 14.5.44-1.6.44,
       23.6.44-22.7.44
MD104  14.12.43-10.6.44 EFB
MD107  14.5.44-22.7.44
MD121  31.1.44-12.6.44 EFB
MD133  22.5.44-19.6.44 EFB
MD182  25.5.44-28.10.44

## Station Flight, Castletown
Spitfire HF VI
BR577  4.12.43-14.6.44

## Station Flight, Peterhead
Spitfire HF VI
BR197  24.12.43-9.7.44
BR297  27.11.43-8.6.44
BR304  24.12.43-7.6.44
BR579  27.11.43-8.6.44

In addition to RAF examples other Spitfire Mk Vs, remained in USAAF hands in June 1944, included:

## 31st Air Transport Group, Grove
AB976  26.5.44-7.7.44 RIW
AR278  31.5.44-25.7.44 RIW
AR295  2.6.44-4.7.44
BL993  31.5.44-23.7.44 RIW

BM526  5.6.44-13.7.44
EP606  13.5.44-7.7.44

## 67th Reconnaissance Group, Membury
W3848  2.11.43-16.6.44 RIE
W3902  7.5.44-18.7.44
A4729  20.12.43 20.6.44 RIW DH
AA882  2.7.43-17.6.44 RIW DH
AB789  22.11.43-19.8.44
AB862  22.11.43-17.6.44 RIW DH
AD118  17.10.43-14.6.44, to AFDU
AD191  6.12.43-17.6.44 RIW Heston
AD288  20.11.43-16.6.44 RIW DH
AD451  20.12.43-16.6.44 RIW DH
AR393  6.1.44-17.6.44 RIW Heston
BM229  6.1.44-12.6.44 RIW DH
BM318  26.1.44-20.6.44 RIW
EP768  20.12.43-11.8.44

## USAAF, Middle Wallop
AA728  8.5.44-18.7.44
AB898  9.5.44-18.7.44
AR390  8.5.44-17.7.44
AR395  10.5.44-15.7.44
BL247  9.5.44-18.7.44
BL368  9.5.44-18.7.44
BL437  9.5.44-17.7.44
BL530  9.5.44-17.7.44
BL729  9.5.44-17.6.44
BL962  9.5.44-15.7.44
BM411  9.5.44-16.6.44 RIW
BM430  7.5.44-17.7.44
EP182  9.5.44-?

## Miscellaneous Spitfire Vs in USAAF hands
AD464  1.10.42-12.7.44 RIW
AR404  9.11.43 to Mt Farm, period uncertain
BL243  17.1.44-18.8.44 RIW
BL670  17.1.44-?
BL888  17.1.44-14.6.44
BL898  12.5.43-16.6.44 used by No. 2 USA
       Sqn
BM512  17.1.44-13.8.44
BM630  1.7.43-10.8.44 used by 335 US Sqn

# The Bristol Beaufighter VI(f)

By June 1944 the Beaufighter had all but left the air defence regime in Britain, and only No. 406 Squadron based at Winkleigh was listed as still operating them. Although No. 68 Squadron certainly held 16 Mk VI(f)s which are reckoned to have remained at Fairwood Common for some weeks after leaving the front-line, the squadron was no longer established with Beaufighters. No. 406 was also already receiving Mosquito NF Mk XIIs.

On the night of 5/6 June No. 406 Squadron mounted four defensive patrols off the south-west coast and a Beaufighter crewed by Flt Lt H.D. McNabb with Flt Sgt P.F. Tindall, flew a *Ranger* to Lannion and Morlaix. Near the latter airfield a shell exploded below the aircraft, making a large hole under the navigator's position, and breaking the elevator trim cable.

Next night four Beaufighters (including *ND223* and *ND225*) flew Channel patrols within Operation *Bigot* while two Mosquitoes of the squadron flew *Rangers* to Morlaix, Lannion and Kerlin Bastard. The last Beaufighter night-fighter operational patrols were flown on 9 August when *KW119* (1/Lt J.M. Purdy, USAAF and Flg Off J.J. Green) and *ND231* (1/Lt S.W. Filkosky USAAF and Flg Off F.L. Hill) patrolled at night over naval vessels off the Brest Peninsula, which activity had already attracted 12 sorties that month. Mosquitoes took over Brest patrols from Beaufighters on 10 August. The last Beaufighters left the squadron on 27 August.

## Beaufighter VI(f)s on squadron strength, 5 June 1944

\* operated on 6 June 1944

### No. 68 Sqn, Fairwood Common

| | |
|---|---|
| *V8568* | 2.4.44-3.7.44 |
| *V8569* | 9.2.43-6.7.44 |
| *\*V8613* | 18.4.44-6.10.44 |
| *V8618* | 21.2.43-22.7.44 |
| *V8620* | 28.2.43-14.8.44 |
| *V8742* | 8.3.43-22.7.44 |
| *MM844* | 11.6.43-23.8.44 |
| *\*MM850* | 15.6.43-6.7.44 |
| *MM883* | 5.5.44-17.8.44 |
| *MM915* | 13.5.44-6.7.44 |
| *MM920* | 18.9.43-16.8.44 |
| *ND211* | 25.9.43-27.8.44 |
| *ND220* | 17.4.44-15.6.44 RIW |
| *ND239* | 23.12.43-11.7.44 |
| *\*ND268* | 9.5.44-11.7.44 |
| *ND169* | 17.4.44-23.7.44 |

### No. 406 Sqn, Winkleigh

| | |
|---|---|
| *KV977* | 4.10.43-26.8.44 |
| *KV980* | 22.10.43-12.6.44 RIW |
| *KW101* | 22.10.43-28.6.44 |
| *KW102* | 24.10.43-2.7.44 |
| *KW105* | 24.10.43-23.7.44 RIW |
| *\*KW119* | 2.12.43-28.8.44 |
| *MM914* | 5.5.44-1.9.44 |
| *MM946* | 5.5.44-1.3.45 |
| *ND216* | 5.10.43-4.6.44 |
| *ND219* | 9.10.43-24.8.44 (ROS 4.6.44-16.6.44) |
| *\*ND221* | 4.10.43-10.8.44 RIW |
| *ND222* | 12.10.43-23.6.44 RIW (ROS 11.4.44-9.6.44) |
| *\*ND223* | 12.10.43-11.6.44 RIW |
| *ND224* | 12.10.43-10.6.44 RIW |
| *\*ND225* | 22.10.43-13.7.44 RIW |
| *ND228* | 26.10.43-13.7.44 RIW |
| *ND226* | 5.5.44-28.8.44 |
| *ND267* | 5.5.44-28.8.44 |

# Taylorcraft Austers: the gunners' eyes

When the British Army went to France in 1939 it relied for air support mainly upon RAF-flown Westland Lysanders. Events in May 1940 proved them to be too large and intractable for the task despite their splendid short-field performance. By 1944,

*Auster AOPs were derived from Taylorcraft Plus D T9120, acquired for field trials in France in 1939.*

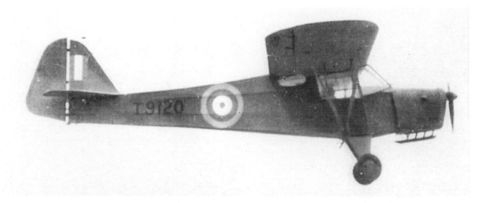

*A line of Auster AOP IVs at Rearsby, with* MT226 *visible. (Auster)*

technology had largely superseded the Lysander's message pick-up hook – although not the physical transfer of documents. Another fundamental change could be found sitting on the pilot's seat for, although Austers were on RAF charge, they were handled and flown by RAF-trained soldiers. While part of the AEAF, the air observation post (AOP) squadrons followed an Army lifestyle even to the extent that the first squadron went ashore in Normandy, via the beach – the hard way – just like the other soldiers. Their mounts, ideal for gunnery observation, were modifications of American pre-war small high-wing Taylorcraft monoplanes revamped in Britain into the Auster family.

One Taylorcraft Plus Model C was field tested in France late 1939. Its value led in 1941 to plans for a militarized 'austerity' version, the Taylorcraft Auster AOP Mk I. Although its de Havilland Gipsy Major

engine was not ideal, the aircraft carrying 10 gal of petrol could, with full flap, unstick in 85 yds and land in 160 yds. In between it could fly hands-off at a mere 55 mph, thus giving it considerable battlefield support potential.

Extended glazing improved the view from the 1,400 lb 1942 version, the AOP Mk III, top speed 144 mph. Highly manoeuvrable and delightfully light to fly, the Auster III could land in 150 yds which meant that it could operate from a meadow adjacent to a gun battery.

Still needed was a superior engine and two Auster Is were experimentally re-engined with the American Lycoming 290. All-up weight increased, but all-round performance improved, so a modified version was put into production in late 1943 as the AOP Mk IV, offering an even better rear view. A&AEE trials showed its still air stalling speed to be a mere 41 mph

*A Walrus's eye-view of an Auster being shepherded to France on D-Day. (IWM)*

**Above** *A splendid view indeed of a Fleet Air Arm Walrus II (HD902?) leading Austers to France. (IWM)*

**Below** *Preparing to cross to France, Auster IVs of No. 652 (AOP) Squadron assemble at Bolt Head. (IWM)*

**Bottom** *No. 652 (AOP) Squadron's very basic mobile Operations Room. (Museum of Army Flying)*

– 34 mph with the flaps fully down – giving it almost hovering ability, thus making it even more ideal for observing artillery shoots. Improved elevator trim, too, led to more positive handling. Fuel capacity had increased by half to 15 gal, normal loaded weight to about 1,600 lb. Squadron delivery began in February 1944, and this was the version the Army took to France in 1944. Just before D-Day several Auster Mk Vs (a refined version of the Mk IV) entered service.

On 2 June 1944 Operation *Bell Weather*, under the overall watch of No. 46 Group, came into play. Seven AOP squadrons holding 102 Auster Mk IVs and allocated to the AEAF came under Old Sarum's control preparatory to moving to France. It was anticipated that 12 Mk IVs of No. 652 Squadron, and perhaps four of 'A' Flight, No. 662 Squadron, might cross to Normandy on D-Day. On D+1 and D+2, formations of Austers would be guided on a 60-mile-long crossing by two navigating Royal Navy Walruses to landing spaces in Normandy. Immediately prior to D-Day these advance Austers were positioned at Selsey, where 662 Squadron arrived on D-Day. Spotting for the artillery was certain to be a desperate, prime need.

Also at Selsey was No. 652 Squadron, acquainted with Austers since November 1942 and which had shown it possible to control 10 'shoots' a day during Exercise *Spartan*, the 1943 major tactical air force mobility trial. At Ipswich in February 1944 the first Auster IVs joined No. 652, and on 29 April 1944 the squadron had entered the invasion concentration area at Cobham to await the call to advance.

On 5 June the squadron personnel embarked and by 12:30 hrs on 6 June personnel of the two Flights of the squadron, aboard landing craft, were in Norman waters. At 02:30 hrs on 7 June 'A' Flight main party went ashore and started marching to their earmarked landing ground at Bény-sur-Mer, only to find the Germans stoutly defending the area. They had, literally, to fight their way through.

'A' Flight's vehicle party disembarked at 04:00 hrs and on approaching Bény was engaged by much small arms fire before having to ward off, and escape from, attacks by infantry and tanks. By radio they advised 'B' Flight – still at sea – of the situation. Since there were no prospects of operating from Bény ALG, with the Germans so close and a radar station a mere 500 yds from the site, when 'B' Flight personnel and vehicles disembarked at 18:30 hrs on 7 June they made for a site by 3rd Division HQ at Plumetot.

By early 8 June the second ALG area had been sufficiently cleared of the enemy to allow four 'B' Flight Auster IVs, shepherded from Bolt Head by a Royal Navy Walrus, to fly in from Britain by 08:15 hrs, making them the first British aircraft to be based in France after the invasion began. That day the pilots spotted for seven artillery shoots during which two batteries firing upon 6th Airborne Division HQ were silenced. Mid-afternoon found the 'B' Flight contingent setting out to their intended ALG. It also saw the arrival of the first No. 662 Squadron aircraft which landed on a 120-yd-long strip near

*An Auster IV hidden in a bulldozed trench covered in camouflage netting. (Museum of Army Flying)*

*Removing the netting from an Auster IV of No. 652 (AOP) Squadron. (Museum of Army Flying)*

Arromanches, from where they were soon in action spotting for the Army and also for the battleship HMS *Rodney*.

On 9 June, with operations still impossible from Bény-sur-Mer, 'A' Flight, No. 652 Squadron pulled out and moved to the second operating ground. Ten shoots were directed that day, the most eventful coming late afternoon when, at around 17:00 hrs, Captain Pugh's *MT105* was set upon by five Fw 190s. He evaded two of their attacks only to be shot down and fatally wounded in a third onslaught. Black and white stripes on the upper surfaces of his aircraft were said to make it too conspicuous from above, for which reason many such markings were soon removed from AEAF aircraft. By the end of D+3 'A' Flight had a new ALG near Reviers.

The effectiveness of the Auster AOPs was such that when they appeared, enemy batteries stopped firing. Little wonder, for on 10 June, by which time the squadron was also carrying out aerial photography, No. 652 three times observed the impact points of hefty shells hurled ashore from the cruiser HMS *Belfast*. By the end of June 1944, four more AOP squadrons were ashore.

## Austers on squadron strength, 5 June 1944

(AOP Mk IVs unless otherwise indicated)

### No. 652 Sqn (landed in Normandy 7 June)

MS950  19.2.44-11.6.44
MS953  19.2.44-26.4.46
MS955  19.2.44-26.4.46
MS957  19.2.44-14.9.44 BFA

*An Auster IV carrying out a Normandy shoot for 25-pounder guns. (Museum of Army Flying)*

```
MT101   19.2.44-19.4.45
MT102   19.2.44-29.8.46
MT103   6.3.44-23.2.45 EFA
MT104   22.2.44-28.4.45 AC FB
MT105   19.2.44-9.6.44 EFB
MT106   22.2.44-18.3.45 B GA
MT107   24.2.44-13.7.44
MT111   24.2.44-23.6.44 BFB
MT172   8.6.44-19.7.45
MT345   12.5.44-12.4.45
MT346   13.5.44-22.2.45
```

## No. 653 Sqn (landed in Normandy 18 June)

```
MS958   21.2.44-30.4.45
MS959   11.2.44-24.10.44 EFB
MS960   17.2.44-10.8.44
MS962   13.2.44-30.8.45
MS968   2.44-12.7.45
MS969   21.2.44-17.7.44 EFB
MS970   21.2.44-16.10.45
MS979   21.2.44-?
MT108   2.44-30.4.45
MT112   24.2.44-2.4.45 EFA
MT113   16.5.44-20.7.44
MT164   8.3.44-26.8.44 EFB
MT165   9.3.44-20.7.44
MT166   14.3.44-8.8.44
MT167   18.3.44-20.7.44
MT168   9.3.44-20.7.44
MT169   21.3.44-19.4.45
```

## No. 658 Sqn (landed in Normandy 18 June)

```
MT132   2.3.44 1.7.44 BFB
MT133   12.3.44-14.9.44
MT134   3.3.44-5.8.44 BFB
MT135   29.2.44-18.7.44 BFA
MT136   3.3.44-14.9.44 BFB
MT137   3.3.44-28.5.45
MT138   3.3.44-25.7.45
MT140   3.3.44-6.7.44
MT141   4.3.44-22.6.44 EA, ground fire,
        21.7.44-3.8.44
MT142   4.3.44-6.7.44
MT143   4.3.44-1.7.44, 17.8.44-12.4.45
MT144   4.3.44-6.7.44
MT145   4.3.44-6.7.44
MT158   12.3.44-1.1.45 EFB
MT270   (Mk IV) 7.4.43-6.7.44
MT391   (Mk III) 11.43-15.6.44
MT405   (Mk III) 10.10.43-23.9.44
MT406   (Mk III) 27.6.43-15.6.44
```

## No. 659 Sqn (landed in France 13 June)

```
MT170   27.3.44-3.5.45
MT171   12.3.44-11.8.44 EFA
MT174   5.4.44-8.8.44 BFA
MT176   22.3.44-18.7.44 BFA
MT177   24.3.44-2.8.44 EFB
MT179   24.3.44-29.6.44
MT180   27.3.44-6.8.44 EFA
MT181   30.3.44-25.7.44 Cat B (enemy ground
        action)
MT182   22.3.44-22.6.44 EFB
MT189   30.3.44-16.6.45
MT191   22.3.44-11.7.44 BFB
MT255   7.4.44-19.3.45
MT256   5.4.44-29.3.45
```

```
MT271   12.4.44-16.6.45
MT273   14.4.44-3.2.45 EFB (shot down by
        Fw 190 near Venlo)
MT274   14.4.44-29.6.44
```

## No. 660 Sqn, (landed in France 9 June; aircraft mostly allocated 8.6.44, in use earlier)

```
MS963   8.6.44-26.3.45 FTR
MS964   8.6.44-9.8.45
MS965   8.6.44-11.4.45
MS966   8.6.44-5.1.45 EFB (damaged by AA
        fire)
MS971   8.6.44-1.5.46
MS973   8.6.44-14.9.44 EFA
MS974   8.6.44-8.2.45
MS975   8.6.44-26.8.45
MS976   8.6.44-22.2.45
MS978   8.6.44-1.5.45
MT114   8.6.44-15.6.44 FA
MT115   8.6.44-25.5.46
MT119   8.6.44-13.9.44 FA
MT120   8.6.44-16.8.44 EFA
```

## No. 661 Sqn (landed in France 18 June)

```
MT121   ?-22.6.44 EFA
MT122   15.6.44-8.6.45
MT124   ?-12.6.44 AC FA
MT125   15.6.44-9.11.45
MT126   15.6.44-21.6.45
MT127   15.6.44-22.6.44
MT130   15.6.44-15.8.44
MT118   10.5.44-15.6.44
MT275   12.4.44-8.11.45
```

## No. 662 Sqn (landed in France 8 June)

```
MT184   3.4.44-22.6.44 BFA
MT186   22.3.44-5.3.45 BFB
MT187   24.3.44-24.8.44 EFB
MT188   24.3.44-28.3.45 EFB (hit by shell
        whilst observing)
MT190   24.3.44-15.7.44, 2.8.44-29.4.45
MT192   27.3.44-14.6.45
MT193   25.3.44-26.4.45
MT195   24.3.44-3.8.44 BFB
MT197   27.3.44-5.6.45
MT199   27.3.44-20.1.45 BFB
MT213   3.4.44-11.9.44 AC FB
MT214   28.3.44-19.6.44 FTR (shot down
        whilst observing)
MT216   28.3.44-28.7.45
MT217   3.4.44-28.4.45 FBB
MT218   28.3.44-24.5.45
MT347   19.5.44-6.2.45
MT348   19.5.44-20.4.45
```

Many AEAF 'fighter' squadrons were allocated an Auster Mk III, IV or V for light transport and urgent communications duties. These other users included:

## AEAF Communications Sqn, Heston

```
MT339   (Mk IV) 11.5.44-14.6.44
MT356   (Mk V, first production a/c) 30.5.44-
        13.6.44
MT364   (Mk V) 8.6.44-3.5.45
```

## SHAEF Communications Sqn, Heston

```
MT340   (Mk IV) 11.5.44-30.8.45
```

*HQ 2TAF Communications Sqn,*
**Hartfordbridge Flats**
    *MT284* (Mk IV) 31.5.44-8.6.44
    *MT389* (Mk III) 5.2.44-23.6.44
    *MK445* (Mk III) 13.4.44-24.6.44

*No. 83 Group Support Unit,* **Redhill**
    *MT357* (Mk V) 6.6.44-19.4.45 BFA

*No. 85 Group Communications Sqn*
    *MT333* (Mk IV) 10.5.44-15.7.44 BFA
    *MT334* (Mk IV) 10.5.44-30.11.44
    *MT335* (Mk IV) 10.5.44-18.9.44 BFA
    *MT336* (Mk IV) 10.5.44-31.8.44 BFA
    *MT337* (Mk IV) 10.5.44-9.4.46

# Fighter reconnaissance Mustangs

During the months immediately preceding D-Day, low-flying Mustangs were responsible for gathering the essential photographs and intelligence material for the Normandy landings. On D-Day the RAF's Allison-engined Mustangs flying low, in pairs, observed the effectiveness of naval gunfire or sought details of enemy troop movements.

Two of the squadrons involved were Nos. 2 and 268, which at first light on 6 June began spotting the effectiveness of gunfire from the cruisers HMS *Belfast*, *Hawkins*, *Kempenfelt* and *Montcalm*. They operated until midday after briefings by Captains Parish and Wilson, RN, then stood by to carry out reconnaissance flights for the 1st Canadian Army. By then over 500 sorties had been flown by the host of assorted aircraft also operating from Lee-on-Solent, with the two RAF squadrons mentioned working to detailed plans in assisting ships firing on shore targets between Le Havre and Port en Bessin.

Thought to be the first eyewitness of the Allied landings in the American sector, was Mustang IA pilot Flt Lt Weighill flying *FD566* who, with Flg Off Shute as his No. 2 in *FD529*, left Gatwick at 05:00 hrs and crossed out over Bournemouth only to enter a very heavy storm. The weather soon cleared and then, to quote his report: 'Through the early mist one could see the flashes of gunfire. Flak over the beaches, of terrific intensity, created a black cloud over the area. We made landfall to the east of Barfleur, and then flew down to Pointe de la Pircée. Inside the Bay the sea was littered with ships of all descriptions ploughing doggedly towards the enemy coast and looking very grim and determined. As we were early we stooged up and down the beaches a few miles inland, but flak soon cured us of that habit.

'I established contact with HMS *Glasgow* which commenced to pound away at a strongpoint. The bombardment was terrific. I could see the shells in the form of red and white lights as they left the ships and flew towards the shore. Halfway through, *Glasgow* asked for progress of the landing craft. I went to 1,000 ft and reported they were about 300 yds off land. We saw the larger vessels turn broadside and belch flames and destruction; a most terrifying sight for as they fired what are now known to have been rockets, a sheet of flame 50 yds long enveloped the ship. By this time the first boat was ashore and I watched it. The front came down and men inside jumped into the water and ran towards the beach. This wonderful moment I reported, the first men had actually landed. Smoke and dust hid the beach from view, but an occasional clear patch enabled us to see more and more.'

At 06:43 hrs the second shoot began with the fighters spotting for the warships HMS *Emerald*, *Flores*, *Ramillies*, *Roberts* and veteran *Warspite*. A third shoot began around 09:00 hrs, this time with HMS *Argonaut*, the Free French cruiser *Gleyques* and the USS *Nevada*.

At 11:00 hrs W. Off. McClean toured the beaches from 5,000 ft, making landfall at Ile de Marcoeuf for a stupendous panoramic view of the whole length of the invasion beaches and the thousands of ships. He reported the beaches to be 'black with landing troops' and 'about three miles inland, big fires near Mere l'Eglise' and 'the whole coastline fire-dotted'. Only Flt Lt Woodward failed to return from a shoot near Ouistreham. He had called his No. 2 saying he could not continue, and was going to try to get home. After lunch a BBC recording team arrived to talk to the Mustang pilots.

In the evening Nos. 2 and 268 Squadrons (i.e. 35 Wing) took over the task performed by the US 67th Reconnaissance Group, flying 14 sorties in their Mustangs and scouring the Cherbourg Peninsula and an area east of Rouen for signs of enemy reinforcement movement.

Other Mustang squadrons had equally eventful days, No. 168 also despatching its first two pairs (Sqn Ldr P.W. Mason in *AM197* with Flg Off J.P.C. Catterns in *AM102* and Flt Lt Richardson in *AP167* with Flg Off J.W. Walker (Australian) in *AP195*) at 05:00 hrs for a Tac/R between Port-en-Bessin and Alençon. During the squadron's fourth operation, again by four aircraft, one of the first casualties occurred when off Lion-sur-Mer Flg Off Barnard's *AM225* suddenly exploded, possibly hit by a shell from a bombarding warship. Around midday two of the squadron's pilots saw, four miles south of Trouville, a dozen unidentified aircraft, thought to be the first enemy fighters seen that day.

But what of the background to the remarkable P-51 Mustang? Invariably presented as America's finest fighter of the 1940s and as much British as American, it was undistinguished until mated with the Rolls-Royce Merlin – except in the low-level fighter-reconnaissance role.

While the Germans were busy seizing Scandinavia in April 1940, a British delegation was visiting North American Inc., with whom a bond existed after pre-war purchase for the RAF of their Harvard trainer. Already the firm had dabbled with fighters and the British asked whether North American was interested in designing one for the RAF. The company jumped at the chance and in a matter of days produced a layout for a superb-looking aeroplane, the NA 73. With faith in the company's claim that the aircraft would be flying in the autumn, the British on 29 May 1940 ordered 230 examples.

In the new design everything possible was done to reduce drag. Smooth and slender lines, radiator tucked well into the fuselage, square wing-tips to improve rate of roll, all were carefully incorporated. So was the then revolutionary laminar wing, with an aerofoil section in which the deepest part was well towards the mainplane trailing-edge to allow smooth air to pass over much of the wing surface. Although ideal at high speed, it meant a longer take-off run, and slow-speed handling was somewhat impaired.

The prototype of what had at the height of the Battle of Britain been named Mustang first flew on 26 October 1940 –

*AG346, the first Mustang I to reach Britain, photographed in November 1941.*

well on time. By then the RAF's order for the dashing American fighter had risen to 620. The first production Mustang I for the RAF flew on 16 April 1941 and, without military load, reached a top speed of 394 mph at 15,000 ft.

September 1941 saw the first RAF Mustangs packed for shipment and on 5 January 1942 No. 26 Squadron became the first recipient. On 24 January 1942 the decision was taken to equip 10 squadrons with Mustang Is – but all were in Army Co-operation Command and not Fighter Command, for the Mustang, after all its great promise, was a disappointing performer. Why? The Allison V-1710 engine which powered it gave a maximum output of 1,150 hp at a mere 12,000 ft, thus precluding the Mustang's use for general combat in Fighter Command.

Nevertheless, testing in Britain showed the V-1710 to run extremely smoothly at low revs; indeed, the Mustang I could fly an acceptable low-level fighter-reconnaissance combat profile for an astonishing 4.1 hrs whereas British fighters were hard put to reach half that time. At 15,000 ft the Mustang, carrying 140 gal of fuel, had a range of 990 miles. Its 11 ft 10 in-wide undercarriage track was another praiseworthy feature; likewise the two nose and wing .50-in guns backed by four .303-in wing guns. Loaded for official trials the aeroplane's take-off weight was 8,625 lb and the recorded top speed was 370 mph, reached at 15,000 ft.

Farnborough's scientists investigated the high performance, attributing it mainly to the 50 lb/100 fps drag ratio compared with 65 lb/100 fps of the average Spitfire. Fine lines and the laminar wing undoubtedly enhanced the performance, making it higher than the Spitfire V's below 25,000 ft although the Spitfire out-turned the Mustang I.

Interim fighter-reconnaissance versions soon appeared, the first being the Mk IA with four 20-mm wing-mounted cannon. Then came the Mustang II with an Allison F4R engine raising the top speed to 401 mph at 4,400 ft. Some examples featured the -F2OR engine which produced 409 mph at 10,000 ft.

On 1 June 1944 the total RAF holding of Mustang I/IIs was 495 of which 306 were airworthy in Britain. Three squadrons employed 58 Mk Is, two squadrons had in total 29 Mk IAs and No. 2 Squadron still had 11 Mk IIs, making a total of 98 for operational employment in the very important tactical fighter-reconnaissance role.

## Operations

Months before the invasion, Mustangs in particular brought back photographs showing beach obstacles and gradients, as well as film of coastal features and gun batteries along the French coast. Oblique photographs were taken at wave top height from three or four miles out to sea, providing recognition photographs for assault force coxswains. More obliques were taken 1,500 yds from the coast and at zero ft to assist platoon commanders. From the same vantage point but 2,000 ft up, photographs were secured of the assault area's hinterland. More photographs showed land forms further inland, and to assist advancing commanders, bridges and river banks needed to be photographed as well as areas suitable for prospective landing strips. Pictures were taken of areas chosen as drop and landing zones for airborne forces and observation was kept for possible preventive defences. All these items were additional to the usual types of military and supply depots, airfields, etc, upon which photo-reconnaissance Mosquitoes, Spitfires and Mustangs kept watch. Assembling Allied landing forces were photographed in Britain to ensure that their camouflage was the best possible. In the two weeks prior to D-Day, one RAF mobile photographic section alone produced no less than 120,000 prints.

Between 1 April and 5 June 1944, AEAF tactical fighter-reconnaissance aircraft flew 3,215 photographic reconnaissance sorties, while the RAF's Benson-based and the USAAF's strategic forces flew another 1,519 sorties attributable to invasion needs. Although Mustangs proved invaluable in the low-level role, it was dangerous work even for such fast aircraft.

Like Nos. 2 and 268 Squadrons, on D-Day Mustangs of No. 430 (Canadian) Squadron played a very prominent part. Their sorties started even before sunrise, Flg Off J.A. Lowndes and Flg Off E. Winiars leaving first, followed by Sqn Ldr F.H. Chesters and Wing Cdr R.C. Waddle. Reconnoitring main roads in the Caen area,

FD502, *a four-cannon Mustang IA about to leave on a tactical-reconnaissance sortie.*

the squadrons met much light AA fire but saw little movement until at about 08:30 hrs when Flg Off J.S. Cox and Flg Off T.H. Lambros spotted transport moving near Bayeux – possibly tanks. Not until mid-morning was confirmation of that obtained by Flt Lt J.V. Prendergast (*AP180-E*) and Flg Off C. Butchart (*AM230-B*). From each pair of aircraft oblique photographs were being taken, one using a 14-in lens and the other an 8-in lens. All flying had to be low because of the very poor weather which, by late morning, was causing some operations to be abandoned.

Mid-afternoon brought No. 430 Squadron its first sighting during the day of enemy aircraft: six Ju 88s spotted by Gordon and Lambros. More serious was a later encounter after enemy fighters had made their first appearance of the day.

Wing Cdr Godfrey (*AM103*) and Flg Off J.S. Cox (*AG645*) were giving cover to Sqn Ldr Chesters (*AP186*) undertaking a Tac/R in the Evreux area when they were intercepted by four Fw 190s. Flg Off Cox was soon shot down, by which time the engagement had attracted another two Fw 190s. Wing Cdr Godfrey climbed into cloud and Sqn Ldr Chesters set course for Le Havre pursued for two minutes by Fw 190s which fired upon his Mustang without securing strikes.

During the operations No. 430 Squadron acquired plentiful photographs showing Allied forces on the beaches, limited enemy road activity and photographs of the state of many bridges in the area. Tactical reconnaissance sorties are known to have been undertaken by the following aircraft and squadrons.

## MUSTANGS TACTICAL RECONNAISSANCE SORTIES, 6 JUNE 1944

| Time | Sqn | Aircraft | Details |
|------|-----|----------|---------|
| 05:00-07:00 | 168 | AM102 + AM197 | Port en Bessin–Caen–Argentan–Alençon |
| | | AP167 + AP195 | |
| 05:05-07:05 | 430 | AM253-N + AP235-A | Port en Bessin–Bayeux–Vire–N of Caen |
| 05:15-07:10 | 430 | AM201-S + AM224-D | Thury Harcourt–Comfront–Alençon |
| 05:20-06:50 | 168 | AL979 + AM210 | Ouistreham–Caen–Mézidon–Cabourg |
| 06:00-08:10 | 430 | AG664-M + AP180-E | N Caen, roads to Caen; photos taken |
| 06:05-07:55 | 168 | AM128 + AP262 | Port en Bessin, around Bayeux |
| 07:05-08:50 | 430 | AM125-W + AM227-L | Villeville–Bayeux; two tanks seen |
| 07:10-08:50 | 430 | AG377-D + AG433-Z | Assault areas, out at Arromanches |
| 07:20-09:10 | 168 | AM219 + AM255 (FTR) | Ouistreham–SW Caen |
| | | AM202 + AM244 | |
| 08:25-10:10 | 268 | FD506 + FD546 | Port en Bessin |

| Time | Sqn | Aircraft | Details |
|---|---|---|---|
| 08:45-10:10 | 430 | *AG627-C + AL986-T* | Port en Bessin–Bayeux and return |
| 08:50-10:45 | 430 | *AM230-B + AP180-E* | Villeville–Caen; 60 tanks seen |
| 09:25-11:20 | 268 | FD501 + FD544 | ? |
| 09:40-11:05 | 168 | *AM159 + AM247* | Courcelles–Falaise–Thury Harcourt |
| 10:50-12:25 | 168 | *AL979 + AM210* | Port en Bessin–Vire–Mortain–Flers–Argentan |
| 10:55-12:15 | 430 | *AM103-O + AP235-A* | Ouistreham, returned (separated) |
| 11:00-12:45 | 430 | *AG433-Z + AG531-H* | Port en Bessin–Caen |
| 11:00-12:50 | 168 | *AG470 + AP222* | Villers–Flers–Domfront–Alençon–Le Mele–Surs; three tanks seen St Silvain, 10–12 possible enemy aircraft |
| 11:00-13:00 | 430 | *AG627-C + AM125-W* | Roads, Falaise–Argentan–Mortague–Alençon–Domfront |
| 11:05-12:45 | 430 | *AG488-V + AG660* | Port en Bessin–Bayeux, return |
| 13:10-14:45 | 168 | *AM202 + AM244* | Ouistreham–Caen; tanks reported |
| 14:40-16:20 | 168 | *AL979 + AP222* | Caen–Falaise–Conde roads |
| 14:40-16:35 | 168 | *AM197 + AP195* | Caen–Falaise; eight AFVs seen, 10 lorries S of Caen; out St Aubin |
| 15:00-17:00 | 168 | *AP167 + AM102 + AM210 + ?????* | Ouistreham–Argentan–Vire–Mortain–Villers Bocage |
| 15:00-17:00 | 430 | *AG664-M + AM253-N* | Port en Bessin–Alençon–Domfront–Villiers; six Ju 88s seen |
| 16:35-18:10 | 430 | *AL986-T + AM201-S* | Trouville–Point de le Vee–Lisieux–Laiga–Gauburge–Gace–Lisieux |
| 16:35-18:10 | 430 | *AM103-O + AP186-Y* | Trouville–Rosemont–Evreux–Tonde. Engaged by Fw *AG645-P* (FTR) 190s, Flg Off J. S. Cox shot down |
| 17:00-18:40 | 168 | *AM202 + AM244* | Bayeux area |
| 17:55-19:50 | 414 | *AG529 + AG618* | Falaise–Argentan–Vire–Mortain–Villers Bocage |
| 18:00-20:05 | 414 | *AG507 + AM186* | Falaise–Argentan–Vire–Mortain–Villers Bocage |
| 18:00-20:10 | 414 | *AM251 + AP239* | Falaise–Argentan–Vire–Mortain–Villers Bocage |
| 18:45-20:30 | 168 | *AM197 + AP195* | Ouistreham-Caen-Bayeux |
| 19:25-21:00 | 268 | *FD506 + FD546* | Reconnaissance of roads leading to the lodgement zone; searches for troop and vehicle reinforcements |
| 19:38-21:13 | 268 | *FD552 + FD557* | |
| 19:40-20:55 | 268 | *FD471 + FD476* | |
| 19:41-21:00 | 2 | *FD501 + FD507* | |
| 19:44-21:14 | 2 | *????? + ?????* | |
| 19:49-20:50 | 2 | *FD502 + FD529* | |
| 19:55-21:40 | 168 | *AL979 + AM128* | Bayeux–Airel–Isigny–Carentan; shot up Vire bridges |
| 21:20-23:00 | 430 | *AG488-V + AP180-E* | Ouistreham–Caen (burning)–Port en Bessin |
| 21:45-23:15 | 168 | *AM244 + AP262* | Ouistreham–Traan–Carbourg–Deauville–Douzule (six lorries seen)–Cabourg |

The other main task allotted to Mustang tactical reconnaissance squadrons was observation for gunners on the warships engaged in pounding defences on the Normandy coast. For this duty two squadrons of Spitfire Vs (Nos. 26 and 63) and two Wings – each of three Mustang squadrons of 2nd TAF – received special training in naval procedures from No. 3 Naval Fighter Wing whose Seafire squadrons also participated in gunnery spotting for the D-Day warships. Operating in pairs, the mixed contingent flew 304 sorties of which 236 were flown by five AEAF squadrons. Each of the two Spitfire squadrons flew 76 sorties before they switched to other duties at noon on 6 June. Liaison with warships bombarding enemy positions was carried out from 6 June to 19 June, by which time 1,318 sorties had been flown by the spotters. Of these the AEAF flew 940 sorties during which five aircraft failed to return from operations. Later in the campaign Mustangs again supplemented naval squadrons.

## MUSTANGS USED DURING 'SPOTTING' FOR NAVAL GUNNERS, 6 JUNE 1944

| Time | Sqn | Aircraft | Notes |
|---|---|---|---|
| 04:55-07:00 | 268 | *FD546 + FD562* | |
| 04:55-07:15 | 414 | *AG529 + AM104* | |
| 04:55-07:25 | 414 | *AG548 + AP213* | |
| 05:00-07:15 | 414 | *AG634 + AP239* | |
| 05:00-07:15 | 414 | *AM186 + AM251* | |
| 05:00-07:30 | 268 | *FD498 + FD507* | |
| 05:00-07:35 | 2 | *FD529 + FD566* | Spotters for first US landing at 06:43 |
| 05:02-07:52 | 2 | *FD474 + FD501* | Met flak from Le Havre |
| 05:05-08:00 | 2 | *FR935* | Other aircraft (*FR908*) u/s |
| 05:30-06:35 | 268 | *FD471 + FD535* | |

| Time | Sqn | Aircraft | Notes |
|---|---|---|---|
| 05:45-08:40 | 268 | FD486 + FD552 | |
| 05:50-07:35 | 268 | FD549 + FD561 | |
| 05:55-08:05 | 2 | FR900 + FR902 | |
| 05:56-07:56 | 2 | FD502 + FD565 | Spotters for warships |
| 05:58-08:43 | 2 | FR919 + FR924 | Naval gun spotters; FR924 damaged by AA fire |
| 06:00-07:50 | 414 | AG595 + AM193 | |
| 06:00-07:55 | 268 | FD544 + FD557 | |
| 06.00-08.00 | 268 | FD477 + FD541 | Intense flak; FD477 FTR |
| 06:00-08:00 | 414 | AG490 + AG514 | |
| 06:00-08:20 | 414 | AG618 + AP220 | |
| 06:10-06:35 | 2 | FD474 + FD567 | Naval gun spotters |
| 08:15-10:35 | 414 | AG529 + AM104 | |
| 08:25-10:10 | 414 | AM186 + AM251 | AM186 aborted at 08:55 |
| 08:25-10:00 | 414 | AG634 + AP239 | |
| 08:30-10:10 | 2 | FD474 + FD501 | Naval gun spotters |
| 08:30-10:30 | 268 | FD488 + FD498 | |
| 08:30-11:00 | 414 | AG548 + AP213 | |
| 08:40-10:40 | 268 | FD480 + FD562 | |
| 09:00-10:50 | 414 | AG618 + AP220 | |
| 09:05-11:15 | 414 | AG490 + AG514 | |
| 09:10-10:40 | 414 | AG595 + AM153 | |
| 09:10-12:08 | 2 | FD484 + FD567 | Naval gun spotters |
| 09:10-11:31 | 2 | FD527 + FD566 | Naval gun spotters |
| 09:12-11:17 | 2 | FD502 + FD565 | Naval gun spotters |
| 09:15-11:35 | 2 | FR900 + FR902 | Naval gun spotters |
| 09:25-11:20 | 2 | FD447 + FD472 | (both 268 Sqn aircraft) |
| 09:25-11:45 | 2 | FR906 + FR919 | Naval gun spotters |
| 09:30-11:04 | 2 | FR907 + FR928 | Naval gun spotters |
| 09:30-11:20 | 268 | FD541 + FD557 | Naval gun spotters |
| 09:30-11:35 | 268 | FD535 + FD561 | Naval gun spotters |
| 10:00-12:10 | 2 | FR908 + FR935 | Naval gun spotters; FR908 early return |

# Mustang I/IA/IIs on squadron strength, 5 June 1944

\* operated on 6.6.44, but not necessarily by the squadron to which the aircraft was assigned. Nos. 2 and 268 Squadrons at Gatwick drew aircraft from a 'pool'.

## No. 2 Sqn, Gatwick

Mk IA:
Operations commenced 12.2.44 using aircraft exchanged with 168 Sqn. Mk IAs passed to 268 Squadron 22.6.44 and replaced by Mk IIs

| | |
|---|---|
| *FD474 | 2.44-22.6.44 |
| *FD484 | 2.44-29.6.44 |
| *FD502 | 2.44-22.6.44 |
| *FD507 | ?-? |
| *FD529 | 2.44-17.6.44 EFB |
| *FD565 | 2.44-16.6.44 FTR |
| *FD566 | 3.44-22.6.44 |

Mk II:

| | |
|---|---|
| FR891 | 5.44-7.12.44 Cat E |
| FR892 | 3.5.44-17.6.44 FTR |
| *FR900 | 3.5.44-30.11.44 |
| *FR902 | 3.5.44-27.6.44 FTR |
| *FR906 | 5.44-18.1.45 |
| *FR907 | 5.44-8.11.44 |
| *FR919 | 4.5.44-28.11.44 |
| FR923 | 6.6.44-1.9.44 BFB |
| *FR924 | 3.5.44-6.6.44 BFB, 29.6.44-12.12.44 FTR |
| *FR928 | 3.5.44-29.8.44 BFB |
| FR930 | 4.6.44-27.7.44, 17.8.44-30.11.44 |
| FR931 | 6.6.44-18.7.44, 17.8.44-3.9.44 |
| FR934 | 6.6.44-23.6.44 FTR |
| *FR935 | 6.5.44-26.6.44, 27.7.44-30.11.44 |
| *FR937 | 4.6.44-15.6.44 |

## No. 168 Sqn, Odiham

Mk I:
Received from No. 2 Squadron; resumed operations 2.3.44

| | |
|---|---|
| AG395 | 28.5.44-13.7.44 |
| *AG470 | ?-18.8.44 |
| AG474 | 3.6.44-24.6.44 FTR |
| AG570 | 5.6.44-9.10.44 |
| *AL979 | 3.44-20.7.44 FTR |
| *AM102 | 11.5.44-15.6.44 |
| *AM128 | ?-9.6.44 FTR |
| AM141 | ?-26.10.44 E MR |
| *AM159 | ?-22.6.44 FTR |
| *AM176 | ?-17.6.44 FBB |
| AM194 | ? 19.8.44 Cat E |
| *AM197 | ?-29.6.44 |
| *AM202 | ?-? |
| *AM210 | ?-22.6.44 |
| *AM219 | ?-9.10.44 |
| AM225 | 27.2.44-8.6.44 FTR |
| AM243 | 8.6.44-12.7.44 |
| *AM244 | 3.44-? |
| *AM247 | 5.44-27.7.44 |
| *AM255 | 5.44-? |
| *AM910 | 3.44-? |
| *AP167 | 3.44-21.9.44 |
| AP175 | 5.6.44-6.7.44 |
| *AP195 | 3.44-? |
| AP202 | 29.2.44-20.10.44 E MR |
| *AP222 | 3.44-? |
| AP230 | 6.44-13.8.44 FTR |
| *AP262 | 6.44-13.8.44 |

## No. 268 Sqn, Gatwick

Mk IA:
Began Mk IA operations 13.8.43 and flew last sorties with them 7.5.45, although it operated Typhoons from 8.8.44. Many Mk IAs came from Nos. 168 and 170

Squadrons and were assigned to 405 ARF until 8.6.44, even though the aircraft were already in squadron service.

| | |
|---|---|
| FD444 | 13.3.44-9.11.44 |
| *FD447 | 22.7.43-19.6.44 FTR |
| *FD471 | ?-? |
| *FD472 | 6.44-30.9.44 |
| FD476 | 9.10.43-14.8.44 |
| *FD477 | 6.44-14.9.44 |
| *FD486 | 15.7.43-19.6.44 |
| FD490 | 22.1.44-20.7.44 |
| FD495 | 7.7.43-6.6.44 FTR |
| *FD498 | 6.44-28.8.44 |
| *FD501 | 6.44-21.8.44 |
| *FD506 | 6.44-19.6.44 |
| *FD507 | 10.7.43-24.6.44 AC FB |
| FD510 | 18.8.43-15.6.44 RIW |
| *FD535 | 6.44-19.4.45 |
| *FD541 | 6.44-10.5.45 |
| *FD544 | 6.44-16.11.44 |
| *FD546 | ?-? |
| *FD549 | ?-? |
| *FD552 | 6.44-15.6.44 FTR |
| *FD557 | 6.44-17.6.44 |
| *FD561 | 6.44-28.9.44 |
| *FD562 | 6.44-14.9.44 |
| FD563 | 6.44-18.6.44 |
| FD967 | 6.44-19.6.44 FTR |

### No. 414 (Canadian) Sqn, Odiham
Mk I:

Although in use long before D-Day the aircraft were in many cases assigned to holding units (examples listed) and not placed on squadron charge until 8 June 1944

| | |
|---|---|
| AG425 | 6.44-21.9.44 |
| *AG490 | 405 ARF 24.10.43, 414 Sqn 8.6.44-18.8.44 |
| *AG507 | 83 GSU 25.4.44, 414 Sqn 8.6.44-23.8.44 |
| AG512 | 25.8.43-31.8.44 |
| *AG514 | 6.44-17.6.44 AC FB |
| *AG529 | 6.44-11.6.44 FBB |
| *AG548 | 6.44-27.7.44 FTR |
| AG552 | 83 GSU 13.5.44, 414 Sqn 8.6.44-4.7.44 |
| *AG595 | 6.44-10.6.44 EFB |

| | |
|---|---|
| AG601 | 6.44-18.8.44 E MR |
| *AG618 | 6.44-26.6.44 FB AC |
| *AG634 | 6.44-24.6.44 |
| AG649 | 6.44-6.7.44 RIW |
| *AL992 | 29.2.44-24.8.44 |
| *AM104 | 16.8.43-14.9.44 |
| *AM153 | 6.44-14.9.44 |
| *AM186 | 6.44-23.8.44 |
| *AM193 | ?-? |
| *AM220 | ?-? |
| *AM251 | 6.9.42-19.6.44 FTR |
| AP211 | 31.5.43-19.8.44 Cat E |
| *AP213 | ?-? |
| *AP220 | ?-? |
| *AP239 | 8.6.44-18.8.44 |
| AP246 | 22.6.44-29.6.44 FTR, but BBOC |

### No. 430 (Canadian) Sqn, Odiham
Mk I:

| | |
|---|---|
| *D-AG377 | ?-? |
| *Z-AG433 | ?-? |
| AG456 | 39 Wing to 430 Sqn 8.6.44-13.8.44 FTR |
| AG465 | ?-7.6.44 FTR |
| *V-AG488 | 28.6.43-28.9.44 (ROS 12.6.44-12.7.44) |
| *H-AG531 | ?-9.6.44 FBB |
| AG553 | 39 Wing 31.5.44, 430 Sqn 8.6.44-22.6.44 EFB |
| *C-AG627 | 19.9.43-27.7.44 |
| *M-AG664 | 409 ARF, 430 Sqn 8.6.44-14.9.44 |
| *T-AL986 | 5.44-4.11.44 |
| *O-AM103 | 8.6.44-16.7.44 |
| *W-AM125 | ?-? |
| AM139 | 29.4.43-12.7.44 RIW |
| *S-AM201 | 8.6.44-23.9.44 FTR |
| *K-AM224 | 8.6.44-1.10.44 Cat E |
| *L-AM227 | 8.6.44-20.10.44 E MR |
| *B-AM230 | 26.1.43-27.7.44 FBB |
| AM237 | ?-6.6.44 |
| *N-AM253 | 8.6.44-1.12.44 |
| AP170 | 8.6.44-21.6.44 |
| AP178 | 8.5.43-30.11.44 |
| *E-AP180 | ?-? |
| *Y-AP186 | 8.6.44-? |
| *A-AP235 | ?-? |

# The spotting Spitfires

To ensure the naval bombardment was effective it was essential to have ample aircraft informing ship gunnery control centres of the accuracy of their fire, particularly since the targets were often relatively small and well camouflaged. Thick reinforced concrete bunkers, so much a part of the vaunted 'Atlantic Wall' proved very difficult to find, and even more difficult to destroy.

The Fleet Air Arm, during early planning, stated that it had insufficient resources to provide enough Seafires for the task, and on D-Day one of its squadrons drew upon the stock of Spitfire Vbs. Therefore, to help, Nos. 26 and 63 Squadrons had their Hurricanes replaced with Spitfire LF Vbs, each squadron holding 21 aircraft. Seconded from ADGB, they were supplemented with the two

Mustang Wings taken from 2nd TAF, the entire force only just large enough for the task set.

Between 6 June and 19 June an overall total of 1,318 gunnery support sorties were flown, 940 of them by the RAF/FAA element, and at a cost of five ALAF aircraft. On D-Day 394 spotting sorties were mounted, including 236 by RAF squadrons, and each of the two Spitfire squadrons, operating from dawn to sunset, managed 76 sorties.

Both Spitfire squadrons, which pooled their aircraft and pilots, operated from RNAS Lee-on-Solent with Seafires and Mustangs.

No. 63 Squadron's surviving records present little detail, whereas No. 26 Squadron prepared a good account upon which the following analysis is based. During 142 hrs of flying some pilots managed four sorties; two aircraft were quite seriously damaged and when opportunity presented itself, pilots engaged in ground strafing.

### SORTIES DESPATCHED BY NO. 26 SQUADRON

| Time | Aircraft | Details |
|---|---|---|
| For HMS Belfast | | |
| 04:45-06:25 | BL545 + BL719 | |
| For HMS Erebus | | |
| 04:45-06:25 | W3423 + AD133 | Abortive sorties |
| 05:25-07:05 | AD204 + EP233 | |
| For HMS Glasgow | | |
| 04:45-06:20 | AB971 + BL589 | |
| 07:40-09:40 | AB971 + BL589 | No hits seen |
| For HMS Hawkins | | |
| 13:40-15:30 | ????? + BL589 | |
| For HMS Orion | | |
| 18:55-20:55 | AB141 + EP233 | Engaged dispersed tanks |
| For HMS Ramillies | | |
| 12:55-14:45 | AD133 + AD204 | |
| For HMS Roberts | | |
| 04:45-06:25 | ????? + W3638 | Eight rounds fired only |
| 05:25-07:10 | BL477 + BM476 | |
| 05:25-07:08 | AD299 + BL772 | |
| 08:25-10:15 | | Ship did not fire |
| 09:55-11:55 | AD268 + BL772 | |
| 10:40-12:05 | W3638 + AA944 | Ship not firing; pilots strafed coastal guns |
| 11:25-13:00 | AB141 + EP233 | Also strafed guns in Trouville |
| 12:10-14:00 | AD204 + AD268 | |
| 13:40-15:10 | AB141 + BL997 | |
| 14:25-16:15 | AA944 + AD268 | |
| 15:10-17:15 | BL545 + BM476 | |

| | | |
|---|---|---|
| 15:55-18:15 | AD204 + EN862 | |
| USS Argonaut | | |
| 07:40-09:20 | BL545 + BL719 | R/T delays; target demolished |
| USS Tuscalosa | | |
| 06:55-08:55 | BM256 + EN862 | |
| 08:25-10:10 | AD204 + EP233 | |
| 09:55-11:55 | BM256 + EN862 | |
| 10:40-12:05 | W3836 + BM476 | |
| 12:45-14:15 | W3462 + BM476 | |
| 12:55-14:45 | BL772 + EN862 | No firing |
| 13:40-15:30 | AD133 + AD299 | |
| 14:25-16:20 | W3638 + AA848 | |
| 15:10-16:45 | W3462 + W3836 | |
| 16:40-18:30 | AD299 + BL477 | |
| 17:25-19:25 | AD204 + BL772 | |
| 18:55-20:35 | ????? + EN862 | |
| 20:25-22:35 | BL579 + BM476 | |
| Controlling vessel uncertain | | |
| 07:40-09:40 | W3462 + W3638 | |
| 08:25-10:10 | BL997 + BM256 | |

## Spitfire Vs used by Gunnery Spotting Pool, 5 June 1944

### No. 26 Sqn, Lee-on-Solent
Spitfire V

| | |
|---|---|
| W3313 | 2.4.44-21.9.44 |
| W3314 | 10.4.44-19.8.44 EFA |
| *W3423 | 2.4.44-25.1.45 |
| *W3638 | 22.5.44-18.12.44 FA, 1.1.45 Cat E |
| *W3836 | 3.4.44-8.2.45 |
| *AA944 | 18.4.44-7.6.44 ROS, 23.6.44-25.1.45 |
| *AB141 | 350 Sqn loan, 10.6.44-19.9.44 Cat E |
| *AB971 | ? – with 26 Sqn 2.8.44-29.3.45 |
| *AD133 | ? – with 26 Sqn 27.7.44-26.1.45 |
| *AD204 | 303 Sqn loan(?), with 26 Sqn 15.9.44-8.2.45 |
| *AD268 | Loaned(?), with 26 Sqn 26.6.44-18.1.45 |
| *AD299 | 12.4.44-26.1.45 |
| *BL477 | ?-? |
| *BL545 | 5.44-8.2.45 |
| BL546 | 17.5.44-8.2.45 |
| *BL579 | 28.4.44-? |
| *BL589 | 26.4.44-25.1.45 |
| *BL719 | 3.4.44-25.1.45 |
| *BL772 | On loan with 26 Sqn 17.7.44-21.11.44 EFB |
| *BL997 | 2.4.44-25.1.45 |
| *BM256 | On loan from 501 Sqn |
| *BM476 | ?-25.1.45 |
| EE644 | 13.4.44-6.7.44 |
| *EN862 | 10.4.44-19.10.44 |
| *EP233 | 5.44-6.10.44 EPA |

### No. 63 Sqn, Lee-on-Solent
Spitfire Vb/Vc: Examples which operated on D-Day unknown

| | |
|---|---|
| W3443 | 22.5.44-11.6.44 |
| W3713 | 1.5.44-8.7.44 FA, also 30.12.44-1.2.45 |
| AA848 | 31.5.44-1.2.45 |
| AB138 | 1.5.44-9.6.44 to AST |
| AD192 | 26.5.44-8.2.45 |
| AR437 | 3.5.44-22.6.44 |
| AR604 | 22.5.44-8.2.45; modified Mk Vc |
| BL688 | 1.5.44-4.11.44 RIW |
| BL698 | 1.5.44-30.6.44 |

| | |
|---|---|
| BL753 | 1.5.44-25.6.44 FTR |
| BL826 | 27.4.44-14.5.44 ROS, 8.7.44-8.3.45 |
| BL965 | 1.5.44-12.6.44 RIW |
| BL987 | 3.5.44-25.6.44 FTR |
| BL990 | 3.5.44-14.5.44, 28.6.44-10.10.44 |
| BM127 | 5.44-18.12.44 |
| BM158 | 17.5.44-1.2.45 |
| BM577 | 1.5.44-8.5.45 |
| BM587 | 1.5.44-2.1.45 |
| BM588 | 1.5.44-1.7.44 RIW; returned, used to 8.2.45 |
| EE626 | 1.5.44-17.5.44 ROS, 23.6.44-2.10.44; modified Mk Vc |
| EP452 | 1.5.44-20.6.44 RIW |

## Supermarine Spitfire PR XIs of 2nd TAF

Details of the variety of PR Spitfires operating in 1944 may be found within the Coastal Command section. Dealt with here are the D-Day activities of the three squadrons of 2nd TAF which, between them, were using 56 Spitfire PR Mk XIs at the time. One, No. 16 Squadron, had a very busy day.

Out of their 16 sorties a dozen were low-level, flown beneath solid cloud. For pilots used to high-level sorties until recently, facing intense light flak was a new experience. Flights to the beachhead area also provided pilots with some of the best views anyone had that day of the invasion, additional excitement coming when a Bf 109 chasing the squadron's CO was shot down by a Spitfire.

At 09:05 hrs Wg Cdr C.F. Webb set out in *PA929* of No. 16 Squadron to try to locate 'message strips' established for the airborne forces between Ouistreham and Caen, to make a visual assessment of the state of bridges in the area and do a quick run over Caen. The bridges he

**Below** *Early Spitfire PR Mk XIs (*EN149 *shown) had the usual-style Spitfire rudder. (Supermarine)*

**Bottom** *Spitfire PR Mk XI* PL775-A *of No. 16 Squadron wearing full invasion regalia had the broad-chord increased area rudder of most Mk XIs. (IWM CH13492)*

photographed from 1,000 ft. Then he found one of the main DZs and circled it, watching heavy shells bursting upon it. Not having found any message strips, he viewed Caen then tried again and dropped a map to some airborne forces soldiers riding in a Jeep – an unusual activity for a high-flying PR Spitfire! They pointed vaguely south which enabled him to find the strips.

Between 13:25 to 14:55 hrs, *PA869* was used over Villers Bocage–Fuchy–Thury Harcourt-Caen and the beaches, taking line overlap pictures. Photographs showed Caen burning, Pegasus Bridge and canal areas; also the night's glider LZ and Ouistreham beach.

Other sorties by No. 16 Squadron were as follows:

| Time | Aircraft | Details |
|---|---|---|
| 06:55-08:55 | PA861 | Rail centres, Loire Valley |
| 07:00-09:00 | EN663 | Railways, Amiens |
| | MB944 | Airfield NE of Paris |
| | MB953 | Landing strip near Tergnier |
| 08:30-10:45 | PA870 | Villages in the Falaise–Thury Harcourt area; damaged by AA fire |
| 08:40-10:00 | PL770 | Sqn Ldr E.M. Goodale, Caen area |
| 09:00 10:40 | PA869 | Flt Lt D.W. Sampson, Coutances–St Lô; 5-in lens, photos through cloud breaks from 10,000 ft |
| 10:10-11:40 | EN654 | Rail centres, Amiens and in Paris |
| 12:45-15:15 | PL770 | Le Treport–Amiens–Fecamp area |
| 13:30-14:55 | PA929 | Wg Cdr P. Stansfield, follow-up to Wg Cdr Webb's sortie; chased by Bf 109 |
| 14:10-16:10 | PA947 | Flt Lt E. Martin, Coutances– St Lô; obliques of beaches |

| | | |
|---|---|---|
| 14:45-16:15 | PA933 | and off-shore shipping Flg Off R.D. Armstrong, Cabourg–Mézidon; met AA fire; using 5- and 20-in lens cameras |
| 14:45-16:45 | PA870 | No details known |
| 17:00-19:05 | PA929 | Caen–Falaise |

Of the other two squadrons No. 4 managed only one sortie, flown to Le Mesnil le Roi (19:30 to 21:25 hrs) by Flt Lt D.E. Mobs in *PA857*. No. 400 (RCAF) Squadron flew only three sorties, using *PA900* (twice) and *PL799*.

## Spitfire PR Mk XIs on squadron strength, 5 June 1944

\* operated on 6 June 1944

### No. 4 Sqn, Gatwick
| | |
|---|---|
| PA852 | 2.2.44-12.4.45 |
| *PA857 | 7.2.44-17.5.45 |
| PA884 | 18.1.44-6.9.45 |
| PA887 | 1.2.44-25.7.44 |
| PA891 | 2.2.44-14.6.44, 20.7.44-22.2.45, 20.4.45-11.5.45 |
| PA897 | 11.2.44-8.7.45 |
| PA899 | 11.2.44-20.7.44 |
| PA931 | 11.3.44-13.6.44, 3.8.44-15.2.45 |
| PA949 | 15.6.44-29.6.44 |
| PL786 | 23.5.44-12.10.44 |
| PL787 | 25.4.44-17.7.44 EFB |
| PL794 | 30.5.44-?.46 |
| PL796 | 15.6.44-24.12.44 EFB |
| PL831 | 30.5.44-9.8.44 EFB |

### No. 16 Sqn, Northolt
| | |
|---|---|
| *EN654 | 21.12.43-24.6.44, 27.7.44-11.9.44 |
| *EN663 | 29.10.43-29.8.44 |
| *MB944 | 20.3.44-8.5.44, 27.7.44-21.9.44, 2.11.44 14.12.44 |
| MB951 | 28.11.43-22.7.44 |
| *MB953 | 22.12.43-6.9.44 |
| MB954 | 22.12.43-28.4.44, 27.7.44-18.9.44 EFB |

*Spitfire PR Mk XI* PL830-G *of No. 16 Squadron with reduced 'invasion markings'. (Ray Sturtivant collection)*

227

```
MB957   5.10.43-27.9.44 AC FA
MB958'  5.11.43-13.8.44 AC FB
 PA838  3.11.43-14.6.45
 PA849  9.12.43-7.6.44, 23.7.44-12.12.44
*PA861  5.12.43-6.9.44
*PA869  ?-?
*PA870  3.1.44-7.6.44 EFB
 PA909  12.3.44-8.6.44 EFB
*PA929  12.3.44-8.6.44 EFB
*PA933  14.3.44-31.8.44 EFB
*PA947  14.3.44-25.7.44
*PL770  6.5.44-28.6.45
 PL823  8.6.44-26.7.45
 PL834  8.6.44-20.9.44 EFB
```

```
 PA871  19.1.44-14.12.44
 PA886  19.1.44-15.2.45
 PA888  25.1.44-12.7.44 B FB
 PA889  24.1.44-4.2.45
 PA894  7.2.44-7.9.44, 19.10.44-1.1.45 E EA
*PA900  11.2.44-28.12.44
 PA903  11.2.44-12.10.44, 24.11.44-2.2.45
 PA939  5.3.44-16.5.44, 8.6.44-10.9.44
 PA942  5.5.44-1.1.45 EA B
 PL797  23.5.44-17.7.44 EFB
*PL799  25.5.44-29.8.45 SOC
 PL824  30.5.44-6.9.45 SOC
 PL829  25.5.44-28.7.44 EFB
 PL833  8.6.44-26.7.44
```

**No. 400 Sqn, Odiham**
```
 EN681  6.5.44-?
```

# The Vickers-Armstrong Wellington GR XIII

On 5 May 1944 a specialized squadron, No. 69, formed at Northolt under Wg Cdr D.M. Channon. The squadron formed part of No. 34 (PR) Wing and was given a night reconnaissance role. Relying upon the light from flares, it was to photograph enemy troop and vehicle movement on roads well behind and leading to the battle area, and also any night activity on airfields. Accurate navigation being called for, specially-equipped Avro Ansons were used for training. The squadron was armed with Wellington GR Mk XIIIs, fitted out for the task by No. 69 Squadron Preparation Flight; part of No. 34 (PR) Wing Support Unit, Northolt. The Wellington's duration and load-carrying ability made it an ideal choice. Operations commenced on 5/6 June 1944, and in September 1944 No. 69 Squadron moved to the Continent to continue operations to the end of hostilities.

## NO. 69 SQUADRON: INITIAL OPERATIONS

| Date | Time | Aircraft | Details |
|---|---|---|---|
| 5 June | 23:55-02:20 hrs | MF231 | Captain: Wg Cdr Channon; Recce Vernon–Beauvais road |
| 6 June | 00:15-01:40 hrs | JA381 | Captain: W. Off W.D. Sheehan; Recce Fleury–Paris |

*Wellington 'NR' Mk XIII* MF280 *of No. 69 Squadron in standard night-fighter colours. (Ray Sturtivant collection)*

|  |  | road intended, aborted due to *Gee* failure |
|---|---|---|
| 7 June | 00:45-03:00 hrs *JA381* | Captain: Sqn Ldr K.G. Wakefield; Flares on Evreux airfield |

## Wellington GR Mk XIIIs on squadron strength, 5 June 1944

\* operated on 5/6 June 1944

### No. 69 Sqn, Northolt

| | |
|---|---|
| HZ761 | 11.5.44-7.10.44 |
| HZ762 | 2.5.44-8.45 |
| *JA381 | 14.5.44-22/23.4.45 BFB |
| JA384 | 11.5.44-5.7.44, 24.8.44-7.2.45 |

| | |
|---|---|
| JA425 | 6.5.44-29.7.44 EFB |
| JA584 | 3.5.44-1.1.45 EA (burnt out during Operation *Bodenplatz*) |
| JA628 | 11.5.44-17.4.45 |
| JA629 | 3.5.44-28.5.44, 22.6.44-8.8.44 FTR |
| JA631 | 3.5.44-28.5.44, 22.6.44-8.8.44 FTR |
| ME902 | 2.5.44-11.6.44 FTR (Laval–Le Mans reconnaissance) |
| ME929 | 2.5.44-26.7.44 FTR (Elbeuf–Lisieux reconnaissance) |
| ME950 | 9.5.44-24.5.44, 23.6.44-1.8.44 |
| MF128 | 8.5.44-11.5.44, 22.6.44-7.9.44 |
| MF129 | 9.5.44-11.5.44, 22.6.44-1.8.44, 30.11.44-1.1.45 (destroyed during Operation *Bodenplatz*) |
| MF130 | 12.5.44-19.11.44, 12.44-5.1.45, 29.4.45-8.45 |
| *MF231 | 2.5.44-15.6.44 FTR (Le Havre area?) |
| MF235 | 3.5.44-16.5.44, 27.5.44-29.7.44 |

# The strikers of 2nd TAF

The strike force of 2nd TAF comprised 11 rocket-firing and seven bomber Typhoon squadrons placed in Nos. 83 and 84 Groups, and the aircraft of No. 2 Group. Three Typhoon squadrons on Air Alert, and under partial control of each Group HQ ship, were to attack tactical targets immediately to the rear of the beach landing zones 20 minutes before troops disembarked. Another nine squadrons were on hand to attack military HQs, defended localities and gun positions as required.

No. 2 Group's first task was to lay smoke screens to conceal both Eastern and Western Task Forces, and shield them from heavy gun batteries near Le Havre and St Vaast respectively. Otherwise, No. 2 Group

would concentrate, at night, on preventing enemy movement on all approaches to the beachhead.

Supplying target information were five tactical reconnaissance squadrons flying Mustang Is and IIs. Two of them, until noon on D-Day, assisted Spitfire Vs of Nos. 26 and 63 Squadrons which, with No. 3 Naval Fighter Wing and all operating from Lee-on-Solent, observed the accuracy of shelling by Allied warships. One Spitfire would observe while its companion protected it.

Operations on 6 June fell into eight distinct phases generating varying responses. The first call for help came at 07:34 hrs when 21st Army Group requested

*Typhoon MN293-D ('D' on engine cowling) pulling away from Thorney Island on a sortie during 6 June 1944.*

an attack on HQ 84th Corps at Château La Meauffe, near St Lô, and a squadron of 'Bomphoons' was despatched.

Although there was no evident enemy troop movement towards the battle area, 21st Army Group at 10:15 hrs asked for armed reconnaissance to make certain. Orders were issued at 10:27 hrs for a squadron of Typhoons to scour the Lisieux-Caen and Bretteville-Caen roads. Another squadron of rocket firers was, at 10:29 hrs, ordered to search between Caen and Thury Harcourt, Bayeux and Beaumont.

At 11:20 hrs 2nd TAF was informed that a radar site on Cap de la Heve was controlling gunfire directed at shipping. Five minutes later rocket-firing Typhoons were given orders to destroy it.

Because of a somewhat confused situation it was 14:15 hrs before the next call came for 2nd TAF assistance. Airborne forces were finding stiff resistance from positions south-west of Cabourg. A special bomb line was prescribed at 14:17 hrs with a call for two rocket-firing Typhoon squadrons to operate.

Half an hour later came reports of general movement towards Bayeux and Caen, so armed reconnaissances by RP-armed Typhoons were at once ordered. At 15:35 hrs HQ 2nd TAF received news of movement from the east. It was then decided to operate continuous armed reconnaissances throughout the rest of daylight over three areas, one Typhoon Wing being allotted to each. The zones

were: a) south of Caen; b) south of a line Lisieux-Caen; and c) south of Bayeux. Operations were then ordered at 15:40 hrs. Night activity by No. 2 Group, it was decided, should also cover these three areas with that south of Caen having priority.

Another special request from 21st Army Group arrived at 18:35 hrs. Enemy transports were moving north from Caen and tanks were trundling west of the city. Again, two squadrons of RP-armed Typhoons were despatched.

There had been two surprises during daylight hours: 1) the lack of expected fierce Wehrmacht response and reinforcement; 2) the almost complete absence of the Luftwaffe. Would they do battle next day?

Armed reconnaissance was therefore again developed in three areas. The first was around rail centres at Caen and Falaise, 10 Typhoon squadrons at Hurn, Holmsley South and Westhampnett being given the task. The other eight, under Thorney Island control, would operate over five target areas, viz, Pont de Vec, Audemar, Courant, Louvier and Evreux/Lisieux. New to the fray would be five fighter-bomber squadrons under Funtington control which would operate in the Argentan-Bueil area.

As soon as the orders were issued AVM Saunders, AOC No. 11 Group, pointed out that Typhoons would be incapable of mounting effective patrols in the areas assigned because their target area duration without long-range fuel tanks would be too

*Typhoon* PR:R *of 609 Squadron taxies out carrying two drop tanks and only four RP rails instead of the usual eight. Note the squadron letters on the fin – there was widespread diversity of positioning of lettering on fighters. (IWM)*

short. Carrying fuel tanks, however, reduced the operational load, but the tasks were so important that reduction had to be accepted. Orders were given by 2nd TAF for two fuel tanks and only four RPs to be carried by each aircraft. The five 'Bomphoon' squadrons would carry one long-range wing tank and one 500 lb bomb only. To achieve the changes aircraft were modified between each turnround, as sorties allowed. No mean problem had been thrown up very soon during the invasion. No. 184 Squadron, with no tanks available, could operate only in the closest area.

During the morning there were losses from increased flak, with No. 440 Squadron losing three aircraft on the route Calais-Caen-Falaise. Balloons protecting the beachhead were also a source of increased concern for all the fighters.

Afternoon on 7 June brought a call for support for the 61st Brigade's attack on Port en Bessin. Not long after, reports were received of Allied troops being bombed. Investigation showed that drop tanks, and not bombs, were landing among them.

As on D-Day the weather remained consistently poor for air operations. It might, it was thought, cloak enemy ground movement and the detrainment of the 17th Panzer Grenadier expected between Ville Dieu and Folligny. No. 2 Group would need to be busy in the four chosen areas: Argentan-Caen, Domfront-Flers-Caen-Mortain-Vire-Caen, Avranchges-Caen-Coutances and Lisieux-Caen. But a foothold had by now been gained, over five miles deep in some places. Breakout would be much harder to achieve. 2nd TAF would have to help make sure that the German army was pestered by night and day.

# Hawker Typhoon

A giant among contemporaries, mighty and boisterous the Sabre which powered it, the pugnacious Typhoon's finest hours came when it slammed rockets into the Panzers, thus prohibiting their flight from Normandy.

Sydney Camm, Hawker's famed designer, was introduced to Napier's massive Sabre engine in 1937, two years after Major Halford began its design. Breathtaking indeed was the mock-up of the 36.65 litre beast, forecast to give over 2,000 hp and in which sleeve valves were being used for the first time in a 24-cylinder inline engine neatly packaged in a drag-reducing H-pattern cross-section.

Camm had soon calculated that the engine might give a fighter a speed as high as 464 mph. Considerable fuel would certainly be needed – maybe 200 gal – and the aircraft's 40-ft-span wing could carry a dozen .303 in machine-guns. That would increase the weight and firing complication, but by using the same ammunition load they could achieve a *coup de grâce* faster than eight guns.

Rolls-Royce also had a new, powerful engine underway, their 24 cylinder 1,920 hp Vulture. Comprising two Kestrel engines, its X-configuration was more difficult to fit into Camm's fighter and he viewed it only as a feasible alternative. Camm was now, and rather privately, advised by the DTD to 'hold your guns'. The Operational Requirements Committee (ORC) had secretly met in April 1937, following Camm's earlier initiative, and been prompted into considering future fighters. They had concluded that high speed was more important than heavy cannon guns, whereas Fighter Command wanted 12-gun fighters able to attain 35,000 ft while, paradoxically, being suitable for ground attack. Ultimately, Camm's new fighter proved ideal for the latter activity.

In September 1937 he presented to the Air Ministry plans for his new fighter, forecasting a top speed of 428 mph at 19,000 ft for a Vulture-powered version. ORC deliberations followed, leading to a call for a 12-gun fighter to attain 400 mph at 15,000 ft. In January 1938 the industry was invited to submit suitable designs, Hawker with a head start presenting the best and most conventional. By giving it the 'go-ahead' the Ministry was unknowingly assuring the company of a long, successful future, which was not to be Supermarine's good fortune.

The Rolls-Royce Vulture was encountering problems whereas, according to Napier, bench tests in March 1938 showed the Sabre producing 2,050 hp. Production, Napier claimed, would reach 30 engines per month by December 1940. As an insurance the Air Ministry decided to order four Hawker F.18/37 prototypes – two of each version – designated 'R' and 'N' types.

Unease soon arose over both engines and in September 1938 Camm was asked to consider another new power source, the Bristol Centaurus. Such installation would, he replied, restrict too much the pilot's view.

On 20 October 1938 Hawker received the third Sabre mock-up engine, and Napier revealed plans for a special Sabre factory. But already the Vulture engine had drawn ahead and on 23 December 1938 the twelfth working example reached Kingston.

By July 1939 a Vulture engine was in airframe *P5219*. No Sabre had materialized at Hawker although an order for '1,000 Camm fighters for delivery by December 1941' was decided upon by the Air Ministry on 4 July 1939. Initially there would be 100 of each version, but beyond that...? Plans of a week later called for 500 of each, the 'R' to be built by Avro at Yeadon and the 'N' at Glosters, Hucclecote, all the firms being part of the Hawker Siddeley Group. With production confirmed, the 'R' (also called 'V') in August 1939 was named 'Tornado', and the 'N' (alias 'S') became the 'Typhoon' on 6 September 1939.

Far in advance of the Typhoon, Tornado *P5219* flew first on 6 October 1939. Its radiator had been positioned well aft but to ease plumbing and improve general aerodynamics it was almost immediately repositioned below the nose, and the new configuration first flew on 6 December 1939. By then a Sabre had arrived at Hawker's Kingston works. Just how much the new fighter meant to Hawker became apparent when on 12 December 1939 the Spitfire was officially given development priority over the Hurricane.

The Sabre-powered Typhoon, *P5212*, flew for the first time on 24 February 1940, and all was far from well. On 9 May the aircraft's fuselage fractured in flight and the prototype was skilfully nursed home. The Battle of Britain, the troubled Sabre and now a structural problem further delayed the whole programme. In June 1940 the Sabre somehow passed the customary 100 hr type test showing a power output of 2,200 bhp. Too many novel items were plaguing the Sabre, it was said, and that Napier 'tinkered too much' with it. An estimate of 29 September 1940 suggested that new fighter production could commence in February 1941, providing the RAF with 166 aircraft by June 1941 and then 40 per month.

Flight trials of Typhoon *P5212* (the Napier Sabre NS 1 giving 2,250 hp at 14,500 ft) showed a top speed of 410 mph TAS at 20,000 ft reached in 4.7 minutes. Fuel load was 155 gal, all-up weight 10,620 lb, but the Typhoon's ceiling was only 32,300 ft. Add full military load and clearly the aircraft was well down on estimates. Air Ministry belief was that had the Sabre been a Rolls-Royce engine it could by now have become reliable.

The second Typhoon, *P5216*, first flew on 3 May 1941 with four cannon – more in favour than machine-guns. Because wing production was well underway, early Typhoons were completed as Mk Ias, each carrying a dozen .303 in machine-guns.

On 26 May 1941 the first production Mk Ia, *R7576,* flew at Hucclecote. Barely had its engine cooled when an incredible official call was received – you must fit 'Universal' wings featuring either six cannon or two cannon and eight machine-guns! Fortunately the Typhoon had a very thick wing which could accommodate not only its sturdy landing gear and guns, but also the necessary items for other features. But changing the wing at this stage would have been disastrous. Officialdom was soon brought to its senses.

Then the Chief of the Air Staff pointed out that the Typhoon must be made suitable for high-altitude operations. That meant devising a blower for a specially developed high-level Sabre, an idea that generated more shock waves. The RAF received its first two Mk Ias in July 1941, subsequent monthly production totalling just 6, 12, 0, 7 and 11 respectively. The Tornado faded, for its engine was in a worse plight than the Sabre. *R7936*, the only production Tornado, flew for the first time on 30 August 1941.

As production of 20 mm cannon increased the Sabre became ever more troublesome. Nevertheless, on 1 September 1941 No. 56 Squadron, Duxford, received its first Typhoon, *R7583*, and was optimistically declared 'reformed on the Typhoon'! Instead it faced problems with engine shafts, oil and coolant pumps and on 1 November *R7592* flown by Plt Off Deck crashed in a dive from 3,000 ft. He had been overcome by leaking carbon monoxide fumes entering the cockpit.

Typhoons were immediately grounded for fitment of longer exhaust manifolds.

Cold starts were difficult and fragments of machined metal were discovered in engine cylinders. Although pleasant to fly, the Typhoon vibrated badly above 4g and by early 1942 many more problems were apparent. Countering complaints about a poor view aft, the 165th and subsequent Typhoons featured a clear-view rear canopy. Not until February 1942 did the four-cannon Mk Ib enter production. Deliveries began in April 1942, to No. 266 Squadron at Duxford, now the ancestral home of RAF Typhoons.

Camm had been reviewing operational uses for his fighter, suggesting its suitability for low-level operations and especially ground attack. Two 43 gal external long-range tanks could easily be added. By July 1942 a trial installation of either a 500 lb or 1,000 lb bomb beneath each mainplane led to what became the 'Bomphoon'. So successful was the conversion that on 18 August 1942 fighter-bomber sets were ordered for 300 aircraft. The first operational example joined No. 181 Squadron at Duxford on 7 September 1942, as Sabre II production was stepped up.

R7646, the bomber trials installation aircraft, weight 12,184 lb with two 500-pounders aboard. A typical Sabre II straight Mk Ia fighter, R7617, carrying warload and 148 gal of petrol tipped the scales at 10,887 lb. By contrast Mk Ib R7700, assessed in August 1942 and armed with four cannon, weighed 11,070 lb when operationally loaded and had a top speed of 376 mph at 8,500 ft and 394 mph at 20,200 ft attained in 8.7 minutes. Climb to 15,000 ft took 6.2 minutes and service ceiling was 32,200 ft. A third development led to the Typhoon Ib carrying eight 60 lb rocket projectiles (RPs) on long rails, four beneath each mainplane.

With airframe production outstripping suitable engines, some Typhoons were placed in engineless 'purgatory store'. Nevertheless, by the end of December 1942 12 squadrons were flying Typhoons. No. 609 Squadron equipped in April-May 1942, followed successively by Nos. 1, 257, 486, 181, 182, 183, 193, 197 and 198. Engine troubles remained throughout 1942. Excessive vibration, eventually largely overcome by fitting a four-bladed propeller, was blamed for a series of disastrous fuselage fractures occurring immediately ahead of the tailplane. Small strengthening plates were fitted around the fuselage of 300 Typhoons to combat the problem. Then came the discovery that it was primarily due to elevator flutter arising from incorrect balancing. Prominent undercarriage fairing doors, extended on the approach, aggravated the situation. A cure came in 1944 when the larger tailplane of the Tempest was applied to the Typhoon. Teardrop clear-view canopies were fitted to 1944/45 production aircraft.

## Operations

On 28 May 1942 Plt Off Elcombe (R7631) of No. 266 Squadron made the first Typhoon operational 'scramble'. His quarry – over Duxford – turned out to be a Spitfire! At 17:34 hrs on 30 May the first operational defensive patrol was flown by Sqn Ldr 'Cocky' Dundas (R7585) and Plt Off Donigher (R8200) between Selsey Bill and St Catherine's Point when responding to German fighter-bombers. Two days later, trouble struck when two Spitfire pilots of No. 401 Squadron mistook the new shapes for Germans, shooting down R7678 and R8199. Special identity markings were quickly introduced on Typhoons. On 20 June 1942 the first offensive Typhoon Ia/Ib operation was undertaken from Duxford, a patrol from Mardyck to Boulogne, and on 9 August the first 'kill' was a Ju 88 credited to No. 266 Squadron. Operation Jubilee, the Dieppe raid of 19 August 1942, brought the first major action for three Typhoon squadrons. After a morning escort of nine Boulton-Paul Defiants of Northolt's Mandrel Flight they patrolled between Le Touquet and Le Treport, and spotted three Do 217s and a dozen Fw 190s making for ships returning from Dieppe. Nos. 266 and 609 Squadrons pitted the Typhoon against the '190 for the first time, and although it could outpace the Focke-Wulf the Typhoon could not out-manoeuvre it. No. 266 Squadron, in the thick of the fight, claimed a Do 217 destroyed and a probable. Plt Off Smithyman (R7813) was probably first to destroy a Fw 190. Flt Lt Johnson followed another from 15,000 ft to sea level and was credited with a probable. But as Dawson and Munro headed home at sea level a Spitfire shot Dawson's R7815 into the sea.

At Duxford on 1 October 1942, and

under Sqn Ldr Denis Crowley-Milling, No. 181 Squadron formed to work-up the Typhoon as a fighter-bomber. Via Ludham on 10 December 1942 four 'Bomphoons' led by Crowley-Milling (*R8877*) set off to attack with bombs and cannon an armed trawler off Ijmuiden. It was left badly mauled. Thereafter 'Bomphoon' *Roadsteads* and bomber escorts became almost a daily event.

A dozen Typhoons of 181 Squadron were on 20 December 1943 probably the first to use the Typhoon's most effective weapon, the 60 lb rocket projectile (RP), when attacking the Bellevue construction works in northern France. No. 182 Squadron used RPs for the first time on 24 January 1944. Typhoons were to the fore in attacks on airfields, radar stations, gun positions, bridges, V-1 launch sites, railway and communications targets and during the preparations for the invasion.

On 6 June 1944 18 Typhoon squadrons – 11 RP-firing and seven bomb-carrying – were available for operations. Three were on Air Alert, one being allocated to each of the British landing groups to attack targets immediately behind the beaches in the 20 minutes before landings began. These squadrons were also available for direction by each HQ ship in case special targets needed attention.

Another nine squadrons were on hand to attack military HQs, defended localities and enemy gun batteries. These squadron delivered very effective attacks upon eight targets.

Two others, Nos. 137 and 263 Squadrons

of ADGB, operated one at either end of the English Channel to engage naval surface craft attempting to enter the area. On D-Day they took off very early, searching for fast patrol boats.

After the Air Alert force operated, and an attack was made on the German HQ in the Château La Meauffe, the confused situation prevented more attacks until mid-morning when targets began presenting themselves and thus generated five major *Ramrod* operations. Two requests for air support were received before midday, one a radar site at Le Havre aiding guns firing at Allied shipping, the other a defended location south-west of Cabourg upon which airborne troops were advancing. Typhoons attacked the latter most effectively. Early in the afternoon the enemy's HQ 84 Korps at St Leu was attacked, just before Mustangs of No. 2 Squadron flying an armed reconnaissance just south of Lisieux found 30 tanks stationary in Caen, well-defended and obvious targets for later attack.

At 14:30 hrs reports reached HQ 2nd TAF of general movement of small enemy parties towards Caen and Bayeux. Responding from mid-afternoon until sundown, Typhoon formations flew 28 armed reconnaissances in three prescribed areas in search of what proved to be very little Wehrmacht invasion response. German fighter reaction was equally limited, but on one operation Bf 109s diving out of cloud bounced the Typhoons and shot down three. Summarising the day's activity, 2nd TAF recorded 107 Typhoon sorties during specially directed

*By 1944 Typhoons presented a hybrid appearance, having three- or four-bladed propellers. Assorted styles of cockpit canopies remained. (Hawker Aircraft)*

*A No. 247 Squadron Typhoon at 'B6' being rearmed with 60 lb RPs. (IWM CL160)*

morning attacks upon 10 targets and 222 armed reconnaissance sorties by Typhoons during 6 June. Six tanks, 12 armoured fighting vehicles and 21 motor transports were listed as destroyed, along with six tanks damaged and 29 vehicles. Losses amounted to five Typhoons and their pilots.

In mid-June Typhoon squadrons began operating from advanced temporary airfields in France, some very close to the front-line. From the French fields clouds of dry dust were hurled into the aircrafts' radiators and engines, necessitating their replacement and withdrawal for repair and the rapid fitment of special filters. Few German fighters tackled the Typhoons, but some of them encountered ground fire which caused serious damage or accounted for most losses, and led to a quick turnover of aircraft. Many returned to England for attention at civilian repair centres run by Marshall's Flying School at Cambridge and Taylorcraft Aircraft at Rearsby, Leicester. On D-Day 151 Typhoons were within the CRO, with over 400 being held ready for action or stored at maintenance units.

With its engine problems largely overcome by 1944 the Typhoon, as a ground attack aircraft, performed extremely well, causing mayhem during the merciless destruction of German forces in the Falaise pocket. As the armies advanced eastward Typhoons, sometimes lining up like a cab rank, gave the troops very close support as well as undertaking deeper daylight *Rangers.* As soon as hostilities ceased so did the Typhoon's association with the RAF. Within a few weeks it had all but become a raucous memory.

# Summary of Typhoon Operations, 6 June 1944

NB: In many cases aircraft identities remain unknown. Times 'up' and 'down' are in some instances supplemented by known time on target (ToT).

| Task | No. A/c + Sqn | Time up ToT + Time down | Notes |
|---|---|---|---|
| Shipping recce, Cap Gris Nez-Flushing | 4/137 | 04:53 hrs 06:10 hrs | No ships seen: *JR327, MN198, MN240, MN460* |
| No. 10 Group shipping sweep 10 miles SW Ushant-Ile de Batz-*Ramrod 973* (bombing) | 8/263 (RPs) | 06:26 hrs ??:?? hrs 07:43 hrs | Uneventful; poor weather |
| Ste Croix Grand Tonne (Chateau le Parc) | 8/197 | 07:05 hrs 07:45 hrs 08:25 hrs | Bombed E/W 1,200 ft, 15 x 500 lb. Two D/H, rest scattered |
| Meivaomes, rocket positions | 8/266 | 07:10 hrs 07:55 hrs 08:30 hrs | Target unseen. Gun position bombed; 16 x 500 lb bombs: *DN562, JR384, MN133, MN184, MN320, MN400, MN493, MN600* |
| Reviers field | 8/174 | 07:24 hrs | 64 x 60 lb RPs on |

| Task | No. A/c + Sqn | Time up / ToT + / Time down | Notes |
|---|---|---|---|
|  | (RPs) | 08:00 hrs / 08:38 hrs | three battery gun positions: JP596, JP602, JR195, JR261, MN141, MN190, MN371, MN577 |
| Tailleville gun battery | 8/245 (RPs) | 07:13 hrs / 07:45 hrs / 08:31 hrs | Flt Off Borden wounded, landed Ford. Target not located – rainstorm. Camp attacked; 64 x 60 lb RPs |
| Periers-sur-le-Dan defended area | 24/181 +12/247 | 07:07 hrs / 07:18 hrs / 08:45 hrs | Aborted; bad weather and smoke. Four of 247 fired 32 x 60 lb RPs at beach guns W of Cabourg. 181 Sqn: R8840, JP579, JP604 (abort), JP916, JR134, JR244, JR297, JR317, JR513, MN208, MN693; 247 Sqn (RP): JP934, JR372, JR524, MN340, MN373, MN421, MN430, MN451, MN710, MN823 and two uncertain |
| RAMROD 974: 'Bomphoons' divebomb Le Hamel (Asnelles-sur-Mer) block-houses overlooking beach | 6/438 | 06:57 hrs / 07:28 hrs / ??:?? hrs | 12 x 500 lb MCs on Le Hamel strongpoint; four hits |
| Vers-sur-Mer strongpoint; support British 50th Div landing | 6/438 | 08:07 hrs / ??:?? hrs / ??:?? hrs | 12 x 500 lb on Vers; two D/Hs |
| Courseulles medium gun battery | 12/439 | 06:55 hrs / 07:29 hrs / 08:16 hrs | 1,000 lb MCs, results smoke-obscured: JR506, MN352, MN356, MN370, MN417, MN435, MN464, MN553, MN581, MN663, MN665 |
| Ouistreham strongpoint, beach at La Breche | 12/440 | 06:55 hrs / 07:25 hrs / 08:10 hrs | 24 x 500 lb; D/Hs and near misses. Attacked 88 mm guns near beach: MN171, MN257, MN307, MN348, MN378, MN403, MN457, MN555, MN583, MN603, MN635, MN644 |
| RAMROD A.32 | 11/198 | 08:28 hrs | 88 x 60 lb RPs, |
| Chateau La Meauffe | (RPs) | 09:00 hrs / 09:46 hrs | many hits on building: P-JP665, T-JR197, C-JR366, J-JR512, K-MN132, N-MN195, D-MN293, E-MN537, S-MN546, B-MN570, M-MN775, A-????? |
| RAMROD A.58 Thin-skinned vehicles, Caen-Lisieux and Caen-Bretteville roads | 12/183 (RPs) | 11:30 hrs / ??:?? hrs / 13:03 hrs | Vehicles hit, tank left blazing. Two locos hit at Mézidon, water tower hit at Argences. Three a/c Cat E; Flt Lt Evans, Flg Off Taylor & Flg Off Gee missing (MN432?) |
| RAMROD A.59 Roads attacked, Caen-Bayeux and nearby | 12/164 (RPs) | 11:24 hrs / 12:00 hrs / 13:00 hrs | Three locos, two lorries, rail trucks, staff car attacked; Fw 190 destroyed on ground: JP909, MJ203, MN177, MN284, MN368, MN419, MN454, MN646 and four more |
| RAMROD A.64 Le Havre/Cap de la Heve, coastal ship watcher (XII/35) | 4/609 (RPs) | 12:07 hrs / 12:38 hrs / 13:02 hrs | 32 x 60 lb RPs and cannon; strikes seen: MN248, MN494, MN520, MN630 |
| RAMROD 975 Armed recce, Troarn-Falaise-Conde | 8/440 | 19:17 hrs / 19:30/20:40 / 21:05 hrs | Bombed two trucks, strafed two vehicles St Laurent: MN171, MN257, MN307, MN378, MN403, MN428 (FTR), MN457, MN583 |

## OTHER OPERATIONS

| Task | No. A/c + Sqn | Time up / ToT + / Time down | Notes |
|---|---|---|---|
| Falaise-Caen road | 7/198 | ??:?? hrs / ??:?? hrs / ??:?? hrs | C-JR366, J-JR512, D-MN293, G-MN410, E-MN537 and two more |
| Gun position W of Cabourg | 12/175 | 15:30 hrs / 16:50 hrs | RP attack: DN267, JR502, MN138, MN185, MN194, MN202, MN353, MN471, MN481, MN582, MN594, MN717 |
| Armed recce, Caen area | 8/181 (RPs) | 16:05 hrs / 17:25 hrs | Seven armoured cars attacked. Flt Sgt Howard FTR (flak, Caen area): R8840, JP604, |

| Operation | Unit | Times | Results |
|---|---|---|---|
| | | | JR134, J-JR317, JR513, F-MN199, MN200, MN648 |
| Armed recce, Caen Bay | 8/182 | 16:15 hrs 17:40 hrs | JP395, JP612, JP913, JR220, JR266, MM995, MN482, MN531, MN681 |
| Armed recce, S of Caen | 8/439 | 16:40 hrs 18:05 hrs | JR362(?), JR506, JR521, MN352, MN401, MN464, MN553 |
| Armed recce, S of Caen | 8/440 | 16:45 hrs 18:15 hrs | 'MJ' (Wg Cdr Judd led), MN115, MN171, MN348, MN366, MN548, MN635, MN663 |
| Armed recce, Caen area | 9/193 | 16:50 hrs 18:05 hrs | Attacked eight tanks at Mondeville, two destroyed; 2,568 cannon rounds, and bombs |
| Armed recce, near Caen | 6/257 | 17:05 hrs 19:25 hrs | Vehicles attacked |
| Armed recce, Caen area | 8/245 | 17:30 hrs 19:00 hrs | MT and AFVs attacked, some burning |
| Armed recce, SW of Caen | 8/174 | 17:30 hrs 18:45 hrs | Attacked MT N of Villars. JP596, JR261, JR495, JR526, MM952, MM968, MN470 and one more |
| Armed recce, Bayeux | 8/164 | 17:34 hrs ??:?? hrs 19:00 hrs | Attacks on railway and Orne bridge; Lorry and tank burning. Sqn Ldr Beake destroyed an Fw 190: JP909, MN130, MN203, MN284, MN419 and one more |
| Sweep S of Caen | 10/438 | 17:55 hrs 18:50 hrs | Three recce cars attacked |
| Armed recce, Bayeux | 8/266 | 18:00 hrs 18:40 hrs 19:25 hrs | Two MTs destroyed, four tankers left burning: MN133, MN184, MN264, MN320, MN493, MN600 and one more. Sgt Donne baled out (DN562) 5 miles NW of Caen |
| Armed recce, S of Caen | 12/247 (8 RPs, 4 ftrs) | 18:20 hrs ??:?? hrs ??:?? hrs | Destroyed six vehicles. Plt Off Loads (P-JR391) damaged by AA fire: DN492, JP934, JR372, JR524, MN340, MN451, MN591, |
| Road convoy, Caen | 2/247 | 18:55 hrs 19:45 hrs 20:20 hrs | Truck blown up (four seen). One Typhoon Cat B |
| Armed recce, roads S of Caen | 10/182 | 19:20 hrs 20:48 hrs | JP395, JP480, JP540, JP612, JP913, JR220, JR255, JR517, JR524, MN303, MN472 |
| Armed recce, S of Caen | 8/193 | 19:45 hrs 21:00 hrs | No engagements |
| Armed recce, Caen area | 8/439 | 19:45 hrs 21:00 hrs | JR362(?), JR506, MN352, MN356, MN370(?), MN417, MN435, MN581 |
| Armed recce, St Leger | 8/257 | 19:45 hrs 21:20 hrs | Bombs and cannon used; St Leger attacked |
| Armed recce, Caen-Falaise | 10/175 | 20:00 hrs 21:35 hrs | Rockets and cannon used DN267, JP382, JP584, JR502, MN202, MN353, MN471, MN594, MN717 and one uncertain |
| No. 10 Group shipping sweep, Western Channel | 8/263 (RPs) | 20:15 hrs 21:50 hrs | 500 ton ship damaged off Granville. First use of RPs by No. 263 Sqn |
| Armed recce, SE of Caen | 8/609 (RPs) | 20:30 hrs 21:15 hrs 22:21 hrs | Eight RPs fired at house. W. Off Martin FTR |
| Armed recce, Balleray-Breteville-Mézidon | 7/174 | 20:20 hrs 21:40 hrs | Bridge attacked: JP541, JP596, JP614, JP671, JR495, MM954, MN190, MN577 |
| Armed recce, Caen area | 6/245 | 20:35 hrs 22:00 hrs | MT and AFV attacked |
| Caen-Argentan, major strafing attack on two convoys | 10/438 | 20:50 hrs 22:00 hrs | Eight bombers dropped 16 x 500 lb bombs on trucks |
| Armed recce, Caen area | ?/266 | 21:10 hrs 22:25 hrs | Four MTs destroyed, two damaged: JP752, MN133, MN320, MN343, MN400, MN493, MN600 |
| Armed recce, S of Caen | 9/164 | 21:15 hrs ??:?? hrs | MN177, MN203, MN419, MN454 and five unknown |
| Armed recce, S of Bayeux | 8/183 | 21:20 hrs 22:50 hrs | Many attacks on vehicles: EK498, JP681, JP790, MN427, MN461, MN573, MN576, MN554 |

Armed recce 8/257 21:40 hrs Vehicles and staff
22:25 hrs car attacked at
T.9447

# Typhoon 1Bs on squadron strength, 5 June 1944

\* operated on 6 June 1944

From mid-April 1944 Typhoons were assigned to support units, although they were flown and operated by squadrons. Many of those remaining were re-assigned to squadrons on 8, 15 or 22 June 1944, and were joined by replacements for any recent losses. There was also some 'unrecorded' transfer of aircraft between squadrons, even between wings, to maintain operations. Considerable battle damage caused a rapid turnover of aircraft. Some Typhoons remained at squadron bases although being repaired by outside units, and appear still to be on squadron strength. A precise listing of Typhoons used around D-Day is thus very difficult!

### No. 137 Sqn, Manston

| EK270 | 18.3.44-25.2.45 EFB |
| EK289 | 27.3.44-18.8.44 |
| JP677 | 31.5.44-25.7.44 |
| JR305 | 22.2.44-1.4.45 |
| *JR327 | 24.3.44-19.8.44 |
| JR328 | 31.5.44-8.7.44 |
| MN126 | ?-18.8.44 EFA |
| MN134 | 3.3.44-31.12.44 |
| MN169 | 30.4.44-28.9.44 EFB, shot down by flak |
| MN191 | 30.3.44-8.89.44 FTR, shot down by flak |

| MN198 | ?-? |
| MN351 | 25.4.44-28.6.44 BFB, RIW |
| *MN429 | 10.4.44-10.7.44 AC FB |
| MN455 | 30.3.44-11.6.44 ROS, 14.7.44-22.3.45 |
| MN460 | ?-9.44 |
| MN468 | 4.6.44-6.7.44 BFB, crashed approaching Manston |
| MN584 | 25.4.44-6.9.44 BFA |
| MN586 | 18.5.44-5.12.44 EFB, shot down by flak |
| MN596 | 18.5.44-27.4 44 EFB, collided with MN156, anti V-1 patrol |
| MN627 | 26.5.44-30.9.44 AC FB |
| MN632 | 26.5.44-19.8.44 |
| MN660 | 22.5.44-31.12.44 EFB, shot down by flak |

### No. 164 Sqn, Thorney Island (to Funtington 17.6.44; Hurn 21.6.44)

| DN432 | 5.44-8.8.44 RIW |
| EJ598 | 5.44-30.8.44 |
| JP500 | ?-14.6.44 |
| JP684 | 5.44-? |
| JP687 | 5.44-20.6.44 AC FA |
| *JP909 | 5.44-6.6.44 AC FB |
| *MN130 | 1.3.44-6.7.44 |
| *MN177 | 6.44-31.8.44 BFA |
| *MN203 | 6.44-27.7.44 |
| *MN284 | 6.44-5.10.44 AC FB |
| MN287 | 8.6.44 (from 257 Sqn) -17.9.44 |
| *MN368 | 8.6.44-15.6.44 |
| *MN419 | ?-14.6.44 AC FB |
| *MN454 | ?-6.6.44 FTR, shot down near Caen |
| MN523 | 8.6.44-6.7.44, 27.7.44-17.8.44 |
| MN593 | 8.6.44-23.8.44 |
| MN631 | 8.6.44-5.7.45 |
| *MN646 | ?-14.6.44 EFB |

*The ultimate 137 Squadron Typhoon – four-bladed propeller, teardrop cockpit canopy and toned-down camouflage in total contrast to D-Day markings (via H.A. Kofoed).*

### No. 174 Sqn, Holmsley South (to 'B2' Bazenville 19.6.44)

| | |
|---|---|
| *JP541 | 29.7.43-2.8.43, 2.12.43-10.8.44 FTR |
| *JP596 | 8.6.44-18.1.45 |
| *JP602 | 8.6.44-1.9.44 |
| JP608 | 29.8.43-13.9.44 |
| *JP614 | 29.8.43-6.7.44 RIW |
| *JP671 | 3.1.44-23.7.44 FTR |
| *JR195 | ?-? |
| JR241 | 15.12.43-30.8.44 |
| *JR261 | 175 Sqn aircraft, used on D-Day |
| JR310 | ?-22.6.44 |
| *JR495 | 8.6.44-28.12.44 |
| JR525 | 12.4.44-5.7.44 |
| *JR526 | 8.6.44-23.9.44 EFA |
| *MM952 | 8.6.44-? |
| *MM954 | 8.6.44-28.10.44 |
| *MM968 | 8.6.44 FTR, shot down by flak |
| *MN141 | 8.6.44-? |
| *MN190 | 8.6.44-2.9.44 |
| MN253 | 8.6.44-6.7.44 |
| MN301 | 8.6.44-2.9.44, to 164 Sqn |
| *MN371 | 8.6.44-8.2.45 |
| *MN470 | 8.6.44-13.7.44 |
| MN525 | 8.6.44-26.7.44 FTR, shot down by flak |
| MN534 | 8.6.44-9.10.44 |
| *MN577 | 5.44-10.5.45 |
| MN608 | ?-31.8.44 FTR, crashed near Albert |

### No. 175 Sqn, Holmsley South (to 'B3' Ste Croix 20.6.44)

| | |
|---|---|
| *DN267 | 6.44-30.7.44 FTR, shot down by flak |
| *JP382 | 6.44-7.8.44 AC FB |
| *JP584 | 6.44-8.2.45 |
| JP651 | 6.44-23.6.44 AC FB |
| JP736 | 18.3.44-13.6.44 BFB |
| JR388 | 8.6.44-14.8.44 FTR, crashed near Falaise |
| *JR502 | 6.44-9.7.44 FTR |
| *MN185 | 6.44-17.7.44 |
| *MN194 | 6.44-21.6.44 |
| *MN202 | 6.44-10.8.44 |
| MN251 | 5.44-12.6.44 |
| *MN353 | 6.44-16.9.44 |
| *MN471 | 6.44-1.7.44 (AC FA on 174 Sqn) |
| *MN481 | 6.44-15.6.44 FTR, crashed in the Channel |

| | |
|---|---|
| MN536 | 6.44-25.1.45 |
| MN549 | 6.44-15.6.44 |
| MN571 | 6.44-11.8.44 AC FB |
| *MN582 | 6.44-? |
| MN594 | 6.44-18.1.45 |
| *MN717 | 6.44-27.9.44 FTR, shot down by flak |

### No. 181 Sqn, Hurn (to 'B6' Coulombs 21.6.44)

| | |
|---|---|
| R8840 | 6.44-5.10.44 |
| JP515 | 17.7.43-12.6.44 RIW |
| JP551 | 24.7.43-29.4.44, FA, ROS, 27.6.44-12.7.44 |
| *JP579 | 26.7.43-10.7.44 RIW |
| *JP604 | 3.11.43-6.6.44 FTR, shot down by flak near Caen |
| JP611 | 23.8.43-24.7.44 |
| JP800 | 5.44-22.9.44 Cat E, burnt out, crashed near Eindhoven |
| *JP916 | ?-24.7.44 |
| JP917 | 30.11.43-12.5.44, AC FB, ?-22.7.44 |
| JP920 | 12.11.43-2.8.44 EFB, re-cat RIW 11.9.44 |
| *JR134 | ?-14.7.44 RIW |
| *JR244 | 21.1.44-20.5.44, ?-7.6.44 EFB |
| JR297 | 6.44-29.5.45 |
| JR317 | 6.44-6.7.44, 27.7.44-19.8.44 |
| JR334 | ?-28.6.44 EFB, crash-landed Normandy |
| *JR513 | ?-? |
| MN186 | ?-25.7.44 EFB (with 186 Sqn when shot down near Caen) |
| MN199 | 15.6.44?-?-? |
| *MN200 | ?-16.6.44 EFB? |
| MN208 | ?-? |
| MN607 | ?-16.6.44 BFB |
| *MN648 | ?-22.6.44, seriously damaged by German artillery when on ground at 'B6' |
| *MN693 | ?-29.6.44 |

### No. 182 Sqn, Hurn ('B6' Coulombs 10.6.44)

| | |
|---|---|
| *JP395 | 14.1.44-8.6.44 FB |
| *JP480 | ?-? |
| *JP540 | 17.8.43-17.6.44 B FB, 25.7.44-20.10.44 |
| JP612 | 6.44-24.7.45 |

*Typhoons of No. 175 Squadron at 'B5', including* MN253 *and* MN354. *(IWM CL153)*

| JP786 | 23.12.43-6.7.44 Cat E, collision with MN821 at 'B6' |

*JP913 17.12.43-26.6.44 RIW
JR193 29.1.44-24.7.44
*JR220 ?-27.7.44
*JR255 ?-8.6.44 EFB, re-cat RIW
*JR266 ?-24.7.44
JR514 ?-14.6.44 B FB
*JR517 ?-20.7.44
*MM995 ?-8.6.44
*MN303 15.6.44-6.7.44 Cat E, ground accident at 'B6'
*MN472 ?-16.8.44
*MN531 ?-17.6.44 B FB
*MN681 ?-6.7.44
MN735 ?-8.6.44 AC FB
MN821 5.6.44-7.7.44 FTR (on 181 Sqn, flak damage, crashed at 'B6')

### No. 183 Sqn, Thorney Island (Funtington 18.6.44; Hurn 22.6.44; Eastchurch 14.7.44; 'B7' Martragny 25.7.44)

R8843 ?-?
B-R8970 ?-17.8.44 FTR, shot down by Bf 109s near Evreux
R8973 ?-6.6.44 FTR, shot down by Bf 109s SE of Caen
EK498 5.44-11.6.44
*JP681 ?-17.8.44 FTR, shot down by Bf 109s near Evreux
*JP790 ?-8.6.44, 26.8.44 RIW
JR145 18.2.44-25.6.44
JR183 6.11.43-22.7.44
JR208 6.1.44-31.8.44
MN262 4.44-6.10.44
MN265 ?-7.6.44 BFB
*MN427 6.44-23.2.45 BFA
MN432 ?-6.6.44 FTR, shot down by Bf 109s near Caen
*MN461 ?-7.6.44 FTR, from a sweep
*MN554 ?-7.6.44 AC FB
*MN573 6.44-21.8.44 AC FB
*MN576 ?-24.6.44 EFB, crash-landed near Bernay
MN742 ?-14.6.44 FTR, shot down by flak
MN806 8.6.44-12.7.44 FTR, shot down by flak, Cap d'Antifer

### No. 184 Sqn, Westhampnett (Holmsley South 17.6.44; 'B10' Plumetot 27.6.44)

JP440 ?-7.6.44 BFB
JP656 ?-?
MN147 ?-5.44, 3.6.44-19.9.44
MN174 6.44-15.6.44 EFB (on 198 Sqn), re-cat RIW
MN205 6.44-?
MN255 6.44-6.7.44, 22.7.44-17.8.44 EFB
MN288 6.44-27.7.44
MN360 ?-15.6.44 AC FA, ROS, 14.7.44-23.7.44
MN486 6.44-12.7.44 RIW
MN529 6.44-31.8.44
MN590 6.44-10.9.44 EFB
MN628 6.44-15.6.44
MN636 6.44-6.7.44
MN642 7.6.44 FTR, shot down by flak, Mézidon area
MN656 6.44-7.6.44 EFB
MN659 6.44-27.6.44, 18.7.44-23.7.44

MN667 ?-7.6.44 EFB, shot down by flak, Mézidon area
MN692 6.44-27.6.44, 22.7.44-26.7.44
MN718 6.44-7.8.44 FTR, shot down by flak near Mortain

### No. 193 Sqn, Need's Oar Point (Hurn 3.7.44; 'B15' Ryes 11.7.44; On D-Day probably drew upon aircraft from other squadrons in four-squadron No. 146 Wing)

JP499 24.3.44-28.6.44
JP842 4.44-10.6.44 BFA
JR376 4.44-8.5.44 AC FB, ROS, ?-7.7.44
MM985 13.3.44-17.7.44 RIW
MN256 25.2.44-15.6.44 EFB
MN364 4.44-8.6.44 AC FB
MB397 4.44-25.5.44 AC FB, ROS, 1.7.44-?
MN462 ?-12.9.44
MN522 5.44-10.6.44 FTR, shot down by flak
MN602 5.6.44-15.8.44 FTR, shot down by flak, Argenta

### No. 197 Sqn, Need's Oar Point (Hurn 3.7.44; 'B3' Ste Croix 17.9.44)

DN543 ?-?
JP682 6.44-13.7.44 AC FB
JP851 18.3.44-8.6.44
JP899 3.6.44-2.9.44
JR248 6.44-26.8.44 AC FB
JR367 3.6.44-24.6.44 BFB
MN125 30.1.44-7.6.44 FTR, shot down by flak, Villars Bocage
MN138 6.44-15.6.44 (possibly used by 175 Sqn)
MN209 6.44-14.7.44 FTR, shot down by Bf 109s near Lisieux
MN269 5.6.44-17.6.44 FTR
MN324 6.44-17.8.44
MN341 6.44-17.8.44 EFB, crashed near Vimoutiers, battle damaged
MN412 4.44-26.6.44
MN423 4.44-7.6.44 FTR, from a sweep, near St Lô
MN463 6.44-18.8.44 FTR
MN484 6.44-17.8.44 AC FB
MN491 6.44-?
MN629 6.44-24.6.44 BFB, serious flak damage, 6.7.44 Cat E
MN634 6.44-26.7.44 AC FB
MN688 8.6.44-18.6.44 BFB
MN759 8.6.44-27.7.44

### No. 198 Sqn, Thorney Island (Funtington 18.6.44; Hurn 22.6.44; 'B5' Camilly/'B10' Plumetot 1.7.44)

R8900 29.3.44-6.7.44
JP503 ?-7.6.44 FTR, crashed near Lisieux
JP655 15.3.44-8.6.44 EFB, crashed near Caen
*JR197 ?-22.6.44, shot down by flak near Cherbourg
JR322 ?-?
*JR366 21.2.44-22.6.44 AC FB, 19.8.44-4.10.44 FTR, shot down near Ederveen
JR512 6.44-14.6.44 EFB
JR527 14.1.44-25.12.44 AC FB

MN128  21.2.44-2.5.44 AC FB, 9.6.44-8.44
*MN132  21.2.44-18.6.44 FTR
*MN195  3.3.44-16.6.44 AC FB
MN241  13.2.44-2.4.44, 31.5.44-7.6.44
*MN293  6.44-6.7.44
MN314  14.3.44-18.6.44 BFB
MN409  8.6.44-8.44
MN410  ? ?
MN425  4.44-18.6.44 AC FB
*MN537  6.44-18.6.44 AC FB
*MN546  6.44-6.8.44 BFB
*MN570  6.44-24.7.44, RIW 3.8.44
MN585  6.44-24.6.44 AC FB
MN694  6.44-8.6.44 AC FB
MN696  6.44-4.6.44 AC FA, 8.6.44 to 84 GSU
*MN775  6.44-18.8.44 BFB

*JR524  ?-12.6.44 FTR
MM925  ?-10.6.44 AC FA
MN317  4.44-?
*MN340  5.44-3.7.44
*MN373  4.44-18.6.44 BFB
*MN421  5.44-8.6.44 BFB
*MN430  4.44-17.6.44 AC FB; returned to use, held to 1.9.44
MN451  6.44-28.10.44
*MN591  5.44-?
MN599  5.44-12.6.44 AC FB
*MN710  5.44-18.6.44 EFB, crashed on take-off, 'B6'
MN795  6.44-6.7.44, collided with MN821, 'B6'
MN809  6.44-17.6.44 FTR, shot down by flak
*MN823  6.44-3.7.44

## No. 245 Sqn, Holmsley South ('B5' Camilly 17.6.44)

JP606  6.44-18.7.44
JP669  6.44-10.8.44, 21.8.44-3.9.44
JP898  6.44-18.8.44 FTR
JR289  4.44-7.6.44 FTR, shot down by flak near Caen
JR429  6.44-14.7.44 AC FA
MM993  6.44-1.3.45
MN319  6.44-18.10.44 FTR
MN325  6.44-20.9.44 RIW
MN376  6.44-7.9.44
MN377  4.44-7.6.44 FTR, shot down by flak, Caen area
MN459  6.44-17.8.44 FTR, crashed near Lisieux
MN490  4.44-15.6.44 FTR, shot down by flak near Falaise
MN530  6.44-7.8.44 AC FB
MN532  6.44-13.7.44 RIW
MN819  6.44-18.7.44
MN863  6.44-10.7.44 RIW

## No. 247 Sqn, Hurn ('B6' Coulombs 20.6.44)

*DN492  4.44-8.6.44 AC FB
JP838  4.44-15.6.44 AC FA
JP934  4.44-8.7.44 (EFB, with 182 Sqn)
JR290  5.44-29.6.44 AC FB
JR362  ?-? (possibly served with 439 Sqn)
*JR372  4.44-8.6.44 BFB, ROS, 14.6.44-?
*JR391  ?-7.6.44 BFB

## No. 257 Sqn, Need's Oar Point (Hurn 2.7.44; 'B3' Ste Croix 15.7.44)

JP975  19.10.43-28.1.44, 16.4.44-29.6.44
JR320  6.44-18.11.44
JR507  14.3.44-18.6.44 (BFB, on 164 Sqn)
MN118  10.1.44-18.6.44 AC FB
MN193  3.2.44-13.6.44 BFA
MN237  4.3.44-8.6.44
MN294  ?-?
MN304  3.3.44-8.6.44
MN354  6.44-14.7.44 AC FB
MN372  4.44-12.6.44 FTR
MN381  6.44-17.7.44 AC FB
MN396  8.6.44-31.8.44
MN405  8.6.44-13.7.44 FTR, shot down by Bf 109s, Cormeilles-en-Vexin
MN408  4.44-8.8.44
MN416  ?-17.6.44 FTR, crashed SW of Caen
MN452  6.44-18.11.44
MN492  6.44-23.8.44 EFA
MN541  6.44-12.7.44 RIW
MN643  6.44-12.7.44, 21.9.44-30.9.44 AC FB
MN652  6.44-11.12.44 EFB
MN682  6.44-6.7.44
MN754  6.44-17.6.44 FTR
MN755  6.44 15.6.44
MN757  ?-8.6.44 BFB

## No. 263 Sqn, Harrowbeer (Bolt Head 19.6.44; Hurn 10.7.44; Eastchurch 23.7.44; 'B3' Ste Croix 6.8.44)

JR312  11.4.44-15.6.44 AC FB, ROS,

*Typhoons of No. 245 Squadron. 'Invasion markings' on Typhoons were soon toned down. (IWM CL449)*

|  |  |
|---|---|
|  | 31.7.44-17.8.44 |
| *JR368* | 25.2.44-6.7.44 |
| *JR441* | 12.12.43-7.6.44 |
| *JR446* | 13.12.43-7.6.44 |
| *JR498* | 11.4.44-14.6.44, 7.7.44-10.8.44 |
| *MN178* | 3.5.44-14.6.44 AC FB, 24.6.44-27.6.44, 7.7.44-30.11.44 |
| *MN245* | 3.5.44-8.44 |
| *MN261* | 3.5.44-19.10.44 |
| *MN282* | 3.5.44-5.11.44 AC FB |
| *MN292* | 3.5.44-15.6.44 EFA |
| *MN300* | 3.5.44-23.6.44 FTR |
| *MN407* | 1.7.44-18.8.44 EFB |
| *MN449* | 21.3.44-16.4.44 ROS, 13.5.44-9.6.44 FTR |
| *MN467* | 26.4.44-14.6.44 AC FB, ROS, 28.7.44-16.2.45 EFA |
| *MN476* | 9.4.44-2.7.44, 10.8.44-13.10.44 EFB |
| *MN477* | 9.4.44-25.8.44 FTR |
| *MN487* | 9.4.44-19.11.44 |
| *MN515* | 10.4.44-7.6.44 FTR |
| *MN524* | 5.44-24.6.44 FTR, shot down off St Malo |
| *MN661* | 27.5.44-14.6.44 EFB, flak damage, crashed at Grantex, Jersey |
| *MN738* | 30.5.44-8.11.44 BFB |

### No. 266 Sqn, Need's Oar Point (Eastchurch 29.6.44; Hurn 13.7.44; 'B3' Ste Croix 17.7.44)

|  |  |
|---|---|
| *DN562* | 5.44-6.6.44 FTR |
| *JP752* | 24.2.44-15.6.44, 22.6.44-27.7.44 |
| *JR306* | 6.44-27.7.44 |
| *JR384* | 6.44-24.6.44 AC FB |
| *MN133* | 23.2.44-19.7.44 FTR, shot down by fighters near Lisieux |
| *MN148* | 28.2.44-21.9.44 |
| *MN175* | 27.2.44-8.6.44, to 198 Sqn |
| *MN184* | 28.2.44-17.7.44 FTR |
| *MN243* | 11.3.44-18.4.44, 8.6.44-21.12.44, 11.1.45-25.1.45 |
| *MN264* | 6.44-? |
| *MN297* | 28.2.44-8.6.44 EF, crashed in Channel |
| *MN320* | 8.6.44-15.9.44 AC |
| *MN343* | 8.6.44-12.10.44 |
| *MN361* | 6.44-28.7.44 EFB |
| *MN400* | 6.44-7.8.44 FTR |
| *MN493* | 6.44-27.8.44 AC FB |
| *MN539* | 6.44-18.7.44 BFB |
| *MN600* | 6.44-31.7.44 BFB |
| *MN651* | 6.44-29.6.44 |
| *MN680* | 6.44-17.8.44 FTR, shot down by Fw 190s |
| *MN773* | 6.44-8.10.44 BFA |

### No. 438 (RCAF) Sqn, Hurn

|  |  |
|---|---|
| *MN150* | 6.44-25.8.44 |
| *MN298* | 6.44-16.6.44 FTR, shot down by Bf 109s near Vendes |
| *MN321* | 6.44-3.8.44 FTR, shot down by flak |
| *MN345* | 4.44-6.6.44 AC FB, ROS, 29.6.44-20.8.44 |
| *MN346* | 4.44-12.6.44 FTR, shot down by flak |
| *MN347* | 8.6.44-18.8.44 FTR, shot down by flak near Orbec |
| *MN375* | 4.44-12.6.44 |
| *MN411* | 4.44-6.6.44 AC FB |
| *MN413* | 6.44-2.8.44 |
| *MN424* | 6.44-6.10.44, 23.11.44-22.1.45 |
| *MN473* | 6.44-25.6.44 AC FB |

|  |  |
|---|---|
| *MN475* | 6.44-6.7.44 |
| *MN482* | 6.44-5.10.44 |
| *MN538* | 5.44-12.6.44 FTR, flak damage, crashed in Channel |
| *MN547* | 6.44-16.9.44, 31.8.44-27.9.44 |
| *MN579* | 6.44-18.8.44 EFB, crashed in Normandy, flak damage |
| *MN626* | 6.44-1.11.44 |
| *MN633* | 6.44-27.7.44 |
| *MN687* | 6.44-12.8.44 FTR, shot down by AA, Le Mesnil Villement |
| *MN715* | 6.44-17.7.44 EFB (with 440 Sqn), flak damage, crashed Maltot, Calvados |
| *MN758* | 6.44-1.3.45 |

### No. 439 (RCAF) Sqn, Hurn

|  |  |
|---|---|
| *R8897* | 29.1.44-16.6.44, oldest Typhoon in front-line service |
| *JR506* | 22.2.44-13.8.44 AC FB |
| *JR521* | 6.44-9.8.44 EFB, force-landed near St Germain d'Ectot |
| *MN316* | 6.44-27.7.44 |
| *MN352* | 6.44-5.10.44 AC FB |
| *MN356* | 6.44-6.9.44 AC FB |
| *MN362* | 4.44-26.7.44 FTR |
| *MN370* | 6.44-31.7.44 |
| *MN379* | 6.44-2.10.44 EFB |
| *MN401* | 6.44-19.8.44 FTR |
| *MN417* | 6.44-15.6.44 EFB, flak damage, crashed on Carpiquet |
| *MN435* | 3.44-7.6.44 AC FB, ROS, 30.6.44-27.7.44 |
| *MN464* | 6.44-8.7.44, flak damage, crashed at Lantheuil |
| *MN553* | 6.44-12.8.44 FTR, shot down by flak, Le Pont de Vers, Calvados |
| *MN569* | 6.44-? |
| *MN574* | 6.44-18.7.44 FTR, shot down by flak, Mesnil-Fremental |
| *MN581* | 6.44-23.6.44 BFB |
| *MN663* | 6.44-23.6.44 FTR, flak damage, ditched in Channel |
| *MN665* | 6.44-2.8.44 |
| *MN716* | 6.44-27.7.44 |
| *MN776* | 6.44-27.6.44 EFB, crash-landed at Camilly |

### No. 440 (RCAF) Sqn, Hurn

|  |  |
|---|---|
| *MM961* | 10.5.44-15.6.44 |
| *MN115* | 6.44-11.1.45 |
| *MN171* | 4.44-23.6.44 FTR, shot down by flak near Juvigny |
| *MN172* | 25.2.44-14.6.44 AC FB |
| *MN189* | 23.2.44-? |
| *MN257* | 2.44-7.6.44 EFB, flak damage near Caen |
| *MN258* | Assigned to 609 Sqn, operated in 6.44 by 440 Sqn |
| *MN307* | ?-7.6.44 FTR |
| *MN348* | 6.44-2.10.44 AC FB |
| *MN366* | 4.44-20.6.44 AC FB |
| *MN369* | 4.44-26.7.44 AC FB |
| *MN378* | 6.44-6.9.44 AC FB |
| *MN403* | 6.44-26.7.44 FTR |
| *MN420* | 3.44-6.6.44 BFB |
| *MN428* | 3.44-6.6.44 FTR |
| *MN457* | 6.44-24.6.44 AC FA |
| *MN528* | 6.44-4.7.44 RIW |
| *MN548* | 3.44-7.6.44 FTR, shot down by flak near Caen |

**No. 609 Sqn, Thorney Island ('B2'**
**Bazenville 18.6.44; Hurn 22.6.44; 'B10'**
**Plumetot 1.7.44)**

# The de Havilland Mosquito FB Mk VI

Adding bombs to the Mosquito fighter was achieved by utilizing belly space aft of the cannon. After No. 23 Squadron confirmed the effectiveness of such an idea when operating from Malta, de Havilland devised a dedicated fighter-bomber which, because the Mk V was planned as the main bomber version, became the FB Mk VI.

A Mk IV airframe, DZ434, completed as the first Mk VI, received a new identity, HJ622, before emerging in May 1942 and lasting only until 10 July 1942. An engine failure at Boscombe Down not only brought about its abrupt end, but also seriously delayed development. Production eventually commenced in February 1943.

First recipients of the FB Mk VI were the two Fighter Command long-range Intruder squadrons, Nos. 418 and 605, equipped respectively in May and July 1943. Long-range tanks and the Mosquito's high performance enabled deep daylight penetrations from Britain as far as Czechoslovakia, which achievement no other Allied aircraft could match. But the FB Mk VIs were to become better known for other reasons.

Having already experienced the Mosquito day bomber's performance, No. 2 Group was eager to employ the Mk VI, similarly, after transferring to Fighter Command prior to joining 2nd TAF. Nos. 21, 464 (RAAF) and 487 (RNZAF) Squadrons congregated at Sculthorpe in late summer 1943 and formed the Mosquito VI-equipped No. 140 Wing, superintended by the famous Gp Capt P.C. Pickard.

Low-level daylight operations began on 30 October 1943 when 24 aircraft staged through Exeter, each to drop four 500 lb HEs (one beneath each wing) on a power station north of Nantes. Famous Mosquito O-Orange (DZ414) filmed the show. More training was needed – and Merlin 25-powered aircraft with improved low-altitude performance. Six 487 Squadron aircraft tried to bomb Hazemeyer Electrics' Hengelo factory on 5 November, then more low-level ventures followed. One of the most courageous was an attempt by Sqn Ldr A.S. Cussons and his navigator to sink a sizeable merchant vessel off Ile de Croix. It cost them their lives and led to calls for the award of two Victoria Crosses.

A second Mosquito Wing, which began forming on 14 October 1943 at Lasham, comprised Nos. 107 and 613 Squadrons, to which was added No. 305 (Polish) Squadron. On 15 March 1944 No. 138 Wing was declared fully operational.

So serious was the build-up of V-1 flying-bomb sites in France that on 21 December 1943 No. 140 Wing began attacking them, before moving to Hunsdon on 31 December 1943. Assorted tactics employed ranged from high-level pathfinder-led sorties to low-level and dive attacks in the face of intense defensive fire. *DZ414* was usually around filming the action, as on 18 February 1944 when Mosquitoes from Hunsdon delivered the famous attack on Amiens prison, breaking its walls and enabling the escape of Resistance members imprisoned there.

By that time the Mosquito FB Mk VI-equipped squadrons were practising for their post-invasion specialized night activity. Starting in February 1944, each squadron would spend a month operating at night, usually against airfields. Daylight sorties were not entirely neglected: Hengelo was raided again on 18 March,

and the Gestapo offices in Schevingsche Wegg, Den Haag were attacked by No. 613 Squadron. Night-flying training and operations were, however, given top priority.

Between 3 October 1943 and 26 May 1944, No. 2 Group Mosquito squadrons managed 155 daylight operations involving some 1,600 sorties. The cost was 36 aircraft missing and 21 seriously damaged.

On 3 June 1944 No. 2 Group Operations Order GO3 outlined the tasks for its Mosquito Mk VI squadrons. At 22:00 hrs on 5 June the first of 98 aircraft set out to operate in a manner to be repeated most nights until the end of hostilities in Europe. The order stated that the Mosquitoes were '. . . to cause maximum delay to the movement by road and rail of enemy forces at night in the area prescribed. All Mitchell and Mosquito squadrons in the Group will be used throughout the hours of darkness.' Operations at first took place in the area Lessay–Caen–Lisieux–Argentan–Domfront –Fourgere–Avranches. Within that zone both Mosquito wings were allocated five more precise locations, each one called a 'tennis court', to be patrolled by a

*Mosquito FB Mk VIs of No. 464 (RAAF) Squadron visiting Hatfield shortly before D-Day. (de Havilland)*

*Nos. 418 (RCAF) and 605 Squadrons strafed ground defences during the night airborne landings on 5/6 June. 418's Mosquito FB Mk VIs had been very active in the intruder role since mid-1943. (de Havilland)*

Mosquito whose crew was, on the night of the invasion, ordered to attack all road movement, particularly by thin-skinned vehicles. Mosquito crews relied upon visual sightings at low-level. They used bombs, cannon and machine-guns, and sometimes attacked by the light of flares dropped by Mitchells. A continuous patrol would be mounted by one aircraft over each 'tennis court', with two other aircraft being held in reserve.

Each patrol would last for 30 minutes, and if no activity was observed a static target would be attacked. Anything that moved chanced its luck. On 5/6 June 90 of the Mosquitoes operating delivered attacks on road and rail targets, although there was little movement. Next night 122 of 129 Mosquitoes operating made attacks, dropping 486 x 500 lb bombs within three areas of operation, *viz*, Bayeux–Carentan–Granville–Avranches– Bayeux; Caen–Lisieux–Evreux–Dreux–Alençon–Caen; and between Argentan and Pontorson. Movement was limited until a few nights later, then the action was piled on. Prisoners were soon telling their captors that night onslaughts by Mosquitoes were more frightening than day attacks when they could at least see what was happening. At night, sometimes in the eerie glow of flares dropped from Mitchells, everything seemed 'more dangerous, more morale-shattering'.

*A trio of Mosquito FB Mk VIs, squadron uncertain.*

*Mosquito FB Mk VI HR250 reached the RAF on 7 June 1944, and served with No. 151 Squadron from 19 July to 17 September 1944. Later used by No. 29 Squadron, and by the CFE post-war, it was sold to Yugoslavia in 1951 and became 8072. (via A.S. Thomas)*

In the first week following D-Day the Mosquito FB Mk VI squadrons achieved a remarkable 93 per cent serviceability level. On 10 June the Army requested an attack on a large assembly of petrol tankers at Chatellerault, 200 miles into France. A dozen aircraft from Nos. 107, 464 and 487 Squadrons soon obliged with an evening assault. Not long after, they reminded the Gestapo that they were still around, leaving a 'calling card' on an HQ at Egletons where, it was believed, the hated Klaus Barbi was hiding. Right to the very end of hostilities, if the Mosquitoes found the enemy they bit him – *hard*.

## Mosquito FB Mk VIs on squadron strength, 5 June 1944

\* One *Ranger* sortie 5/6 June
\*\* Two *Ranger* sorties 5/6 June

### No. 21 Sqn, Gravesend

| | |
|---|---|
| *HR194 | 6.44-19.8.44 EFB, crashed returning from ops |
| HX952 | 29.3.44-17.9.44 FTR, Arnhem support, Nijmegen barracks |
| HX969 | 27.12.43-15.6.44 |
| \*\*LR291 | 2.1.44-19.10.44 |
| *LR348 | 1.2.44-8.11.44 |
| \*\*LR356 | 5.44-4.12.44 |
| *LR373 | 20.1.44-25.6.44 EFB |
| \*\*LR381 | 20.1.44-8.7.44 |
| *LR382 | 20.1.44-31.8.44 FTR |
| *LR402 | 23.1.44-24.8.44, 3.10.44-4.1.45 |
| *NS837 | 22.3.44-23.6.44 EFB |
| \*\*NS889 | 30.4.44-2.10.44 AC FB |
| NS903 | 28.5.44-1.3.45 |

| | |
|---|---|
| \*\*NS935 | 20.3.44-31.7.44 FTR |
| \*\*NS938 | 30.4.44-14.6.44 FTR |
| *NS959 | 26.5.44-10.7.44 EFB |
| *NS978 | 12.5.44-8.8.44 FTR |
| *NS989 | 1.5.44-25.6.44 EFB |
| \*\*NS990 | 30.5.44-27/28.2.45 FTR |
| *NT124 | 22.5.44-30.7.44 BFB |
| NT170 | 29.6.44-1.11.44 AC FB |
| *NT174 | 19.5.44-4/5.2.45 AC FB |
| NT182 | 17.5.44-21.6.44 EFB |
| E-NT200 | 28.5.44-21.6.44 |

### No. 107 Sqn, Lasham

| | |
|---|---|
| *J-HJ771 | 5.44-3.9.44 |
| HJ772 | 11.2.44-15.8.44 |
| HJ824 | 19.2.44-15.6.44 |
| U-HX901 | 11.2.44-26.6.44 EFB |
| *U-HX905 | ?-? |
| *F-LR257 | 14.23.44-25.8.44 FTR |
| LR264 | 4.3.44-31.7.44, 7.9.44-17.9.44 |
| LR384 | 17.3.44-22.7.44 |
| *P-NS820 | 24.2.44-8.8.44 FTR |
| *O-NS831 | 4.44-1.8.44 BFA |
| NS836 | 15.3.44-27.1.45 FTR |
| NS852 | 28.3.44-4.9.44 |
| *L-NS853 | 30.4.44-24.9.45 |
| *V-NS883 | 20.3.44-22.6.44 |
| *Q-NS886 | 28.3.44-5.7.44 FTR |
| *B-NS902 | 18.5.44-8.6.44 FTR |
| *N-NS908 | 17.3.44-22.11.44 |
| *T-NS910 | 7.5.44-29.11.44 BFB |
| *C-NS912 | 4.44-2.9.44 FTR |
| *K-NS934 | 30.4.44-4.11.44 EFB |
| S-NS952 | 27.5.44-25.8.44 EFB |
| NS953 | 19.3.44-29.10.44 FTR |
| *D-NT115 | 4.44-24.11.44 |

### No. 305 (Polish) Sqn, Lasham

| | |
|---|---|
| HX939 | 9.2.44-3.7.44 |
| *O-HX980 | 1.2.44-11.1.45 |
| LR261 | 7.2.44-21.7.44 |
| *Q-LR262 | 2.2.44-24.9.44 EFA |
| *R-LR275 | 13.3.44-8.6.44 FTR |

| | |
|---|---|
| *D-LR295 | 24.12.43-20.10.44 |
| LR298 | 24.12.43-31.8.44 |
| *N-LR300 | 24.12.43-10.7.44 FTR |
| *A-LR303 | 5.44-8.3.45 |
| *J-LR365 | 12.2.44-11.1.45 |
| *H-MM422 | 6.44-8.11.44 FTR |
| NS824 | 11.2.44-22.11.44 |
| *V-NS841 | 6.44-27.8.44 EFB |
| *B-NS846 | ?-? |
| *S-NS873 | 20.3.44-11.7.44 FTR |
| *R-NS887 | 17.5.44-15.12.44 |
| *M-NS888 | 5.4.44-21.9.44 |
| NS909 | 20.3.44-1.7.45 |
| *T-NS913 | 10.4.44-16.6.44 FTR |
| *C-NS927 | ?-? |
| *E-NT175 | 5.44-? |
| LR518 | (T Mk III) 20.2.44-20.6.44 |
| LR556 | (T Mk III) 5.5.44-31.8.44 |
| *Z-??143 | ?-? |

## No. 464 (RAAF) Sqn, Gravesend

| | |
|---|---|
| HJ776 | 4.44-6.7.44 |
| HJ993 | (T Mk III) 6.44-31.8.44 |
| *HP934 | 6.44-27.11.44 FTR |
| *HX858 | 24.8.43-5.8.44 FTR |
| *HX913 | 7.9.43-7.44 |
| *HX914 | 7.9.43-8.7.44 |
| *HX919 | 19.9.43-14.9.44 |
| HX920 | 9.9.43-22.2.45 FTR |
| HX921 | 9.9.43-11.11.44 |
| *HX976 | 6.44-21.6.44 |
| *HX977 | ?-? |
| *LR256 | 21.10.43-6.10.44 |
| LR332 | 15.12.44-12.6.44 EFB |
| *LR334 | 9.1.44-27.7.44 |
| **LR383 | 20.1.44-22.6.44 AC FB |
| LR535 | (T Mk III) 8.5.44-6.7.44 |
| *MM403 | 23.1.44-18.1.45 EFB |
| *MM407 | 25.1.44-? |
| *MM243 | 11.3.44-8.8.44 FTR |
| MM427 | 11.3.44-22.12.44 FTR |
| NS890 | 28.3.44-1/2.2.45 FTR |
| *NS893 | 30.3.44-11.6.44 EFB |
| NS896 | 28.3.44-10/11.2.45 AC FB |
| *NS897 | 22.3.44-5.6.44 FTR |
| *NS926 | 5.4.44-8.7.44 |
| *NS937 | 30.4.44-5.7.44 FTR |
| NT144 | 22.5.44-1.3.45 |
| NT177 | 19.5.44-31.8.44 |

## No. 487 (RNZAF) Sqn, Gravesend

| | |
|---|---|
| HJ967 | (T Mk III) 27.9.43-12.7.44 |
| T-HP924 | 20.3.44-31.8.44 |
| HP925 | 5.2.44-16.5.44, 3.7.44-10.8.44 |
| *U-HP933 | 4.44-22.2.45 FTR |
| *Q-HX855 | 6.9.43-6.11.44 |
| *E-HX917 | 7.9.43-5.7.44 FTR |
| HX953 | 2.10.43-14.6.44 |
| B-HX963 | ?-? |
| *J-HX974 | 8.1.44-26.7.44 |
| *V-LR299 | 5.2.44-13.10.44 |
| *F-LR332 | (464 Sqn aircraft) |
| *R-LR333 | 2.44-9.9.44 EFA, overshot on landing, Thorney Island |
| *D-LR335 | 6.44-22.6.44 |
| *K-MM412 | 6.44-19.7.44 |
| *N-MM418 | 22.3.44-1.8.44, 21.9.44-18.11.44 |
| *W-NS829 | 24.2.44-13.10.44 |
| *G-NS834 | 14.3.44-4.1.45 |
| NS840 | 22.3.44-2.45 |
| *L-NS891 | 28.3.44-8.6.44 |
| *H-NS963 | 30.4.44-6.1.45 |
| *S-NS964 | 17.5.44-27.3.44 |
| NS988 | 26.5.44-30.9.44 FTR |
| A NT135 | 18.5.44-30.7.44 FTR |
| *Y-NT180 | 27.5.44-1.8.44 AC FB |
| NT184 | 6.44-25.12.44 |

## No. 613 Sqn, Lasham

| | |
|---|---|
| *HJ666 | 4.44-20.1.45 |
| *HP927 | 14.2.44-1.1.45 |
| *HP930 | 15.2.44-23.12.44 FTR |
| *HX828 | 5.44-18.5.45 |
| *S-LR302 | 26.11.43-17.1.45 EFB |
| *C-LR351 | 20.1.44-3.5.45 |
| LR354 | 10.1.44-25.12.44 EFB |
| *H-LR355 | 6.1.44-1.8.44 EFA, overshot landing |
| *X-LR368 | 8.1.44-6.8.44 FTR |
| T-LR369 | 20.1.44-15.2.45 |
| *W-LR374 | 8.2.44-31.3.45 |
| NS822 | 24.2.44-22.6.44 |
| **NS827 | 19.2.44-8.3.44, 13.5.44-25.12.44 |
| *Q-NS848 | 24.3.44-8.6.44 |
| *P-NS859 | 30.3.44-1/2.3.45 FTR |
| *Z-NS898 | 31.3.44-17.9.44 |
| **A-NS899 | 5.44-6.8.44, 21.9.44-22.2.45 FTR |
| *NS907 | 3.6.44-31.7.44 FTR |
| NS927 | 24.3.44-8.1.45 |
| *R-NS977 | 7.5.44-11/12.2.45 FTR |
| *Y-NS987 | 1.5.44-28.7.44 EFA |

# The Douglas Boston IIIA

On D-Day the two Boston squadrons performed significantly, laying smoke to screen the Allied landing force closing upon Normandy's shore. This was no new task; Bostons had performed similarly during the August 1942 Dieppe raid, and during Operation *Starkey* in September 1943. Nor were they relative newcomers to the area for in 1939 the French government had recognized the Douglas DB-7 as one of the best American warplanes and ordered some. When France fell, Britain inherited many of those on order. By November 1940 150 DB-7s were in Britain and more were under contract. The early versions, powered by Pratt & Whitney Twin Wasp engines, were so short on range that the British converted them into night-fighters and later applied them to a night intruder campaign.

Not until 1941 did the superior Wright Cyclone-powered DB-7Bs reach Britain and, appearing logical successors to its Blenheims, were placed in No. 2 Group which in March 1942 began using them as day bombers, usually in medium-altitude formation attacks screened by RAF fighters and as bait for the enemy. Early Boston IIIs still had only an 800-mile range whereas later examples had this boosted to 1,050 miles at 16,000 ft when operating on 66 per cent power. Their other refinements included ejector exhausts which, although they provided better engine cooling and added 15 mph to the speed, produced many maintenance problems. Occasionally the three Boston squadrons operated at low level, relying upon speed and good manoeuvrability to attack special targets such as power stations. The number of aircraft involved was limited because many Bostons were diverted to the Mediterranean war, served as night-fighters or were used by the USAAF. Indeed, the US 8th AF opened its European bombing campaign with Boston IIIs lent by the RAF.

Boston IIIA deliveries began on 13 October 1942 when *BZ196* and *BZ203* flew into Britain. Boeing-built, the Mk IIIA – wing span 61 ft 4 in, length 47 ft 4 in, loaded weight 21,700 lb when carrying a 2,000 lb bomb load and 400 gal of fuel – represented a further refinement with its two 1,600 hp Wright Cyclone GR-2600-23 engines fitted with a further-modified ejector exhaust system. A&AEE trials showed the Mk IIIA to be faster still, with a maximum speed of 309 mph TAS at 1,800 ft in MS gear, 320 mph TAS at 10,500 ft in FS gear. Boston IIIA operations began on 1 May 1943, the somewhat lengthy incubation period arising because more troubles with the complex ejector exhaust system needed solving, and fresh crews were needed to replace those operating Boston IIIs flown to North Africa. More, mainly medium-level and some low-level operations followed, interspersed by periods of training with the Army which occasionally involved smoke-laying from up to three canisters fitted in the bomb bay and from which smoke was expelled through tubes. Naturally, that involved

accurate low flying and ensuring that the surface wind did not spoil the smoke curtain.

A new Boston IIIA squadron, No. 342 manned by Free French crews and formed at West Raynham on 7 April 1943, made use of Sculthorpe and Great Massingham and on 6 September 1943 moved to Hartfordbridge Flats (later called Blackbushe) to join Nos. 88 and 107 Squadrons which had moved in on 19 and 1 August 1943 respectively. Together they formed No. 137 Wing. On 9 September Bostons of No. 88 Squadron provided smoke cover for the HQ ship in the large convoy making a feint towards France during Operation *Starkey*, designed to tempt enemy air response and try out tactics to be used during Operation *Neptune*.

Eventually No. 2 Group worked its way through 134 Boston IIIAs, only five of which were reported missing. Another 41 were variously written off due to battle incidents. The three Boston IIIA squadrons carried out numerous day raids on military and transport targets, also Channel ports, before, at the end of 1943, they switched to bombing V-1 sites in France. February 1944 saw No. 137 Wing reduced to two Boston-equipped squadrons and an establishment of 36 aircraft, after No. 107 Squadron left for Lasham to rearm with Mosquito FB Mk VIs. Consequently the Boston IIIAs were shuffled around, and by D-Day the squadrons had been virtually re-equipped. That is not revealed by official aircraft history records because the Bostons were (on paper) held by the units designed to provide rapid replacement for expected high losses. Many Bostons were not placed on squadron strength until 22 June 1944.

Other newcomers, the Boston Mk IVs, were then crossing the Atlantic. Featuring a two-gun Martin dorsal turret, the first Mk IV arrived in Britain on 19 March 1944. More powerful 1,700 hp Wright Cyclone engines boosted the speed to a creditable 327 mph at 10,600 ft, despite the loaded weight increase to 24,000 lb. Three Mk IVs were with squadrons for trials and conversion training in June 1944 but their presence was always limited, No. 2 Group only receiving 49 examples.

As the invasion approached, Nos. 88 and 342 Squadrons operated particularly against coastal batteries, airfields (including important Evreux), and rail installations which included Hirson and Cambrai. Early May 1944 had seen No. 88 again practise smoke-laying and late that month both squadrons began, unusually for them, night-flying training, during which they practised working to very precise instructions. On 28 May No. 88 was treated to a demonstration, on Salisbury Plain, of the Army producing smoke to indicate targets. Next day AM Sir Arthur Coningham, AOC-in-C 2nd TAF, addressed the Boston crews of No. 137 Wing, telling them of a very important operation awaiting them.

## Operations

During the evening of 5 June Smoke Curtain Installation (SCI) equipment was fitted to the Bostons, already decorated with invasion stripes. At 01:00 hrs on 6 June squadron aircrew were called, the main briefing coming at 02:00 hrs. No. 88 Squadron would, from off Le Havre, stream smoke westwards, while No. 342 Squadron would fly along the eastern side of the Cherbourg Peninsula to shield from coastal defence gunfire the approaching US forces. The squadrons held 36 Boston IIIAs, four of them unserviceable.

Wg Cdr Maher and crew (BZ382) were first away to lead the show, and on time at 05:00 hrs began smoke-laying from 1½ miles east of the monitor, HMS Roberts, the third warship in the fleet from the north end. Maher approached at 300 ft, descending almost to sea level before starting to release smoke off Cap Barfleur. The ships being slightly east of the prescribed position meant that the Bostons had to fly closer to shore than expected. E-boats raced out of Le Havre trying, in vain, to shoot at the ships and also the Bostons. In the general confusion W. Off Boyle and crew were shot down. To requite its operational task No. 88 Squadron needed to borrow three aircraft from No. 342 Squadron: E, H and S. On return, Flt Lt Smith (BZ214) was forced to make a downwind landing and overshot into a sandpit. His gunner was hurled through the floor of the aircraft and killed. All others of the 19 crews involved completed their tasks without injury. The strong wind soon had the smoke shifting, but it mattered little because it had been renewed every 10 minutes to take account of the forward movement of ships closing in on the shore.

The Free French squadron, which undertook smoke training on the morning of 5 June, despatched their first two aircraft (BZ206 and BZ332) at 05:23 hrs. The task was to start the 10,000-yd-long screen from near the Isle St Noricons. The necessary smoke screen required twice the possible smoke load of one aircraft, and so a second Boston had to slot in ahead of the first. The runs were commenced two minutes apart, the second aircraft starting to generate smoke just before the first had completed its release. Five more pairs followed the first, taking over smoke production at 10-minute intervals, the last getting airborne at 06:04 hrs. One Boston crashed into the water halfway through its run and another

*A Boston III of No. 88 Squadron during its smoke-laying sortie to screen the dawn approach of the Allied invasion force. Repeatedly, and wrongly, portrayed as D-Day participants are Boston IIIs of No. 88 Squadron with white noses, the paint being applied for their part in September 1943's Operation Starkey. Such markings were featured by a number of participants, along with chordwise black-and-white bands painted around the outer mainplanes. In June 1944 some Dakotas, initially, and wrongly, bore similarly-placed bands. (IWM)*

smashed into the sea some way north of the laying area, due to unknown causes.

Once home the Bostons' tanks were replenished, in case more smoke was needed. All through 6 June and well into 7 June, the squadrons waited for a call that never came. Later that day the SCI gear was removed and the Boston crews were briefed for night interdictor bomber operations close to the bridgehead. Lack of radar meant they could only operate in fair weather, in good visibility, by moonlight, to supplement No. 2 Group's Mosquitoes and Mitchells in preventing all German troop movement by night – but the weather was consistently bad. Low-level bombing of special and often small targets was needed – but not low enough for bursting bombs to destroy the attackers, as could readily happen at night.

On 7/8 June the Boston crews tried to find Mézidon railyards. Out of 12 crews at No. 88 Squadron operating only two located the target, for the weather was very bad. By daylight, though, the Boston squadrons, almost to the end of the war, would play an effective part in No. 2 Group's formation bombing raids, and usually in relatively close support of ground forces. Evidence of the effectiveness of their raids came on 12 June when the Forêt de Grumborg, HQ of the 21st Panzer Group, was battered in a raid led by Wg Cdr Maher, who, in *BZ412*, was introducing on to operations the Boston IV fitted with the Mk. XIV bombsight and which next day led a heavy raid on the 21st Panzers south-east of Caen. The Mk IV had only just missed a part in the D-Day operations.

## Bostons on squadron strength, 5 June 1944

(Mk IIIAs unless otherwise indicated)
* operated on 6 June 1944

### No. 88 Sqn, Hartfordbridge Flats

| | | |
|---|---|---|
| *E-BZ196 | 5.44-9.44 | |
| *A-BZ210 | 5.44-1.8.44 | |
| *T-BZ214 | 5.44-7.6.44 | |
| *U-BZ229 | 5.44-9.44 | |
| *K-BZ239 | 4.44-22.9.44 | |
| *N-BZ243 | 24.8.44-7.6.44 | FTR |
| .*O-BZ262 | 5.44-8.7.44 | EFB |
| *B-BZ264 | 24.8.43-27.7.44 | |
| J-BZ274 | 11.8.44-23.6.44 | |
| *G-BZ286 | 3.44-13.12.44 | |
| *L-BZ292 | 4.44-21.11.44 | |
| *R-BZ301 | 3.44-3.12.44 | |
| *H-BZ326 | 24.2.44-12.1.45 | |
| D-BZ331 | 9.2.44-17.11.44 | |
| *Q-BZ336 | 5.44-22.8.44 | |
| *S-BZ357 | 3.44-4.1.45 | |
| *F-BZ377 | 3.44-24.2.45 | |
| C-BZ382 | 26.4.43-13.8.44 | FTR |
| BZ398 | 22.8.43-19.8.44 | |
| BZ411 | (Mk IV) 5.44-14.3.45 | |
| M-BZ412 | (Mk IV) 25.4.44-5.11.44 | AC FB |

### No. 342 (Free French) Sqn, Hartfordbridge Flats

| | | |
|---|---|---|
| BZ198 | 6.44-5.8.44 | FTR |
| *G-BZ206 | 6.44-5.4.45 | |
| A-BZ208 | 29.4.43-10.8.44 | |
| *J-BZ213 | 9.2.44-6.6.44 | FTR |
| *S-BZ259 | 6.44-23.11.44 | |
| *L-BZ261 | 17.10.43-5.8.44 | EFB |
| *N-BZ270 | 5.5.43-23.6.44 | RIW |
| *K-BZ284 | 4.44-5.4.45 | |
| *Q-BZ285 | 13.2.44-17.9.44 | |
| *B-BZ302 | 25.9.43-29.8.44 | |
| F-BZ303 | 9.2.44-6.7.44 | |
| *E-BZ312 | 1.44-9.9.44 | RIW |
| *C-BZ332 | 8.6.43-10.8.44 | |
| *H-BZ334 | 5.44-17.8.44 | |
| *P-BZ338 | 4.44-29.9.44 | |
| *R-BZ372 | 5.44-14.9.44 | |
| *T-BZ376 | 8.6.43-? | |
| *O-BZ394 | 10.2.44-21.9.44 | |
| X-BZ422 | (Mk IV) ?-? | |

# The North American Mitchell II

By 1941 the search for a No. 2 Group Blenheim replacement was desperate. The only feasible British design in view was an untried de Havilland novelty, and the need for such an aeroplane was being increasingly questioned. Bomber Command could see little value in providing little more than bait for enemy fighters during *Circus* operations.

Switching to Vultee Vengeance dive-bombers was mooted, or for No. 2 Group to become a mainstream bomber formation.

But the Army expressed a need for bomber support during any campaign in northern Europe. No. 2 Group was therefore retained and operated such aircraft as it could acquire, mainly 'small' American bombers of which the North American B-25 Mitchell was one.

The first awaited example (*FL164*) arrived on 15 June 1942 and a month later another two joined No. 21 Squadron at Bodney for operational assessment, while the A&AEE carried out full service trials. The hope was that the Mitchell might prove to be far superior to the Boston; apart from having two Wright Cyclone GR-2600 engines they had little in common. Indeed, for No. 2 Group the Boston was a better aeroplane, although the Mitchell's 4 x 1,000 lb bomb load was superior. With a wing span of 67 ft 6½ in and a length of 54 ft 1 in it was no small aeroplane, and its loaded weight of 26,000 lb could, if really necessary, be pushed to 30,000 lb and into the Wellington class. Normally loaded, the Mitchell II – on offer – had a top speed of 294 mph TAS at 14,800 ft using full supercharger (FS). Cruising at 15,000 ft, its operational range could be as high as 1,230 miles, its ceiling 26,700 ft.

Quite serious problems were soon encountered with the engines, guns and dorsal gun turret. After adjustments, delivery of Mitchells to squadrons at West Raynham began with No. 98 Squadron, reformed on 12 September 1942. Next day it received its first example. Second recipient was No. 180 Squadron, reformed on 13 September 1942 and which took on charge its first Mitchell on 29 September.

By then No. 2 Group knew the way ahead rested with small bombers flying fast and low to avoid radar detection, fighter interception and heavy AA fire. The Boston could perform like that, but it was questionable whether the heavier, less agile Mitchell was suitable. It looked just possible and so the Mitchell squadrons were ordered to participate in the Philips Eindhoven raid of December 1942 – until training revealed the bombers as still inadequate for such a venture. The dorsal .50 in guns were jamming after a dozen rounds of firing.

On 22 January 1943 an operation was attempted. Both squadrons would field six aircraft, one group attacking the Perfine oil tanks, the other the Sinclair oil refinery, both targets located alongside the Ghent–Terneuzen Canal. All the Mitchells flew in low, climbing to 1,000 ft as they approached the targets prior to release. The somewhat unwieldy, large Mitchells presented easy targets for AA gunners whose fire immediately shattered one aircraft. No. 180 Squadron leader's aircraft was badly damaged then brought down by Fw 190s which picked off another Mitchell before Mustang Is of No. 169 Squadron came to the rescue of the bombers, each of which had been carrying a sizeable load for No. 2 Group aircraft: 2 x 1,000 lb and 4 x 500 lb HE bombs. Such a load-carrier was well worth having – but how should it be operated?

The answer was in daylight, in formation, at medium altitudes for carpet bombing, and strongly escorted – which was the manner in which No. 2 Group

*Mitchell II* FV914-A *of No. 98 Squadron. (Ray Sturtivant collection)*

employed its Mitchells to the end of the war. With supplies sufficient a third squadron, the Royal Netherlands Navy's No. 320 Squadron, in exile, reformed in March 1943, receiving its own Mitchells which it began operating from Lasham the following August. On D-Day it was still using these special examples. The fourth squadron, No. 226, reluctantly bade farewell to its Bostons at Swanton Morley in May 1943. Completing the quartet was No. 305 (Polish) Squadron, which began arming with Mitchells in September 1943 and which in November 1943 joined No. 226 Squadron at Lasham. During autumn and winter 1943 the four squadrons hammered away at airfields, military targets and communications items in France, as well as attacking V-1 sites, before indulging in carpet bombing during the run-up to the invasion.

By then examples of the Mitchell II srs ii were in use, featuring a rear fuselage similar in layout (but without tail guns) to that of the Mk III, which was better armed but heavier and less responsive. Although the first Mk IIIs arrived in May 1944, none joined the squadrons until November 1944.

## Operations

The main task for the four Mitchell squadrons at the start of Operation *Neptune* was night bombing of static, tactical targets. *Gee-H*-equipped Mitchells acted as pathfinders, dropping up to 24 x 5 in flares either for Mosquito VIs or other Mitchells. On moonlit nights they could operate individually. These tasks were practised in April during Exercise *Nightlight*. No. 226 Squadron's 'Special Signals Flight' – alias 'C' Flight – flew high-level patrols over central France along specified routes, maintaining radio liaison with Resistance forces. On the evening of *Neptune* the four squadrons claimed to have 66 serviceable Mitchell bombers between them out of 82 on strength.

Despite the poor weather on 5/6 June, at 23:50 hrs 12 Mitchells of No. 226 Squadron set out to bomb the road-rail junction at Villers Bocage, upon which, aided by the pathfinders, they directed 32 x 500 lb HEs. No. 180 Squadron's turn came at 01:15 hrs when 12 aircraft – of which five did not bomb – set out to damage roads and railway features at Argentan. Next away were 12 of No. 320 Squadron, intending to destroy the railway bridge at Dives. For them the weather was so bad that none located the target. All brought their loads back. Rounding off the first night's bombing, the first of 11 crews of No. 98 Squadron set off at 02:16 hrs to conduct individual sorties, of which eight were effective, and attacked the railway at Conde-sur-Vire and nearby railway cuttings. Patrolling between Chartes and Orleans, *FV948* of No. 226 Squadron's Special Signals Flight operated between 00:05 and 04:00 hrs, contacting French Resistance forces to complete the night's Mitchell activity.

During daylight on 6 June the four squadrons rested; then, after darkness, and with the expectation of plentiful movement

*A trio of No. 226 Squadron Mitchell IIs photographed soon after D-Day. FW130-A (dominant) was a long-service machine which on 6/7 June 1944 raided Villedieu rail junction, a troop detraining point. Beyond is FW152-V. (IWM CL107)*

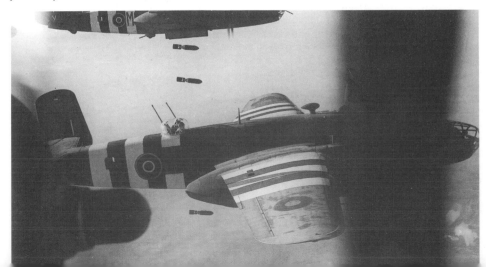

*Mitchell II FW172 of No. 180 Squadron pulls away from Dunsfold's Runway 26 on 7 August 1944. (Canadian Armed Forces)*

by German ground forces, 60 Mitchells were despatched of which 49 dropped 204 x 1,000 lb bombs on transport facilities at Villers Bocage and Falaise, the bridge at Dives and a defile in Thury Harcourt.

Enemy movement on 6/7 June was far less than expected, but on 7/8 June Mitchell crews were liberally supplied with tempting targets. Troops detraining at Flers, Villedieu and Vires came under attack, while Bostons dropped 20 lb anti-personnel bombs at Folligny. More of their number joined Mitchells bombing Mézidon. The night's activity was a combined effort by No. 2 Group, for Mosquitoes of Nos. 21, 464 and 487 Squadrons attacked troops and their transports in a disc centred on Argentan and extending to Domfront and Lisieux. The remaining Mosquito squadrons operated further west, sealing approaches to the battle zone. Next night it rained, halting such activity.

Although committed mainly to night operations, for a while the Mitchells were still available for daylight operations and proved it on the evening of 10 June when 71, Spitfire-escorted, followed 40 rocket-firing Typhoons of Nos. 181, 182, 245 and 247 Squadrons to demolish the Château de la Caine, HQ of Panzer Group West. In a very effective attack the force killed Gen von Dawans and his staff. The Mitchell crews then rested briefly before another busy night's operations. Similar activity occupied the weeks ahead, particularly as German forces retreated and bridges ahead

of them needed to be destroyed. While their activities were never headline-grabbing, the Mitchell squadrons contributed most amply to the end of the war in Europe.

## Mitchell IIs on squadron strength, 5 June 1944

\* operated on 5/6 June 1944

As with other 2TAF aircraft, Mitchells were assigned to the reserve (from March 1944), even if they were in squadron hands. Many were 'reassigned' to squadrons on 8 June 1944. The following listing includes many initial dates relating to when the aircraft are known to have been operational with the relevant squadron.

### No. 98 Sqn, Dunsfold

| | |
|---|---|
| B-FL176 | 21.9.42-9.9.44 (flew a record 125 operational sorties between 22.1.43 11.8.44) |
| J-FL182 | 4.44-2.11.44 |
| G-FL186 | 17.9.42-23.7.44 FTR (flew 93 operational sorties) |
| FL675 | 5.44-17.8.44 |
| FV916 | 5.44-10.8.44 |
| *H-FV931 | 13.9.43-23.7.44 Cat E |
| P-FV969 | 5.44-1.2.45 |
| *L-FV976 | 5.44-19.11.44 |
| FV981 | 6.44-4.7.44 |
| FV982 | 6.44-22.6.44 |
| *S-FV985 | 5.44-24.7.44 FTR |
| *M-FW102 | 5.44-20.8.44 |
| *X-FW107 | 5.44-21.12.44 |
| K-FW115 | 19.1.44-19.10.44 |
| *R-FW122 | 6.44-23.7.44 FTR |
| P-FW129 | 2.44-13.6.44 FTR |
| Q-FW167 | 6.44-13.9.44 FTR |
| U-FW168 | 6.44-2.1.45 BFA |
| FW170 | 6.44-17.8.44 |
| *D-FW184 | ?-13.6.44 FTR |
| FW189 | 6.44-23.11.44 |

```
*C-FW201   6.44-12.11.44 FB AC
 T-FW203   6.44-27.1.45 FB AC
*V-FW215   6.44-2.11.44, 12.12.44-11.4.45
 O-FW228   5.44-12.6.44, 22.6.44-12.11.44
*F-FW253   5.44-13.7.44 EFB
 W-FW256   5.44-19.1.45
```

### No. 180 Sqn, Dunsfold
```
     FL210   5.44-10.8.44 FB AC
     FL679   28.6.43-15.8.44
    *FV924   ?-?
     FV928   5.44-19.12.44 EFB
    *FV967   19.1.44-22.6.44
    *FV998   ?-20.6.44 FTR
    *FW101   6.44-28.6.44 BFB
     FW113   1.2.44-10.8.44 FTR
     FW118   5.44-23.7.44 FTR
    *FW124   5.44-21.8.44 EFB
    *FW125   5.44-11.9.44 FTR
    *FW135   5.44-2.11.44
    *FW158   5.44-23.11.44
     FW161   5.44-9.11.44
    *FW190   5.44-24.7.44 BFB
    *FW191   5.44-1.1.45
     FW206   5.44-2.11.44
     FW207   5.44-31.8.44
     FW240   5.44-14.6.45
    *FW249   5.44-6.10.44
    *FW269   5.44-6.11.44
```

### No. 226 Sqn, Hartfordbridge Flats
```
  Q-FL192   5.44-18/19.6.44 FTR, from flare drop
    FL680   3.44-17.8.44
    FV905   25.6.43-18.10.44
  M-FV919   29.2.44-21.9.44
    FV920   30.3.44-17.3.45
 *G-FV936   28.8.43-13.7.44, 17.8.44-10.9.44 EFB
  D-FV958   15.12.43-28.9.44
 *J-FV989   5.44-18.8.44 FTR
 *C-FW105   5.44-31.8.44 EFB
 *T-FW111   5.44-18.8.44 FB AC
 *U-FW112   5.44-6.7.44 BFB
 *X-FW116   3.1.44-25.7.44
 *W-FW127   3.44-18.8.44 FTR
```

```
*H-FW128   5.44-20.6.44 BFB
*A-FW130   2.44-6.11.44
 P-FW134   5.44-23.6.44 FB AC
*B-FW144   5.44-30.6.44 BFA
 V-FW152   5.44-26.11.44 FTR
 F-FW153   5.44-5.4.45
*E-FW160   5.44-7.9.44
 Y-FW163   5.44-5.11.44 BFB
*Z-FW181   5.44-5.4.45
 S-FW210   5.44-26.7.44 FTR
```

**Special Signals Flight:**
```
     FV900   9.6.43-3.8.44
     FV943   6.44-26.7.44
     FV947   27.7.43-5.44, 6.44-3.8.44
     FV948   6.44-3.8.44
     FV960   14.3.44-14.8.44
     FV966   6.44-5.7.44
     FV973   14.3.44-3.8.44
```

### No. 320 (Dutch Navy) Sqn, Dunsfold
```
     FR143   24.3.43-9.8.44 FTR, Fôret de Lyons;
             ditched in Channel
   N-FR149   24.3.43-12.6.44 FTR
   W-FR150   6.43-8.6.44 EFA
  *C-FR151   13.9.43-20.6.44 FTR
  *Y-FR156   18.7.43-6.10.44
  *J-FR160   5.44-10.8.44
  *D-FR164   5.44-27.12.44
  *V-FR167   5.44-21.11.44
     FR168   24.3.43-27.1.45
   P-FR176   10.11.43-26.11.44 FTR
     FR179   15.11.43-8.6.44 FTR
  *R-FR182   12.11.43-8.6.44 EFA
   Z-FR185   16.11.43-27.7.44
  *H-FR188   ?-12.4.45
  *F-FR189   ?-30.12.44
  *E-FR190   ?-5.9.44 EFA
  *A-FR191   26.11.43-13.6.44 FTR
  *G-FR202   ?-26.4.45
  *S-FR204   ?-24.6.44 FTR
   Q-FR205   ?-14.6.44 FTR
   U-FR207   ?-14.6.45
     FV970   5.44-22.1.45
```

# The Air-Sea Rescue force

Expectation of heavy losses during Operation *Neptune* gave the Air-Sea Rescue (ASR) force an important role. By 1944, well-organized and experienced, it showed just how much things had changed since the outbreak of war, when no RAF ASR force existed. Then, airmen whose aircraft crashed at sea had to be rescued by civilian lifeboats or ships; a chancy affair. During the Battle of Britain the Germans displayed their well-organized rescue service, using seaplanes and launches, and in autumn 1940 the British introduced Lysanders to locate survivors; then, if necessary, drop them dinghies, provide limited sustenance and guide rescue launches – but only around Britain's shores.

Refinement of tactics and equipment followed, including the introduction of Supermarine Walrus biplane amphibians able to land on water to effect rescue. Their vulnerability and slow speed led to modified lighter aircraft both to protect

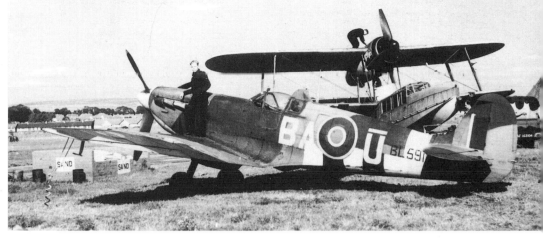

*Air-Sea Rescue Spitfire LF Mk Vbs – mostly with clipped wing-tips – were very active on D-Day. BL591-U, with only under fuselage stripes, was used by No. 277 Squadron, Shoreham, one of whose Sea Otters is visible too. (A.S. Thomas collection)*

them and also to make faster sea searches. Boulton Paul Defiant fighters were tried, but eventually favour fell upon Spitfire Mk IIs and by D-Day LF Mk Vbs, usually operating in pairs, partly for their own protection.

None was suitable for deep sea search, so standard bombers were employed to assist Coastal Command which used Lockheed Hudsons for the task. To save lives far out to sea a novel idea was the dropping of a 1,630 lb lifeboat. Designed by Uffa Fox, of Cowes yachting fame, the airborne lifeboat drifted down beneath a group of parachutes and on hitting the water deployed lifelines for crash survivors to seize. The lifeboats carried sails as well as food, rescue equipment, etc, and were being carried on D-Day on yet another aircraft type with as chequered a history as any: the Vickers-Armstrong Warwick.

## Vickers-Armstrong Warwick

In January 1935 the DTD had recommended developing a bomber design, the B.1/35, to follow the Hampden and Wellington. It was to carry a 3,000 lb bomb load for 1,500 miles at 230 mph. Four companies produced schemes, Vickers in July 1935 proposing a 288 mph twin Bristol Hercules-powered enlarged Wellington, the favoured submission, a prototype of which was to fly in July 1937.

Then came 1936 specifications calling for much superior bombers, like the Halifax and Stirling. To improve B.1/35, the Air Ministry now called for a 2,000 mile range. Therefore, in January 1937, Vickers – busy refining the Wellington – began redesigning their B.1/35 and re-engining it with Rolls-Royce Vultures, forecast to raise its speed to 332 mph.

On 8 November 1937 the Air Staff informed Vickers that they would also like a Napier Sabre-engined prototype. Then on 13 December the Air Ministry decided to withdraw support from the Hercules version, substituting a call for a layout using the untried new 18-cylinder 2,000 hp Bristol Centaurus. The performance requirement was also increased, calling for a 5,000 lb bomb load to be carried during a 2,000 mile sortie.

Such repeated changes played havoc with the design phase, which changed yet again in January 1939 when the Sabre scheme was halted. Thus the first Vickers B.1/35 would have Vultures, the second the Centaurus. On 13 August 1939 the prototype, *K8178*, first flew and the second example, *L9704*, took to the air on 5 April 1940. In July 1940, with the Vulture in trouble, and Centaurus production impossible before 1942, the Air Ministry authorized the adaptation of the design to take American Pratt & Whitney R2800-5-A4-G Twin Wasps, and on 27 October 1940 Vickers received the go-ahead to re-engine *L9704*. Production of 250 examples was

*Lifeboat-carrying Warwick ASR Mk Is were at high readiness during Operation Neptune, among them BV591 of No. 276 Squadron wearing AQP in Dull Red aft of the fuselage roundel superimposed on the AEAF stripes. (A.S. Thomas collection)*

agreed on 28 December 1940, delivery to begin in November 1941. Designated Warwick I/P1, the production specification was issued on 23 June 1941, although it was 25 July 1941 before the Twin Wasp-powered aircraft flew. The Air Ministry had originally envisaged 'a large Wellington', believing commonality of parts to be feasible. That was not really possible, and matters were made more complex by repeated calls for change.

The Warwick – wing span 96 ft 9 in, length overall 72 ft 8 in, wheel track 22 ft 10 in – was large for a 'twin'. On 1 May 1942 the first production Warwick B Mk I (*BV214*) flew; but during protracted trials the A&AEE found it to possess unsatisfactory power-weight ratios, and to be unable to maintain height when loaded and flying on one engine. Taking off at

46,000 lb, it could convey a 5,800 lb bomb load for 3,500 miles while cruising at 206 mph, and showed a top speed of 255 mph at 14,000 ft. The Centaurus prototype had reached 290 mph at 15,000 ft.

In August 1942 the Air Ministry considered employing Warwicks for personnel transport duties, which later came about. But in July 1942 deliveries of Twin Wasp-engined bombers had begun. The Directorate of Operational Requirements further considered the aircraft's potential. Bomber Command having no use for the Warwick, its use as a long-range ASR aircraft was proposed but not agreed without protracted discussions. On 7 May 1943 details were agreed whereby 113 examples (substantially bombers) would be converted into ASR aircraft, leaving the remainder as freighters.

*Warwick ASR Mk I HF944-K of No. 282 Squadron in full AEAF trim.*

On 22 June another of the many plans required 54 (later 40) bombers to be fully converted into ASR Mk Is; another 10 to be partially converted as ASR Mk I Stage A, able to carry a Mk I airborne lifeboat; 20 ASR Mk I Stage B, also fitted with ASV Mk II radar; and 179 ASR Mk I Stage C (the norm), able to carry the enlarged 3,600 lb lifeboat.

Eight years after the aircraft's inception it entered service when the Warwick Training Unit formed at Bircham Newton on 28 June 1943, to join Hudsons of No. 279 Squadron already carrying lifeboats. No. 280 Squadron, first with Warwicks, began receiving the ASR Mk I in October 1943. Nos. 279, 280, 281 and 282 Squadrons – all using Warwicks by D-Day – were Coastal Command squadrons whereas No. 276 and 278 Squadrons (which operated only a few examples) were AEAF-directed. By D-Day, 368 Warwicks of assorted types had been delivered to the RAF.

## Supermarine Walrus

Apart from the Spitfire, able to drop a dinghy, AEAF ASR squadrons used Supermarine Walrus amphibians mostly built for, and transferred or diverted from, the Fleet Air Arm. As the Seagull V, the type had first flown on 21 June 1933. A dozen, called Walrus Is, were ordered for the FAA in 1935 and more in 1936, and were intended for use as shipborne amphibians. Early in the war, production was switched to Saunders-Roe at Cowes,

Isle of Wight, where 461 Walruses were built, 190 of them Mk IIs with wooden hulls which were easier to repair than metal ones. All of the *HD*-serialled Walruses were Mk IIs. Examples modified for ASR use had a railing around the forward fuselage to enable survivors to climb aboard more easily. The Walrus had a top speed of about 135 mph, a maximum range of some 600 miles, and it alighted at 57 mph.

A modified, longer-range version of the Walrus, the Sea Otter ASR Mk I, was entering service at the time of D-Day. Whereas the Walrus had a pusher traction system and a 750 hp Bristol Pegasus, the Sea Otter had a more conventional powerplant configuration, its 965 hp Bristol Mercury XXX engine enabling it to lift heavier loads.

## Aircraft assigned to Air-Sea Rescue squadrons, 5 June 1944
* operated on 6 June 1944

NB: Some squadrons had Flights on more than one station, and squadrons flew a mixture of aircraft types, actual strength uncertain. Numbers in parentheses indicate total strength listed on Returns to HQ AEAF on 5 June 1944.

### *No. 275 Sqn,* **Warmwell**
Spitfire Vb (7):
    *AA846  25.5.44-20.2.45 SOC
     AA978  13.4.44-8.4.44, 26.5.44-30.12.44 Cat
               B MR
    *AD475  4.44-20.2.45 SOC
    *BL294  26.4.44-8.12.44, 14.12.44-20.2.45
             SOC
    *BM653  3.6.44-31.7.44 ROS, 8.9.44-? SOC(?)
    *EP507  4.5.44-20.9.44, 13.10.44-20.2.45 SOC

*Although design of the Supermarine Sea Otter (based upon the Walrus) commenced in 1936, the type did not enter RAF service until 1944.*

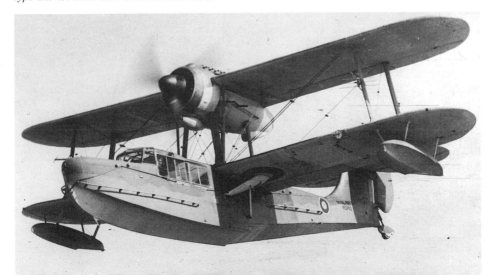

*??488   ?-? (possibly *BM448*)
Walrus I/II (5):
    *L2282   5.44-26.2.45
    *W2746   11.5.44-19.8.44
    *HD925   12.5.44-2.45
    HD929   7.3.44-2.45
    HD930   5.4.44-2.45
Anson I (1):
    ??645   ?-?
    ??539   ?-?

## No. 276 Sqn, HQ and 'A' Flight (Warwick), Portreath; 'B' Flight (Spitfire and Walrus), Bolt Head

Spitfire Vb (6):
    *E-BL379   ?-?
    *BM474   26.4.44-10.8.44 RIW
    *BL616   1.5.44-28.9.44
    *I-BL933   26.4.44-14.9.44
    *L-BM474   26.4.44-10.8.44 RIW
    *O-EN841   1.5.44-23.7.44 EFB
Warwick ASR I (4)
    *BV527   6.4.44-2.11.44
    *BV531   13.5.44-2.11.44
    HP398   6.4.44-2.11.44
    *HF940   6.4.44-2.11.44
Walrus I/II (6)
    *P5658   10.4.44-4.12.45
    W2780   6.6.44-11.45
    W3083   21.4.44-19.3.45
    *HD908   21.4.44-8.6.44
    *HD931   2.4.44-16.8.44
    HD934   ?-?
Anson I (1):
    EG499   ?-?

## No. 277 Sqn, 'A' Flight (Spitfire/Walrus/Sea Otter) Shoreham; 'B' Flight (Spitfire), Hawkinge

Spitfire Vb (22):
    *W3528   10.6.44-4.3.45
    *W3641   25.3.44-9.7.44 RIW
    *W3647   4.3.44-10.11.44 ROS, 24.11.44-
             17.2.45 SOC
    AA930   17.5.44-29.7.44 RIW
    AB814   6.5.44-20.2.45 SOC
    *AB925   5.6.44-17.2.45 SOC
    *AB975   26.5.44-25.6.44 Cat E
    *AB185   12.5.44-19.7.44 RIW DH
    *AD199   4.3.44-17.8.44 RIW
    *AD366   26.5.44-26.6.44, 16.7.44-13.2.45 Cat
             E
    AR453   19.5.44-14.6.44, 16.7.44-13.10.44
    *BL377   6.5.44-16.8.44 RIW (FA)
    *BL445   6.5.44-21.11.44 RIW
    *BL591   12.5.44-22.9.44

*BL725   17.5.44-1.3.45
BM273   26.5.44-13.10.44
*BM510   19.5.44-?
*EP435   5.6.44-1.3.45
*EP522   14.1.44-8.6.44, 21.7.44-28.9.44
*??361   ?-?
*??448   ?-?
*??875   ?-?
*??877   ?-?
Walrus I/II (12):
    L2289   ?-9.44 Cat E
    W2735   ?-?
    *X9563(?)   25.3.44-15.7.44
    HD877   2.5.44-8.4.45
    HD912   7.5.44-27.10.44
    HD923   8.5.44-9.11.44
    HD936   25.4.44-4.11.44
Sea Otter I (5):
    JM746   ?-?
    JM759   ?-?
    JM764   ?-?
    JM796   ?-?

## No. 278 Sqn, 'A' Flight (Warwick), Bradwell Bay; 'B' Flight (Spitfire and Walrus), Martlesham Heath

Spitfire Vb (10):
    *W3330   18.4.44- crash-landed, Warwick
             7.6.44, 30.6.44- to 275 Sqn 12.7.44
    W3368   18.4.44-26.2.45 SOC
    *U-W3893   4.44-23.4.44, 10.5.44-8.7.44 AC FB,
             ROS, 21.7.44-13.10.44
    *N-W3948   23.5.44-13.10.44
    AB786   18.4.44-14.6.44
    AD562   24.4.44-22.2.45
    *Q-BL376   18.4.44-18.1.45
    *Y-BM418   26.5.44-26.11.44
    *X-BM491   23.5.44-14.11.44
    BM532   24.4.44-22.2.45
Walrus II (6):
    W3076   9.5.44-12.3.45
    HD830   6.6.44-19.8.44 sunk
    *HD918   ?-?
    *HD926   ?-?
    *HD935   13.4.44-23.11.44
Warwick ASR I Stage C (5):
    *BV475   5.4.44-29.11.44
    *BV478   5.4.44 26.3.45
    *BV528   5.4.44-15.11.44 EFA
    BV529   5.4.44-10.3.45
    *HF968   1.3.44-10.3.45
Anson I (5):
    EG543   ?-?
    DJ617   ?-?
    ??539   ?-?
    ??606   ?-?
    ??645   ?-?

# Part Four
# The Seekers

# Coastal Command

Immediately before, and during the Normandy campaign, Coastal Command's primary task was to prevent submarines and surface ships from infiltrating the English Channel. This was achieved by mounting continuous patrols by day and night within five prescribed sea areas in the western approaches. Every portion of these was visited every half hour by Coastal Command, for which purpose No. 19 Group was reinforced to 21-squadron strength. The expectation was that, as shipping assembled for the invasion, U-boats would creep into the Bristol Channel and operate off south coast ports too. Coastal Command and the Royal Navy combined to frustrate that. As Allied troopship convoys sailed along the west coast and into the English Channel, swarms of light naval craft protected them. Coastal Command was ordered to deliver rapid attacks on any U-boat seen, kill it if possible and then rapidly continue patrol in case a pack was operating. *Rover* patrols would take care of German surface ships.

Throughout hostilities, Coastal Command's particular adversary was the U-boat, an ingenious prey never easy to find, and by 1943 fighting back when attacked. At the start of June 1944 49 normal-type U-boats were assigned by the Kriegsmarine to anti-invasion duty, 24 of them lurking in the port of Brest and 19 in St Nazaire. An additional nine had air-breathing snorkel equipment, but none was a large ocean-going vessel.

Facing them on D-Day were 286 Allied 'sub-seekers' – corvettes, destroyers, sloops, etc, operating in four anti-U-boat zones set between Eire, Land's End and the Brest Peninsula.

Another threat taken seriously was the possibility of attacks on invasion shipping by E- and R-boats: fast torpedo/patrol boats and minesweepers operating from ports along the north coast of France. Bomber Command therefore mined sea lanes and entrances to these ports. ACM Sir Sholto Douglas, AOC-in-C Coastal Command, in his 18 April 1944 overall plan for Coastal Command, placed in No. 16 Group seven squadrons to deal with small boats, and also listed four No. 19 Group reinforcement squadrons available to No. 16 Group should a U-boat enter the Channel from the east. At night No. 415 (RCAF) Squadron, operating ASV radar-equipped Wellington GR Mk XIIIs out of Bircham Newton, and No. 524 Squadron, Davidstowe Moor, similarly equipped, sought and attacked these small ships off the Low Countries and north-west France. No. 415 (RCAF) Squadron was half-equipped with ex-Fleet Air Arm Fairey Albacore light bombers, the Albacore Flight being split between Manston, Winkleigh and Thorney Island for D-Day operations. On 6 June it gathered again at Manston. Each Albacore was able to carry 6 x 250 lb HE bombs. Relatively slow but manoeuvrable, Albacores were ideal for seeking out the E-boats at night, close to the enemy coast, and scored notable successes.

The AEAF, too, was available to attack E- and R-boats, and ADGB placed a squadron of Typhoons at each end of the English Channel for Operation *Channel*

*Stop.* Instituted in 1941, it was still there preventing enemy surface vessels from entering those waters. After D-Day AEAF was taken off this commitment, leaving the task to Coastal Command Beaufighter strike squadrons escorted by ADGB Mustang III squadrons.

While the main Coastal Command effort was directed against U-boat penetration, on 5/6 June, to help protect invasion shipping, four Albacores searched for E-boats off Dunkirk, but without sightings. Next night two Wellingtons up from Docking, *JA635-A* (23:07-04:31 hrs) and *HZ650-M* (22:15-05:35 hrs), each armed with 4 x 500 lb bombs and many flares, attacked four E-boats, capsizing one and seriously damaging another. On 7/8 June E-boats ventured out in strength from Le Havre and Bologne, and three attacking the Eastern Task Force managed to torpedo the Norwegian destroyer *Svenner*. They certainly posed a threat, and some were set upon by Beaufighters which, that night, claimed to sink two E-boats and damage another three. Up from Winkleigh, Flg Off H.L. Parker flying an Albacore scored near misses on E-boats off Dieppe, while Wellington *HZ650-M* of No. 415 (RCAF) Squadron drew more blood by sinking one and damaging another early on 8 June. Two more were sunk by Wellington *L* of the same squadron.

With the E-boat threat remaining, Bomber Command, asked to attack their 'nests', at dusk on 14 June rained heavy blows upon their shelters. Led by 18 *Oboe*-equipped Mosquitoes, 333 Lancasters dropped 1,026 tons of HE and 22 x 12,000 lb 'Tallboy' Deep Penetration bombs on Le Havre dock area, destroying 11 E/R-boats. Next evening, 285 bombers and 12 Mosquitoes meted out similar treatment at Boulogne where 27 patrol boats were destroyed.

Coastal Command had long been playing a most vital part in the invasion preparations, for its 106 Group-administered, Benson-based Mosquito and Spitfire photo-reconnaissance squadrons which in particular watched ports and naval activity. They are probably better known for their amazing lone penetrations to literally all parts of Hitler's empire. Almost ignored in post-war literature, each daylight sortie to a distant target like Berlin in a very high-flying Spitfire was an astounding achievement. Uncomfortable, extremely hard going, dangerous and demanding, every intelligence-gathering sortie was wrapped in strict secrecy. Two-man Mosquitoes often went further, sometimes roaming southern Europe and the Balkans, and returning after the crew and their aircraft had refreshed themselves during a Maltese call. Not surprisingly the strategic reconnaissance squadrons, over a long period, played an extremely important part in the preparations for Operation *Overlord* and its successful outcome.

In the days immediately preceding the invasion the photo-reconnaissance squadrons maintained a careful watch on Biscay ports to assess which surface naval vessels might attempt to intervene. On 2 June two *Elbing* Class destroyers were spotted, one in Le Havre, the other at Brest, and there were seven E- and R-boats in Cherbourg. Next day 15 assorted boats were in Le Havre, and when the Biscay ports were reconnoitred on 3 June five destroyers were found. Two *Seetier* Class vessels were tied up at Bordeaux, another was at La Pallice, and one in Royan was keeping company with the small captured ex-Dutch destroyer *Tjerk Hiddes*. By next day the latter had sailed for Brest. All five vessels seemed very likely to attempt some action.

Coastal Command's large, relatively slow aircraft, although well defended, were vulnerable to west coast-based German fighters. Therefore, a constant watch on their bases was maintained – particularly now that Coastal Command had to ensure that no U-boats entered the assault region. Additionally, patrols by Mosquitoes and Beaufighters were repeatedly flown along the coast from Biscay to the Low Countries in search of shipping and, in the west, German heavy fighters.

At the end of May three Ju 88s flew a Channel reconnaissance, and on 4 June a heavy fighter reconnoitred the south-west approaches; otherwise – apart from daily *Zenit* flights and shipping search patrols well away from land by Ju 88s of F/123 – German aircraft were rare commodities. On 3 June reconnaissance discovered seven Fw 200s at St Jean d'Angerly, and three Ju 52s with mine degaussing rings were, as usual, at La Rochelle. At Cazaux there were at least 15 Ju 88s, possibly 21 of them, with more at Kerlin Bastard where an He 177 was found. That base was visited several times on D-Day by Cornish-based Spitfire IXs, and devastated on 7 June by 132 US 8th AF bombers. Cognac also accommodated Fw 200s and a few Ju 52s, but the main base for heavyweights was Bordeaux/Merignac where nine He 177s, Fw 200s and Ju 88s were available for operations on D-Day. By contrast, the seaplane bases at Biscarosse and Brest were almost empty. There was some flying by 1./ZGI on 4 June and a *Zenit* flight rounded Ireland, but the only enemy aircraft seen flying were Ju 88s of F/123, easing the task set for the RAF maritime operations.

Apart from within the designated Channel area, Nos. 15 and 18 Groups, Coastal Command, were maintaining constant watch for U-boats slipping by NE of the Shetland Isles. On 3 June they succeeded in sinking seven of 22 U-boats attempting to break out into the Atlantic, and in the 24 hrs beginning at noon on 5 June three Liberators, a Sunderland, two RAF and two RCAF Catalinas keeping watch observed only one submerged U-boat. Patrol over the south-west approaches was well under way by June, and the Fleet Air Arm was lending a hand, seven of the 18 Grumman Avengers of No. 849 Squadron night-flying *TFN* patrols on 5/6 June, assisted by Swordfishes of Nos. 816 and 838 Squadrons. The US Navy was helping too, using Consolidated PB4Y-1s from Dunkeswell flown by squadrons VP-103, VP-105 and VP-110.

The No. 19 Group bases at Predannack and St Eval were each expected to generate up to 10 patrols a day using Liberator GR Mk Vs supplemented by as many as possible of the better defended latest model, the GR Mk VI, just entering service. Night operations were particularly the province of the four Chivenor-based Leigh Light-equipped Wellington GR Mk XIV squadrons. Sunderlands from Mount Batten and Pembroke Dock operated by day and night, seeking U-boats by means of ASV radar and, like the others, attacking them with depth charges.

Summarising its 5 June effort, No. 19 Group listed 57 anti-U-boat operations, one anti-shipping sortie, and two long-range meteorological reconnaissance flights by Halifax Vs out of Brawdy; 343 hrs flying in total. An evening operation took two 'Tsetse' heavy-gun Mosquitoes of No. 248 Squadron to the mouth of the Gironde to search for warships and U-boats. After dark on 5 June three Wellingtons, three Sunderlands, four Halifaxes, two PB4Y-1s and a Swordfish patrolled within the prescribed area. At 00:46 hrs, position 45° 35'N/08° 10'W, Wellington N/172 Squadron obtained a radar contact and homed on to the U-boat 11 miles away, reaching it just after it submerged. Possibly it was the same one spotted at 01:08 hrs from Sunderland Mk III *ML763-J* of No. 228 Squadron. As the flying-boat made its attack run the bomb doors refused to open, so the crew could only machine-gun their fast-disappearing foe. Halifax IIs also operated, reporting only three small ships – two of them coasters observed from a No. 58 Squadron aircraft.

Anti-U-boat patrols maintained throughout D-Day produced increasing evidence that the German submarines were hell-bent on penetrating forbidden territory. Six at least made a determined effort to

*A US Navy PB4Y-1 Liberator operated from Dunkeswell crosses the Devon coast. (IWM)*

cause big trouble. Among their seekers were 11 Liberators, a Wellington, 18 Swordfishes, four PB4Y-1s and a Sunderland, all working in a confined area. There might have been more Sunderlands had Plymouth Sound not been so packed with shipping which prevented No. 10 (RAAF) Squadron's Sunderland Mk IIIs from operating. At 14:15 hrs the crew of a US Navy PB4Y-1 at position 48° 55'N/04° 57'W spotted a Ju 88 flying south three miles away, probably one of the usual F/123 patrols. At 16:25 hrs and at 49° 26'N/05° 25'W, a Sunderland crew saw another Ju 88 and turned towards it, but the flying-boat was too slow for the chase.

During the morning, six Beaufighters flew anti-shipping patrols and another six carried out an armed reconnaissance, while two Avengers similarly operated to the south-west. Two formations of Mosquito Mk VIs of No. 248 Squadron seeking any further Ju 88s off the Brest Peninsula, merely glimpsed two entering cloud at 09:06 hrs, position 48° 26'N/05° 27'W.

Coastal Command's most spectacular D-Day operation came late in the day. Three of the west coast destroyers – Z24 and Z32, both 2,400 ton *Seetier* Class vessels, and the ex-Dutch *ZH-1*, the *Tjerck Hiddes* – sailed north from the Gironde. Their movements were reported by midday and a strike force gathered comprising 17 cannon-firing Beaufighters of No. 144 Sqn to strafe the warship defenders and 14 RP-carrying Beaufighters of No. 404 Squadron to sink the ships. Eight Mosquito Mk VIs of No. 248 Squadron were prepared as escort, and around 18:55 hrs the strike force set forth. The Mosquitoes fired at targets on the way, Flg Off Green with Flt Sgt Studdard in *F/248* Squadron at 22:03 hrs picking off a Ju 88 before the three destroyers were found. The strike damaged them, forcing the ships to shelter in Brest.

On the evening of 7 June *T.24*, an *Elbing* Class destroyer, joined them and then they sailed once more. Off the Brest Peninsula they were intercepted by British destroyers led by HMS *Tartar*. The *Tjerck Hiddes* was sunk, also *Z32*. The other two, further damaged, returned to Brest.

As D-Day ended Coastal Command had 29 aircraft flying anti-U-boat patrols over the south-west (10 Wellingtons, nine Liberators, six Halifaxes and four Sunderlands) and another 11 NE of the Shetland Isles. Seeking enemy surface ships in the English Channel or North Sea were 44 Beaufighters, six Swordfishes, five Wellingtons and three Avengers. During the night Flt Lt Carmichael of No. 53 Squadron achieved the 'first' success by sinking U-55. Five U-boats were damaged during the night, but their return fire brought down four of their attackers. For Flg Off K. Moore of No. 224 Squadron, 7/8 June brought remarkable success when he sank U-269 and U-373 – one to the left, one to the right. That same night, U-970 was sunk by a Sunderland. Early on 9 June it was the turn of No. 120 Squadron, No. 18 Group, helping out from its Ballykelly base. Twice its Liberators tackled U-boats and succeeded in destroying one off the Scilly Isles. Not to be outdone, Mosquitoes caught U-821 and damaged it before a Liberator crew finished it off near Ushant, close to where a No. 304 Squadron Wellington sank U-441. Naval vessels also had successes, two British frigates sinking a submarine on 15 June.

U-boats had tried to operate in the forbidden zone and, despite the patrols, one is thought to have penetrated late on 6 June. But submarines did not sink one Allied vessel. Over 600 sorties had been directed against the U-boats by the end of June 1944 and 80 sightings had been reported off the assault area. During those, 46 attacks were mounted (three in co-operation with the Royal Navy) and damage was claimed on 18 occasions.

By mid-June 1944 the demand for Channel operations was much reduced and the squadrons switched to shipping protection elsewhere. As in 1940, Coastal Command was still performing in all operational roles – bomber, fighter, reconnaissance, transport. They required a most diverse assortment of aircraft, many uniquely equipped or modified. Just how varied they were may be seen from the following census of British-based squadrons and units of Coastal Command at 18:00 hrs on the eve of D-Day.

## OCEAN PATROL

| Type/Mark | Sqn | Estab | | Serviceable | | |
| | | | | Op | Non-Op | Un |
| --- | --- | --- | --- | --- | --- | --- |
| Liberator IIIA | | | | | | |
| | 86 | - | | 4 | 5 | 3 |
| Liberator V/VI | | | | | | |
| | 53 | 15 | { VI | - | - | 3 |
| | | | { V | 9 | - | 3 |

| | | | | | |
|---|---|---|---|---|---|
| 59 | 15 | V | 7 | 3 | 7 |
| *86 | 15 | - | - | - | |
| 120 | 15 | V | 10 | 1 | 3 |
| 206 | 15 | VI | 5 | 2 | 3 |
| 224 | 15 { | VI | 1 | 1 | - |
| | | V | 9 | 1 | 4 |
| 311 | 15 | V | 12 | 1 | 3 |
| 547 | 15 { | VI | 2 | - | 3 |
| | | V | 4 | 1 | 5 |
| **Totals** | **8** | **120** | **59** | **10** | **36** |

* 86 Sqn re-equipping

Wellington XIII

| | | | | |
|---|---|---|---|---|
| *172 | - | - | - | 1 |
| *179 | - | - | - | 1 |
| *304 | - | - | 1 | - |
| +415 | 10 | 5 | 3 | 2 |
| 524 | 10 | 6 | - | 4 |
| **Totals** | **1½** | **20** | **11** | **4** | **8** |

* re-equipping with Wellington XIV
+ established on Wellington XIII/Albacore

Wellington XIV

| | | | | |
|---|---|---|---|---|
| *172 | 15 | 9 | 3 | 5 |
| *179 | 15 | 11 | 1 | 3 |
| *304 | 15 | 10 | 2 | 3 |
| 407 | 15 | 8 | 3 | 4 |
| 612 | 15 | 12 | 2 | 1 |
| **Totals** | **5** | **75** | **50** | **11** | **16** |

* re-equipping with Wellington XIV

Sunderland III

| | | | | |
|---|---|---|---|---|
| 10 | 12 | 10 | 2 | - |
| 201 | 12 | 11 | 3 | 2 |
| 228 | 12 | 10 | 2 | 4 |
| 330 | 9 | 3 | 1 | 4 |
| 422 | 12 | 4 | 6 | 5 |
| 423 | 12 | 1 | 6 | 6 |
| 461 | 12 | 10 | 2 | 2 |
| **Totals** | **7** | **81** | **49** | **22** | **23** |

NB 461 Sqn testing one Sunderland V

Catalina IV

| | | | | |
|---|---|---|---|---|
| 202 | 16 | 15 | - | 1 |
| 210 | 12 | - | 1 | 9 |
| **Totals** | **2** | **28** | **15** | **1** | **10** |

Halifax II

| | | | | |
|---|---|---|---|---|
| 58 | 15 | 9 | 3 | 4 |
| 502 | 15 | 6 | 1 | 8 |
| **Totals** | **2** | **30** | **15** | **4** | **12** |

## ANTI-SHIPPING STRIKE FORCE

Beaufighter X

| | | | | |
|---|---|---|---|---|
| 143 | 20 | 18 | - | 2 |
| 144 | 20 | 17 | - | - |
| *235 | 20 | 12 | 2 | 1 |
| 236 | 20 | 17 | - | 1 |
| 254 | 20 | 20 | - | 2 |
| 404 | 20 | 13 | 4 | 1 |
| 455 | 20 | 15 | - | 4 |
| 489 | 20 | 15 | 1 | 3 |
| **Totals** | **8** | **160** | **127** | **7** | **14** |

Beaufighter XI *
* 235 Sqn re-arming with Beaufighter X

Mosquito IV

| | | | | |
|---|---|---|---|---|
| (Training) 618 | 20 | - | 14 | 11 |

Mosquito VI

| | | | | |
|---|---|---|---|---|
| (Operational) 248 | 20 | 16 | 3 | 1 |

Mosquito XVIII

| | | | | |
|---|---|---|---|---|
| (Operational) 248 | 4 | 2 | 1 | 2 |
| **Totals** | **2** | **44** | **18** | **18** | **14** |

Albacore

| | | | | |
|---|---|---|---|---|
| 415 | 15 | 13 | 2 | 6 |

## PHOTOGRAPHIC RECONNAISSANCE

Mosquito IX/XIV

| | | | | | |
|---|---|---|---|---|---|
| 540 | 20 { | IX | 10 | - | 1 |
| | | XVI | 4 | 1 | 1 |
| 544 | 20 { | IX | 9 | - | 3 |
| | | XIV | 2 | 1 | 3 |
| **Totals** | **2** | **40** | **25** | **2** | **8** |

Spitfire

| | | | | | |
|---|---|---|---|---|---|
| | - | IV | - | - | 1 |
| | 5 | X | 5 | - | - |
| 541 { | 10 | XI | 8 | 11 | 1 |
| | - | XIII | 2 | - | - |
| | 5 | XIX | 5 | - | - |
| | 5 | X | 5 | 1 | - |
| 542 { | 10 | XI | 13 | 3 | 2 |
| | - | XIII | 2 | - | - |
| | 5 | XIX | 5 | - | - |
| **Totals** | **2** | | **40** | **45** | **15** | **4** |

## METEOROLOGICAL RECONNAISSANCE

Gladiator II

| | | | | |
|---|---|---|---|---|
| 520 | - | - | - | 1 |
| 521 | 5 | 2 | - | 2 |
| 1402 Flt | 5 | 4 | - | 1 |

Halifax V*

| | | | | |
|---|---|---|---|---|
| 517 | 23 | 4 | 1 | 5 |
| 518 | 14 | 4 | 2 | 6 |
| 520 | 7 | 1 | - | 6 |

Hudson III

| | | | | |
|---|---|---|---|---|
| 1407 Flt | 6 | - | - | 1 |
| 519 | 14 | - | - | - |
| 521 | 4 | - | - | - |

Hurricane II

| | | | | |
|---|---|---|---|---|
| 520 | 3 | 2 | - | - |

Spitfire VI

| | | | | |
|---|---|---|---|---|
| 1402 Flt | 3 | 1 | - | 2 |
| 519 | 3 | 3 | - | 1 |

Ventura V

| | | | | |
|---|---|---|---|---|
| 519 | - | 8 | - | 6 |
| 521 | - | 5 | - | 2 |
| **Totals** | **7** | **87** | **34** | **3** | **33** |

* Of 48 Halifaxes allocated to these squadrons, 19 were in store.

## AIR-SEA RESCUE

Hudson III

| | | | | |
|---|---|---|---|---|
| 279 | 6 | 4 | 1 | 2 |

Walrus

| | | | | |
|---|---|---|---|---|
| 280 | 3 | 2 | - | 1 |

Warwick I

| | | | | |
|---|---|---|---|---|
| 280 | 20 | 13 | 1 | 7 |
| 281 | 20 | 10 | 1 | 9 |
| 282 | 20 | 9 | 2 | 10 |
| **Totals** | **4** | **69** | **38** | **5** | **29** |

## SPECIAL DUTIES

Catalina

| | | | | |
|---|---|---|---|---|
| 333 | 3 | 3 | - | - |

| | | | | |
|---|---|---|---|---|
| Mosquito VI | | | | |
| 333 | 6 | 5 | 1 | 1 |

| **Totals** | **1** | **9** | **8** | **1** | **1** |
|---|---|---|---|---|---|

## COASTAL COMMAND PREPARATION POOLS

| | Serviceable | Unserviceable |
|---|---|---|
| Beaufighter X | 23 | 24 |
| Liberator V | - | 2 |
| Liberator VI | - | 4 |
| Mosquito VI | 1 | 4 |
| Wellington XIII | - | 2 |
| Wellington XIV | 1 | 17 |

## ANTI U-BOAT PATROLS, SOUTH-WEST APPROACHES 13:00 HRS 5 JUNE–02:00 HRS 7 JUNE 1944

| Time/Day | Sqn | Aircraft | Notes |
|---|---|---|---|
| 00:15/5-05:03/6 | 179 | B | |
| 13:21/5-02:14/6 | 206 | A-EV871 | |
| 16:55/5-08:22/6 | 120 | Z | |
| 18:40/5-08:56/6 | 228 | J-ML763 | U-boat seen at 45° 41'N/08° 15'W; bomb doors failed to open |
| 19:33/5-22:22/5 | 461 | A-ML735 | |
| 19:58/5-16:05/6 | 172 | M | Patrol area E |
| 20:50/5-07:05/6 | 58 | D-JP165 | Reported 2 flak ships at 46° 12'N/ 01° 42'W |
| 20:57/5-06:07/6 | 612 | F | |
| 21/25/5-07:16/6 | 407 | A-HF302 | |
| 22:05/5-08:24/6 | 224 | C | Patrol area E |
| 22:44/5-06:15/6 | 502 | F | |
| 23:15/5-07:30/6 | 58 | A-HR792 | |
| 23:16/5-09:50/6 | 53 | J-BZ774 | Patrol area E |
| 23:28/5-06:27/6 | 179 | C | |
| 23:34/5-09:50/6 | 224 | G | Patrol area E |
| 23:40/5-07:23/6 | 502 | A | |
| 23:41/5-07:16/6 | 502 | G | Four armed trawlers seen at 47° 24'N/ 03° 29'W |
| 23:52/5-10:30/6 | 53 | U-BZ820 | Patrol area G |
| 00:30/6-07:00/6 | 612 | V | |
| 00:40/6-16:04/6 | 120 | L | |
| 00:50/6-11:21/6 | 224 | L | Patrol area G |
| 01:09/6-11:57/6 | 53 | C | |
| 02:06/6-06:45/6 | 58 | R-HR983 | Unidentified warships seen |
| 04:42/6-20:20/6 | 59 | T | |
| 05:03/6-15:20/6 | 311 | L-BZ717 | |
| 05:20/6-16:03/6 | 547 | M | |
| 05:21/6-17:25/6 | 10 | W-JM721 | |
| 05:44/6-16:20/6 | 311 | E-BZ745 | |
| 05:58/6-16:50/6 | 206 | C-EV874 | |
| 06:20/6-16:35/6 | 311 | Q-BZ741 | |
| 06:34/6-17:21/6 | 547 | B | |
| 08:31/6-11:43/6 | 120 | Q | Abortive |
| 11:03/6-01:07/7 | 120 | S | |
| 13:29/6-15:23/7 | 59 | M-FL946 | |
| 13:31/6-23:26/6 | 311 | Z-BZ751 | |
| 14:11/6-00:03/7 | 311 | X-FL975 | |
| 14:39/6-01:35/7 | 206 | E-EV947 | |
| 14:47/6-01:05/7 | 547 | R | |
| 15:05/6-01:35/7 | 206 | J | |
| 16:10/6-01:48/7 | 53 | E-BZ781 | Two U-boats seen |
| 17:25/6-04:26/7 | 179 | K-HF189 | |
| 18:04/6-09:36/7 | 120 | F | |
| 18:30/6-07:40/7 | 461 | M-ML747 | |
| 18:50/6-09:44/7 | 120 | M | |
| 19:22/6-06:34/7 | 502 | F | Unidentified ships seen |
| 19:40/6-08:49/7 | 201 | S-ML760 | Attacked U-boat at 45° 13'N/08° 30'W |
| 20:29/6-04:09/7 | 120 | H | |
| 21:15/6-07:10/7 | 407 | L-HF286 | |
| 21:26/6-08:14/7 | 53 | N | |
| 21:39/6-??:??/? | 224 | M | FTR |
| 21:42/6-07:35/7 | 172 | Z-NB800 | |
| 21:43/6-08:34/7 | 172 | S-HF446 | |
| 21:50/6-07:14/7 | 224 | J | |
| 22:01/6-06:42/7 | 53 | R | |
| 22:07/6-03:03/7 | 172 | B | |
| 22:14/6-08:15/7 | 612 | R | |
| 22:18/6-06:33/7 | 53 | L-BZ944 | |
| 22:20/6-08:55/7 | 58 | Z-JP167 | |
| 22:26/6-08:25/7 | 502 | Y | |
| 22:35/6-08:36/7 | 304 | B-HF421 | |
| 22:35/6-??:??/? | 407 | C | FTR |
| 22:50/6-09:26/7 | 304 | X-HF397 | |
| 22:54/6-00:55/7 | 502 | J | Fuel problems, early return |
| 22:55/6-09:20/7 | 58 | J-HR675 | |
| 22:59/6-09:38/7 | 224 | E | |
| 23:10/6-08:19/7 | 502 | U | Attacked a U-boat |
| 23:12/6-06:07/7 | 524 | D | E/R-boat search |
| 23:35/6-??:??/? | 524 | F | FTR |
| 23:57/6-??:??/? | 53 | M-BZ778 | FTR |

# The Bristol Beaufighter – Torpedo Fighter

The 'Beau' fighter somewhat disappointed the RAF, for a top speed higher than about 320 mph had been expected. But its nose featured four cannon, the wings held six machine-guns, it was roomy and possessed good duration. A year before the Beaufighter entered service, Blenheim fighters were given a maritime role, arousing Coastal Command interest in the newer Bristol product. On 23 April 1940 Bristol was informed of official interest in a Beaufighter variant for Coastal Command.

Proposed was a basic fit for the 51st and subsequent Bristol-built Beaufighters and 26th and subsequent Fairey-produced machines. The events of summer 1940 blew that scheme off course.

When the Battle of the Atlantic opened in earnest, and Fw 200 Condors began attacking shipping off Ireland, something better than long-range Blenheim IV(f)s was needed. Therefore, No. 252 Squadron was, on 21 November 1940, reformed within Coastal Command and equipped with standard Beaufighter I(f) fighters. Another Mk I, R2152, featuring items required in the Coastal Command Beaufighter, was officially inspected on 25 November. After immediate approval 80 Mk I(c)s were ordered with additional fuel tanks in the fuselage centre section. From R2269, the 217th Beaufighter built and delivered in February 1941, the basic maritime fit was introduced – a year after the idea had been seriously mooted. Very soon, half the Beaufighters built were equipped for possible maritime use, Fairey and the Weston factory producing these while Bristol's Filton works built standard fighters. An early intention was to fit the Beaufighter with two Bristol Hercules H.E.6SM (or Mk VI) engines which performed best at over 15,000 ft. Instead, early Beaufighters had Hercules II and III engines peaking at around 10,000 ft and giving less power.

Pressure was applied and Bristol had the Hercules VI flying in R2130 by March 1941, but not until November 1941 did the first production Mk VI Beaufighter, X7542, appear. A&AEE trials showed it to weigh 19,750 lb when operationally loaded, and to have a top speed of 327 mph MS TAS at 8,500 ft and 333 mph FS TAS at 15,600 ft; a height attained in 7.5 minutes. To reach 25,000 ft took 19 minutes, and its service ceiling was 28,000 ft. Production Beaufighters were designated Mk VI(f) as fighters, or Mk VI(c) when intended for Coastal Command. Based on the Mk I, the Beaufighter VI incorporated 358 basic modifications, to which another 38 were added at MUs to make it a front-line Fighter Command night-fighter; or 43 to change it into a long-range maritime fighter, in which role it was soon performing extremely well. Most Beaufighters had basic maritime features to prevent too much production interference.

Dedicated Coastal Command aircraft featured different radio and wiring, a chart table and navigation instruments. Additional fuel tanks could only realistically be fitted in the centre planes and outer mainplanes, adding 152 gal and increasing range by 450 miles. Machine-guns were removed to make way for the fuel tanks, and it was not long before wing guns were generally no longer fitted, to allow for one type of production mainplane. For pure fighters, increased duration was equally useful.

Impressed by the speed, strength and endurance of his Beaufighter I(c) fighters, ACM Sir Philip Joubert de la Ferté, AOC-in-C Coastal Command, suggested that they could, indeed should, be converted into 'torpedo fighters'. Bristol Beauforts currently delivered torpedoes – and the Beaufighter was derived from the Beaufort. The newcomer was much faster, which posed release problems, had better engines and superior single-engine performance, carried four cannon, had no rear defence and was less spacious. Nevertheless, January 1942 saw a possible 'torpedo fighter' explored at HQ Coastal Command and by Bristol. For simplicity the torpedo would be carried externally, leaving ample space for the internal torpedo drum and launch gear. Wind tunnel tests showed a likely speed reduction of only 7 or 8 mph and duration cut by 10 per cent; all translating into a 1,720 mile practical range at 5,000 ft. Ammunition would be reduced to 27 rounds per cannon.

Sir Philip Joubert presented his idea to the Air Ministry in February 1942 and was abruptly told that only fighter 'Beaus' were needed, and that his performance calculations were 'too optimistic'. Crew accommodation would be too cramped, there was no rear defence, longitudinal stability was poor even with the latest dihedral tailplane, and the aircraft was too fast in the attack profile. In short, its virtues were limited; and in any case, torpedoes were in short supply. Coastal Command would have to be satisfied with the new Beaufighter Mk VI(c)/P1, the production specification for which was agreed on 9 April 1942.

Somewhat disheartened, Coastal Command enquired of the Americans as to whether they could spare any torpedoes, either 18 in or their 22.44 in, the latter known to the RAF as the Mk XIII. They were only too ready to be of help, having 'ample stocks'!

Suddenly the Air Staff gave their support, stating that the proposed aeroplane would be far superior to the Beaufort! The pilot's view was good, and dive brakes could cut the speed from 230 mph to 170 mph in 20 seconds. AM Sir Ralph Sorley stated that 'the idea appears very promising', adding that it 'might be very useful', especially in the Far East. He strongly advocated a Mk XII torpedo TI Beaufighter.

On 13 April 1942 Bristol was given permission to convert *X8065* into a torpedo fighter, hurriedly prepared it and presented it for official inspection on 8 May. Trial flying at TDU Gosport quickly proved its worth, which was fortunate because the aircraft subsequently crashed due to engine failure. Full approval from the Air Ministry for what was now loosely known as the Beaufighter (Stage II) followed in June 1942, and Bristol was told to convert another 15 Beaufighter VIs into torpedo fighters, the first becoming available in July 1942. Clearly, it was a good idea requiring refinement – and good enough for 60 Mk VI (Interim Torpedo Fighters) to follow at the rate of 20 per month between October and January 1943.

Torpedoes being naval weapons, the Admiralty was asked for its view of the torpedo fighter idea which it readily accepted, considering the Beaufighter very suitable. Bristol's other new design, the Buckingham, flying in small numbers by D-Day, would not be sufficiently manoeuvrable, their Lordships reckoned. Instead, an entirely new version was prescribed, the 'Stage III' H.7/42, of which four prototypes were ordered on 4 September 1942 of what became the Bristol S.7/42, later named the Brigand.

On 7 August Ministerial recommendation for full-scale production of the 'Beau' torpedo fighter was reached, and on 13 August 1942 N.E. Rowe informed Bristol that it was to proceed, basing the aircraft upon a Mk VI(c) carrying externally one 1,425 lb 18 in Mk XII, or the larger Mk XIII, torpedo. Those existed in various forms, the 1,605 lb Mk XIIB being 194.03 in long and the newer 1,790 lb 'XII Z' 203.03 in in length. The 2,127 lb US Mk XIII torpedo was only 161 in long, all of which somewhat complicated conversion work. A stronger structure was needed between keel members carrying the torpedo release fittings, as was torpedo steadying equipment, a stronger undercarriage, dihedral tailplane as standard and ultimately air brakes to slow the aircraft on its drop run-in.

Although initially intended to carry a Mk XII torpedo, Mk VI(c) *EL329* was used to try out wing-mounted 3 in 'UP' rocket projectiles which squadrons later used widely and very effectively. Bomb loads

*EL223/G, an early Beaufighter TF Mk X carrying a torpedo. (Bristol)*

comprising 4 x 500 lb HEs were also frequently used. *EL223*, a standard fully-loaded Mk VI(c) weighing 23,250 lb, showed a top speed of 296 mph TAS at 2,000 ft, torpedo release taking place at 170 kts. Carrying 550 gal of fuel, the normal range would be 1,350 miles; 610 gal would give 1,490 miles. By removing wing guns, tankage could be increased to 682 gal, translating into a 1,690 mile range.

So successful was the conversion that on 5 November 1942 AMSO wanted all Weston-super-Mare production – 80 aircraft a month – to be TF Mk VI(c)s by early 1943. The Mk VI(c) being slower at low level than the old Mk I(c), further improvement was achieved by cropping the impeller and blower on the Hercules VI, thus producing the Hercules XVII engine which gave 1,735 hp at 500 ft and a new Beaufighter model, the TF Mk X, the trial installation aircraft for which was *EL290*, first flown in November 1942. A&AEE trials showed the 24,000 lb aircraft to have top speeds of 297 mph TAS at 200 ft and 307 mph at 10,000 ft linked to a normal range of 1,240 miles. The non-torpedo carrying version, the Mk XI(c), like the Mk X, at last had a rearward-firing Browning gun fitted in the dorsal cupola. A fin fillet to improve directional control was not tested on a Mk X (*NV251*) until November 1944.

## Operations

Coastal Command suggested that Beaufighters be used in Strike Wings comprising cannon-armed fighters, bomb-carrying Beau-bombers and torpedo-carrying 'Torbeaus', all operating in cohesive formations. Cannon-armed aircraft would open and close any attack by strafing ships' gunners to prevent them interfering. The first was the North Coates Strike Wing comprising No. 143 (fighters), No. 236 (Beau-bombers) and No. 254 ('Torbeaus') Squadrons.

A large convoy off the Netherlands was selected as the first target, but when Nos. 236 and 254 Squadrons attacked they were set upon by Fw 190s which shot down three Beaufighters and seriously damaged four others. More training and better planning were needed.

Not until 18 April 1943 did a Strike Wing operate again. No. 254 Squadron once more provided 'Torbeaus', No. 236 Squadron the bombers and No. 143 Squadron the strafing fighters, in an attack that went very well and heralded many more.

For D-Day eight squadrons holding 150 Beaufighter TF Mk Xs were held ready to tackle any E-boats entering either end of the English Channel and operating off northern France. Bad weather made finding the small ships difficult, but No. 143 Squadron claimed to sink three and No. 489 Squadron attacked others. Plt Off M.W. Dixon of No. 143 Squadron brought *LX972* home badly damaged by return fire, and Nos. 455 and 489 Squadrons operated from both Langham and Manston. *M* of 489 Squadron attacked a group of eight E-boats. All operated as Beau-bombers,

*'Beau-bomber'* NE788 *of No. 489 (RNZAF) Squadron at Langham. (IWM MH6457)*

*Rocket projectiles being fired from Beaufighter TF Mk X* NE549-E *of No. 455 (RAAF) Squadron. (Bruce Robertson collection)*

flying very low and each carrying 2 x 500 lb GP and 2 x 500 lb MC bombs.

Although busy trying to find and sink E-boats, the most spectacular Beaufighter operation on D-Day came early in the evening when three German destroyers were attacked by the Davidstowe Moor Strike Wing led by Wg Cdr Lumsden. A force of 14 RP-carrying Beaufighters of No. 404 Squadron led by Sqn Ldr R.A. Schoales and 17 cannon-armed Beaufighters of No. 144 Squadron, escorted by eight Mosquitoes provided by No. 248 Squadron, flew near to Ushant, then turned south-east in search of their prey.

Tempting targets soon presented themselves, but the Strike Wing was briefed to attack only one. At 19:48 hrs, position 48° 10'N/05° 10'W, six 'M' Class minesweepers were spotted, and they hurled light flak at the strike force continuing to search for the bigger fish. At 47° 27'N/03° 40'W four of 144's aircraft peeled off, heading, mistakenly, for what turned out to be three more minesweepers, so the quartet rejoined the main force. A surfaced U-boat, flanked by two tunnymen, was seen in position 47° 28'N/03° 43'W at 20:15 hrs and was attacked by two Mosquitoes as it crash-dived.

At 47° 03'N/03° 08'W (near Belle Ile) at 20:27 hrs, more ships were spotted heading north at 15 kts and line abreast. At first there was uncertainty over identification but Flg Off S.S. Shulemson DSO, soon identified them and called 'It *is* the target. Attack, attack!' and the three destroyers were immediately tackled.

Flying from out of the sun the Beaufighters, achieving maximum surprise, strafed the warships, then 404 Squadron rammed rocket salvoes into the vessels. Flg Off Wainman in *NE825-P* held his fire until he was only 800 yds from one of them, then launched two rockets followed by another pair from 300 yds away, before raking the vessel with cannon fire. To reduce the chance of misses, others attacked from quite close range. Some underwater hits were scored and cannon fire smashed into the superstructure. Then came No. 144 Squadron, strafing the vessels with heavy weapons. Within seconds the onslaught was over. A large explosion rocked the middle destroyer, black smoke billowed forward of the bridge and then the rearmost ship stopped. As the Beaufighters regrouped the leading destroyer was seen to be lower in the water and the centre one was on fire.

Not until the attack was almost over did AA guns on the ships open up. No. 404 Squadron was by then drawing away as No. 144 Squadron again strafed the warships. Hydraulics in *LZ180* (Flg Off Dalman) were hit and although it belly-landed at base the crew were unhurt. *NE823* (Plt Off

Bainett), hit by cannon fire, landed safely at Predannack. Flt Sgt Chapman, the navigator, had injuries and was taken to the Royal Cornwall Infirmary, Truro. Flt Sgt Morton's *NE208* was less fortunate and ditched soon after the attack. Both occupants climbed into their dinghy while Weyman in *P*/404 Squadron circled above, broadcasting helpful advice before dropping a marine marker which failed to ignite. He spotted this and called up a Liberator and saw it 'waggling its wings' – before its gunners opened fire! A Warwick brought an airborne lifeboat to the crew, who boarded it and headed for the English coast. For them, safety remained some way off, and it was two days before a Canadian destroyer picked them up. The operation was the most spectacular carried out by Coastal Command on D-Day.

## SUMMARY OF BEAUFIGHTER TF X OPERATIONS, 5–6 JUNE 1944

Unless stated otherwise, all sorties were E-boat searches

| Date | Time | Sqn | Aircraft | Notes |
|---|---|---|---|---|
| 5/6 | 22:09-00:25 | 455 | *D-KW277, B-NE202, V-NE774, X-NE775, Q-NE798* | |
| | 22:05-00:19 | 489 | *T-LZ540, J-NE209, M-NE224, V-NE427, S-NE429, W-NE433* | Flushing–Ijmuiden |
| 5/6 | 23:05-03:25 | 254 | *R* | Search 53° 06'N/02° 02'E to 52° 07'N/04° 05'E |
| 5/6 | 23:39-00:38 | 254 | *V, X* | |
| 6 | 00:01-02:42 | 254 | *D, B* | |
| 6 | 00:50-04:25 | 254 | *L* | |
| 6 | 01:02-04:12 | 254 | *A, S* | |
| 6 | 04:30-05:10 | 143 | *H-LX957, E-LX972* | |
| 6 | 05:00-05:50 | 143 | *D-LX848* | |
| 6 | 06:30-09:20 | 143 | *D-LX848, U-LX943, F-NE223, Z-NE666, V-NE764, S-NE770* | |
| 6 | 07:55-09:25 | 143 | *T-LX822, A-LX847, R-LX973, Q-NE685, M-NE768, C-NE772* | |
| 6 | 13:10-14:05 | 143 | *Q-NE685, Z-NE666* | |
| 6 | 15:29-19:54 | 235 | *P, R, V, Z* | |
| 6 | 18:34-22:35 | 144 | *U-JM346, F-LX851, T-LZ180, D-LZ219, O-LZ225, P-LZ538, V-LZ542, Q-NE208, M-NE227, S-NE423, W-NE430, B-NE435, K-NE578, S-NE740, X-NE747, N-NE823, J-NE829* | Rocket attack on destroyers |
| | | 404 | *Q-LZ189, Z-LZ295, V-LZ441, M-LZ451, R-NE198, U-NE339, O-NE341, F-NE354, H-NE355, K-NE426, J-NE431, L-NE744, P-NE825, S-NT916* | Strafing attack on destroyers |
| 6 | 20:48-23:05 | 455 | *J-LZ402, O-NE326* | Ship recce from Langham |
| 6 | 21:55-00:10 | 455 | *D-KW227, B-NE202, F-NE348, V-NE774, X-NE775* | From Manston; *NE202* suffered a tyre burst and belly-landed |
| 6 | 22:00-01:00 | 489 | *T-LZ540, J-NE209, M-NE224, V-NE427* | Attacked 8 E-boats, Flushing–Fecamp |
| 6 | 23:00-01:00 | 143 | *U-LX943, H-LX957, Z-NE666, V-NE764, S-NE770* | |
| 6 | 23:06-23:50 | 254 | *C* | Abandoned; bad weather |
| 6 | 23:00-23:55 | 455 | *L-NE340* | Ship recce, from |
| | | 489 | *W-NE433* | Manston; four 500 lb bombs each off Dunkirk |

269

# Beaufighter TF Mk X/XI(c)s on squadron strength, 5 June 1944

* operated on 5/6 June 1944

## No. 143 Sqn, Manston
*Z-LX808  7.5.44-16.11.44
*T-LX822  235 Sqn aircraft
A-LX847  7.5.44-17.6.44 FA, RIW
*D-LX848  7.5.44-27.8.44 FTR
*U-LX943  235 Sqn aircraft(?)
*H-LX957  7.5.44-2.12.44
*E-LX972  7.5.44-1.7.44, (battle damage 7.6.44,
          then RIW)
*R-LX973  7.5.44-9.11.44
G-LZ406  7.5.44-5/6.9.44 FTR
Y-NE205  7.5.44-29.5.44 FA, RIW 10.6.44
N-NE211  20.1.44-20.6.44 FA, RIW
*F-NE223  12.5.44-17.9.44 EFB, ditched shortly
          after take-off
NE531  8.4.44-14.8.44, (ROS 6.6.44-16.6.44)
*Z-NE666  5.44-1.9.44 AC FB
J-NE667  11.3.44-17.7.44 RIW
*Q-NE685  12.3.44-14.6.44 EFB, flak damage,
          crashed at Manston
NE690  16.3.44-11.5.44 EFA, crashed during
       bombing practice
*V-NE764  3.44-18.11.44
M-NE768  25.3.44-16.12.44
*S-NE770  25.3.44-13.6.44 EFB
*C-NE772  25.3.44-26.8.44 FTR
NE813  17.5.44-30.11.44
I-NE822  17.5.44-7.9.44 EFB

## No. 144 Sqn, Davidstowe Moor
JM340  29.10.43-9.8.44 (ROS 3.6.44-30.6.44)
*U-JM346  24.12.43-5.4.45 FTR
LX849  3.1.44-11.1.45 FTR, Flekkefiord
*F-LX851  16.9.43-10.1.45 FTR
*T-LZ180  22.9.43-6.6.44, belly-landed after
          operations
A-LZ182  21.9.43-20.2.45 EFA (ROS 19.5.44-
         16.6.44)
LZ216  3.9.43-7.3.45 (ROS 21.4.44-7.6.44)
*D-LZ219  3.9.43-12.9.44 (ROS 6.6.44-16.6.44)
LZ222  18.9.43-18.8.44 RIW
*O-LZ225  4.9.43-13.6.44 EFA, crashed off Jurby
*P-LZ538  25.12.43-17.3.45
*V-LZ542  23.1.44-9.8.44 RIW
*Q-NE208  13.3.44-6.6.44 FTR, ditched in
          English Channel
*M-NE227  30.1.44-14.6.45
*S-NE423  25.2.44-14.11.45
*W-NE430  8.4.44-5.10.44
*B-NE435  2.4.44-26.6.45
NE437  2.4.44-19.9.44 FTR (ROS 7.4.44-
       21.7.44)
*K-NE578  30.4.44-20/21.3.45 FA, SOC
*S-NE740  31.5.44-6.8.44 RIW
*X-NE747  31.5.44-13.7.44 RIW
*N-NE823  22.5.44-18.7.44 RIW
*J-NE829  31.5.44-9.10.44

## No. 235 Sqn, Portreath
JM107  (Mk XIc) ?-?
JM117  (Mk XIc) ?-?
JM280  (Mk XIc) 7.5.44-8.7.44 (ROS
       15.5.44-16.6.44)
JM281  (Mk XIc) 7.5.44-11.7.44 (ROS
       17.5.44-16.6.44)

JM287  7.5.44-28.6.44
LX805  12.2.44-25.6.44
LX807  25.6.43-29.6.44
LX809  6.1.44-25.6.44
LX817  9.7.43-5.7.44
LX822  8.7.43-24.6.44
LX933  7.7.43-12.8.44
LX936  7.7.43-24.6.44 (ROS 13.5.44-4.6.44)
LX943  5.7.43-5.7.44
LX944  5.7.43-5.7.44
LX947  9.8.43-21.6.44 Cat E
LZ181  15.8.43-1.8.44
LZ410  7.10.43-22.6.44
NE575  19.3.44-22.6.44

## No. 236 Sqn, North Coates
KW280  24.12.43-27.12.44
LX821  19.10.43-12.6.44 RIW (FA 18.5.44)
LX824  30.6.43-27.7.44 RIW (FA 6.7.44)
LX827  16.7.43-18.10.44 Cat E (ROS
       30.5.44-21.7.44)
LX854  16.7.43-24.6.44 FA, RIW
LX856  9.7.43-16.5.45
LX941  9.7.43-25.4.45
LX942  9.7.43-6.8.44 EFB, crashed after take-
       off, Perranporth
LX980  16.7.43-27.1.45 battle damage
LX981  16.7.43-28.6.45 SOC on squadron
LZ188  17.8.43-8.7.44 (ROS 9.6.44-16.6.44)
LZ288  20.10.43-19.5.45
LZ293  16.3.44-11.8.44 Cat E
NE193  7.12.43-13.6.44 EFB
NE194  2.12.43-24.8.44 FTR from attack on
       warship off Le Verdon
NE195  30.11.43-24.8.44 EFB, crash-landed,
       Vannes
NE432  7.2.44-28.12.44
NE441  7.5.44-23.6.44 B FB
NE442  6.5.44-30.4.45 (ROS 15.5.44-30.6.44)
NE443  6.5.44-5.7.44 FTR (ROS 11.5.44-
       9.6.44)
NE746  26.5.44-12.9.44 FTR, shot down off
       Texel
NE794  28.3.44-15.5.45 (ROS 27.4.44-9.6.44)
NE828  18.5.44-18.4.44 FTR from operations
       off the Netherlands
NT917  30.5.44-14.6.45
NT923  27.5.44-22.6.44

## No. 254 Sqn, North Coates
JM215  (XIc) 12.5.43-13.8.44
JM339  28.6.43-10.11.44 RIW
LX806  28.12.43-17.9.44 EFB, ditched off
       Lincolnshire
LZ217  8.9.43-29.8.44 FTR, ditched off
       Heligoland
LZ221  6.9.43-8.7.44 Cat E
LZ223  9.9.43-13.4.45 RIW (Cat B FB
       27/28.3.45)
LZ224  6.9.43-13.12.45
LZ418  10.1.44-1.4.45 FTR
LZ436  26.10.43-8.11.44 EFB
NE218  19.2.44-11.3.45 EFA
NE225  29.1.44-20.7.44 FTR
NE428  31.3.44-7.6.45
NE436  28.3.44-30.4.45
NE438  27.5.44-24.12.44
NE439  9.4.44-12.9.44 FTR, shot down off
       Texel
NE465  14.4.44-17.1.45 FTR, collided with

NV197
NE481  6.5.44-13.8.44 B FB
NE576  8.5.44-2.12.44 FTR
NE577  6.5.44-24.8.44 EFB
NE801  11.5.44-8.6.44 FTR, sweep off
      Netherlands
NE802  12.5.44-6.9.44 EFA, crashed on take-
      off
NE808  30.5.44-23.6.44
NT924  12.5.44-8.4.45

## No. 404 Sqn, Davidstowe Moor
Y-LX940  6.9.43-1.4.45, FA 21.5.44 (ROS
      16.6.44)
X-LZ176  23.8.43-28.6.44 Cat E (FA 28.5.44,
      ROS 9.6.44)
*Q-LZ189  28.8.43-2.10.44 EFB
LZ291  19.9.43-6.6.44 RIW (FA 18.5.44)
*Z-LZ295  19.9.43-13.8.44 FTR, shot down off
      Royan
*V-LZ441  22.10.43-12.8.44 FTR, shipping
      strike, Ile de Re
E-LZ444  26.10.43-2.10.44 EFA
D-LZ449  4.11.43-10.5.45 (battle damage
      30.3.44, ROS 7.6.44)
*M-LZ451  26.10.43-28.2.44
*R-NE198  27.11.43-27.8.44 FTR from Gironde
      Estuary
NE199  16.12.43-13.6.44
*U-NE339  20.12.43-24.3.45 FTR, shipping
      strike, Egersund; ditched
*O-NE341  22.12.43-13.10.44 FTR, ditched
*F-NE354  3.1.44-.8.8.44 FTR, shipping strike,
      Belle Ile; shot down
*H-NE355  30.12.43-24.5.45 RIW
NE425  18.2.44-24.8.44
*K-NE426  18.2.44-2.1.45 RIW
*J-NE431  7.2.44-17.9.44
A-NE669  8.4.44-31.3.45
NE684  10.4.44-13.6.44 RIW (B FB 19.5.44)
NE686  17.5.44-28.5.45
B-NE687  9.4.44-24.4.45
*L-NE744  26.5.44-7.7.44 Cat E
NE793  11.5.44-25.10.44
C-NE800  7.5.44-24.4.45 (battle damage
      19.5.44, ROS 9.6.44)
*P-NE825  31.5.44-24.8.44 FA RIW
*S-NT916  31.5.44-25.4.45

## No. 455 Sqn, Langham
*D-KW277  1.2.44-19.8.44 FTR
H-LZ192  28.12.43-29/30.6.44 FTR, off
      Netherlands (FA 28.5.44, ROS
      16.6.44)

U-LZ194  28.12.43-6.7.44 FTR, ditched off
      Nordeney
*J-LZ402  28.12.43-13.6.44 RIW
T-LZ407  28.12.43-23.6.45
S-LZ409  28.12.43-15.4.45
R-LZ537  18.1.44-24.9.44 EFA
A-NE200  11.12.43-8.6.44 FTR, ditched off
      Netherlands
*B-NE202  11.12.43-6.6.44 EFB, tyre burst on
      take-off, Manston, belly-landed
N-NE207  11.12.43-5.4.45 EFB, collided with
      NT920 off Haried Island, Norway
*O-NE326  20.12.43-24.8.44 Cat E
*L-NE340  17.1.44-10.8.44 FTR, shot down by
      flak during convoy attack
G-NE342  22.12.43-7.4.45 EFB, fighter damage,
      crashed at Dallachy
K-NE347  29.12.43-15.4.45 (FA 3.5.44, ROS
      16.6.44)
*F-NE348  ?-6.7.44 FTR, shot down by flak off
      Nordeney
Z-NE668  24.3.44-13.6.44 FTR, ditched while
      attacking convoy off Netherlands
C-NE773  21.3.44-1.7.44 Cat E
*V-NE774  24.3.44-30.8.44 battle damage
*X-NE775  25.3.44-15.6.44 battle damage
*Q-NE798  30.3.44-26.9.44

## No. 489 Sqn, Langham
LZ419  19.5.44-28.6.45
LZ448  10.11.43-7.12.44 FTR
LZ458  17.4.43-20.3.45 (FA 20.4.44, ROS
      9.6.44)
LZ539  16.3.44-18.12.44 FA
*LZ540  24.11.43-21.9.44
LZ541  11.12.43-19.6.45 SOC
LZ543  11.12.43-14.6.44 FTR, shot down off
      Schelde Estuary
*NE209  7.12.43-26.10.45 Cat E
NE210  13.12.43-27.7.44
NE212  2.12.43-9.4.45
NE213  2.12.43-6.12.44 FTR
*NE224  29.12.43-21.9.44 EFB, crashed at
      Little Snoring
NE325  9.2.44-20.6.45
*NE427  19.4.44-21.4.45
*NE429  8.4.44-15.3.45
*NE433  1.5.44-1.11.44 FTR, collided with
      NT945 off Norway
NE434  6.5.44-17.6.44 FTR, flak damage,
      ditched off Ostend
NE826  16.5.44-7.4.45 EFB, overshot
      Sumburgh

# The Consolidated Catalina IV

Catalinas, which had done so well in the Battle of the Atlantic, played only an indirect part in the Normandy invasion. Operating from Sullom Voe, they sought out U-boats attempting to break into the Atlantic via the northern route. Most of the RAF's Catalinas were, in 1944, based overseas, and a high proportion of such Mk

IVs as reached Britain exhibited a serious problem.

In 1943 a new specification for fuel tank sealing was introduced, following the raising of the aromatic content in petrol, to eliminate cockling of metal plating and to hasten production. After a few hours flying the new coating was found to crack readily, even dissolve. Laborious resealing of joints had to be undertaken as soon as Mk IVs arrived, the task being performed by Saunders-Roe at Beaumaris.

By January 1944 48 unsatisfactory Catalina Mk IVs had reached Britain, and only half of them had been modified – at a rate of two or three a month. By February 1944 the situation had improved, for all the Catalinas being delivered – all Boeing-built – arrived with tanks already modified. The general outcome was, however, that few Mk IVs were used by Coastal Command from home bases in 1944. Fuel tank problems were not solely responsible for that, for the Liberator was proving an excellent aeroplane for maritime patrol, and

the large number of operating strips available meant land-based aeroplanes were increasingly favoured by the RAF.

## Catalina GR Mk IVAs on squadron strength, 5 June 1944

### No. 210 Sqn, Sullom Voe

| | |
|---|---|
| JX202 | 19.1.44-18.9.44 |
| JX203 | 19.1.44-9.7.44 |
| JX223 | 19.1.44-8.8.44 |
| JX224 | 19.1.44-28.6.44 |
| JX246 | 19.1.44-4.7.45 |
| JX247 | 27.5.44-2.7.45 |
| JX255 | 11.2.44-26.10.44 |
| JX256 | 30.5.44-2/3.4.45 FTR |
| JX264 | 3.44-15.4.45 |
| JX267 | 23.1.44-17.8.44 |
| JX268 | 29.4.44-22.7.45 |
| JX574 | 19.1.44-9.6.44 FTR |

### No. 333 (Norwegian) Sqn, Woodhaven

Mk IB:

| | |
|---|---|
| D-FP183 | 3.2.44-23.11.44 Cat E |
| A-FP314 | 1477 Flt 5.3.43, 33 Sqn 6.6.43-20.12.44 Cat E |

Mk IVA:

| | |
|---|---|
| C-JA933 | |

# The Consolidated Liberator

'The B-17 Flying Fortress was America's best wartime bomber.' Wrong, very wrong! That title belongs to the B-24 Liberator, the aeroplane that also sealed 'the Atlantic gap'. Of all American types used by the wartime RAF the Liberator was the most outstanding, and, not surprisingly, the AOC-in-C Coastal Command in 1943 expressed a desire for all general reconnaissance squadrons to be armed with Liberators.

Design of the B-24 began in January 1939, making it a second-generation four-engined American bomber. Its most striking feature was the narrow, high-aspect ratio Davis wing, much responsible for the Liberator's amazing duration. The dumpy fuselage indicated transport potential, while a look under the engine nacelles revealed exhaust-driven turbo-superchargers to boost high altitude performance as well as climb and speed. The prototype flew on 29 December 1939 after rapid design work,

and the LB-30 (Liberator, British derivative) soon showed itself capable of 324 mph, making it faster than many fighters. Its fuel consumption indicated a range of over 2,000 miles when carrying a 3,000 lb load. Yet the USAAC – committed to the B-17 – ordered only 32 examples whereas the Europeans, spotting a good thing, wanted many more – the French some 120 and the RAF 114. Not until 1941 could the foreigners be supplied – too late for some – and the first examples were for the RAF.

The Liberator was inferior to its peers in one respect: its defences were primitive. They made the British, desperate in 1940 for aircraft, express reservations about the operational value of the LB-30. Some reassurance came on 21 December 1940 when the US Government informed the Air Ministry that because delivery of the LB-30 would begin in March 1941, the RAF could instead have the superior LB-30A (intended for the US Navy) with its twin hand-held .300 in guns instead of a useless tail gun turret. That was a slight advance. Despite its penetrative qualities, brought about partly by light equipment loading, the aircraft remained useless for bombing operations over Europe. So just after the first LB-30A flew on 17 January 1941, six LB-30As (*AM258-AM263*) of the British contract were converted into transports for the transatlantic ferry service. They would convey crews across the Atlantic to collect American aircraft for British use; frequently so after 11 March 1941 when the Lend-Lease Act became effective.

The six LB-30As were soon joined by a score of B-24A Liberator Mk Is (*AM910-AM929*). By the time of their arrival the decision had been made to place them in Coastal Command as reconnaissance bombers. Tests had revealed that by cruising at 150 kts and carrying a 2,000 lb load the B-24As could fly for 16 hrs. To operate them, No. 120 Squadron reformed on 2 June 1941, at Nutts Corner, Northern Ireland. There, on 8 June, *AM913*, *AM914* and *AM922* arrived for use as crew trainers.

Scottish Aviation at Prestwick, an ideally situated airfield for use as the eastern Atlantic ferry terminus, was appointed Civilian Repair Organization and modification centre for Liberators. By June 1941 it was equipping the first 20 Liberator Is for long-range maritime escort and anti-submarine warfare.

## Operations

Liberator I operations commenced on 20 September 1941 with a patrol by *AM924-D*, and during convoy escort on 4 October the same aircraft became the first Liberator to confront an Fw 200 Condor; and not only with machine-guns, for a belly-mounted 20 mm four-cannon gun pack had been fitted by the British to the squadron's aircraft. A second fierce encounter involved *AM926-F* on 22 October, the aircraft being flown by Flt Lt Bulloch, later awarded the Victoria Cross after attacking a submarine. During the sortie he sighted a U-boat conning tower near position 51° 30'N/16° 00'W, and quickly swung the Liberator around. Three depth charges were dropped which straddled the submarine, soon overcome by an underwater explosion.

When autumn 1941 came, so did the Liberator Mk II, the first version featuring a traversing tail gun turret. A shortfall in British heavy bomber production led to the Air Ministry deciding to re-equip Wellington-armed No. 1 (Bomber) Group with Liberator IIs. In November 1941 No. 150 Squadron at Snaith began rearming, and at Polebrook No. 1653 Conversion Unit soon commenced training Liberator crews. A second squadron, No. 159, formed at Molesworth and a third at Thurleigh. By then a scheme had been devised to place these units in a new Group, No. 8. It came to nothing and the squadrons instead moved overseas.

On 25 November 1941 No. 120 Squadron received the first of a small quota of Mk IIs to supplement – not replace – its Mk Is. The operational scene, not to mention the international one, was ever-changing. The débâcle in the Far East brought major disturbance to the Liberator supply policy, leading to fears that supplies could become too erratic for Bomber Command to ever operate them. Many examples reaching Britain would now pass overseas, where their long range would be as valuable as it was to Coastal Command.

As U-boat attacks multiplied, the need for long-duration maritime aircraft became ever greater, so the Air Ministry, through AVM J.C. Slessor, made a special appeal to the US Government for Liberator supplies under Lend-Lease in addition to Direct Purchase.

Such was Coastal Command's Liberator need that in April 1942 Bomber Command released six of its precious Mk IIs for No. 120 Squadron. Later that month, Liberator Mk IIIs began reaching Scottish Aviation. Release of Mk IIIs to Coastal Command came on 15 May and after minimum modification for maritime service the first example, *FL910*, was passed to No. 224 Squadron, the second GR Liberator squadron, and stationed on Tiree. No. 120 Squadron began receiving Mk IIIs the following month, by which time the squadron held only five precious Very Long Range Mk Is able to escort convoys 800 miles out into the Atlantic. Not until 17 October 1943 was the last Mk I retired. Defended by two gun turrets and carrying additional equipment, the Mk IIIs were heavier and their normal endurance was reduced to 11.6 hrs when carrying a 3,000

*The second long-range Liberator variant was the Mk IIIA, typified by* FK222.

lb offensive load. Some were later modified to carry 600 gal of fuel more than the Mk Is, which changed them into VLR Liberators – designated Mk IIIAs. Some 330 gal of fuel were carried in self-sealing bays, and six 2 x 350 gal tanks could be accommodated in fuselage bomb cells. Like the Mk Is, most carried ASV Mk II search radar.

Liberator Mk IIIs joined two new operators, Nos. 59 and 86 Squadrons, in October 1942. By then the patrolling aircraft were carrying shallower-bursting Torpex depth charges, but to remain effective the Mk IIIs needed ASV radar that the enemy could not detect. The answer soon came from America in the form of the shorter wavelength, 10 cm narrow-beam ASV G Mk III radar. Its introduction was hastened by converting H2S navigation radar sets, the first 40 production examples of which were switched to Coastal Command despite Bomber Command's strong resistance to

*Liberator GR Mk Vs like* BZ291 *carried ASV Mk VI radar in a retractable ventral 'dustbin'.*

the idea. The Americans also agreed to fit their version of this equipment in Liberators destined for Coastal Command, and in January 1943 operations with ASV G Mk III commenced.

Next came the fitting of the Leigh Light airborne searchlight. Housed in a specially-designed 870 lb nacelle unit, it was provided with a control link allowing an operator to switch on the brilliant, narrow beam when the Liberator was about a mile from weapon release. Wing mounting had to be undertaken because fitting the light in the nose meant that the crew would be looking ahead into the 19 million candle power glow. Bomb bay mounting would have much reduced the depth charge load, and lowering the light would have cut the run-in speed by a precious seven kts. Focusing could narrow the beam from 12° to 3°.

For the use of four squadrons in Britain, 60 sets of wing-mounted searchlights were ordered, fitment taking many months. During 1943, Leigh Lights were added only to ASV G Mk III-equipped Liberators. By D-Day three squadrons – Nos. 53, 120 and 224 – were operating searchlight-equipped Liberators of a later type, the Mk V.

During April 1943, by which time Liberators were flying out to patrol escorting convoys as far west as 20°, a revised version of the Mk III, the GR Mk V began arriving. This offered 15.3-hr duration when carrying a 1,500 lb offensive load and cruising at 150 kts. Plans called for 46 to be in Coastal Command squadrons by the end of 1943, by which time 171 general reconnaissance Liberators had been delivered to Britain. Normal range of the GR Mk V carrying 2,560 gal of fuel and 6 x 250 lb AS bombs was 3,440

miles – dramatically reduced if the fuel load was reduced to 2,224 gal and a Leigh Light added, which shows the critical nature of operating Liberators far out to sea. Fitting a .50 in machine-gun in the nose was tried, but every addition imposed a weight penalty. Variations in armour and armament included removal of tail turrets from some Mk Vs, thus allowing an additional 375 gal of fuel to be carried in outer wing tanks – 2,935 gal in all. Carrying 6 x 250 lb AS bombs and cruising at 170 mph at 5,000 ft, such aircraft had a range of about 3,890 miles.

Quickly fed into Coastal Command, Liberator GR Mk Vs first went to Nos. 53, 59 and 86 Squadrons. Most Mk Vs featured ASV radar held in a ventral retractable 'dustbin', and some – as well as some Mk IIIs – were shorn of dorsal turrets to reduce weight and increase range. Once the U-boats were forced to operate in mid-Atlantic, where German aircraft were absent, additional range was more important than unnecessary defence. Because of the limited endurance of Coastal Command's Wellingtons the Air Ministry in September 1943 decided that they must be replaced, and that the Liberator GR Mk V should become the standard GR type. Both well-defended day and Leigh Light-equipped night Liberators were envisaged, although nacelle searchlight supplies limited their use to the three chosen squadrons. Scheduled Liberator production did not allow for all that many diversions to Coastal Command. Instead, two squadrons of Halifaxes were added, while the Wellington squadrons soldiered on to the end of hostilities in Europe.

In further attempts to extend range,

*Liberator GR Mk V BZ791 with the ventral ASV radome extended. Alternatively, some Mk Vs had a chin radome.*

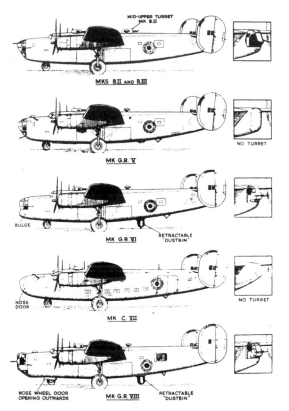

MID-UPPER TURRET MK B.II

MKS B.II AND B.III

NO TURRET

MK G.R. V

BULGE

RETRACTABLE "DUSTBIN"

MK G.R. VI

NOSE DOOR

NO TURRET

MK C. VII

NOSE WHEEL DOOR OPENING OUTWARDS

MK G.R. VIII

RETRACTABLE "DUSTBIN"

*Everyone makes mistakes, as this page from the wartime Liberator handbook shows! The 'GR VI' is really a Mk V with chin radome. Some Mk Vs had tail turrets removed. Liberator GR Mk VIs were externally similar to GR Mk VIIIs except for the inward-opening nosewheel doors.*

turbo-superchargers were removed from some Mk Vs. Coastal Command was concerned about that because the Liberators sometimes needed to be able to quickly take cover in cloud, which often involved a rapid climb from close convoy cover to about 6,000 ft. Arming them with 60 lb RP weapons carried on racks flanking the nose met with far more support, and in March 1944 modification of 25 Mk Vs was put in hand. Some of the modified aircraft were with No. 311 Squadron by D-Day.

The first example of a much-revised Liberator, the GR Mk VI, arrived in Britain (for trial purposes) on 10 December 1943, with main deliveries starting the following month. The Mk VI was the first version to feature a nose turret as well as dorsal and tail gun turrets – Emerson, Martin and Boulton Paul-built respectively. By D-Day

89 Mk VIs, all needing maritime fitment, had arrived in Britain. A further 178 were delivered by the end of 1944.

With their wealth of experience in anti-submarine warfare, the Liberator and Wellington squadrons of Coastal Command were well-suited to sealing the Channel from U-boat intrusion before, during and after Operation *Neptune*. Liberator squadrons in No. 19 Group were No. 311 at Predannack and Nos. 53, 206, 224 and 547 at St Eval. Nos. 59 and 120 Squadrons (No. 18 Group) at Ballykelly were also available. That left No. 86 Squadron, at Reykjavik and already using Tain, watching for U-boats attempting a northern transit into the Atlantic. As the invasion fleet crossed the Channel on 5/6 June, 10 Liberator anti-U-boat sorties were flown and another 27 patrolled during D-Day. These were supplemented by seven sorties undertaken by the 33 available US Navy PB4Y-1 Liberator squadrons – VP-103, VP-105 and VP-110 – based at Dunkeswell and under the operational control of RAF Coastal Command.

## Liberators on squadron strength, 5 June 1944
* operated on 5/6 June 1944

### No. 53 Sqn, St Eval
Mk V:

| | | |
|---|---|---|
| N-BZ769 | 3.2.44-4.8.44 | |
| *J-BZ774 | 30.12.43-8.8.44 | |
| *M-BZ778 | 2.2.44-7.6.44 EFB | |
| BZ781 | 13.3.44-7.9.44 | |
| G-BZ788 | 30.7.43-23.7.44, (ROS 23.5.44-13.6.44) | |
| BZ793 | 26.7.43-8.8.44 | |
| B-BZ814 | 20.10.43-26.10.44 | |
| D-BZ815 | 9.10.43-11.7.44 | |
| *U-BZ820 | 20.10.43-24.7.44 | |
| Q-BZ870 | 13.4.44-3.8.44 | |
| *E-BZ871 | 11.11.43-22.9.44 | |
| V-BZ875 | 31.1.44-14.7.44 | |
| BZ919 | 3.1.44-7.8.44 | |
| *L-BZ944 | 4.12.43-7.9.44 | |

Mk VI:

| | | |
|---|---|---|
| H-EV895 | 8.5.44-18.11.44 EFB, crashed off Stagi Peninsula, Iceland | |
| W-EV899 | 12.5.44-27.8.44 | |
| F-EV953 | 8.5.44-31.1.45 | |

### No. 59 Sqn, Ballykelly
Mk V:

| | | |
|---|---|---|
| D-BZ712 | 30.4.43-10.1.45 | |
| K-BZ716 | 13.5.44-12.10.44 | |
| P-BZ724 | 6.1.44-18.8.44 EFB, crashed near Pelmadale, Scotland | |
| C-BZ742 | 1.5.44-12.10.44 | |

FL944    25.4.44-15.10.44
M-FL946    29.12.43-19.1.45
E-FL972    31.5.44-28.6.44
H-FL977    7.5.43-24.6.44 EFB, crashed
           Binevenagh while returning from
           sortie
X-FL978    8.5.44-16.9.44
B-FL981    31.3.44-21.10.44
Z-FL982    14.5.44-22.10.44
S-FL984    12.4.43-14.1.45
F-FL985    7.4.44-9.12.44
R-FL988    11.4.43-3.2.45
L-FL989    7.5.43-19.6.44 EFB, crashed soon
           after take-off, on Glengod Head, Eire

## No. 86 Sqn, Reykjavik
Mk III:
FK225    22.12.43-7.11.44(?)
*G-FK226    18.12.43-17.8.44 RIW
B-FK229    5.4.43-20.2.45
FK233    5.43-25.9.44
J-FK244    20.12.43-21.9.44
F-FL907    11.3.43-19.7.44 FTR
*N-FL916    7.2.43-19.10.44
*R-FL930    ?-?
M-FL931    7.2.43-27.6.44 FTR
*L-FL943    2.4.44-23.8.44
FL951    14.3.43-?.44(?)

## No. 120 Sqn, Ballykelly
Mk V:
BZ714    21.5.44-13.9.44
BZ719    28.3.44-31.1.45
BZ768    28.3.44-15.1.45
BZ771    16.12.43-26.12.44
BZ782    3.44-15.1.45
BZ787    5.1.44-24.8.44
BZ801    12.4.44-17.12.44
BZ804    8.11.43-29.12.44
BZ876    14.12.43-4.1.45
BZ881    16.1.43-20.1.45
BZ911    28.3.44-29.12.44
BZ912    8.11.43-26.12.44
BZ916    11.11.43-13.1.45
BZ917    11.11.43-26.12.44
BZ920    11.11.43-29.12.44
BZ921    10.12.43-10.1.45
BZ941    8.12.43-30.7.45
Mk III.
FL932    2.10.42-19.8.44
FL933    27.1.43-12.8.44 (Cat FB AC 21.6.44)

## No. 206 Sqn, St Eval
Mk VI:
B-BZ972    20.4.44-19.11.44
BZ975    23.5.44-5.12.44
BZ984    5.6.44-3.3.45
G-EV828    28.4.44-28.2.45
*A-EV871    20.4.44-29.8.44 (ROS 8.6.44-1.7.44)
D-EV873    20.4.44-20.7.44 EFA
*C-EV874    20.4.44-31.8.44
EV882    6.5.44-12.8.44
EV884    27.4.44-22.1.45 (ROS 22.5.44-
         13.6.44)
EV885    11.5.44-29.9.44 FTR (ROS 18.5.44-
         13.6.44)
EV887    28.4.44-31.12.44 FTR (ROS 17.5.44-
         24.6.44)
O-EV888    28.4.44-6.7.44
F-EV898    28.4.44-23.11.44

L-EV943    2.5.44-4.3.45 (ROS 19.5.44-30.5.44)
*E-EV947    28.4.44-16.7.44 FTR
EV954    11.5.44-6.7.44, (ROS 5.6.44-25.6.44)
P-EV985    15.5.44-4.3.45
EV988    14.5.44-20.6.44

## No. 224 Sqn, St Eval
Mk V:
BZ721    13.6.43-22.6.44
BZ766    30.6.43-11.8.44
BZ772    7.12.43-21.8.44
BZ783    31.1.44-20.8.44
BZ789    29.12.43-26.10.44
BZ792    31.8.43-5.9.44
BZ799    4.1.44-11.8.44
BZ803    2.1.44-18.8.44
BZ877    4.1.44-28.8.44
BZ914    30.11.43-22.8.44
B-BZ915    11.11.43-7.6.44 FTR
BZ918    16.11.43-6.9.44
S-BZ940    3.12.43-12.6.44.FTR
BZ942    6.12.43-17.6.44 FTR(?)
BZ943    4.12.43-28.8.44
Mk VI:
BZ985    21.5.44-5.12.44
EV890    13.5.44-11.3.45

## No. 311 Sqn, Predannack
Mk V:
*L-BZ717    6.3.44-14.7.44 EFB
G-BZ720    8.5.44-29.10.44 EFB
H-BZ723    11.5.44-12.3.45
*Q-BZ741    31.3.44-7.7.45
BZ743    5.6.43-26.1.45
*E-BZ745    6.5.44-13.8.44
*Z-BZ751    29.4.44-12.3.45
J-BZ754    20.4.44-29.6.44 EFB
D-FL948    18.7.43-11.3.45
M-FL953    17.2.44-12.11.44
W-FL956    25.4.44-16.3.45
V-FL960    25.4.44-21.3.45
FL961    13.4.44-12.3.45
B-FL966    25.4.44-8.3.45
*X-FL975    26.4.44-17.1.45 B FA
Mk VI:
BZ987    14.2.44-22.6.44
BZ999    19.2.44-31.7.44

## No. 547 Sqn, St Eval
Mk V:
BZ763    22.4.44-30.9.44
BZ784    9.3.44-8.8.44
BZ790    7.3.44-8.9.44
BZ794    10.3.44-9.12.44
BZ797    6.3.44-13.9.44
BZ798    28.3.44-18.9.44
BZ821    7.1.44-18.9.44
BZ874    7.1.44-16.9.44
BZ879    13.4.44-28.9.44
FL941    6.12.43-4.7.44
Mk VI:
BZ979    23.5.44-14.9.45
EV881    7.5.44-20.9.44 EFA
EV883    8.5.44-11.8.44
EV897    22.4.44-10.6.44 FTR
EV923    7.5.44-29.7.45
EV933    7.5.44-9.4.45
EV995    26.4.44-4.12.44
EV996    9.5.44-20.4.45 (ROS 28.5.44-13.6.44)

# The de Havilland Mosquito fighters

Although the Mosquito fighter's range, ample weaponry, high speed and excellent manoeuvrability made it ideal for Coastal Command, only one squadron and one flight were operational with the type on D-Day. As early as December 1940 the Mosquito fighter was earmarked for maritime patrol, but production rates and Fighter Command's needs delayed its introduction until May 1943.

First to operate Mosquito fighters in Coastal Command were, because of their personal knowledge of their country's coastline, a group of Norwegians serving in the RAF. They were posted to a special unit, No. 1477 Flight, tasked with watching

**Below** *Mosquito FB Mk VIs* K-King *and* Q-Queenie *of No. 333 (Norwegian) Squadron which reconnoitred the Norwegian coast.*

**Bottom** *Various second-line RAF aircraft likely to enter the invasion area wore 'invasion stripes'. Mosquito FB Mk VI PZ190, depicted with the Coastal Command Development Unit, joined No. 44 MU on 2 June 1944 and almost immediately went to No. 3504 SU, where it probably acquired its neat striping.*

enemy ships sailing along the Norwegian coast and using its ports.

At Leuchars on 10 May 1943, No. 1477 Flight became No. 333 (Norwegian) Squadron, and also operated Catalinas from Woodhaven. Using a few Mosquito F Mk IIs and mainly F Mk VIs, No. 333 (Norwegian) Squadron flew its first reconnaissance, between Stavanger and Lister Light, on 27 May 1943. Thereafter it contributed much to Coastal Command's activity off Norway, moving to Banff on 3 September 1944 to act in a pathfinder role for the Banff Strike Wing. On D-Day, however, it was far away from any action. That was left to the other Coastal Command Mosquito fighter squadron, No. 248.

Heavy calibre guns were a novel, unusual feature of a number of wartime aircraft. de Havilland reviewed the feasibility of wedding a 3.7 in anti-aircraft gun to their Mosquito for demolition of special targets such as U-boats. Maybe knowledge of that caused MAP to pre-empt such a submission by proposing, in late March 1943, the installation of a 6-pdr field gun in a Mosquito's belly and dangling the proposition that 30 production aircraft would follow. De Havilland's response was rapid, and on 8 June 1943 *HJ732*, the heavily-armed 6-pdr gun Mosquito FB Mk XVIII prototype, made its first flight.

Development was not easy for, although the aircraft's structure could cope with the recoil, the Molins 57 mm gun was a hefty weapon to feed and operate by remote control. It soon transpired that the RAF order was being cut to just three production FB Mk XVIIIs which were not intended to sink U-boats entering Biscay ports. What brought about the reduction of what became popularly called the 'Tsetse' was the limited chance of finding those vessels suitably placed for attack.

On 22 October 1943, the first two Mk XVIIIs joined No. 248 Beaufighter Squadron based at Predannack and two days later flew their first operation. The risk to a lone Mosquito crew attacking any ship was considerable, and on 4 November, when carrying out a very courageous attack, one was shot down. The 'punch' these Mosquitoes could pack encouraged the Germans to provide well-armed escorts for Biscay shipping.

In June 1944 Coastal Command was holding another specialized Mosquito anti-shipping squadron, No. 618, specially formed on 1 April 1943 to sink the *Tirpitz* using *Highball*, a small edition of the 'bouncing mine' which Sir Barnes Wallis had devised to breach German dams. As with its big brother, the casing of the smaller weapon persistently shattered on bouncing. The dams raid and the *Tirpitz* attack were intended to take place simultaneously for security reasons, but *Highball* was not ready in time. By the time it was perfected, targets in European waters were few and No. 618 Squadron – holding 25 Mosquitoes on D-Day – was being prepared for use in the Far East where targets were plentiful. The fear was that the innovative Japanese would quickly copy the idea, with devastating effect upon Allied warships. *Highball* was simply too good to use!

To No. 248 Squadron came news in November 1943 that its Beaufighters were to be replaced in January 1944 by 20 Mosquito FB Mk VI fighter-reconnaissance aircraft for Biscay patrols; in particular, to combat Ju 88s tormenting Allied flights. Mosquitoes were also to operate in areas where Beaufighters were no longer used, namely those defended by single-engined fighters. Operational flying began on 20 February, three days after the squadron had moved to Portreath. In use were FB Mk VIs whose range was extendable using long-range tanks instead of wing bombs. At first 50 gal tanks were carried, but soon they were replaced by 100 gal drop tanks. Although these increased range by 300 miles, they reduced economic cruising speed by 15 mph to 245 mph. At this time discussion began as to the feasibility of a Mosquito VI torpedo-bomber. With a likely top speed of 318 mph, its development was shelved for later consideration and use in the Far East.

On 10 March came the first major operation. A German naval convoy had been discovered and two Mk XVIIIs, protected by four Mk VIs, set off to attack. While the 'Tsetse' aircraft tackled the convoy the fighters engaged protecting Ju 88s in a classic, tough fight, resulting in three of the enemy being shot into the sea. All of the Mosquitoes returned safely. The ensuing weeks saw similar operations, No. 248 Squadron carrying out many effective offensive patrols in its allotted area. Included were many Mk XVIII sorties, mounted until their retirement in January 1945. D-Day saw the FB Mk VIs of No. 248 Squadron extremely active, flying between 04:45 hrs and 22:15 hrs, during which time five operations were undertaken. Three main tasks were set, *viz*, prevention of U-boats and surface vessels attacking Allied shipping; mounting a blockade of Biscay and nearby Channel ports; and providing cover for the Strike Wings. The following summary lists sorties flown:

### OPERATIONS BY NO. 248 SQUADRON, 6 JUNE 1944

| Time | Aircraft | Operation |
|---|---|---|
| 04:45-??:?? | P-HP908, Z-HR134, T-LR347, Q-MM430 | Yellow patrol; no enemy activity |
| 08:25-13:19 | D-HP866, K-LR340, M-LR352, N-LR360 | Yellow patrol; two Ju 88s glimpsed |
| 08:45-09:10 | H-MM424 (Mk XVIII) | Recalled |
| 12:00-16:34 | R-HJ828, V-HP907, Y-HR138, W-HR158 | Yellow patrol |
| 12:10-15:58 | H-MM424, O-NT225 (both Mk XVIIIs) | Found two freighters, Gironde Estuary; no attack |
| 19:45-22:15 | P-HP908, G-HR120, Z-HR134, F-LR339, | Beaufighter escort, details |

| T-LR347, B-LR377, C-LR378, S-MM399 | under Beaufighter entry |
|---|---|

## Mosquito VI/XVIIIs on squadron strength, 5 June 1944

* operated during 5/6 June 1944

### No. 248 Squadron, Portreath

Mk VI:

| | | |
|---|---|---|
| R-HJ828 | 27.11.43-5.9.44 AC FB | |
| D-HP866 | 31.1.44-11.9.44 | |
| *V-HP907 | 31.3.44-27.6.44 | |
| *P-HP908 | 31.3.44-2.8.44 FTR | |
| HP922 | 21.2.44-31.12.44 FTR | |
| *G-HR120 | 26.4.44-5.12.44 FTR | |
| *Z-HR134 | 11.5.44-30.6.44 FTR | |
| *Y-HR138 | 5.5.44-20.2.45 | |
| *W-HR158 | 26.5.44-23.6.44 AC FB | |
| *F-LR339 | 23.12.43-4.7.44 EFB | |
| *K-LR340 | 6.1.44-13.10.44 FTR | |
| LR346 | 22.12.43-25.1.44, 6.4.44-14.8.44 FTR, in the sea | |
| *T-LR347 | 23.12.43-11.7.44, 31.8.44-10.7.45 | |
| *M-LR352 | 14.1.44-21.8.44 EFA | |
| *N-LR360 | 14.1.44-4.7.44 BFB | |
| LR363 | 14.1.44-27.3.44, 7.6.44-4.11.44 EFB | |
| *B-LR377 | 8.2.44-12.7.44 RIW | |
| *C-LR378 | 23.1.44-8.2.45 | |
| *S-MM399 | 8.2.44-31.12.44 EFB | |
| *Q-MM430 | 4.2.44-27.3.44, 30.3.44-21.7.44, 9.8.44-10.1.45 | |

*Operational on D-Day, Mosquito FB Mk XVIII NT225-O of No. 248 Squadron. (IWM CH14114)*

Mk XVIII:
*H-MM424*  26.2.44-16.3.45 (to 254 Sqn)
*L-MM425*  26.2.44-29.2.44, 4.3.44-17.10.44 RIW
*E-NT224*  2.6.44-7.12.44 FTR
*O-NT225*  5.6.44-6.11.44 RIW

***No. 333 (Norwegian) Sqn,* Leuchars**
Mk VI:
*O-HP858*  17.9.43-*circa* 2.45

*R-HP860*  7.10.43-16.6.44 EFB
*K-HP862*  6.3.44-*circa* 3.45
*H-HP864*  27.12.43-23.6.44 FA, 15.9.44-
        30.10.44
*E-HP904*  15.5.44-25.10.44
*L-HP910*  28.2.44-10.4.45

# Photographic Reconnaissance Mosquitoes

It was, surprisingly, Coastal Command that on 20 September 1941 first despatched a Mosquito into enemy airspace. Within a short time Mosquitoes were prying into every corner of Europe from Narvik to Nice, from the Baltic to Biarritz – and usually with impunity. Such was the aircraft's performance that in June 1942 a Benson-based Mosquito in one sortie spied upon Lyons, Marseilles and La Spezia. In seeking the *Tirpitz* another Mosquito flew to Murmansk and back in a day, a track of over 3,000 miles.

These operations were being flown from Benson or Wick by early, relatively unsophisticated Mosquito PR Mk I and PR Mk IV variants (some with long-range tanks) operated by No. 1 Photographic Reconnaissance Unit (PRU). On 19 October 1942 No. 1 PRU split into four squadrons, its Spitfires equipping Nos. 541 and 542 Squadrons and the Mosquitoes Nos. 540 and 544.

To increase the aircraft's operational effectiveness, Merlin 61 engines had already been wedded to a Mosquito Mk IV conversion designated Mk VIII. Two of the five built joined No. 540 Squadron and on 19 February 1943 commenced operational flying. Their higher operational ceiling proved very useful, but the Mosquito also needed even longer range. A great advance came on 29 May 1943 when two Mosquito PR Mk IXs, *LR405* and *LR406*, joined No. 540 Squadron at Benson from where the former, flying the first effective Mk IX sortie, photographed Munich and

Augsburg. Having two-stage supercharger Merlin 72/73 engines, the PR Mk IX was a production version of the PR Mk VIII conversion. On 13 September 1943 No. 544 Squadron began night operations with its Mk IXs, and also flew them during many distant daylight sorties. January 1944 saw the introduction of the Merlin 76/77-powered version of the Mk IXs, allowing them even higher, faster, longer-range operational flights.

The second mainstream PR Mosquito had, by then, entered service. This was the PR Mk XVI, featuring a 2 lb/psi pressure cabin conferring an even higher flying capability, and bringing additional comfort to the crew during lengthy sorties. The Mk XVIs were first placed in Nos. 140 and 400 Squadrons of 2nd TAF which concentrated upon photographing northern and central France during the run-up to D-Day. No. 140 Squadron received its first PR XVI on 12 December 1943, and on 4 February 1944 introduced *MM279* to operations. Nos. 140 and 400 Squadrons were joined in their task by No. 544 Squadron. Between them, the three squadrons also had to photograph the extensive V-weapons undertakings spreading through much of northern France.

While tactical demands increasingly attracted much of the PR Mosquito effort, and particularly that of the new squadrons, Mosquitoes of No. 540 Squadron also tried to photograph the effectiveness of the heavy bombing raids being made upon Berlin. The task proved difficult because of persistent cloud. This was the squadron that from Benson flew amazing sorties to Breslau, Munich, Peenemünde and Posnan. By using San Severo in Italy as a terminus, 540's Mosquito IXs surveyed Venice, Vienna, Klagenfurt, Zagreb and many other distant localities. Less usual for the squadron were short-range missions, such as famed Sqn Ldr John Merifield's low-level run to Limoges in *LR422* and coverage of the Caen coastal area on 20 March 1944. To increase range two underwing drop tanks could be carried, the 50 gal type affording a 2,180 mile sortie, the 100 gal type – which Nos. 540 and 544 Squadrons began using in April 1944 – boosting range to 2,450 miles. During August 1944 200 gal tanks were introduced, and that led to the later PR Mosquito, the Mk 34.

Shortly before D-Day, PR Mosquitoes of Nos. 4 and 400 Squadrons completed their contribution to *Overlord*. The early months of 1944 had seen the Mosquito PR Mk XVIs equipping 'B' Flight, No. 4 Squadron concentrating upon photographing northern France. In March they had moved to Sawbridgeworth from where they flew their first high-level PR sortie on 20 March (using *MM313*) and their last Mosquito sortie (using *MM309*) on 20 May. Then, 'B' Flight received PR Spitfires. No. 400 Squadron, whose six Mosquitoes had concentrated upon photographing rivers and bridges in France, had ceased Mosquito operations on 12 May. Its aircraft came off strength on 29 May. No. 140 Squadron, however, remained very busy and from 4 May carried out a lot of night photography over France. Military targets, towns, villages, roads, railways, bridges, airfields, V-weapon sites and much more were superbly photographed by the Mosquitoes.

## Operations in June 1944

The two main tasks carried out by PR Mosquitoes were photography by day of rail centres to assess reinforcement activity and, by night, the photography of troop movements. The former task was mainly given over to No. 544 Squadron, which secured the photographs used to prepare No. 617 Squadron's 'Tallboy' bombing of the Saumur tunnel, after which the Mosquitoes took damage assessment

photographs. Tactical duty was in the main the task allotted to No. 140 Squadron. At night, Mk II and Mk III photoflashes were dropped from 3,000 ft to 5,000 ft, to provide sufficient light for the Fairchild K.19 camera fitted with a 6 in, 10 in or 12 in lens.

The D-Day sorties were not without drama. Flg Off G.H. Ardley's aircraft, *MM250*, had its cockpit cover come adrift during a morning sortie, but was nevertheless operating again in the afternoon. Greater catastrophe claimed *MM279*, the first PR Mk XVI to fail to return from an operation.

### SORTIES FLOWN BY PR MOSQUITOES, 5-7 JUNE 1944

| Date | Time | Sqn | Aircraft | Notes |
|------|------|-----|----------|-------|
| 5/6 | 23:00-03:00 | 140 | *MM282* | Granville–St Lô–Vire |
| 5/6 | 23:30-02:50 | 140 | *MM305/G* | Châteaudun, Freteval |
| 5/6 | 23:35-02:35 | 140 | *MM312* | Evreux, Lisieux |
| 5/6 | 23:35-02:40 | 140 | *MM281* | Verbuil, Chartres |
| 6 | 06:35-09:50 | 140 | *MM280* | Rouen–Pontoise |
| 6 | 06:56-09:00 | 140 | *MM250* | Abbeville–Amiens |
| 6 | 06:50- – | 140 | *MM279* | Montdidier–Cambrai; FTR |
| 6 | 06:50-09:20 | 140 | *MM301* | Abbeville–Amiens, low-level |
| 6 | 08:20-12:05 | 544 | *MM234* | Saumur, from 4,000 ft |
| 6 | 09:10-12:50 | 544 | *LR417* | Saumur, from 2,000 ft |
| 6 | 13:35-16:30 | 544 | *NS500* | Saumur, from 3,500 ft |
| 6 | 15:30-19:45 | 544 | *LR431* | Toulouse |
| 6 | 15:30-20:05 | 544 | *LR425* | Toulouse |
| 6 | 16:00-20:35 | 544 | *MM246* | Toulouse |
| 6 | 16:05-19:55 | 544 | *MM240* | Saumur, from 2,000 ft |
| 6 | 16:45-18:15 | 140 | *MM250* | Beachhead, Trouville–St Vaast |
| 6 | 17:00-20:50 | 544 | *LR417* | Saumur, from 1,000 ft to 2,000 ft |
| 6/7 | 23:40-02:35 | 140 | *MM281* | St Lô |
| 6/7 | 23:50-02:05 | 140 | *MM312* | To rear of beachhead |
| 6/7 | 23:55-02:00 | 140 | *MM282* | To rear of beachhead |
| 6/7 | 23:55-02:03 | 140 | *MM305/G* | Lisieux |

## PR Mosquitoes of strategic squadrons, 5.6.44

* one mission
** two missions on 5/6 June 1944

### No. 540 Sqn, Benson

Mk IX:
  *LR406*  29.5.43-?.44(?)
  *LR413*  11.8.43-26.6.44 EFB, crash-landed in

Corsica (PR Lyons area)
LR414   4.7.43-13.7.44, 17.9.44-24.2.45
LR415   4.7.43-24.2.45
LR422   15.8.43-19.6.44, 7.7.44-2.45
LR426   1.9.43-24.3.45
LR427   14.8.43-20.8.44, 18.10.44-25.10.44
LR428   26.8.43-16.12.44
LR429   1.9.43-?.44
LR433   1.9.43-8.8.44 FTR, Bavaria
LR435   24.9.43-9.8.44 FTR, landed in Sweden

Mk XVI:
MM354   5.5.44-19.8.44 FTR, crashed in Normandy
MM355   3.44-23.8.44 FTR
MM358   8.5.44-13.11.45
MM360   14.5.44-21.8.44 FTR
MM365   4.44-22.6.44
MM397   25.5.44-26.11.44
NS504   1.5.44-6.8.44 FTR
NS525   24.4.44-13.11.45

### No. 544 Sqn, Benson
Mk IX:
**LR417   4.44-20.7.45
LR423   11.10.43-7.2.45
*LR425   23.10.43-23.7.44 EFA
*LR431   9.10.43-18.7.44 FTR, Brunswick area
LR432   8.10.43-22.1.45
MM231   11.10.43-18.9.44 FTR
MM233   16.10.43-2.9.44 FTR
*MM234   17.11.43-8.12.44
*MM240   25.10.43-2.8.44, crash-landed, Manston, SOC 13.8.44
MM245   5.11.43-11.8.44 FTR from low level oblique sortie, Foret de Nieppes
*MM246   23.10.43-10.9.44 EFB, crashed on

take-off, Benson
Mk XVI:
MM272   26.1.44-6.7.44 FA, crash-landed, Benson
MM327   22.2.44-12.6.44
MM352   18.4.44-9.6.44 FTR, southern France
NS500   23.5.44-12.4.45 FTR

## PR Mosquitoes of 2nd TAF squadron, 5.6.44

### No. 140 Sqn, Northolt
Mk IX:
LR479   11.11.43-30.4.44, 8.6.44-4.7.44
MM249   8.11.43-15.7.44 EFB, force-landed, Windsor Great Park
**MM250   5.11.43-3.12.43, 17.2.44-28.6.44
MM251   11.1.43-?
Mk XVI:
MM274   23.12.43-8.8.44 EFB, overshot Northolt
MM278   6.1.44-19.3.44, 8.6.44-6.3.45 Cat E, crashed on take-off, Lille/Vendeville
*MM279   23.12.43-7.6.44 FTR
*MM280   23.12.43-21.9.44
**MM281   6.1.44-26.12.44, crashed on take-off, Melsbroek
**MM282   22.2.44-1.1.45 EA Cat C
MM298   28.1.44-31.7.44
*MM301   1.2.44-14.12.44
MM302   28.1.44-20.7.44
*MM304   1.3.44-10.6.45 EFA, crashed on take-off, Eindhoven
**MM305   1.3.44-7.7.45
**MM312   19.2.44 EFB, crash-landed, Amiens/Glisy

# The General Reconnaissance Handley Page Halifax

In Bomber Command, the planned replacement for the Whitley was the Stirling. Instead, it turned out to be the Halifax. The need to replace obsolescent Whitley Mk VIIs in Coastal Command's Nos. 58 and 502 Squadrons, and ever increasing U-boat activity well out in the Atlantic, led in late 1942 to the release from Bomber Command of sufficient Merlin-engined Halifaxes to arm and support both squadrons. BD427 on 11 December 1942 was the last No. 58 Squadron Whitley to operate, before the squadron moved to Holmsley South to convert. From St David's on 23 February

1943 the Halifax Mk II srs ia first operated, and began making anti-U-boat and anti-shipping patrols over Biscay.

No. 502 Squadron flew its last Whitley Mk VII sortie on 16 February 1943 and on 2 March made its way to Holmsley South also to convert. Squadron strength for each unit was set at 12 IE + 3 IR Halifax Mk II srs ias, and on 31 March No. 502 Squadron was declared operational at St Eval. The first U-boat attack by a Halifax came on 1 April 1943.

Maximum patrol duration with useful offensive load being the prerequisite for any general reconnaissance aircraft, an assessment of the Halifax's minimum safe patrol envelope was required. An aircraft of No. 502 Squadron was selected for trials from Holmsley South, flown by a crew from A&AEE Boscombe Down. On 11 June 1943 Halifax *J*, laden with 6 x 600 lb depth bombs, and weighing 61,400 lb at take-off, was test-flown by Flg Off McClintock. Applying +14 lb boost, producing 3,500 revs for take-off in the 12 to 15 mph surface wind, the aircraft became airborne in 1,500 yds as IAS reached 110 kts. Climb out was at 115 kts on +12 lb/2,850 revs, eventually reduced to +6 lb/2,650 revs. Cruise at 1,000 ft/135 kts followed, although at 1.98 mpg the fuel consumption was high, partly due to a rapid and early return as bad weather set in.

A second, more thorough trial – this time flown from St Eval – took place on 25 June. *HR815*, its engines again specially cleaned to accept +14 lb boost, was to fly at the lowest feasible cruising speed (1,800 revs/IAS 140 kts) and, if possible, land with two hrs fuel remaining, thus allowing for diversion. Carrying 2,732 gal of petrol at take-off and with a full operational load, and lightened by the removal of 350 lb of armour plating, the Halifax's all-up weight was 61,750 lb. In a 10 mph wind, *HR815* became airborne in 1,400 yds, then course was set for the Fastnet Rock. A cruising speed of 135 kts, achieved using +3$^{1}$/2 lb boost/2,200 revs, was increased to 140 kts after two hrs, subsequent to which revs were cut first to 1,850 and then 1,800 and boost eventually to +1 lb as the weight fell during the flight at an average height of 2,000 ft, dictated by cloud levels. Careful weighing after landing at Boscombe Down showed the aircraft (with crew aboard) tipping the 'scales' at 43,822 lb. Then it was refuelled with 2,399 gal of fuel. According to a flow meter, 2,361 gal had been used, indicating 333 gal remaining at the end of the flight. Calculations showed a rate of fuel consumption of 140 gal per hour. Bomb bay tanks in this GR aircraft held 230 gal. Very detailed calculations concerning the quantity of fuel remaining led to the conclusion that the Halifax Mk II had a very creditable 16-hr maximum endurance at 140 kts, but that 13 hrs should be the norm – 12 hrs for Halifaxes with three bomb bay tanks.

Throughout the rest of 1943 both Halifax squadrons based at Holmsley South, but often using forward bases, operated mainly over Biscay and to the south-west of Eire. In December 1943 the squadrons moved to St David's, joining No. 517 (Met Recce) Squadron. All three squadrons operated from here and Brawdy until September 1944.

## ANTI-U-BOAT SORTIES FLOWN BY HALIFAXES, 5–7 JUNE 1944

| Day | Time | Sqn | Aircraft | Notes |
|-----|------|-----|----------|-------|
| 5/6 | 20:50-07:05 | 58 | *JP165-D* | Fire exchanged with two minesweepers, from beam guns and rear turret; aircraft hit in starboard wing-tip |
| 5/6 | 22:44-06:15 | 502 | *F* | No action |
| 5/6 | 23:15-07:30 | 58 | *HR792-A* | Trawlers seen |
| 5/6 | 23:41-07:16 | 502 | *G* | Trawlers seen |
| 5/6 | 02:06-06:45 | 58 | *HR983-R* | Warships seen, identity uncertain |
| 6/7 | 19:22-06:34 | 502 | *F* | *Ranger* patrol, uncertain sighting of ships |
| 6/7 | 22:20-08:55 | 58 | *JP167-Z* | Patrol *F*, no sightings |
| 6/7 | 22:26-08:25 | 502 | *Y* | No sightings |
| 6/7 | 22:54-00:55 | 502 | *J* | Fuel problem, abortive |
| 6/7 | 22:55-09:20 | 58 | *HR675-J* | *Ranger* patrol |

The most effective patrol was flown by Lt Powell (USAAF) in *U*/502 Squadron, which took off at 23:10 hrs on 7 June. At 04:30 hrs a fully-surfaced U-boat was detected 18 miles away. Only one of the two high-intensity flares dropped ignited as the Halifax circled to port and entered an up-moon attack profile. At 04:33 hrs 3 x 600 lb AS bombs were released, straddling the vessel which opened fire as it dived and escaped a few moments later.

The following night, Flg Off Spurgeons flying *F*/502 Sqn, found a surfaced U-boat slowly moving. His first run-in was poorly positioned, and the bombs hung up on the second; but on the third, 4 x 600 lb AS bombs exploded around the U-boat, whose fierce return fire crippled the aircraft's port inner engine and damaged the tailplane and elevators. The same night, Sqn Ldr Brook in *HX177-F* of 58 Sqn attacked a submarine, and Flt Lt Aldridge in *JD178-V* of 58 Sqn did likewise on 9 June. Both squadrons operated Halifaxes to the end of hostilities, Mk IIIs coming into use in February 1945.

HR744, *a 'white' Halifax GR Mk II series ia of No. 58 Squadron. (Ray Sturtivant collection)*

## Halifax GR Mk II srs ias on squadron strength, 5 June 1944
\* operated on 5/6.6.44

### No. 58 Sqn, St David's
| | |
|---|---|
| *\*J-HR675* | 5.44-? |
| *HR744* | 29.4.43-12.8.44 |
| *\*A-HR792* | 20.5.43-13.1.45 EFA, crashed Stornoway |
| *\*R-HR983* | 17.9.43-30.11.44 SOC |
| *M-HX152* | 18.9.43-8.2.45 SOC |
| *F-HX177* | 24.11.43-20.7.44 EFA, crashed on take-off, St David's |
| *Y-HX178* | 12.12.43-16.10.44 FTR, crashed at sea off Wester Ross |
| *P-HX224* | 28.11.43-25/26.2.45 FTR from Skaggerak patrol |
| *V-JD178* | 15.9.43-6.8.44 Cat E |
| *\*D-JP165* | 21.5.44-9.4.45 EFA |

| | |
|---|---|
| *\*Z-JP167* | 17.5.44-10.11.44 FTR |
| *H-JP173* | 27.5.44-20/21.2.45 FTR |
| *T-JP255* | 16.5.44-16.4.45 SOC |
| *L-JP257* | 2.6.44-21.7.44, 20.9.44-8.10.44 |
| *JP297* | 5.3.44-9.6.44 SOC |
| *K-JP300* | 5.6.44-16.1.45, 28.3.45-16.4.45 SOC |
| *JP319* | 6.6.44-31.7.44 |

### No. 502 Sqn, St David's
(known aircraft):
| | |
|---|---|
| *HR686* | 18.2.43-3.10.44 FTR |
| *HX222* | 3.12.43-13.3.45 SOC |
| *JD895* | 7.5.43-13.8.43, 26.9.43-1.11.44 |
| *JB901* | 11.5.43-22.3.45 SOC |
| *JD218* | 25.7.43-6.9.44 |
| *JP164* | 4.6.44-30.8.44 FTR |
| *JP169* | 28.5.44-30.11.44 SOC |
| *JP172* | 27.5.44-? |
| *Y-?????* | ?-22.6.44 FTR |

# The weather reconnaissance team

Weather reconnaissance by Coastal Command squadrons and Flights throughout hostilities provided a vital service upon which weather forecasting was based. On D-Day, weather reconnaissance sorties were flown as follows:

**Aldergrove:**
Gladiator (4); Spitfire (2)
**Bircham Newton:**
Gladiator (4); Ventura V (2)

**Brawdy:**
Halifax V (2)
**Tiree:**
Halifax V (2)
**Wick:**
Spitfires (2); Ventura V (2)

## Handley Page Halifax

The most common aircraft in use at the time were the Halifax Vs flown by three meteorological reconnaissance squadrons.

Of these, the closest placed to the Normandy invasion was No. 517 Squadron based at St David's and which also flew its 10-hr-long *Epicure B* weather reconnaissance sorties over the Atlantic from Brawdy. The squadron formed from No. 1404 (Met) Flight on 11 August 1943 at St Eval, from where it operated Fortress IIs until 8 November 1943. After rearming with Halifaxes, the first sortie was flown (from St Mawgan) on 15 December 1943. No. 517 Squadron had moved to St David's in late November 1943.

On D-Day a reconnaissance sortie flown by Flg Off Eveling and crew ended in disaster. Halifax *LL144-L* left Brawdy at 01:45 hrs and at 07:33 hrs, position 43° 33'N/17° 07'W, serious engine trouble was reported and the aircraft ditched soon after. An air-sea rescue search was mounted by two Warwicks of No. 282 Squadron, and at 11:55 hrs Sqn Ldr Fox set out from Brawdy in Halifax *LL299-M* on an 11 hr 45 min search. Next day, two more 517 Squadron Halifax Vs, *LL220-F* and *LK707-D*, searched. Near the position from where the Halifax crew had reported trouble a dinghy was sighted. No trace of the crew was ever found.

Many of Coastal Command's meteorological reconnaissance squadrons were only indirectly associated with Operation *Neptune*. Included were the Handley Page Halifax Vs of No. 517 Squadron:

### No. 517 Sqn, St David's
```
  O-DK256  6.6.44-21.10.44   EFB, crashed in
                             Morocco
  D-LK707  11.12.43-19.6.45
  E-LK745  29.1.44-31.7.44
  J-LL117  19.12.43-24.4.44 ROS, 11.6.44-?
 *K-LL144  20.12.43-6.6.44 FTR
   LL145   20.12.43-21.11.44 FA
  B-LL188  21.2.44-19.7.44
  A-LL216  29.2.43-21.7.44
  F-LL220  12.2.44-24.7.44
  H-LL295  19.3.44-24.7.44
  N-LL297  10.4.44-30.7.44
  L-LL298  26.3.44-16.7.44
  M-LL299  29.3.44-15.7.44
```

## Lockheed Ventura
Among the unusual aircraft to be found in the squadrons were a handful of Lockheed PV-1 Ventura

Mk Vs used by No. 519 Squadron, based at Wick and including:

### No. 519 Sqn, Wick
```
  FN962  25.9.43-19.8.44
  FN966  29.10.43-13.10.44
  FN969  ?-?
  FN994  29.10.43-19.8.44
  FP614  20.11.43-10.8.44
  FP661  6.1.44-12.9.44
```

A few more were with No. 521 Squadron, Docking, including *FN984* (26.10.43-30.9.44) and *FN985* (29.10.43-20.11.44).

## Gloster Gladiator
Worthy of mention here are surely the handful of Gloster Gladiator biplanes of the type introduced to weather reporting in 1939 and better known for the particularly courageous flying by their pilots in Malta and Norway early in the war. Among those remaining on D-Day (all Mk IIs) was *L8032*, under overhaul at Marshall's Flying School, Cambridge, between 14.2.44 and 28.9.44 (and now part of the Shuttleworth Collection). Another with a long history was *N5594*, which on 1.6.39 had joined the Mildenhall Met Flight, and which after overhaul served from 4.2.41 at Bircham Newton, there passing through the hands of No. 401 Flight, subsequently renamed No. 1401 (Met) Flight, before joining 521 Squadron on 3.9.43 and crashing at Docking on 14.9.44. Five Gladiator Mk IIs were based at Aldergrove:

### No. 1402 (Met) Flight, Aldergrove
```
  N5576  18.3.42-28.4.43, 16.1.44-22.11.44
  N5591  23.1.41-21.3.45
  N5592  23.1.41-21.3.45
  N5637  25.3.42-27.1.43, 1.6.43-9.2.45
  N5902  15.2.44-?, to 521 Sqn 7.4.44-?
```

Gloster Gladiators undertook temperature and humidity recording flights to about 23,000 ft for much of the war, and another four, including *N5630*, were still being used at the time of the D-Day invasion by No. 520 Squadron at Gibraltar. Several others were still flying with No. 61 OTU at Rednall or being overhauled at Cambridge. *N2311* was in Gloster's hands 17.4.44–27.9.44.

# The Short Sunderland GR III

Seven UK-based flying-boat squadrons in June 1944 held 94 Sunderland GR Mk IIIs, 50 of them serviceable on D-Day. Calls in 1940 for revised Sunderlands had led to the building of 407 Mk IIIs for RAF use by D-Day, but the need for superior engines which had dogged the Sunderland's career remained.

Any notions of fitting Rolls-Royce Merlins in a Sunderland Mk II had quickly faded in favour of Bristol Pegasus XVIIIs on tubular mountings, *T9042* being chosen

as the trial installation aircraft. The intention was to incorporate even more major modifications including a better streamlined forebody and step, additional fuel tankage, retractable wing floats and greater wing span. All were intended to improve the Sunderland for the increasingly bitter Atlantic war ahead. As the Battle of Britain ended, hull modifications on *T9042* were 90 per cent complete and the intention was to fly it in December 1940. Instead, repeated changes

**Below** *Second mainstream Sunderland was the Mk II, like* W3986-U *of No. 10 (RAAF) Squadron seen in April 1942 carrying ASV Mk II aerials. (Shorts)*

**Bottom** T9042, *pictured in June 1941, became the Sunderland Mk III prototype. (Shorts)*

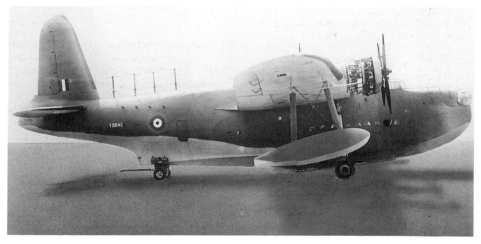

287

brought delay and the aircraft did not fly until 28 June 1941. Meanwhile an interim Sunderland, a simpler Mk II, went ahead, it being a Mk I with two-stage supercharged Pegasus XVIIIs, an FN 7 dorsal turret, FN 4A tail turret, and ASV Mk II radar with an impressive array of *Yagi* aerials.

Although *T9042* did not feature all of the initially proposed major changes, it had a more streamlined step – previously tested using *P9624* in attempts to improve airborne performance by reducing aerodynamic drag. To take-off seaplanes first need to rise onto the central step, then begin lift-off from the water. Unfortunately the new step impaired water performance, causing the boat to 'porpoise', a condition further aggravated by its refined afterbody. As weight continued to increase, the entire hull was affected, making rough water handling tricky.

Including advances already scheduled for 52 production Mk IIs, *W3999*, the first production example of this newer version and designated Mk III, flew on 15 December 1941 and joined No. 10 (RAAF) Squadron at Mount Batten on 29 January 1942. No. 201 Squadron, first to fully equip with Sunderland Mk IIIs, had already received *W4000* on 9 January 1942. The most numerous type of Sunderland, the last Mk III delivered before D-Day was *NJ176* which joined the RAF at 57 MU, Wig Bay, on 29 May 1944. Production was completed in September 1944.

With a structure weight of 33,000 lb, and taking off at 58,000 lb, the Mk III took one minute and 1,530 yds to unstick. Maximum speed was 170 kts at 3,000 ft and most economical cruising came at 127 kts and 5,000 ft. Still-air range was 2,030 sea miles, although a practical range of 1,620 sea miles during a 12.7 hr flight was more representative. At sea level its rate of climb was 540 fpm, and it took some 9.8 minutes to attain 5,000 ft.

As the Sunderland Mk III entered service the battle against U-boats in the Atlantic was at its height. Using ASV Mk II to seek surfaced submarines, particularly in Biscay, Sunderlands achieved good results – until the U-boat crews managed to detect their ASV radar transmissions. Undetectable ASV G Mk III was introduced late 1943, although U-boats caught on the surface now responded by using their gun defences, thus making attacks by the relatively slow Sunderlands hazardous. German fighters had also to be faced, so the defensive armament of Sunderland Mk IIIs steadily improved. Twin Brownings were carried in the nose turret and Vickers K-guns in ports on either side of the galley. Twin belt-fed .50 in Brownings were also installed in beam positions in the hull of some aircraft. A twin Browning mid-upper FN 7 turret was standard, and by 1944 Sunderland Mk IIIs also featured two fixed forward-firing Browning guns on either side of the bow to discourage U-boat defenders. Some Mk IIIs were carrying as many as 18 machine-guns. By August 1944 all Sunderland Mk Is and IIs had left Coastal Command, and been replaced in the OTUs by ASV Mk II-equipped Sunderland IIIs.

The Sunderland was, by any reckoning, a remarkable aeroplane. By the end of hostilities its all-up weight had risen from the 50,100 lb of early Mk Is to over 65,000 lb in the Mk V being tried out by D-Day, and to over 70,000 lb in the ultimate version, the Mk IV, renamed the Seaford. Before the war, the realization was that the aircraft's structure could accept considerable additional weight, but that demanded far more engine power than was available. Anti-ship weapon stowage was unsatisfactory, the load unnecessarily limited. But additional weight inevitably dragged the hull deeper into the water, producing unacceptable spray patterns.

Nevertheless, the AOC-in-C Coastal Command, on 29 March 1942, expressed to his superiors a wish to see the Sunderland 'improved like the Spitfire', pointing out that very little had been similarly done to any aircraft type in his Command. The Pegasus XVIII engine uneconomically remained in production only for Sunderlands, over-occupying production sources, so he suggested a new wing carrying more powerful powerplants – preferably the Bristol Hercules, the Wright Cyclone or maybe the forthcoming Bristol Centaurus. Such engines would raise the cruising speed to 140 kts, endurance to 16 hrs. More speed meant faster transit to patrol station.

The MAP accepted this need for updating, particularly of the mainplanes, and in May 1942 seaplane tank tests commenced to assess the take-off characteristics of a modernized Sunderland, loaded weight 56,000 lb to 66,000 lb. They showed that spray would hit the existing tailplanes and enter the propeller discs.

Running at 17 kts/56,000 lb, the propellers became marginally clear and were all free by 32 kts. Loaded to 66,000 lb, spray still touched the tailplane tips at 32 kts, so it would not be easy to make improvements, especially when at 65 kts/66,000 lb very heavy spray still seemed certain to hit the tailplanes mid-span; if anything, worsening at 70 kts.

As the war progressed, Pegasus XVIIIs were wearing out because they frequently ran at combat power. New engines would need ample reserve power, which problem generated a novel suggestion in November 1942 from No. 10 (RAAF) Squadron: why not fit American 1,200 hp Pratt & Whitney R-1830-30-90B or -90C Twin Wasps? Forecasts suggested they would raise the tare weight to 36,381 lb, give a top speed of 229 mph at 5,000 ft and a cruising speed of 150 mph at 5,000 ft, which implied a fuel load of 2,129 gal. A range of 2,530 miles equalled an endurance of 17.18 hrs. Suggestions that the new engines wedded to the Sunderland Mk III would be too powerful were soon dismissed, but because of ideas surrounding the use of Hercules engines, instructions for trials were not given until late 1943. *ML765* on the Rochester line was then ordered to be converted. Mountings and engines for a second example were sent to Mount Batten to be fitted in Mk III *ML839* of No. 10 (RAAF) Squadron.

The former first flew in March 1944. The latter, first flown on 4 May 1944 by G/C Alexander OBE (RAAF), was fitted with a velocity and gravity recorder to assess the likely life of the aircraft's structure. The newcomer had a higher cruising speed than the Mk III, and could fly with only two engines functioning on one mainplane; a very desirable improvement. Although the tare weight of 28,290 lb in the Mk I had risen to 35,915 lb for the Mk V, its operational range carrying 2,142 gal of fuel and a 1,700 lb weapon load was 1,760 miles. Optimum cruising speed was 126 kts TAS, top speed 186 kts TAS. At 60,000 lb weight take-off was accomplished in 52 seconds. Pratt & Whitney Twin Wasps were introduced on the production line starting with *ML796* which also carried ASV Mk VIc whose scanners were carried in radomes beneath the outer wings. From May 1944 Mk IIIs were also completed with these changes, and some previous aircraft were retrospectively modified. As for the Mk V, with a 2¹/₂-hr-long extension to patrol times, *ML839-A* of No. 10 (RAAF) Squadron operated for the first time, between 07:22 hrs and 20:51 hrs in the hands of Flt Lt Chilcott, on 12 September 1944. The Sunderland Mk V was more generally introduced from February 1945 and served post-war until 1957. Mk IIIs re-engined with Twin Wasps were officially designated Mk VR to distinguish them.

*Sunderland Mk III* ML739-N *of No. 201 Squadron at Pembroke Dock. (Ray Sturtivant collection)*

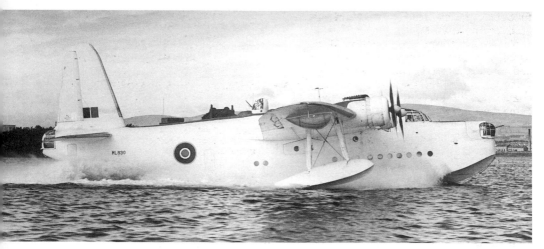

*Few aviation sights equal that of a large seaplane, such as Sunderland III ML830 of No. 10 (RAAF) Squadron, during a take-off run. (Shorts)*

Coastal Command's 1942 request for a radical new Sunderland was answered by Specification R.8/42, calling for the Sunderland Mk IV (Hercules VI engines) of which only two prototypes (*MZ269* and *MZ271*) and 30 production examples were ordered in September 1942. It featured a 3 ft longer forebody, 5 ft 6 in longer aft body, and a further refined step widened by 11½ in at the chine.

All-up weight rose to 71,500 lb, fuel tankage by 620 gal, the wing was strengthened and the tailplane had 6½ dihedral. Although *MZ269* was completed in May 1944, it did not fly until September 1944. Intended by then for the Pacific war, it was so different from the Sunderland that it was renamed Seaford, with the eight production examples all subsequently modified into Solent airliners. Thus the Seaford never entered squadron service; the Sunderland Mk V was quite adequate.

## Operations

Despite their numbers, Sunderlands of Coastal Command flew only eight operational sorties on 6 June 1944, not all of them in direct support of the invasion forces. Lengthy sorties entailed low-level flying, 71 being undertaken by No. 201 Squadron alone during June 1944 (55 of them during the peak period 9 to 23 June), calling for 882 hrs of operational flying. The most eventful of them involved the crew of *ML760*-S, one of No. 201

Squadron's ASV Mk VIc-equipped aircraft.

Airborne from Pembroke Dock at 19:40 hrs on 6 June, *ML760-S* and her crew had been flying for an hour when a radar contact was obtained at nine miles, so they descended to 250 ft to disguise their approach. The 'blip' disappeared when they were ½ mile away. At 00:04 hrs, position 45° 17'N/08° 25'W, a swirl in the water was seen, but its maker quickly disappeared. Sunderland *ML747-N* of No. 461 Squadron then joined the search. At 02:44 hrs the 201 Squadron crew obtained another contact, 11 miles distant. Again they homed in at 250 ft. At 45° 13'N/08° 30'W at 02:49 hrs they encountered flak from the port side, so they turned steeply to starboard, dived and dropped (for the first time) 1.7 in flares which were also allowing night photography for the first time and which illuminated a fully surfaced U-boat about 10° to port, range 600 yds. As *S-Sugar* swung sharply right, guns on the U-boat again opened up, then the Sunderland ran in with forward and mid-upper guns blazing away for six seconds and scored hits around the conning tower. Dropped from 100 ft, six 250 lb Torpex depth charges straddled the victim, two bursting close to its tower. Nothing more was seen of the vessel although the Sunderland orbited the area for 58 minutes. No. 201 Squadron had scored their first 'kill' of 1944. For their spirited action, Flg Off H.L. Baveystock received a Bar to his DFC and the eagle-eyed radar operators,

Flt Sgt D.J. Currie and Flt Sgt D.E. South, each received a DFM.

No. 461 Squadron, also Pembroke Dock-based, managed 78 sorties (931 hrs) in June and attacked three U-boats, two at night using the new flares. On 8 June one radar contact led to flares and depth charges being dropped from *ML741-P* at 300 ft, but the results were inconclusive. Attacking U-boats was a hazardous task and they took their revenge on 11/12 June when *ML760-S*, being flown by Sqn Ldr W.D. Ruth DFC and Bar, was shot down as it ran in on an attack.

# Sunderland GR Mk IIIs on squadron strength, 5 June 1944

\* operated on 6.6.44

### *No. 10 Sqn, (RAAF)* Mount Batten
| | |
|---|---|
| DD852 | 24.5.43-2.9.44 EFA |
| DD865 | 2.8.43-5.1.45 |
| DW113 | 4.12.43-30.11.44 |
| EK573 | 14.8.43-17.5.45 |
| EK586 | 6.10.43-7.12.44 |
| JM678 | 11.5.44-15.6.44 EFA |
| \*W-JM721 | 4.12.43-6.11.44 |
| ML730 | 10.11.43-28.7.44 |
| ML839 | 8.12.43-12.10.44 EFA |
| ML848 | 22.2.44-5.1.45 |
| ML856 | 19.3.44-30.11.44 |

### *No. 201 Sqn,* Pembroke Dock
| | |
|---|---|
| DD829 | 22.12.42-10.6.44 |
| W-EJ150 | 30.3.44-3.7.45 |
| EK579 | 29.8.43-16.6.44 |
| N-ML739 | 6.4.44-11.11.44 |
| Q-ML742 | 13.1.44-3.7.45 |
| T-ML759 | 17.4.44-12.12.44 |
| \*S-ML760 | 24.4.44-12.6.44 EFB |
| V-ML764 | 22.4.44-4.8.45 |
| ML768 | 23.5.44-15.6.44 |
| ML769 | 23.5.44-16.9.44(?) |
| Y-ML813 | 22.4.44-10.11.45 |
| U-ML814 | 24.4.44-1.12.44 |
| M-ML875 | 10.4.44-10.1.45 |
| O-ML876 | 17.4.44-3.7.45 |
| P-ML881 | 18.5.44-7.3.45 |
| ML882 | 18.5.44-8.3.45 |

### *No. 228 Sqn,* Pembroke Dock
| | |
|---|---|
| DD835 | 27.5.44-10.6.44 |
| DD847 | 29.3.43-12.6.44 |
| DV958 | 19.10.43-12.6.44 |
| EJ151 | 20.4.44-11.11.44 |
| JM684 | 28.5.43-18.6.44 |
| ML745 | 27.4.44-1.10.44 FA |
| ML749 | 22.4.44-5.9.44 |
| ML762 | 30.4.44-10.6.44 FTR |
| \*J-ML763 | 4.5.44-23.7.44 |
| ML766 | 22.5.44-14.11.44 EFA, taxiing accident, Pembroke Dock |
| ML767 | 24.4.44-28.10.44 |
| ML770 | 22.5.44-21.2.45 EFA, taxiing accident |

| | off Scilly Isles |
|---|---|
| ML815 | 10.4.44-5.4.45 |
| ML877 | 10.4.44-5.4.45 |
| ML878 | 27.4.44-20.2.45 |
| ML879 | 10.5.44-2.11.44 |

### *No. 330 (Norwegian) Sqn,* Sullom Voe
| | |
|---|---|
| N-W6027 | 26.5.44-8.7.44 |
| T-W6067 | 16.3.43-6.8.44 |
| Y-DD844 | 20.3.44-15.7.44 |
| Z-DD851 | 25.4.44-20.7.44 |
| G-DD856 | 6.6.43-21.7.44 Cat E |
| F-DP184 | 6.6.43-6.7.44 |
| H-DV992 | 23.9.43-21.7.44 |
| W-EJ133 | 12.4.44-8.7.44 |
| JM667 | 3.43-11.9.44 (B FB ROS 16.5-31.7.44) |

### *No. 422 (RCAF) Sqn,* Castle Archdale
| | |
|---|---|
| B-DD845 | 5.5.43-25.6.44 |
| H-DD850 | 18.5.43-14.7.44 |
| P-DD854 | 30.5.43-25.6.44 |
| Y-DD855 | 12.2.44-12.7.44 |
| L-DP178 | 15.1.44-7.6.44 |
| T-DV970 | 15.5.44-14.7.44 |
| D-DV988 | 15.5.44-6.7.44 |
| Q-EK576 | 20.8.43-23.7.44 |
| U-EK591 | 3.10.43-22.7.44 |
| W-EK594 | 6.4.44-24.6.44 |
| EK595 | 6.4.44-30.9.44 |
| E-JM679 | 20.5.44-29.8.44 |
| S-ML836 | 22.11.43-25.6.44 |

### *No. 423 (RCAF) Sqn,* Castle Archdale
| | |
|---|---|
| DD838 | 12.5.44-28.7.44 |
| DD843 | 10.5.43-25.6.44 |
| DD849 | 28.7.43-18.7.44 |
| DD853 | 27.12.43-30.8.44 |
| DD862 | 19.12.43-31.5.45 EFA |
| DD867 | 20.8.43-2.8.44 |
| DP191 | 24.10.43-29.7.44 |
| DP193 | 1.12.43-3.8.44 |
| DV978 | 15.5.44-31.7.44 |
| DV980 | 11.5.44-4.8.44 |
| DW111 | 13.5.44-29.8.44 |
| EK575 | 12.5.44-14.8.44 |
| EK583 | 15.11.43-3.8.44 |

### *No. 461 (RAAF) Sqn,* Pembroke Dock
| | |
|---|---|
| DP196 | 16.2.44-16.9.44 |
| O-DP199 | 27.3.44-19.6.45 |
| X-DP200 | 24.3.44-26.1.45 |
| H-DV960 | 24.7.42-14.6.44 |
| F-DV989 | 3.9.42-27.10.44 |
| J-EJ138 | 6.11.43-28.12.44 |
| EK590 | 14.5.44-7.6.44 |
| \*A-ML735 | 18.3.44-15.10.44 FTR |
| P-ML741 | ?-17.2.45 |
| O-ML743 | 24.3.44-14/15.3.45 EFB, crashed into a hillside in Donegal soon after take-off |
| B-ML744 | 6.4.44-11.3.45 |
| R-ML746 | 17.3.44-18.12.44 |
| \*M-ML747 | 24.2.44-20.3.45 |
| C-ML748 | 6.4.44-11.6.44 EFB |
| Z-ML757 | 5.4.44-26.3.45 |
| E-ML758 | 6.4.44-2.5.45 |
| G-ML771 | 28.5.44-? |

# The Vickers-Armstrong Wellington

Of greater importance than numbers suggest, Wellingtons, despite being considered obsolescent, made a considerable contribution to Operation *Neptune*. Like its 1930s Vickers stablemate, the Spitfire, the Wellington by 1944 had undergone considerable modification, particularly in respect of engine power and armament. As a trainer it remained active into the early 1950s. Although withdrawn from the Bomber Command offensive in 1943, Wellington OTU *Bullseye* large-scale night exercises almost to the end of hostilities were planned to provide effective 'feints' to deceive enemy defensive radar.

First of the dedicated maritime Wellingtons was the GR Mk VIII, introduced in 1941. A 30,000 lb, 2,000 mile range Mk Ic variant, it was fitted with ASV Mk II radar and was able to carry two depth charges. Following the 1941 introduction of Hercules XI-engined Wellington Mk IIIs, and later the Hercules VI- and XVI-engined Mk X, more maritime editions were prepared. Many carried a quite spectacular item – an airborne searchlight.

For maritime night strike, assistance flares were unsuitable due to their inevitably low release, fast burn and rapid drift. A more enterprising idea was to locate the target using ASV, then floodlight it during the run-in. Such an airborne searchlight had been proposed by Sqn Ldr H. de V. Leigh, a 1940 officer in 'personnel' at HQ Coastal Command. Encouraged by ACM Sir Frederick Bowhill, AOC-in-C Coastal Command, with whom he had long been friends, Leigh developed his idea. Bowhill obtained for Leigh *P9223*, a DW 1 Wellington which, having earlier served for magnetic mine 'busting', carried a powerful generator. Messrs Savage and Parson were persuaded to build an experimental 24 in searchlight which, by January 1941, had been fitted in *P9223* where once there had been a ventral turret.

The idea was effectively tested in March, and in May 1941 tried out using a surfaced Royal Navy submarine first located by radar. Although the latter barely revealed the vessel among sea 'returns', at low-level the searchlight soon sorted out the picture. It was a most suitable item, but batteries would have to replace the too-heavy generator.

Very different was another airborne searchlight, the Helmore Turbinlite, also under development. Fitted into the nose of a Douglas Havoc, it was intended to illuminate an enemy aircraft, allowing a satellite fighter to close in for the 'kill'. Nose-mounted, heavy, and not really manoeuvrable, the Turbinlite produced diffused light and not a beam, rendering it of little value at sea. Official backing, and the support of AM Philip Joubert, ACAS (Radio), gave it an advantage, and the Leigh Light proposition was strongly opposed at high level. Even worse for Leigh, two Wellingtons were then each fitted with a Turbinlite; but undaunted, Leigh pressed on with his idea. He privately managed to persuade Savages to build a production prototype of his searchlight.

Two months passed, then a joint Royal Navy-Coastal Command team reported that the Turbinlite was completely useless for picking out surfaced U-boats. Joubert, aware of the value of Leigh's device, promptly changed his mind and backed this other contender! Bowhill immediately requested that Leigh Lights be fitted to six Wellingtons and six Catalinas – and urgently. That request came in August 1941, and with no movement by November he decided to ask for 30 Wellingtons to be so fitted. The Air Staff wanted more trials, and also told him that 20 aircraft would be sufficient – and only if the first six Wellingtons proved the idea worth pursuing. The British were exercising one of their most precious skills: unwarranted caution to delay the introduction of a highly successful idea. With what to the players seemed like regret, and after reluctantly deciding that the Leigh Light seemed to be of some use, authorization was given for 'one squadron' of Wellingtons to operate with searchlights.

Production of Wellington GR Mk VIIIs at the start of 1942 amounted to six a month. Equipping No. 1417 Leigh Light Trials Flight, formed on 8 March 1942 at Chivenor, with the now proposed 16 aircraft was expecting a lot. Nevertheless, in March 1942 GR Mk VIII production was at least increased to 20 a month. After seven months the Wellingtons – Mk VIIIs each with a retractable ventral searchlight – were at last arriving at Chivenor, at the rate of one a month. By May only five were available.

ACM Joubert replaced Bowhill as AOC-in-C Coastal Command in June 1942 and, knowing the saga of the Leigh Light, in sheer exasperation ordered Chivenor-based No. 172 Squadron (formed on 4 April 1942 from No. 1417 Flight) to start operating. Late on 3 June, four of its five Wellingtons were dispatched and, using their ASV Mk II, easily found and illuminated small ship contacts. Best of all, *ES986-F* flown by Sqn Ldr J.H. Creswell returned after illuminating two surfaced U-boats. One of them was an Italian Navy boat which had been attacked with depth charges and was to be sunk three days later by a Sunderland of No. 10 (RAAF) Squadron. The other was machine-gunned, doubtless giving the crew an amazing tale to relate. Submarines thereafter were quick to avoid night lights. As for Joubert, he demanded more Leigh Lights, and fast!

Wellington Leigh Light operations were not all that simple. Without an accurate altimeter for low flying it was easy to fly into the sea – especially with the light 'on'. But after July 1942, when a Leigh Light Wellington made the first 'kill', the decision was made to form a second squadron, along with development of underwing nacelle lights for Liberators and Catalinas. The new risks in night surfacing forced the well-defended U-boats to surface more by day, but only briefly to charge their batteries. Of 27 U-boat sightings in Biscay during June 1942, only seven involved searchlight illumination. In July French tunny fishermen put to sea in Biscay, greatly increasing the difficulty of finding (by using ASV Mk II) the small radar 'blips' made by submarines. Next month, U-boats began to be fitted with an ASV detector, range up to 30 miles.

August 1942 saw seven Wellingtons of No. 172 Squadron move to Skitten, satellite station of Wick, which led, on 1 September, to the formation of the second squadron, No. 179, based at Wick for night search sorties towards the north-east. In November the squadron moved to Gibraltar to operate by night off Portugal and over southern Biscay in support of Operation *Torch*. Ultimately 58 Wellington Mk VIIIs (Temperate) were fitted with Leigh Lights. Also available, from January 1943, were Hercules-powered maritime Wellingtons; first the GR Mk XI (Hercules VI and ASV Mk II) and then 40 Leigh Light-fitted Mk XIIs (Hercules VI and ASV Mk II) supplied initially to No. 172 Squadron which introduced the type to operations on 6/7 March 1943. Disappointment with results at the time came mainly because U-boat commanders were playing safe. Their crews, staying surfaced, also started to fight back, but when in March ASV G Mk III came into use radiating emissions which U-boat equipment could not detect, the advantage again tilted in Coastal Command's favour. No. 172 Squadron proved that by sinking the *U-665* on 20 March.

By 1943 the Wellington Mk X, a generally improved Mk III in which the Hercules XI engines were replaced first by Mk VIs and then Mk XVIs to improve climb rate, speed and ceiling, was in full production. Maximum take-off weight rose to 34,500 lb, but the bomb load remained only 4,500 lb. Adaptation of the Mk X for a general reconnaissance role resulted in the Mks XIII and XIV. The former, all-up weight 36,500 lb, entered production in April 1943 and when fitted with Hercules XVII engines to enhance low-level attack performance, had a top speed of 245 mph at 500 ft. The 36,000 lb Mk XIV, like the Mk XII, carried a retractable Leigh Light amidships, and featured a prominent nose radome encasing ASV G Mk III and nose contours similar to those of the Wellington Mk I. The GR Mk XIV, which entered production in May 1943, had a top speed of 248 mph at 500 ft, and carrying a 4,950 lb offensive load had a cruising range of 1,365 miles. No. 172 Squadron first operated Mk XIVs on the night of 19 August 1943, by which time four No. 19 Group Leigh Light Wellington Mk XII/XIV squadrons (Nos. 172, 179, 407 and 612, each holding 12 + 3

*Some Wellington GR Mk XIVs of RAF Coastal Command acquired black 'invasion stripes' on the lower fuselage.* NB772 *is shown as* P-Peter *of No. 524 Squadron. (via A.S. Thomas)*

aircraft and soon joined by No. 304 Squadron) were operating over the Bay of Biscay and between Gibraltar and Cape Finistere. Maritime Wellington production was still limited, only 364 being built between July and the end of December 1943, many of them fitted out for overseas use. In November 1943 the Air Staff outlined improvements for the Mk XIV for introduction in 1944. These included a single .300 in front gun, useful during an attack profile and to be retrospectively fitted; also 2 x .300 in guns for production aircraft. ASV Mk VI radar would be tried in six aircraft at Defford, then at 32 MU 10 aircraft would be converted monthly. On the production lines, Wellington XIVs were by late 1943 being built at the ratio of 15 Tropical to five Temperate examples. There remained a need for balance in production of the two types.

Wellington Mk XIV squadrons were, in April 1944, ordered to help prevent U-boats entering the English Channel to sink ships assembling for the forthcoming invasion. For the purpose four squadrons gathered at Chivenor: No. 172 Squadron joined by No. 407 Squadron from St Eval, by No. 304 Squadron on 19 February 1944 and by No. 612 Squadron on 5 March. By then there were over 60 Wellington Mk XIVs and another 15 of No. 179 Squadron at Predannack, where they arrived from Gibraltar on 24 April. In August 1943 the Air Staff had asked for Liberators to replace all these Wellingtons, but Lend-

Lease deliveries were insufficient to permit that. Instead, 11 Wellingtons patrolled at night on 5/6 June, and 16 the following night when No. 407 Squadron's *HF149* flown by Sqn Ldr D.W. Farrell failed to return. The success of the Leigh Light Wellingtons and others should not be measured by the number of submarines attacked; the very fact that the U-boats could not break through at this most important time was Coastal Command's greatest success.

## Wellington GR Mk XIVs on squadron strength, 5 June 1944

* operated on 5/6.6.44

### No. 172 Sqn, Chivenor

|  |  |
|---|---|
| HF147 | 8.5.44-22.7.44 |
| HF183 | 7.10.43-14.11.44 Cat E |
| HF197 | 15.9.43-8.5.44, 13.6.44-23.9.44 |
| HF246 | 27.5.44-17.8.44 EFB |
| HF335 | 30.5.44-15.4.45 |
| HF392 | 2.3.44-16.9.44 |
| HF411 | 9.4.44-12.6.44 |
| HF422 | 28.4.44-22.3.45 |
| *S-HF446 | 28.2.44-15.6.44 FTR |
| HF449 | 27.4.44-29/30.7.44 FTR |
| MP724 | 7.10.43-3.3.44, 3.6.44-8.6.44 |
| MP789 | 3.5.44-19.4.45 |
| Z-NB800 | 19.5.44-24.3.45 |
| NB801 | 15.5.44-16.6.45 |
| NB804 | 27.5.44-10.4.45 |
| NB805 | 13.5.44-25/26.6.44 FTR |
| NB808 | 25.5.44-25.7.44, 9.9.44-22.4.45 |
| NB809 | 27.5.44-29.7.44 EFB, burnt |

### No. 179 Sqn, Predannack

|  |  |
|---|---|
| HF123 | ?-25.10.44 |

*A main base for Wellington GR Mk XIVs was Chivenor where this example of No. 304 Squadron was photographed. (IWM HU4067)*

| | |
|---|---|
| J-HF143 | 26.7.43-24.6.44 FTR |
| IIF154 | 13.9.43-21.6.45 |
| *K-HF189 | 8.5.44-12.6.44 FTR |
| HF195 | 30.11.43-5.12.44 |
| HF222 | 16.10.43-6.44 |
| HF225 | 11.11.43-16.9.44 |
| R-HF309 | 11.1.44-14.6.44 FTR |
| HF312 | 16.2.44-20.9.44 |
| HF361 | 4.3.44-31.10.44 |
| HF394 | 4.3.44-8.1.45 |
| HF406 | 1.4.44-6.12.44 |
| HF408 | 31.3.44-8.6.44 AC FA |
| MP741 | 30.7.43-21.10.43, 19.12.43-26.8.44 |

## No. 304 Sqn, Chivenor

| | |
|---|---|
| E-HF303 | 6.4.44-? |
| G-HF304 | 20.4.44-30.5.44, 25.6.44-27.6.44 |
| Y-HF329 | 6.4.44-22.4.45 |
| N-HF330 | 11.4.44-9.5.44, 10.6.44-31.5.45 |
| M-HF334 | 10.4.44-13.6.45 |
| W-HF386 | 10.4.44-20.6.44 |
| K-HF388 | 10.4.44-17.5.45 |
| *X-HF397 | 10.4.44-17.5.45 |
| HF420 | 26.4.44-5.6.45 |
| *B-HF421 | 20.4.44-31.5.45 |
| V-HF448 | 26.4.44-13.6.45 |
| S-HF451 | 26.4.44-17.5.45 |
| NF767 | 27.4.44-20.3.45 EFB |
| NB779 | 30.5.44-10.7.44 |
| NB806 | 28.5.44-22.6.45 |

## No. 407 Sqn, Chivenor

| | |
|---|---|
| HF134 | 11.4.44-6.9.44 |
| HF135 | 31.5.44-19.7.44 |
| HF144 | 23.12.43-21/22.6.44 FTR |
| HF145 | 30.3.44-19.6.44 Cat E |

| | |
|---|---|
| HF149 | 4.5.44-6/7.6.44 FTR |
| IIF152 | 7.10.43-29.1.44, 25.3.44-30.5.44, 1.7.44 31.7.44 |
| HF169 | 18.12.43-19.3.44, 24.6.44-6.9.44 |
| HF171 | 7.10.43-19.7.44 |
| HF184 | 18.8.43-19.7.44 |
| HF269 | 27.3.44-21.7.44 |
| HF280 | 31.5.44-21.7.44 |
| HF286 | 29.1.44-21.7.44 |
| *A-HF302 | 7.2.44-9.8.44 |
| HF305 | 24.2.44-21.7.44 |
| HF363 | 31.5.44-31.7.44 |
| HF382 | 31.5.44-8.9.44 |
| HF410 | 5.6.44-28.7.44 |
| HF412 | 8.5.44-7.7.44 EFB |
| HF413 | 4.5.44-25.6.44 |

## No. 612 Sqn, Chivenor

| | |
|---|---|
| HF148 | 10.2.44-6.7.44, 22.7.44-21.12.44 |
| HF227 | 17.1.44-17.11.44 |
| HF250 | 24.11.43-15.5.44, 25.6.44-29.11.44 |
| HF270 | 1.12.43-2.12.44 |
| HF333 | 27.2.44-18.5.44, 20.6.44-1.10.44 |
| HF385 | 27.3.44-21.6.44 BFA |
| HF387 | 26.3.44-9.11.44 |
| HF389 | 26.3.44-5.8.44 |
| HF390 | 27.3.44-2.1.45 |
| HF391 | 30.3.44-22/23.6.44 FTR |
| HF393 | 27.3.44-13.11.44 |
| HF395 | 25.3.44-16.11.44 |
| HF396 | 24.3.44-7.11.44 |
| HF398 | 27.3.44-27.11.44 |
| HF399 | 26.3.44-29.8.44 |
| HF447 | 24.4.44-21.10.44 |
| MP714 | 30.12.43-15.5.44, 17.6.44-19.9.44 |
| NB807 | 27.5.44-23.9.44 BFA |

# Coastal Command's photographic reconnaissance Spitfires

The early days of the photographic reconnaissance (PR) Spitfires are described in *Aircraft for the Few* (PSL). By D-Day, development of these specialized aircraft had reached its peak, for on 30 April 1944 the RAF's first two Griffon-engined PR Mk XIXs arrived at Benson. Five distinct PR Spitfires were then in use.

Whereas the early PR Spitfires had virtually been 'one-off' modified MK Is, by 1942 standardization had been reached in the PR Mk IV, a production reconnaissance version of the Mk V. Only one Mk IV – non-operational – remained at Benson on D-Day. The mainstream PR Spitfire by then was the PR Mk XI, a derivative of the Merlin 60-series-engined Mk IX fighter redesigned to accommodate two cameras in a special 'universal' mounting in the rear fuselage. Delivery began in early 1943 and *EN343* of No. 542 Squadron flown by Flg Off F.G. Fray on 17 May 1943 secured the first photographs showing the broken Mohne and Sorpe Dams. Next day Flg Off D.G. Scott flying *EN411* secured photographs showing the extent of flooding. By D-Day deliveries had reached *PL847*, then at Benson.

At that time the two Benson squadrons also held 12 of the 16 PR Mk Xs, converted Spitfire F Mk VII airframes powered by the Merlin and differing from the Mk XI by having a pressure cabin installed. Although adding to pilot comfort on long flights, the new cabin significantly added to the weight of the aircraft and thus affected performance.

There were also four PR Mk XIIIs in use, modified PR Mk IVs fitted with Merlin 32 engines for low-level operations. By D-Day both Benson-based squadrons each held five Griffon-engined Spitfire PR Mk XIXs, of which 22 had by then been delivered. The first operational sortie by a Mk XIX was undertaken by *RM628* of No. 542 Squadron on 24 May 1944.

On 6 June the following sorties were flown by 542 Squadron from Benson:

**Spitfire PR Mk XIX**
| | | |
|---|---|---|
| 08:50-10:30 | *RM632* | PR of *Noball* sites, Cherbourg area |
| 14:40-16:20 | *RM638* | PR of invasion area, photos around Caen |
| 14:45-16:20 | *RM632* | PR of invasion area, photos around Caen |
| 18:00-19:45 | *RM632* | PR of invasion area, Caen area |

**Spitfire PR Mk XI**
| | | |
|---|---|---|
| 06:50-08:30 | *EN396* | PR of *Noball* sites, Boulogne–Amiens area |
| 10:05-11:35 | *EN667* | PR of gun positions, Calais |
| 16:30-17:50 | *EN652* | PR of coastal guns, Calais to Le Touquet |

Only one sortie was flown by No. 541 Squadron, by Gp Cpt Beamish, who in *RM629* tried to secure photographs of the invasion area but was defeated by dense cloud.

## Coastal Command PR Spitfires (PR Mk XI unless otherwise stated)

### No. 541 Sqn, Benson

| | |
|---|---|
| EN662 | 10.7.43-18.6.44 |
| Q-EN664 | 26.7.43-18.6.44 |
| EN666 | 22.7.43-11.9.44 |
| EN683 | 22.9.43-18.6.44 |
| EN906 | (Mk Vb) 13.10.43-18.6.44 |
| EN907 | (Mk Vb) 13.10.43-12.7.44 |
| T-MB787 | 31.6.43-30.8.44 |
| E-MB903 | 10.10.43-18.6.44 |
| Z-MB907 | 13.10.43-12.7.44 |
| PA859 | 26.3.44-1.1.45 B EA |
| PA864 | 29.12.43-7.11.44 |
| H-PA868 | 12.43-5.7.44 B FB |
| G-PA942 | 14.3.44-15.6.44 |
| V-PA943 | 14.3.44-7.11.44 |
| PL775 | 14.5.44-8.9.45 |

PR Mk X:
| | |
|---|---|
| MD191 | 23.5.44-12.2.45 |
| MD193 | 8.5.44-11.8.44, 23.9.44-25.8.45 |
| MD195 | 23.5.44-5.12.44 |
| MD197 | 25.5.44-15.7.44 RIW |
| MD199 | 23.5.44-13.1.45 B FB |

PR MK XIII:
| | |
|---|---|
| W3135 | 25.4.43-14.9.44 |
| AR319 | 25.4.43-26.8.44 RIW |

PR MK XIX:
| | |
|---|---|
| *RM629 | 2.6.44-5.7.44 |
| RM631 | 2.6.44-9.3.45 FTR |

# To sink the E-boats: No. 415 (RCAF) Squadron and the Fairey Albacore

The Canadian Government most certainly did *not* approve. Their airmen had not crossed the Atlantic to fight the Germans by using antique Albacore biplanes. No. 415 (RCAF) Squadron, the RCAF's Air Marshal Breadner emphasized, should be a bomber squadron. He waged an uphill fight!

Why indeed were they flying Albacores, which the Fleet Air Arm viewed as obsolescent? From 1942 until March 1943, two squadrons of FAA Albacore biplane torpedo bombers flew anti-E-boat sorties over the North Sea and English Channel. Then in June 1943 the Admiralty had to embark other squadrons, leaving shipping off the south and east coasts of England at the mercy of the E-boats. By August 1943, with the approach of longer dark nights, the importance of an anti-E-boat force was stressed by Fighter Command which, because it operated suitable radars, controlled the operation.

Well positioned to take on the task was No. 415, the Canadian-manned torpedo bomber squadron based at Thorney Island. Operating within the anti-U-boat force, it was primarily intended to use its Hampden TBR Mk Is against Biscay blockade runners. Being few in number, they generated little profitable work for a torpedo bomber squadron in the area; and in any case, other aircraft could tackle them. Of the four torpedo bomber squadrons in Britain No. 415 (RCAF) Squadron could most readily be switched to other tasks. Such was the supply rate that it could not in any case have converted to Beaufighter torpedo bombers before May 1944.

When the Canadian Government learnt of a plan to replace the Hampdens with early-war Albacore 'antique torpedo bomber biplanes', there were harsh words. Yet on dark nights, carrying 250 lb bombs, they could seek out and very effectively dive-bomb E-boats. In October 1943 Albacores were firmly chosen for No. 415 (RCAF) Squadron. Then came another surprise – only half the squadron would have Albacores and would be based at Manston to operate over the English Channel; the rest would equip with what the Canadians somewhat unfairly called 'obsolescent' Wellington GR Mk XIIIs, to be operated from Bircham Newton/Docking and used to search for E-boats at night as far as 60 miles out from the East Anglian coast. The squadron would remain part of No. 16 Group, Coastal Command, although No. 11 Group, Fighter Command, would control Albacore

Channel operations. During October Albacores (some from No. 841 Squadron, FAA, at Manston) began joining the squadron, along with Wellington XIIIs.

The possibility of E-boat attacks during the forthcoming invasion was taken very seriously. Two were made on Channel shipping during December 1943 and that led to urgent requests from the Royal Navy for the RAF Albacores to be positioned at Thorney Island, which meant forming a detached servicing echelon.

By February 1944 No. 415 (RCAF) Squadron's HQ and 10 aircraft of Wellington Flight were at Bircham Newton/Docking to carry out flare-dropping for 'Torbeaus' and bombing attacks on shipping off the Dutch coast. If E-boats were sighted, AC HQ Chatham was informed and despatched surface forces to engage them. Wellingtons shadowed the operation, guiding the naval craft. Nine Albacores fitted with ASV Mk II radar and VHF were detached to Manston as 'Albacore Flight'. There they came under the control of Vice-Admiral Dover. Three more Albacores were at Thorney Island under C-in-C Portsmouth, and another three at Bircham Newton came under the control of AC HQ Chatham while awaiting transfer to Winkleigh and C-in-C Plymouth. Although the squadron structure

was complex and fragmented, its importance was considerable; so much so that late February 1944 brought a suggestion that the Wellington Flight become a new No. 210 Squadron and the Albacores equip a 'Special Albacore Flight'. Instead, a second Wellington GR Mk XIII squadron, No. 524 and 10-aircraft strong, formed at Davidstowe Moor on 7 April to seek E-boats operating in the run-up to and during the invasion. The Air Ministry repeatedly pointed out to the Canadians the value of their squadron's work, and did not consider the Wellington GR Mk XIII 'obsolescent'. Yet by 25 February there had been only one E-boat sinking attributed to Albacores. On 21 December 1943 six had been attacked, but only one received a direct hit. On six occasions Albacores had attacked surface ships during 113 sorties.

Employing such aircraft in a possible fierce fight during Operation *Neptune* was now reviewed, the fear being that only Wellingtons might survive. That implied arming the whole of No. 415 Squadron with Wellingtons – and that the Canadians would not accept. Instead they stated their preference even for the Albacore! On 2 March 1944 the British gave way; yes, No. 415 could reform in Bomber Command – but not before September. That, too,

*An all-black Albacore of No. 415 (RCAF) Squadron at Thorney Island. No. 119 Squadron later operated 'NH'-marked Albacores. (IWM CL1635)*

annoyed the Canadians, who then said that in the meantime their crews must fly only the Albacores; not Wellingtons, which had long before been replaced in their bomber squadrons. But the British continued planning; 415's Wellingtons would be switched to No. 425 Squadron on 19 July 1944 and Albacore Flight (concentrated at Manston) would become No. 119 Squadron.

No. 415 Squadron, in the period immediately preceding D-Day, flew three types of operations. *Deadly* patrols, undertaken against small surface warships, began on 3 November 1943, and by 31 March 1944 159 sorties had resulted in sightings of over 40 E-boats and seven attacks. *Gilbey* patrols, flown by Wellingtons, had taken place on 15 nights. During the 17 sorties there had been nine sightings, and two attacks using 500 lb bombs. *Dutch Coast* patrols began on 1 March 1944, and during 11 over seven nights two attacks led to two Wellingtons being lost.

Coastal Command again reminded the RCAF of the importance of the Albacores' work, but limited *Channel Stop* success was rated insufficient to deter enemy E-boats from operating in force, as seemed likely, during *Neptune*. Yet rearming the whole squadron with Wellingtons would have taken at least two months – and at a very unsuitable time. The naval view was that the Albacores remained quite suitable; but since the RAF wanted more Wellingtons, it proposed another, third Flight using Wellingtons.

That suggestion soon led to final agreement. Only RAF aircrews would be posted to No. 415 Squadron from 1 April 1944, and when the proportion of RCAF personnel fell below 50 per cent those would then be posted to Bomber Command's No. 6 (RCAF) Group. Approval was given for No. 524 Squadron to move to Bircham Newton in mid-July to take over the 10 ASV Mk II radar/Mk XIV bombsight Wellington GR XIIIs of No. 415 Squadron. Although using Leigh Light-equipped Wellington GR Mk XIVs was suggested it was not favoured, for the area of illumination produced by the searchlight was too limited and approach with light exposed too hazardous. The new squadron's role remained that of seeking ships at sea, reporting their whereabouts,

then illuminating them for a strike force.

During June 1944 No. 415 Squadron was very active, its first D-Day success coming at 23:59 hrs on 6 June when Wellington *HZ649-M* of 415 Squadron, Docking, attacked four E-boats, capsizing one and causing an explosion aboard another. Two more were damaged off Cap Gris Nez by an Albacore operating from Manston early on 7 June, and that night two Wellingtons probably sank two more. One was credited to Wg Cdr C.G. Ruttan DSO and crew. Albacores were particularly successful on 23 June when *V* scored a direct hit on an E-boat, *Y* damaged two and *M* tackled a small warship. By then the end for No. 415 (RCAF) Squadron in Coastal Command was near and on 2 July 1944 personnel of No. 524 Squadron began arriving at Bircham Newton to take over 415's tasks. The last Albacore sorties controlled by 415 were flown on 20 July 1944 when eight from Manston laid smoke during daylight to protect a Channel convoy, then carried out supporting patrols. Not until January 1945 did Albacores (with No. 119 Squadron) cease to be operational, and after a busy career. Luckily the Canadians did not have to handle their replacement – that even more aged design, the Fairey Swordfish!

## OPERATIONS BY NO. 415 (RCAF) SQUADRON, 5/6 JUNE 1944

**Wellington Flight (usual weapon load 4 x 500 lb MC HE plus 32 reconnaissance flares):**

| Time | Aircraft | Notes |
|---|---|---|
| 22:07-05:22 | B-HZ649 | Visual, anti-E-boat |
| 22:59-03:13 | A-JA635 | Patrol Z |
| 23:00-04:24 | M-HZ650 | Crossover patrol |
| ??:??-??:?? | L-????? | Patrol W |

**Albacore Flight (usual weapon load 2 x 250 lb GP HE):**

| Time | Aircraft | Notes |
|---|---|---|
| 23:52-02:39 | ?-????? | From Manston, Dunkirk-Berck patrol |
| 23:55-02:25 | E-????? | From Manston, Channel search |
| 01:47-04:03 | L-????? | From Manston, Channel search |
| 01:50-04:05 | H-????? | From Manston, Channel search |

## OPERATIONS BY NO. 415 (RCAF) SQUADRON, 6/7 JUNE 1944

**Wellington Flight:**

| Time | Aircraft | Notes |
|---|---|---|
| 22:15-05:35 | M-HZ650 | Crossover patrol |
| 23:07-04:31 | A-JA635 | Crossover Patrol B |
| 23:13-04:43 | C-????? | Crossover Patrol Z |

**Albacore Flight:**

| | | |
|---|---|---|
| 23:35-00:17 | *X-?????* | Channel patrol |
| 23:52-00:50 | *E-?????* | Attacked seven small vessels off Cap Gris Nez |
| 01:30-01:53 | *J-?????* | Abortive |
| 01:20-03:20 | *E-?????* | Channel patrol |
| 02:40-04:10 | *H-?????* | Attacked E-boats off Cap Gris Nez |

## Albacores & Wellingtons on squadron strength, 5 June 1944

\* operated on 5/6 June 1944

### No. 415 (RCAF) Squadron, Bircham Newton/Docking/Manston

Wellington Mk XIII

| | |
|---|---|
| *HZ639* | 4.10.43-7.44 |
| *O-HZ644* | 25.10.43-17.7.44 |
| *\*B-HZ649* | 15.10.43-13.6.44 FTR |
| *M-HZ650* | 28.9.43-17.7.44 |
| *HZ653* | 28.9.43-17.7.44 |
| *H-HZ659* | 15.10.43-13.6.44 FTR |
| *HZ702* | 28.9.43-17.7.44 |
| *J-HZ721* | 28.9.43-17.7.44 |
| *\*\*A-JA635* | 20.2.44-17.7.44 |
| *\*D-MF213* | 3.2.44-17.7.44 |
| *MF233* | 26.5.44-17.7.44 |

Albacore

| | |
|---|---|
| *C1-L7123* | 6.4.44-25.7.44 |

| | |
|---|---|
| *T9150* | ?-25.7.44 |
| *X8940* | ?-25.7.44 |
| *X8949* | 29.3.44-25.7.44 |
| *X8951* | 30.5.44-25.7.44 |
| *X9074* | 1.5.44-25.7.44 |
| *X9186* | 1.5.44-25.7.44 |
| *X9215* | ?-25.7.44 |
| *X9220* | 10.5.44-25.7.44 |
| *A1-X9222* | ?-25.7.44 |
| *X9257* | ?-25.7.44 |
| *X9281* | ?-25.7.44 |
| *X9290* | ?-25.7.44 |
| *BF586* | ?-25.7.44 |
| *BF593* | 20.4.44-25.7.44 |
| *P1-BF600* | ?-25.7.44 |
| *BF651* | 5.44-25.7.44 |
| *BF730* | 3.5.44-25.7.44 |

NB: Although the Albacores became part of No. 119 Squadron from 19.7.44, their handover date was 25.7.44.

Vickers Armstrong Wellington GR Mk XIIIs used by No. 524 Squadron on anti-E-boat sorties from April 1944 included:

### No.524 Sqn, Davidstowe Moor

| | |
|---|---|
| *MF234* | 2.6.44-1.9.44 |
| *C-MF320* | |
| *MF373* | 22.4.44-3.2.45 |
| *MF374* | 24.4.44-13.7.44 FTR |

# The Air-Sea Rescue force

## Vickers-Armstrong Warwick ASR Mk I

The Warwick's development is outlined elsewhere in this volume, and the type formed the backbone of Coastal Command's deep-sea rescue force, supplementing the Lockheed Hudsons of No. 279 Squadron still based at Bircham Newton. All played a subsidiary role in Operation *Neptune*, Coastal Command's aircraft including the following:

### No. 280 Sqn, Strubby

| | |
|---|---|
| *BV290* | 14.9.43-9.10.44 FTR |
| *BV304* | 6.9.43-9.11.44 EFA, burnt out |
| *BV308* | 4.12.43-1.10.44 EFA |
| *BV311* | 4.12.43-18.11.44 |
| *BV313* | 7.9.43-19.10.44 |
| *BV314* | 6.9.43-28.9.46 EFA |
| *BV335* | 10.43-16.2.45 |
| *BV337* | 17.11.43-29.6.44 EFB |
| *BV338* | 5.12.43-18.11.44 |
| *BV340* | 5.12.43-2.11.44 |
| *BV341* | 6.10.43-15.10.44 |

| | |
|---|---|
| *BV345* | 4.12.43-22.5.45 FA AC |
| *BV349* | 15.9.43-8.12.44 |
| *BV351* | 6.11.43-16.1.45 |
| *BV352* | 10.11.43-12.12.44 |
| *BV367* | 15.9.43-25.10.43, 25.1.44-8.4.45 |
| *BV368* | 14.9.43-7.10.44 FTR |
| *BV384* | 13.9.43-26.11.44 |
| *BV385* | 16.9.43-3.3.45 |
| *BV386* | 25.11.43-6.4.45 |
| *BV471* | 19.12.43-31.7.44 B FB |
| *HF947* | 8.3.44-8.12.44 |
| *HF981* | 7.5.44-17.11.44 |

### No. 281 Sqn, Tiree

Gave cover over seas around northern half of Britain, using Lindholme gear until May 1944 when use of airborne lifeboat began.

| | |
|---|---|
| *BV284* | 5.12.43-28.6.44 FA, RIW |
| *BV303* | 25.1.44-25.5.45 |
| *BV309* | 25.1.44-18.3.45 |
| *BV392* | 29.12.43-17.11.44 |
| *BV401* | 15.4.44-17.11.44 |
| *BV404* | 9.12.43-17.11.44 |
| *BV405* | 9.12.43-?.44 |
| *BV407* | 13.12.43-15.5.45 |
| *BV411* | 11.12.43-2.7.44, 26.8.44-14.9.44 EFA |

BV413  11.12.43-17.11.44
BV414  29.12.43-26.9.44, 28.11.44-7.12.44
BV417  30.12.43-3.8.44 Cat E, during MR
BV419  29.12.43-17.11.44
BV440  1.1.44-17.11.44
BV474  19.12.43-3.11.44
BV481  3.1.44-18.5.45
BV516  31.12.43-17.11.44

### *No. 282 Sqn*, **Davidstowe Moor**

Moved to Davidstowe Moor 2.44; resumed operations 15.4.44. First rescue using lifeboat 27.4.44.

BV286  29.3.44-18.3.45
BV288  29.3.44-18.3.45
BV316  4.6.44-10.9.44 EFA, burnt out
BV410  26.4.44-23.11.44
HF942  15.3.44-29.8.44 AC FB
HF944  8.3.44-12.5.45
HF950  3.3.44-12.9.44 EFA
HF952  3.3.44-3.4.45
HF959  3.3.44-8.6.44 FTR, crashed at sea
HF961  18.3.44-30.10.45
HF962  18.3.44-23.7.45
HF963  3.3.44-23.11.44
HF964  16.2.44-4.11.44
HF967  18.5.44-26.11.44
HF969  3.3.44-3.45
HF974  23.3.44-23.11.44

HF975  3.3.44-23.11.44
HF976  18.3.44-23.7.44
HF977  8.3.44-27.11.44
HF978  5.3.44-6.6.44 AC FB, 23.6.44-2.5.45
HF979  23.3.44-26.11.44
HG130  19.3.44-3.7.44 BFB

## Lockheed Hudson III/VI

On 5 May 1943 Hudson W/279 Squadron was the first aircraft to drop an airborne lifeboat operationally, when it released *W.N.5* to the crew of a ditched Halifax of No. 102 Squadron. On 31 July the sixth lifeboat was dropped, to the crew of Mitchell Q/226 Squadron. The squadron continued this duty, using a variety of Hudsons until late 1944, and even made drops close to the Dutch coast. Examples of Hudsons in use in June 1944 include these:

V9118  (Mk III) 22.1.44-21.10.44
V9161  (Mk III) 22.1.44-24.8.44
AE533  (Mk III) 10.6.43-13.9.44
EW914  (Mk VI) 14.3.43-7.11.44
FK450  (Mk VI) 17.3.43-30.11.44

# The Naval contribution

Throughout the war, home-placed shore-based Fleet Air Arm squadrons operated against German shipping, sometimes in conjunction with RAF Coastal Command, quite often with Fighter Command. During December 1943 the Air Ministry asked the Admiralty whether the FAA could loan any squadrons to RAF Coastal Command, for *Channel Stop* and anti-E-boat operations.

In response, 30 Corsairs and 30 Barracudas were offered, then on 29 January 1944 complete squadrons, each of 20 aircraft, and a total of 1,500 ratings, were proposed. This was further defined as comprising eight squadrons of fighters (probably Seafire IIcs, Corsairs and Hellcats). Spotting for naval gunners would involve another 72 Seafires. Two squadrons of Barracudas were available for the anti-E-boat task, and two squadrons of Avengers for daylight shipping strike. The Air Ministry replied that the latter two types would need to be attached to Coastal

Command about two months before D-Day in order to work-up.

During February 1944 a plan was conceived whereby Nos. 808, 886 and 897 Squadrons, Fleet Air Arm, would be discharged, then reform as No. 3 Naval Fighter Wing at Lee-on-Solent to become gunnery spotting squadrons. These, along with Nos. 26 and 63 Squadrons (RAF) would form an Air Spotting Pool.

There were, however, no particular roles for Corsairs and Hellcats, nor for the Barracudas. Therefore the FAA suggested substituting Swordfishes, a type long used operationally by squadrons shore-based in Britain. A new agreement was reached on 29 March 1944 to make six squadrons available, from 20 April, for Operation *Neptune*. The force would be composed of two Avenger squadrons using Perranporth or St David's, a Swordfish squadron at Perranporth and another at Harrowbeer, and at Manston (under No. 16 Group) one

*A Fleet Air Arm Seafire L Mk III used as a gunnery observation aircraft. (IWM CL520)*

Avenger and one Swordfish squadron. First task for the four squadrons in the south-west (No. 19 Group area) would be to afford day and night cover and close escort to invasion convoys in passage from the Bristol Channel to Portland. The two squadrons at Manston would similarly protect convoys sailing North Foreland to Beachy Head. In addition, Swordfishes would carry out anti-E- and R-boat sorties at night.

Avengers in Britain were still comparatively few. No. 846 Squadron was trained and already allocated to HMS *Tracker*, but No. 852 would not complete training until 15 June and was earmarked for HMS *Nabob*; No. 854 Squadron was in early training and listed for HMS *Trumpeter*. Eventually the Fleet Air Arm contributed the following squadrons to Operation *Neptune*:

### Avengers

| | | | | | |
|---|---|---|---|---|---|
| 848 | Manston | 20.4.44-14.6.44 | Thorney Island | 14.6.44-24.8.44 | 12 Avenger I |
| 854 | Hawkinge | 23.5.44-7.8.44 | Thorney Island | 7.8.44-27.8.44 | 12 Avenger II |
| 855 | Hawkinge | 31.5.44-6.8.44 | Thorney Island | 6.8.44-7.9.44 | 12 Avenger II |
| | Docking | 7.9.44-21.10.44 | | | |
| 849 | Perranporth | 20.4.44-5.8.44 | St Eval | 5.8.44-26.8.44 | 12 Avenger I |
| 850 | Perranporth | 23.4.44-1.1.8.44 | | | 12 Avenger I |

### Swordfish II (ASV Mk X): Anti-shipping and anti-U-boat strike force

| | | | |
|---|---|---|---|
| 819 | Manston | 18.4.44-7.8.44 | Belgium, Swingfield and Bircham Newton to 2.45 |
| 816 | Perranporth | 20.4.44-1.8.44 | Each squadron equipped with 12 Swordfish IIs |
| 838 | Harrobeer | 20.4.44-8.8.44 | |

### Seafires, 3rd Naval Fighter Wing, Lee-on-Solent: Air Spotting Pool, No. 34 Reconnaissance Wing, 2nd TAF

| | | |
|---|---|---|
| 808 | 14.5.44-19.7.44 | 10 Spitfire L Mk Vbs |
| 885 | 13.5.44-19.7.44 | 885 absorbed 897 on 15.7.44 and 886 on 19.7.44.12 Seafire L Mk IIIs |
| 886 | 20.5.44-19.7.44 | Disbanded 19.7.44, 10 Seafire L Mk IIIs |
| 897 | 21.5.44-15.7.44 | Disbanded 15.7.44, 10 Spitfire L Mk Vbs |

### Wildcats

| | | | |
|---|---|---|---|
| 881 | HMS *Pursuer* | 5.6.44-11.6.44 | 881 absorbed 896 on 12.6.44 |
| 896 | HMS *Pursuer* | 5.6.44-11.6.44 | Fighter protection for convoy escort groups, western end of English Channel |

### Avengers and Wildcats

| | | | |
|---|---|---|---|
| 846 | HMS *Tracker* | 5.6.44-11.6.44 | A-S/fighter cover, south-west approaches to English Channel |

### Hellcats

| | | | |
|---|---|---|---|
| 800 | HMS *Emperor* | 7.6.44-18.6.44 | Fighter protection for convoy escort groups, western end of |
| 804 | HMS *Emperor* | 7.6.44-18.6.44 | English Channel |

The No. 19 Group Avenger squadrons commenced *TFN* patrols in daylight on 4 June, and were very active on the afternoon of 5 June.

Swordfishes operated in darkness. The agreement was for these squadrons to serve with Coastal Command until 1 August 1944, although U-boat activity in the English Channel caused some extensions and replacement by other squadrons.

## PATROLS IN NO. 19 GROUP AREA, 6 JUNE 1944

| Sqn | Aircraft | Time up/Day | Time down/Day |
|-----|----------|-------------|---------------|
| 816 | G, P | 19:57 | 23:05 |
| 838 | L | 20:06 | 23:06 |
| 838 | R | 21:56/5 | 01:05 |
| 838 | T | 22:10/5 | 02:05 |
| 816 | A | 22:15/5 | 01:03 |
| 816 | K, L | 23:55/5 | 02:50 |
| 838 | A | 00:07 | 03:10 |
| 816 | B, V, Q | 01:02 | 04:07 |
| 838 | H | 01:53 | 05:16 |
| 838 | C | 02:08 | 05:00 |
| 816 | M | 02:20 | 04:50 |
| 838 | B | 03:55 | 07:02 |
| 838 | Z | 04:04 | 07:02 |
| 816 | F | 04:14 | 06:52 |
| 849 | G, F, H | 06:10 | 09:12 |
| 849 | M, A, C | 08:30 | 11:39 |
| 849 | L, P, Q | 10:45 | 14:20 |
| 850 | G, A, H | 13:04 | 16:34 |
| 850 | K, C, M | 15:25 | 18:35 |
| 850 | F, Q, R | 17:50 | 21:50 |
| 816 | F | 19:50 | 22:50 |
| 838 | L | 20:01 | 23:35 |
| 816 | G | 20:08 | 22:46 |
| 816 | H | 21:54 | 01:45/7 |
| 838 | M | 22:28 | 01:58 |
| 816 | K | 23:40 | 06:19 |
| 838 | A | 23:59 | 03:05/7 |

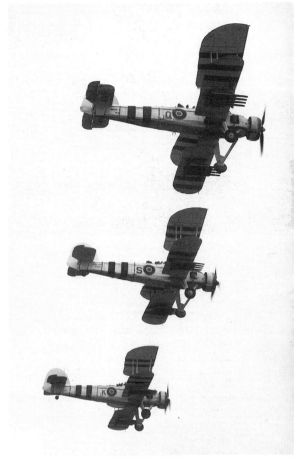

*Fairey Swordfish IIs of the Fleet Air Arm, including* NF249-S. *(IWM A24986)*

# Appendix One

## OCCUPANCY OF BRITISH ADVANCED LANDING GROUNDS IN NORMANDY – JUNE–AUGUST 1944

B.1 Asnelles  
49.20N/00.34W — no squadron use

B.2 Bazenville  
49.18N/00.34W — No 174 Sqn, Typhoon, 19 June – 27 August  
No 609 Sqn, Typhoon, 18 June – 22 June  
No 403 Sqn, Spitfire IX, 17 June – August  
No 414 Sqn, Mustang – first used on 14 June  
No 416 Sqn, Spitfire IX, 16 June – August 1944  
No 421 Sqn, Spitfire IX, 16 June – August 1944 (first used on 14 June)

B.3 Ste Croix-sur-Mer  
49.19N/00.31W — No 175 Sqn, Typhoon, 20 June – 24 June  
Used from 10 June by ADLS Hurricanes  
First 4 Spitfires to land in France (442 Sqn), also 412 Sqn, here 10 June  
No 441 Sqn, Spitfire IX, 15 June – 14 July  
No 442 Sqn, Spitfire IX, 15 June – 14 July  
No 443 Sqn, Spitfire IX, 15 June – 28 August

B.4 Beny-sur-Mer  
49.18N/00.25W — Some use by Auster AOP IVs of 651 Sqn  
No 401 Sqn, Spitfire IX, 19 June – August  
No 411 Aqn, Spitfire IX, 19 June – August  
No 412 Sqn, Spitfire IX, 19 June – August

B.5 Camilly/Le Fresnoy  
49.16N/00.16W — No 175 Sqn, Typhoon, 24 June – 2 September

B.6 Coulombs  
49.14N/00.35W — No 181 Sqn, Typhoon, 20 June – 11 August  
No 182 Sqn, Typhoon, 20 June – 22 June  
No 247 Sqn, Typhoon, 20 June – 23 June, 28 June – 30 August

B.7 Martragny  
49.16N/00.37W — No 19 Sqn, Mustang III, 25 June – 15 July  
No 65 Sqn, Mustang III, 25 June – 17 July  
No 122 Sqn, Mustang III, 25 June – 16 July  
No 440 Sqn, Typhoon, briefly here in June

B.8 Sommervieu  
49.18N/00.40W — No 168 Sqn, Mustang FR, 29 June – 14 August

B.9 Lanthieul  
49.16N/00.32W — No 438 Sqn, Typhoon, 27 June – August  
No 439 Sqn, Typhoon, 27 June – August  
No 440 Sqn, Typhoon, 27 June – August

B.10 Plumetot  
49.17N/00.22W — No 184 Sqn, Typhoon, 27 June – 14 July  
No 310 Sqn, Spitfire IX, used on 28 June only  
No 312 Sqn, Spitfire IX, used on 28 June only  
No 313 Sqn, Spitfire IX, used on 28 June only

B.11 Longues  
49.20N/00.41W — No 602 Sqn, Spitfire IX, 25 June – 13 August  
No 453 Sqn, Spitfire IX, 25 June – September

B.14 Amblie  
49.18N/00.30W — No 132 Sqn, Spitfire IX, 25 June – 13 August

B.17 Caen/Carpiquet — Not used until August, after breakthrough

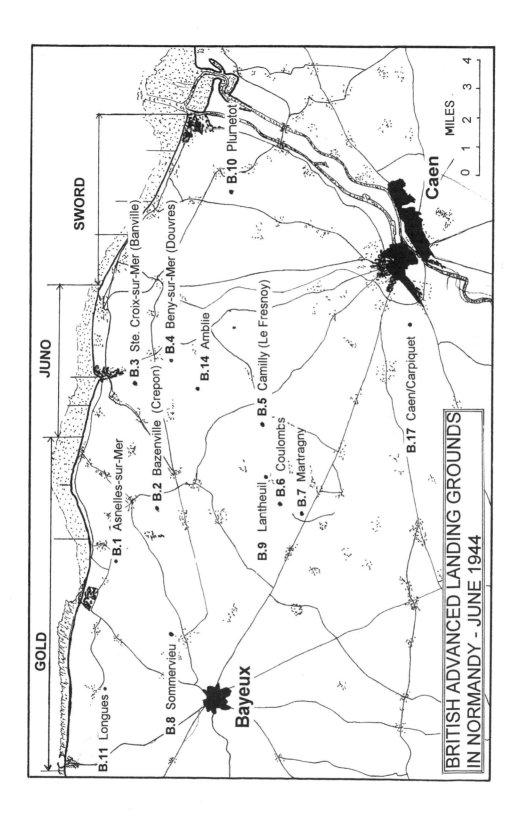

BRITISH ADVANCED LANDING GROUNDS
IN NORMANDY – JUNE 1944

GOLD

JUNO

SWORD

MILES

0 1 2 3 4

B.11 Longues

B.8 Sommervieu

Bayeux

B.1 Asnelles-sur-Mer

B.2 Bazenville (Crepon)

B.3 Ste. Croix-sur-Mer (Banville)

B.4 Beny-sur-Mer (Douvres)

B.14 Amblie

B.10 Plumetot

B.9 Lantheuil

B.6 Coulombs

B.7 Martragny

B.5 Camilly (Le Fresnoy)

B.17 Caen/Carpiquet

Caen

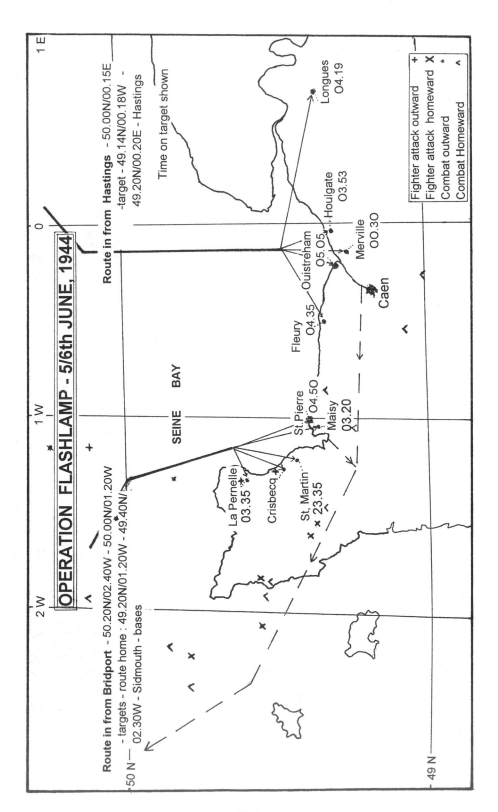

OPERATION FLASHLAMP - 5/6th JUNE, 1944

Route in from Bridport - 50.20N/02.40W - 50.00N/01.20W
- targets - route home : 49.20N/01.20W - 49.40N/
02.30W - Sidmouth - bases

Route in from Hastings - 50.00N/00.15E
-target - 49.14N/00.18W -
49.20N/00.20E - Hastings

Time on target shown

| | Fighter attack outward | + |
| | Fighter attack homeward | X |
| | Combat outward | * |
| | Combat Homeward | ^ |

SEINE BAY

Longues 04.19
Houlgate 03.53
Merville 00.30
Ouistreham 05.05
Caen
Fleury 04.35
St. Pierre 04.50
Maisy 03.20
La Pernelle 03.35
Crisbecq
St, Martin 23.35

2 W    1 W    0    1 E

50 N

49 N

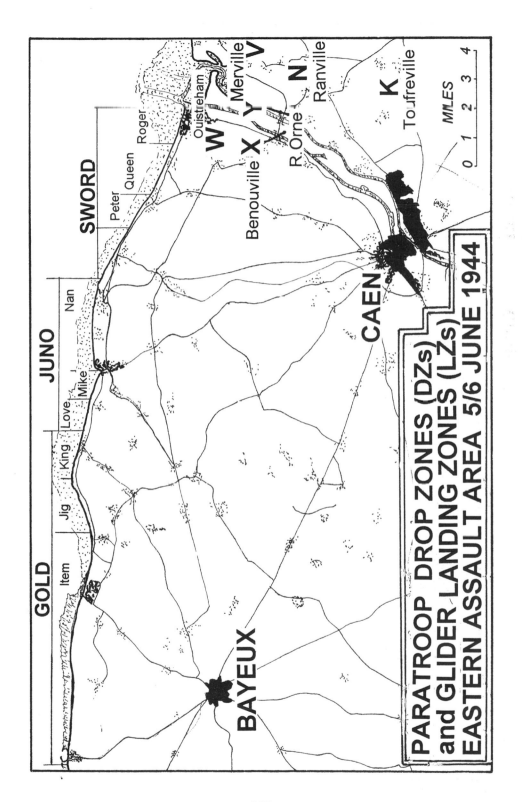

PARATROOP DROP ZONES (DZs)
and GLIDER LANDING ZONES (LZs)
EASTERN ASSAULT AREA 5/6 JUNE 1944

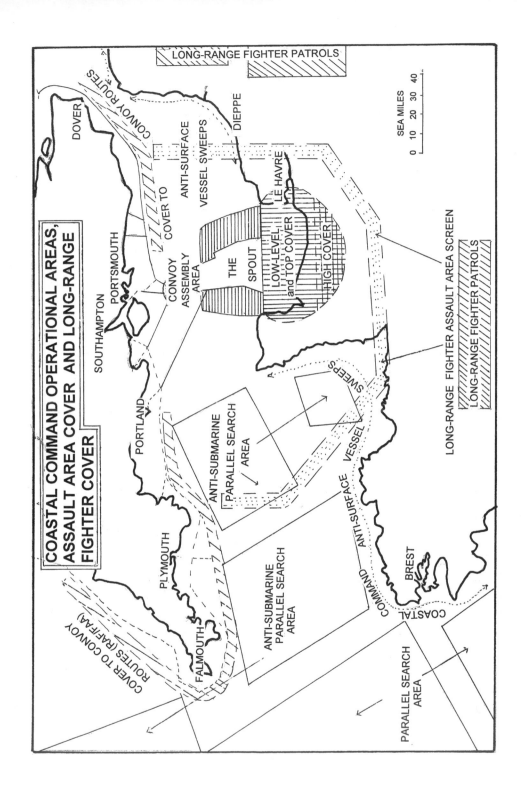

COASTAL COMMAND OPERATIONAL AREAS, ASSAULT AREA COVER AND LONG-RANGE FIGHTER COVER

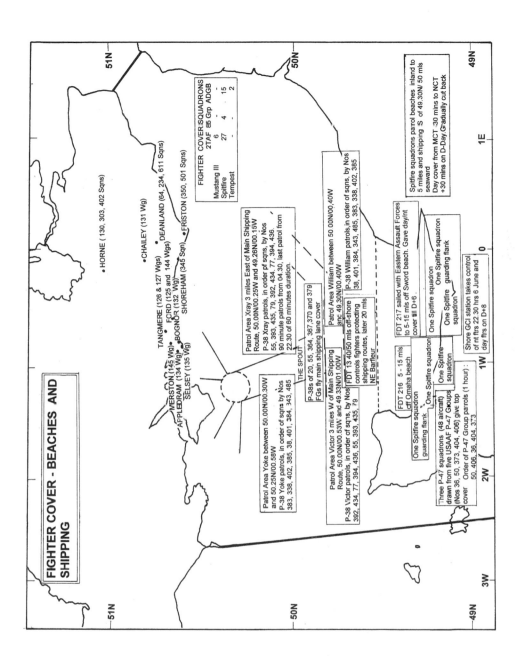

# FIGHTER COVER - BEACHES AND SHIPPING

HORNE ( 130, 303, 402 Sqns)

CHAILEY (131 Wg)

DEANLAND (64, 234, 611 Sqns)

TANGMERE (126 & 127 Wgs)
FORD (125 and 144 Wgs)
MERSTON (145 Wg)
BOGNOR (132 Wg)
SHOREHAM (345 Sqn)
APPLEDRAM (134 Wg)
FRISTON (350, 501 Sqns)
SELSEY (135 Wg)

| FIGHTER COVER SQUADRONS | | |
|---|---|---|
| 2TAF | | ⑤ Grp ADGB |
| Mustang III | 6 | - |
| Spitfire | 27 | 4 - 15 |
| Tempest | - | 2 |

Patrol Area Xray 3 miles East of Main Shipping Route, 50.00N/00.25W and 49.26N/00.15W
P-38 Xray patrols, in order pf sqns, by Nos 55, 393, 435, 79, 392, 434, 77, 394, 436. 90 minute patrols from 04.30, last patrol from 22.30 of 60 minutes duration.

Patrol Area William between 50.00N/00.40W and 49.30N/00.40W
P-38 William patrols, in order of sqns, by Nos 38, 401, 384, 343, 485, 383, 338, 402, 385

THE SPOUT

P-38s of 20, 55, 364, 367,370 and 379 FGs fly main shipping lane cover

FDT 13 40/50 mls off-shore controls fighters protecting shipping routes, later 20 mls NE Barfleur

Patrol Area Yoke between 50.00N/00.30W and 50.25N/00.58W
P-38 Yoke patrols, in order of sqns by Nos 383, 338, 402, 385, 38, 401, 384, 343, 485

Patrol Area Victor 3 miles W of Main Shipping Route, 50.00N/00.53W and 49.33N/01.00W
P-38 Victor patrols, in order of sqns, by Nos 392, 434, 77, 394, 436, 55, 393, 435, 79

Spitfire squadrons parol beaches inland to 5 miles and shipping ⑤ of 49.30N/ 50 mls seaward
Day cover from MCT -30 mins to NCT +30 mins on D-Day Gradually cut back

FDT 217 sailed with Eastern Assault Forces to 5-15 mls off Sword beach. Gave day/nt cover till D-6.

One Spitfire squadron

One Spitfire guarding flank

One Spitfire guarding flank squadron

Shore GCI station takes control of nt ftrs 22.30 hrs 6 June and day ftrs on D+8

FDT 216 5 - 15 mls off Omaha beach

One Spitfire squadron

One Spitfire squadron

One Spitfire squadron guarding flank

Three P-47 squadrons (48 aircraft) drawn from five USAAF P-47 Groups (Nos 36, 50, 373, 404, 406) give top cover. Order of P-47 Group parrols (1 hour):
50, 406, 36, 404, 373

309

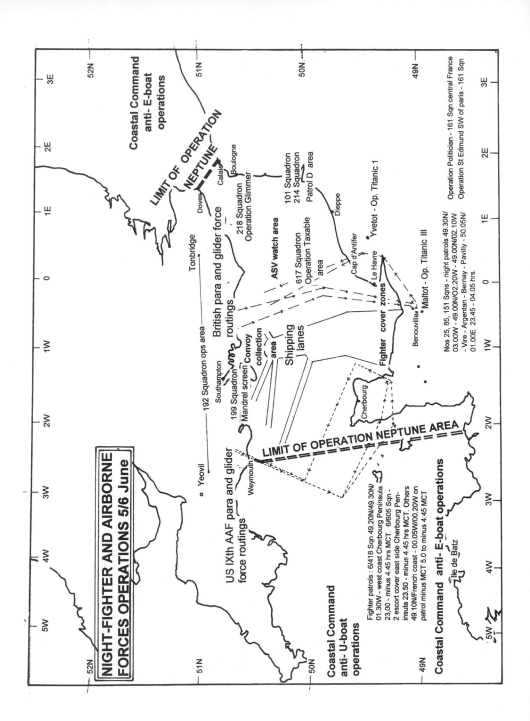

**NIGHT-FIGHTER AND AIRBORNE FORCES OPERATIONS 5/6 June**

Coastal Command anti- E-boat operations

LIMIT OF OPERATION NEPTUNE

Dover
Calais
Boulogne
218 Squadron Operation Glimmer
101 Squadron
214 Squadron Patrol D area
Dieppe
Yvetot - Op. Titanic 1
Cap d'Antifer
Le Havre
Maltot - Op. Titanic III
Benouville

Tonbridge

British para and glider force routings

ASV watch area

617 Squadron Operation Taxable area

Fighter cover zones

192 Squadron ops area

Southampton
199 Squadron
Mandrel screen
Convoy collection area
Shipping lanes

Cherbourg

Nos 25, 85, 151 Sqns - night patrols 49.30N/03.00W - 49.00N/02.20W - 49.00N/02.10W - Vire - Argentan - Bernay - Pavilly - 50.05N/01.00E 23.45 - 04.05 hrs.

Operation Politician - 161 Sqn central France
Operation St Edmund SW of paris - 161 Sqn

Yeovil

US IXth AAF para and glider force routings

Weymouth

LIMIT OF OPERATION NEPTUNE AREA

Coastal Command anti- U-boat operations

Fighter patrols : 6/418 Sqn 49.20N/49.30N/01.30W - west coast Cherbourg Peninsula 23.00 - minus 4.45 hrs MCT. 6/605 Sqn - 2 escort cover east side Cherbourg Peninsula 23.50 - minus 4.45 hrs MCT. Others 49.10N/French coast - 00.05W/00.20W on patrol minus MCT 5.0 to minus 4.45 MCT

Coastal Command anti- E-boat operations

Ile de Batz

# Appendix Two

## Part One: Aircraft stocks on 1 June 1944

During the war years, a monthly census was undertaken by the Organization and Statistics Branch of the Air Ministry covering the entire stock of aircraft held in the United Kingdom and overseas, including naval aircraft. By 1944 the monthly average total was around 50,000 aircraft. The following listing is but a sample of the census of 1 June 1944, the closest census date to D-Day. In essence the figures correlate well, despite the enormity of the task which compilation presented. There are some slight discrepancies, evident in the case of Spitfires and also because of the manner of dividing Beaufighters into day and night fighters; something the compilers found difficult. The aircraft are titled as they were for the census in 1944: 'Mustang X' refers to Merlin-powered Mustang prototype conversions at Rolls-Royce; '(SO)' refers to Special Operations aircraft of Nos. 138 and 161 Squadrons whose Halifaxes were specially prepared; '(SD)' refers to Special Duties aircraft of No. 100 Group; and the Ju 86s had been taken over from the South African Air Force and placed on RAF charge. 'Beechcraft' mentioned in Part Four probably refers to Beechcraft 18 Expeditors; and to distinguish them, the DH 89 entry includes Rapides and the DH 90 entry relates to the Dragonfly. Although promulgated as the Petrel, wartime official records appear generally to entitle the aircraft 'Percival Q.6'. In the naval listing 'Helldiver/SBC-4' may not refer to the biplane Cleveland (four of which were still with the RAF), but the monoplane SB2C/SBW-1B, a few of which were flying from Burscough.

LEGEND:
a) Serving in the Metropolitan Air Force
b) In MAP hands
c) In transit in the UK or to overseas
d) Overseas
e) Total

| Role/Type | a | b | c | d | e |
|---|---|---|---|---|---|
| **Airborne forces:** | | | | | |
| Albemarle | 225 | 47 | 1 | - | 273 |
| Halifax | 74 | - | - | - | 74 |
| Stirling | 253 | - | - | - | 253 |
| **Heavy bombers:** | | | | | |
| Halifax | 1,039 | 135 | 10 | 105 | 1,289 |
| Lancaster | 1,015 | 206 | 7 | 2 | 1,230 |
| Liberator | - | - | - | 314 | 314 |
| Stirling | 353 | 100 | 6 | - | 459 |
| **Medium bombers/GR:** | | | | | |
| Marauder | - | 3 | 56 | 165 | 224 |
| Mitchell | 261 | 129 | 22 | 2 | 414 |
| Warwick/ASR | 226 | 26 | 18 | 54 | 324 |
| Wellington I, II, III, IV, VI, X, XIV, XVI | 872 | 200 | 49 | 483 | 1,604 |
| Wellington VIII, XI, XIII | 435 | 61 | 25 | 497 | 1,018 |
| Ventura | 98 | 54 | 22 | 321 | 495 |
| **Light bombers:** | | | | | |
| Baltimore | - | 4 | 36 | 729 | 769 |
| Boston | 99 | 82 | 19 | 50 | 250 |
| Mosquito | 283 | 111 | 19 | 67 | 480 |
| Vengeance | - | - | 77 | 404 | 481 |
| **Long-range GR:** | | | | | |
| Fortress | *53 | 38 | - | - | 91 |
| Halifax GR | 49 | - | - | - | 49 |
| Liberator | 143 | 83 | 106 | 47 | 379 |
| **Flying-boats:** | | | | | |
| Catalina | 78 | 75 | 20 | 124 | 297 |
| Catalina amphibian | 7 | - | - | - | 7 |
| Coronado | 1 | 2 | - | - | 3 |
| Sunderland | 199 | 31 | 12 | 56 | 298 |
| **Short-range GR:** | | | | | |
| Beaufort | - | - | 1 | 122 | 123 |
| Hudson | 220 | 72 | 2 | 46 | 340 |

| Role/Type | a | b | c | d | e |
|---|---|---|---|---|---|
| **Single-seat fighters:** | | | | | |
| Hurricane II, IV, X | 723 | 43 | 8 | 1,597 | 2,371 |
| Kittyhawk | - | 1 | - | 421 | 422 |
| Mustang I, II, X | 306 | 71 | - | 118 | 495 |
| Mustang III | 218 | 148 | 81 | - | 447 |
| Spitfire V, VI, VII, VIII, IX, XII, XIV, 21 | 2,350 | 481 | 187 | 2,185 | 5,203 |
| Spitfire PR | 221 | 18 | - | 72 | 311 |
| Tempest | 73 | 18 | - | - | 91 |
| Typhoon | 735 | 260 | - | 2 | 997 |
| Thunderbolt | - | - | 204 | 81 | 285 |
| Welkin | 2 | 3 | - | - | 5 |
| **Multi-seat fighters:** | | | | | |
| Beaufighter (day) | 584 | 56 | 19 | 85 | 744 |
| Beaufighter (NF) | 371 | 181 | 35 | 644 | 1,231 |
| Mosquito | 846 | 164 | 5 | 49 | 1,064 |
| Mosquito PR | 104 | 12 | 4 | 34 | 154 |
| **Others:** | | | | | |
| Auster AOP | 428 | 24 | 26 | 166 | 644 |
| Vigilant | 8 | - | - | - | 8 |

\* Includes 10 B-17 (SD) aircraft used by Bomber Command.

# Part Two: Distribution of operational aircraft types in Britain

Legend:
a) In squadron hands
b) In OTUs or conversion units
c) In FTCs or TTCs
d) In miscellaneous units
e) In transit in the British Isles
f) In servicing units

| Role/Type: | a | b | c | d | e | f |
|---|---|---|---|---|---|---|
| **Airborne Forces:** | | | | | | |
| Albemarle | 124 | 20 | - | 15 | - | 66 |
| Halifax | 74 | - | - | - | - | - |
| Stirling | 151 | 29 | - | 1 | 6 | 66 |
| **Heavy bombers:** | | | | | | |
| Halifax | 525 | 336 | - | 54 | 2 | 88 |
| Halifax (SO) | 33 | - | - | 1 | - | - |
| Halifax (SD) | 27 | 6 | - | - | - | 16 |
| Lancaster | 856 | 78 | 1 | 20 | 4 | 56 |
| Stirling III | 62 | 213 | 6 | 5 | - | 47 |
| Stirling (SD) | 20 | - | - | - | - | - |
| B-17 (SD) | 10 | - | - | - | - | - |
| **Medium bombers:** | | | | | | |
| Wellington X and XV, XVI transports | - | 697 | - | 17 | 2 | 148 |
| Wellington (SD) | 8 | - | - | - | - | - |
| Mitchell | 78 | 30 | - | 32 | - | 91 |
| **Light bombers:** | | | | | | |
| Boston | 38 | 7 | 4 | 14 | - | 36 |
| Mosquito | 236 | 22 | - | 11 | - | 9 |
| Mosquito (SD) | 5 | - | - | - | - | - |
| Ventura | - | 4 | - | 19 | - | 75 |

| Type | a | b | c | d | e | |
|---|---|---|---|---|---|---|
| **Long-range GR:** | | | | | | |
| Liberator | 121 | 10 | - | 2 | - | 10 |
| Fortress II | 20 | 7 | - | 16 | - | - |
| **Medium-range GR:** | | | | | | |
| Warwick | - | 10 | - | 85 | - | 131 |
| Wellington XIII, XI, XIII, XIV | 116 | 54 | 82 | 31 | 2 | 150 |
| **Short-range GR:** | | | | | | |
| Hudson | - | 8 | 5 | 57 | 3 | 142 |
| Hudson (SO) | 7 | - | - | - | - | - |
| **Single-seat fighters:** | | | | | | |
| Hurricane II, IV, X | 35 | 211 | - | 280 | 1 | 196 |
| Mustang I, II | 95 | 25 | - | 25 | 2 | 159 |
| Mustang III | 130 | - | - | 23 | 1 | 64 |
| Spitfire V, VI, VII, IX, XII | 1,148 | 122 | - | 436 | 29 | 619 |
| Tempest | 36 | - | - | 1 | - | 36 |
| Typhoon | 376 | 43 | - | 96 | - | 220 |
| Welkin | - | - | - | 2 | - | - |
| **Multi-seat fighters:** | | | | | | |
| Beaufighter (day) | 158 | 96 | - | 38 | 9 | 283 |
| Beaufighter (NF) | 36 | 1 | 4 | 1 | 8 | 83 |
| Mosquito | 337 | 96 | 2 | 103 | - | 174 |
| Mosquito (SD) | 133 | - | - | - | - | - |
| **PR:** | | | | | | |
| Mosquito | 54 | 45 | - | 4 | - | 1 |
| Spitfire | 113 | 14 | 13 | - | 1 | 81 |
| **Flying-boats:** | | | | | | |
| Catalina | 26 | 30 | - | 8 | - | 11 |
| Catalina (SO) | 3 | - | - | - | - | - |
| Catalina amphibian | - | 7 | - | - | - | - |
| Coronado | - | - | - | - | - | 1 |
| Sunderland | 93 | 46 | - | 4 | - | 56 |
| **Others:** | | | | | | |
| Auster AOP | 112 | 37 | 7 | 123 | - | 149 |
| Vigilant | - | - | 7 | - | - | 1 |

# Part Three: Aircraft undergoing repair, modification, trials

Legend:
a) Within Civilian Repair Organization
b) Under Controller Research & Development
c) Having on-site modifications/repairs

| Type | a | b | c |
|---|---|---|---|
| Albemarle | 24 | 7 | 5 |
| Auster | 16 | 6 | 2 |
| Baltimore | 2 | 1 | - |
| Beaufighter\* | 21 | 4 | 31 |
| Beaufighter NF | 91 | 30 | 16 |
| Boston | 40 | 5 | 4 |
| Catalina | 6 | 4 | 6 |
| Fortress | 8 | 3 | - |
| Halifax | 51 | 32 | 39 |
| Hudson | 20 | 2 | 8 |
| Hurricane | 90 | 18 | 5 |
| Kittyhawk | - | 1 | - |
| Lancaster | 16 | 55 | 51 |

| | | | |
|---|---|---|---|
| Liberator | 12 | 9 | 22 |
| Marauder | - | 2 | - |
| Mitchell | 26 | 8 | 4 |
| Mosquito bmr | 26 | 15 | 15 |
| Mosquito ftr | 66 | 29 | 46 |
| Mosquito PR | - | 7 | - |
| Mustang I, II | 34 | 10 | 6 |
| Mustang III | 20 | 12 | 4 |
| Spitfire ftr | 318 | 80 | 52 |
| Spitfire PR | 14 | 3 | 1 |
| Stirling III, IV | 34 | 21 | 45 |
| Sunderland | 8 | 5 | 18 |
| Tempest | 5 | 13 | - |
| Typhoon | 44 | 36 | 18 |
| Ventura | 4 | 4 | 24 |
| Warwick | 10 | 8 | 4 |
| Wellington X, XV, XVI, | 132 | 9 | 52 |
| Wellington VIII, XI, XII, XIV, | 21 | 13 | 27 |
| Welkin | 2 | 1 | - |

*Another 21 Beaufighters were on the census, but it was not specified whether they were for day or night use and their whereabouts were uncertain.

# Part Four: Obsolescent aircraft types remaining in service

Although by June 1944 some prominent types of aircraft remained on charge, their numbers had dramatically fallen as this listing shows.

Legend:
a) In the British Isles in RAF hands
b) In MAP hands
c) Overseas

| Type | a | b | c |
|---|---|---|---|
| Beaufort | 382 | 61 | - |
| Blenheim | 202 | 18 | 205 |
| Hurricane I | 223 | 16 | 113 |
| Ju 86 | - | - | 4 |
| Lysander | 24 | 22 | 50 |
| Maryland | - | - | 7 |
| Mohawk | 1 | - | 50 |
| Spitfire I, II | 424 | 54 | 1 |
| Stirling | 66 | - | - |
| Tomahawk | 10 | - | - |
| Wellington I, IV | 536 | 128 | 13 |
| Whitley I, II, III, IV, V, VI, VII | 366 | 42 | - |
| Whitley (airborne forces) | 53 | - | - |

# Part Five: RAF principal holding of miscellaneous transport and light communications aircraft

Legend:
a) In the British Isles
b) In the Mediterranean theatre
c) In SEAC

| Type | a | b | c |
|---|---|---|---|
| Argus | 91 | 172 | 76 |
| Beechcraft | - | 14 | 3 |
| DH 86 | 1 | 3 | - |
| DH 89 | 17 | 2 | 7 |
| DH 90 | 3 | - | - |
| Envoy | 3 | - | - |
| Flamingo | 3 | - | - |
| Harrow | 20 | - | - |
| Hudson | - | - | 59 |
| Lockheed 12a | 5 | - | 4 |
| Lodestar | - | 23 | 1 |
| Percival Q.6 | 7 | 2 | - |
| Reliant | 50 | - | - |
| Vega Gull | 13 | 1 | 2 |
| Wellesley | - | 8 | - |

# Part Six: Total holdings of types within OTUs and FTC/TTC in the Metropolitan Air Force

| Type | OTU | FTC/ TTC | Total Stock |
|---|---|---|---|
| Anson | 100 | 115 | 1,898 |
| Blenheim | 4 | 117 | 202 |
| Defiant TT | - | - | 52 |
| Dominie | 7 | 44 | 144 |
| Harvard I | 9 | 2 | 20 |
| Lysander TT | - | - | 12 |
| Magister | 8 | 37 | 394 |
| Martinet | 198 | 256 | 1,000 |
| Oxford | 21 | 1,884 | 3,318 |
| Proctor | 5 | 210 | 384 |
| Tiger Moth | 10 | 1,632 | 2,527 |

NB Also with OTUs were: 62 Beauforts, 272 Spitfire I/IIs, 112 Wellington Ic/IVs and 126 Whitleys. Only nine Fairey Battles remained, within miscellaneous units.

# Part Seven: Fleet Air Arm aircraft in the British Isles

Some older aircraft were flying in the Fleet Air Arm, and some operational aircraft were attached to Coastal Command for Channel operations. Others remained at alert states. The following listing summarizes the FAA holding on 1 June 1944.

Legend:
a) First-line squadron strength
b) Operational from bases in the British Isles
c) In training units
d) Classified 'Reserve'

| Type | a | b | c | d |
|---|---|---|---|---|
| Avenger I, II | 85 | 85 | 33 | 269 |
| Barracuda II, III | 108 | 108 | 165 | 534 |
| Corsair II, III | 29 | 29 | 21 | 311 |
| Firefly I, II | 38 | 38 | 13 | 92 |
| Hellcat | 48 | 48 | 10 | 107 |
| Helldiver/SBC-4 | - | - | - | 4 |

| Type | a | b | c | d |
|---|---|---|---|---|
| Hurricane IIc | 14 | 14 | 31 | 57 |
| Seafire II, III | 101 | 101 | 14 | 280 |
| Sea Otter | - | - | 4 | 42 |
| Spitfire LF Vb | 19 | 19 | - | 35 |
| Swordfish II, III | 147 | 47 | 44 | 303 |
| Walrus | 2 | - | ? | 47 |
| Wildcat V, VI | 85 | - | 2 | 178 |

Among the aircraft held in training squadrons were: 67 Albacores, 4 Chesapeakes, 65 Fulmars, 11 Gladiators, 2 Hurricane Is, 5 Kingfishers, 30 Seamews, 5 Sharks, 14 Skua/Rocs, 46 Spitfires and 171 Swordfishes.

Miscellaneous aircraft on naval charge 1 June 1944 included: 16 Austers, 75 Ansons, 17 Beaufighters, 77 Blenheim I/IVs, 2 Dauntlesses, 121 Defiant I/IIIs, 3 Expeditors, 9 Firebrand II/IIIs, 64 Hurricanes, 47 Lysanders, 123 Martinets, 98 Oxfords, 217 Reliants, 3 Sikorsky YR-4B helicopters and 49 Tiger Moths.

# Index

317

**Targets**

**US forces:**